# FERNAND
# LÉGER

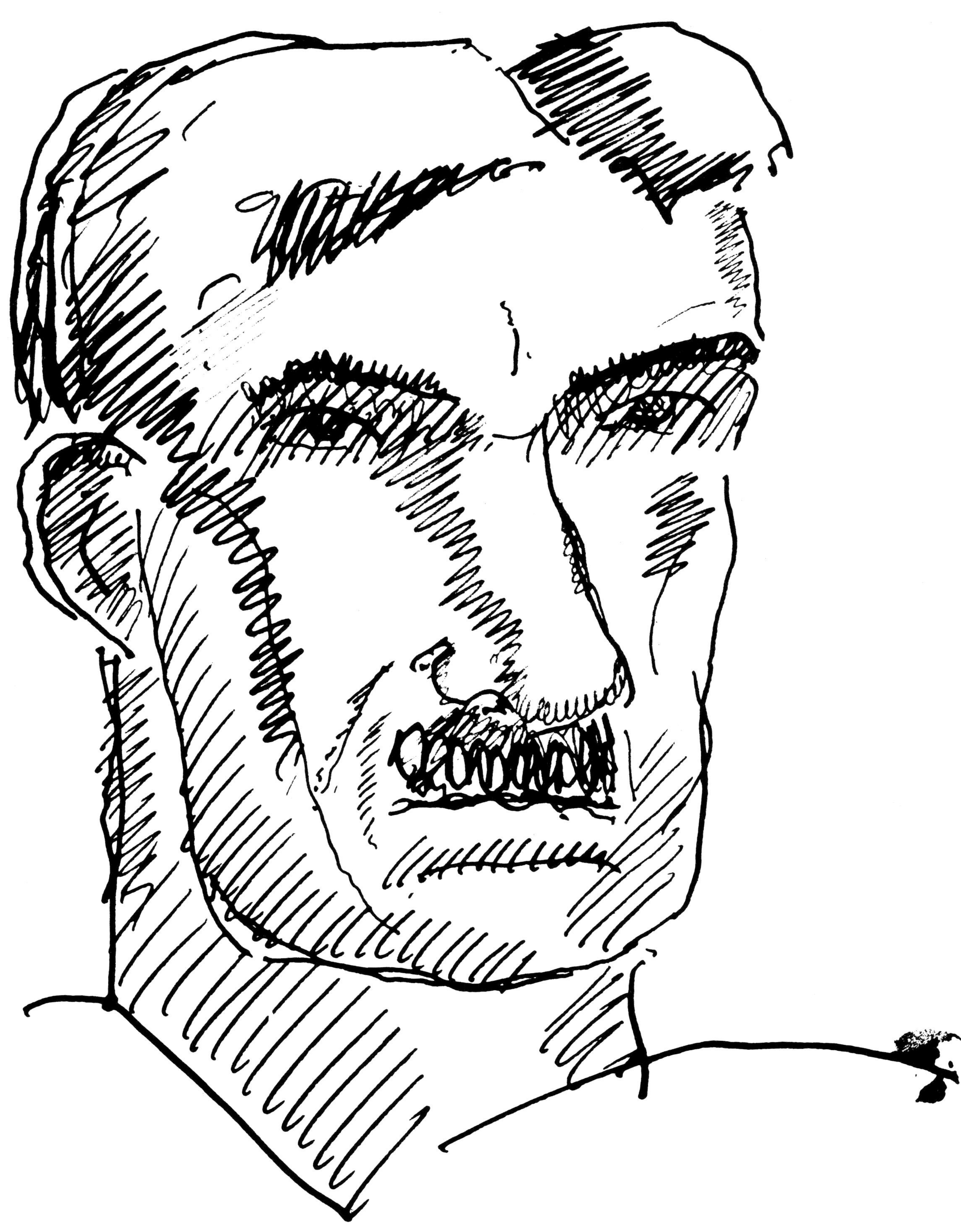

1. SELF-PORTRAIT
Around 1930—Ink drawing, 24 × 13 cm
Musée national Fernand Léger, Biot, France

# F. LEGER

by

GILLES NÉRET

*Translated by Susan D. Resnick*

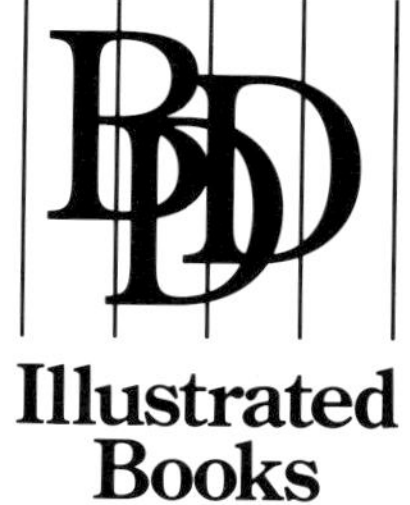

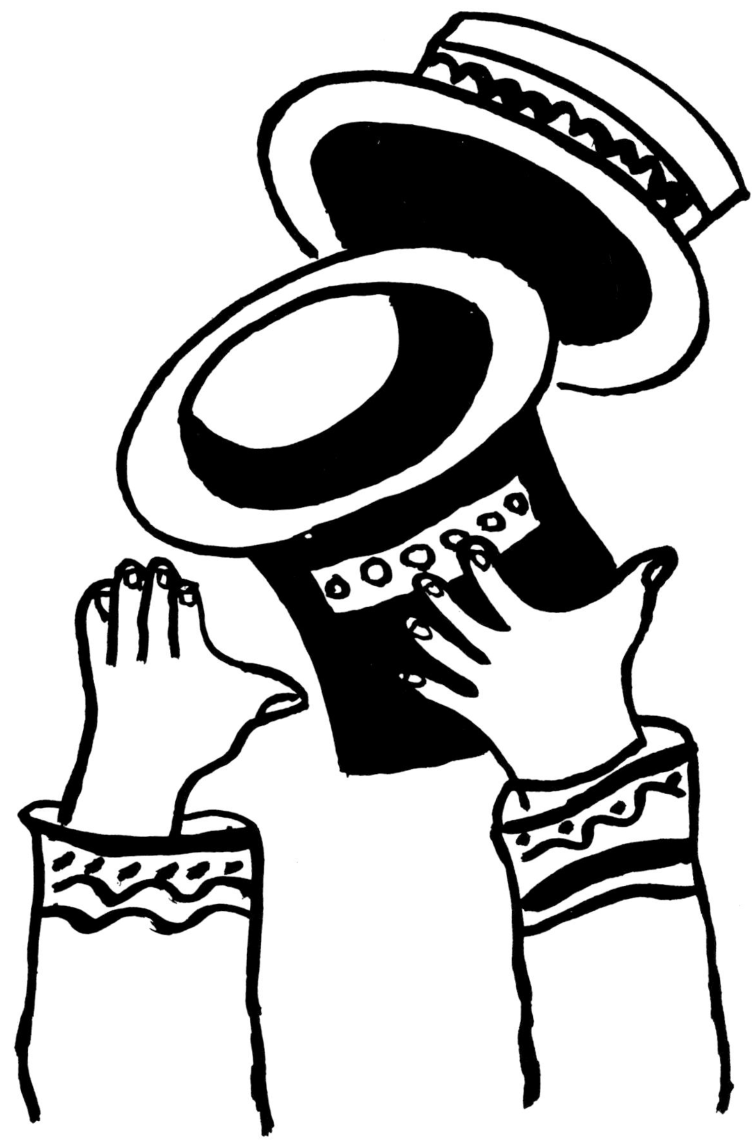

From "The Circus"
1949-Text and drawing by Fernand Léger

BDD Illustrated Books
An imprint of BDD Promotional Book Company, Inc.
1540 Broadway
New York, N.Y. 10036

BDD Illustrated Books and the accompanying logo are trademarks of the BDD Promotional Book Company



First Published in the United States of America in 1993 by BDD Illustrated Books



ISBN 0-7924-5848-6

Printed in Hong Kong

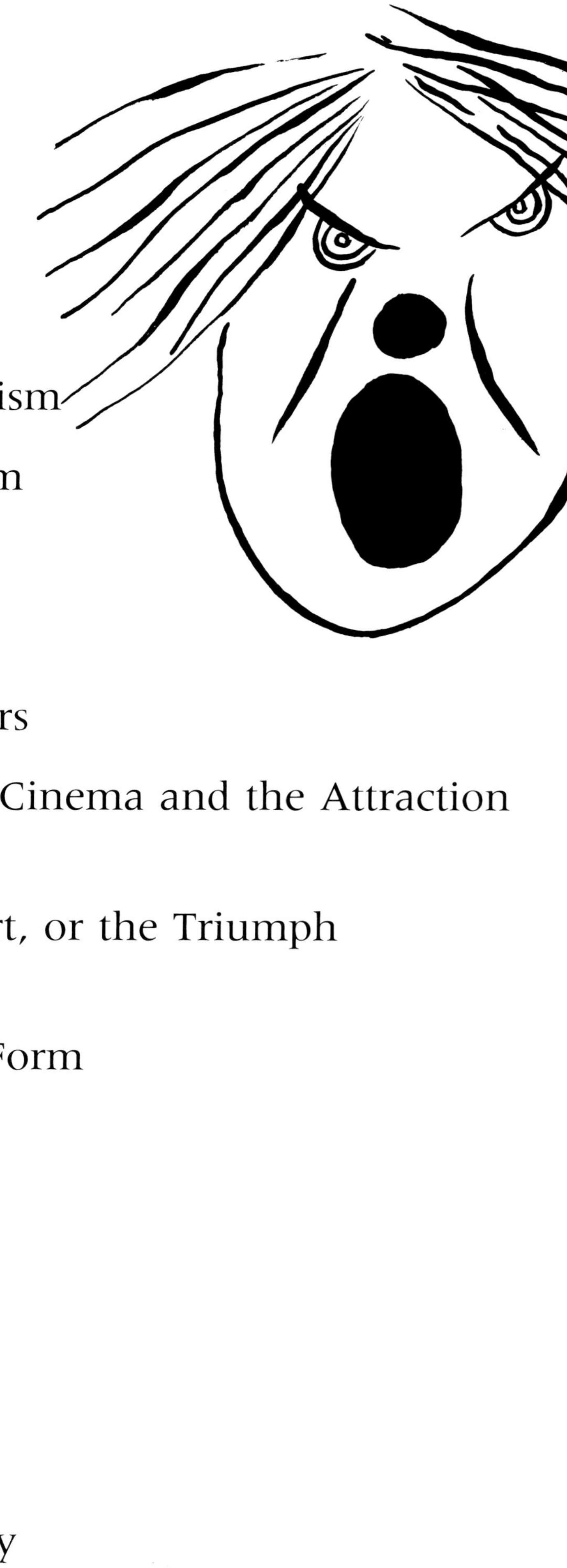

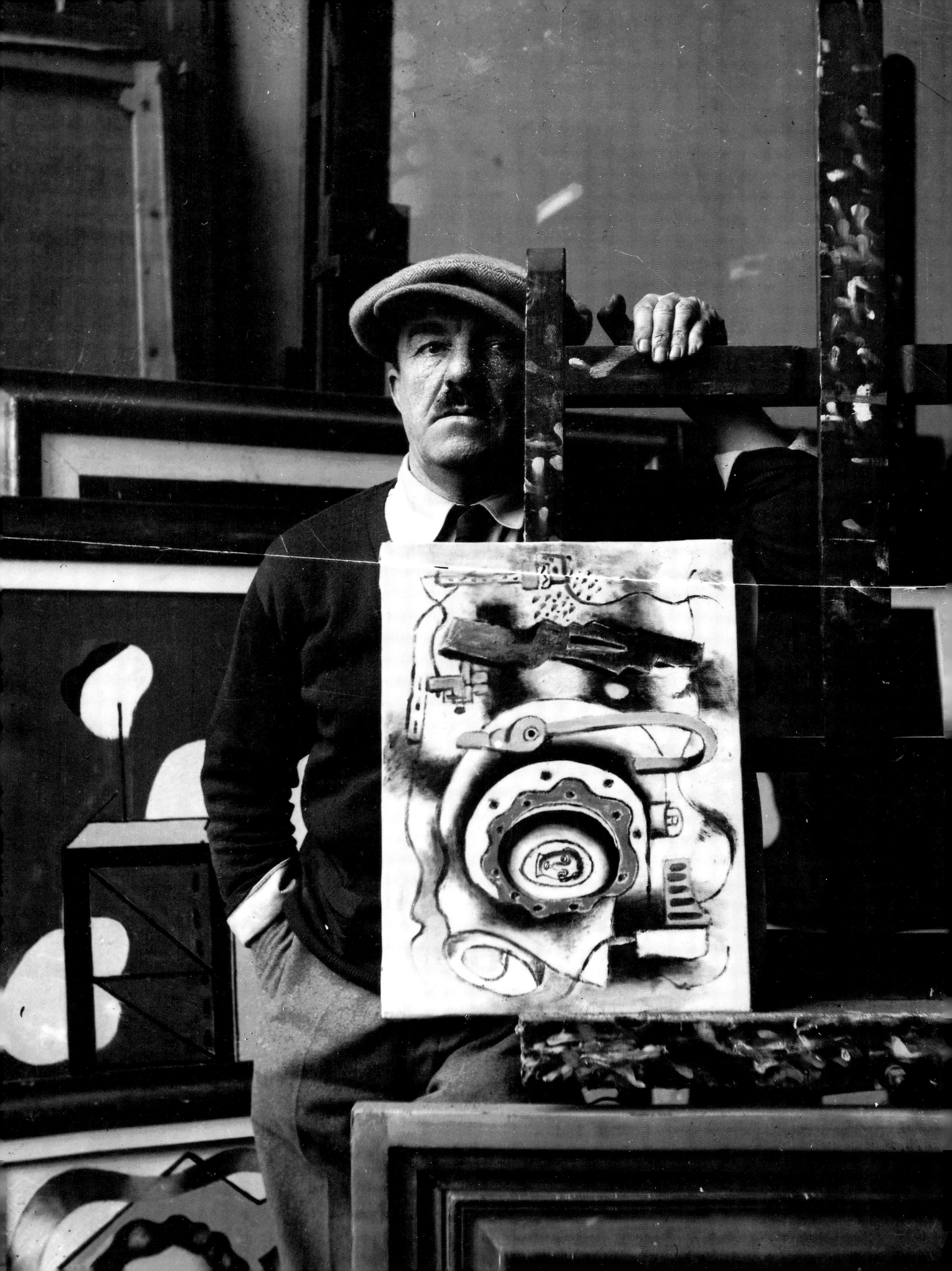

# The Fourth Great One

It is no surprise that both the working class and the bourgeoisie disliked Fernand Léger. Throughout his artistic life he shocked everyone with his relentless search for truth. His art reflects a truth that is ours as well as his. It is a mirror of our times.

Like it or not, the moment will come when we justly acknowledge Léger as the great "early master of contemporary art," a true pioneer. Picasso spent his time undoing reality. Malevich searched for God with strokes of squares and crosses, and Duchamp substituted his "ready-mades" for works of art. Unlike his peers, Léger was a builder, an engineer of sorts. There was also a spark of the Promethean in him. He singlehandedly tried to define and trace the rules and practical applications that govern all contemporary art.

"All artists are marked by the time in which they live," said Matisse in 1908, "but it is most deeply ingrained in great artists." To quote from Roger Garaudy at the beginning of an essay he wrote, "Twentieth-century realism is a posthumous dialogue with Fernand Léger." Léger, however, was not satisfied with being "marked by his time." He also left his own profound mark, both as a painter and as a theoretician. For Garaudy he was "the artistic conscience of his day." *Conscience*—what a formidable word! Who in the world relishes listening to the voice of his conscience? No one enjoys any kind of change that rocks the status quo. Nonetheless, Léger explained, "If pictorial expression changed, it is because modern life made this change necessary. Take, for example, the commercial billboards that disrupt the natural landscape. This is one of the many changes that caused an outburst of protest in people of 'good taste.' It even led to the establishment of the 'Association for the Protection of Natural Landscapes.' Is there anything more ridiculous than this group of decent folks taking on the solemn task of stating what is and what is not good for the environment? We might as well go one step further and get rid of telegraph wires and houses in order to maintain the harmonious integrity of the trees! . . . Cultivated people, those with so-called good taste, have never been able to accept contrast. Nothing is more dreadful than habit, and the people who adamantly protest in front of the commercial billboards are the same ones you see at the Salon des Indépendents doubled over with laughter in their inability to understand modern painting."

Léger considered the yellow or red posterboard that howled out in the timid countryside the most beautiful new pictorial source. "It hobbles all sentimental and literary notions, and announces the advent of pictorial contrast." *Contrast* is the basis of Léger's entire artistic work. Today, automobiles and trains cutting through the countryside are "contrast." What has been lost in descriptive value has acquired synthetic value. "Train and car windows, along with the speed that has been attained, have changed the habitual aspect of things," explained Léger. "Modern man registers one hundred times as many impressions as did artists in the eighteenth century. It is even reflected in the language we speak, which is full of abbreviations and nicknames. The condensed aspect of modern painting with its variety of interrupted forms is a consequence of all this."

Where does a landscape begin, and where does it end? For Léger the natural landscape ends as soon as a house, a telegraph pole, a gas station, or a billboard appears. This is also the point at which the adventure of modern painting begins: these steel towers find their *natural contrast* in clouds. . . "Life today is so different from what it was a century ago. Art must express this in a total way."

Léger was severely criticized for having used the mechanistic elements of modern life for their pictorial possibilities. In 1918 and 1919 he was the very first to incorporate these elements, using them as "a means and not as an end," as "primary materials," just as other artists used the natural landscape or the still life. He invented his own pictorial process, which many after him would borrow from. For Léger, "the state of organized pictorial intensity" to which he applied this "law of contrast" was the only valid means of rendering life. It was the very same means that allowed men like Shakespeare and Molière to transcend their particular eras and endow their work with lasting relevance. Instead of contrasting comic and tragic characters or contrasting scenic backdrops, Léger organized contrasting values, lines, and curves. He cited many illustrious forerunners in his efforts, but credited their toying with contrast to a random choice of subjects rather than to a determined plastic organi-

4. FERNAND LÉGER IN HIS STUDIO WITH *COMPOSITION WITH MEDALLION*, 1931. Photo by Choumoff

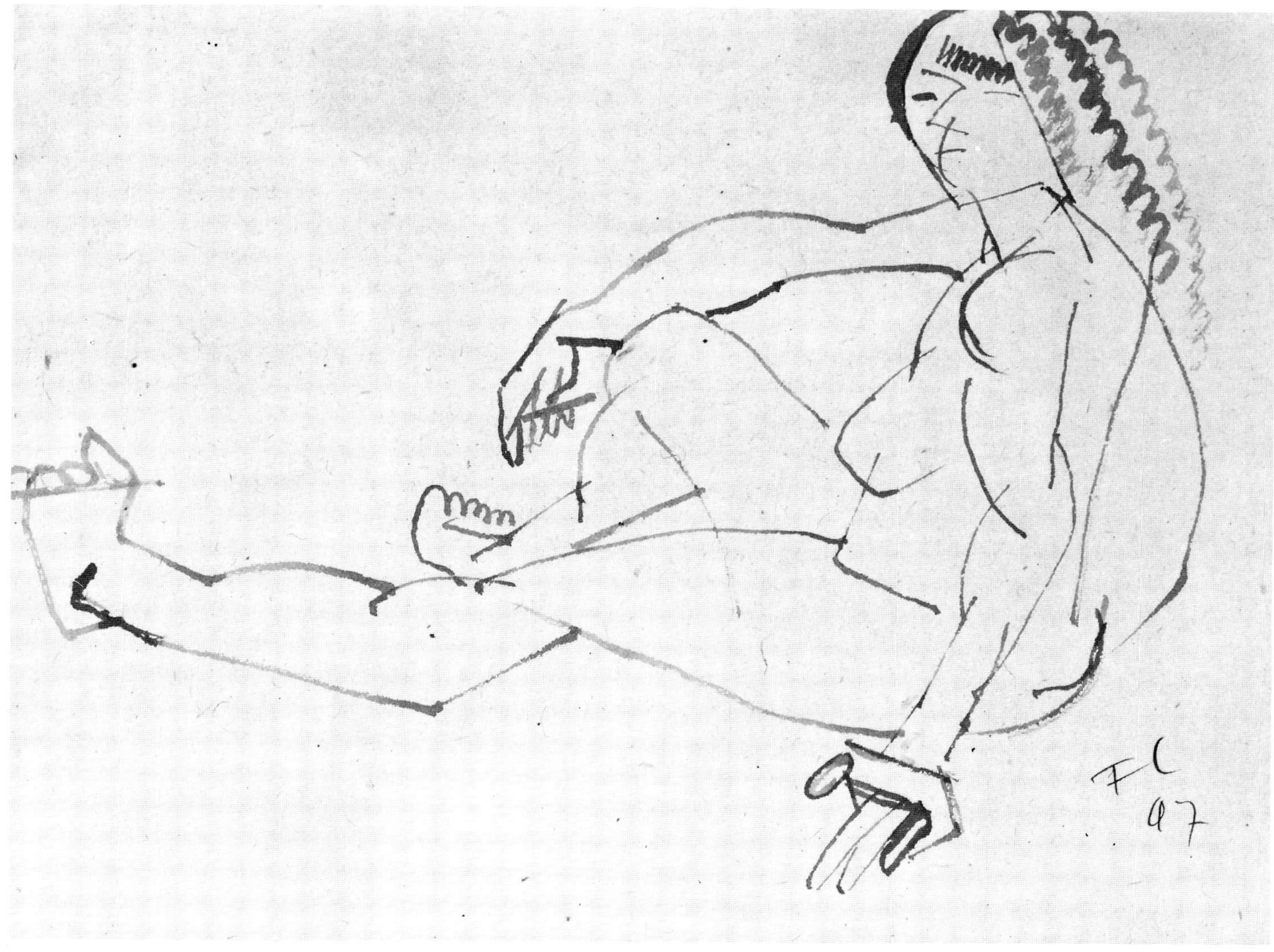


5. SEATED NUDE
1907—Ink on paper, 20.5 × 26.2 cm
Collection of Mr. and Mrs. Adrien Maeght

zation. There is contrast in Giotto and Poussin (the opposition of people and architecture). There is another type of contrast in the paintings of Delacroix when the subject is clearly dominated by plastic expression, in a canvas like *The Crusaders' Entry into Jerusalem* ("L'Entrée des Croisés à Jérusalem"), in particular. A more direct influence on Léger was the contrast in Cézanne, who was the only Impressionist to "clumsily" crush the houses into the trees of his landscapes. "He instinctively knew that was where the truth lay, but he wasn't able to formulate it into a concept," commented Léger.

It was in the footsteps of Cézanne that Léger began to apply what he considered the only method capable of rendering the modern world. He contrasted curves and straight lines, flat surfaces and modulated forms, "pure local colors and nuanced grays," men and machines—It was always a carefully balanced mix, an "equivocal state" between two polarities: that which is real and that which is imagined. "To address the problem by choosing only one of these, to venture into pure abstraction or into imitation, is too easy and avoids the problem in its totality."

For this reason, Léger reacted with surprise and rebellion when his critics accused him of addressing the mechanistic elements in the artistic expression of his times. He justified his method: "Let's take a look at how painting began. I think that they discovered a blue sky and then the white clouds within it and the trees beneath it. Then they painted houses, and then highways with telegraph wires; all of this was painted, and then modern industry created machines. Why at this juncture of human evolution do people start to rant and rave that this must be stopped, that it is forbidden to paint machines or to use them as subject matter? This is absurd."

In his quest for the "shock of contrasts," Léger went directly to the prime sources in the world around him: the esthetics of the machines themselves, the geometric order of streets and cities, the human body looked upon as an object. He found contrast in primary colors, in architecture; he looked at a wall as a

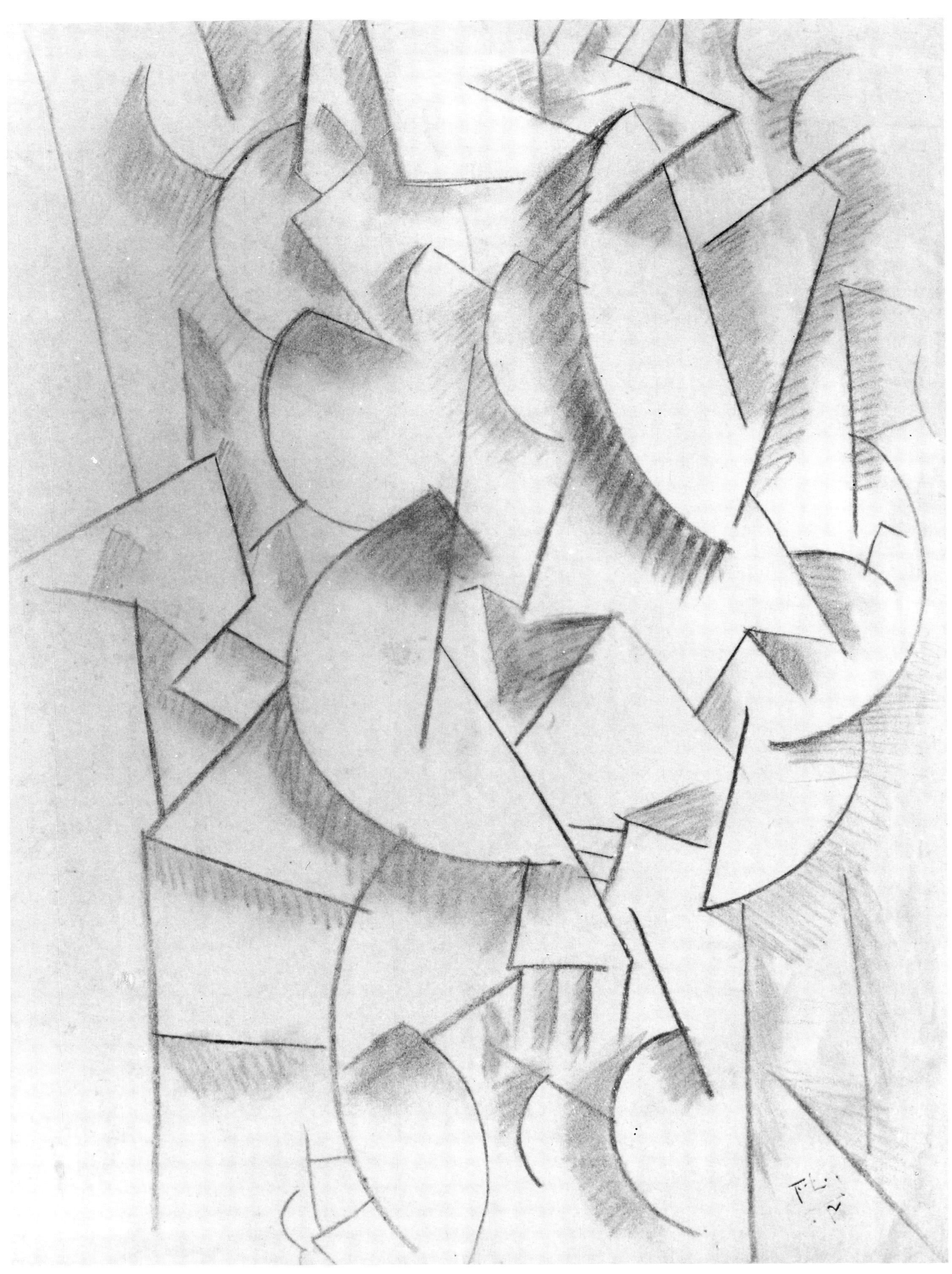

6. COMPOSITION
About 1912—Pencil drawing
Private collection

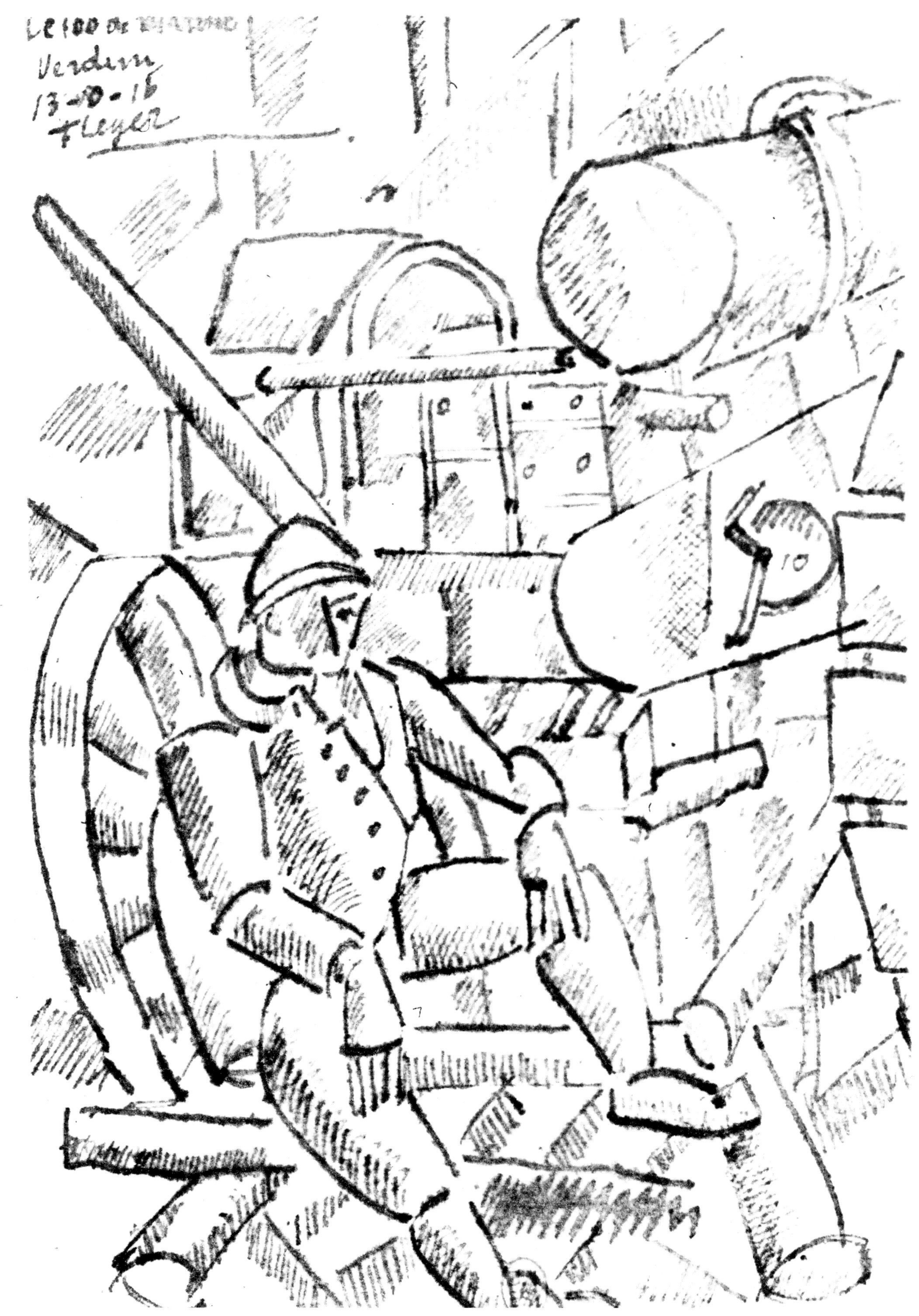


7. THE 100TH MARINE DIVISION, VERDUN, OCTOBER 13, 1916
1916—Ink drawing
Private collection

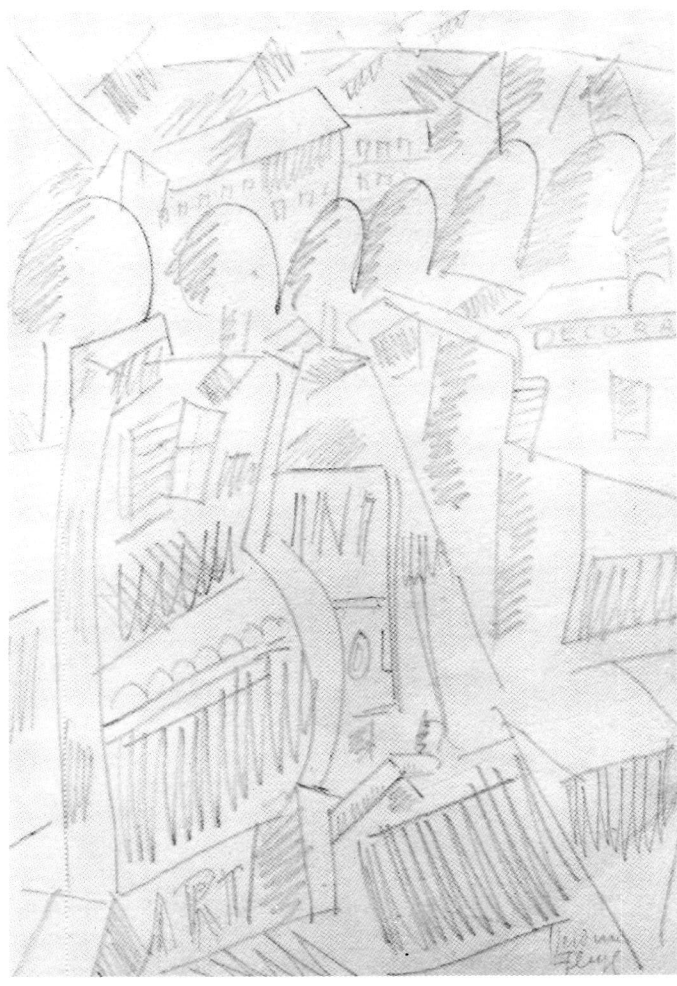


8. VERDUN
1916—Pencil sketch, 19.5 × 14.5 cm
Private collection

9. VERDUN, MAZEL STREET
1916—Pencil sketch, 19 × 14 cm
Private collection

new, vital space. There was contrast in space itself, in the mechanics of motion pictures, in the spectacle of ballet, in the spectacle as "object" and in the object as spectacle.

With Léger, it is futile to draw a line between the two basic orientations of painting: easel painting that arrived during the Italian Renaissance, and mural painting that adapted itself more to architecture. All of Léger's work is monumental. In common pursuit of a "new space," he even worked with Le Corbusier on large-scale murals in primary colors and without subjects. Léger believed that abstract art, synonymous with complete freedom, was problematic for easel painting, but that it had unlimited potential for mural painting. There, too, Léger encountered resistance: the assembly line worker at Renault could not appreciate the wonderful gift that Léger wanted to bestow on him.

Murals that depicted relationships between color and form had no appeal for the worker. Things had not changed all that much since the time when people who could not read or write were educated, and learned to reflect on life, via the figurative stories depicted in frescoes and on the walls of cathedrals and convents. Yet Léger's idea of covering walls with color in order to create a distancing visual effect or an opposite, drawing-in effect (what Léger referred to as "the destruction of the wall" or "the elastic wall") was beyond the scope of the average worker. "Nonetheless, *humanity is the poet,*" blurted out Léger, sorely vexed. "The masses have created slang, a language that is authentic poetry (the bourgeoisie has never invented a single word of slang). Our painting is also slang, but has no contact with this other slang. . . ."

When Vaillant-Couturier, president of the Commission of Fine Arts during the period of the Popular Front, suggested to Léger that he "reveal the riches of art to the common man," Léger went off to Lille in the industrial north to talk on art to the proletariat. "I got there and found about a hundred people in the audience. They were all engineers. Not one worker. The result: a big zero." Léger went on to enumerate all the factors that went against workers having contact with art: museums that closed at five in the evening, the only time when workers could go. On the rare occasions when the museum did stay open late by order of the Ministry, the workers did come,

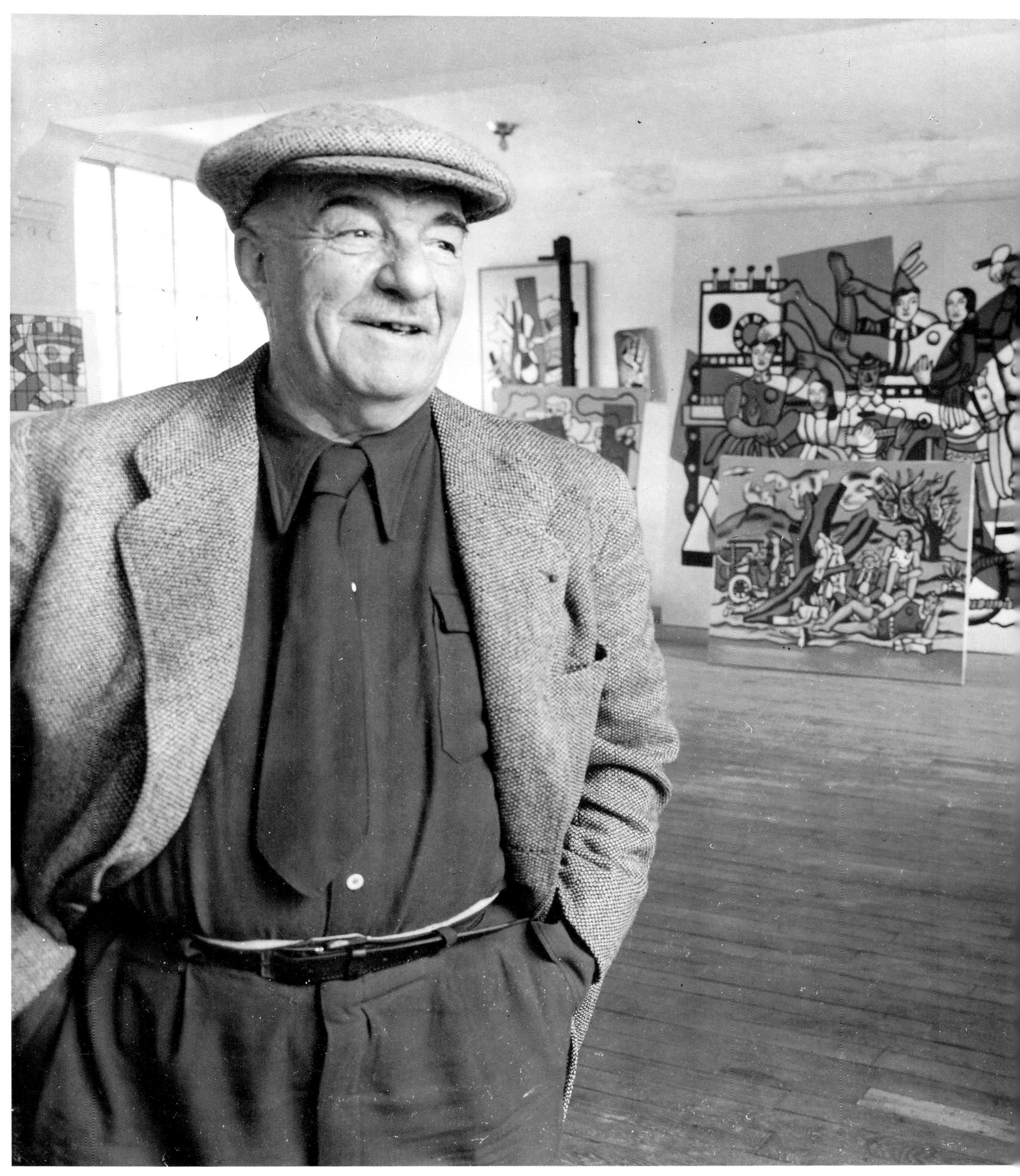

10. FERNAND LEGER IN HIS STUDIO AT GIF-SUR-YVETTE IN FRONT OF *COUNTRY OUTING* (SECOND STAGE) AND *THE BIG PARADE*
1953—Photo by Robert Doisneau

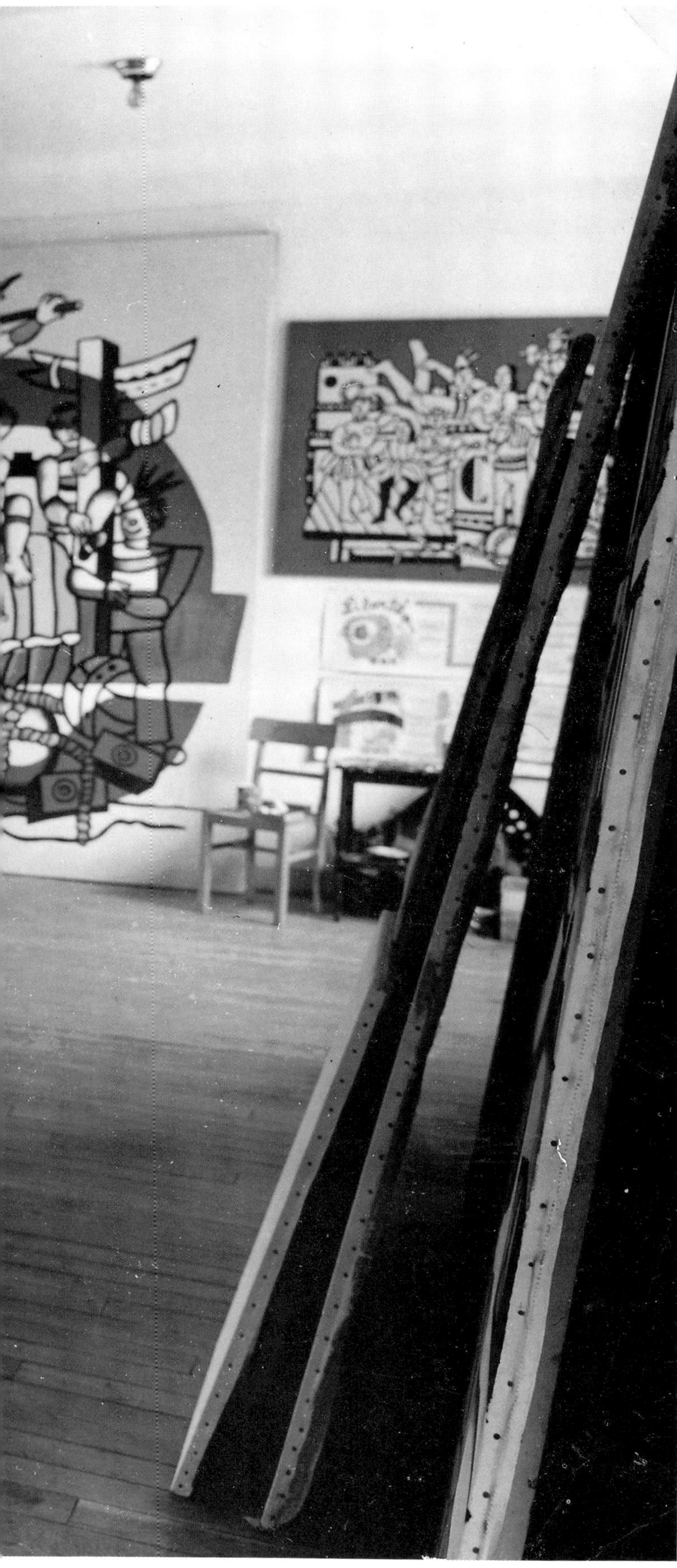

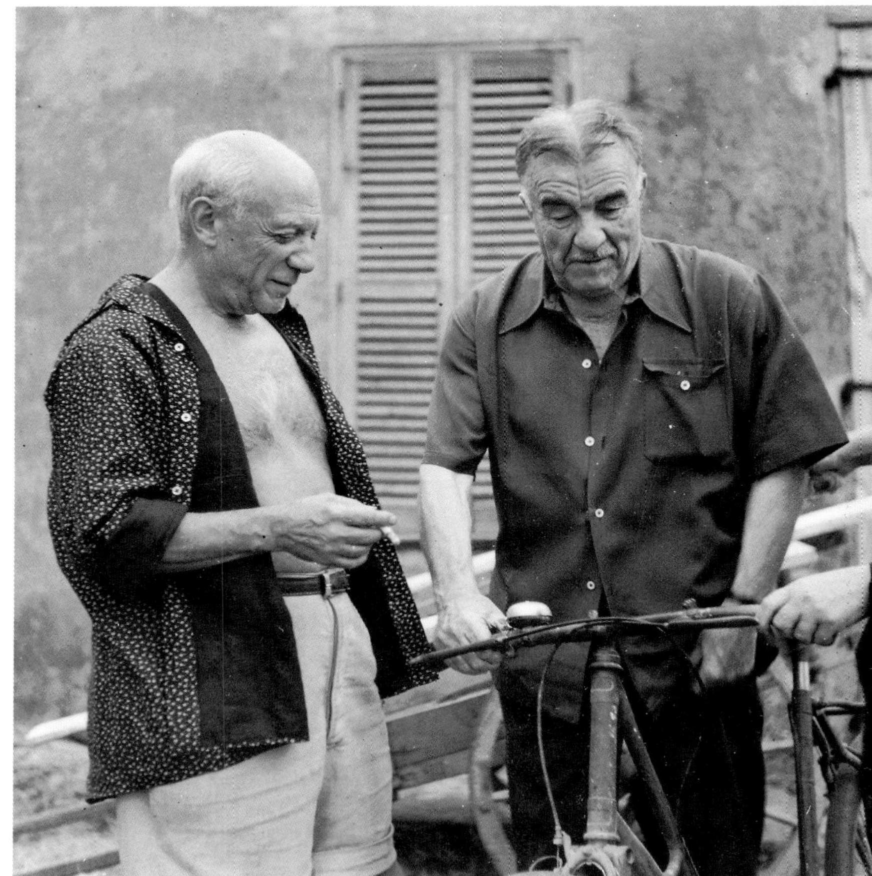

11. LEGER, WITH HIS BIKE, AT PICASSO'S HOME IN VALLAURIS, IN 1952

but they only saw one painting: "They stand in a long line to see the Mona Lisa, who sits there on the wall like a movie star. The result: a big zero." Léger took revenge on the "star" by painting her next to a can of sardines and a set of keys. This was not done to please the Surrealists, but to prove that, for him, the Mona Lisa was just another object. . . There were also "certain mediocre painters" that "throw together some big gimmicks" and "create a stir." The ordinary man judges by comparisons. For such a man, "the best imitated hand is the most beautiful." This was a total travesty, as far as Léger was concerned. Ill. 222

Léger discovered a wealth of new figurative resources, however, when he did set design for film. The most beautiful ornament he found was "the human fragment, the moving close-up of a hand, an eye, a face." He directed the first film, *Le Ballet Mécanique,* without a screenplay. Man Ray's photography was used, and a moving image was the main character. After making a "star" of the machine, Léger noticed that "a human fragment enlarged to one hundred times its real size confronts us with a *new realism* that must be the starting point in modern plastic evolution." The outgrowth of this, of course, was Pop Art, as well as the movement that the critic Restany referred to as the New Realism of Léger, Ill. 138 to 140

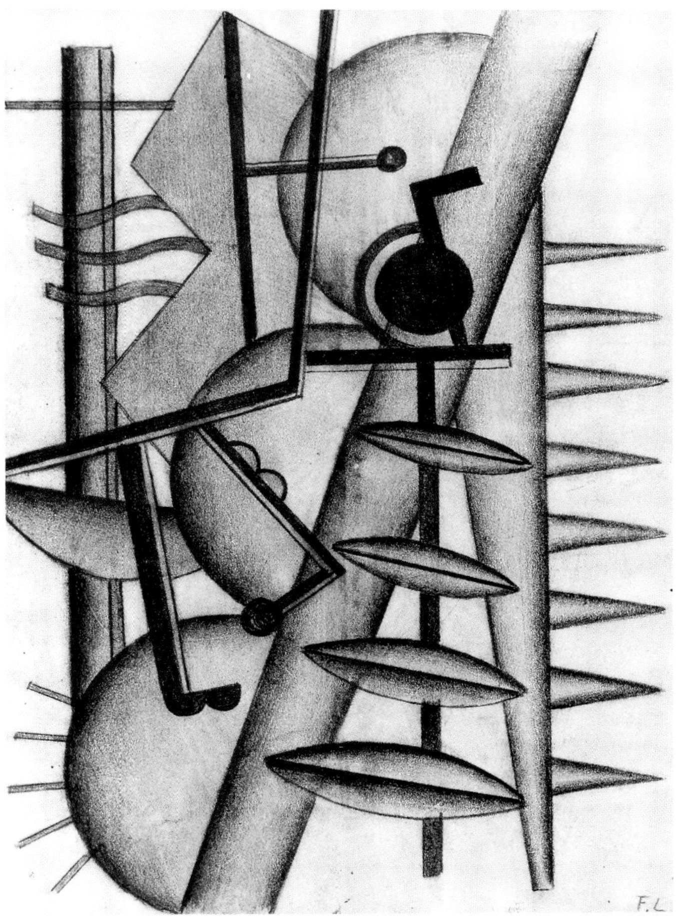

12. MECHANICAL ELEMENTS
Black-lead pencil on paper, 31.9 × 24 cm
Musée National d'Art Moderne, Centre Georges Pompidou, Paris

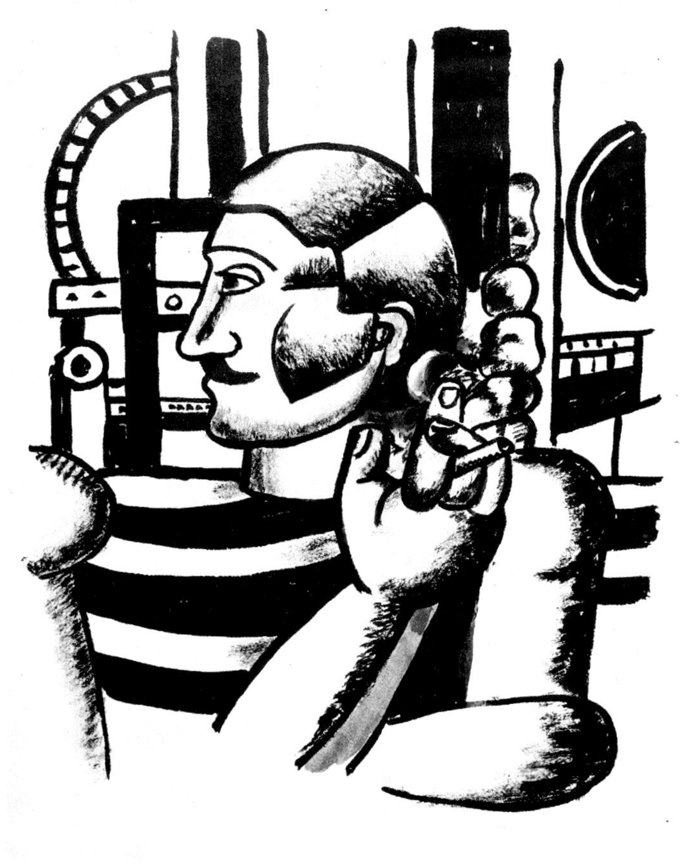

13. THE MECHANIC, STUDY FOR *THE CITY*
1955—wash and drawing, 42 × 32 cm
Private collection

Klein, César, Arman, Tinguely, and others. For Léger (and too bad for the working class and the bourgeoisie) one thing remained certain: modern art was about invention, and not about copying. The Italian Renaissance came the closest to the imitation of nature and was responsible for the confusion. Léger believed that although Michelangelo could sublimely imitate a muscle, and Raphael had a gift for copying a face, neither progress nor a hierarchy in art was achieved by them. "It is not because the artists of the sixteenth century imitated the human form that they were superior to the high periods of Egyptian, Chaldean, Indochinese, Roman, or Gothic art, which interpreted form through stylizing it and not through imitation." Be it poetry or painting, art must be free to invent. It must take us beyond our everyday reality. This is its goal.

Léger went on to affirm his belief in invention by quoting the famous passage from Victor Hugo's *Notre-Dame de Paris,* in the chapter entitled "This Will Kill That": "In the fifteenth century, human thought not only discovered a more durable and resistant architectural form, but another form as well, something even simpler and easier: the letters of Orpheus carved in stone will be replaced by the printed letters of Gutenberg. . . . The book will kill the edifice." Léger felt that the cinema would do in the twentieth century what Gutenberg did in the era of cathedrals, and he questioned the claims made by the over-polished, photographically precise paintings that were in abundance at the French Salon. Film screens were taking over. Visual realism had never been rendered with such intensity before the advent of the first film screen. "With regard to humanity's expession, I don't want to compare what is happening now in science with the revolution that took place at the end of the Middle Ages with the invention of Gutenberg. I do want to mention, however, that modern mechanical marvels such as color photography and cinematography, along with the profusion of pulp novels and the popularization of theaters, are efficiently replacing the development of visual, sentimental, and popular subjects in the figurative arts. They are rendering them obsolete." The working man, dear to Léger, has stopped going to the Louvre, if indeed he has ever gone. Instead of looking at a painting of the marriage of Napoleon and Josephine by David, today people watch Caroline of Monaco's

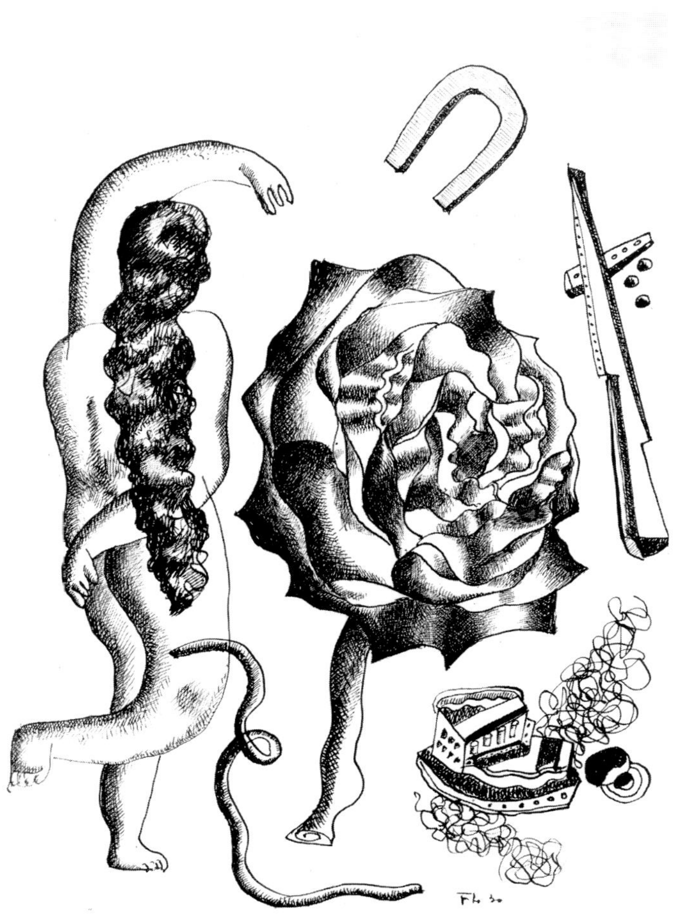

14. WOMAN WITH A ROSE
1930—Pen drawing, 36 × 26 cm
Private collection

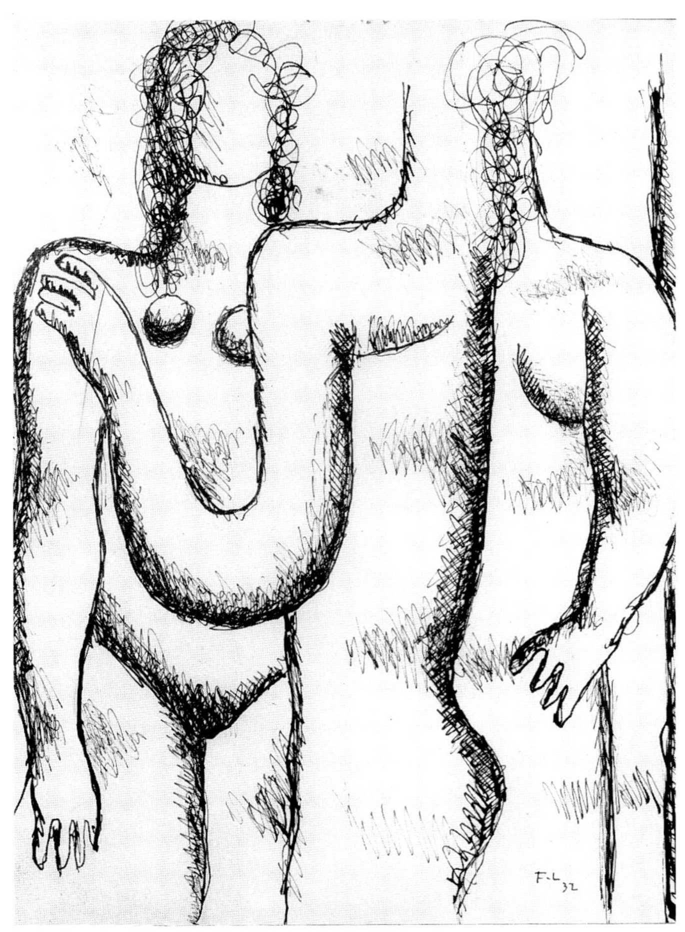

15. TWO FEMALE NUDES
1932—Pen drawing, 17 × 31 cm
Private collection

wedding on television. There is no more need whatsoever for painters like Meissonier or Detaille to illustrate a battle. Television reporters have long since delivered bloodier and more terrifying battle images. Léger believed that modern painting is made up of the harmonious relationship between volume, line, and color. These three elements alone must govern the work of art. If in the harmonization process certain objects or elements of reality find their way into the composition, they can have an enriching effect. They must, however, be subordinate to these three essential elements. The point of view of modern art opposes the academic viewpoint.

Even Léger's machines were invented. "The manufactured object is a polychrome absolute, neat and precise, beautiful as is; it is the most dreadful competition an artist was ever confronted with, but it's so new! I never enjoyed copying a machine. I invent images of machines, like others paint landscapes from the imagination." (Duchamp, who had arrived at the same conclusion, was content to sign manufactured items and thus render them "works of art.") Léger delivered his dreams of machines like a good workman delivers the parts he has made: precise, polished, burnished, in one piece. According to Léger, "Painting is judged in decimeters, and mechanics in tenths of a millimeter." The only difference is the artist's sensitivity in the service of his work. (Duchamp refused to do this, either because he was too lazy, or simply because he preferred to dedicate his time to chess.) Painters were also workers and engineers: "Rousseau is a worker. Cézanne is a little engineer."

When Léger kept returning to his radical concept of the object-form and unintentionally kept offending people by doing so, he admitted that he had no other choice. He interpreted Poussin's *Rape of the Sabine Women* ("L'Enlèvement des Sabines") in terms of abstraction: the "battle of contrasting straight and curved lines" that was so dear to him; the concentration of characters, who are radically contrasted with geometrical elements of construction. The shadow of the painter David was also lurking in the background. Léger dedicated his series entitled *Leisure* Ill. 318 to 325
("Les Loisirs") to David. In "Regarding the Human Form Considered as an Object," Léger wrote: "Without wanting to play the prophet, I see no other way out for art other than *powerful* and human *painting*

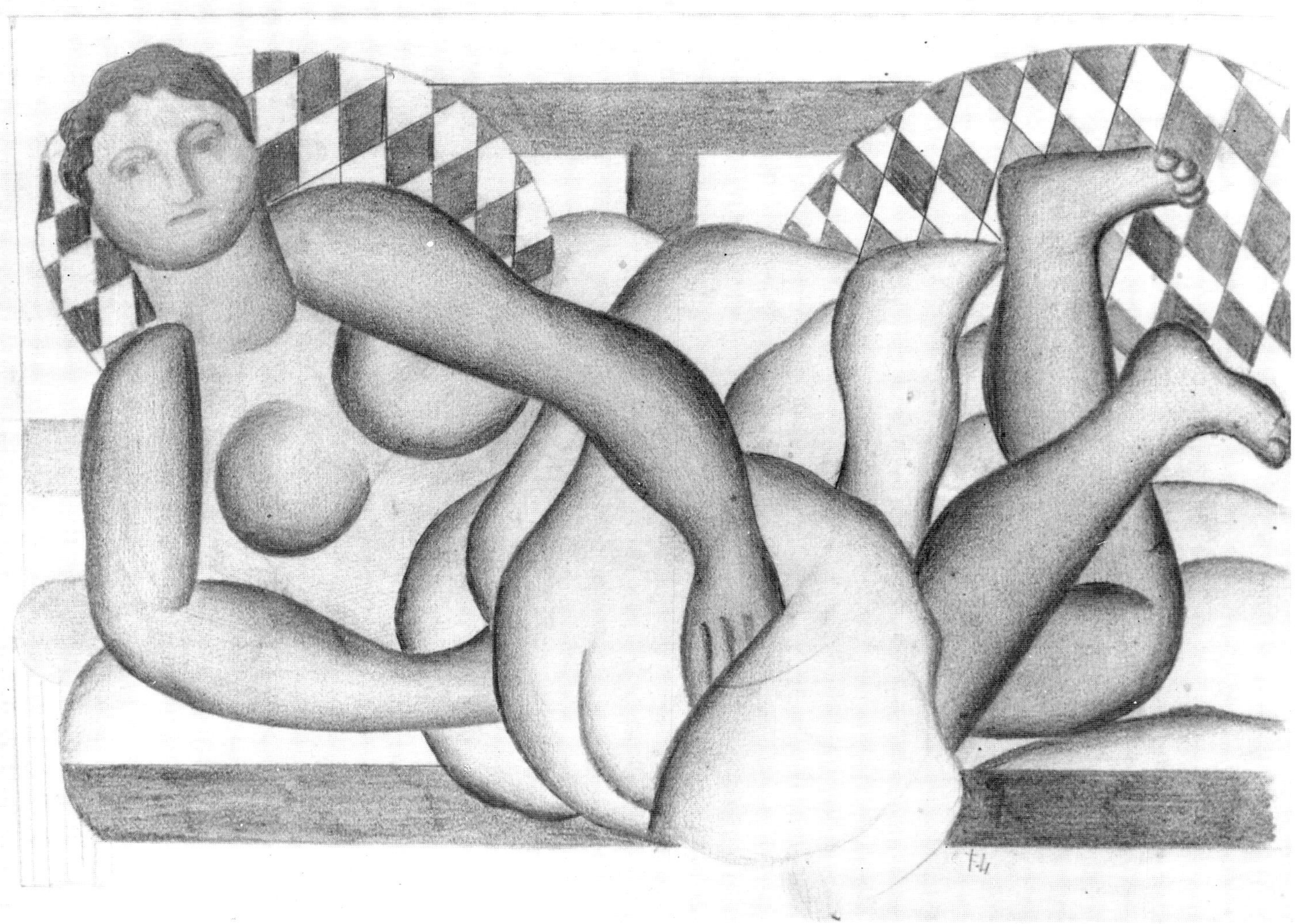

16. WOMAN RECLINING ON A BENCH
1921—Pencil drawing, 79 × 107 cm
Private collection

capable of encompassing all known and new artistic means. This must be carried out in total order and guided by a calm and knowing will." The human form has a purely plastic value in these "powerful paintings." All prior sentimental aspects of it have been eliminated. From the early years beginning in 1905 to the end of his artistic life, Léger's human forms remained deliberately "inexpressive." One can speak of a bicycle or a set of keys in Léger's work in the same way one speaks of his human forms: "the human form has no more importance than a bike or a set of keys. All three are valid artistic objects for me to choose from and use as I wish."
Such words are not far from those of Cézanne: "I want to paint human beings like objects." In his later works, Cézanne achieved a new synthesis of form and setting, and enhanced the monumental presence of the image, as well. The people in his *Card Players* already seem like robots composed of spheres and cylinders. In defining physical traits devoid of obvious individuality, Cézanne was attempting to achieve a characterization of the human type of form. Léger did this with consistency, unity, and power, contrasting the volumes of objects moving in space with architectural and monumental human forms. His point of departure was the individual model. This is evident in his sketches. He ended with a general model, a "standard type." His roots, trees, stones, machines, cyclists, divers, and acrobats were standard models.
The objects are not only "plastically valid" but also often have varying degrees of practicality: "I don't know what is a new subject or what is an old subject; I only know that I have a new way of interpreting it. Trains, cars, and billboards are all good for the application of forms in movement; all my research, as I've often said, comes from the world around me. For a nude model in a studio and thousands of other obvious subjects, it is possible to substitute locomotives and other modern engines that you can't bring into your studio to pose. All of these things are means to an end; what is interesting is the way they're used."
Cinema has a major role in the story of how *object* and pure color became "a valid replacement" for the destroyed *subject*, from the time the Impressionists

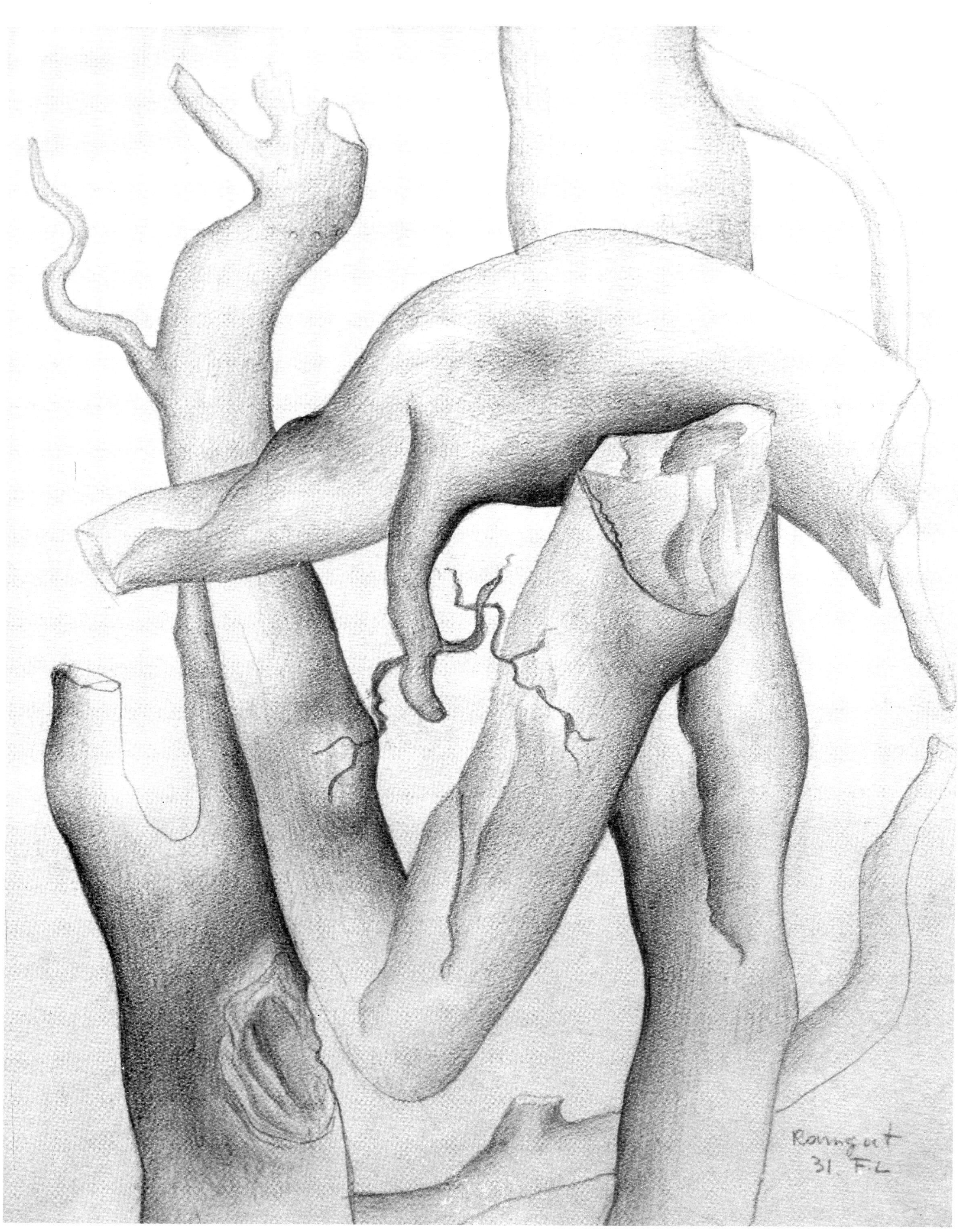

17. BRANCHES
1931—Pencil drawing, 29 × 21.5 cm
Claude Bernard Gallery, Paris

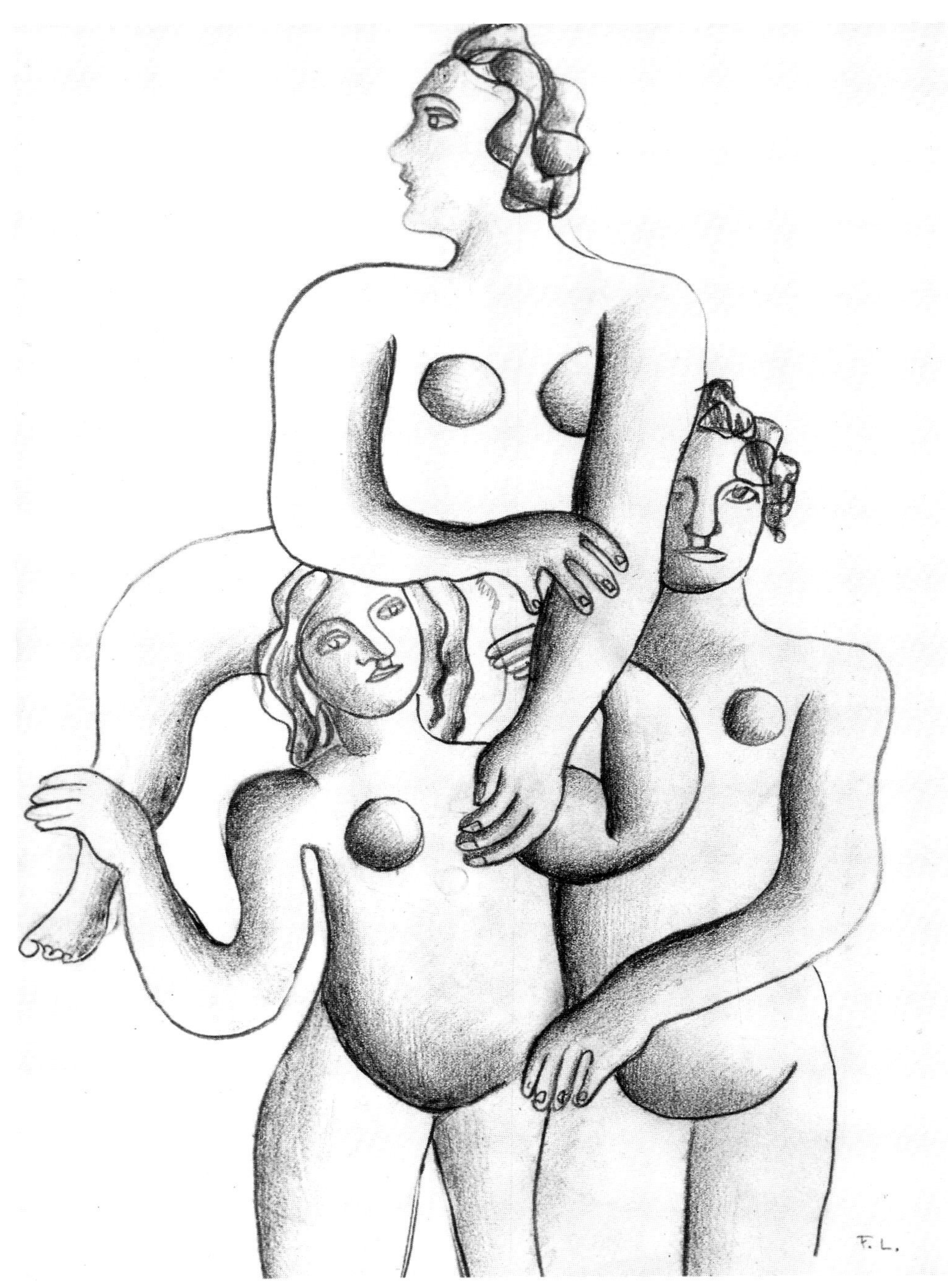


18. THE ACROBATS
1932—Pencil drawing, 36.5 × 26.5 cm
Private collection

chose to favor two tones of green and red instead of a green apple on a red carpet. The film close-up allowed Léger to "accelerate."

In film, Léger projected fragments of the face in close-up onto the screen—an eye, a mouth, a nostril. The film medium allowed him to unleash his artistic interest in the figurative to the point where he actually considered giving up painting to direct full-time, just as Jean Renoir had done. "A foot in a shoe or under a table that is projected ten times its size onto the screen becomes a surprising thing that you've never noticed before," explained Léger. "It takes on a new reality that never existed when you mechanically looked down at the bottom of your leg while walking or sitting. An isolated cloud removed from a blue sky takes on a richness in shape and dimension that can't be seen when it's part of a landscape. Scientific research has enabled artists to release this new reality. Marine plant life, minute animal life, and a drop of water with the microbes magnified thousands of times under the microscope are becoming new pictorial possibilities that have allowed the decorative arts to develop. The outcome is realizing that *everything* is of equal interest, that the human face and body are of no greater plasticf interest than a tree, a plant, a piece of rock, or a rope." This statement is Léger's manifesto. It is the key to the entire body of his work. It is the moving testimony of a

man who decided once and for all to see and celebrate the joys of the modern world.

This did not stop the neophyte standing in front of a Léger painting from asking, "What does this mean?" Picasso once responded to a woman who stood puzzled before one of his own paintings with noses in the middle of cheeks and eyes coming through foreheads: "Madame, do you speak Chinese? No? Well, madame, Chinese can be learned." Léger's desire to educate the masses led him to a more explicit response to this question. He realized that when he composed a picture using fragments of tree bark and a butterfly wing, combined with purely imagined forms, in all probability the public would recognize neither the bark nor the butterfly wing.

In response to the question asked by the public, "Is this an abstract painting?" Léger replied, "No. It is a representational painting. What you refer to as an abstract painting doesn't exist. There is no such thing as 'abstract' and 'concrete.' There are good paintings and bad paintings. There are paintings that move you and paintings that leave you indifferent. One must never judge a painting *through a comparison* of more or less natural elements. A painting has value in itself, just like a musical score or a poem. Reality is infinite and extremely varied."

It was now time for Léger to ask his own "absurd" questions: What is reality? Where does it begin? Where does it end? How much of it should painting contain? To answer these questions, the painter imagined projecting a woman's carefully manicured nail, and made-up eye and mouth, each of which was magnified to one hundred times its actual size. "I would tell one person that it represented a fragment of planetary evolution. To another person, I would say: It is an abstract form. Both would be surprised and enthusiastic and would take my word as truth. Then I would tell them: No, what you have

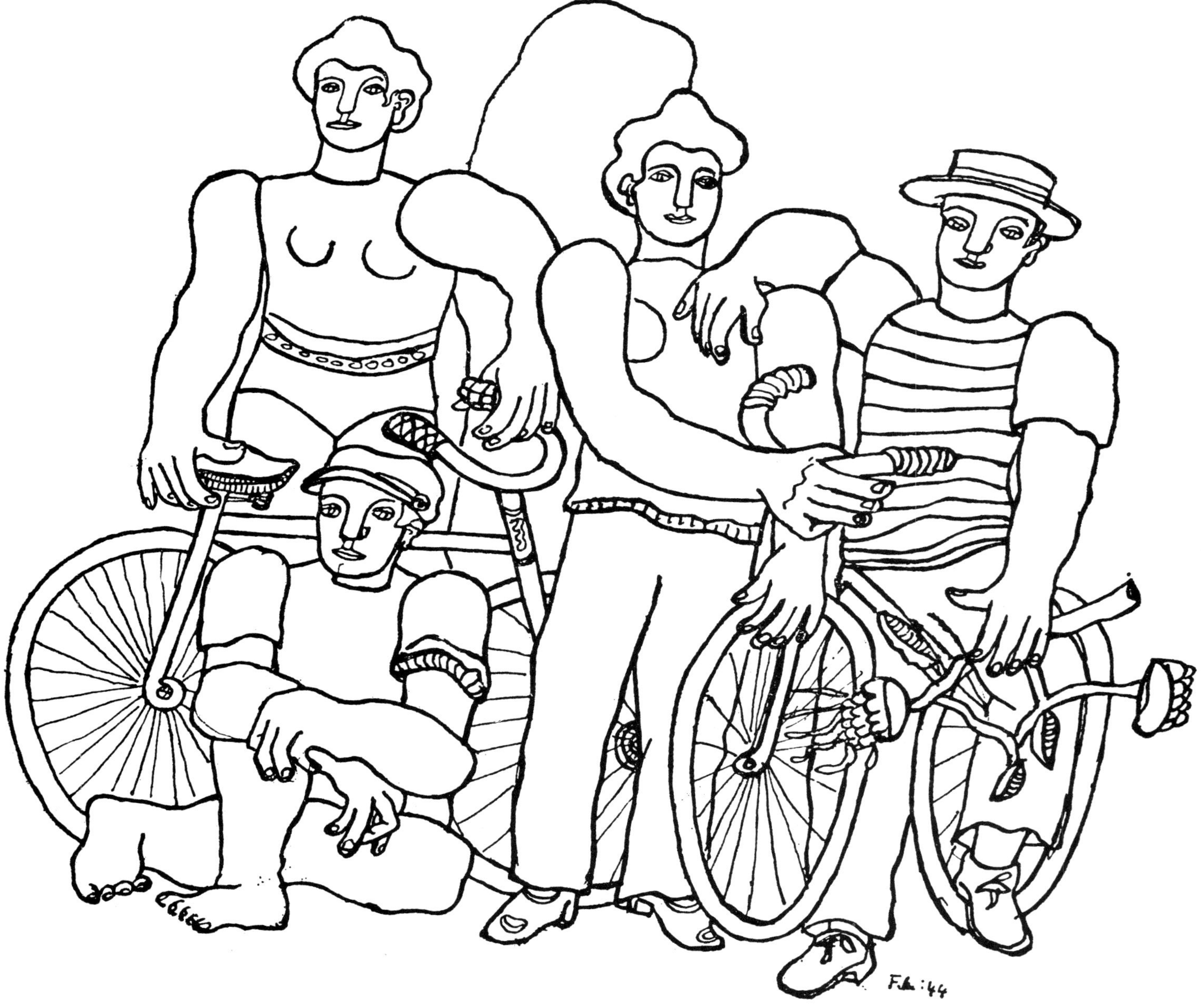


19. THE CYCLISTS
Invitation card for the opening of the Fernand Léger Exhibit
National Gallery of the Grand Palais, Paris, October 15, 1971

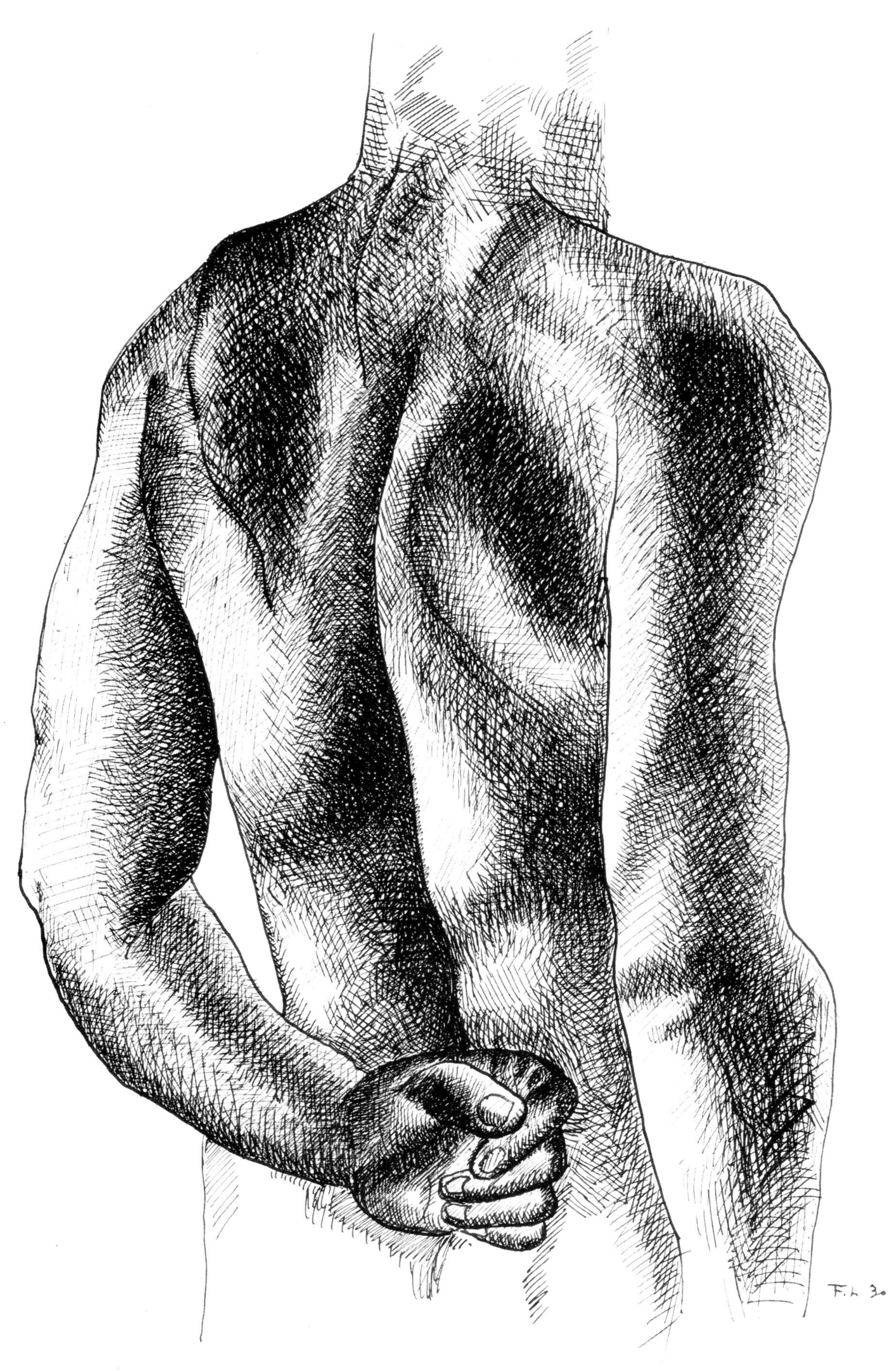

20. MALE NUDE FROM BEHIND
1930—China ink drawing, 37 × 26 cm
Private collection

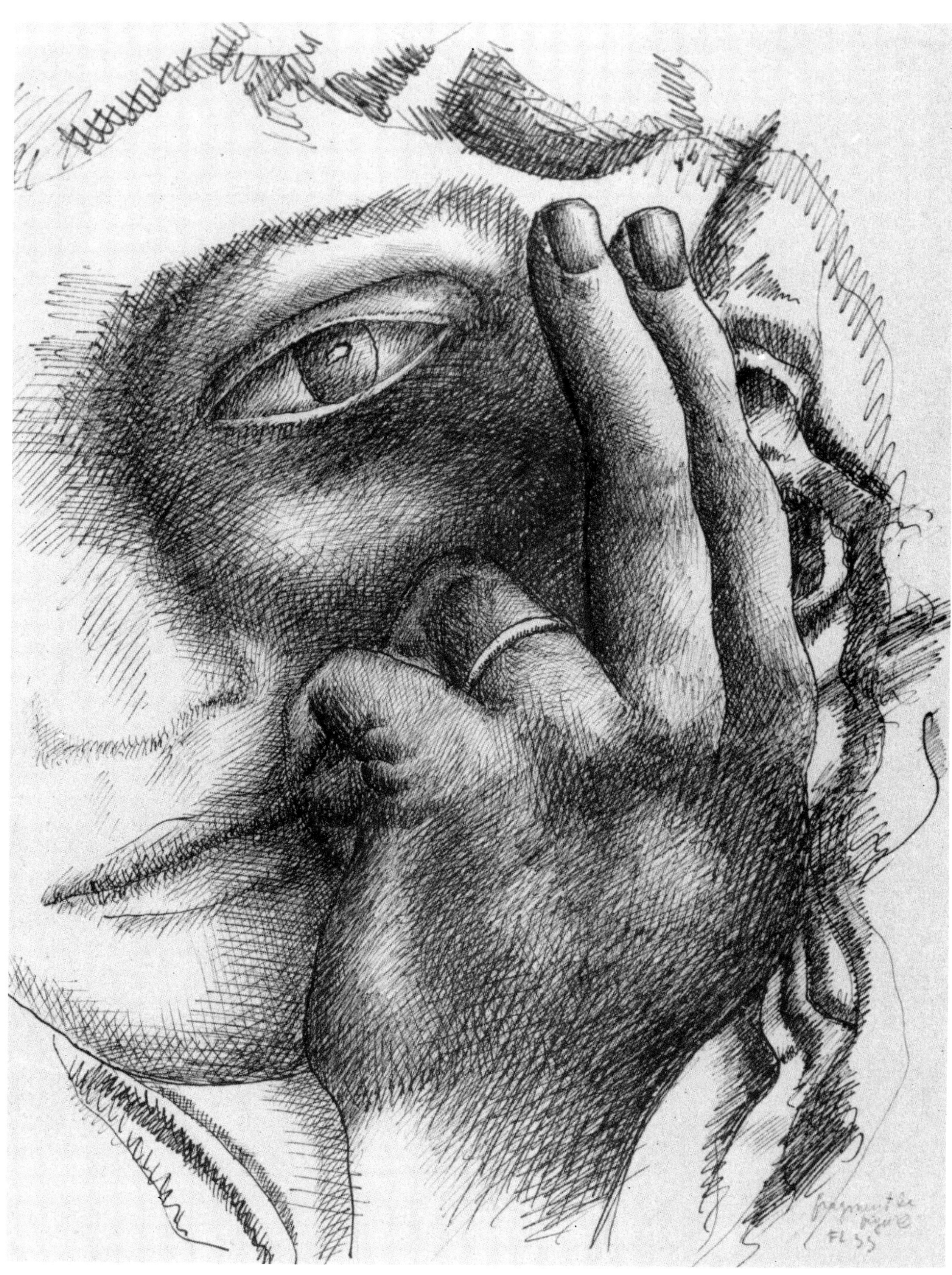

21. FRAGMENT OF A FACE
1933—China ink drawing, 33.5 × 30.5 cm
Private collection

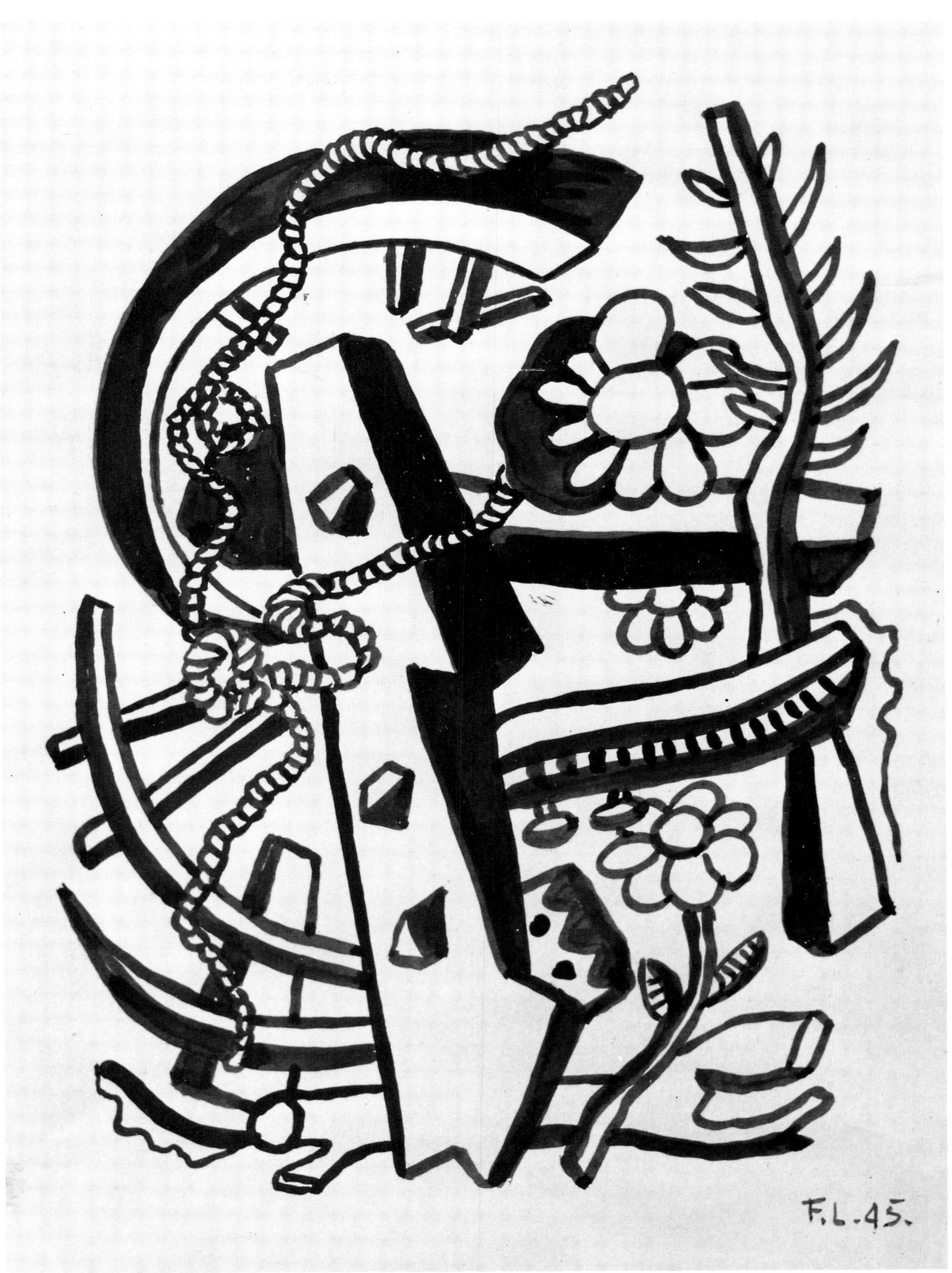


22. LANDSCAPE WITH ROPE
1945—China ink, 33 × 27 cm
Private collection

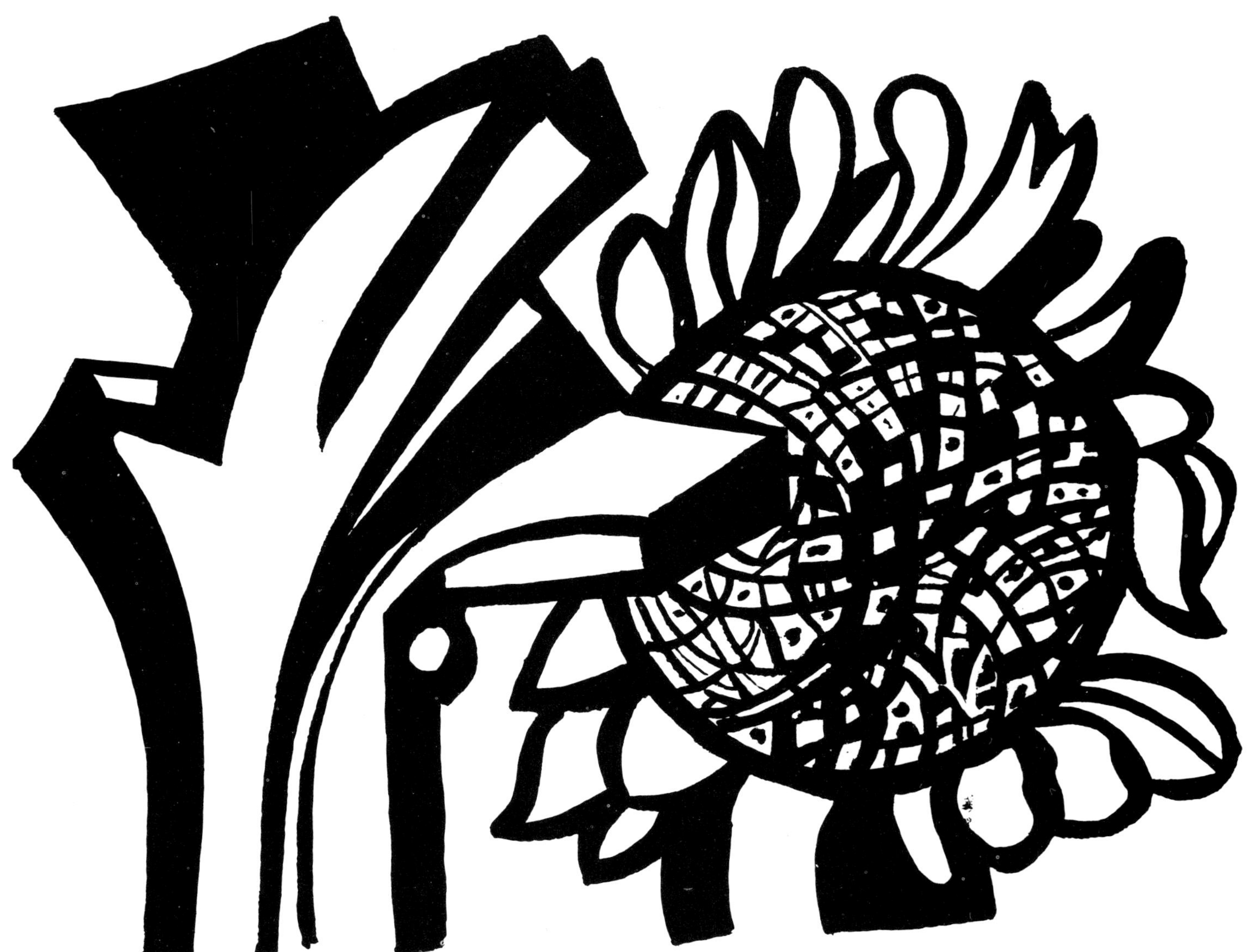

23. SUNFLOWER
About 1952—China ink, 41 × 50 cm

been looking at is the nail on my wife's left pinky. These two people would go away annoyed or chagrined, but would never again ask the question, What does this represent?"

Beauty was everywhere for Léger, whether it was in objects, in fragments, or in purely invented forms. One must simply "learn Chinese." In other words, one must develop one's sensitivity to be able to distinguish what is beautiful from what is not beautiful. Intelligence, like logic, has no role in this. Léger quoted the French physicist Jean Perrin who once told him that "pure sensitivity accounts for as much as 80 percent of all our scientific discoveries."

Color was the other favorite source for Léger's panoply of objects, which are always more or less the same and which he relentlessly deformed, abstracted, multiplied, magnified, and incorporated into his compositions. Unlike André Malraux, who preferred white, Léger was unfailing in his championing of color. He wanted to repaint entire cities in color: a red street, a yellow street, a blue lane, a white avenue, some polychrome monuments. . . "While travelling by sea I would often stand at the ship's rail and stare out over the immense watery surface. I often thought of how surprising it would be to see a luminous and colored sea serpent more than a hundred meters long suddenly emerge." In the United States, Léger's discovery of shop windows, displays, traffic lights, and illuminated signs was the realization of his dream. Just like his friend Le Corbusier, Léger considered a naked wall a "dead surface," which, when colored, became "a living surface." Before one could transform the walls it would be necessary to "liberate" color. "Color is as essential to life as water and fire. People have associated color with joy, action, and pleasure from time immemorial and are therefore prepared to receive it. People bring flowers full of color into their homes, and parrots, dresses, hats, and makeup, too."

Léger exerted great energy in liberating color, and

Puisque la terre
est ronde..
Comment voulez-vous
jouer carré?
Depuis la tête d'un homme
et le corps d'une femme
et la forme
d'un arbre
qui s'inscrivent dans un
Jeu de courbes

24. EXCERPT FROM THE BOOK *THE CIRCUS*

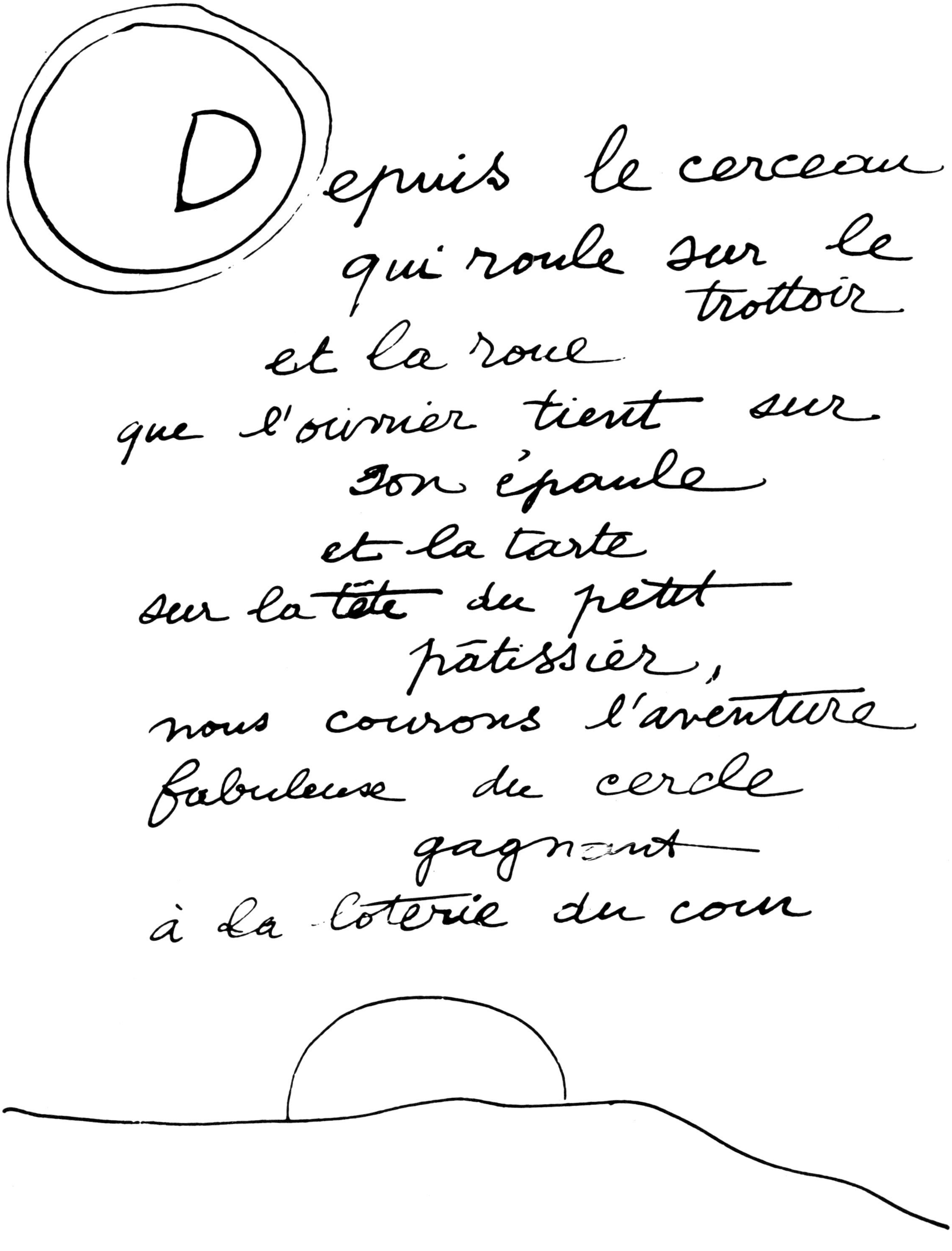

Depuis le cerceau
qui roule sur le
trottoir
et la roue
que l'ouvrier tient sur
son épaule
et la tarte
sur la tête du petit
pâtissier,
nous courons l'aventure
fabuleuse du cercle
gagnant
à la loterie du coin

25. EXCERPT FROM THE BOOK *THE CIRCUS*

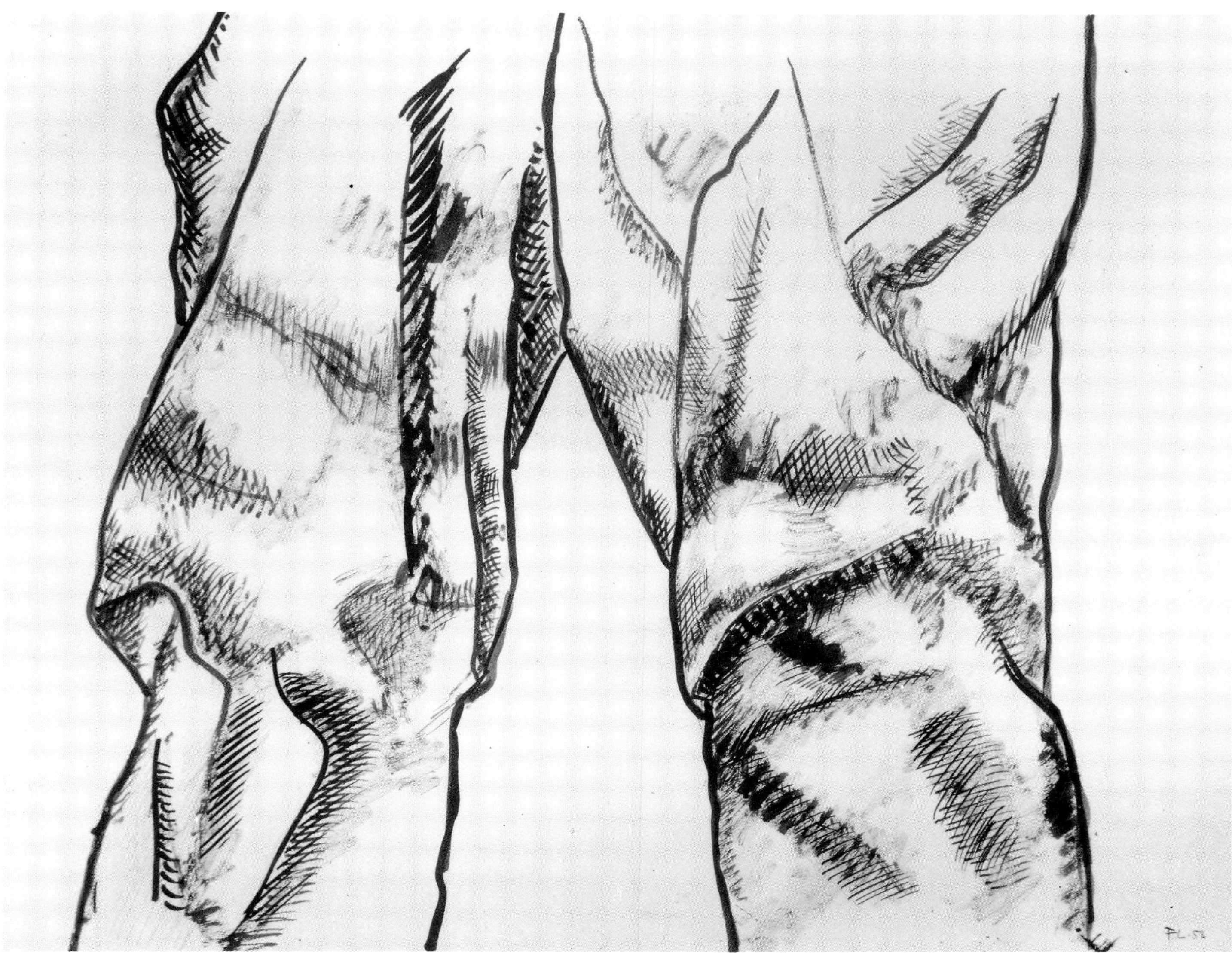

26. STUDY OF LEGS FOR *THE BUILDERS*
1951—Pen drawing, 50 × 64 cm

towards its rational use of serving humanity in the twentieth century. First, through his painting. With
Ill. 41 *Woman in Blue* ("La Femme en bleu") painted in
Ill. 92 1912, pure color is inscribed in a geometric form. In 1919 he painted *The City* ("La Ville") using only unmixed, flatly applied colors. He said of this painting, "Technically it is an artistic revolution. In it I achieved depth and dynamism, and I did it without chiaroscuro or modulation. Advertising was the first to adopt the results of this. Pure colors—reds, blues, and yellows—have escaped from the canvas and are slipping onto billboards, into display windows, onto signs that line the highways, and into traffic signals. Color has been liberated. It is a self-contained reality. Color has a new action that is completely independent of the objects that before now had been responsible for containing or carrying it."

Léger was clearly aware of the importance of what he was doing and of the ensuing consequences. Before him, Cézanne was intimately aware of the geological nature of his painted landscapes. Cézanne had said, "I am the first to arrive on the path that I discovered." Léger, clearly conscious of the implications of "constructive" color, took great pleasure in paraphrasing Cézanne: "I am the first in an era that has not yet arrived."

It was Léger's persistent intention that this revolution should benefit the average person. Through the work of architects like Mallet-Stevens and Le Corbusier, he hoped that buildings and factories would soon reflect this new liberty of color. He proudly cited the example of a depressingly dark factory in Rotterdam that was rebuilt according to the new criteria of color, light, and transparency: "This is what happened. . . Without anyone saying a word to the factory workers, their outward appearance started to change. They looked cleaner, took better care of themselves. They had unconsciously realized that an important event had taken place. They were entering a new phase of existence. The interplay of color and light went far beyond the surface. When rationally developed, color and light can transform

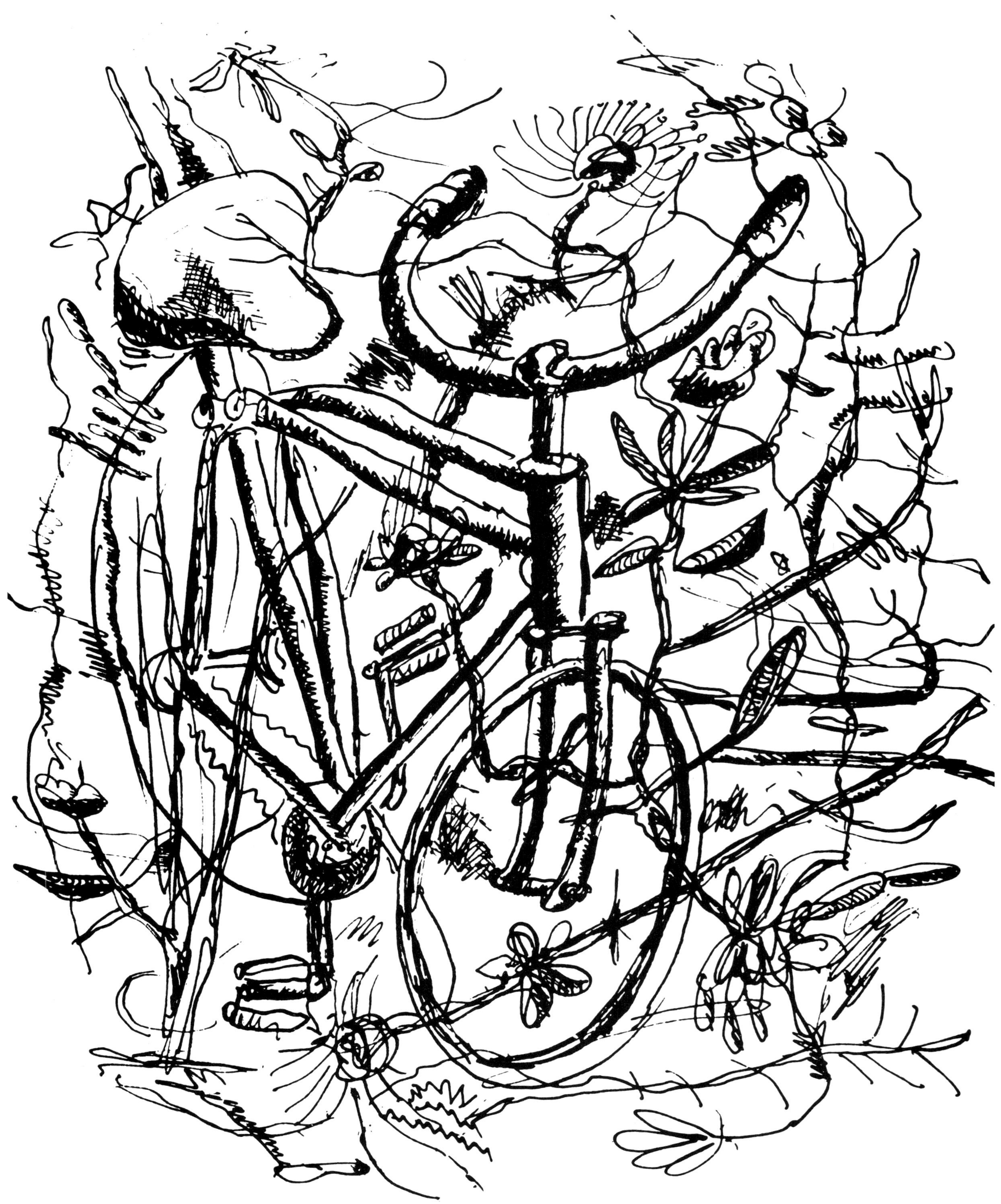

27. DRAWING FROM THE BOOK *THE CIRCUS*

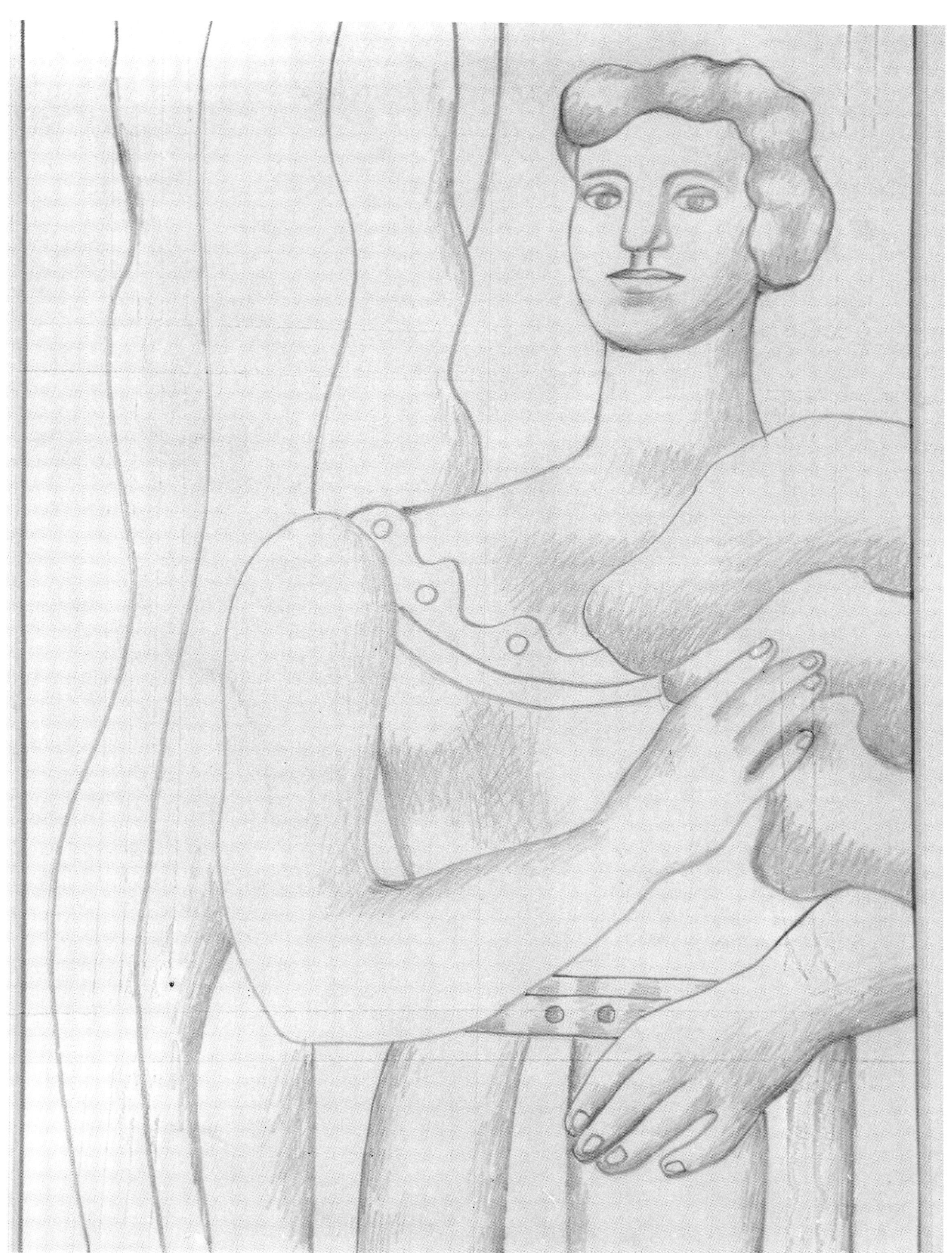

28. WOMAN WITH A SCARF, NO. 3
1945—Pencil drawing, 65 × 50 cm
Private collection

an entire society." Léger's quest went as far as the possibility of "polychrome hospitals" where diseases could be cured through colors— peaceful greens and blues for nervous disorders, yellow rooms for those who were depressed, red rooms for those suffering from anemia. Alas, the era in which painting is reimbursed by medical insurance has still not arrived. Like all good magicians, Léger tried to decorate the monotony of everyday reality with distracting elements of festivity and circus life. In addition to being a great artist, he doubled as a great utopian. He dreamed of being a conductor of great architectural feats with an orchestra of colors to edify new monuments and express people's needs and desires. He hoped in this way to achieve an equilibrium of new "plastic forces." The danger in this dream lay in the fact that he assumed his utopian idea of happiness for the people was their idea as well. This presumptuous attitude was the Orwellian "Big Brother" aspect in Léger's personality. The same trait was also clearly apparent in his friends, those of "L'Esprit Nouveau" and "Purism." Take, for example, Le Corbusier, for whom people and things could be reduced to equations.

Le Corbusier developed a type of "man-machine" to inhabit his "modulars," which were units conceived as boxes for his "Radiant City" ("Ville radieuse"). In 1923 he wrote in *Towards an Architecture* ("Vers une architecture"): "The art of our time is in its proper place when it is addressed to the elite. Art is not for the masses, and even less a prostitute of wealth; art is uniquely a fuel for the elite who must join together to become a guiding force; art essentially belongs to the subject of composition." In this particular context, the notion of a "guide" conjures up dark memories of tyranny, "guides" who were to take charge in Germany, Russia, and China.

When Léger returned to France from visiting New York in the 1930s, his desire to color cities was stronger than ever. "Fifth Avenue, Red; Madison Avenue, Blue; Park Avenue, Yellow. . . ." He went so far with this idea as to propose "forcing clothes merchants to sell entire lines of suits and dresses in green" to compensate for the lack of greenery. Pedestrians would become a sort of ambulatory vegetation. In his *Function of Painting,* he dictated colors of the week or the season: a blue quarter, a pink fortnight! Dictator of color is an unfortunate choice of words for a utopian.

Not since the Middle Ages had the world been so inundated with color. Léger felt the anarchic potential of color, and also, no doubt, the need to control it like a dictator, a "dictator of art." (During the Reign of Terror, at the end of the eighteenth century, the "dictatorship of art" was in the hands of David.) "Streets and countrysides, as well as the gentle and melodious landscapes of the Impressionists, were all of a sudden invaded by billboards advertising

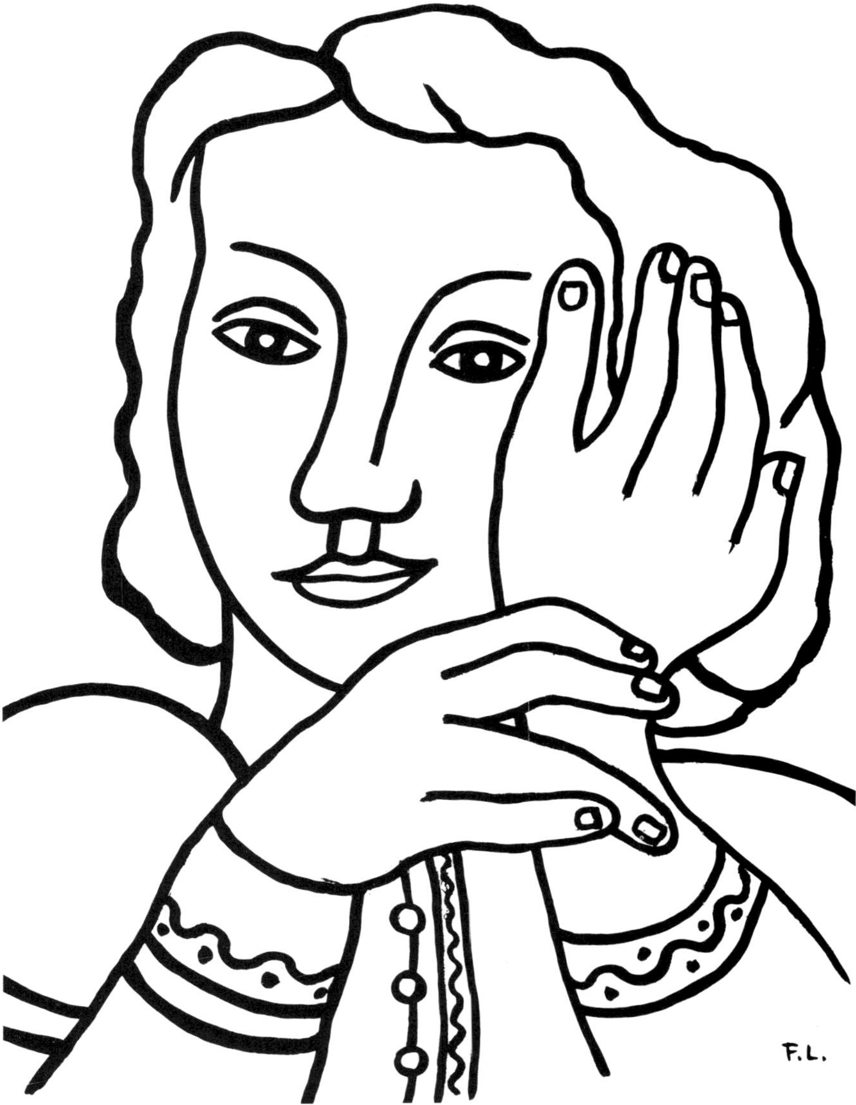


29. PORTRAIT OF NADIA
About 1948—Ink drawing, 65 × 50 cm
Musée National Fernand Léger, Biot

Dubonnet. These billboards broke the melody by cutting into the trees and blocking the clouds. We live in a totally contrasted landscape, and it is the environment of our time." Léger could be ironic, but there was also a hint of hypocrisy in his efforts to shun responsibility: "Art critics have said that one of these days the environmentalists are going to condemn me, because I'm the one who unleashed all this color into the environment. But I have nothing to do with it. Sure, there are a lot of strong colors in my paintings, and I have a lot of students who earn their livings by making posters and displays for windows. I, however, have never done a poster or a display window. I didn't know that the street was my element!"

Léger seemed to take pleasure in portraying himself as a decent fellow: "It has nothing to do with the publicity I've gotten. It's just that the advertising business jumped on the idea of primary colors and used it for commercial purposes. . . ." Léger relentlessly furrowed a path with his "imagery": from

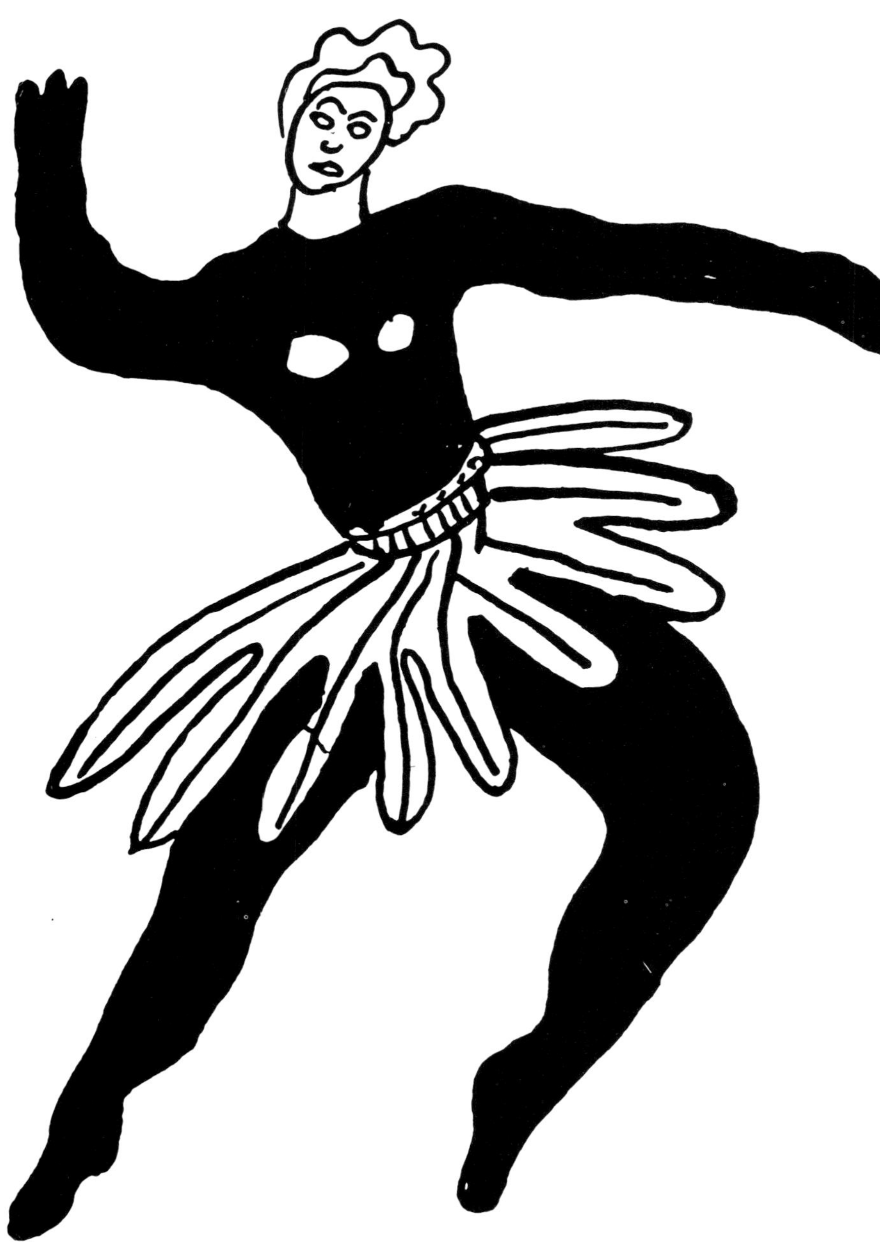

30. DRAWING FROM THE BOOK *THE CIRCUS*

"Cubism" to "Tubism," from "contrasting forms" to "mechanical elements," from "animated landscapes" to "country outings," from the poetics of machinery to the robotics of people, and to the "purism" of objects expressed in monumental style with primary colors. A whole variety of both European and American contemporary art came out of Léger's new language. Nothing was the same. His passage through art radically transformed so many visual habits that he left many disoriented and even hostile people in his tracks.

The public strongly disliked *The Builders* ("Les Constructeurs") with its little men strewn about the steel beams of buildings in progress. These paintings cannot be understood without knowing that they are a direct outcome of Léger's cult worship of the object and of color. Léger realized that his work would continue to be misunderstood by the humble masses whose happiness his art aspired to create. Ill. 311

Despite this, Léger was the clearest communicator of the mini-revolutions that continue to filter through contemporary art. "I'm taking away the table that Braque and Picasso kept. . . . Separate objects that the choice of color makes retreat or advance over the canvas, along with background color, create a new space through movement without the effect of perspective: space is an imagined space, which comes out of rhythm. It is up to the painter to vary the rhythms and colors in order to obtain the desired expression. A transparent space can be suggested by keeping distinct lines and colors. In *The Builders* I tried to achieve more violent contrast by contrasting human figures against clouds and metal structures. I don't know if I succeeded, but I think it was worth it to stir up a brawl."

With his broad shoulders and chiseled face, Léger's peasant appearance made it easy to believe that he was more capable of getting into a fight than of teaching in American universities and writing splendidly on art. He certainly was not opposed to Dalí's type of provocation, but his intention did not have the commercialism of Dalí's soft clocks. Léger used provocation to get his ideas on modern art out. Then he would hammer them in like nails, nails of his own forging.

His statements did have shock value, but above all they were intended to explain what he was doing. He made it clear in *The Function of Painting* that he preferred a state of war to a state of peace. Was this an effective means of getting his point across?: "It depends, of course, on how you look at it. You're either the hunter or the game. If I look at it from the sentimental point of view, I am a monster. I have chosen throughout my life to ignore the sentimental viewpoint. It is an unbearable piece of baggage for anyone in the plastic area. It is an opiate with negative effects, like rhyme in poetry. If I confront life's possibilities face to face, it is because I prefer

what is referred to as the 'warrior viewpoint.' For me, that simply means *life at an accelerated rhythm.* A state of peace is a slowed-down pace, a type of situation where you sit tight indoors behind closed shutters. Everything is taking place in the streets, however, and that's where the *artist* belongs."

From two men transporting large golden letters to be placed above a store, to the latest in elegant fashions parading up and down, the spectacle of modern life was to be found everywhere on the streets. It was in the movies, in the music halls, in the circuses, at the ballet, and at the street fairs where the working class wandered about in search of a distraction from the everyday dreariness: "They flock to this kind of event like flies to light. It is a prime source of fascination for them. It puts them into an inebriated state, somewhere between the state you get into from sitting around at a café and the way you feel when you take drugs. Something inside people, too, leads them to seek out these events. It's something more obscure, but very real; a need for Beauty."

Léger retained a lesson he had learned from the acrobats: "There are more 'figurative passages' in ten minutes of an acrobatic performance than in several scenes of a ballet. . . . Most of the acrobats have the same gracefulness as the dancers, but they know that the streets surrounded by houses and buildings can provide us with a grace and charm that have nothing to do with the curving sweep of arms, pliés, and dainty smiles." The tumblers and mountebanks also played with objects. What could be more perfect than the plastic value of a luminous and colored wheel, sphere, or juggler's ball? What could be more beautiful than the contrast between ten phosphorescent yellow acrobats somersaulting across a stage against a sumptuously colored, static background?

In Léger's world—our world, if we merely open our eyes—bicycles come to life like "willful animals that refuse to move forward or backward and that people must reckon with." "Go to the circus," Léger advised. "Leave your rectangles and geometric windows behind, and enter the world of moving circles. . . . The round form is a free form. It has neither beginning nor end."

Was Léger the painter of the people he so wanted to give happiness to? Today's average person still does not know him, even if the world he or she inhabits is colored with the traces of Léger's brushwork. André Malraux predicted that the twenty-first century would be a religious one. Léger wanted it to be one of *beauty.* "It is a religion like any other one. I think it is useful and beautiful. . . . Our eyes, which for centuries have remained closed to realistic beauty and to the objective phenomena that surround us, are now starting to open: something is ending and something else is beginning. We are at a crossroads, in the middle of a transition that is cruel and thankless, and where every possible mistake and reaction come into play. But in this total confusion of desire and error, there's one certitude: the cult of Beauty. I confront this with the theories that Ozenfant held dear: the demand for what is Beautiful is present everywhere on a daily basis. No doubt about it. It has reached the point of obsession. Seventy-five percent of the details and gestures of everyday life are concerned with Beauty, and we need to become aware of this. We need things to be organized, from the spaces we live in to the discrete way a lock of hair is adjusted under a hat. The desire for harmony penetrates our lives. . . . This is no vague prophecy. We can already touch tomorrow's reality. We are quite clearly moving towards a society in which frenzy has no place, where calm and order exist, and where we know how to live in Beauty without the need for romantic hyperbole."

There is no doubt that Léger made the beauty of the modern world visible. Guillaume Apollinaire, also a great poet of modern times and a contemporary of Léger's, affirmed early on, "When I look at a painting by Léger I feel very good." Léger has indeed been able to give happiness to people.

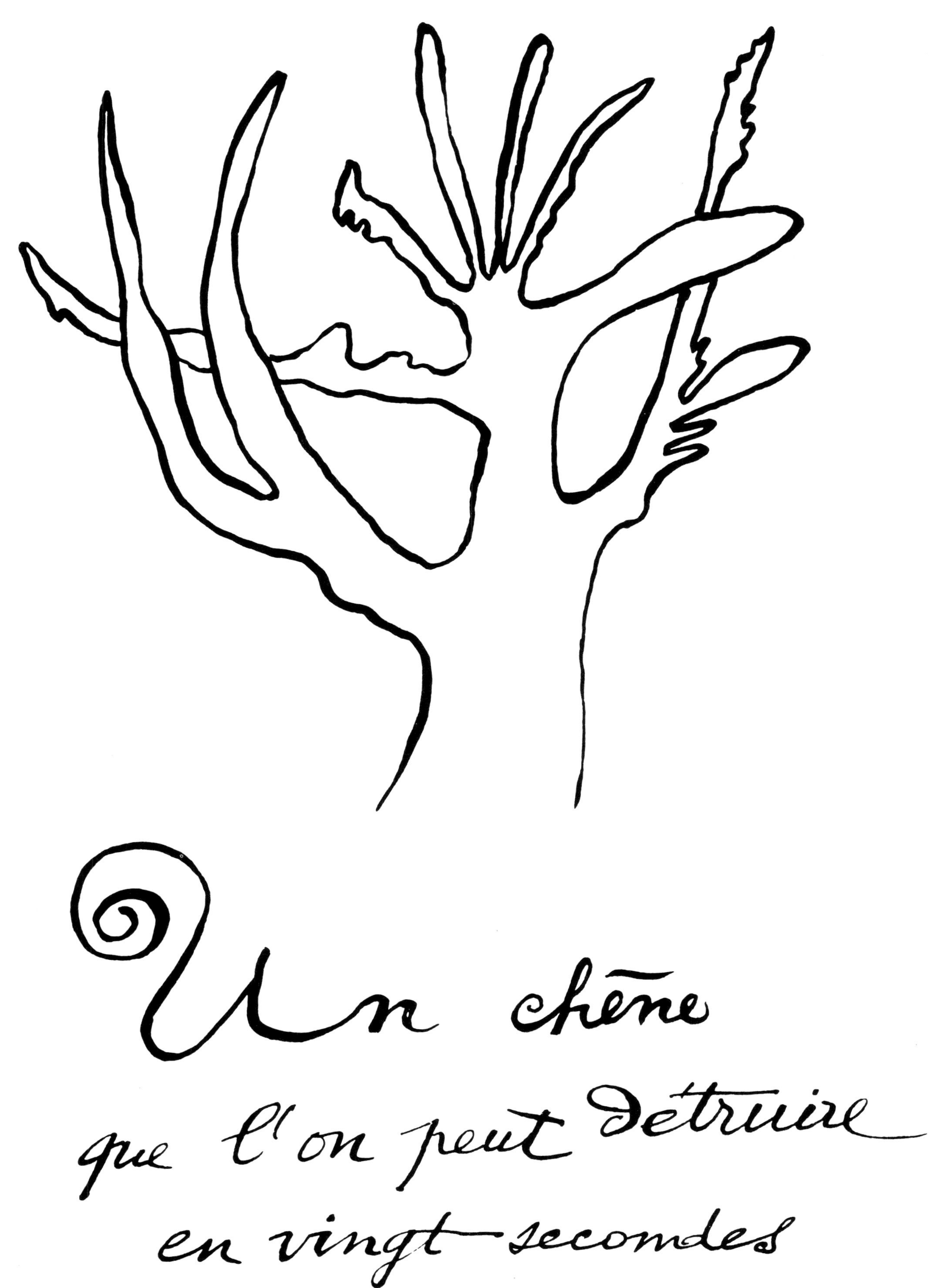


31. EXCERPT FROM THE BOOK *THE CIRCUS*

met un siècle à
repousser.
Les oiseaux sont toujours
merveilleusement habillés,
le progrès est un mot
dénué de sens, et une
vache qui nourrit le monde
fera toujours
trois
Kilomètres
à l'heure

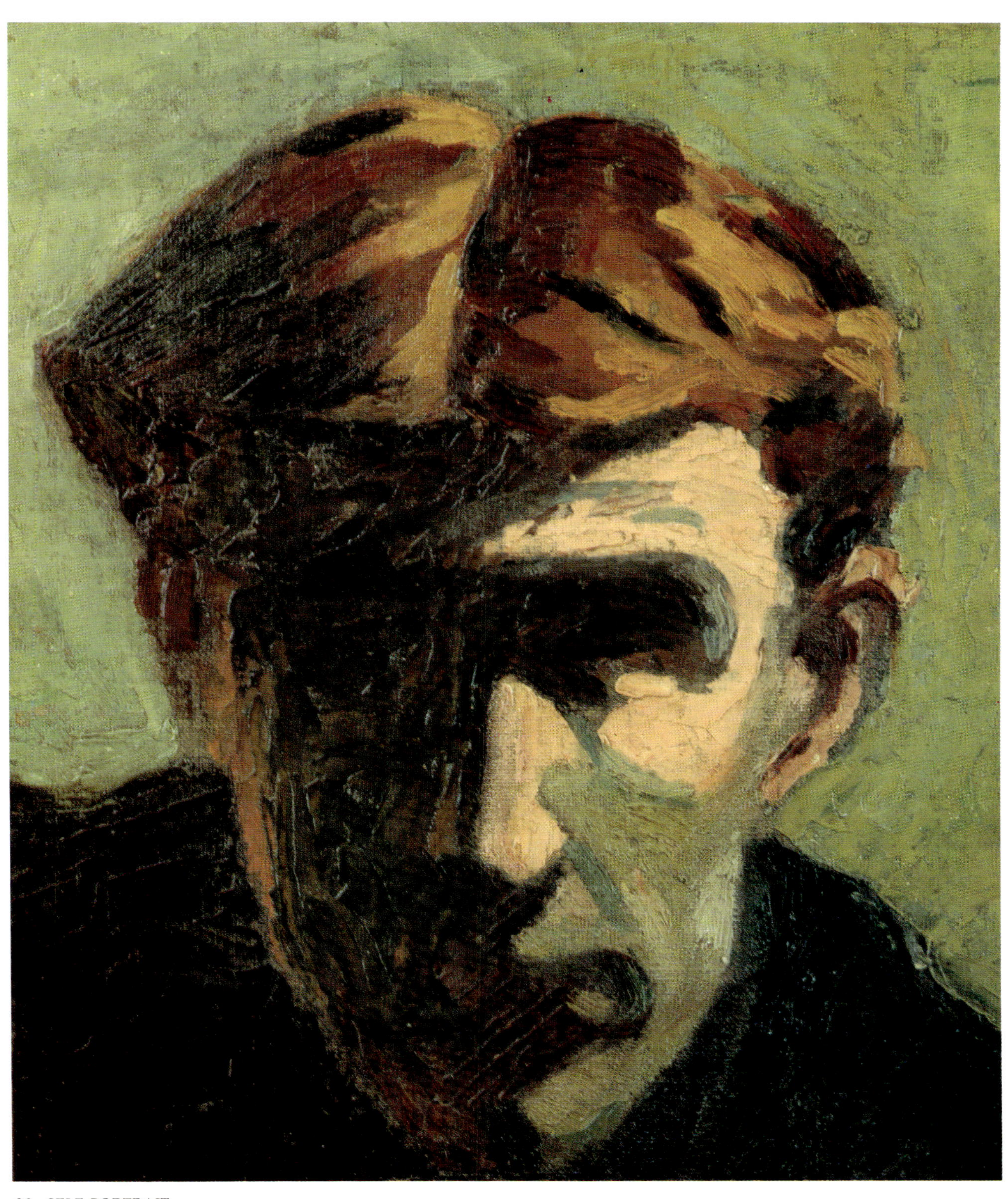

32. SELF-PORTRAIT
1905—Oil on canvas, 28 × 23 cm
Collection of Mr. and Mrs. Adrien Maeght

# Farewell to Impressionism

"All of us started from Cézanne." The modern world began with Cézanne for Fernand Léger, but he would never forget the lesson of freedom he had learned from Impressionism.

In the preface to a monograph that art critic Pierre Descargues dedicated to Léger in 1955, the year that he died, the painter again expressed this notion of freedom: "The artist, the poet, and the creator of beauty are all dedicated to this heroic destiny—*to proceed in freedom.* The price paid for this freedom is high. It demands perpetual risk, day in and day out. These paintings were conceived and realized in a constant state of readiness for war with society." Léger had maintained his belief and his warlike defiance from the very outset. He was of the race of builders and "brawlers." His motto was "the will to live with truth," but he also exemplified the dictum "to thine own self be true." His work evolved with a rare logic, and with rare integrity as well. Truth for Léger was represented in the everyday reality of machines, speed, and color, and also the social world of the work environment where hand and tool confronted each other.

The continuity for Léger's work is remarkable. It is there from his earliest known sketches and paintings
Ill. 337 (around 1905) to his *Birds against a Yellow Background* ("Oiseaux sur fond jaune") in 1955, the very last painting he worked on. "There was no remorse and not one trace of contradiction in this *plastic conscience of our time* (Garaudy)." It was as if Léger was a master of his art from the outset, without passing
Ill. 5 through the apprenticeship years. The first *Nudes*,
Ill. 33 which he sketched between 1900 and 1907, already have the monumental character, the quality of the subject as object, and the large integrated forms of his last paintings. Even his preoccupation with contrast is there at the beginning, expressed in the battle of curves and straight lines. His human forms are a composition of cylinders and circles intersected by angles. They are disjointed and disconnected, just
Ill. 46 like his *Contrasting Forms* ("Contrastes de formes") would be many years later, which fully accomplish the synthesis of rhythm and structure that would be his constant preoccupation.

Léger was born the same year as Pablo Picasso. His father raised livestock. After apprenticing for a time with an architect in Caen, he came to Paris in 1900 and lived hand to mouth. He was accepted into the School of Decorative Arts, but rejected at the École des Beaux-Arts, although he frequented the ateliers of Gérôme and Ferrier as a free student during the time he worked at the Académie Julian. He spent the
winter of 1906–07 in Corsica, and painted canvases Ill. 34
"in the Impressionist style." Two events marked him profoundly, however: the Cézanne retrospective at the Salon d'Automne in 1907, and his move to the "Ruche" (beehive) the following year. The Ruche was a veritable phalanstery, out of which came a good part of modern art. "Without Cézanne, I sometimes wonder what the fate of painting would have been," said Léger. "Cézanne taught me the love of form and volume; he made me concentrate on drawing. Then I started to feel that the drawings had to be rigid, not at all sentimental. . . . Cézanne was the only *rebuilder* in the watered-down landscape of Impressionism."

On December 11, 1919, Daniel Kahnweiler was asking Léger some questions for an essay that he was planning to write about him. Léger responded with an analysis of his work up to the point he had reached at that time. He did this not only with precision but with prophecy. Léger explained with lucidity how he had moved from Impressionism to Cubism, and he also put forth the entire itinerary he had established for himself and that he would relentlessly develop, step by step, in the future. In this respect, the letter to Kahnweiler takes on major importance.

"Born in 1881 in Argentan, Normandy. Spent three empty and useless years at the Beaux-Arts school. I didn't start to work seriously until I was twenty-five, a bit late as you can see. I was at the Beaux-Arts school between the ages of twenty-one and twenty-five. I started around 1900–1902. Impressionism was still the big influence, and, like most other Frenchmen, I poked around in it for a time without coming up with anything personal. Then Cézanne appeared and allowed me to direct my effort in a more conscious way. For several years I worked in a very laborious way. In my confusion I felt that Impres-

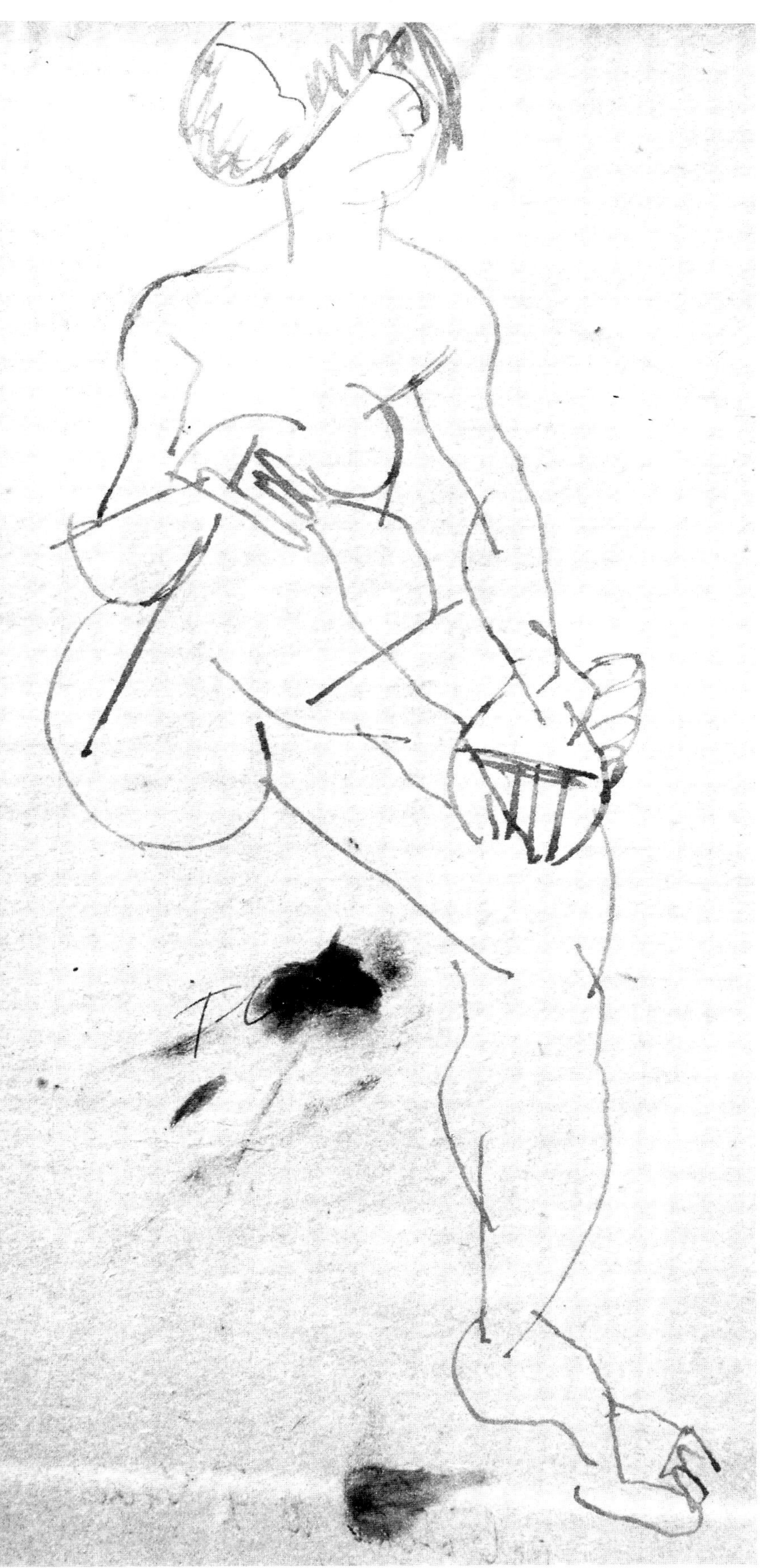
33. STUDY FOR NUDE
1906—Sketch, 35 × 25 cm
Musée National Fernand Léger, Biot

sionism was an ending and not a beginning—even though I was engulfed in the experience—and that Cézanne was a beginning. That was happening without my really knowing where I was going. Everything that I painted between 1902 and 1908 was destroyed along the way. It was the most difficult period of my life, but I guess that all painters have to go through it. It is the time when you're under the influence of something; then comes the transition period, and the creative part. At the Salon des Indépendents in 1910 I showed *Nudes in a Forest*, which Ill. 39
you own. It was influenced by David, by Rousseau, and it was also a reaction to the diffuseness of Neo-Impressionism. I was exasperated by volume and form, the elements that are still the basis of my current work. You know about that phase. I pushed it as far it could go in disconnecting the forms and by neglecting color. When I found my form and got it under control (modulated volume), then the color started coming back. First it was gray, Cézanne-like; then, little by little, it regained its importance.

"To sum it up, I didn't react against the excesses of color in Impressionism, but I'm against its lack of constructive form. My painting will always have a dynamic tendency, that same northern influence that they had. Composition through the assemblage of surfaces, the prime trait of Cubism, was never my forte. For me, it is volume in motion colored in local tones, and the accentuation of movement through contrasting opposition. The smoke series (contrasting soft forms and hard forms), and the women—it's all the same. Then there's the series of abstract canvases in pure contrasts. You've got those, as well. Then I returned to subjects while continuing to oppose plastic contrasts. I rarely depart from the subject, and it's still that way. I'm holding on to it for as long as my desire for renewal allows me to. If I kill it, it's only to get more intensity from it. If you consider that a canvas must be the material contrast of the wall on which one hangs it, it must personify the full force of movement and life. Everything must be dull in relationship to the painting. Today this is possible, since we've gotten away from imitative art. It's possible to achieve plastic intensity and it's important to avoid dead surfaces on the canvas. For me, this issue of live surfaces and dead surfaces is what makes or breaks a painting. I think there are real geographical boundaries involved. There are men from the North and men from the South, and they represent two contrary pictorial tendencies. The entire history of painting revolves around a line that runs through the south of France, below Venice, and then back up through Russia. It would be a curious line to trace, but I think it's easy enough to discern. Impressionism is definitely a northern phenomenon. The reaction to this is magnified by painters from the South. It was only a momentary thing with me. Even

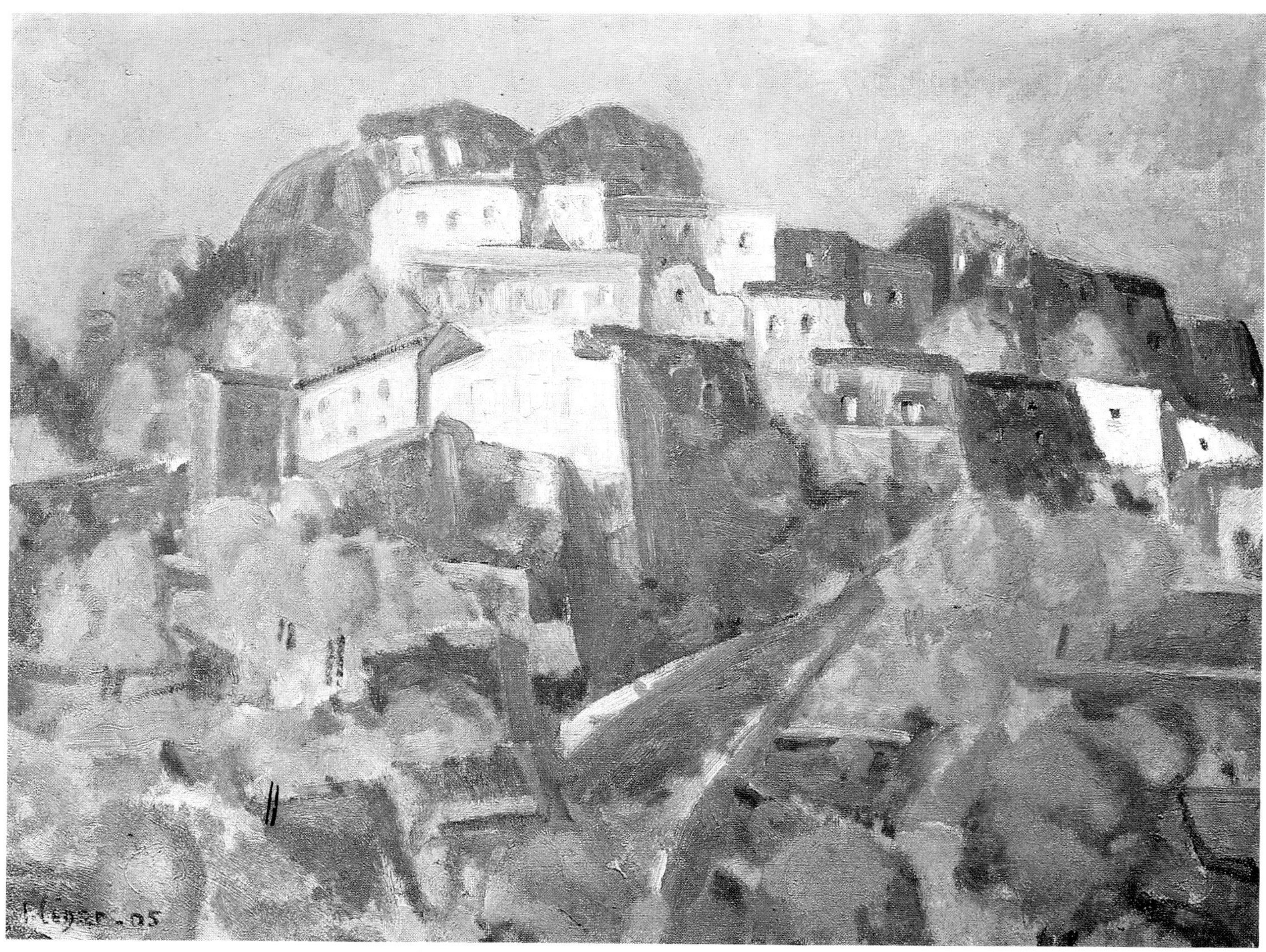

34. CORSICAN VILLAGE AT SUNSET
1905—Oil on canvas, 49.5 × 64.7 cm
Perls Gallery, New York

though I'm far removed from a Renoir or a Sisley, when I stand before their paintings I truly feel that I'm part of their family. I feel the same way with Delacroix and Courbet, but less so with Ingres and Corot.

"Over the past couple of years, I've used a lot of mechanical elements in my paintings. My current forms adapt well to that, and I find a source of variety and intensity in them. . . . Modern life is a treasurehouse of elements. You just have to know how to use them. Every era has its new elements, which are there to serve us. The great challenge is to translate this plastically, and to avoid the mistakes the Futurists have made."

"What is striking in Léger's letter to me," commented Kahnweiler, "is that he speaks tenderly about the luminist art that he's fighting against. He's even claiming kinship to it. Neither Picasso nor Gris ever leaned towards Impressionism, and if Braque perhaps kept a vague attachment to it after he abandoned Fauvist painting, it is clear that he kept it under control during the years of his Cubist formation. With Léger, it is a reaction *against* 'the lack of constructive form in Impressionism,' and 'the diffuseness of Neo-Impressionist painting.' His reaction is manifested in exacerbated volumes and shapes. In this respect he differs from Braque, Gris, and Picasso."

For Léger and his contemporaries, the merits of Impressionism were its rebellion against academic art, its rejection of pompous or mythological subjects, and its focus on the simple things in life. Léger was strongly impressed by this. His professor at Beaux-Arts, the painter Gérôme, a "pompous academician if there ever was one," poked fun at the influence Impressionism had on his students' passion for complementary colors. He referred to Monet and his group of friends as the "red-and-green gang." Léger's future preoccupations were clearly apparent during those early years, even while he poked about in the field of Impressionism and found nothing more in objects than "relationships of color."

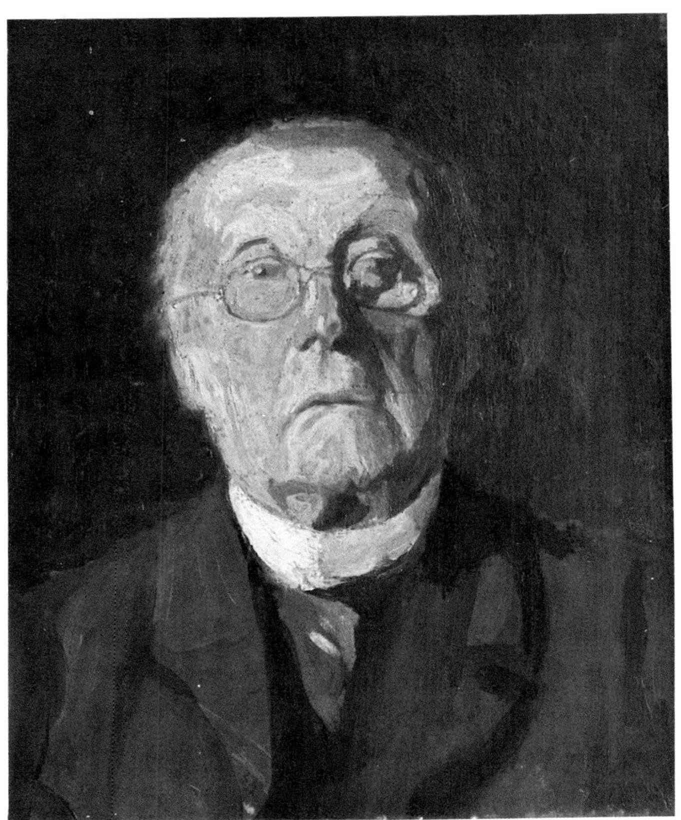

35. PORTRAIT OF THE ARTIST'S UNCLE
1905—Oil on canvas, 44 × 35 cm
Musée National Fernand Léger, Biot

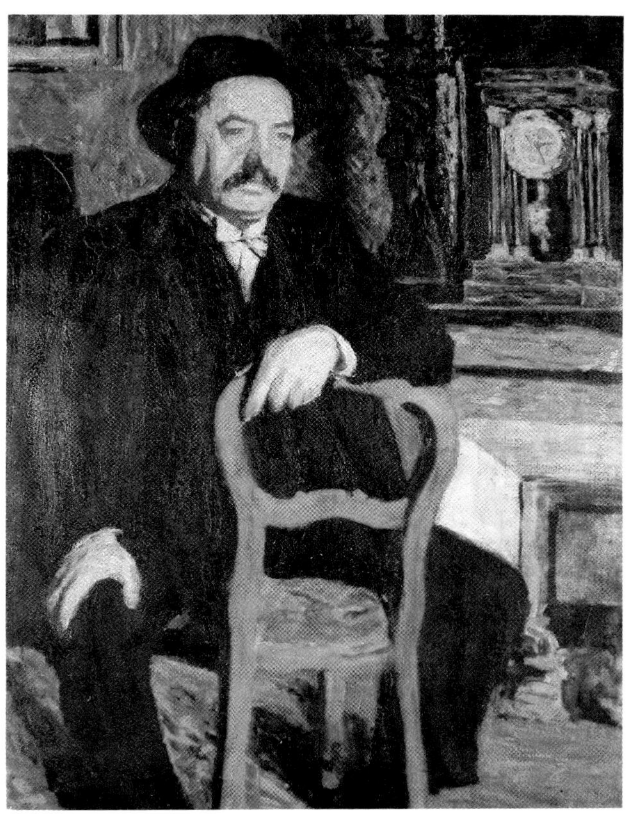

36. PORTRAIT OF MR. BLASINI
1907—Oil on canvas, 64 × 54 cm
Private collection

### The "anti-melodious" source

Ill. 32 Mastery and craftsmanship are aleady evident in
Ill. 35 Léger's early portraits (*Self-Portrait, The Artist's Uncle,*
Ill. 36 *Blasini,* etc.), where there is no trace of any particular stylistic influence. Even before he focused his attention on the effect of light and color, his simplified shapes and carefully modeled forms were already present in these paintings.

Ill. 37 In *My Mother's Garden* ("Le Jardin de ma mère"), painted in 1905 in the midst of his intoxication with color, one can see a first contrast in the rhythm of the composition: the curves of the flowerbeds and the straight lines of the building at the end of the path are opposing circular and vertical lines. Léger gave a moving homage to the Impressionists during a lecture he delivered at the Sorbonne in 1924: "I started painting in the Impressionist style. Immediately afterwards I had a strong reaction to this, but I could only do something about it in relationship to my own work. What led to this reaction was my feeling that the environment of the Impressionist period was naturally melodious, and that my environment was not. When I think back to those years now, I realize that the Impressionists had carried out an extraordinary revolution. They had overthrown chiaroscuro! Their revolution was much greater than ours. What pure interplay of colors! Those five or six courageous painters, who were starving, managed to pull through much tougher circumstances than we were in. . . . I'm not saying that things were easy for us, but you just can't compare the two situations. The Impressionists provided the groundwork for our own revolution, and that's very important."

Working from one painting to the next in reaction to his previous work was a constant trait in Léger's creative process. He moved away from the "melodious" environment of Impressionism and adopted the "anti-melodious" principles of Cézanne: "Between 1905 and 1908, the *battle* of my generation was in full swing. We had to break with Impressionism at all costs, because we were sinking in their fragmented stroke techniques and their separation of tones—that hopeless pulverization of color."

Léger's discovery of Cézanne allowed him to bid farewell to Impressionism so he could pursue the discipline of drawing and the geometry of volume.

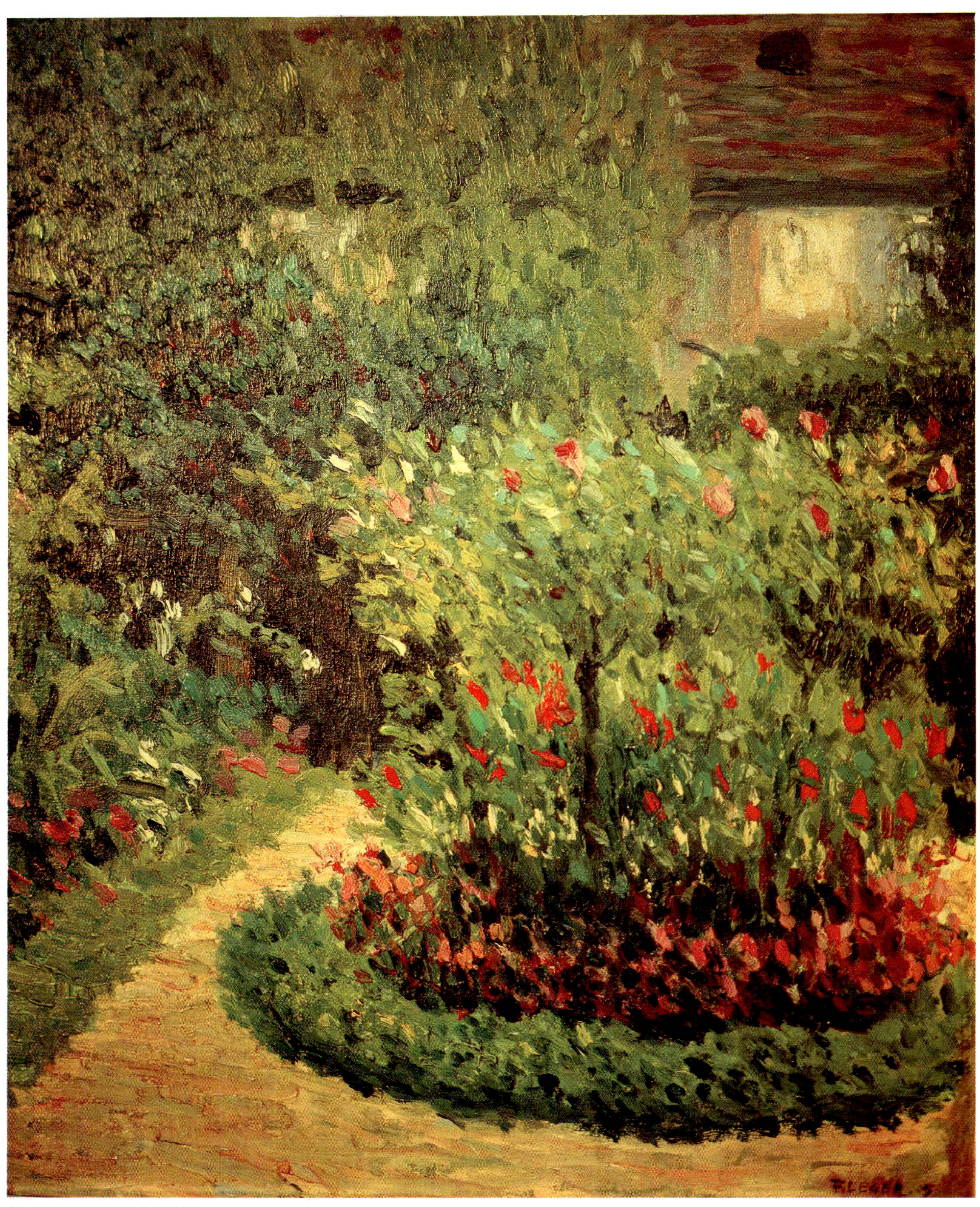

37. MY MOTHER'S GARDEN
1905—Oil on canvas, 46 × 38 cm
Musée National Fernand Léger, Biot

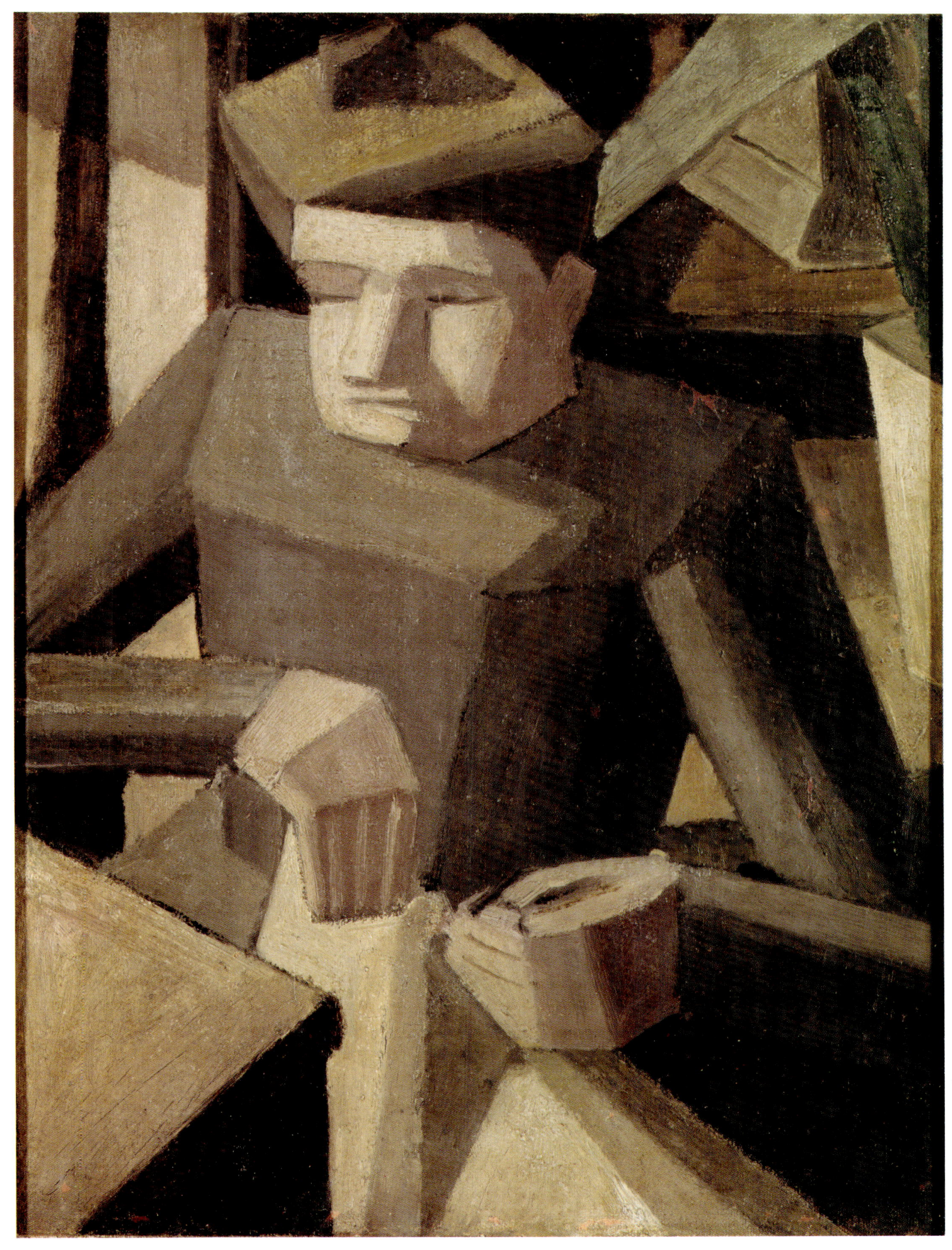

38. THE SEAMSTRESS
1910—Oil on canvas, 73 × 54 cm
Musée National d'Art Moderne, Centre Georges Pompidou, Paris
Gift of Louise and Michel Leiris

# From Cubism to Tubism

Ill. 38 In the transition between *The Seamstress* ("La Cous-
Ill. 39 euse") and *Nudes in the Forest* ("Nus dans la forêt") Léger became Léger. *The Seamstress* is his only truly Cubist painting, in the Cézannian sense. It is the painting that is closest to the technique that Picasso, Braque, or Gris used. It is almost monochromatic, an aggregate of geometrical lines and cubes resembling quartered pieces of wood, in which Léger tried to push Cézanne's asceticism of form and color to the extreme. Roger Garaudy spoke about how Léger watched the sculptor Archipenko at work in the Ruche and exclaimed, "How marvelous to bring wood and iron into play with each other." Léger's *Seamstress* is a pictorial transposition of this same kind of interplay, as well as a "contrasting of material elements." "Analytical Cubism" was too sterile for Léger. It came and went in his work faster than a bolt of lightning. He would spend many years working on *Nudes in the Forest.* It was the outcome of the painter's personal struggle to find is own path, his own voice. It was the decisive moment when he used "dislocation." Traces of discontinuity and disconnection that we can see in his *Nudes* sketches in 1905–06 Ill. 33
henceforth become systematic. Each element attained plastic autonomy. Geometrical volumes were no longer static or joined like they were in *The Seamstress.* Instead, they became autonomous bodies subject only to the laws of motion.

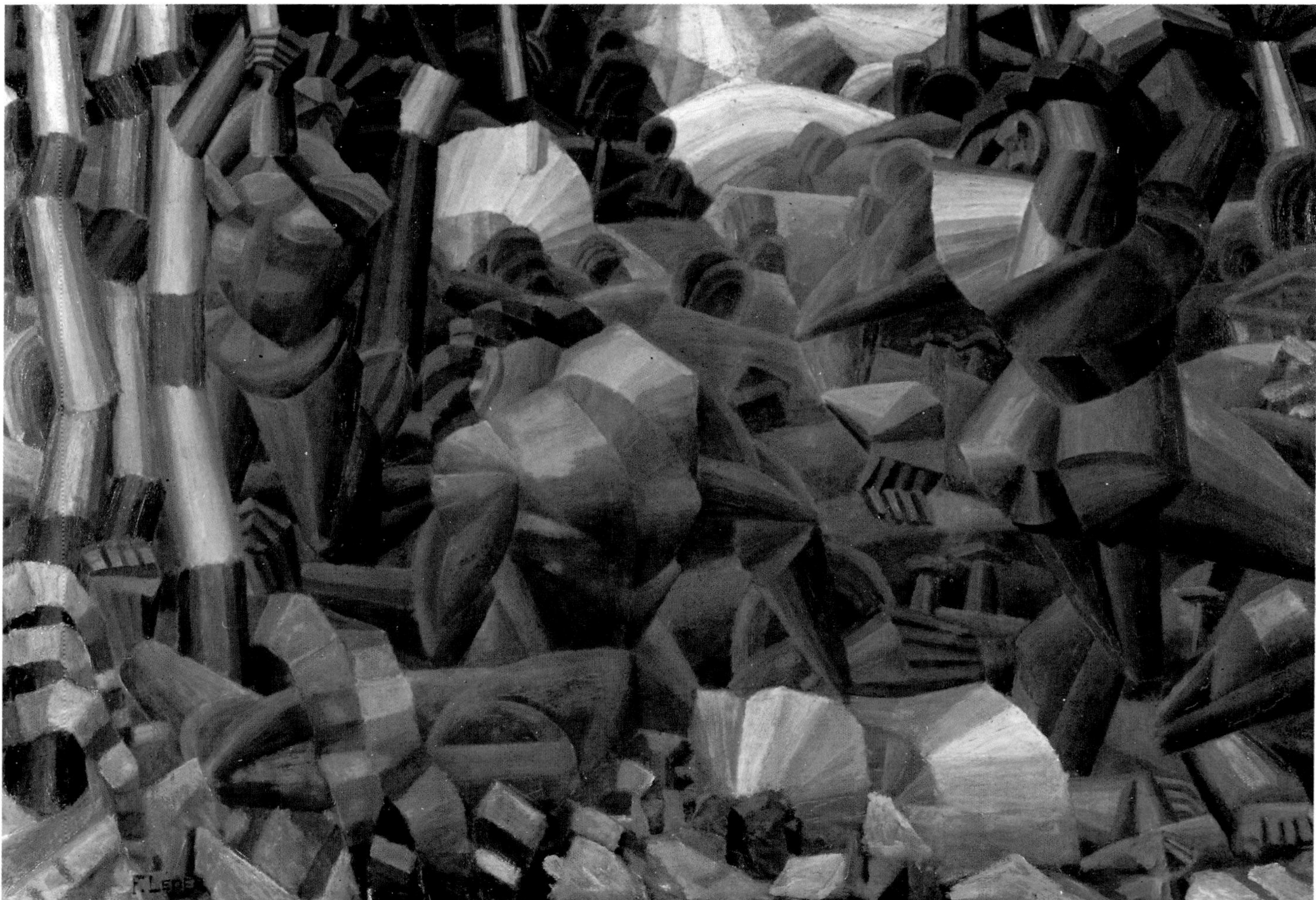


39. NUDES IN THE FOREST
1909–10—Oil on canvas, 120 × 170 cm
Rijksmuseum Kröller Müller, Otterlo

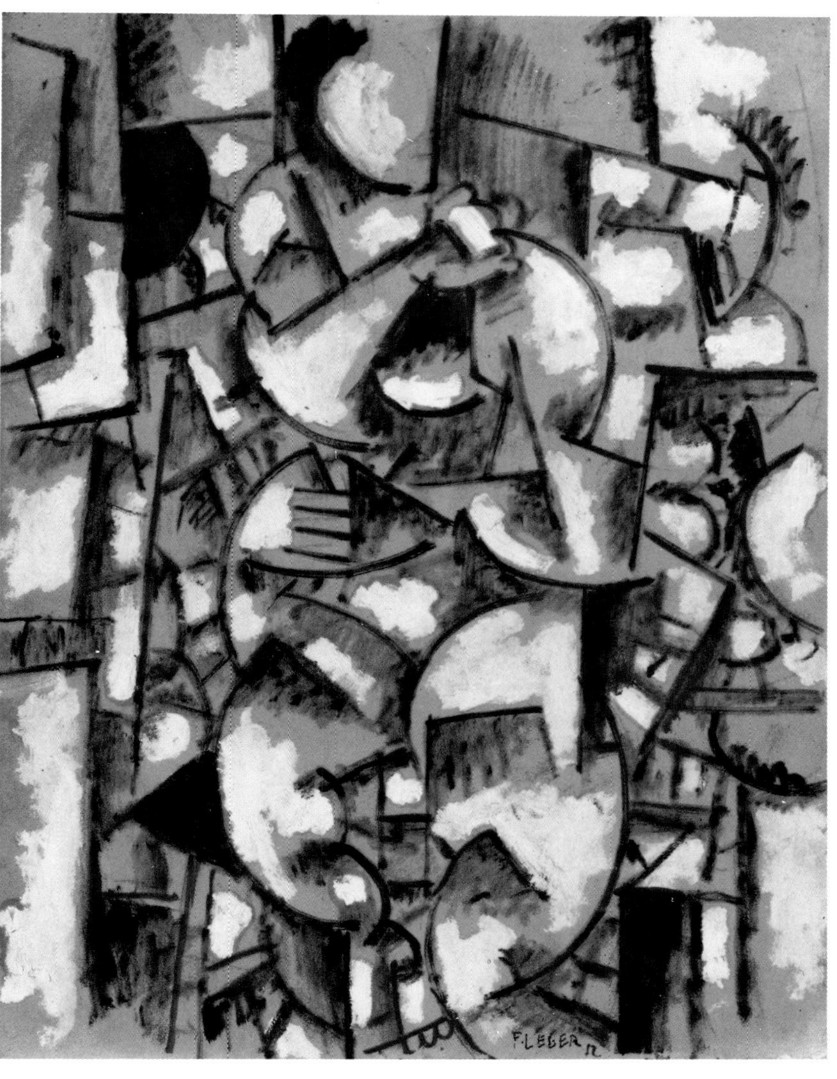



40. STUDIO NUDE
1912—Oil and China ink, gouache, 61 × 50 cm
Musée National d'Art Moderne, Centre Georges Pompidou, Paris
Gift of Louise and Michel Leiris

### Ill. 39 *Nudes in the Forest*

It can be said that *Nudes in the Forest* marked a turning point in Léger's artistic development in the same way that the *Demoiselles d'Avignon* marked a turning point for Picasso. All comparison between the two painters stops here, however. From the historical point of view, Léger is one of the four great Cubists. His form of cubism was different from that of Braque, Picasso, and Gris, who were still passionately involved with "the precise representation of the form of objects" and who tried to faithfully render these objects as they knew them, using their sensations as their guides ("Analytical Cubism"). They later abandoned analysis for the invention of "symbols" (*signes*) and "types" that "evoked" objects rather than described them. Léger, however, was faster. He bypassed the analytical phase and went directly to "Synthetic Cubism." Kahnweiler underlines this essential difference: "While his peers remained stuck in the conflict that resulted from their stubborn willfulness to incorporate within the rectangular perimeters of the canvas everything they knew about an object," Léger focused his attention on "exacerbating the volumes and forms." During the period that Léger was flirting with "abstract painting" he had already resolved the problem of deformation. In 1913 and 1914, his paintings grew out of "lived experience," and paintings like *Studio Nude,* for exam- Ill. 40
ple, are variations on a theme rather than deliberate "abstractions."

*Nudes in the Forest* is a landmark painting because Léger started to liberate himself not only from Cézanne, but from Cubism as well. His adversaries called his efforts "Tubism." The expression was coined by art critic Louis Vauxelles during the 1911 Salon des Indépendents. He intended it to designate a painting that resembled Cubism, but in which we "see" cylinders, and not cubes. Of the cubes, spheres, and cylinders that Léger had inherited from Cézanne, he favored the cylinders most of all. Guillaume Apollinaire, poet and contemporary of Léger, wrote of this painting: "The woodcutters bear the traces of the marks that their hatchets made on the trees, and the overall color has that same deep, greenish light that emanates from the foliage." The painting bears traces of Cézanne in its forms, but there are also traces of Rousseau in the monochrome colors, which create an atmosphere in the Douanier manner.

Léger was only partially conscious of this: "I used all my energy to go to the opposite extreme of Impressionism. I was obsessed with the need to disconnect the human form. They called me a 'tubist.' *Nudes in the Forest* is the outcome of my two-year battle with volume. I wanted to push volume as far as I could. I finished the painting in 1910. People said there were influences of the Douanier Rousseau in the painting. It's possible, because I was looking at Rousseau's work during that period. If I was influenced by it, it wasn't anything conscious or deliberate. . . . For me, *Nudes in the Forest* was merely the battle of volumes. I had felt that I wouldn't be able to get color to hold its own, and that's why I concentrated on volume."

### *The Woman in Blue* Ill. 41

"Once I was in control of my form (contoured volume), color came back again. . . ." After *Nudes in the Forest,* the dealer Kahnweiler bought all of Léger's paintings, and was the first to sign an exclusive contract with him. Now that "the battle with volume" had ended, it was time to start, with *The Woman in Blue,* "the battle with color." Léger was moving further and further away from Cubism: "Between 1909 and 1912, Robert Delaunay and I led the onslaught to liberate color. . . . Cubism had been born out of the need for change. It started with gray tones, and colors were brought in several years later."

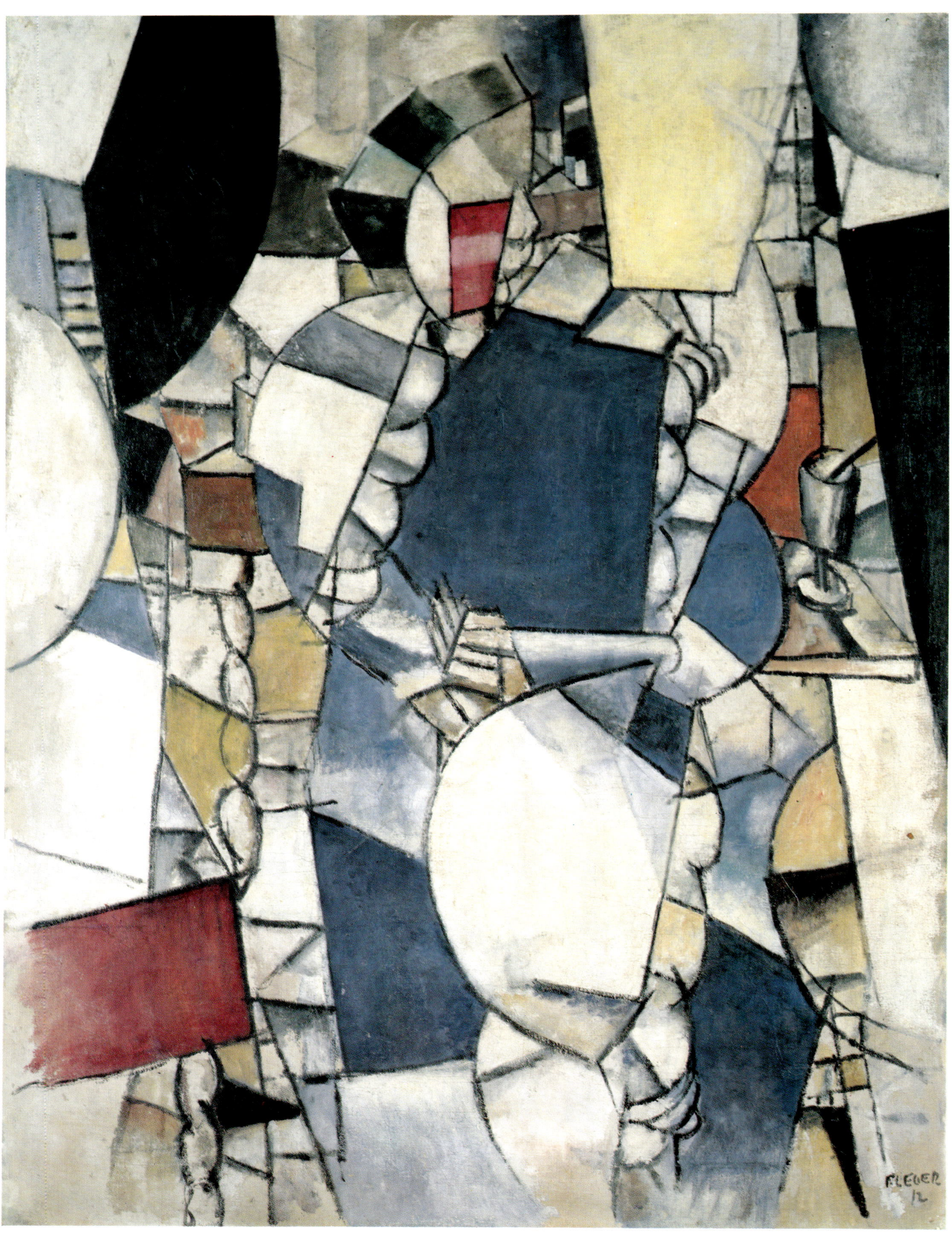


41. WOMAN IN BLUE, STUDY
1912—Oil on canvas, 131 × 99 cm
Musée National Fernand Léger, Biot

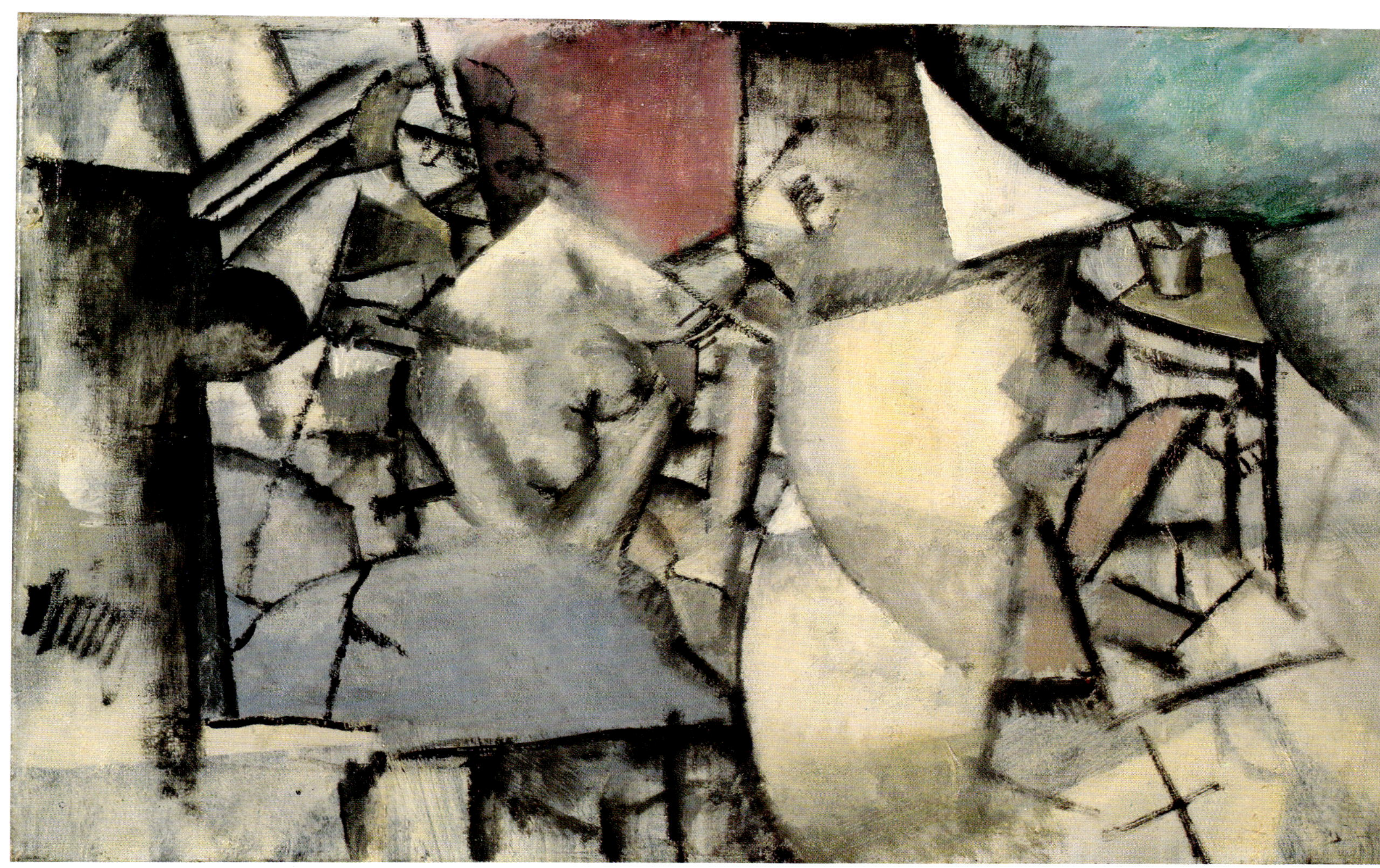

42. RECLINING WOMAN
1911–12—Oil on canvas, 41.7 × 65.5 cm
Private collection

Ill. 43 **_The Wedding_ ("La Noce")**

Léger took a keen interest in Delaunay's paintings, especially *The City* ("La Ville") and his series *Towers* ("Tours"). They influenced his own paintings at the time: *Three Figures* ("Trois figures") in 1910, *The Smokers* ("Les Fumeurs") in 1911, and *The Wedding* in 1910, which would ultimately be his most revo-
Ill. 39 lutionary painting in the period between *Nudes in the*
Ill. 92 *Forest* and *The City*, painted in 1919. Apollinaire baptized the style of Léger and Delaunay with the poetic name of "Orphic Cubism." Apollinaire, the author of *Alcools*, was captivated by Léger, but afraid that the painter would not take his work as far as it could go. In the March 20, 1912, review *Le Petit Bleu*, he made these comments about *The Wedding*: "Léger's canvas emerges from pure painting. There is no subject in this painting, but a great deal of talent. Still, there is always the danger that if the veins of this painter do not flow freely with thought, they could soon collapse."

A painter who only thinks. . . It is true that Léger's paintings were more complex than the still lifes the other Cubists preferred. His well-known "law of contrasts" had some surprising ideas in it; so did his studies of movement and depth. The very personal way he had of mixing the abstract forms he invented with his realistic forms was unsettling. From one painting to the next, Léger moved further and further away from natural laws. He abandoned pictorial likeness and perspective, as well as the proportions of volume and the realism of color. He was moving forward at top speed toward what he considered the most essential: unity and rhythm.

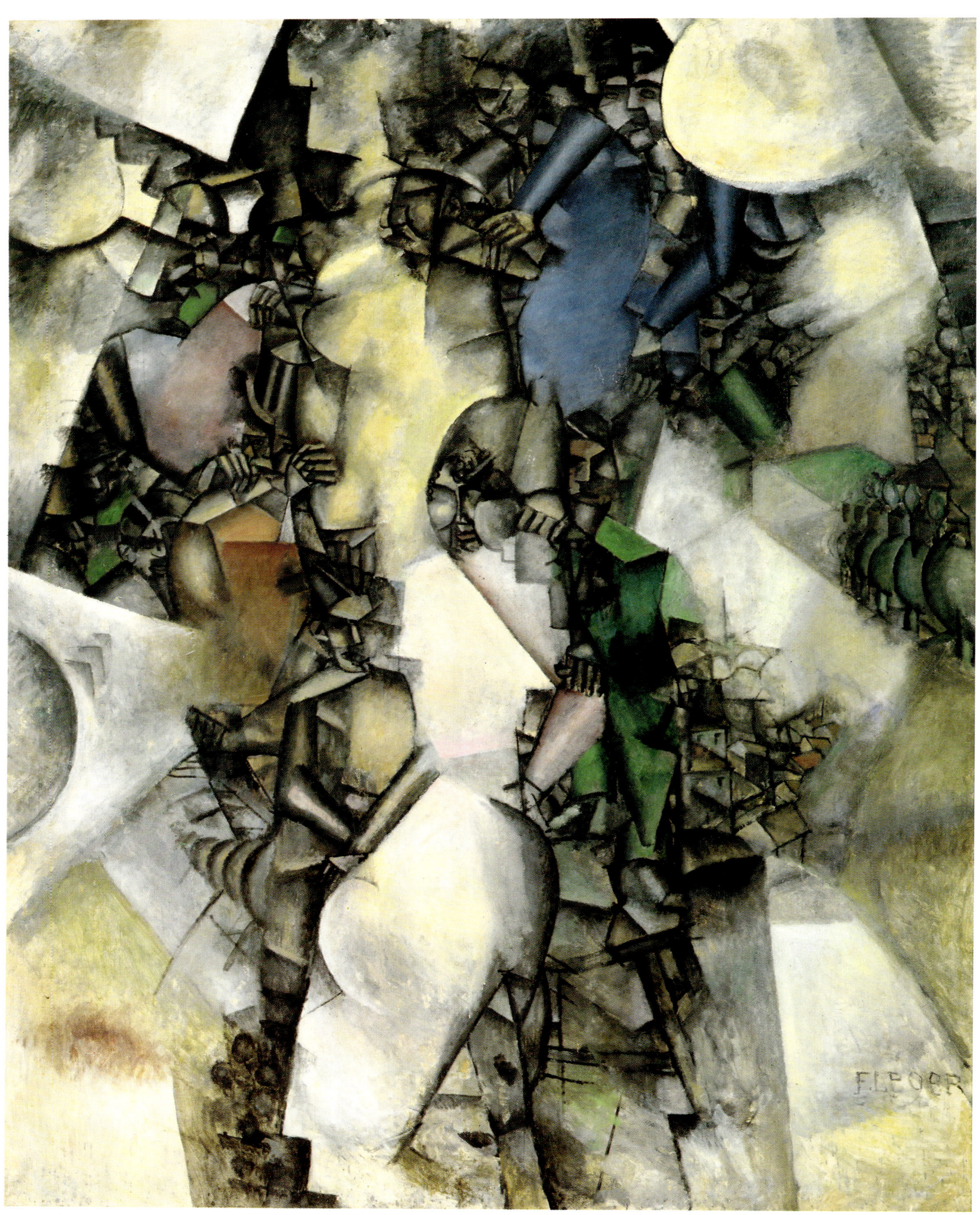

43. THE WEDDING
1910—Oil on canvas, 257 × 206 cm
Musée National d'Art Moderne, Centre Georges Pompidou, Paris
Gift of Alfred Flechtheim

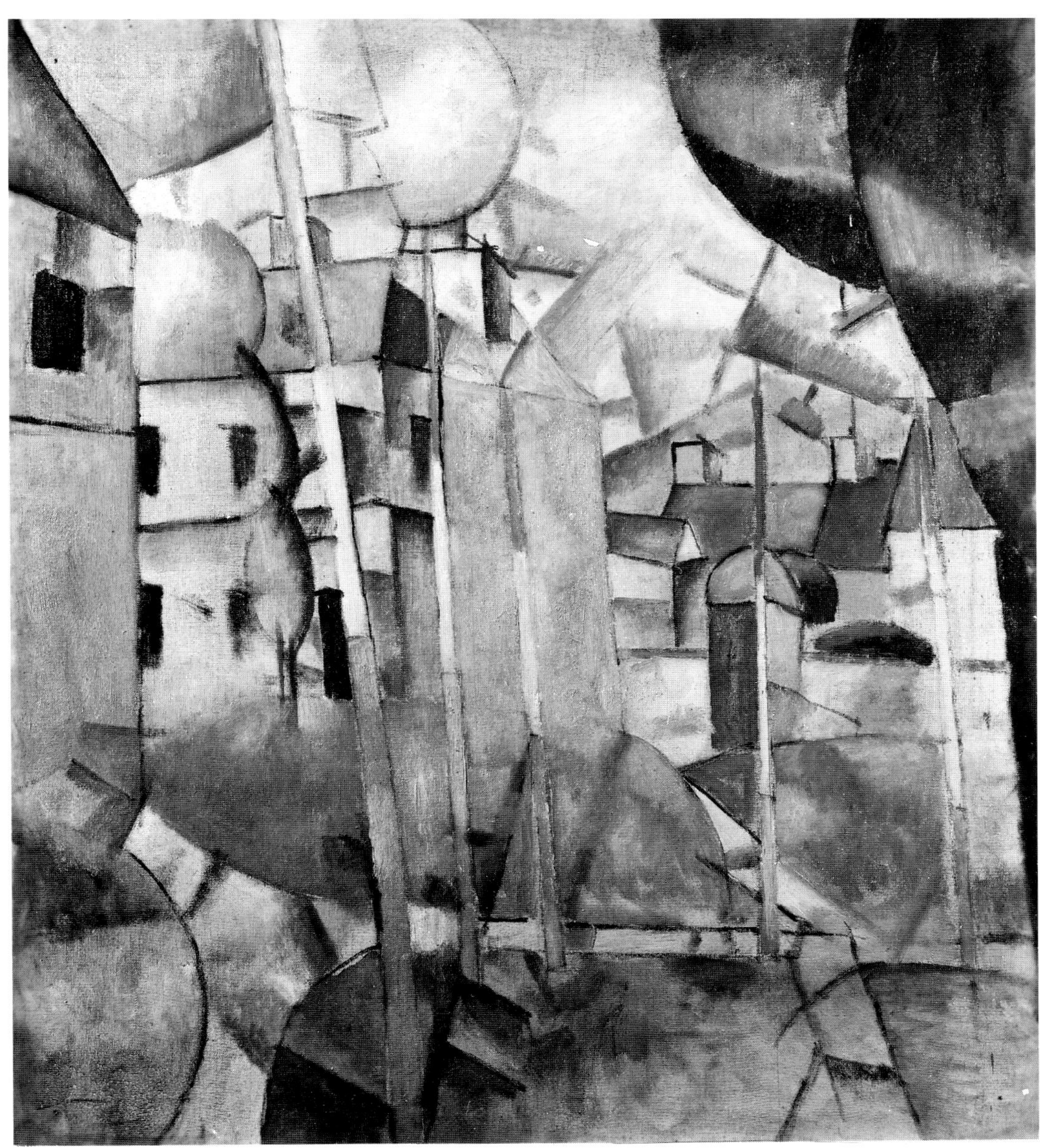

44. LANDSCAPE
1911–1912—Oil on canvas, 92 × 81 cm
Knusthistorisches Museum, Vienna

Ill. 45 ***Grade Crossing***

Later on, Léger would explain how he used abstraction to move towards his own artistic goals; but it is surprising to look back and see how this painter, who attached so much importance to the object, ignored it during the period he preferred geometric forms that had no apparent relationship to reality. "In 1912 and 1913 I was struggling to leave Cézanne behind me. Cézanne's hold on me was so strong that in order to break away I had to go all the way to abstraction." Léger's abstractions were really abstractions disguised in real objects. In *Grade Crossing* (1912), the frothy tree forms modulated in contrasted light, and the spires with their rhythmic sweeps had the same unreality as the forest of lances in Uccello's *Battle.*

Once he had mastered colors that had nothing to do with Impressionism, Léger was ready to attack his next phase, his next revolution. He rendered homage to Cézanne in the form of a farewell: "In his sensitivity to the contrast of forms, Cézanne is the only one of all the Impressionists who touched on the profound meaning of pictorial life."

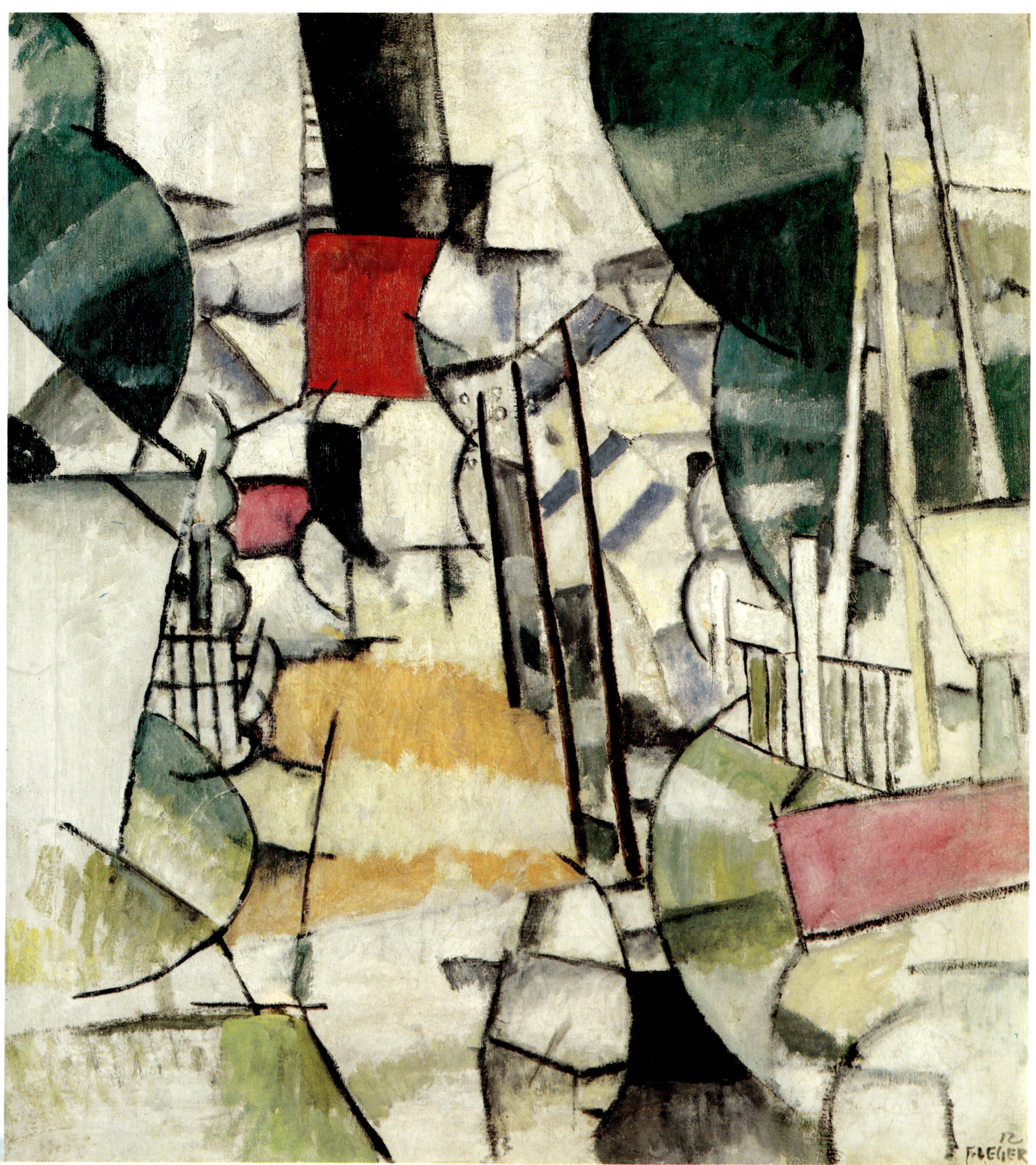


45. GRADE CROSSING
1912—Oil on canvas, 93 × 81 cm
Beyeler Gallery, Basel

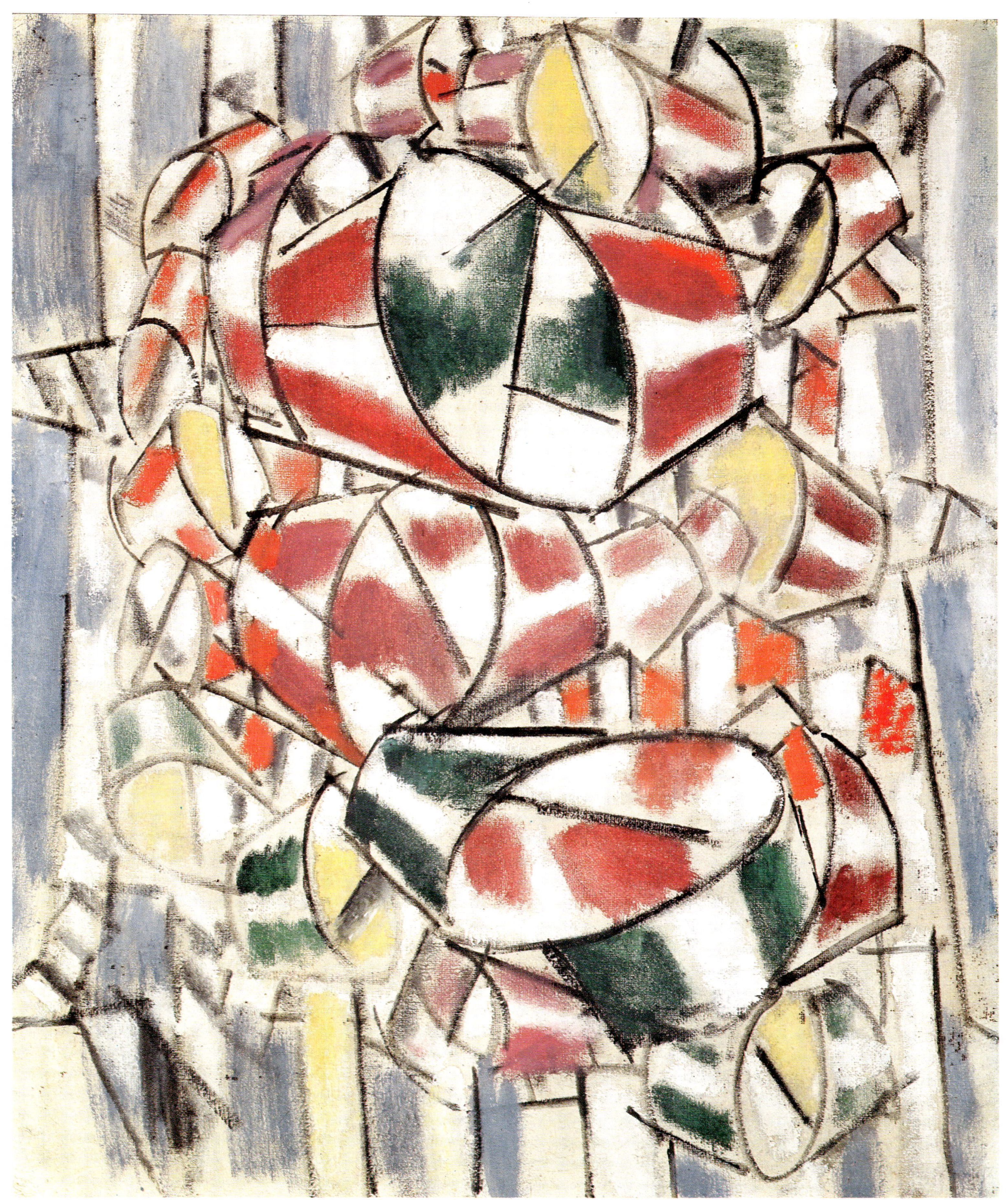

46. CONTRASTING FORMS
1913—Oil on canvas, 100 × 81 cm
Musée National d'Art Moderne, Centre Georges Pompidou, Paris
Gift of Jeanne and André Lefèvre

# Ill. 46 to 76 Contrast of Form

Picasso, Braque, and Gris still continued to put all their efforts into form at the (temporary) expense of color. Their paintings had a rare chromatic austerity. In reaction to this, Delaunay tried to suppress the importance of line and concentrated solely on color; Léger went from one shore of color to the next and did not want to sacrifice any of the elements. He used everything, "contrasted" everything, and continued to build the body of his work step by step.

In the lectures he gave at the Wassilieff Academy in Paris, he defined his present and future esthetics with the precision of a good mechanic. "Pictorial realism is the simultaneous arrangement of three large plastic quantities: Line, Form, and Color. If any one of them is sacrificed to the detriment of the other two, the work cannot qualify as *a classic* in the strict sense of the word; i.e., a work that transcends the historical period in which it was created." In this sense, the flat, monochrome guitars of Picasso and his friends rank among the nonqualifiers. So do the paintings of Léger's friend Delaunay, with his concept of "simultaneous contrasting colors." Léger threw them all into the same category of transgressor, and added, with reference to Delaunay (although he did not mention him by name): "To intentionally want to eliminate essential means of expression such as line and form, and treat them as insignificant except for their color value, is childish and reactionary. . . . A painter who calls himself a modernist and who rightfully considers perspective and sentimentality negative and unusable, must know how to replace them with something more than one continual relationship; pure colors, for example."

At a certain point, Léger even disagreed with Delaunay about color: "For Delaunay and me, color was a necessary tonic. Even there, Delaunay and I were apart from the others. They painted in monochromes, and we painted in polychromes. Then came my battle with Delaunay himself. He was keeping the Impressionist tradition of using complementary colors, one color next to the other, green next to red. I wanted to arrive at tones that stood alone, a very red red, a very blue blue."

For Léger, "compositions with multiplied contrasts" were the only way to truly express the dynamics of modern life. In the series of lectures at the Wassilieff Academy, he affirmed that "all things can work towards an intensive realism obtained through purely dynamic means. Pictorial contrast used in the strictest and most broadly accepted way (complementary colors, forms, and lines) is henceforth the framework for modern painting." Why is this?

"Life today is much faster and more fragmented than it used to be. It must undergo dynamic *divisionism* as a means of artistic expression." Léger had very clear ideas about the "recipe" for this process. "In order to build through color (because this is essential and fundamental), the two tones must balance or neutralize each other. If, for example, the green surface is more important than the red surface, there is no more construction. If composition through multiplied contrasts uses all the pictorial means available, it allows for a wonderfully realistic experience, and for variety as well. As a matter of fact, instead of opposing two expressive means in a sudden and additive way, you compose one canvas with groups of similar forms that contrast with opposing groups of similar forms. If you distribute your colors in the same spirit—i.e., by adding similar tones, coloring one of these groups of forms against a contrasting group—you will wind up with multiple sources of tones, lines, and colors acting against other contrary and dissonant sources. Contrast = dissonace. This must be maximized for expressive effect."

It was characteristic of the period to search for and find the formula that could best represent "modern art." Marcel Duchamp, Léger's contemporary, was integrating decomposed movement into Cubism. His famous *Nude Descending a Staircase* was shown at the 1912 Section d'Or exhibit in Paris, and indicated a convergence with Futurism that was more technical than intellectual. The same painting, exhibited one year later at the New York Armory Show, provoked a major scandal: one critic thought it looked like "an explosion in a tile factory."

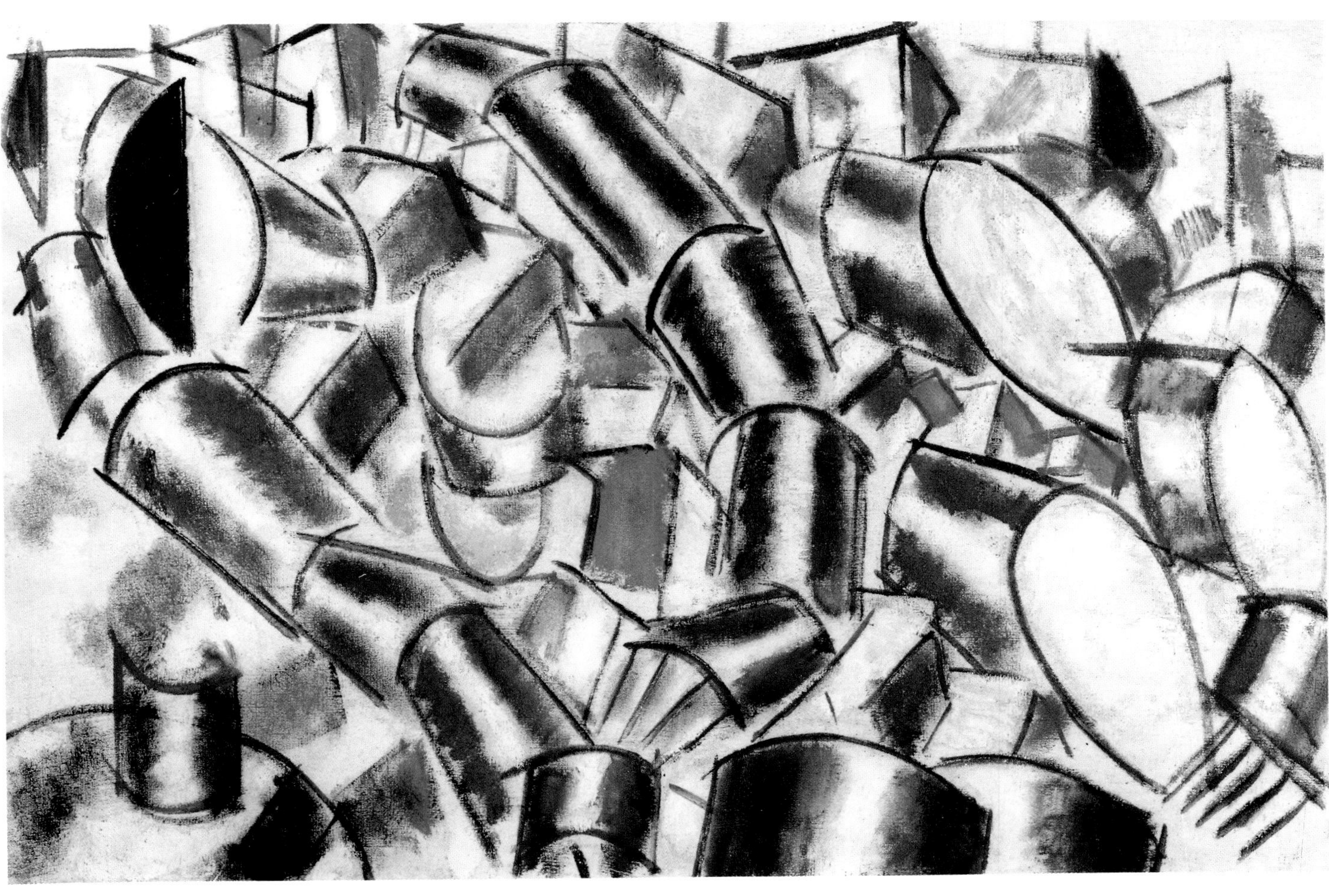

47. RECLINING WOMAN
1913—Oil on canvas, 66 × 100 cm
Musée National d'Art Moderne, Centre Georges Pompidou, Paris
Gift of Paul Rosenberg

## Duchamp's nude and Léger's woman-robot

Duchamp's vision dissolved reality even more. He wanted to go further in accomplishing the decomposition of form into volume than Cézanne had sought to do and than the Cubists continued to do. Duchamp, however, used color towards a different goal and used monochromatic color with a neutral, golden-yellow dominant underscored here and there by brownish or greenish shadows. His interest in traditional painting rapidly waned. He was aware of the technological challenge to esthetics, and in 1914 he chose to abandon painting. He replaced his canvases with "ready-mades," manufactured objects on which he was content to put his signature and thus elevate them to the level of art. Besides a common love for stairs in the plastic vocabularies of Duchamp and Léger, it is noteworthy that Duchamp's first ready-made was *Bicycle Wheel,* fixed to a stool in a way that allowed it to turn freely.

In response to Duchamp's *Nude Descending a Staircase,* Léger presented a woman-robot built from a hundred flights of stairs, and an alarm clock (a hitherto unknown element in modern art) as part of a bicycle wheel. The alarm clock is still painted on Ill. 58
the canvas, however, and with brushes and colors, just as Giotto had done centuries earlier. There is a major difference, though. Léger's clock is represented by a minute fragment of a clock. It is the strident sound of the alarm that spreads across the entire canvas with large, almost gestural forms. In place of melodic, Hispano-Cubist guitars, Léger preferred the alarm clock as the signal of the infernal cadences that Charlie Chaplin made the subject of his film *Modern Times.* Ill. 46 to 54

From *Contrasting Forms* to *Staircase,* Léger clarified his Cubist itinerary. Unlike Delaunay, he finally accepted a return to the object, which he rebuilt in a pictorial space. Instead of presenting the object simultaneously from different angles, as Duchamp had done and Picasso and consorts did, Léger employed *his own* "dynamic contrasting" process. This involved the simultaneous integration of line, form, and color, and a personalized interpretation of Futurist doctrines that he filtered through his own deep attachment to real things.

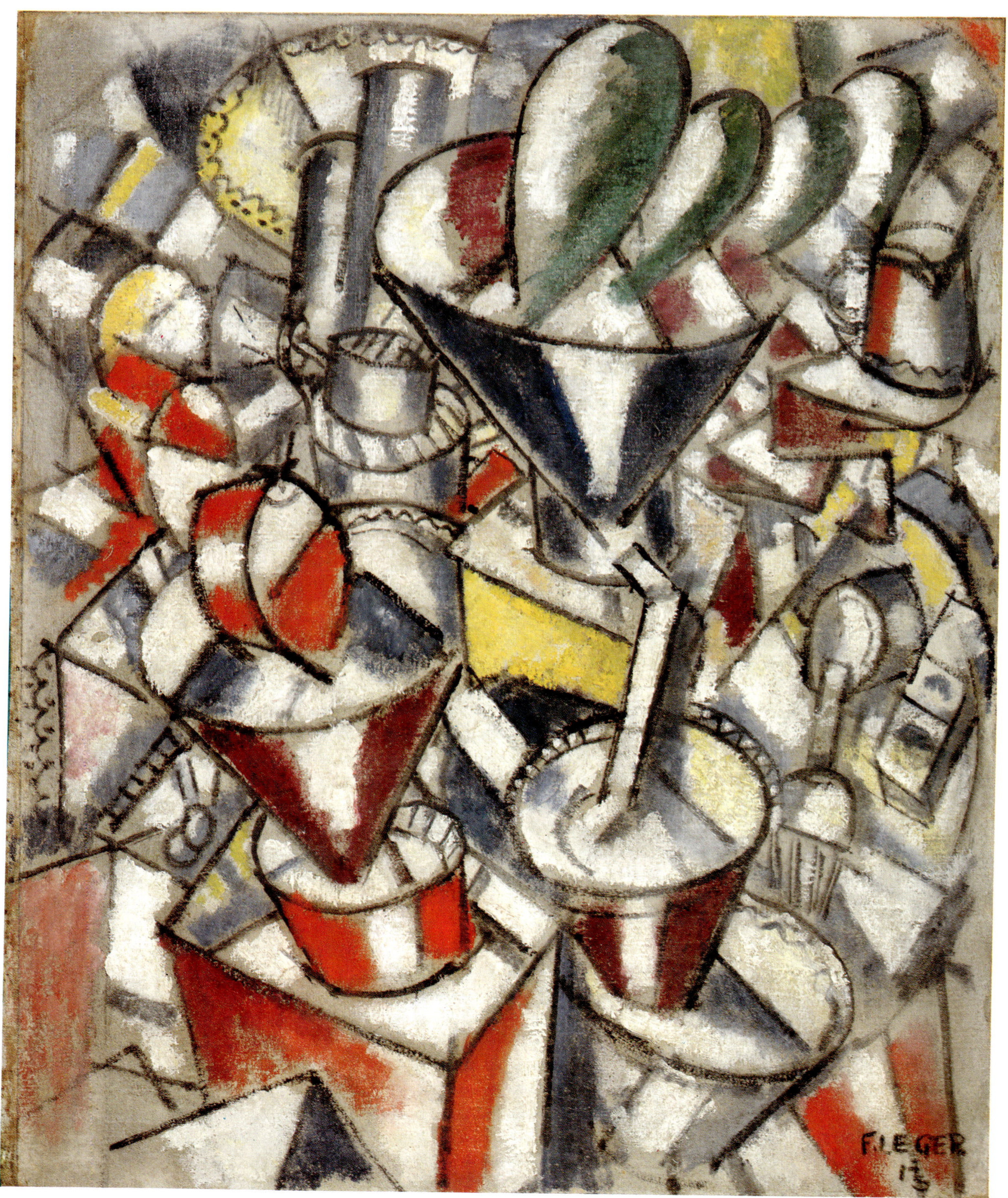


48. STILL LIFE WITH COLORED CYLINDERS
1913—Oil on canvas, 90 × 72 cm
Beyeler Gallery, Basel

### Futurism versus Cubism

Futurism, which started in Italy in 1909, was the movement that rivaled Cubism. The differences between the two great movements were irreconcilable, but there were several aspects of Futurism that initially appealed to Léger. Marinetti, the leader of the movement, urged the overthrow of icons in order to celebrate the dynamism of the modern world in all its many forms. Machines were exalted, especially the automobile, the locomotive, and the airplane, as well as all forms of macho violence that related to war or to the industrial revolution. The technical foundation for this avant-garde movement was "divisionism," inherited from Segantini and Previati. "Dynamic sensation" was favored at the expense of the static image and the laws governing perspective and density. The conflict between the Cubists and the Futurists that started in 1912 grew out of two incompatible artistic goals: the Cubists were devoted to rendering the essence of the painting; the Futurists, on the contrary, conceived of the painting as an ideal space for the contradictions and tensions of the modern world that Léger baptized as "contrasts."

In Douglas Cooper's book *Fernand Léger and the New Space*, the author insists that "Léger is the only one to represent movement, with the exception of the

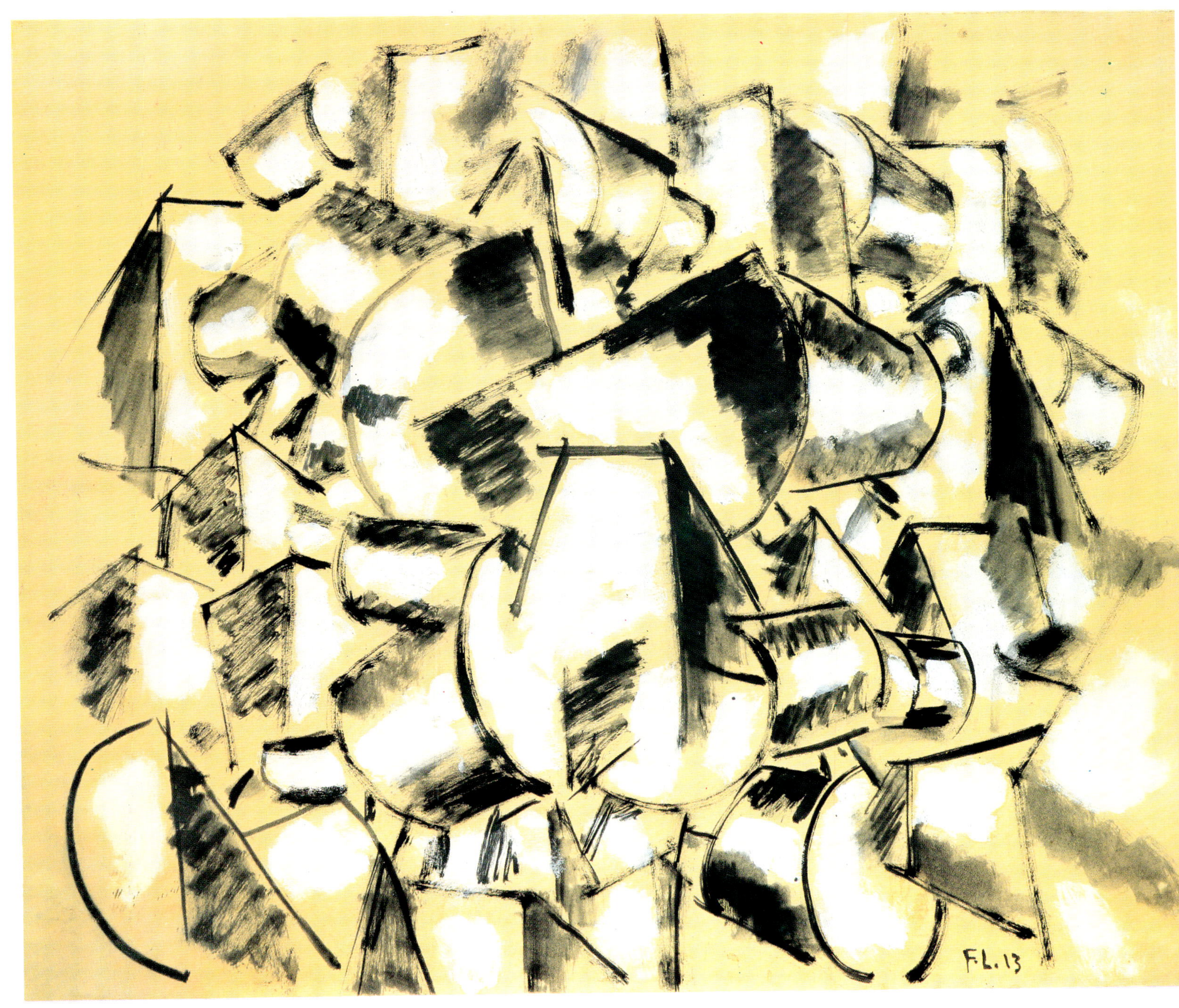


49. CONTRASTING FORMS
1913—Ink, gouache, and touches of white paint, 41.5 × 49 cm
Lionel Prejger collection, Paris

Futurists and of Marcel Duchamp." But Léger worked in a totally different way than they did: his images were always simple, and communicated the sensation of movement through the dynamic rhythm of the forms. During the same period, Léger was avoiding decorative elements just as much as pure abstraction, although he admitted that his first paintings were somewhat abstract: his forms and his colors represented partial qualities and aspects of things that were willfully detached from the *whole thing*. (This process is different from the one Léger used later on when he used fragments of objects.) This was done in such an arbitrary manner that many of the canvases of this period appear nonfigurative at first glance, although they are actually based on a visual experience of reality. Léger found it superfluous to introduce anecdotal and recognizable elements of reality into his canvases, such as printed letters and collage. He held fast to visual experience, and tried to produce an immediate visual effect. If the theories and intellectual concepts are removed from his paintings, we are left with direct communication via the shock value obtained through purely plastic means. One must be caught up in the painting, and led to an understanding of it through lines, colors, rhythms, and contrasts; emotions and intellect are not supposed to intervene. There is no mystery or mysticism to be found.

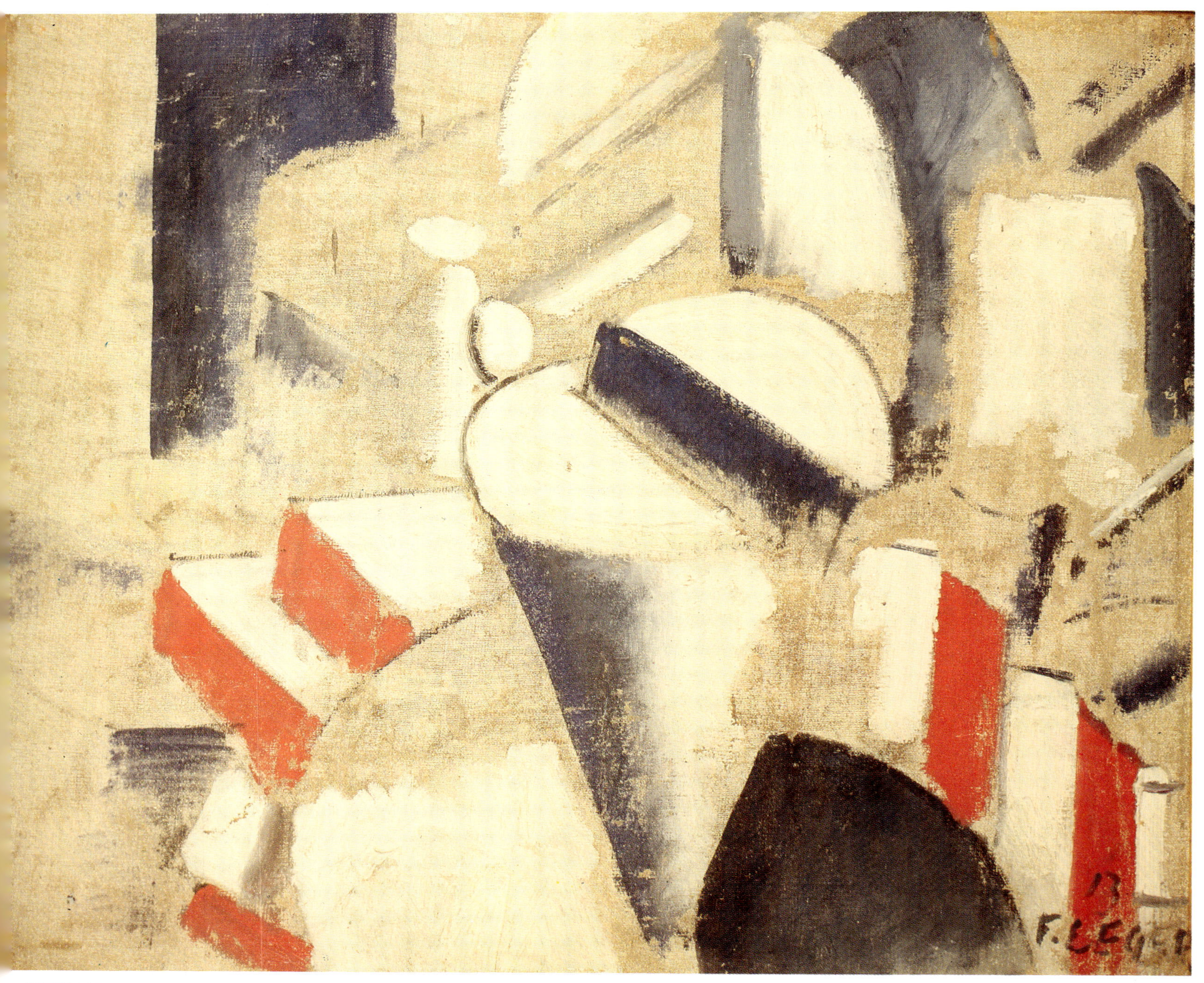

CONTRASTING FORMS
1913—Oil on canvas, 46 × 55 cm
Musée National Fernand Léger, Biot

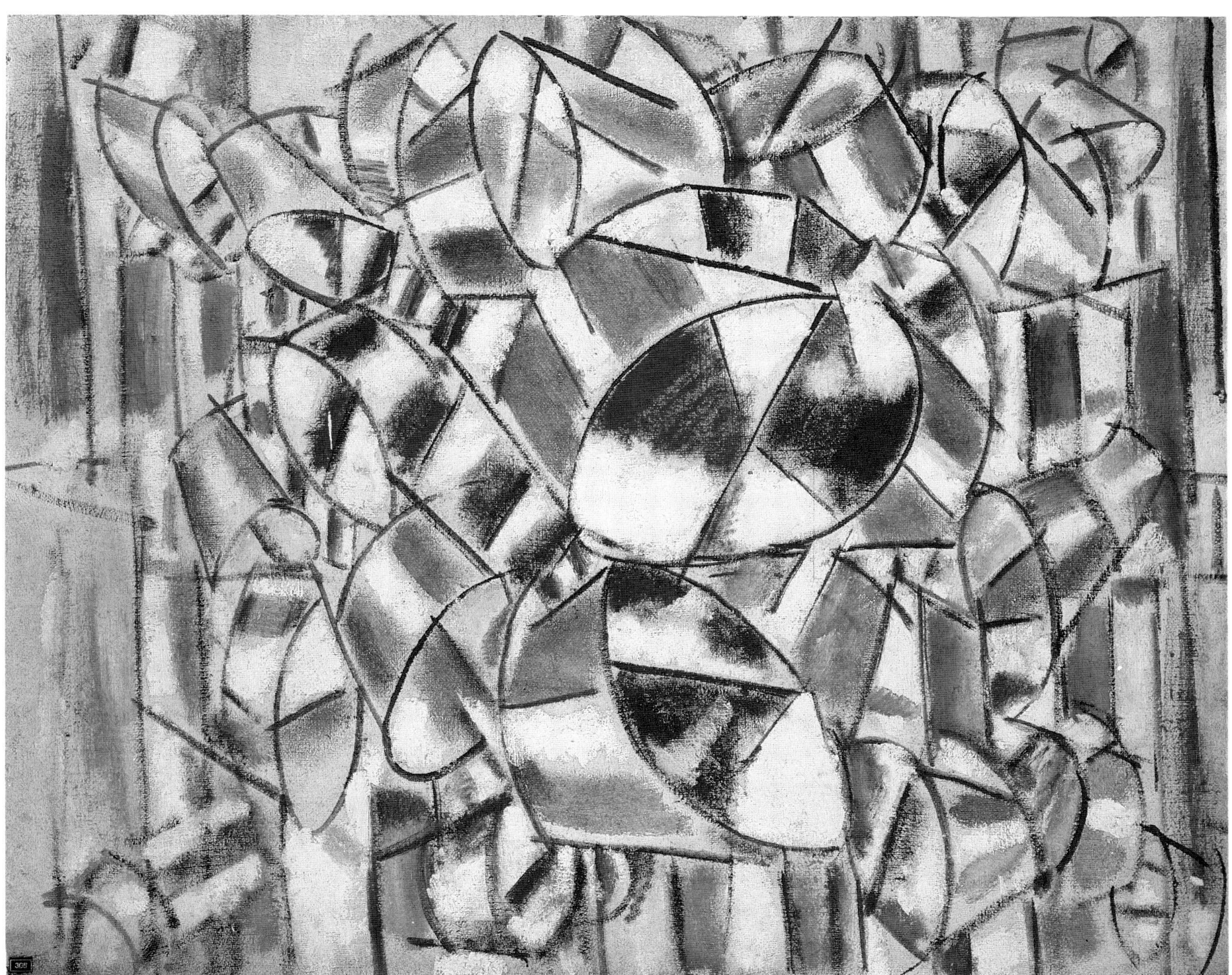

51. GEOMETRICAL ELEMENTS
1913—Oil on canvas, 81 × 100 cm
Staatsgalerie, Stuttgart

## The Cubo-Futurism of Malevich and the contrasts of Léger

Everybody tried to prove that "intellect" and "emotion" were not "supposed to" intervene. "Mystery" and "mysticism" were even more insignificant. There is something suspicious about this "call to order," in the same way that the Stalinist regime saw nothing other than the formal aspects in the works of Malevich. At the time, Malevich (who would become the father of Suprematism) was working with the same sort of tubular condensation of objects and characters that Léger was. Malevich painted *Woodcutter* in 1912 using an interplay of circles and cylinders that resulted in interlocking volumes with a strong mechanical effect reinforced by metallic colors.

Both Léger and Malevich were fighting their own separate battles with form and color, but it is difficult to accept that neither intellect nor emotion found its way onto their canvases. Léger was thinking about the visual effect of his "contrasting forms," and Malevich was focused on "Cubo-Futurism." What good is a machine that has no function? Were these painters robots without a soul?

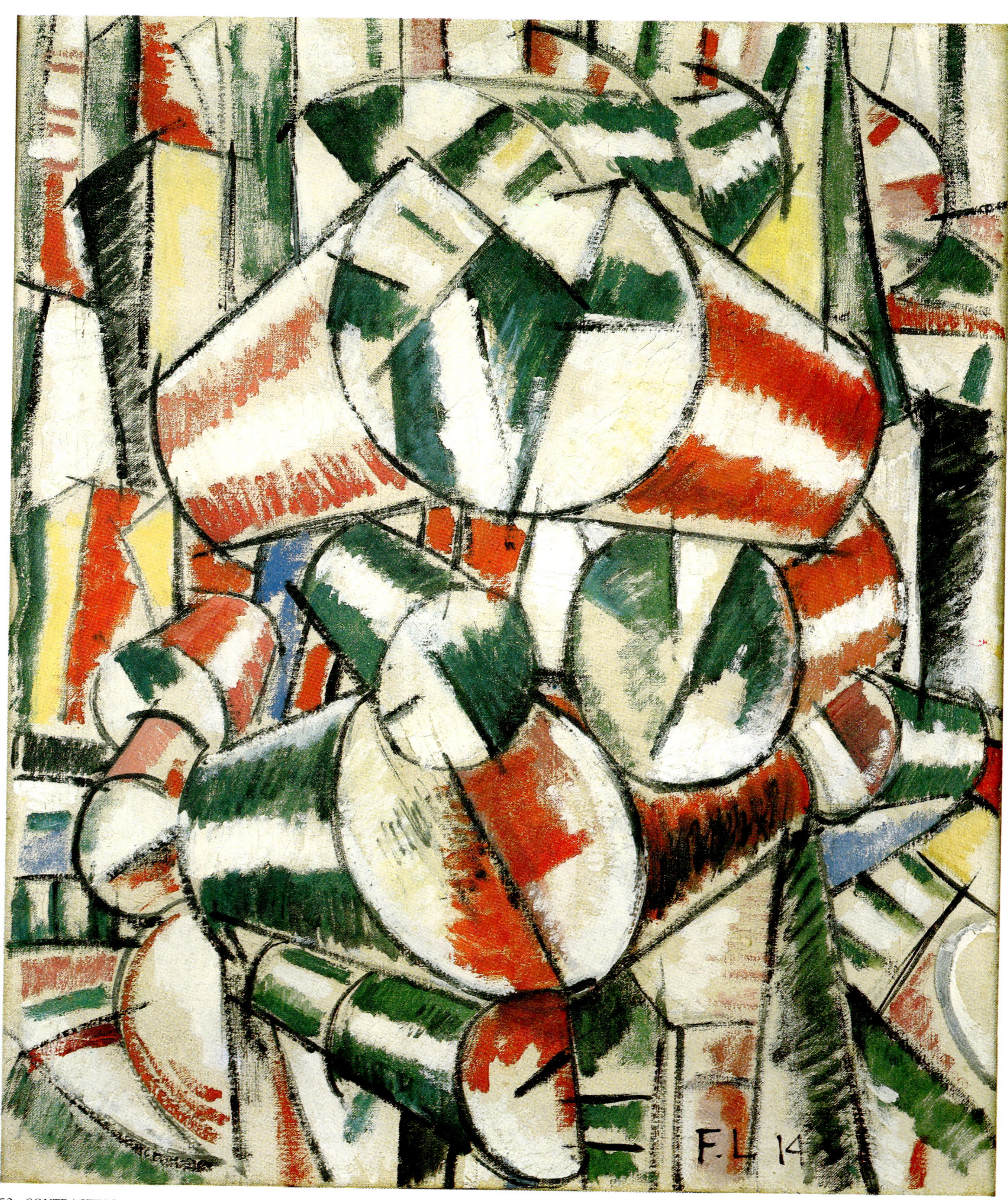


52. CONTRASTING FORMS
1914—Oil on canvas, 61 × 50 cm
Beyeler Gallery, Basel

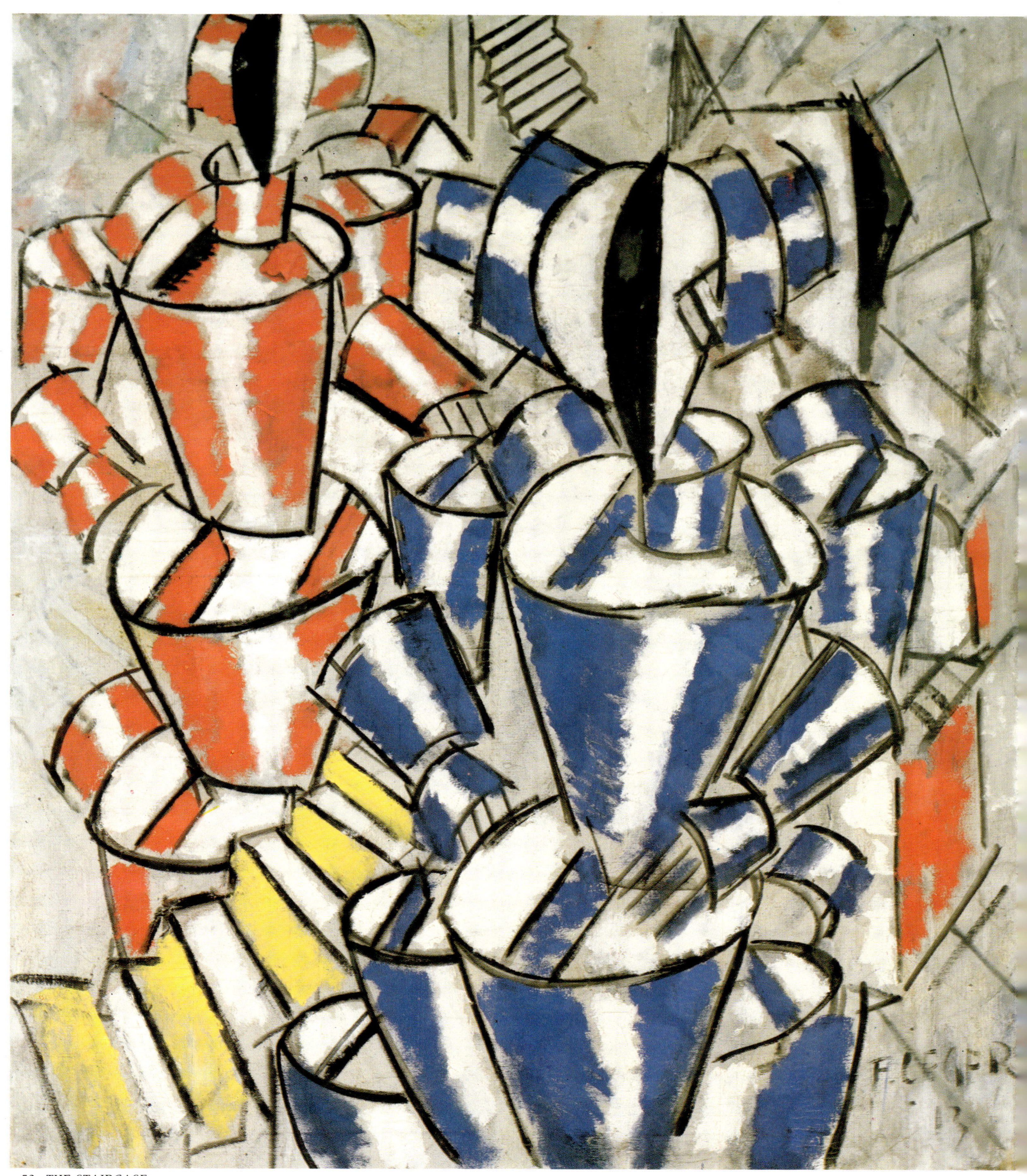

53. THE STAIRCASE
1913—Oil on canvas, 144 × 118 cm
Kunsthaus, Zurich

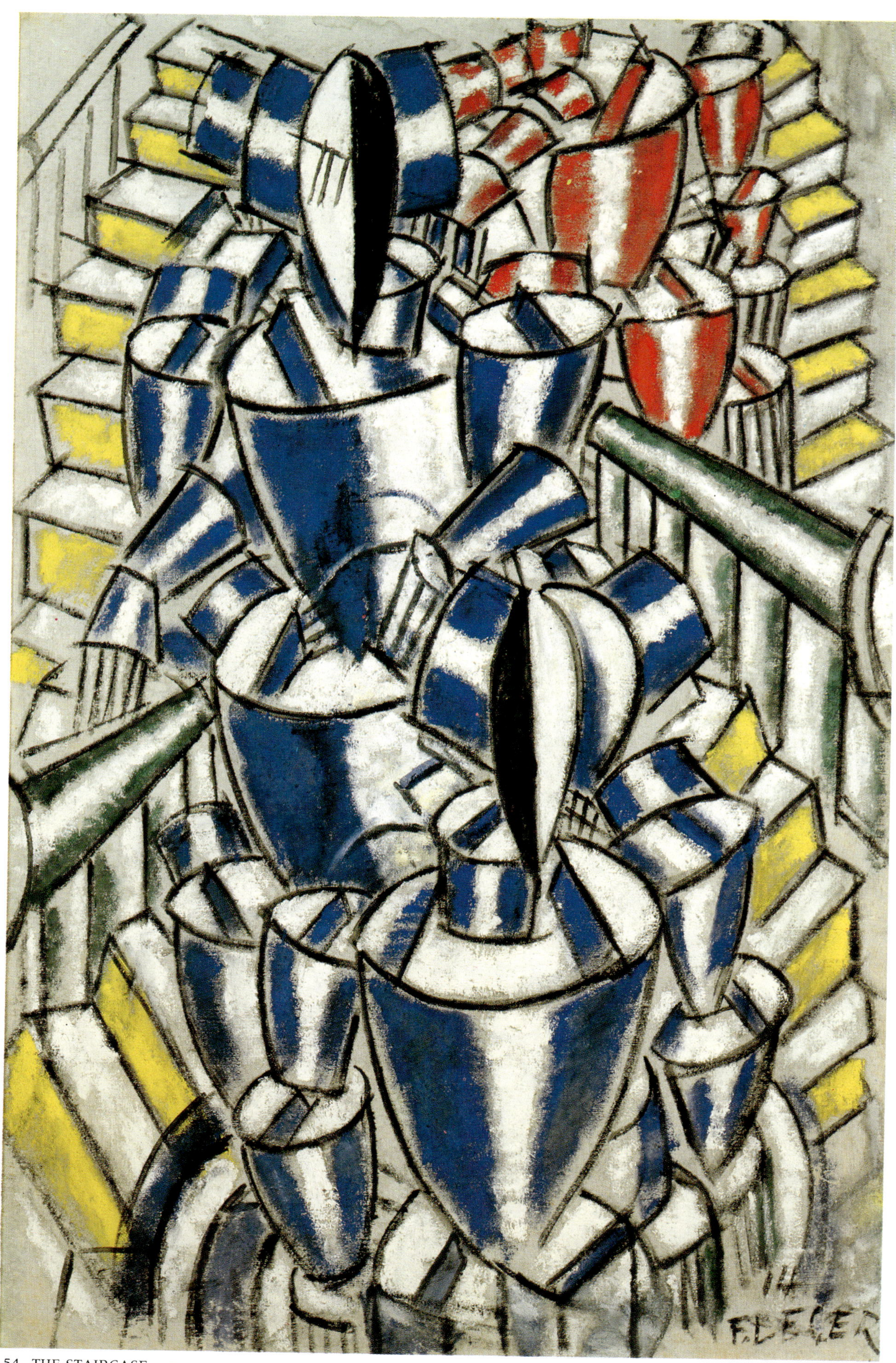

54. THE STAIRCASE
1914—Oil on canvas, 144.5 × 93.5 cm
Moderna Museet, Stockholm

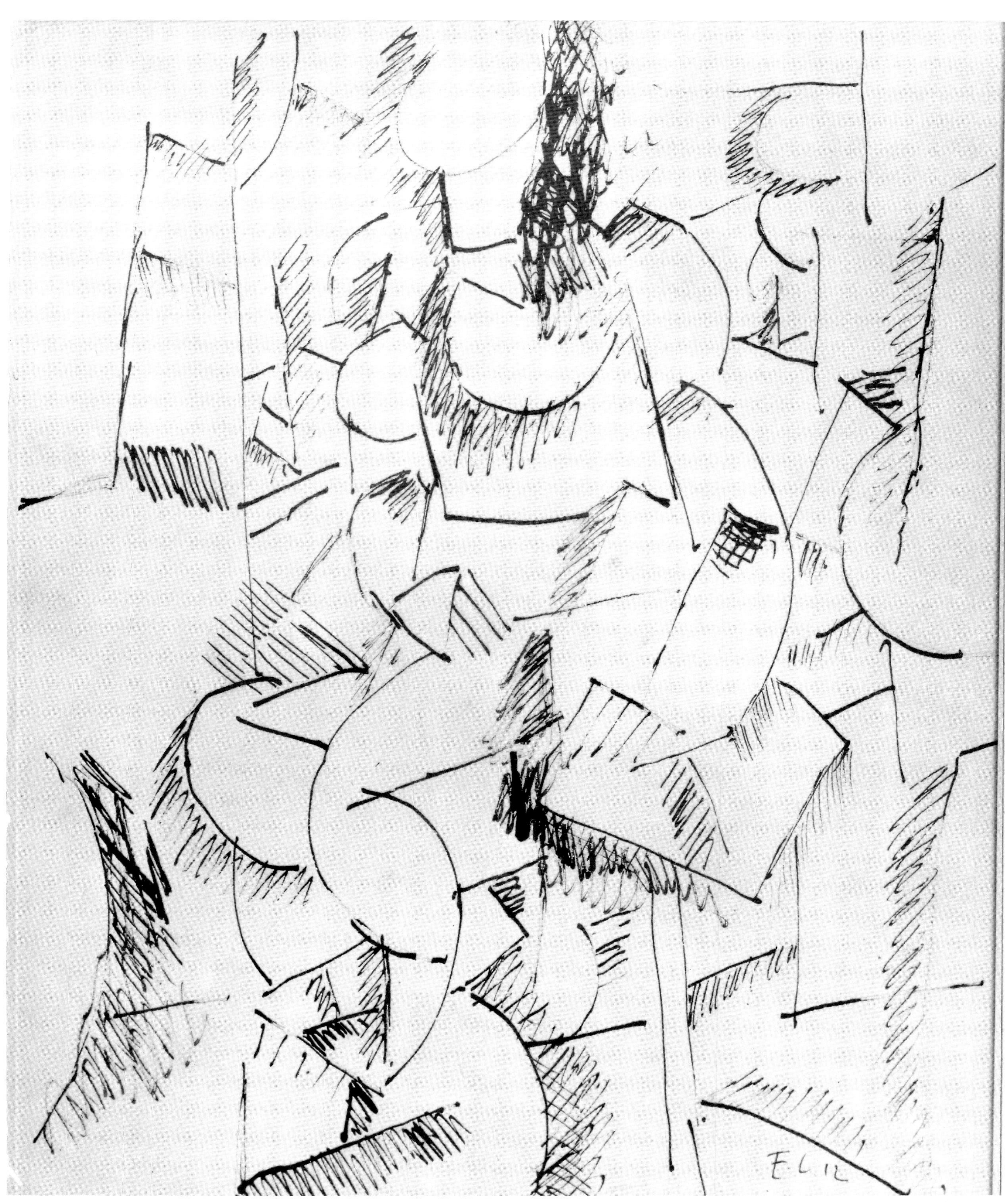


55. WOMAN
1912—Ink drawing
Private collection

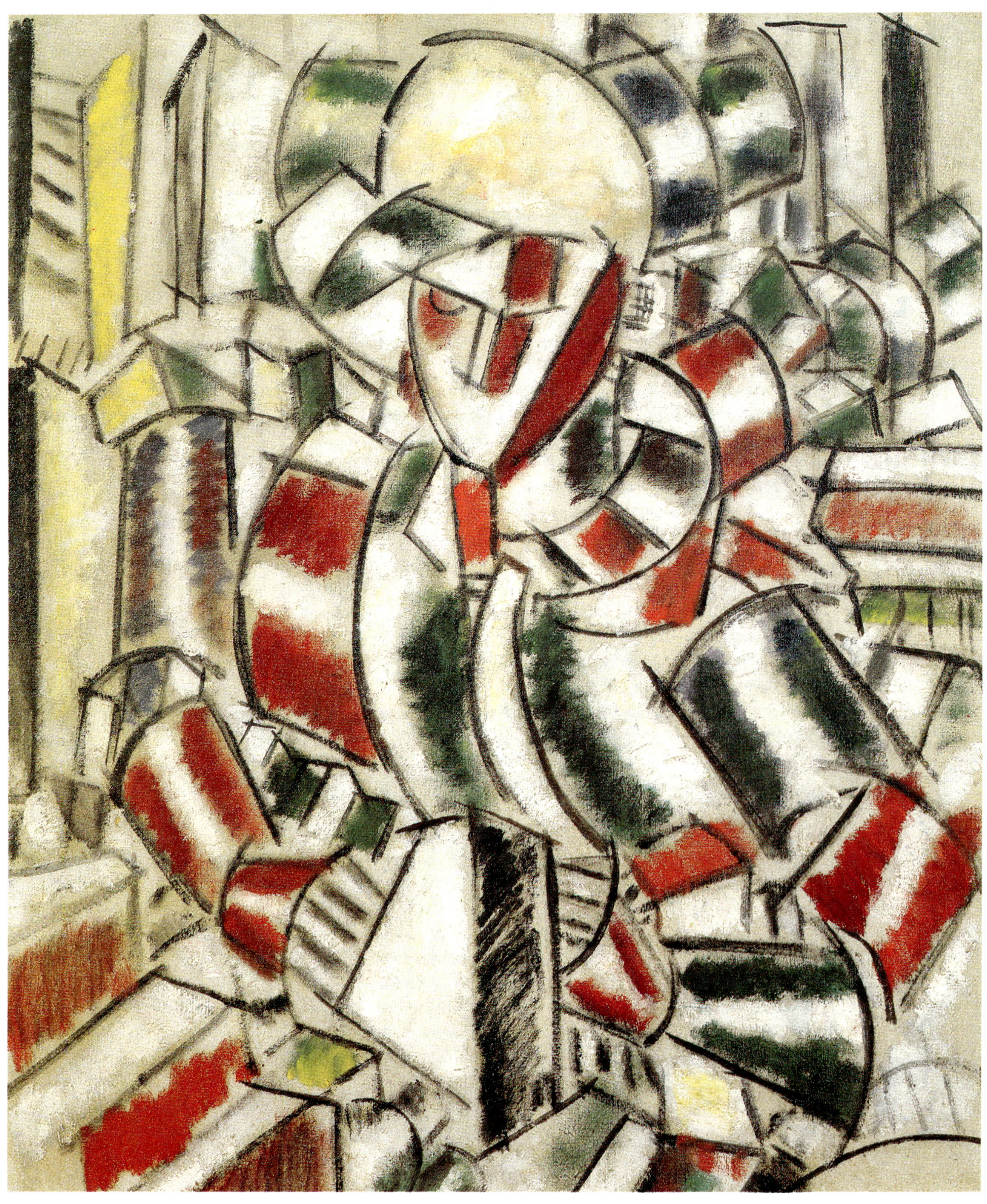

56. WOMAN IN RED AND GREEN
1914—Oil on canvas, 100 × 81 cm
Musée National d'Art Moderne, Centre Georges Pompidou, Paris

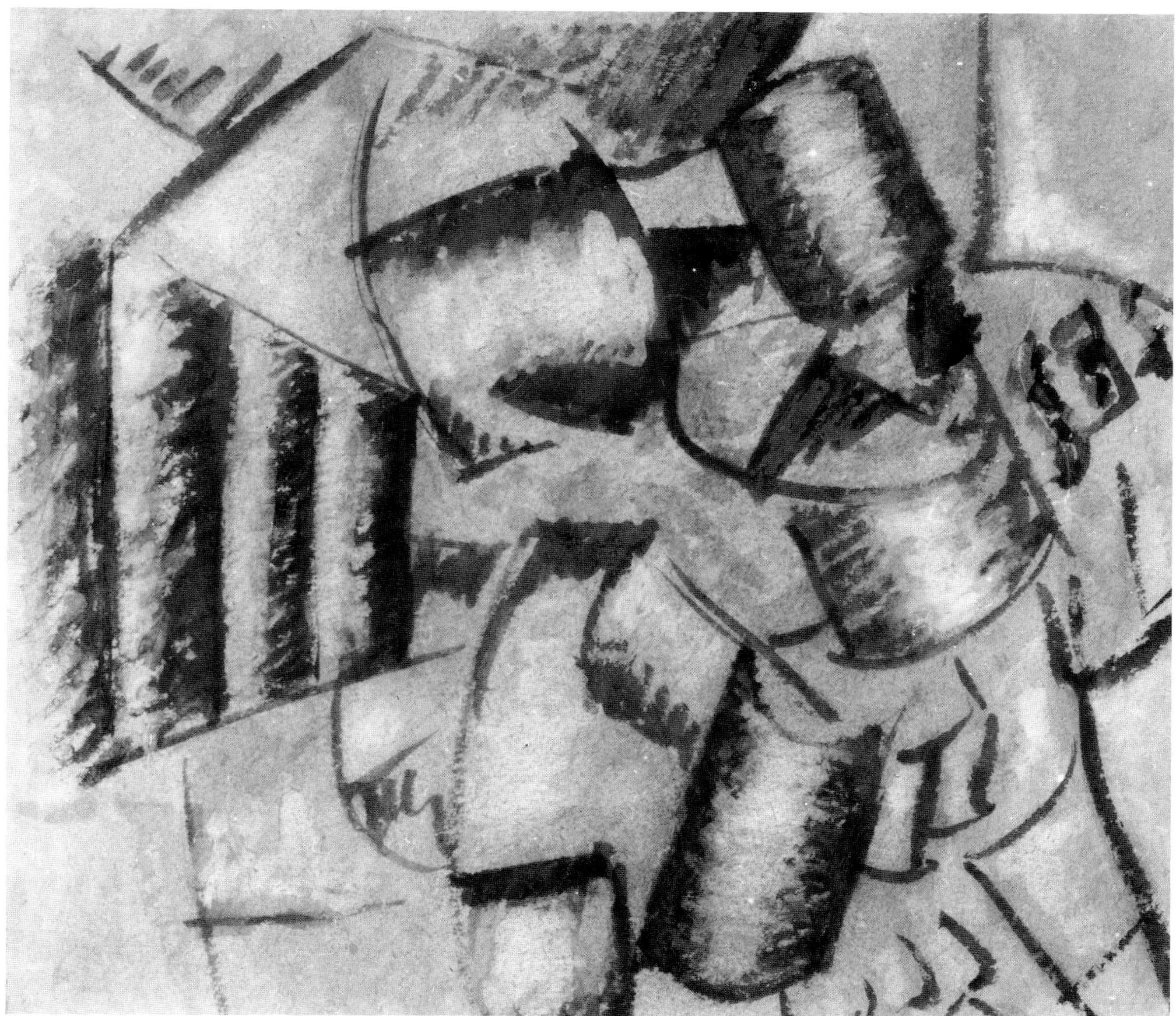

57. STUDY FOR *THE SMOKER*
1914—Gouache, 18 × 20 cm
Private collection

## Constructive abstraction

Roger Garaudy, as a member of the Central Committee of the French Communist Party and a Marxist in good standing who authored works such as *The Materialist Theory of Knowledge* and *God Is Dead*, insisted on the formalistic aspects of Léger's work. He considered it devoid of all philosophical speculation. Garaudy's sole focus was on plastic construction: "Léger would readily smirk at those who see Léger's work as a channel for metaphysical knowledge, or as a mystical key to reality, or even as a key to the mystery of things. He has no intention of discovering God's thought, the laws of nature, or the inner forces that move heaven and earth. Léger sees himself as a builder, not as a man of letters. In his abstract forms, he is looking for immediate visual reality, pure figuration separated from the pictorial matrix and even from the object. Line relationships have been an issue for as long as there have been architects. Léger situates the issue at the center of his work as a painter, but in terms of contrasts.

"It is for this reason that abstraction is a constant leitmotif throughout the body of his work: the orchestration is abstract, but the expression is concrete; 'the object' takes on its plastic value and importance to the extent that the abstract action of the forms, volumes, flat tints, reliefs, and colors are expressed concretely. Each time that Léger gravitated back towards large 'subjects' and monumental realism, the conjunction of geometrical forms, the figurative contrast of curves (be they clouds or human figures) with the straight lines and angles of a metal framework, the work became constructive abstraction. *The Builders* is an example." Ill. 311

Léger's atheism is well known. Nonetheless, there is a dimension beyond the formal side of his work.

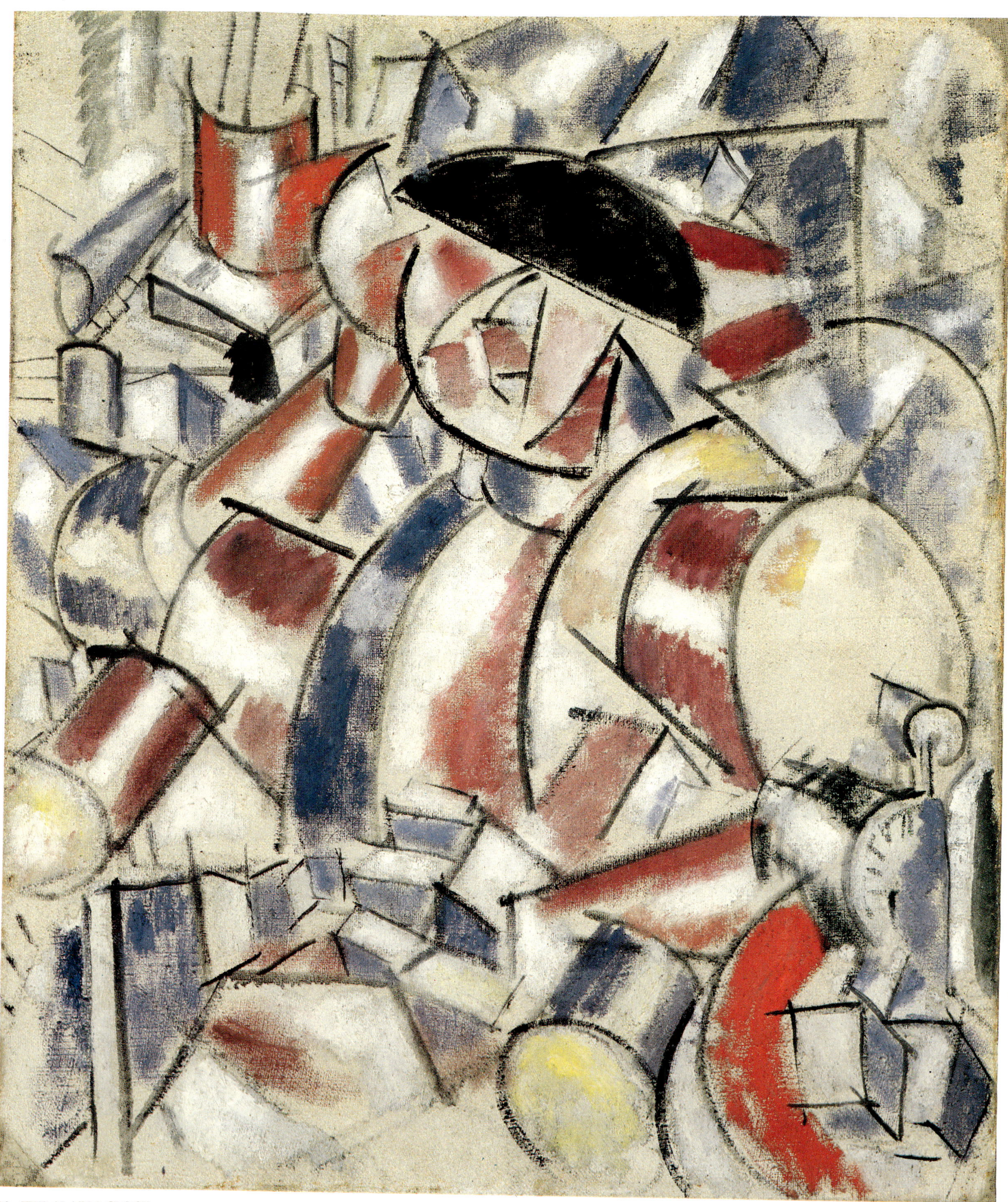

58. THE ALARM CLOCK
1914—Oil on canvas, 100 × 81 cm
Musée National d'Art Moderne, Centre Georges Pompidou, Paris
Gift of Jeanne and André Lefèvre

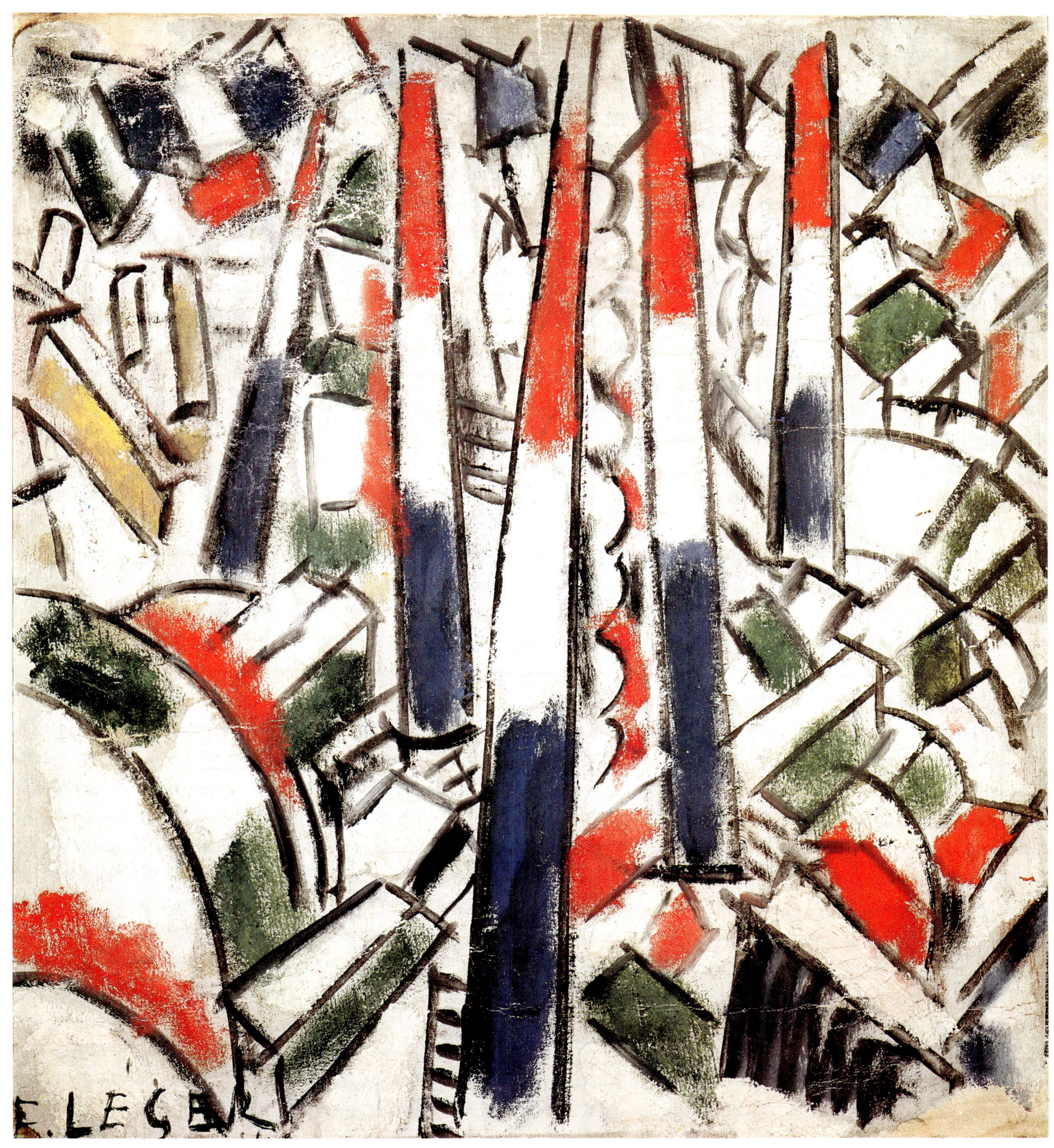


59. THE FOURTEENTH OF JULY 1914
1914—Oil on canvas, 73 × 60 cm
Musée National Fernand Léger, Biot

Léger as "medium," as all great artists are, was searching for that "naïveté of vision" in the manner of Cézanne. This did not mean "primitive." It meant the rediscovery of simplicity. Color, form, and contrast have no meaning if they do not engender beauty, joy, and light.

For Léger, people were the "poets" and "artists," but God was the only "creator." When André Verdet expressed surprise that an atheist like Léger was decorating a church, the painter replied: "There's no contradiction or hypocrisy in what I am doing. When I magnify sacred objects, the nails, the ciboria, the crown of thorns, the elements that depict the Passion of Christ, I am not deviating from my objectives. My spirit is healthy, and I don't need to rely on any kind of crutch. I quite simply had the undreamed-of opportunity to decorate vast surfaces in strict keeping with my plastic concepts. My only desire was to bring an evolving rhythm of form and color to everyone, believers and nonbelievers alike, something that could be useful and widely accepted because *it spreads joy and light in the hearts of everyone.*"

The more one gets to know the works, words, and writings of Léger, the more it becomes clear that he is closer to the geometric pantheism of Spinoza and the "constructive flame," the "artistic spark" of the Stoics, than he is to the Marxist-Leninist brand of Stalinism.

On the eve of World War I, Léger's forms became more visible within the "contrasting forms." Traces of women's portraits appeared with dresses and hats. From time to time a feature would be sketched, such as an eye or a nose right in the middle of a conical face. The shock of war would push Léger in the direction he had already been leaning towards.

### The flags of the Fourteenth of July

Ill. 59 There are "Fauve" touches in Léger's *Fourteenth of July 1914* that remind us of his rooftop landscapes of four years earlier: the landscapes of Paris painted from his window at 13 Rue de l'Ancienne-Comédie
Ill. 61 in the Latin Quarter. The paintings are full of spirit,
Ill. 62 despite the rumblings of war. His city landscapes are joyous movements on the canvas: cube houses and circles of trees, sweeping kaleidoscopes that show none of the tragic confrontation of Cézanne's houses crushed into the trees. Léger explained: "I take the visual effects of trees, the curves and circles moving skyward between the houses and whose plastic value must be translated onto the canvas. This is the best example of the application of my research: multiplied intensity. Concentrate your curves with the greatest possible variety without disconnecting them; surround them by the dry, hard surfaces of the houses, which are dead surfaces that will come to life and become mobile when you paint them in colors that are in opposition to what surrounds them. This maximizes the effect." It sounds easy, but you have to be Léger to make the recipe work! Apollinaire, being a great admirer of what Léger cooked up on canvas, wrote in "The Cubist Painters: Esthetic Meditations": "Look at you, beautiful tints, light colors, and bubbling forms! The pleasant fumes are the emblem of civilization. The sky that is awry is the ceiling over our streets that has been cut apart and placed upright. The infinite sweetness of raspberry-colored roofs. It wouldn't matter if a man had a hand with six fingers, or if he had three legs. I love Léger's art because there's not a trace of disdain in it. There's no vulgarity either, and he's not a man of contradictions." Apollinaire plays with the word *léger*, which means "light and airy," to praise the artist and the artist's use of color: "Oh, how I love your airy colors [*couleurs légères*], Fernand Léger. Fantasy will never elevate you to fairyland, but it will furnish you with all your joy. Your painting is liquid: the sea, blood, rivers, rain, a glass full of water, and our sweat and tears from major efforts and long fatigues that could also fill a glass; the humidity of kisses, too."

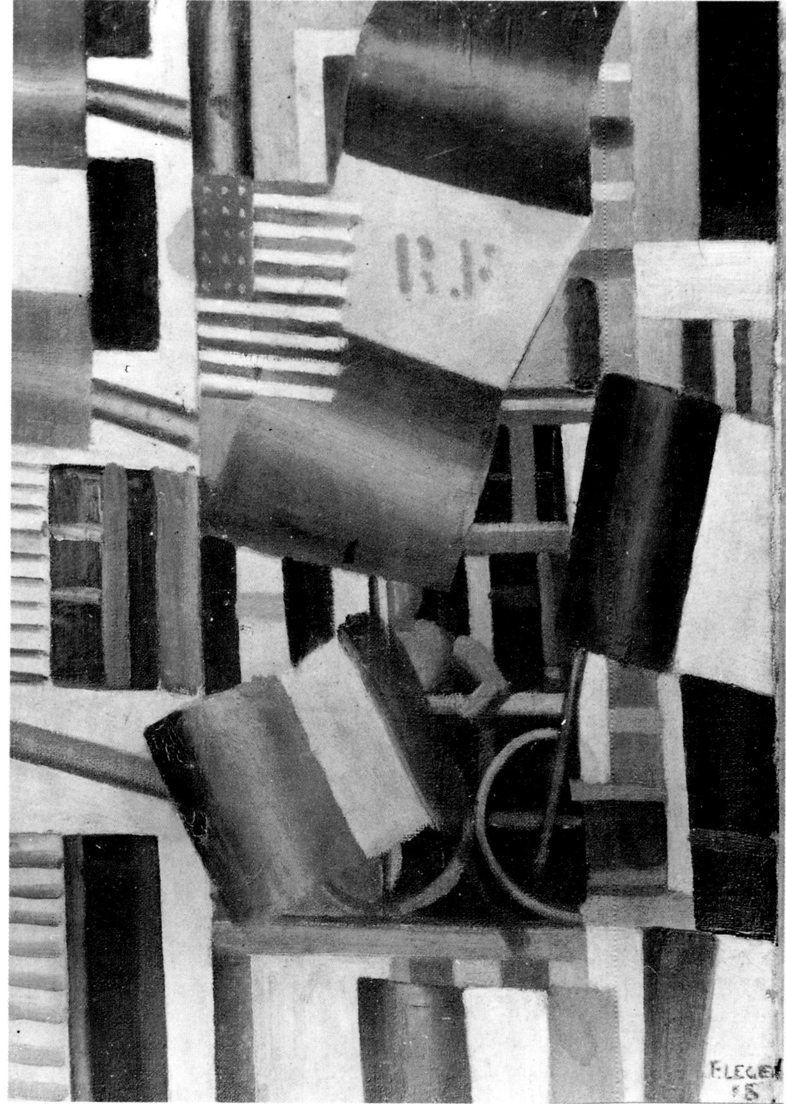

60. THE FLAGS
1918—Oil on canvas
Private collection

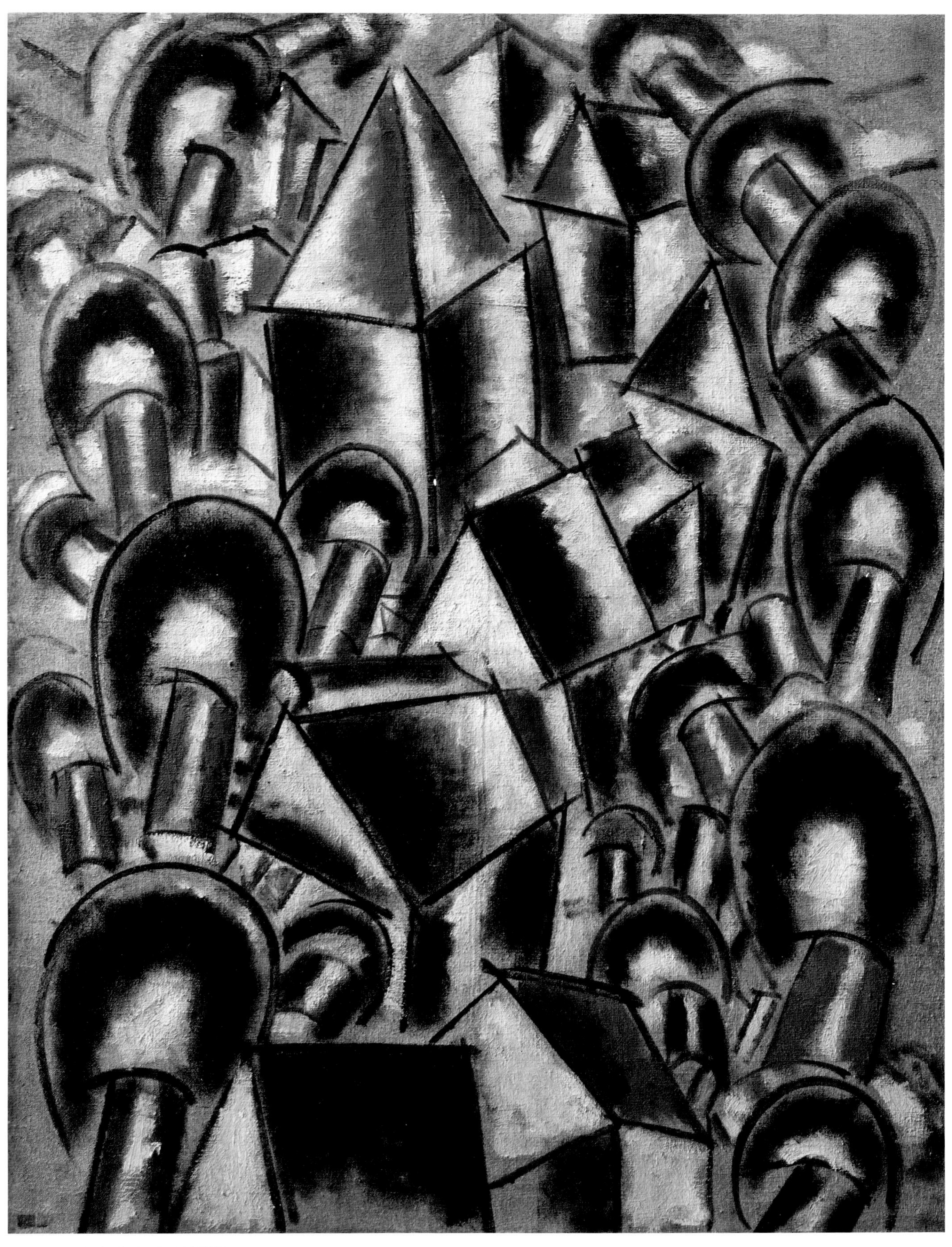

61. THE HOUSES IN THE TREES
1914—Oil on canvas, 130 × 97 cm
Oeffentliche Kunstsammlung, Kunstmuseum, Basel

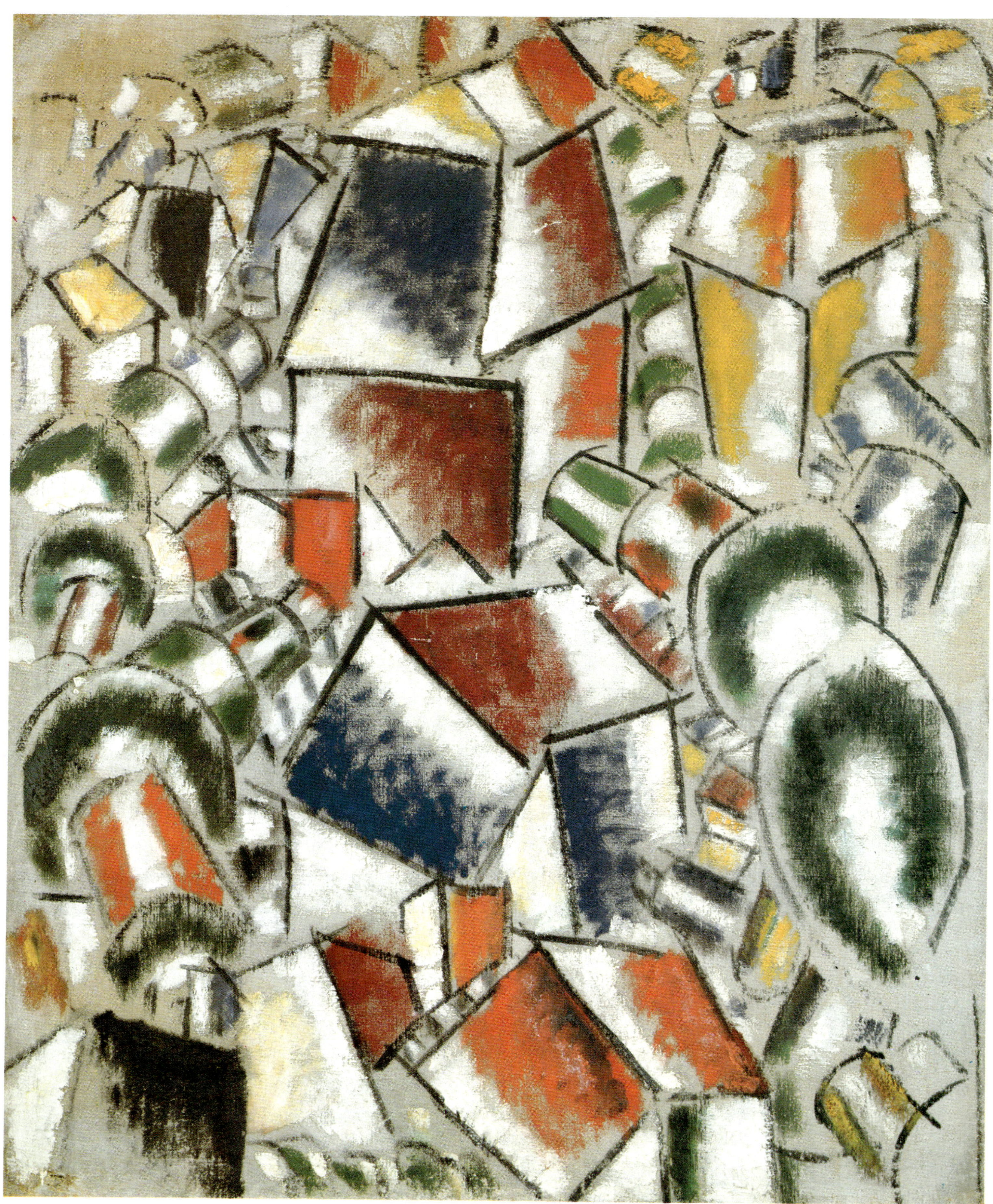

62. LANDSCAPE
1914—Oil on canvas, 102 × 83 cm
Musée d'Art Moderne, Villeneuve-d'Ascq
Gift of Geneviève and Jean Masurel

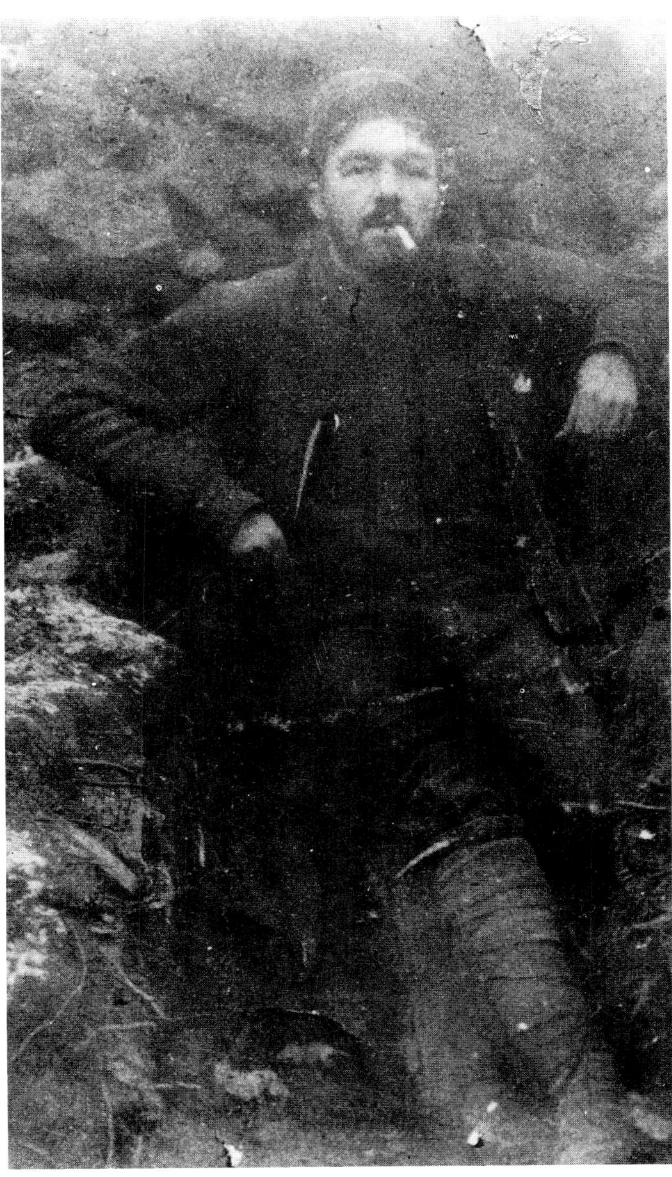

63. FERNAND LEGER AT THE "FOREST HOUSE" IN 1915

## A breech of a 75mm cannon in sunlight

August—1914. At the age of thirty-three, Léger was mobilized. As a soldier he was gassed in 1916, and then finally discharged at the end of 1917. "The war was a major event for me," he wrote. "There was a supra-poetic atmosphere at the front. It excited me to the core. Good God! What faces! And then there was the mud, the corpses, the artillery. I had never sketched a cannon before, but I had them right in front of my eyes. The war allowed me to sink my feet into the dirt. . . . I had left Paris in the throes of abstraction, a period of pictorial liberation. Without any transition I was suddenly among the whole French people; my new buddies were miners, laborers of the earth, artisans of wood and iron. . . . At the same time I was stunned by the sight of the breech of a 75 millimeter in the sunlight. It was the magic of light on the white metal. That's all it took for me to forget the abstract art of 1912–1913. The crudeness, variety, humor, and downright perfection of certain men around me, their precise sense of utilitarian reality and its application in the midst of the life-and-death drama we were in, and even more than that. . . These poets and inventors of everyday poetic images made me went to paint in slang with all its color and mobility. Once I had taken a bite out of this reality, I would never forget the objects that populated it. In terms of my plastic evolution, I learned more from the breech of a 75 in the sunlight than from all the museums of the world. When I returned from the war, I continued to use what I had experienced at the front."

## The Verdun sketches Ill. 64
Ill. 69

When Léger first began his military duty and was Ill. 70
unable to paint, he sketched the soldiers in the Ill. 73
trenches, the corpses, and the devastated cities and towns. It was not long, however, before the painter's incorrigible optimism took over, and his Verdun sketches became charming Cubist landscapes. Instead of battle scenes, he sketched scenes of soldiers during their leisure time. He portrayed them relaxing, smoking a pipe, or playing cards. In 1938, Léger declared to a group of workers: "A work of art has no place on the battlefield. On the contrary, it must be a source of relaxation from the exhaustion of your daily struggles." He would also say: "Between us, do you really think that a working-class man would want to have a painting on the wall of his home in which he saw himself sweating inside a factory? He would prefer to have a bouquet of flowers or a nice landscape hanging on his wall. It's a matter of waiting until he, too, can be liberated and elevated to a higher artistic level."

64. ARTILLERY HORSES
1915—China ink drawing, 14.5 × 18.5 cm
Private collection

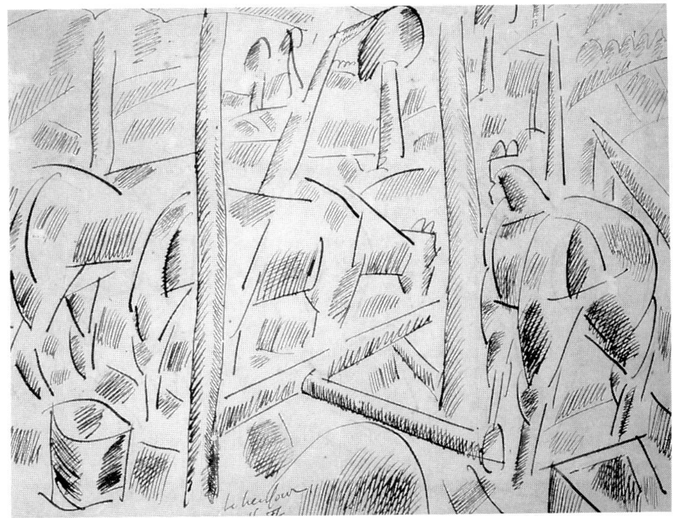

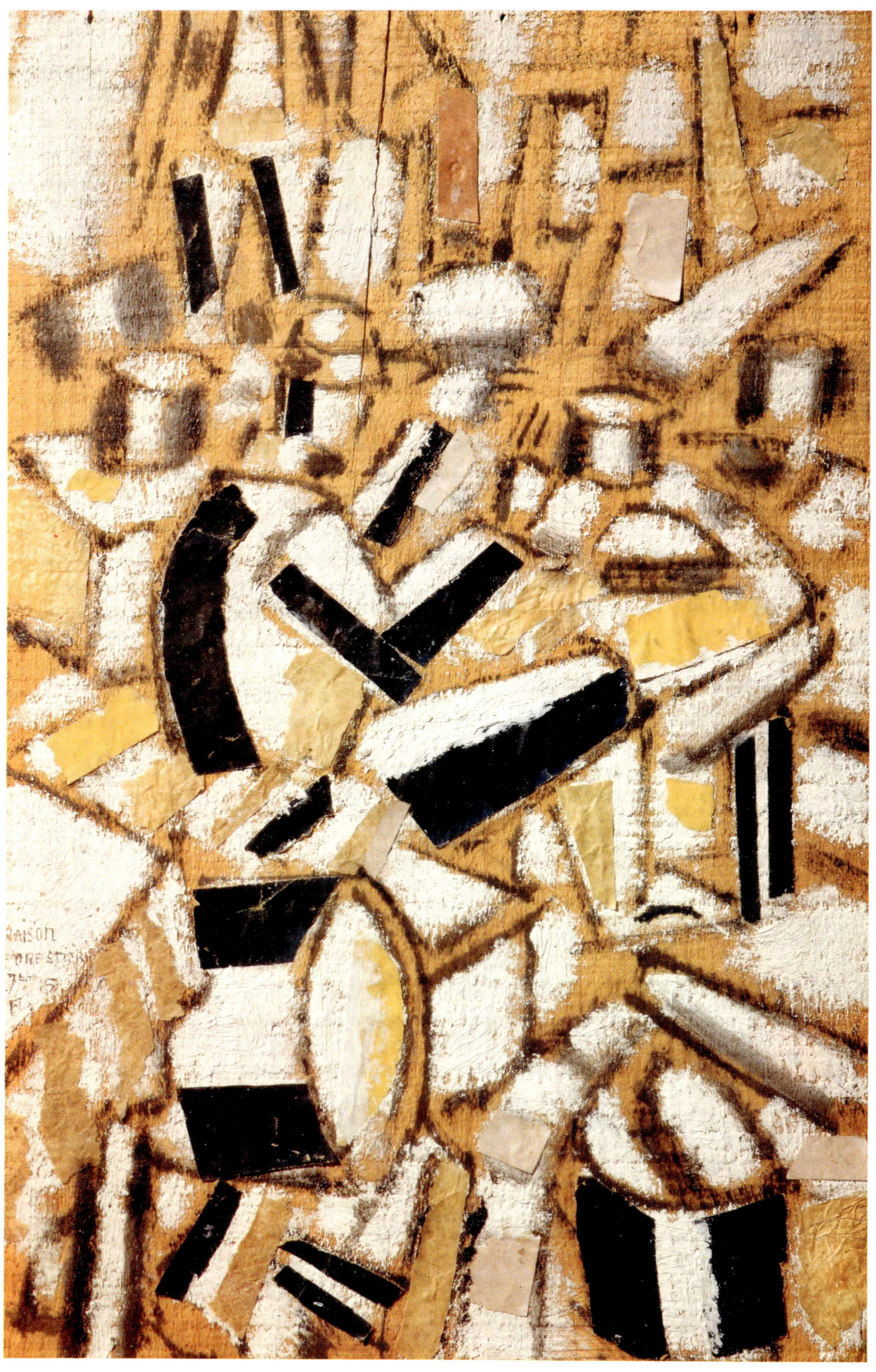

65. THE CARD GAME
1915—Oil on posterboard, 39 × 26 cm
Private collection, Baltimore

66. THE CARD GAME
1917—Oil on canvas, 129 × 193 cm
Rijksmuseum Kröller Müller, Otterlo

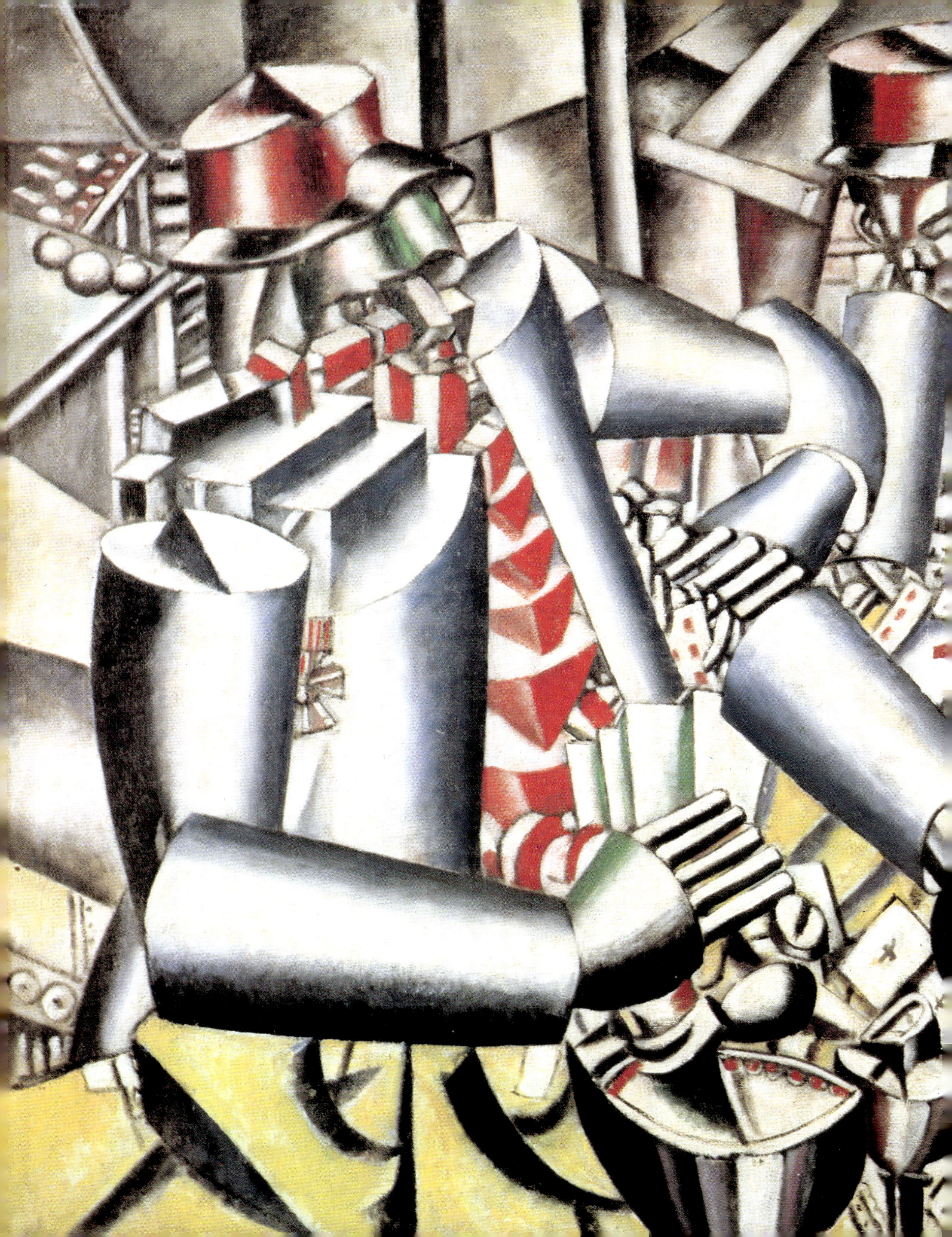

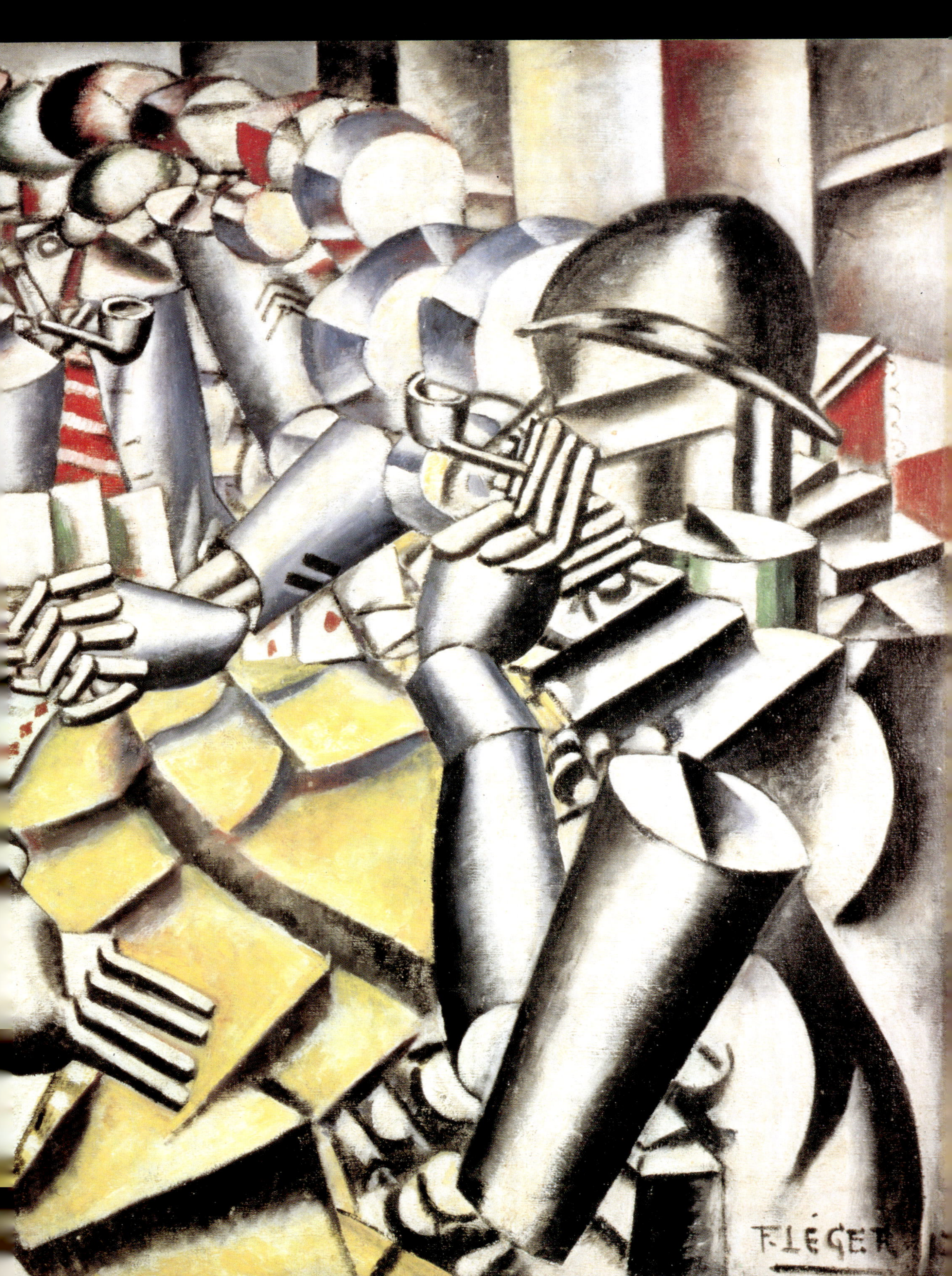
F. LÉGER

Ill. 66 ***The Card Game***

In 1917, Léger was immobilized at the Villepinte Hospital and had his revenge by painting *The Card Game,* a large war canvas that was astonishing in its gaiety and color. It was a monumental work (129 by 193 centimeters). The format was similar to that of
Ill. 43 *The Wedding,* but the palette differed. Léger replaced the earlier contrasting primary colors with a metallic, toned palette in the manner of Malevich. Léger's "card players," which preceded his "mechanical period," were already beginning to take on the aspects
Ill. 39 of his robots. They remind us of his "woodcutters" from 1909–10, except that he used the kind of cold, metallic patina that was very characteristic of the forms he would create in the early 1920s. "Sunlight on cannon barrels and the very nudity of objects are what influenced me and shaped my work."

There is no doubt: *The Card Game* marks a new phase in Léger's evolution. Léger spoke of it as "the first painting in which I deliberately took my subject matter from current events." He loved the soldiers. They were his buddies. "It's the war that brought me down to earth. . . Gosh, were those guys big! I was pretty hardy myself, and I wasn't scared. I became buddies with them. So much so that when I was offered the chance to go into the safety of camouflage, far from the front, I didn't want to leave them. 'I'm staying,' I said. While the guys were playing cards, I'd stay nearby and watch them. I did pencil drawings and sketches because I wanted to capture those moments. Those fellows really made an impression on me, and the desire to sketch them was a spontaneous thing. Later on, that's what turned into *The Card Game.*" Curiously enough, all this warmth and camaraderie Léger expressed turned into cold and metallic forms in *The Card Game.* It was as if the painter had drawn on his actual experiences, his discovery of men in their diversity, their bonding, and their slang that was "so expressive that it even impressed Apollinaire," and then had undergone some revelation as he contemplated all this in the very real context of a life-and-death situation. As Léger delved into the essential experience through these men, they were transformed into monstrous robots on his canvas. The painting is as much a protestation against war as it is an expression of war. It is a condemnation and an exaltation of the mechanical world revealed through the barrel of a cannon. At the same time, it is the affirmation of the beauty of mechanical things, and Léger's certitude that a new relationship between man and the machine was possible, that a period of destruction was first and foremost a time for building, as well. According to Roger Garaudy, "It's an angry outburst against war, which compels men to become uniform and mechanical robots, and at the same time it's a tribute to the power of man, who is able to create these machines whose very rhythm exalts man's power to direct and control them. This mechanistic force in a state of war crushes men. In war, it is an atrociously *alienated* expression of power, but it is power, nonetheless."

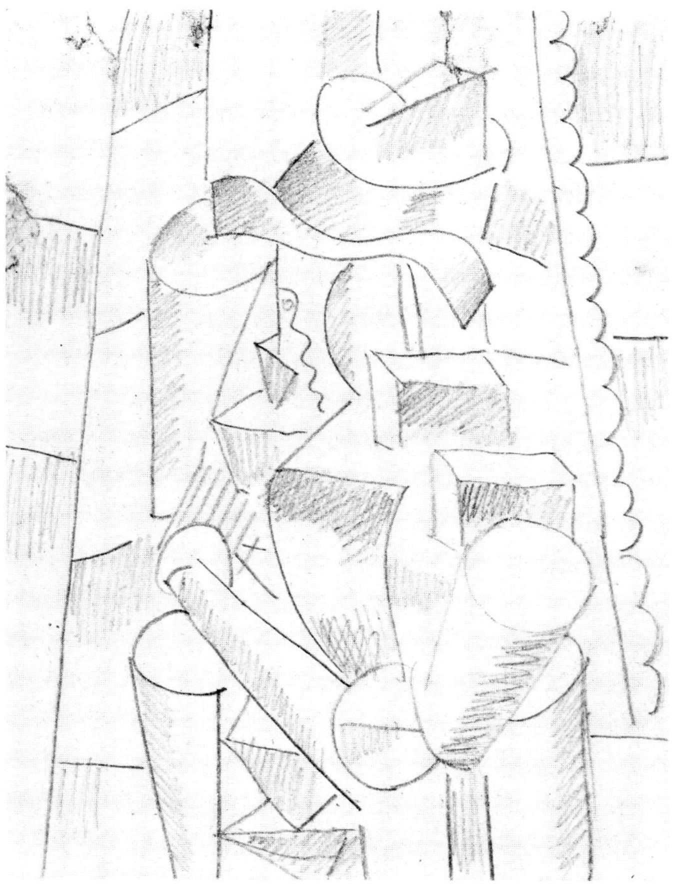

67. STUDY FOR *THE SOLDIER WITH A PIPE*
About 1916—Pencil sketch on paper, 17 × 12.2 cm
Musée National d'Art Moderne, Centre Georges Pompidou, Paris

***Soldier with a Pipe*** Ill. 68

While Léger was on furlough in 1916 he painted *Soldier with a Pipe.* The soldier is a hierarchical form that came straight out of his "spontaneous" sketches. It is one of his first powerful effigies. In this particular instance it was rooted in the tragic reality of war, and captured in its fullness during a moment of leisure. It is one of those effigies that, in the words of Pierre Abraham, made Léger "a herald of the common man."

Léger did not like war. It singularly lacked color. He complained about this: "War was gray and camouflaged. Anything with light, color, or even tone was forbidden and punishable by death. It was a life of the blind, where everything that was perceivable and detectable to the eye had to be hidden and made to disappear. Nobody saw the war. It was masked, dissimulated, crawling, and earth-colored. The useless eye saw nothing. Everyone 'heard' the war. It was a symphony so enormous that no composer or musician has ever been able to equal it: *Four years without*

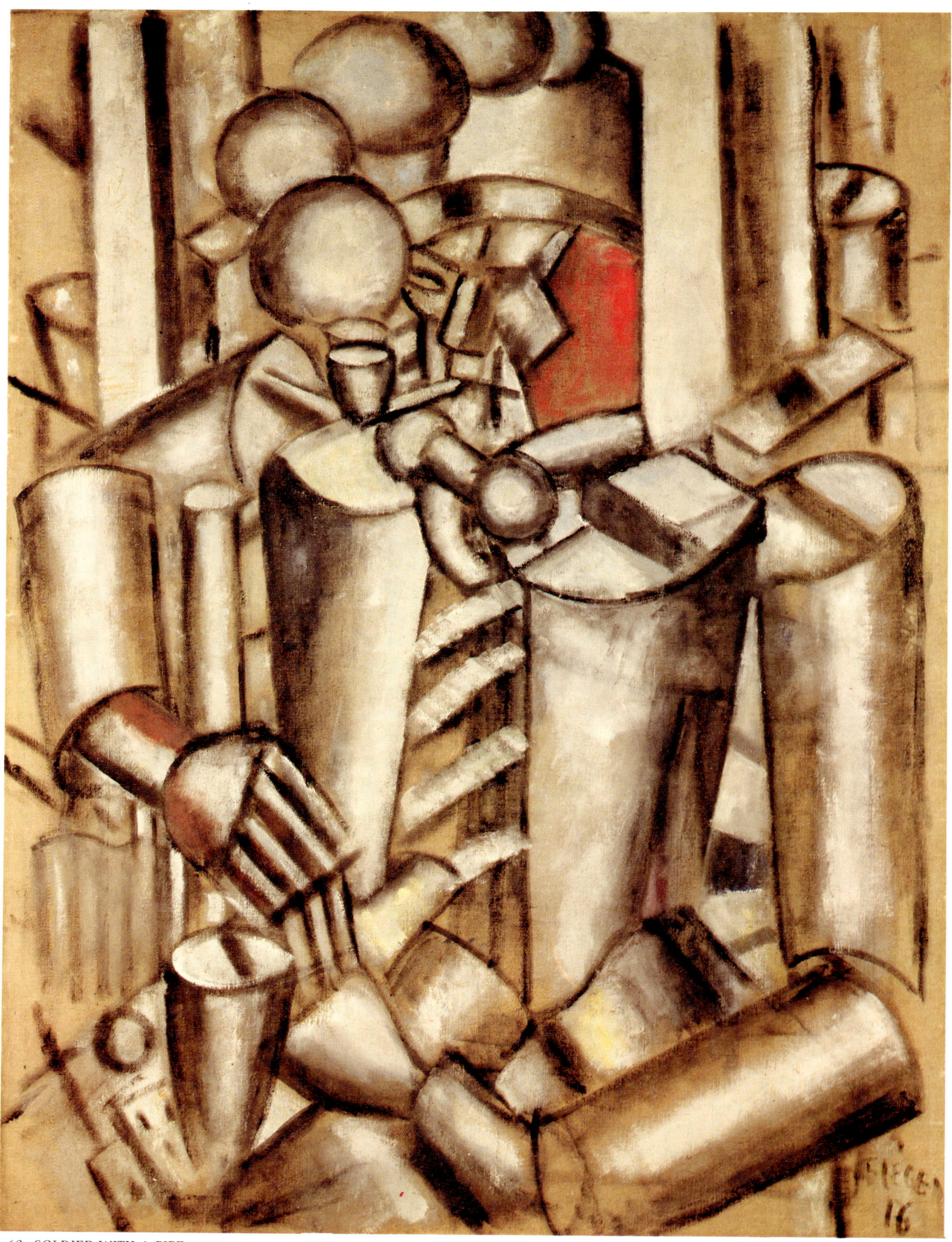

68. SOLDIER WITH A PIPE
1916—Oil on canvas, 130 × 97 cm
Kunstsammlung Nordrhein Westfalen, Düsseldorf

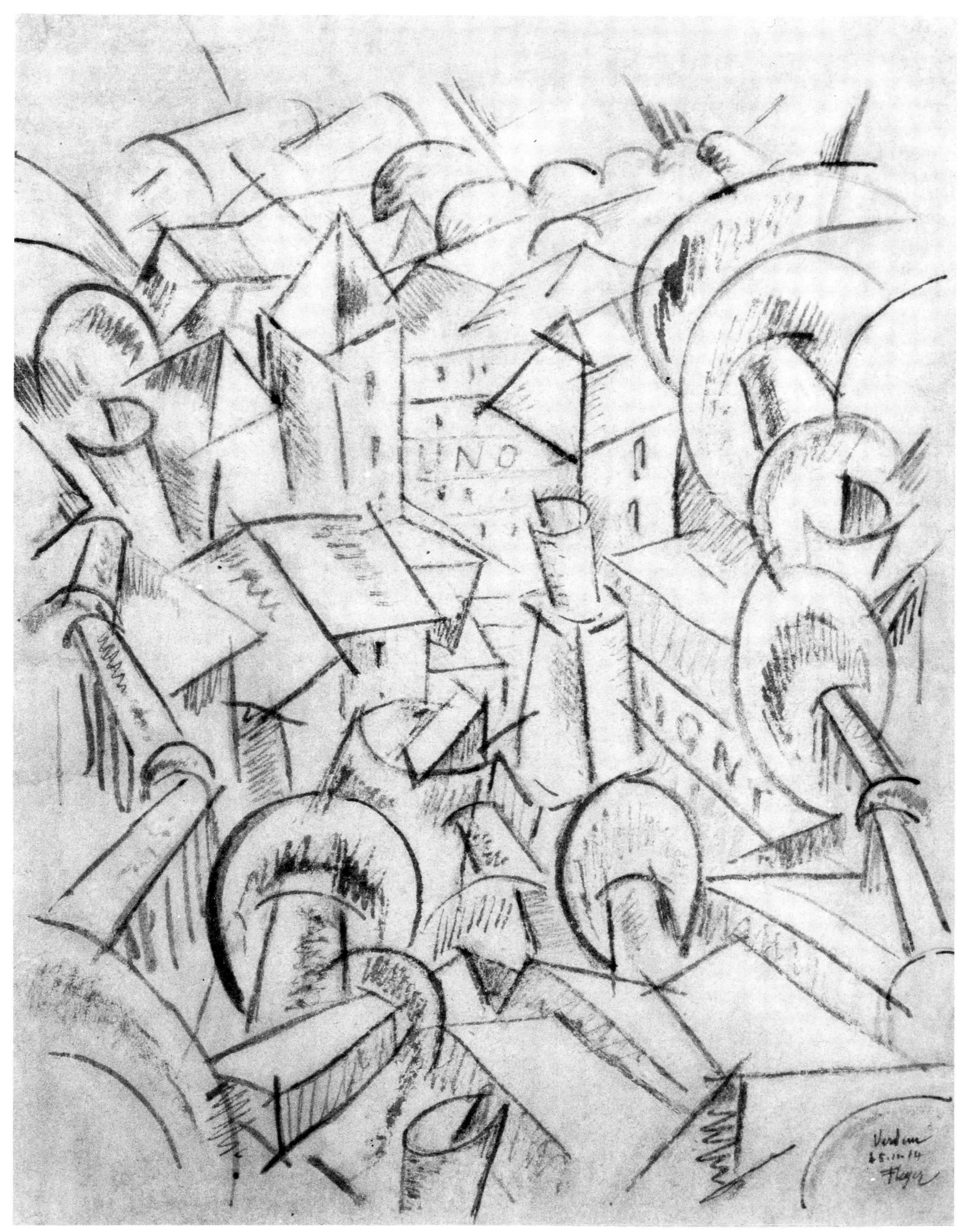


69. VERDUN, OCTOBER 25, 1914
1914—Pen drawing, 31 × 23.5 cm
Private collection

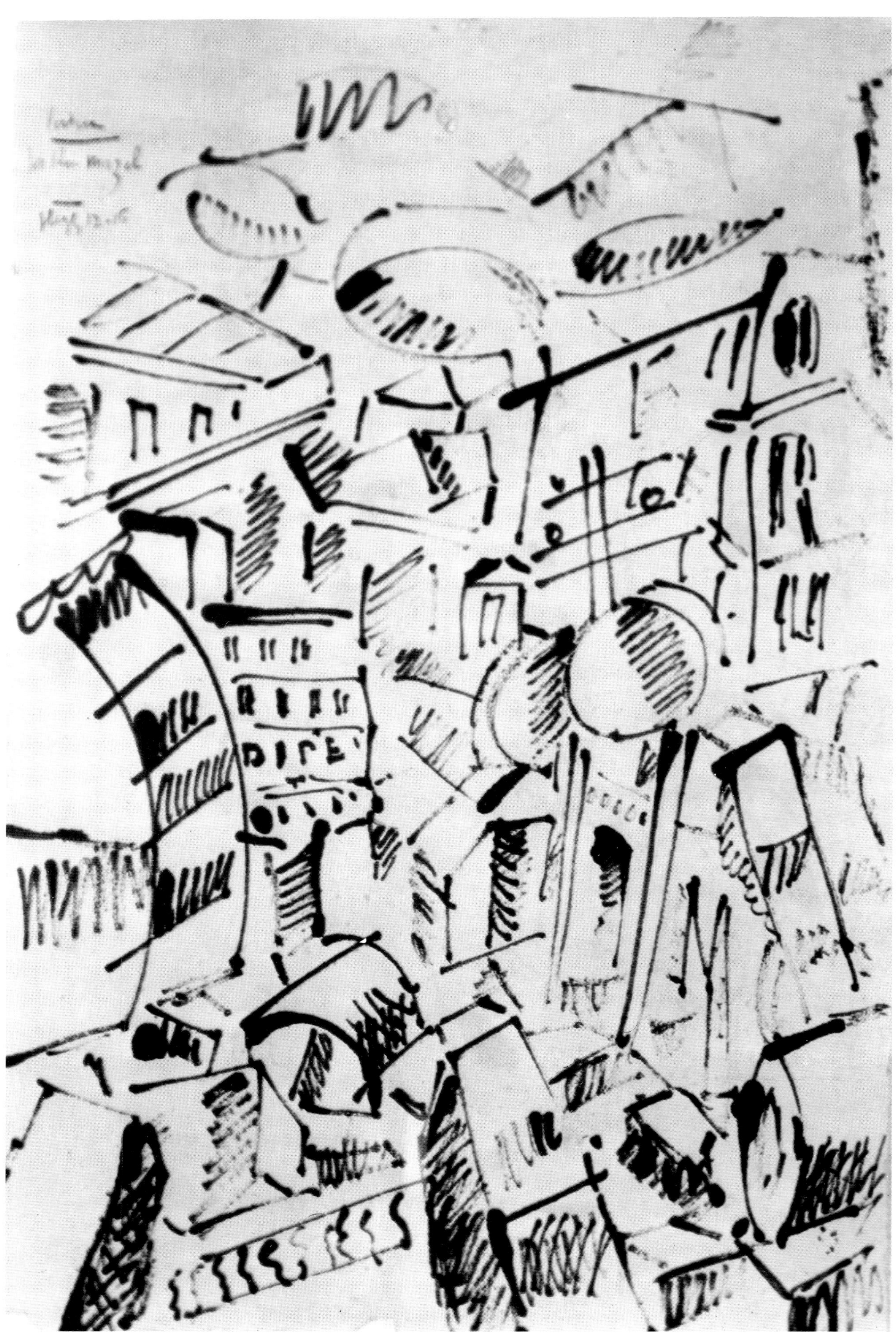

70. VERDUN, MAZEL STREET
1916—Ink drawing on paper, 30 × 19 cm
Private collection

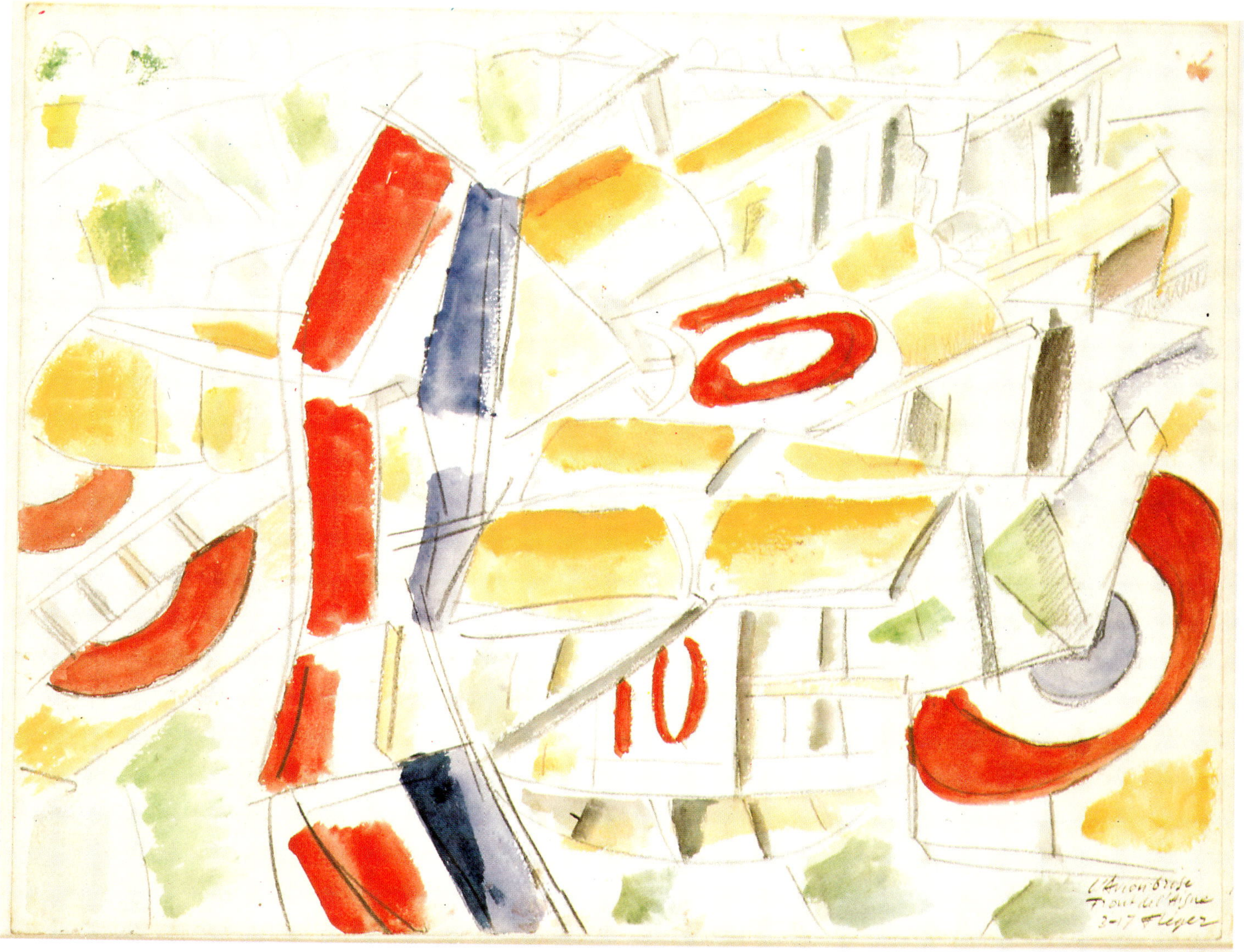

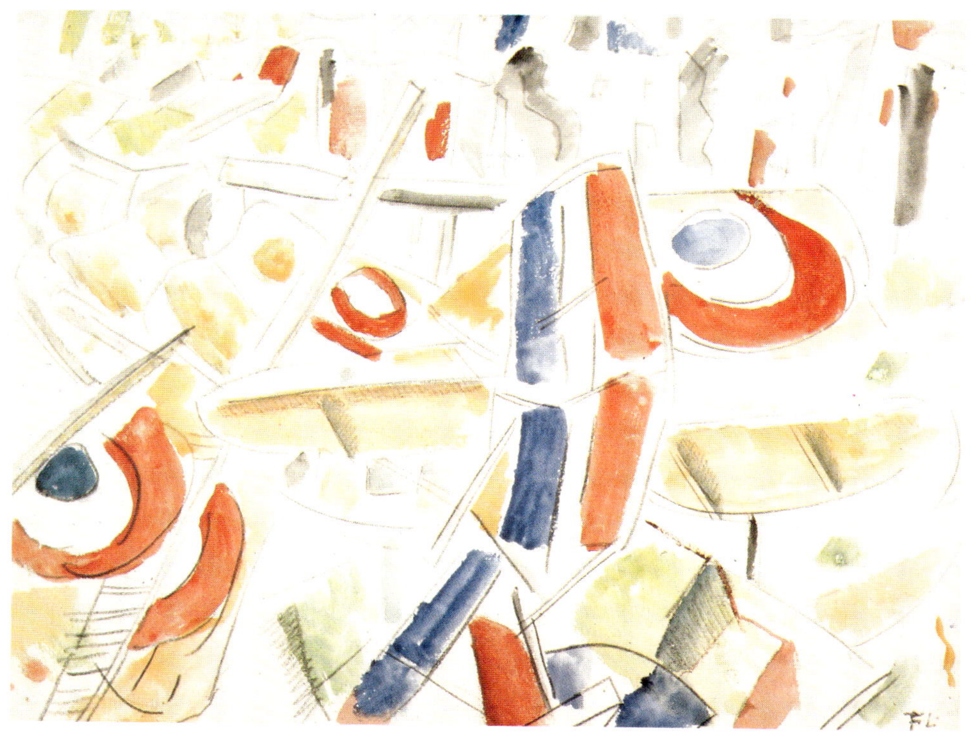

71. *THE CRASHED AIRPLANE: THE AISNE FRONT*
1917—Gouache, 22.5 × 28.5 cm
Private collection

72. AIRPLANE
1916—Watercolor, 23 × 29 cm
Private collection

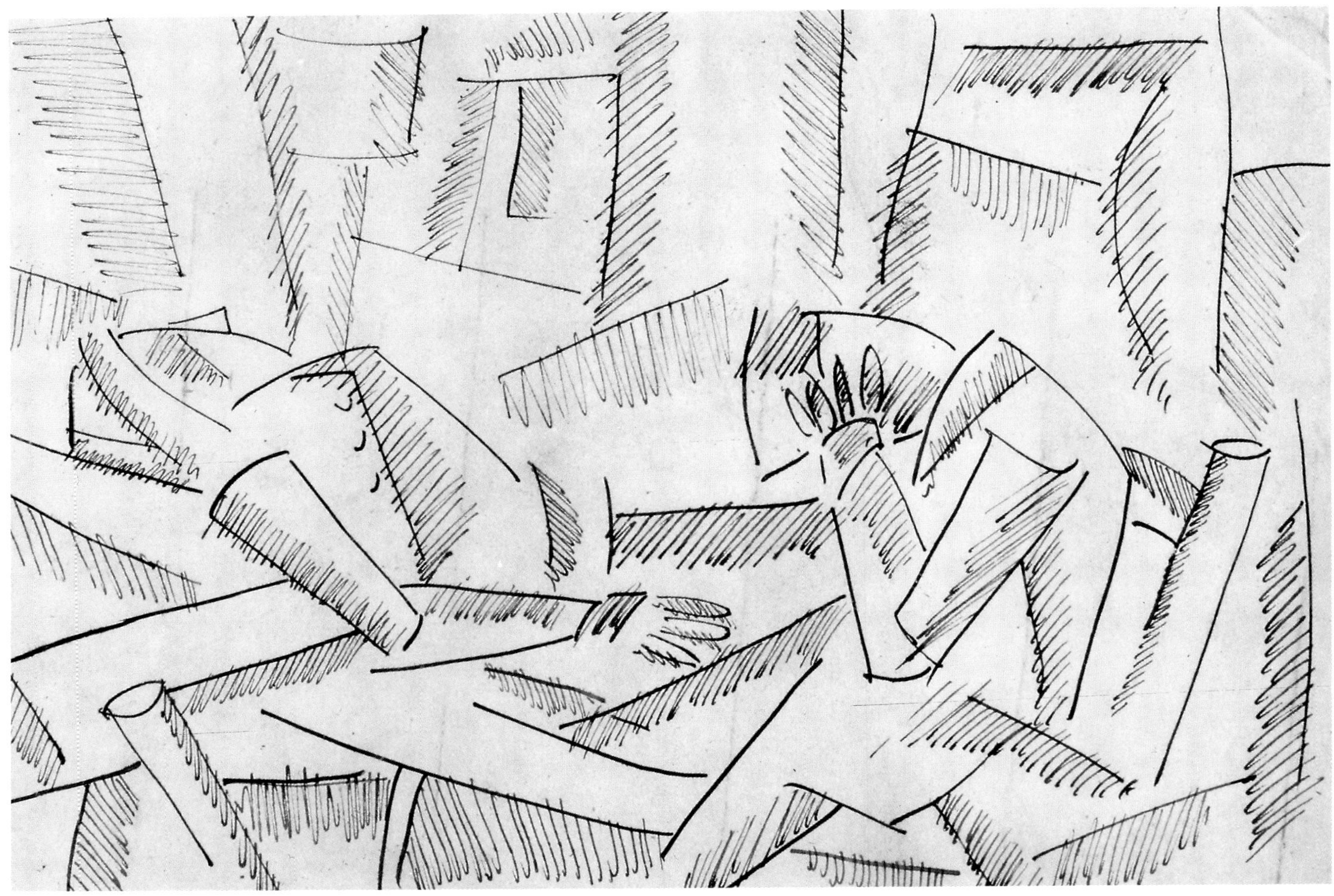

73. TWO SOLDIERS
1915—China ink drawing, 17 × 24.5 cm
Private collection

*color!"* During this same period, Malevich was painting *Woman with Buckets* and *The Glasscutter* in an analogous style. There were flattened bodies with cylindrical limbs, and hands that evoked machine parts, like those painted by Léger, whose cardplayers are an aggregate of cylindrical parts with hands like steel hooks. The figures are ensconced in metal armor and seen to be both pioneers and victims of the new era. The machines that they have created seem to have molded to their flesh. They are already the
Ill. 311 beginnings of what will become *The Builders*, where Léger's objective would henceforth be to acknowledge urban and industrial civilization, characterized by efficiency, speed, and violence. One can see the enormous distance travelled since Cézanne's *Cardplayers* (1890–92), in which nature was expressed through the sphere, the cylinder, and the cube; it is now the confrontation of man against man, even in play. Léger moved forward to the "mechanical period," in which man confronts machine, resulting not only in beauty but in the terrible constraints the machine imposes on man.

The revelations of war were twofold for Léger: the world of beautiful and implacable machines, and the world of men who work these machines and are in turn crushed by them. It would, however, be a major injustice to portray Léger, who was optimistic about the humanity of the machine, as a masochistic painter who depicted the mechanization of mankind.

The return of color in Léger's work takes on a liberating role in the context of suffocating reality, as if the artist wanted to prove that it was not necessary to submit to the grayness of the everyday modern world. Léger's painting rebelled against the heaviness that stifled man, and attempted to provide people with a reason to rejoice: "Man must be distracted from everyday trials and tribulations. He must be enveloped and made to live in a new and preponderant plastic order. Even in times of greatest doubt, no artist can be permitted to latch onto past constraints. He must assume his destiny; it's an immense solitude. Every man that has ever been cursed with inventiveness, creativity, or the need to build has experienced this."

74. THE CIRCUS
1918—Oil on canvas, 58 × 94.5 cm
Musée National d'Art Moderne, Centre Georges Pompidou, Paris
Gift of Eva Gourgaud

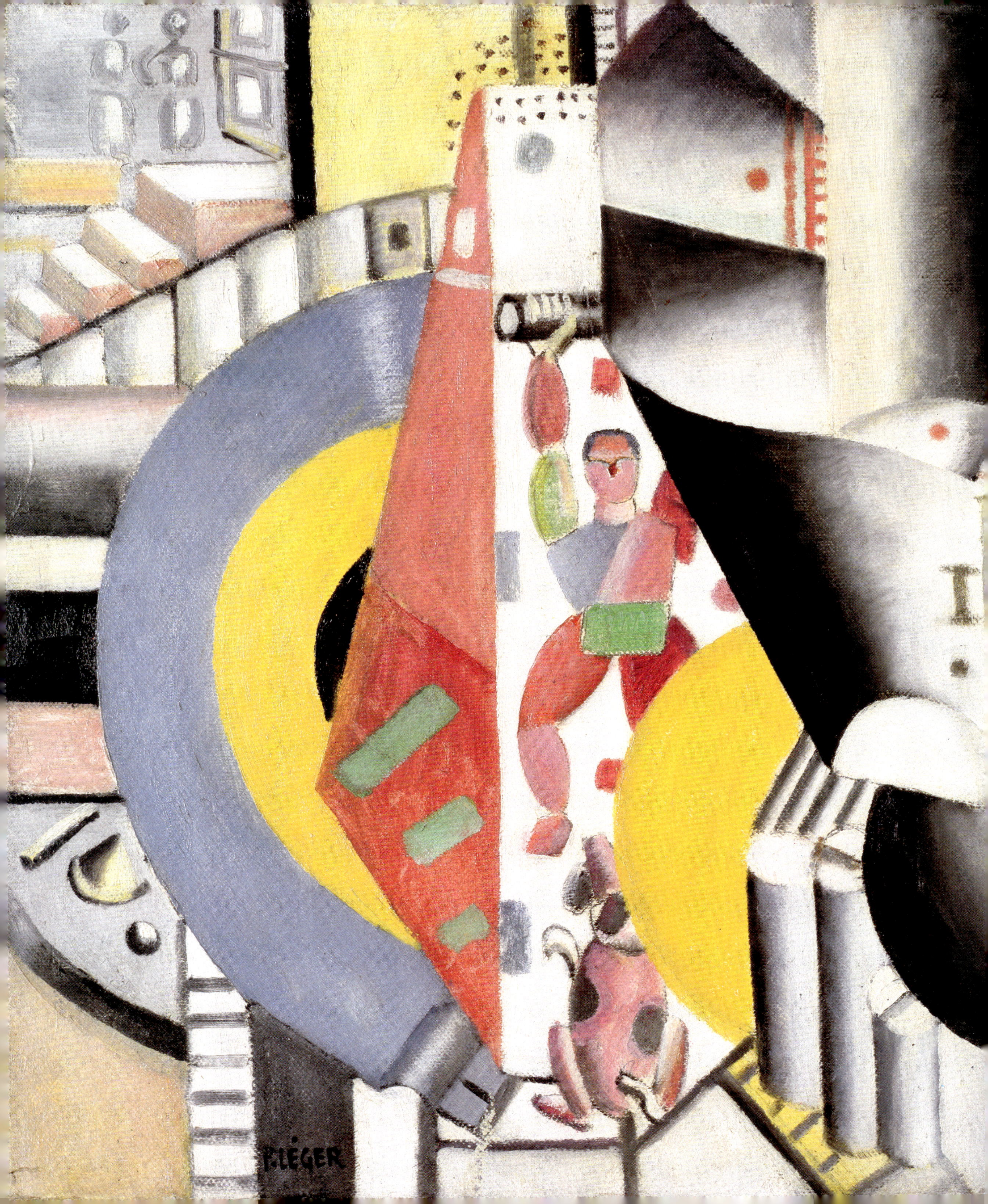
F.LÉGER

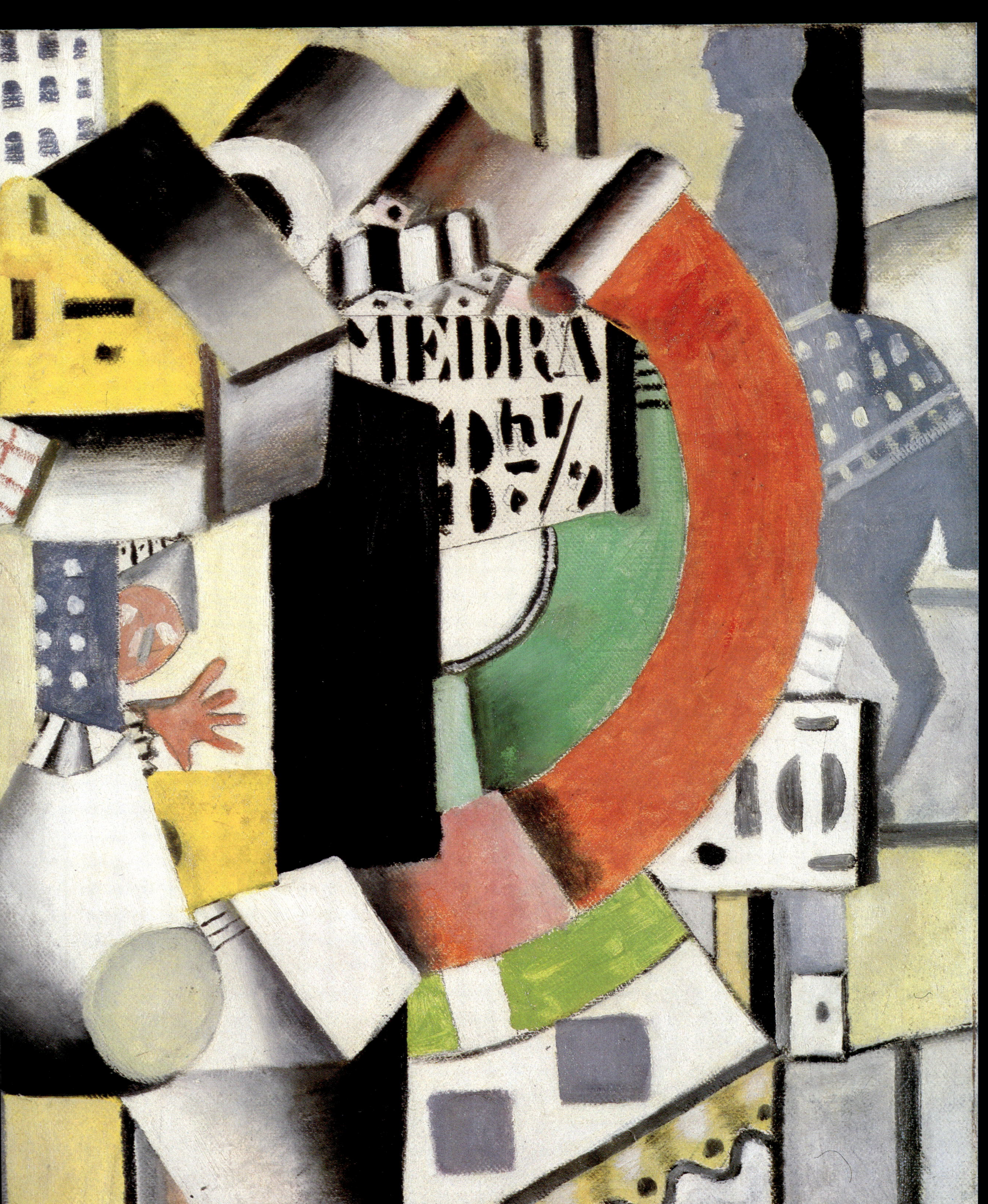

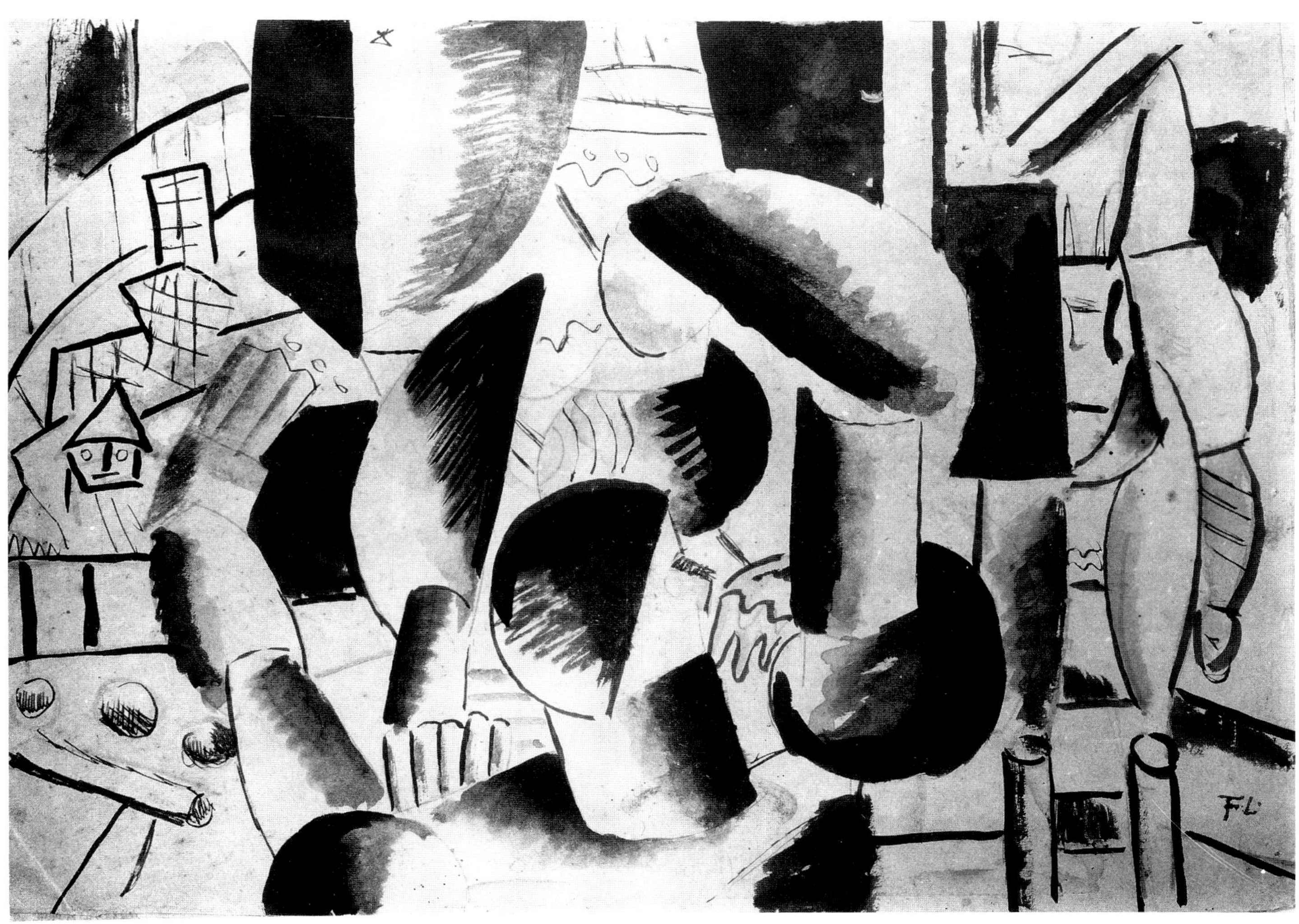

75. THE CIRCUS
1919—China ink drawing, 23.5 × 32 cm
Louise Leiris Gallery, Paris

## Ill. 74 The warrior at rest: *The Circus*

What better means of engendering "distraction" than the circus! The Circus was a leitmotif throughout all of Léger's work. It has been said that after Léger made Cézanne's *Cardplayers* a contemporary
Ill. 66 statement through his own *Card Game*, that he went on to do the same with Seurat's *Circus.* All the early painters of modern art favored the circus as a figurative model. It inspired masterpieces from Degas, Renoir, Seurat, and Toulouse-Lautrec, as well as great works from Archipenko, Calder, Chagall, Laurens, Picasso, Rouault, and van Dongen. In her book *Picasso and His Friends*, Fernande Olivier, Picasso's companion, wrote that before the outbreak of World War I poets and painters would gather at the Médrano Circus in Paris.

*Le Cirque Médrano* and *Circus Acrobats* ("Acrobates dans le cirque") further extended the experience that began with *Nudes in the Forest* and continued with *The Card Game*, where the human face, as well as the objects, has borrowed from the structure and geometry of the machine. The soldiers in *The Card Game* are robots in shining armor. Léger's acrobats are reduced to marionettes, but the theme has changed. The warrior at rest became the vehicle through which Léger introduced dazzling color. Peace has returned and people were rediscovering the simple joys of theater and street shows. It was the beginning of Léger's methodical construction of the magical elements of the circus: "*The White Ballet* ["Le Ballet blanc"] is one of my most vivid memories of the nights that Apollinaire, Max Jacob, Blaise Cendrars, and I spent at the Médrano Circus. To be a painter and see that spectacle provoked a feeling of impotence in terms of how to translate it all onto the canvas. . . . Children knew that the arrival of the circus in their town was a great event. The circus is an adventure in the extreme . . . the magic of freedom is extraordinary: a moving, transportable edifice that is built up in the space of one night, that appears and disappears like something miraculous, fleeting, and free. I'll always remember when, as a child, I saw the poster on the walls of my little town in Normandy announcing the arrival of the circus, the marvelous, miraculous circus."

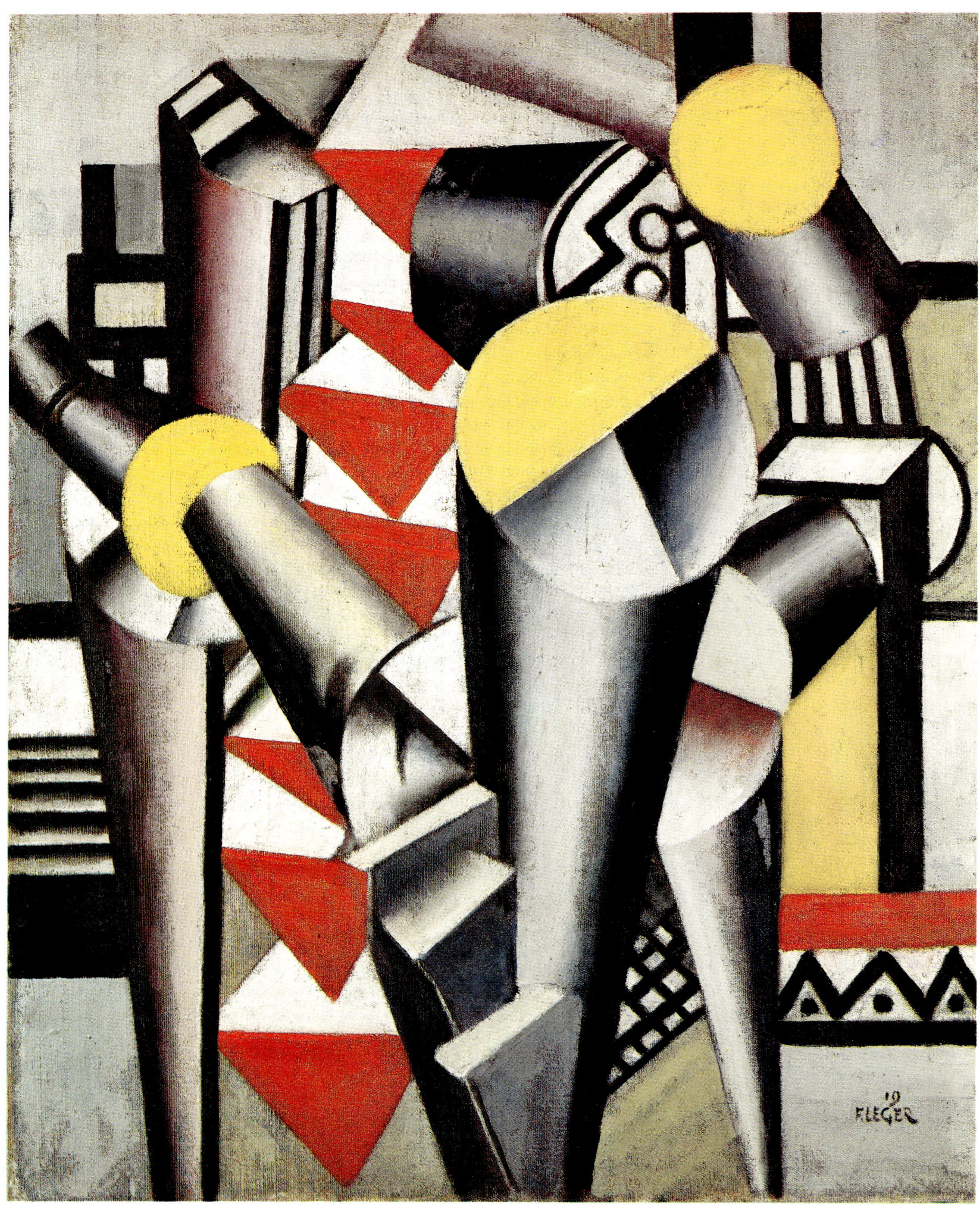

76. STUDY FOR *THE CARD GAME*
1919—Oil on canvas, 92.4 × 73.2 cm
Staatsgalerie, Stuttgart

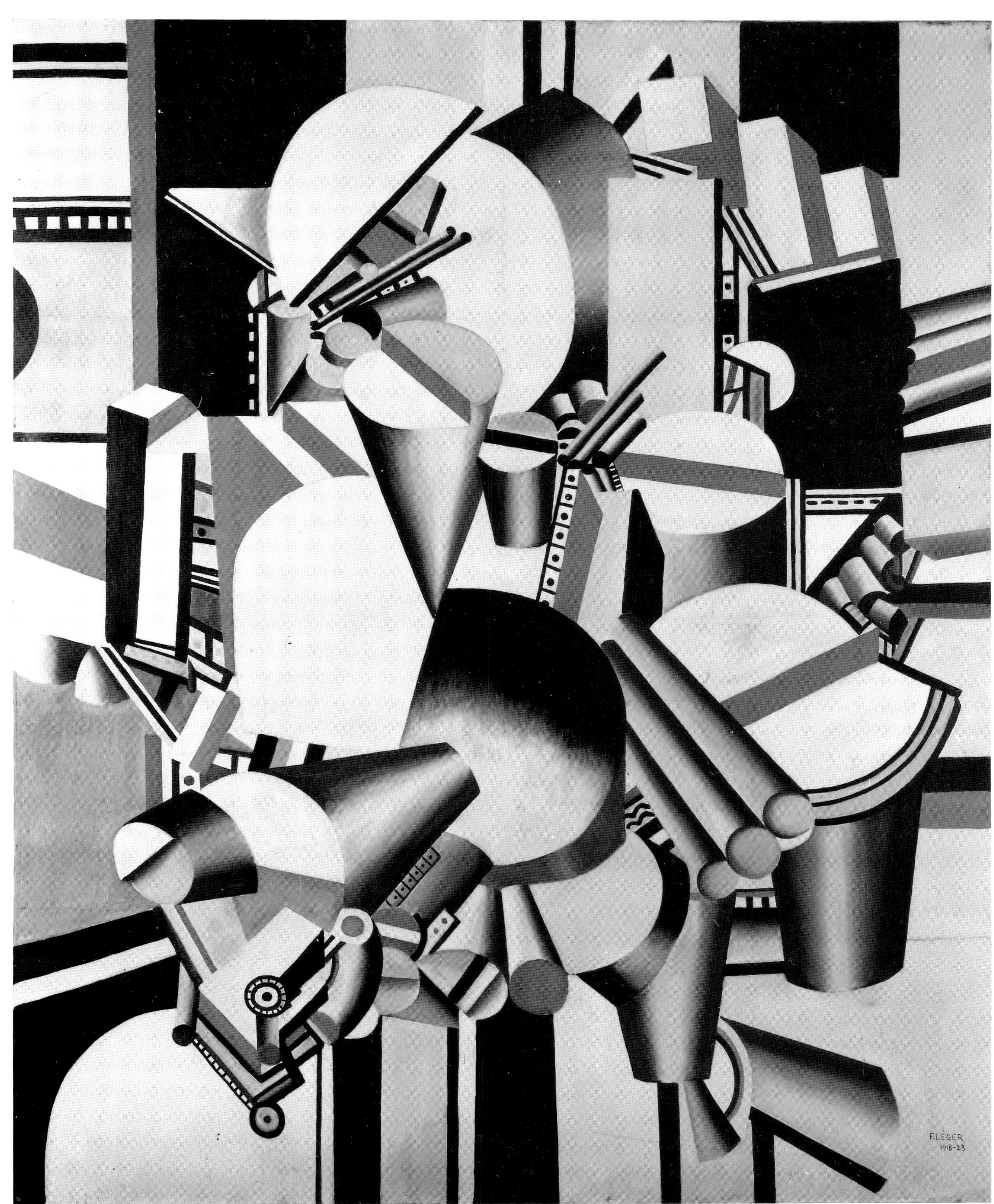


77. MECHANICAL ELEMENTS
1918–23—Oil on canvas, 211 × 167.5 cm
Oeffentliche Kunstsammlung, Kunstmuseum, Basel

# Poetics of the Machine

The year 1919: Léger had returned from war forever marked by "reality": "Once I had taken a bite of this reality, it was to stay with me. When I returned from the war, I continued to use what I had felt at the front. For three years I used geometric forms, a period that will be called the *mechanical period.*"

The titles of the paintings of this period are a striking revelation of machine society and the urban, industrial life that Léger was an enthusiatic witness of. He saw motors, helices, scaffoldings, grade crossings, and smokestacks as sublime elements of representa-
Ill. 77 tion that found their way into paintings like *Mechan-*
Ill. 87 *ical Elements, Tugboat* ("Le Remorqueur"), *Train*
& 96 *Station* ("La Gare"), and *Discs in the City* ("Les
Ill. 98 Disques dans la ville").

Ill. 99 Léger returned from the United States with an anecdote that reveals what he was looking for, and found, during this period: "I brought back a lot of memories from the United States, but I'll never forget the Negroes. Their simplicity, childlike kindness, and prodigious sense of rhythm impressed me greatly. Among the mechanistic canvases I showed there was *Discs.* Black people would stand for a long time in front of this painting, and then they would say: 'We need this kind of thing, man. It's great! It's the kind of thing that inspires us to invent new music, a new kind of jazz. It already makes us want to dance.' Then one of them started to improvise a rhythm. He was dancing in front of the canvas. I should have offered the painting to them right then and there. The painting was acquired by the Petit Palais in Paris, but it would have been much better off with the black people. They wanted to take it back home with them to the South. Yeah. . . If I had been as free as they were, I would have offered it to them as a gift. . . . I could feel that they needed that painting as much as they needed to eat and drink. I gave them a dynamically colored watercolor instead. They were happy with it, but it's really the painting that they wanted."

Beneath the unintentionally condescending tone of the European intellectual who came to bring civilization to the "good savages," we can sense the emotion and satisfaction Léger felt. His work was finally being understood and enthusiastically received by the people. He had found in the warmth and communication of American blacks what he had always sought but never found in France. The white Parisian bourgeoisie continued to react coldly to his poetics of the mechanical elements in life. Although Léger's countrymen did not appreciate him as the prophet of his time, he was certain that the future would prove him right. Although Léger saw himself as a painter for the masses, he knew very well that only a few unprejudiced eyes could be seduced by his work. Black people, along with avant-garde artists pursuing a similar path, were his only audience, but he was hopeful for the future. All his great predecessors had been terribly alone. He thought that one day he could make Cézanne's words his own: "A painter like me comes only once every two centuries."

Léger endowed people and machines with qualities that he felt in his heart and guts. So what if his contemporaries did not realize it: "Posterity may place my art in the category of 'artificial paradises,' but I don't think so. This kind of guideline is dominated by a desire for total freedom and perfection that makes for saints, heroes, and crazies. It's an extreme state that only the very few, creators and admirers alike, can sustain. The speed and tumult of modern life threaten this type of elevated state, this fragile and luminous edifice that has emerged from the chaos. Leave it alone; it is there; it had to be made; it will endure."

The obstacle that Léger thought he was up against was the poor visual education of the masses, and a preconceived idea of the "art object." He felt that people were blindfolded, that the mania to classify things stemmed from "a fear of free choice." And yet free choice was essential for seeing beauty: "People are victims of an era that is critical, sceptical, and intellectual, and that stubbornly tries to understand things at the expense of sensitivity. They are blinded by professional titles and honors instead of opening their eyes to Beauty. My goal is to try to impose the following ideas: that a hierarchy of Beauty does not exist; nor can Beauty be catalogued. Beauty is everywhere. It is in the arrangement of your pots and pans, and on the walls of your kitchen, to a greater degree, perhaps, than in the official museums."

## The art of "appearances"

The animation in the city streets was certain proof for Léger that his notion of "self-contained beauty" was a valid one. He gathered multiple "snapshots" that he referred to as "the art of appearances" or "window displays." They result from the syndrome that we call "keeping up with the Joneses." Léger and his friend Maurice Raynal were keen observers of how people labored like ants to assure that everything was perfect. Take the clothes retailer who spent hours decorating his store window, arranging the waistcoats, the shirt cuffs, the neckties. He adjusted each item a millimeter to the right or to the left, and would constantly go outside to verify that every last detail was correct. He organized his window with the adroitness of a master arranger organizing a spectacle; as if his life depended on it. Léger couldn't help comparing this with certain pictorial output, past and present: "When I think of the slipshod and undisciplined works of painters, some of whom are well-known and whose work sells for a lot of money, we can only admire the *courageous craftsman* who forges ahead with great difficulty and painstaking care. The craftsman is much more valuable than the others, but he is also an endangered species. He must constantly repeat his efforts with the same dexterity and skill. There is an undeniable artistic sense in the craftsman, as well as a plastic event of a new order. It is closely tied to commercial goals, and it rivals all existing artistic display."

The École de Beaux-Arts in particular and the world as a whole considered the Mona Lisa to be the artistic summit, the ideal to be aimed for. Léger thought this was a colossal error. Léger preferred the Paris Fair with its inventiveness, billboards, fountains of light, sparkling letters, and wild machines. He thought of the organizers of this fair as the true artists of modern times: "They've upset all the accepted plastic givens . . . and they didn't even know it. Ignorance in this case was a good thing, but the problem of the unconscious in artistic creation is painfully conflicting, and will trouble those who explore this mystery for a long time to come."

78. COMPOSITION
1919—Pen drawing
Private collection

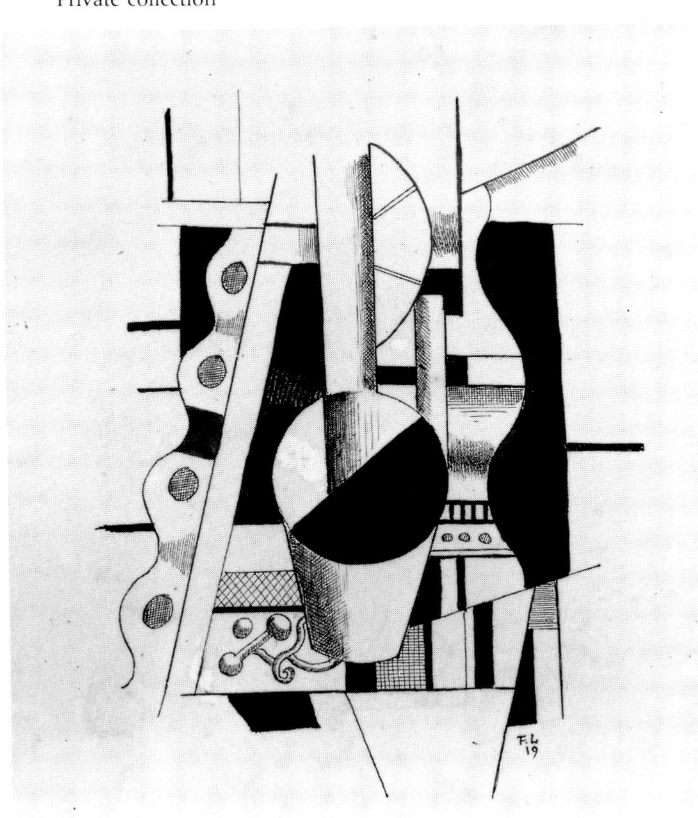

79. COMPOSITION WITH MECHANICAL ELEMENTS
1918—Pen drawing, 26 × 19 cm
Private collection

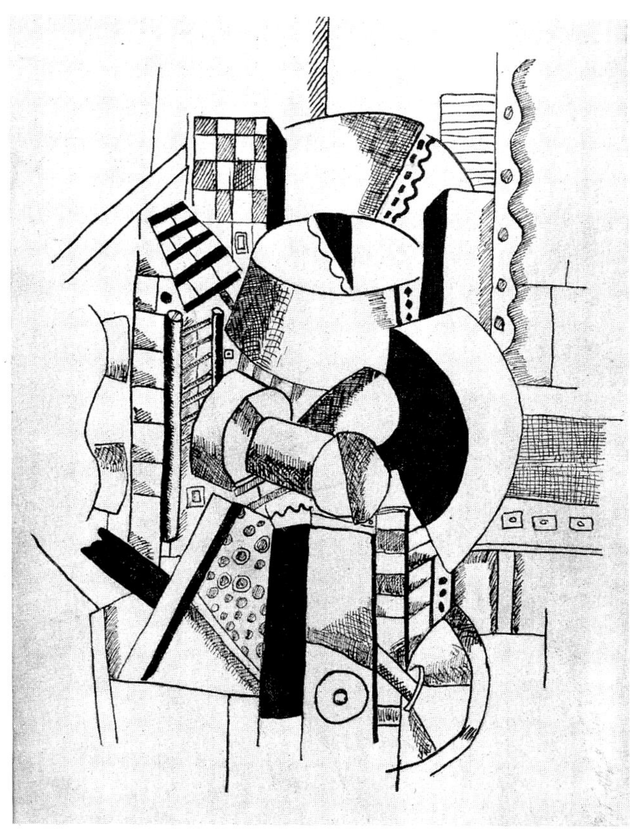

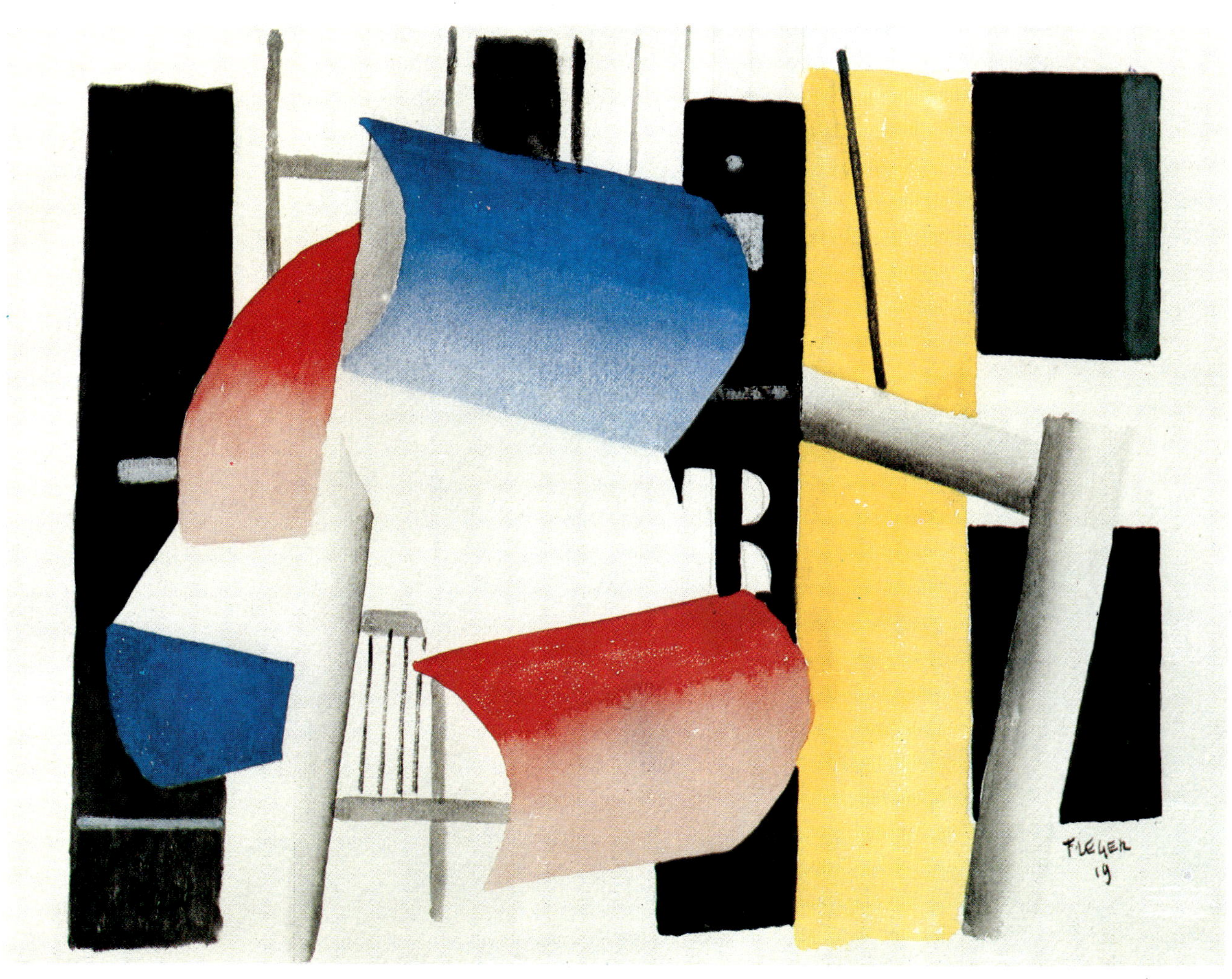


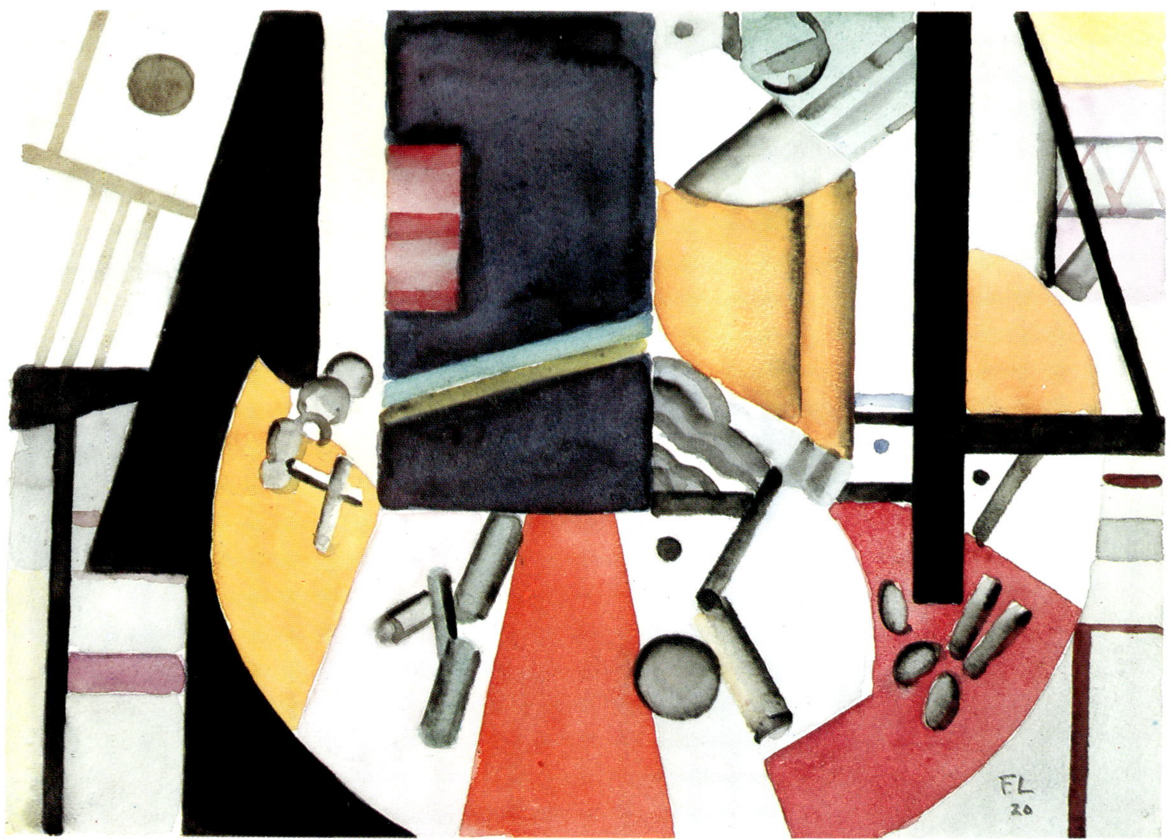


80. COMPOSITION, FLAGS
1919—Watercolor on paper,
25 × 30 cm
Lionel Prejger collection, Paris

81. MECHANICAL COMPOSITION
1920—Watercolor, 23.3 × 31.4 cm
Private collection

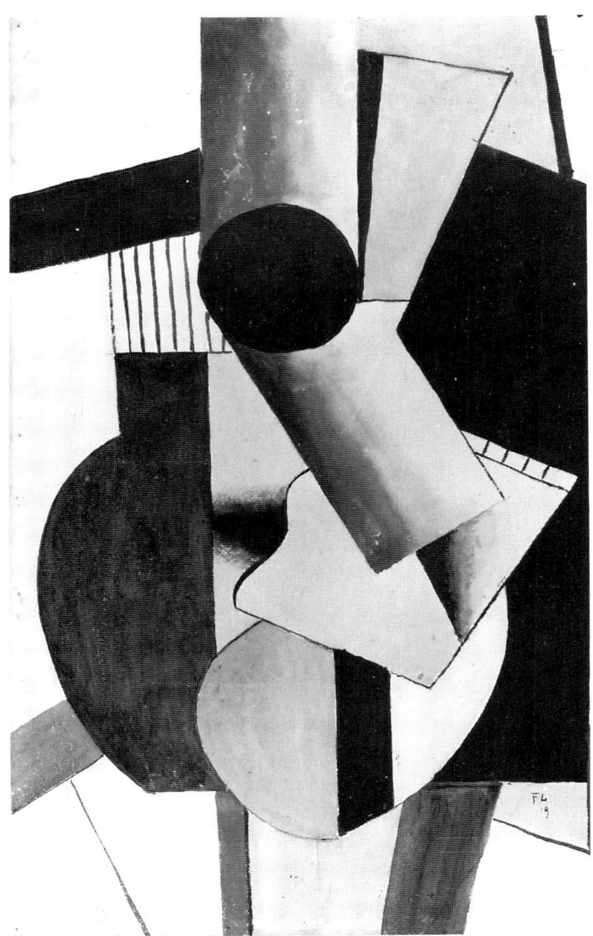

82. COMPOSITION
1919—Watercolor, 39 × 28 cm
Private collection

## The Machine Show beats going to the Louvre

"If the engineers, factory workers, window dressers, and shop owners were aware of the beauty they were producing and amid which they lived, everything would be so simple that there would be no more need for professional artists. Each person would easily find his Mona Lisa: The farmer would find it in his beautiful polychrome tractor, the salesman in his concerto for vests and neckties, the car owner in the melody of shiny chrome fenders. . . Why in the world do all these decent folks go every Sunday to gasp at the dubious paintings in the Louvre, or in any other museum for that matter? Maybe there are two in a thousand paintings that are beautiful." Instead of going to the Louvre, Léger thought they would be better off taking a walk around the Machine Show, the Automobile Show, or the Aviation Show!
Has the washing machine become the Mona Lisa of the twentieth century? Those who now demand the umbrella of Léger, or that Duchamp exhibit some trash cans or other symbols of our civilization at the Pompidou Center in Paris, have either completely misunderstood Léger, or are merely trying to make a fast buck. Léger, however, was very clear on the subject: these objects, machines, automobiles, boats, traffic lights, train stations, and streets are only the raw material. Léger did not copy these things. He invented them. He felt there were "very few whose plastic concept elevates the craftsman's skill to the highest level of Beauty. Both the artisan's work and the work of nature become the raw materials that are arranged, absorbed, and integrated in the artist's mind, and result in the perfect balance of conscious and subconscious, objective and subjective values. Provocation is always present in art. No criterion is possible, and there is no arbitrating body to settle the dispute regarding Beauty."

83. MECHANICAL COMPOSITION
1919—Wash and drawing, 31.5 × 26 cm
Louise Leiris Gallery, Paris

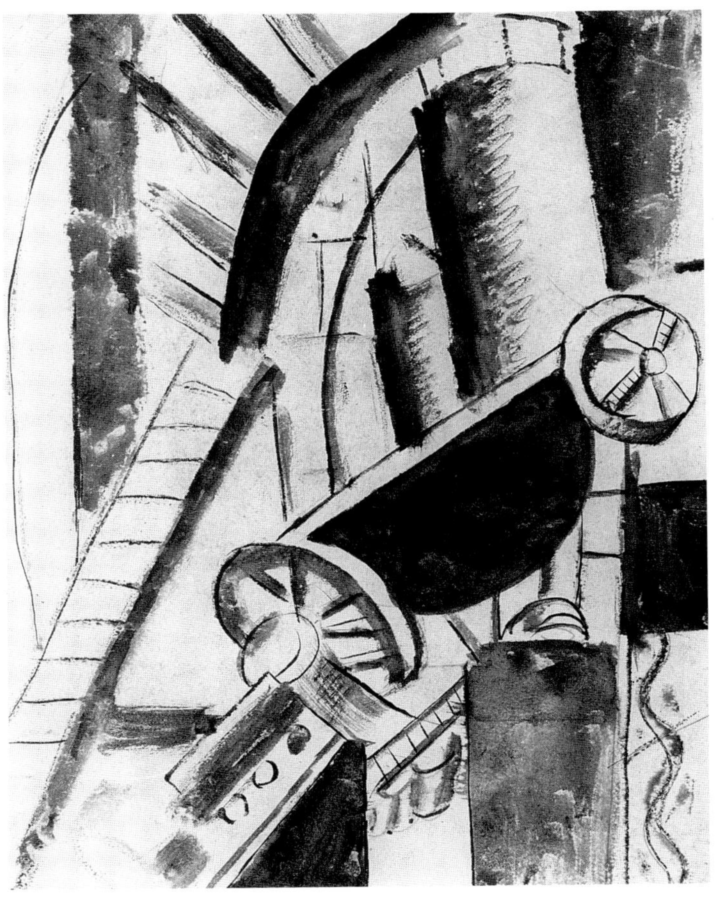

84. MECHANICAL COMPOSITION
1918—Sepia wash and China ink, 40 × 30.5 cm
Private collection

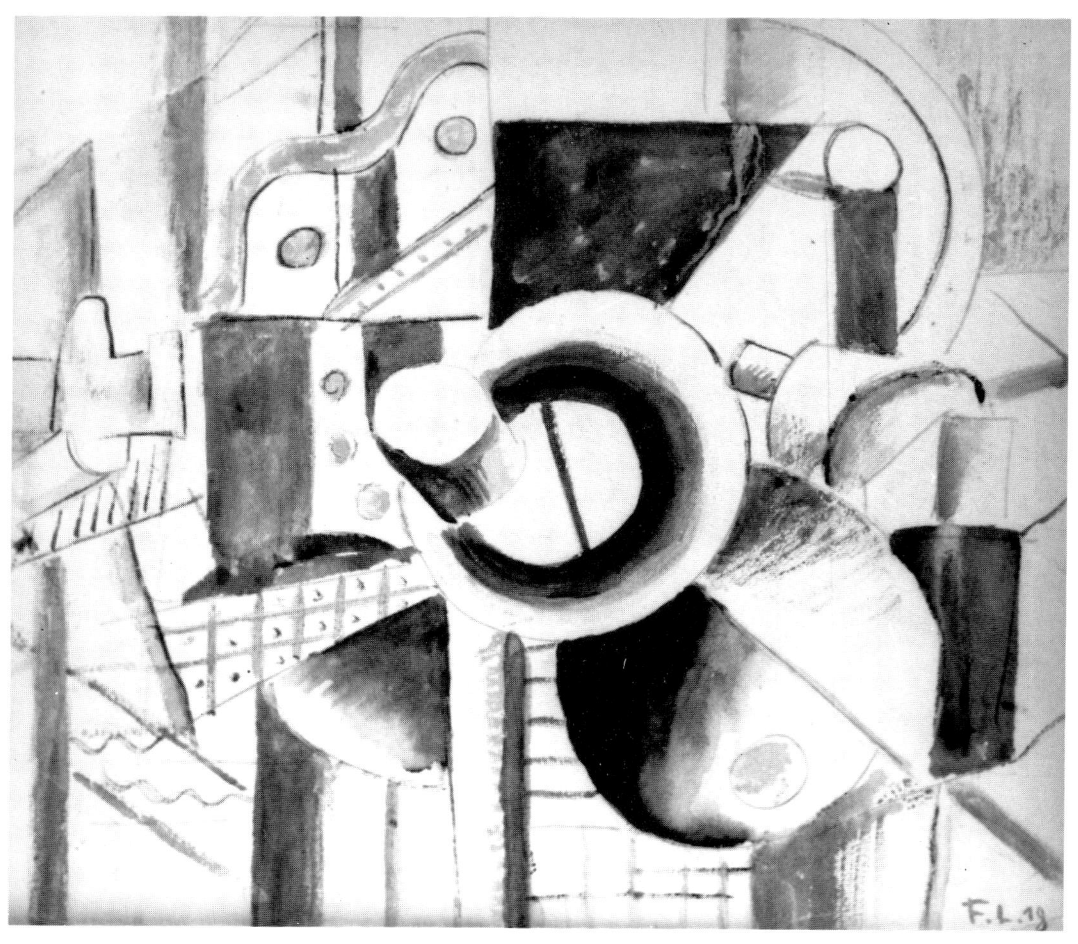


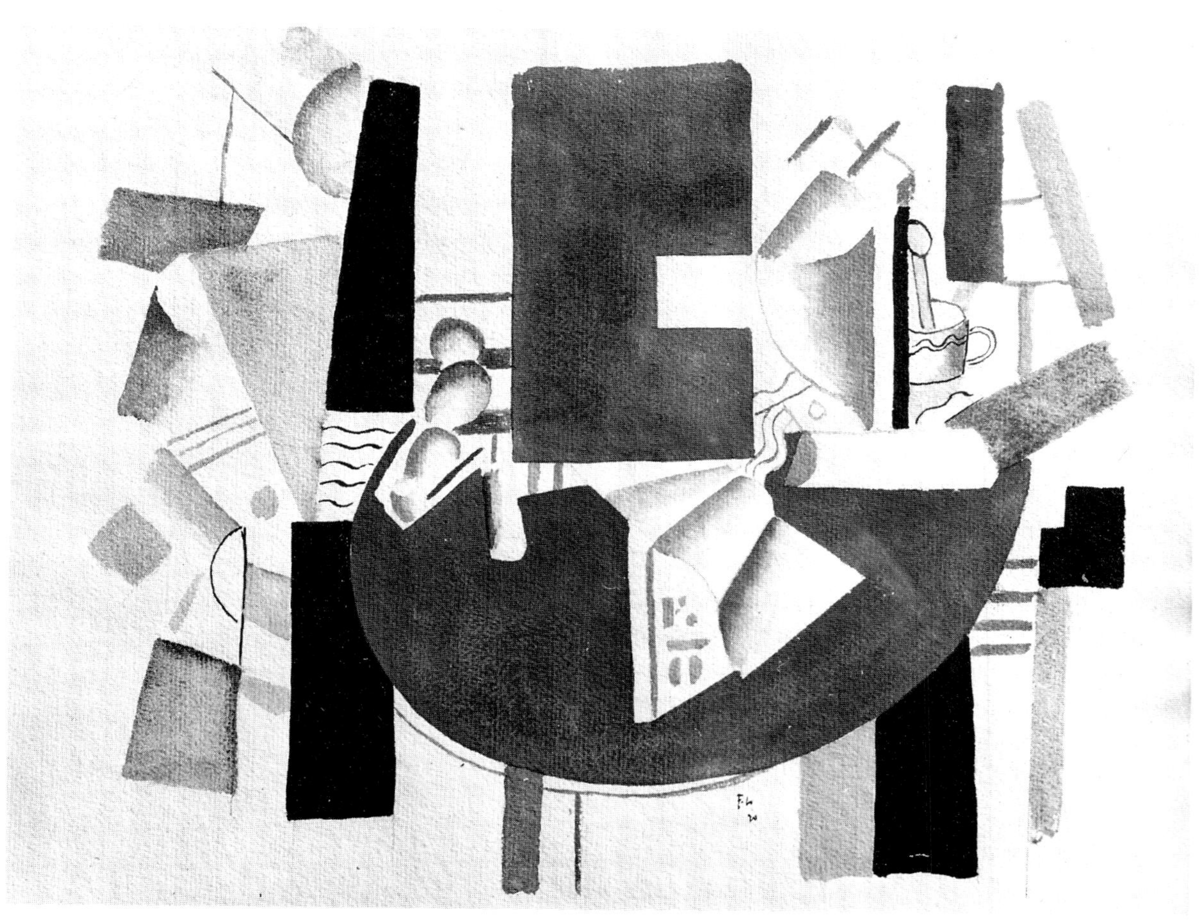

85. RED TABLE STILL LIFE
1920—Gouache on paper, 30 × 34.5 cm
Musée d'Art Moderne, Villeneuve-d'Ascq
Gift of Geneviève and Jean Masurel

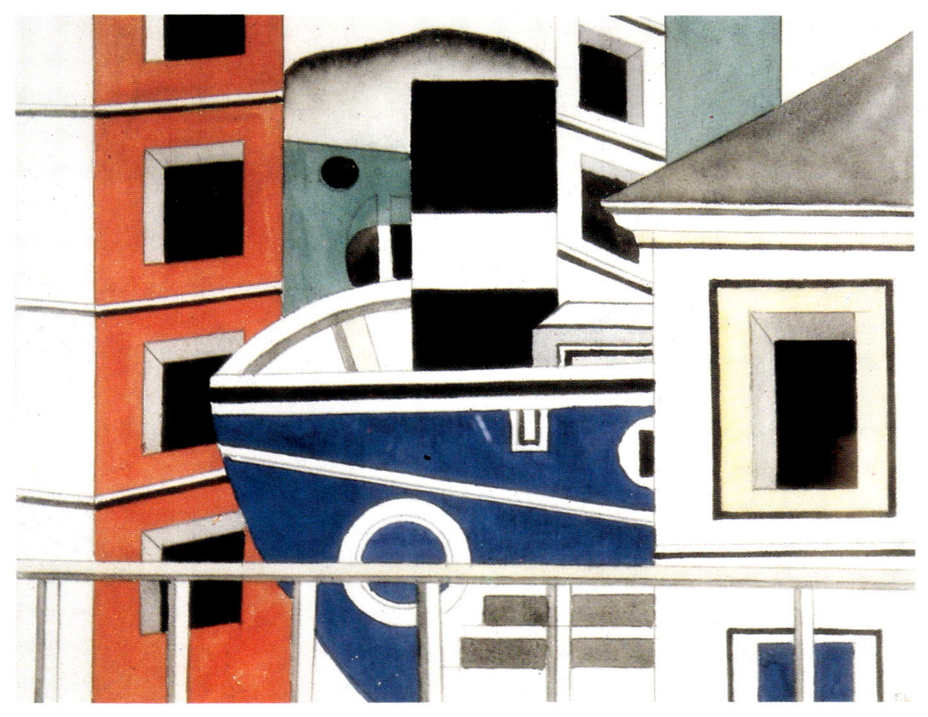

86. IN PORT
1922—Gouache, 26 × 31.5 cm
Private collection

87. THE DECK OF THE TUGBOAT
1920—Oil on canvas, 96 × 130 cm
Musée National d'Art Moderne, Centre Georges Pompidou, Bequest of Eva Gourgaud

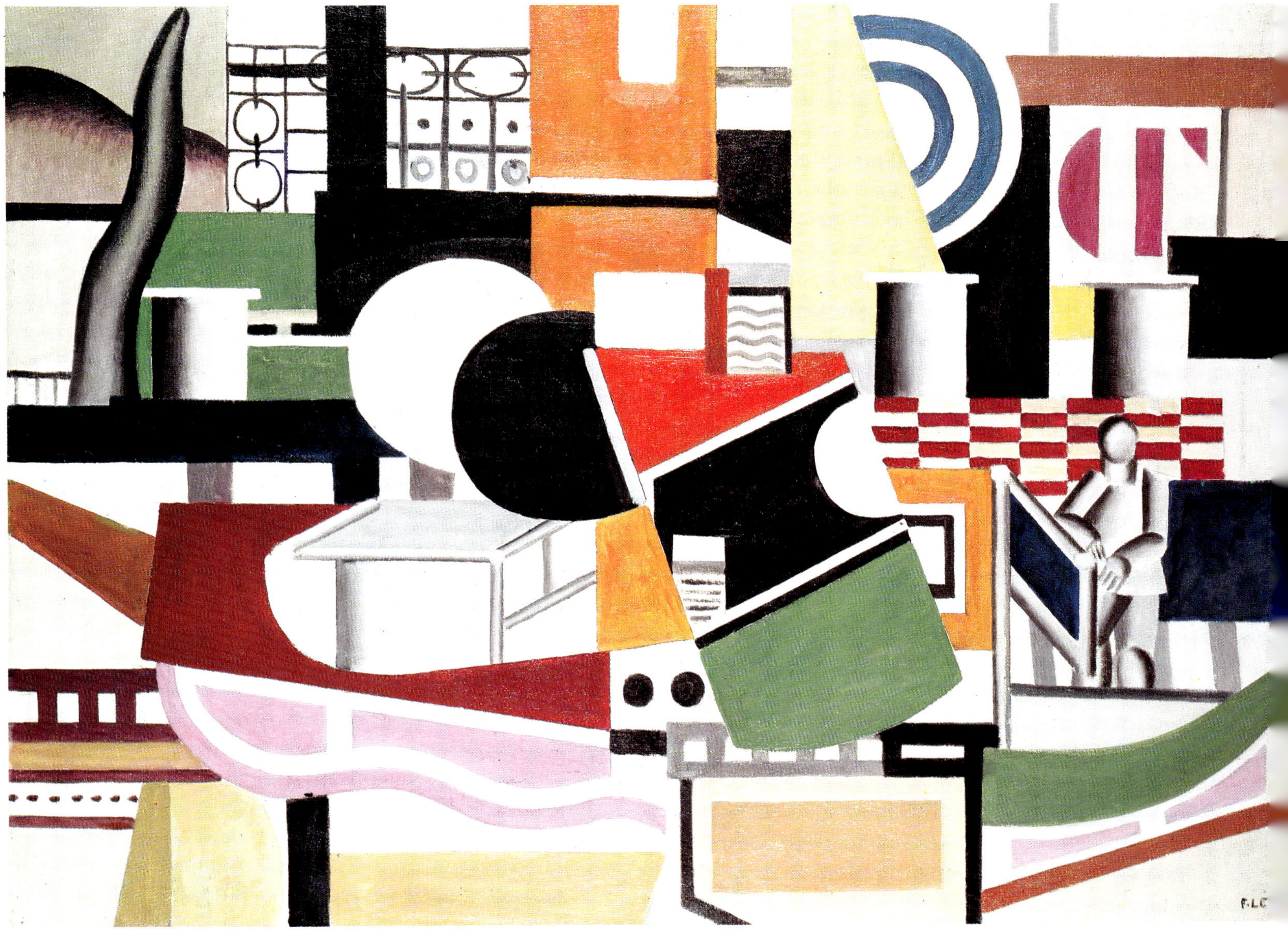

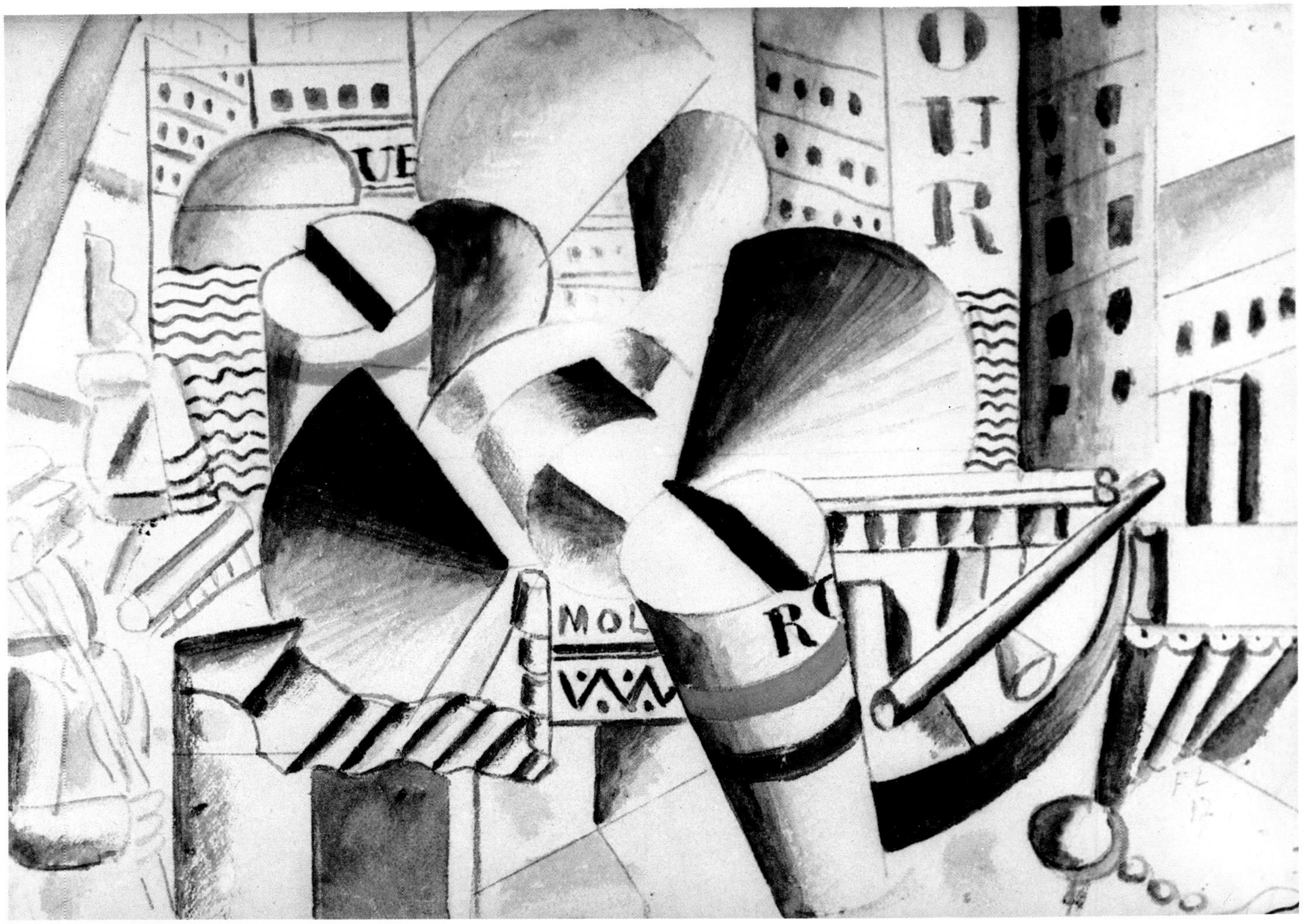


88. TUGBOAT
1917—Watercolor, 17 × 24 cm
Private collection

## Ill. 92 The staccato of machinery

Léger's *City* portrays the megalopolis with the fascination of someone who has just arrived from the countryside, but Léger was not the only one to purify industrial and urban reality into poetry. His friend Blaise Cendrars expressed equal enthusiasm in books like *Transiberian Prose* ("La Prose du Transsibérien"), published in 1913, in which the poet favors heterogeneous, snapshot images of the urban landscape. Cendrars wrote *Kodak* (1924) as a collection of "mental photographs." Delaunay celebrated the Eiffel Tower, soccer stadiums, airplanes, and billboards in his paintings. His style of Orphic Cubism called for the cultivation and application of color as a symbol of light, whereas Léger pursued the colors of urban gaudiness and the staccato of machinery. Picasso, who continued as usual to be guided by his own genius and fantasies, had no need to search urban reality to find what he was looking for. Léger, however, was conscious of his mission: "to carve a path to truth" through his art and his writings. We have chosen to quote the painter frequently in this book because his "ethos" demands expression in words as well as in painting. For Picasso, art was one adventure and explosion after another, but for Léger it was a continuous and persistant task. To quote Werner Schmalenbach on Léger: "From the first moment on he vowed to integrate the reality of his century . . . he was committed to the cause of the working class and its milieu, whereas Picasso surrounded himself with artists, toreadors, Harlequins, and pretty women." Léger's commitment puts him more in the company of the artists who from Berlin to Moscow via Paris and Amsterdam set themselves the task of transforming the everyday aspects of modern life, be it through German Bauhaus, Russian Constructivism, Dutch Stijl, or French Purism.

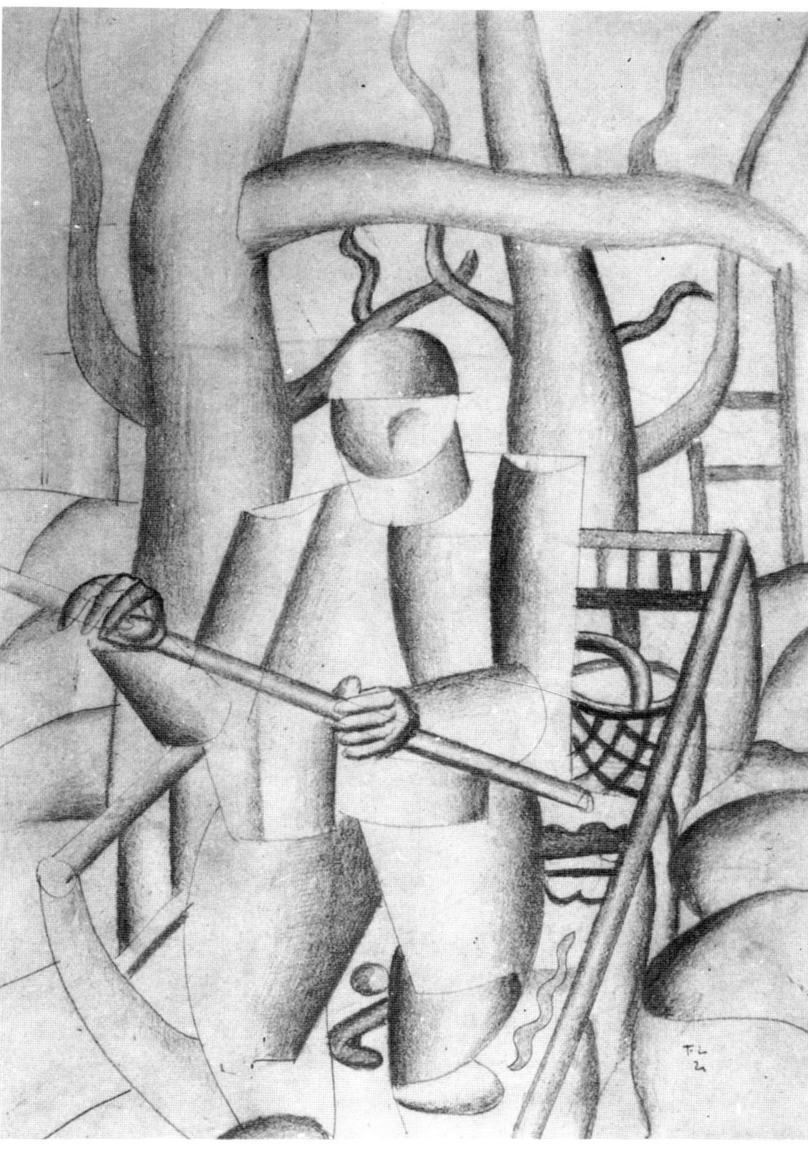

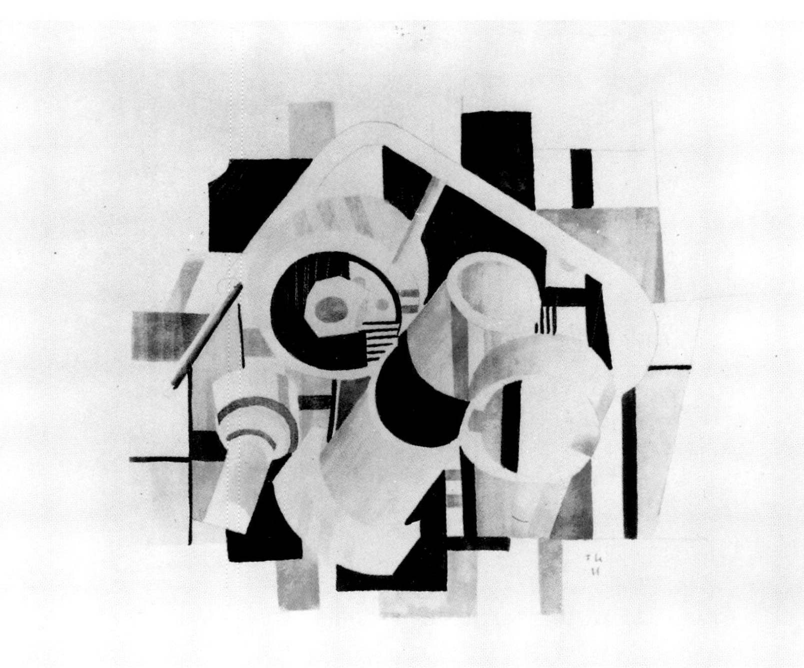

89. FISHERMAN
1921—Pencil drawing, 39 × 27 cm
Private collection
90. COMPOSITION
1921—Wash and watercolor
Private collection

## Decorative silhouettes

*Mechanical Elements* and *Discs* were both inspired by "a breech of a cannon in the sunlight." Human beings, who are absent from these paintings, gradually start to reappear in Léger's work: on boats, in train stations, and in *The City* In 1924 Léger wrote, "Modern man is increasingly living in a predominately geometric order. All human mechanical and industrial creation is dependent on geometrical dictates." The machine is the first fruit of the application of the "laws of geometry" that Léger so greatly valued. In *Mechanical Elements* and *Discs*, Léger did not reproduce one particular machine. He did not even invent one. Instead, he rendered what he referred to as "the predominant geometrical order." The circles of color as symbols of light that Delaunay utilized became multicolored discs in Léger's paintings. They are elements of machine rather than the machine itself. They turn on their axles like mysterious gears in a well-ordered mechanical world. The pure light in Delaunay's paintings is turned into traffic lights or train signals on Léger's canvas. "Today, there's an unprecedented invasion of useful, multicolored objects. Farm equipment is taking on the colors of butterflies and birds. Color is such a vital necessity that it is recapturing its rightful place." Man as creator gave way to his creation. He disappeared from the canvas to give the complex conglomeration of mechanical parts center stage. The eclipse was only momentary. When Léger brought human beings back into his paintings, they were no longer the dominating power, but they were at least given equality with the rest of the objects.

Ill. 77 Ill. 99 Ill. 91 Ill. 92

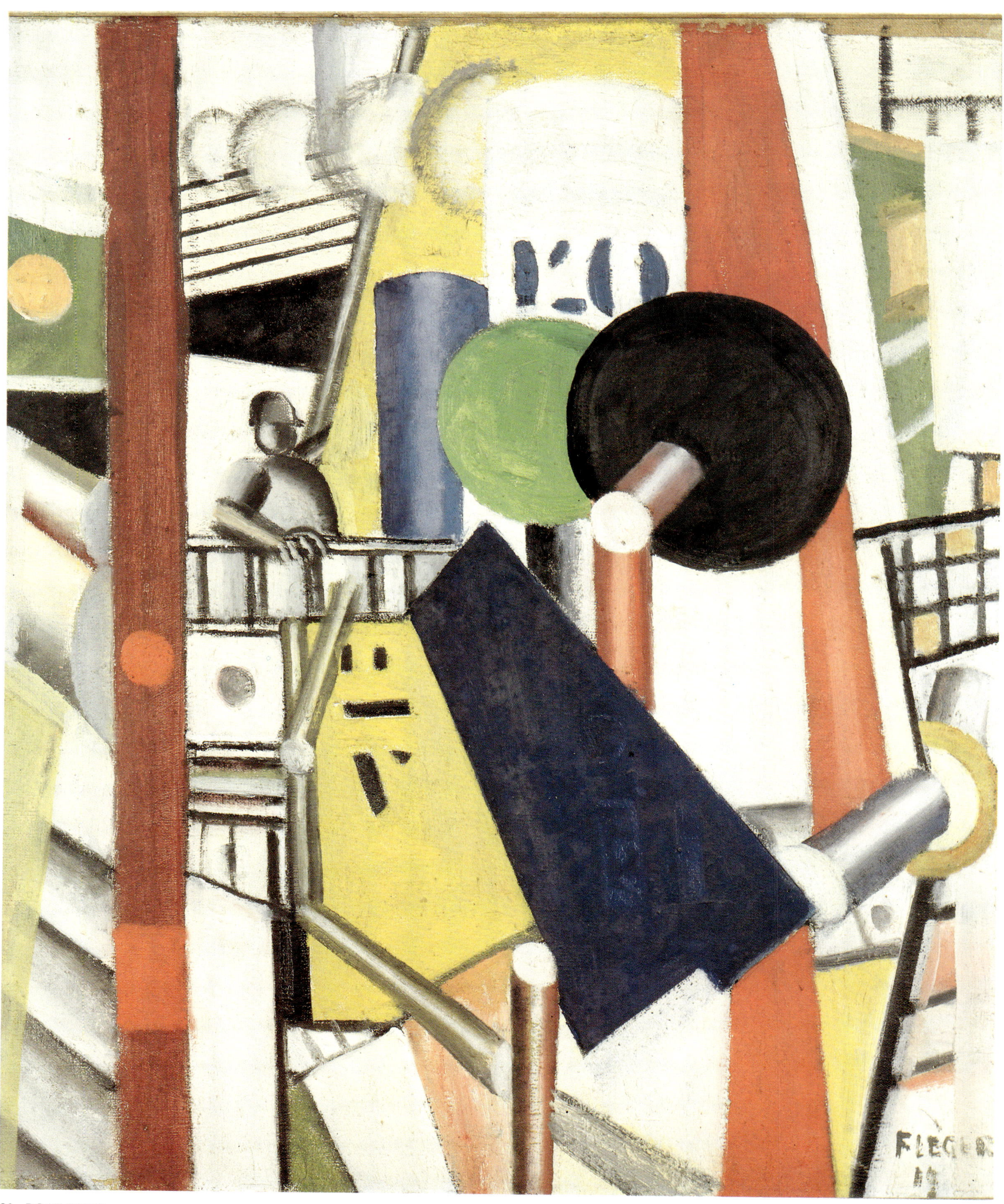


91. BOAT DECK
1919—Oil on canvas 65 × 54 cm
Moderna Museet, Stockholm

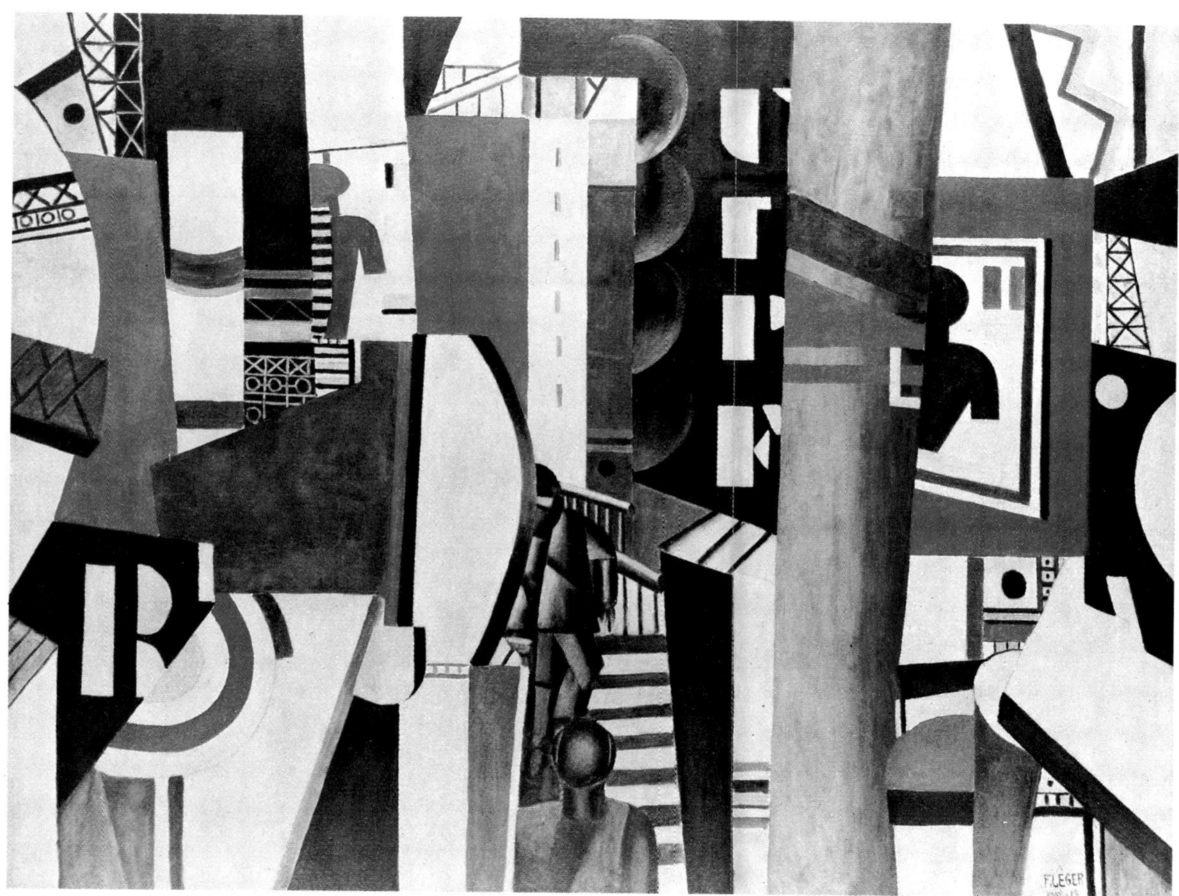

92. THE CITY
1919–20 Oil on canvas, 230 × 297 cm
Museum of Art, Philadelphia

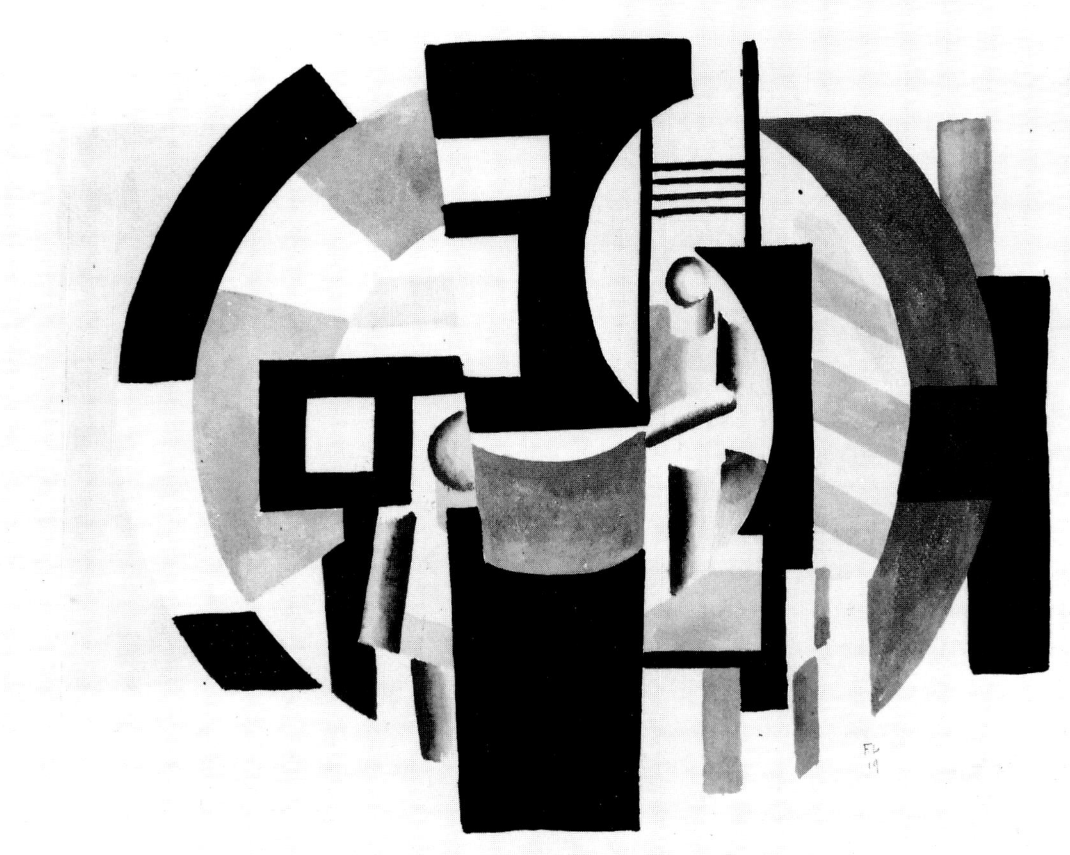

93. COMPOSITION WITH FORMS
1919—Wash with watercolor, 28.5 × 36.5 cm
Private collection

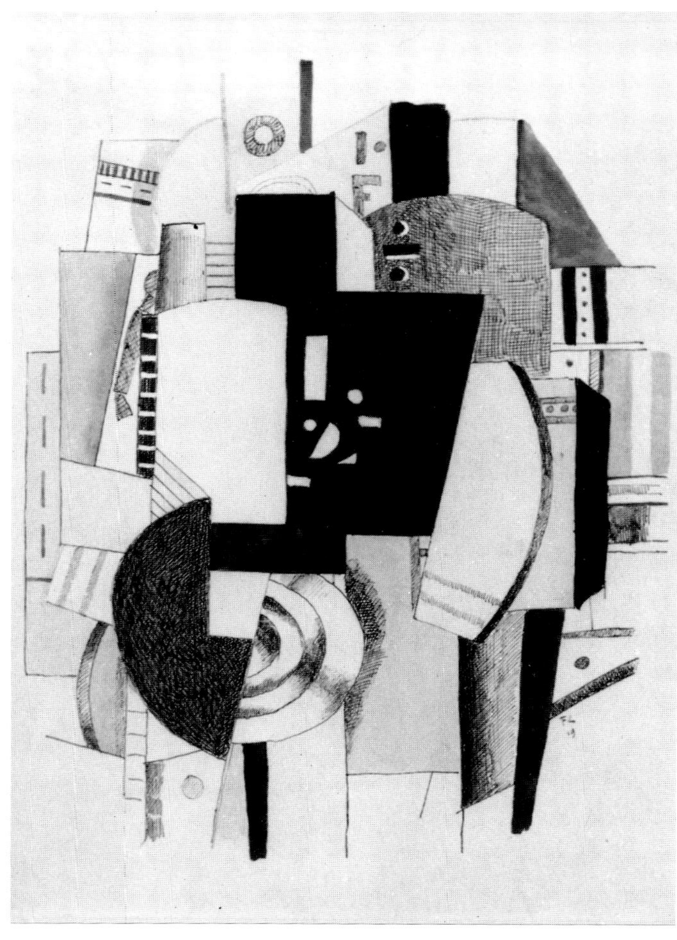

94. STUDY FOR *THE CITY*
1919—Ink and watercolor, 40 × 30.5 cm.
Private collection

## The enlightened state

Ill. 99 *Discs in the City* (1920–21) perfectly illustrates Léger's
work style: he relies on his past paintings. *Discs*
Ill. 92 (1918–19) and elements of *The City* are examples of
how Léger used "preexisting elements" to build a different painting. Léger used the elements like a figurative alphabet with a complete range of tones and forms. With this alphabet he composed geometric symphonies orchestrated to control the chaos of modern life, and yet allow the lights of this reality to shine forth. Like his friend Le Corbusier, Léger focused on order. He knew that the ideal way "to use a plastic order to oppose the confusion of street advertising and publicity was to create *a sensation of beauty, harmony, and physical and moral satisfaction.*" It is obvious that the world Léger painted was uninhabitable and that the machines were not made to function. What the artist did was replace the traditional still life with an "action painting" full of joy and color: "In my search for impact and intensity I used the machine like others use the nude or the still life." From one canvas to the next, his spheres responded to his discs and, in turn, tubes to rope, diagonals to cutouts, flat surfaces to color modulations, products of man's labor to man himself. The human form remained in the background because the artist preferred to represent man through man's creations. Man as a colored form was Léger's primary concern during the mechanical period, but eventually he reintroduced man in his entirety and in a monumental way. "My job is to put man together sketch by sketch, part by part, just like someone who builds a motor or a house. . . . The fog has lifted. No more chiaroscuro. The state of enlightenment has arrived."

95. STUDY FOR *THE CITY*
1918–19—Gouache, China ink, and watercolor, 48.5 × 50.5 cm
Private collection

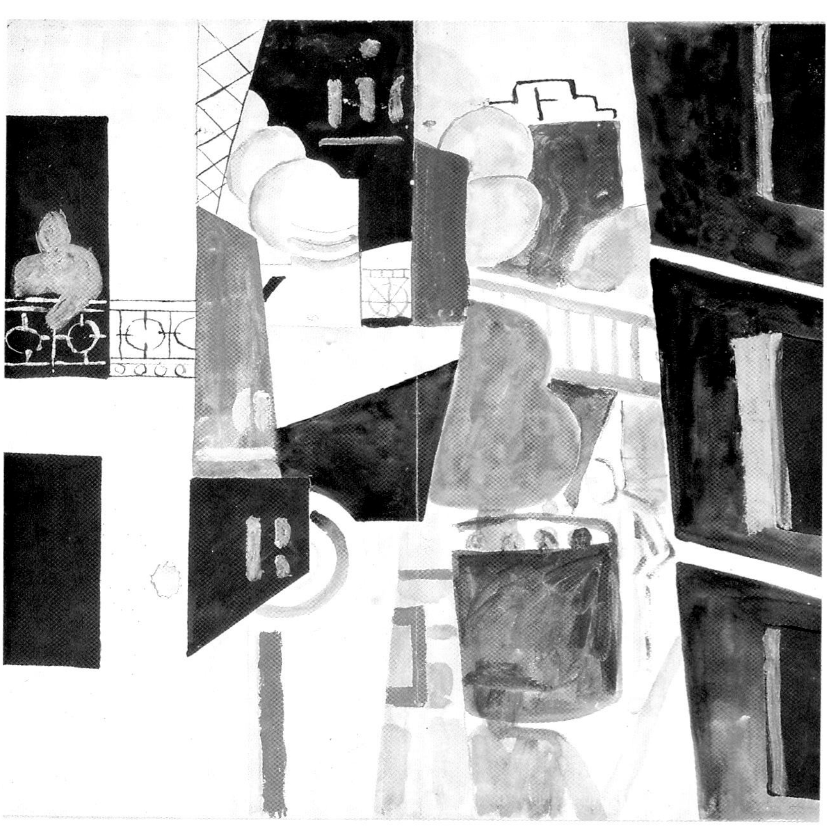

96. THE BIG TUGBOAT
1923—Oil on canvas, 125 × 198 cm
Musée National Fernand Léger, Biot

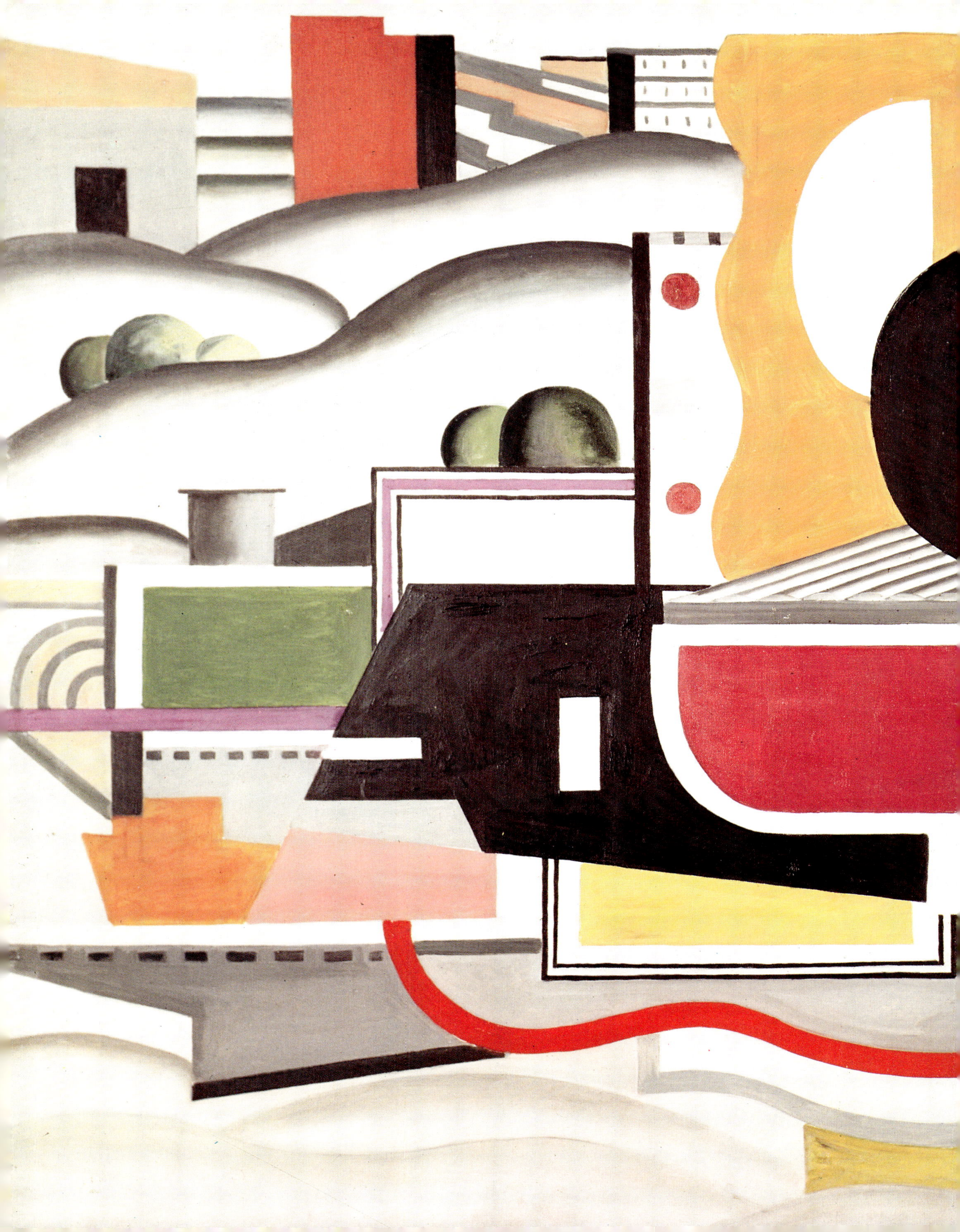

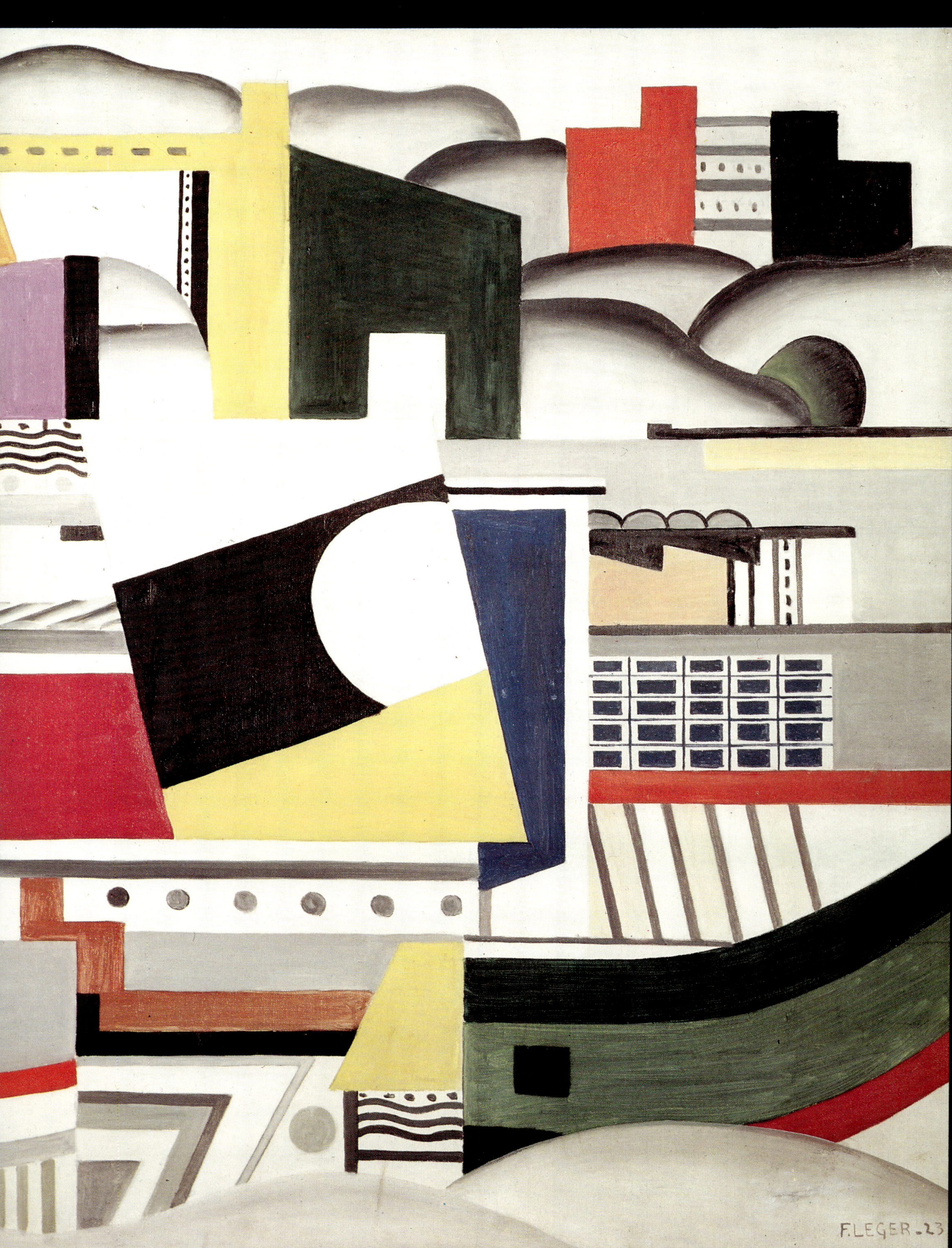
F.LEGER.23

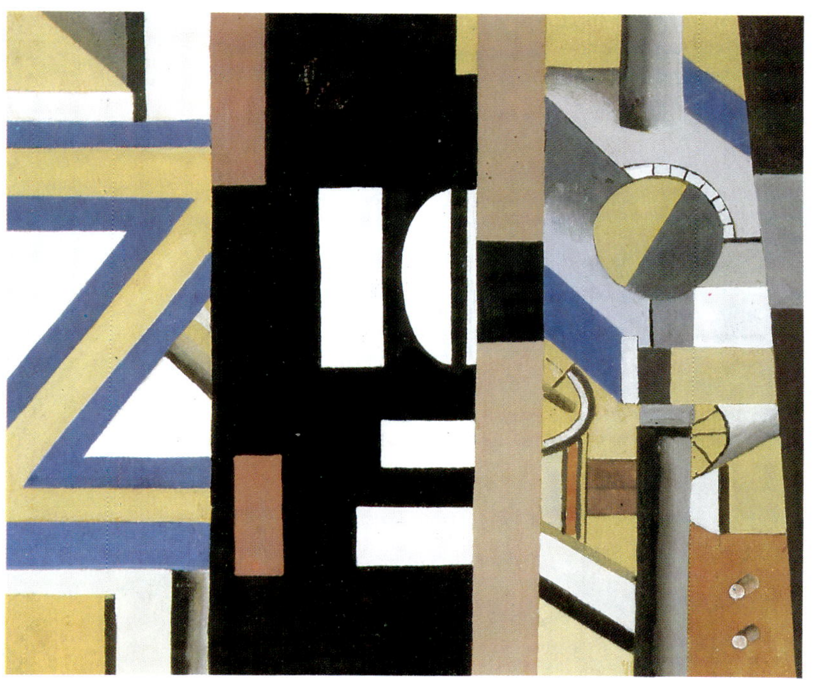

97. STUDY FOR *THE TRAIN STATION*
1918—Gouache, 35 × 40 cm
Private collection

98. TRAIN STATION
1923—Oil on canvas, 81 × 115 cm
Louis Carré Gallery, Paris

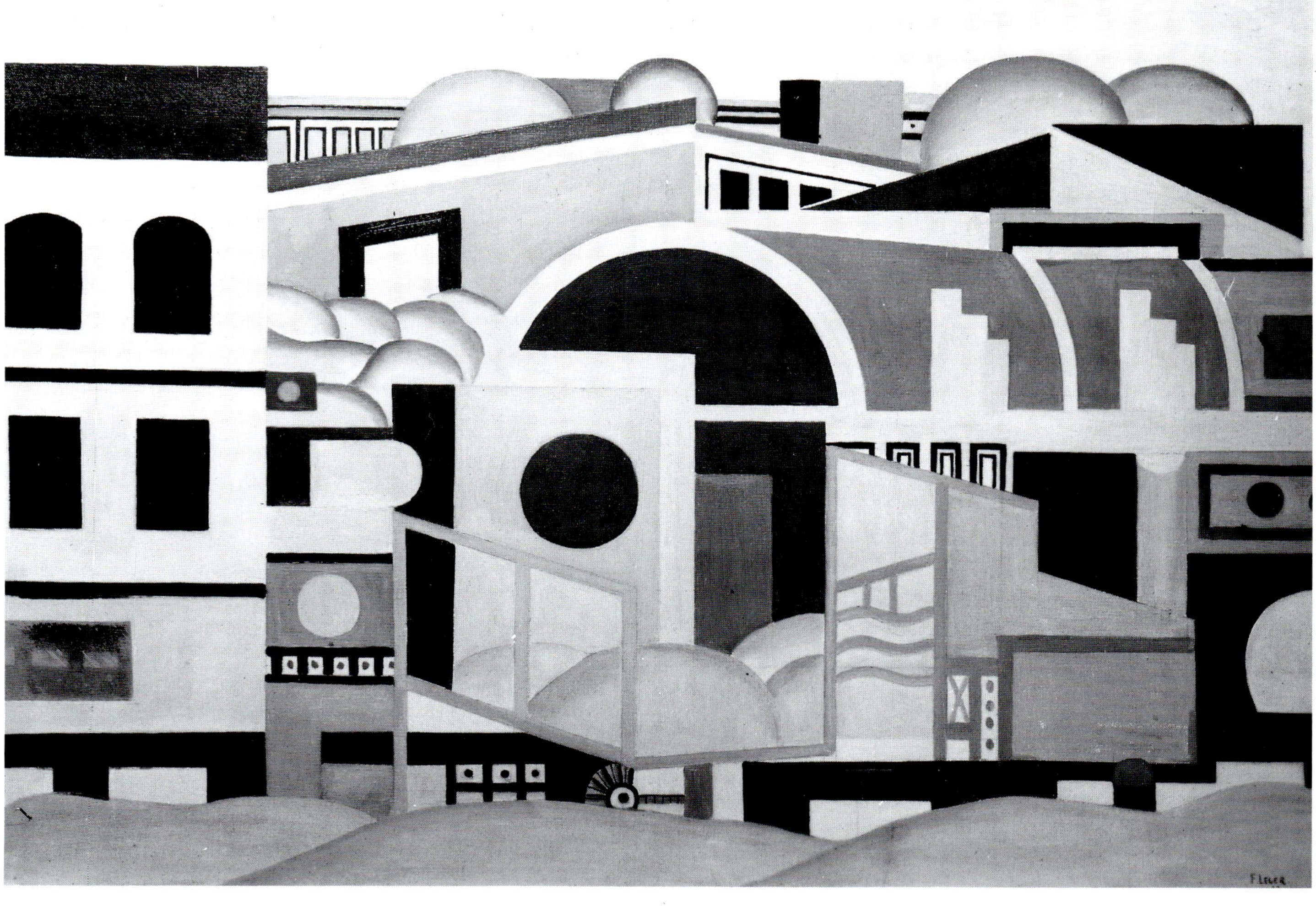

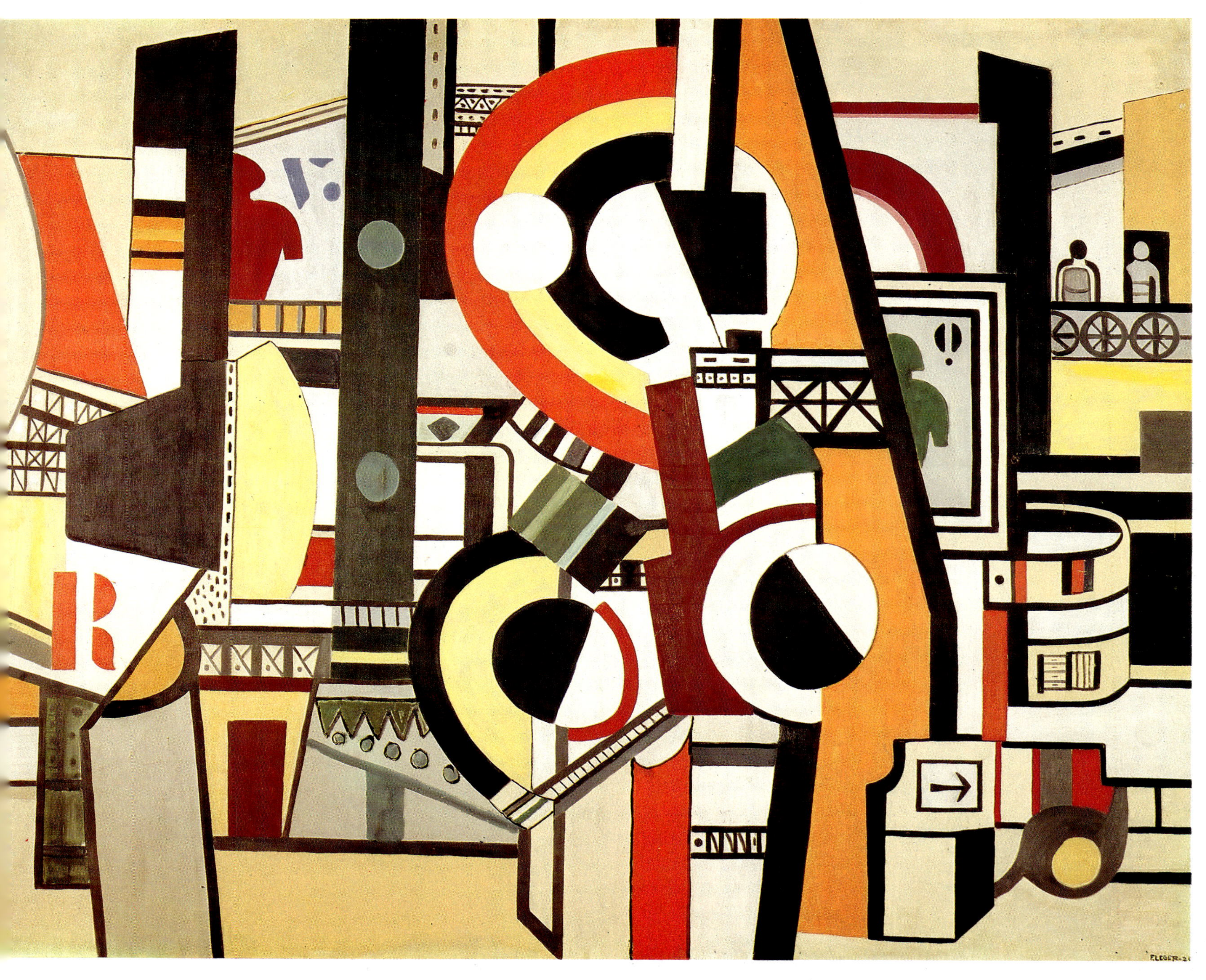


99. DISCS IN THE CITY
1920–21—Oil on canvas, 130 × 162 cm
Musée National d'Art Moderne, Centre Georges Pompidou, Paris
Gift of Louise and Michel Leiris

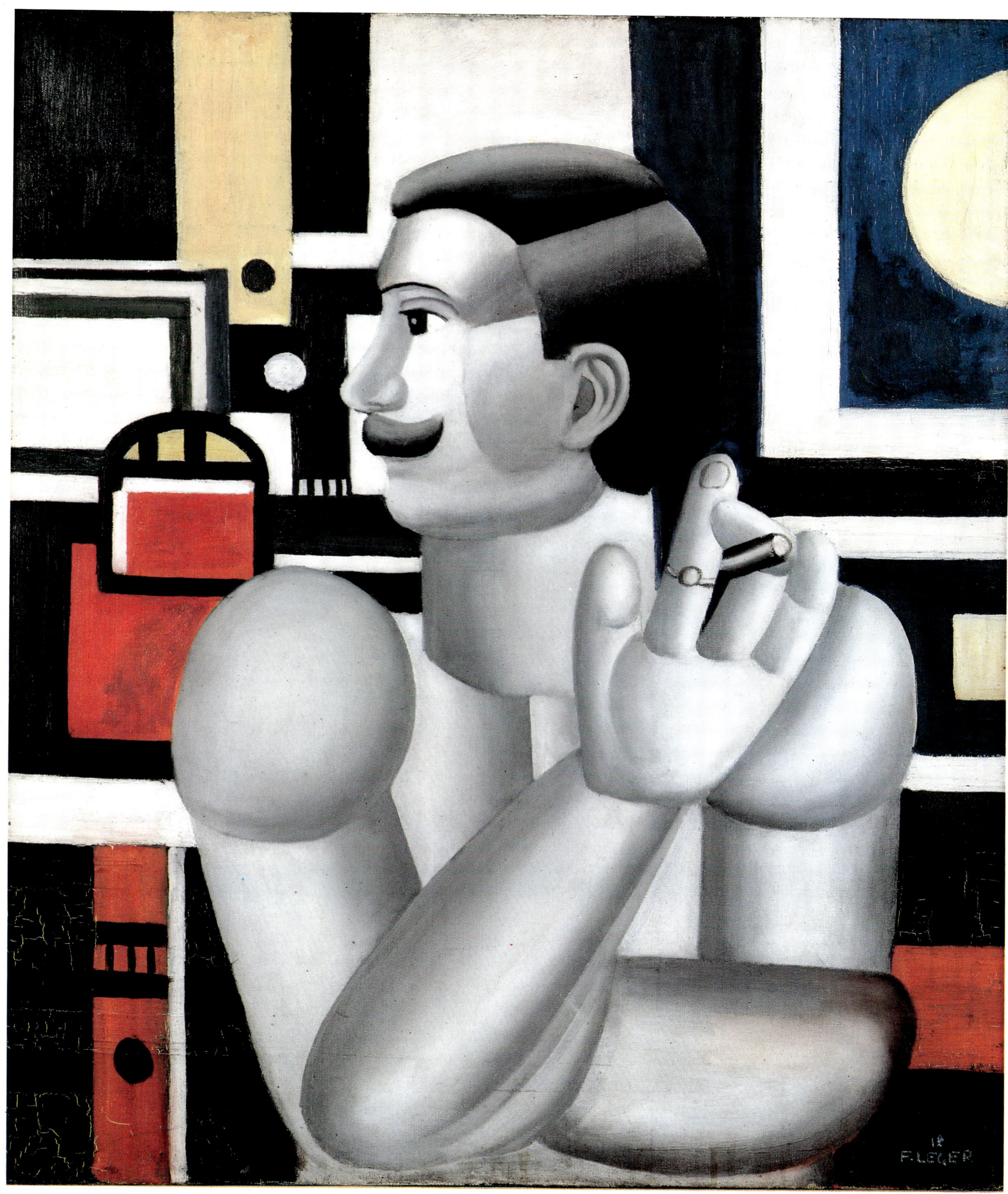


100. THE MECHANIC
1918—Oil on canvas, 65 × 54 cm
Musée d'Art Moderne, Villeneuve-d'Ascq
Gift of Geneviève and Jean Masurel

# A Robotics of Characters

Léger needed a breather after the dynamism of the "mechanical period," and he turned his attention to monumental human forms in stasis. After breaking, disconnecting, and pulverizing the human form like a plaything, he needed to rebuild and recompose it. The result was totally in keeping with his artistic pursuits. The "mechanical period" was of capital importance in this sense. It laid the groundwork for a plastic expression in which architectural values corresponded to the evolution of modern art as Léger understood it. All past emotional connotations of the human form gave way to the "human form as object." It was monumental, stereotypical, and inexpressive.

Ill. 100 In *The Mechanics*, painted in 1918 and 1920, the man
Ill. 101 is an outgrowth of the machinery he has created, but he is portrayed in a less schematic fashion than
Ill. 67 the *Soldier with a Pipe* (1916). Not only is the me-
Ill. 68 chanic himself more realistic, but the objects that surround him as well. He is no longer a technical composition of discs, ovals, and cylinders. He has become a figurative object with monumental characteristics. In Léger's credo of line, form, and color, this time he gets carried away with volume. The dy-
Ill. 92 namism that culminated in *The City* gave way to a static concept in which the immobile human form has a mainly architectural significance. It is a first monument to the worker himself, as opposed to the worker's product. Other monuments would follow, more carefully modeled, and consisting entirely of women. The mechanic stands erect, thanks to the vigorous "contrast" between the geometric background and the recognizably smooth, modulated forms of his body. Léger's rendering of the man's muscles, and the sense of detail in the mustache, ring, and arm tattoo, as well as the frozen profile, make us think of the "naive" paintings of the Douanier Rousseau. For Werner Schmalenbach they recall Charlie Chaplin. Both references are valid. Delaunay had introduced Léger to Rousseau, and Léger wrote about Chaplin: "Apollinaire took me to see Charlot during one of my army leaves. . . . I was completely captivated: that little man is not a little man at all, but a kind of *living object*, dry and mobile in black and white. There's nothing theatrical about his acting . . . he was the first 'man of the screen' (man as screen image). . . . He's part of the great tradition of ancient and primitive peoples who invented the mask. This jumps right out of the screen at you." Chaplin made his films in the same way that Léger made his paintings, and he would be the subject of many Léger paintings, especially in Léger's illustrations for Ivan Goll's book *Chaplinade*. Chaplin also appears in a sequence of *Le Ballet Mécanique* (1924). "Charlot is universal because he is visual," proclaimed Léger. Léger's point of departure was *Charlot as a machine*.

101. THE MECHANIC
1920—Oil on canvas, 116 × 89 cm
National Gallery of Canada, Ottawa

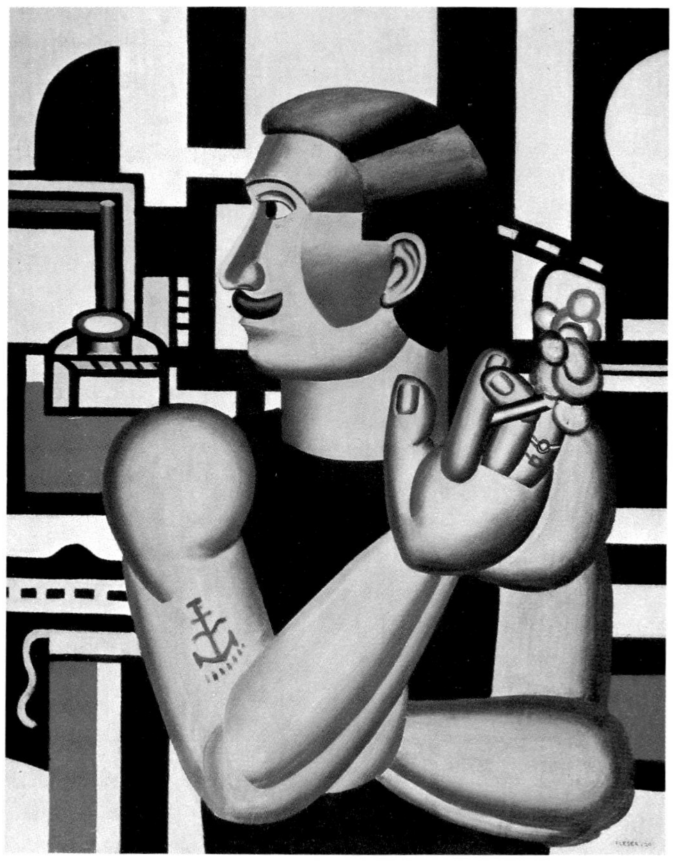

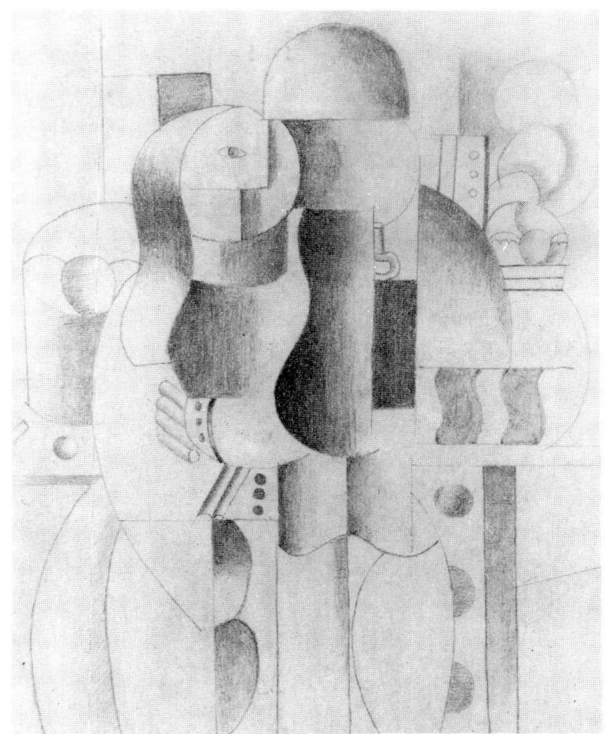

102. UNTITLED (MAN AND WOMAN)
1918—Pencil drawing, 37 × 30 cm
Private collection

## Ill. 104 *Woman at the Mirror:* the plastic value

Nadia Léger spoke about walking with her husband past fifteenth- and sixteenth-century portraits of men and women when they were in Italy. Léger was astonished to realize that the viewer's attention was so totally drawn to the color and textures of velvet, the lace embroidery in the clothes, and the way the hair was coiffed that the faces themselves went completely unnoticed. What one saw was an enormous, beautiful painting. In turn, Léger wanted to teach his students to paint portraits of twentieth-century men and women: men wearing gray suits, women in simple dresses with flexible hairstyles. "We no longer wear rich and colorful clothes, which in the past enhanced painting. But we have objects all around us. Thus, we must represent this man and woman surrounded by modern objects. . . . Why not paint a twentieth-century hand that is predominant because of its technological achievements? Why not paint a man next to a machine? After all, it is a painting of our time." Nadia finished the anecdote with her own personal conclusion: "You can find your own means of expression through looking at the works of the Old Masters, or the works of Léger. Since there were twelfth, and fifteenth centuries, there's no reason at all why there shouldn't be a twentieth, too."

Léger wrote in "Regarding the Human Form Considered as an Object" (1945): "The *object* in modern painting must become the *main character* and overthrow the subject. If, in turn, the human form becomes an object, it can considerably liberate possibilities for the modern artist. He would then be free to use the law of contrasts, which is a constructive law in the fullest sense." In his 1949 essay "How I Conceive the Human Figure," he is even more precise: "In the preceding pictorial tradition, *the human figure and the landscape* were heavy with meaning. Why? It was the landscape in which people lived, and the human figures and portraits that decorated the walls of their homes. That is how they acquired sentimental value, which has led to such a quantity of good, bad, or debatable paintings. To clearly see this, the modern artist needed to detach himself from the hegemony of sentimental art. We have liberated ourselves by allowing the object to replace the subject. Abstract art came as a complete liberation, and then we were able to consider the human figure as a plastic value, not as a sentimental value. That is why the human figure has remained willfully inexpressive throughout the evolution of my work from 1905 to the present. I am aware that this very radical concept of the figure-as-object is offensive to a great many people, but there is nothing I can do about it."

103. STUDY FOR *THE DANCE*
1919—Pencil on paper, 38 × 31 cm
Private collection

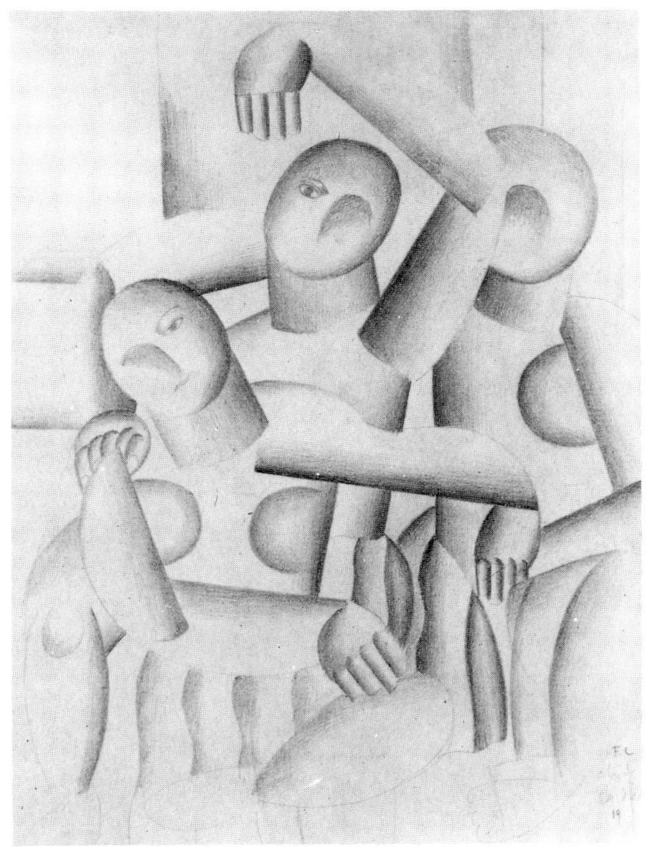

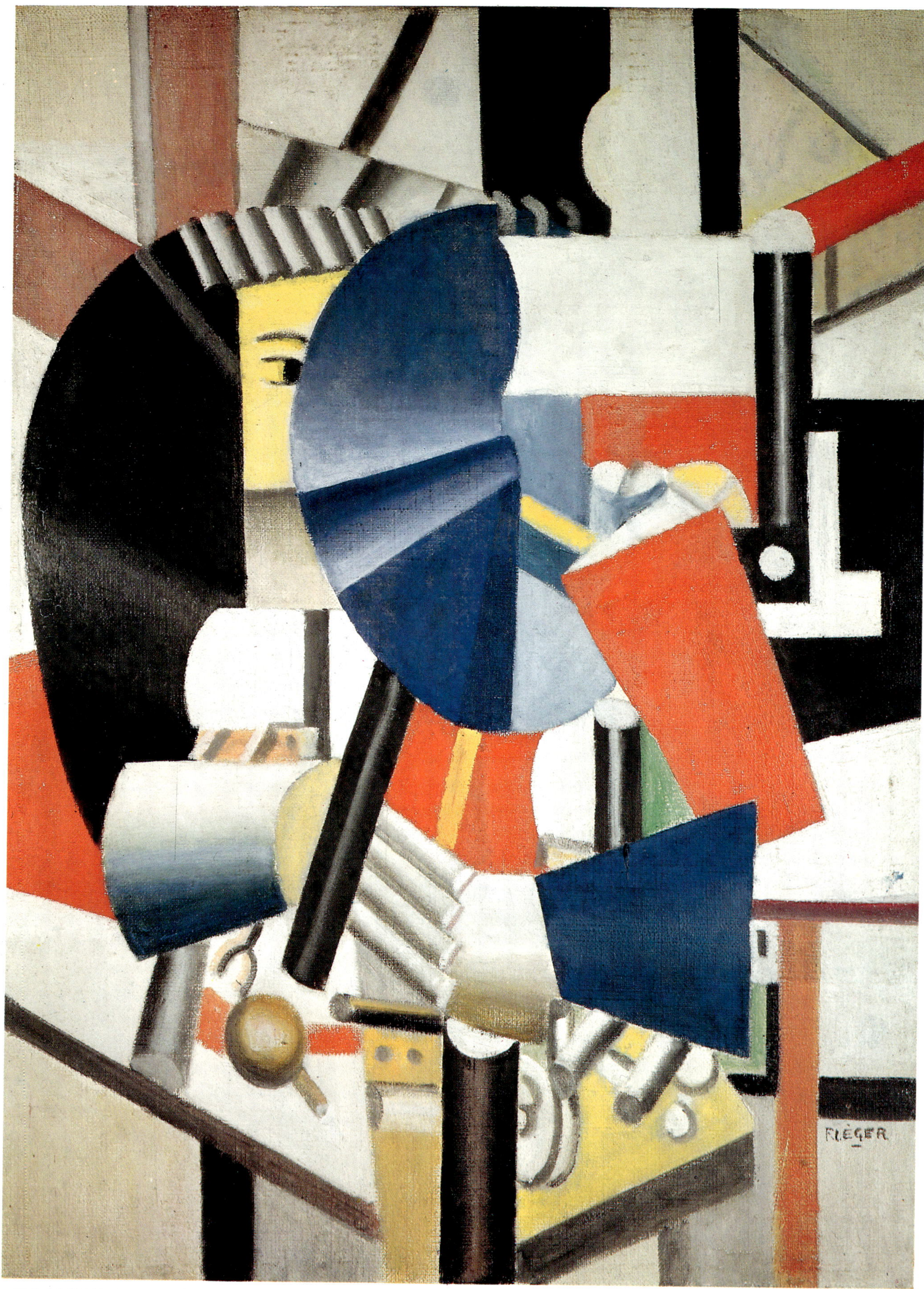


104. WOMAN AT THE MIRROR
1920—Oil on canvas, 91.5 × 64.5 cm
Moderna Museet, Stockholm

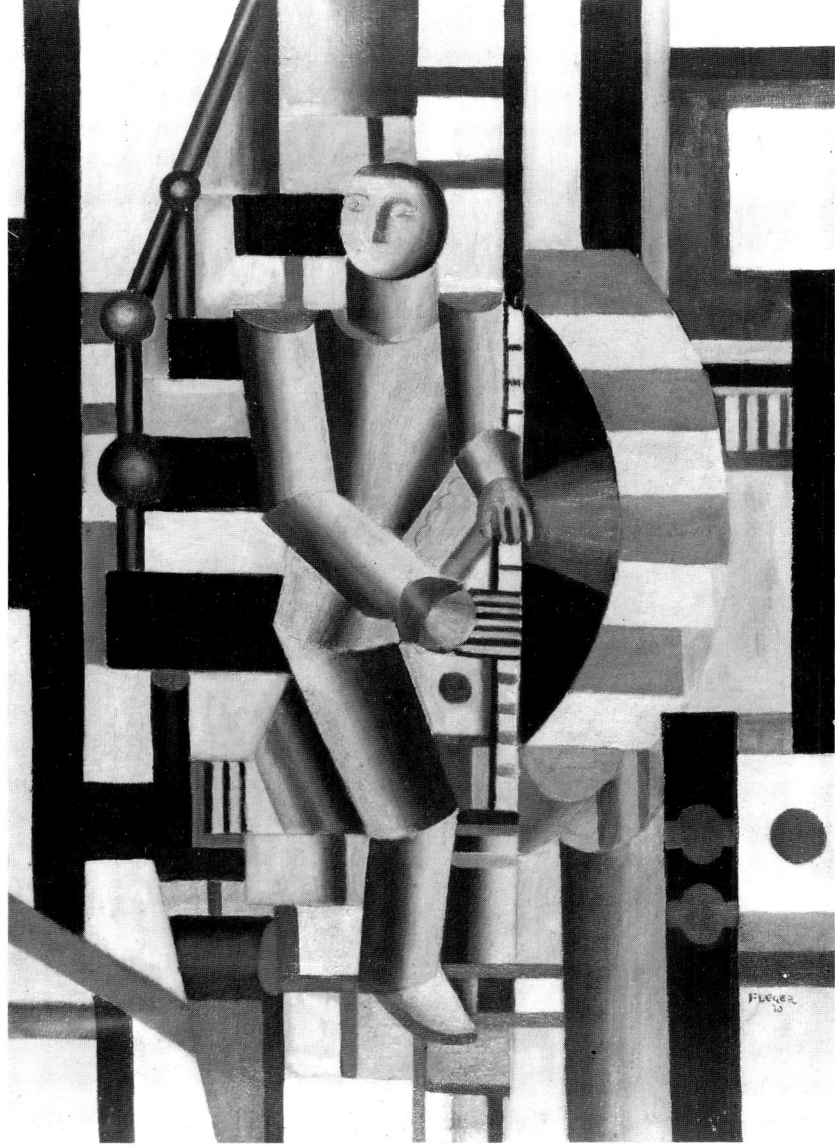

105. DRAFT FOR THE *MAN WITH A DOG*
1920—Oil on canvas, 65 × 46 cm
Museé d'Art Moderne, Villeneuve-d'Ascq
Gift of Geneviève and Jean Masurel

## *The Staircase*, a youth brought forth by a farm machine

Ill. 106
Ill. 105

It is quite clear by now that Léger was not motivated by public approval. Nonetheless, public disapproval of his work methods cruelly hurt him. He found his rewards elsewhere: the satisfaction of knowing that he had translated his plastic intentions onto the canvas. The following anecdote illustrates his transition from the mechanical world to the adaptation of depersonalized human beings used as emblems:

One year it so happened that the Aviation Show was about to open just next door to the Salon d'Automne where Léger was exhibiting his work. The art show was filled with "enormous gray, mournful surfaces, which were utterly pretentious." The Aviation Show was filled with "beautiful metallic objects that were hard, stable, and useful, with natural and pure colors. There were infinite varieties of steel, which interacted with the vermillions and blues. All this was dominated by the geometric strength of the forms." It is as if Léger were describing his own canvases from the metallic period.

The machinists who were working on the Aviation Show had never seen an art show before, and they decided to see what it was like. Léger arranged for their visit, but was "terribly saddened to see them get so excited in front of paintings that aren't even worth mentioning."

He did, however, have one experience that warmed his heart, via his painter's vision of life: "I'll always see that young lad of sixteen with bright red hair and a new blue vest, orange pants, and a hand with a spot of Prussian blue on it, as he contemplated the nude women framed in gold; that young, modern working man exploded with color and killed all the art on the walls, reducing it to vaporous shadows in decrepit frames. That marvelous kid seemed like he had been brought forth into this world by a farm machine. He was the symbol of the world to come, the show next door, the tomorrow when *Prejudice* would be no more." What a lively "contrast"! That young polychrome man gained direct entry into Léger's world.

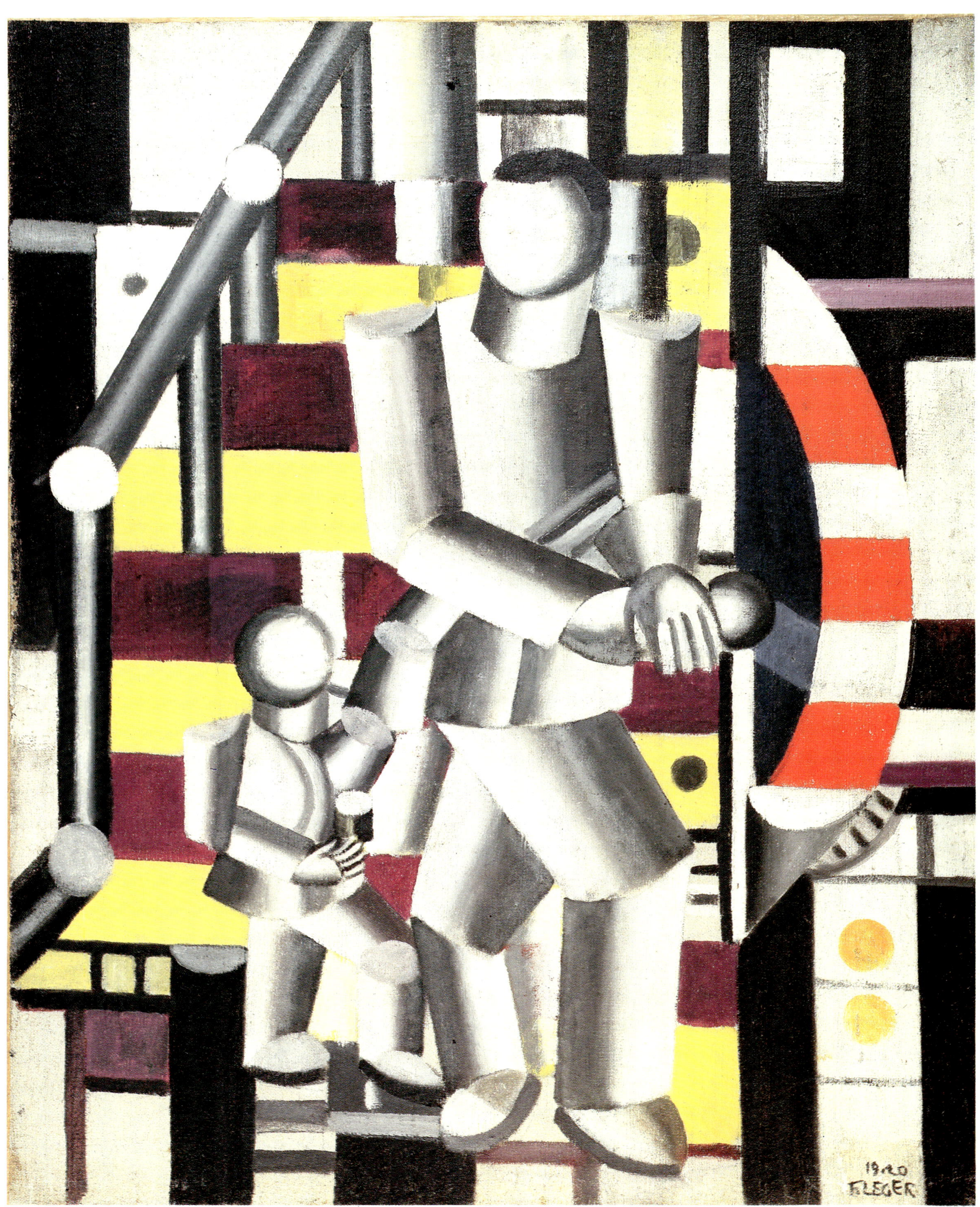


106. THE STAIRCASE
1919–20—Oil on canvas, 74.6 × 60 cm
Rosengart Gallery, Lucerne, Switzerland

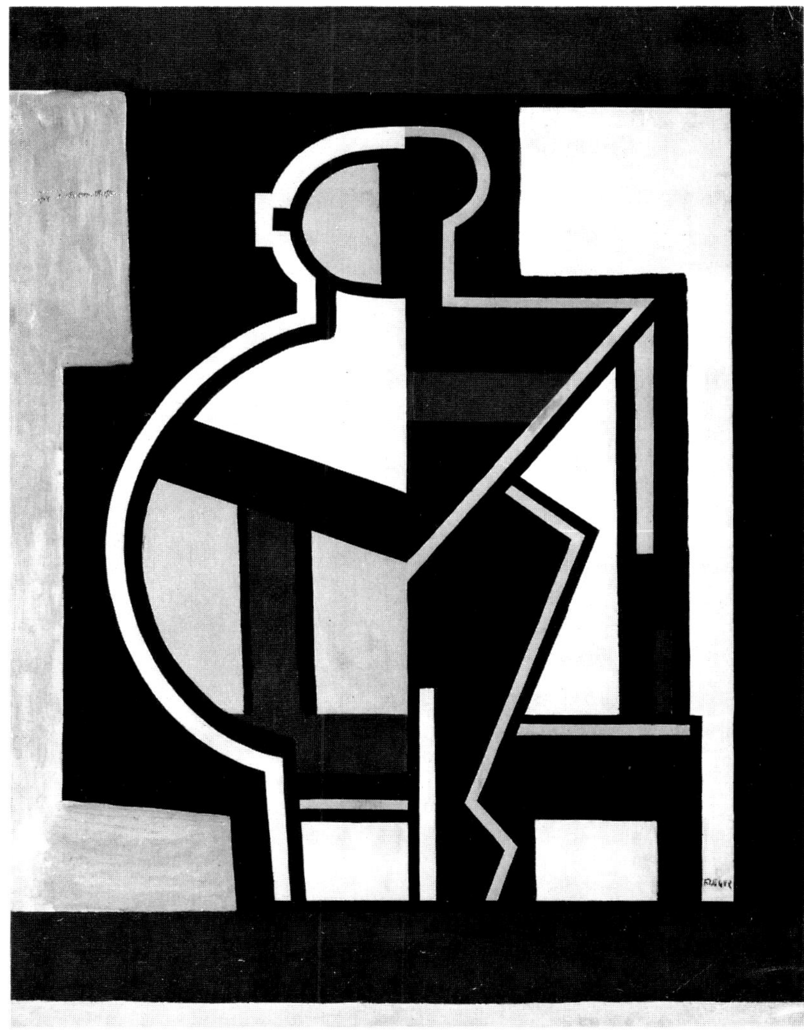

107. ABSTRACT COMPOSITION
1919—Oil on canvas, 156 × 114 cm
Musée Nationale Fernand Léger, Biot

## Herald of the common man

Léger as "Herald of the comman man"—this title was never more appropriate than during the period
Ill. 100 of *The Mechanic, Three Comrades* ("Les Trois Cama-
Ill. 108 rades"), *Man with a Dog* ("L'Homme au chien"), *The*
Ill. 105 *Staircase* ("L'Escalier"), *The Waiter* ("Le Garçon de
Ill. 106 café"). These characters are "stuck" against back-
Ill. 111 grounds that represent the modern environment. An entire inventory of recognizable objects is enumerated to identify the characters in terms of their function, activity, and occupation. One character wears a sailor's cap; another descends a metallic staircase that could be on a ship or inside a factory; a third is identified by a tray and glass. It is clear that *Three Friends* represents working-class men, anonymous sailors, ordinary laborers. Most of the time they are represented in the painter's favorite way: on a break, smoking a pipe, relaxing.

Contrary to the Cubists, Léger never used collage as a technique. His characters do, however, seem "stuck" to the background. It is one more use of "contrast," another card in the player's hand, except for the fact that Léger has replaced the king of hearts and the jack of clubs with anonymous workers. The contrast between physical reality and the expressionless characters who are deprived of personality gives value and presence to the painting itself. It also reenforces another desired contrast: the grayness of the characters and the polychrome decor on which the characters are "stuck."

During this period of Léger's work, the body and clothes of the characters seem to melt together in tubular monochromatics, accentuating the contrast with the color-saturated decors. The characters are represented with physical integrity. They have hair, noses, mouths, and eyes, but rarely do they ever have an expression. It is as if they are wearing primitive masks inherited from some foregone age, those same elements Léger used to describe Chaplin in the film *Modern Times*.

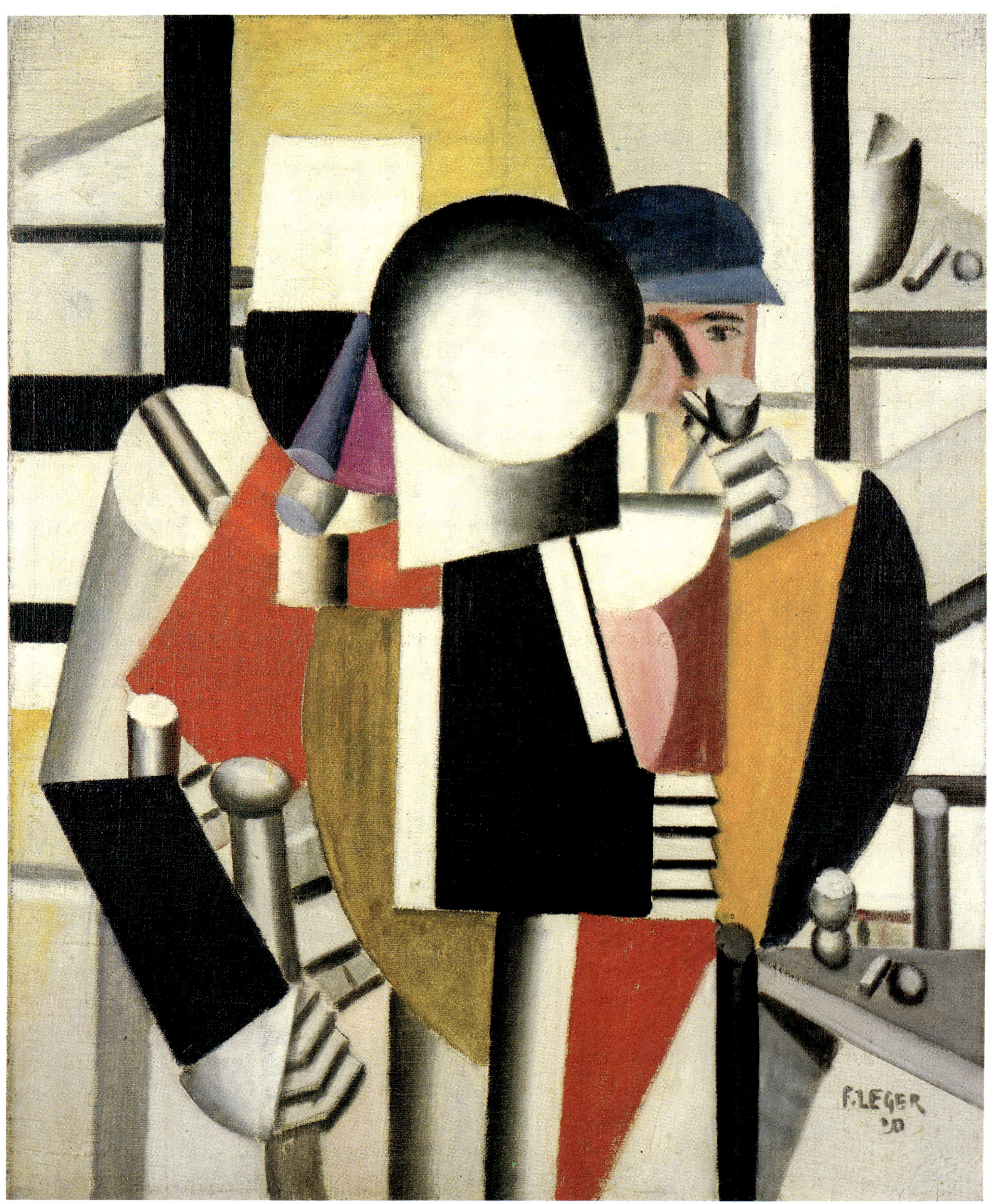


108. THREE COMRADES
1920—Oil on canvas, 92 × 73 cm
Stedelijk Museum, Amsterdam

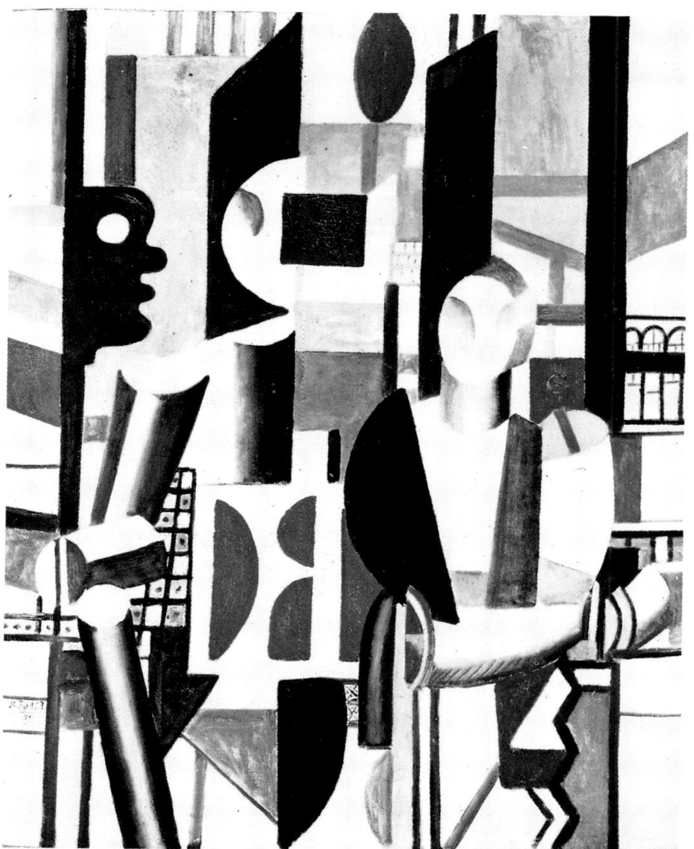

109. MAN IN THE CITY
1919—Oil on canvas, 145.5 × 113.5 cm
Peggy Guggenheim Foundation, Venice

## Builder of a twentieth-century realism

Léger's period of robotization in which his characters become statues is one of synthesis as well as transition. It fits perfectly into the context of his consistent evolution. Applying his mastery of contrast, he reunited rounded bodies and decorative geometrical lines, robots and everyday objects, still life and characters, landscapes and elements of industrial architecture. In the years that followed, he would again disconnect these elements in order to deal with them separately, and simplify them to the extreme in terms of form and color until he could once again reunite them in their finished form and definitive color. The final synthesis would include the same thematic subjects he dealt with from the beginning, be they personified objects, characters-as-objects, monumental abstractions, the circus, builders. . . All of this was first expressed through pure dynamism with the spatial freeing of objects, and ultimately through soothing and deliberate ornamentation. After confronting the human form in its robotic manifestation, Léger would draw up an inventory of objects in the modern environment. In this sense Garaudy refers to Léger as the "builder of a twentieth-century realism," who even branched into architecture—then gradually returned to a more humanized and vital form of representation.

Shortly before his death, Léger again said to Nadia: "I painted forms. During the Cubist years we started out by destroying these forms. Now I'm restructuring them with eyes and mouths. But these forms are static and I must go beyond this. A national form of painting is called for." If Léger had lived on and been able to go full circle, he may have even rejoined Raphael: a passage through the modern world into the atemporal world. This is the essential drama of modern art. Early on it wanted to break with the monotony of a nose in the middle of a face, only to discover after a long exploration that the nose is best just where it has always been.

110. COMPOSITION WITH TWO CHARACTERS
1920—Wash on paper, 30.5 × 27.5 cm
Private collection

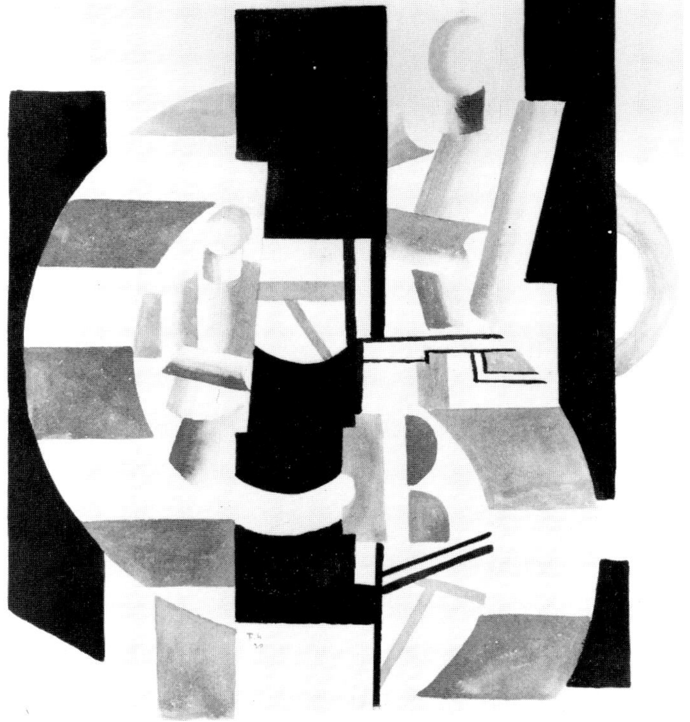

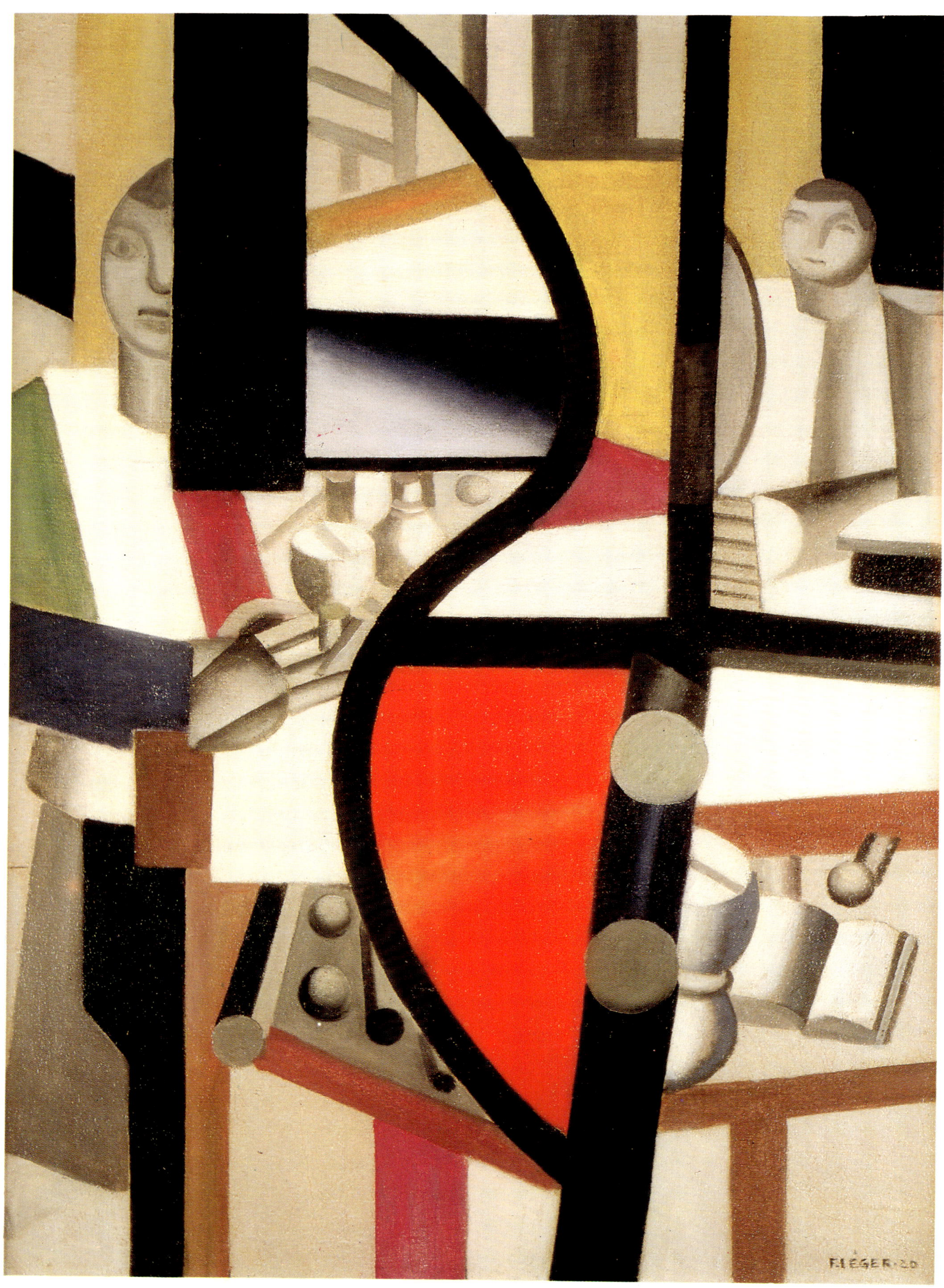


111. THE WAITER
1920—Oil on canvas, 93 × 65 cm
Private collection

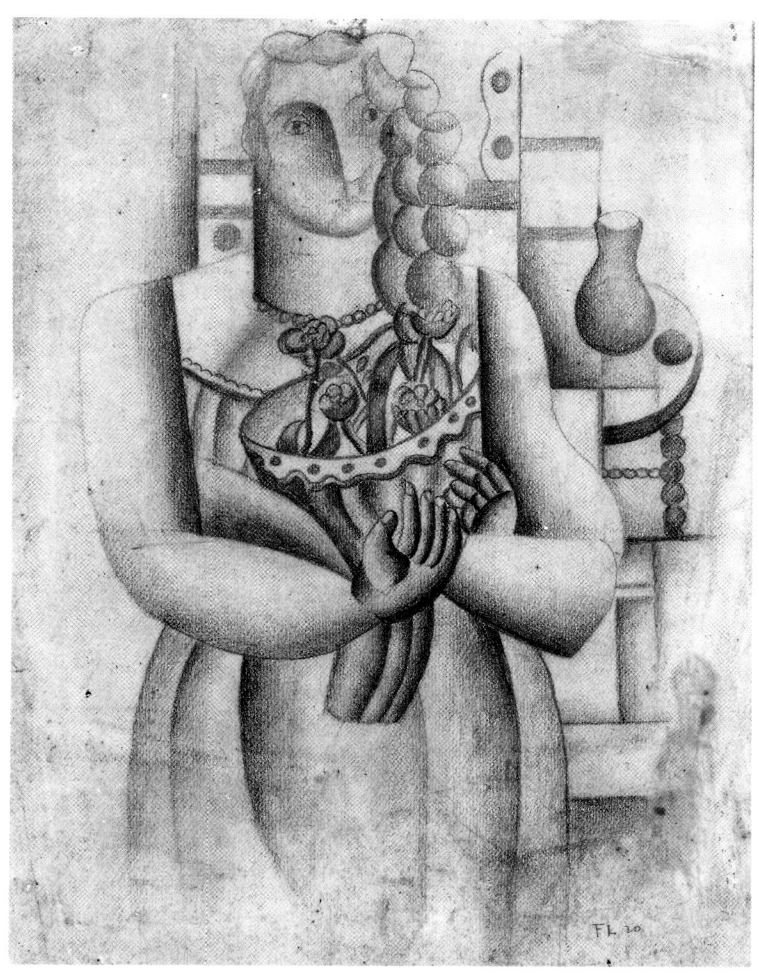

112. WOMAN WITH FLOWER BOUQUET
1920—Pencil on paper, 38 × 29 cm
Collection of Mr. and Mrs. Adrien Maeght

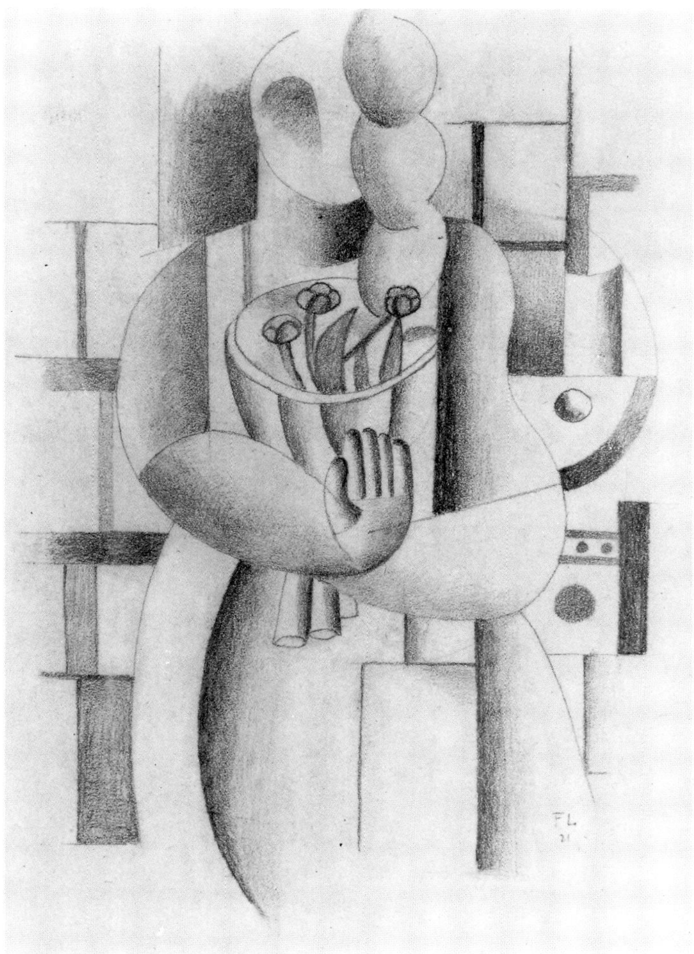

113. WOMAN WITH A FLOWER POT
1921—Pencil on paper, 35 × 25 cm
Private collection

**The anatomy of objects and the statuary figurines**

Léger did entire series of sketches before arriving at the final composition of a painting. These sketches served to simplify and integrate forms. He also painted different versions of the same subject, each of which progressed with stylistic concerns leading to a formula for the simplest ornamental value: "When I transpose a sketch onto the canvas, I simplify it; I submit the form to the general idea of the canvas, I remove everything from it that is not useful, I liberate it from all the parasites that might disturb the purity of the manner in which the canvas receives it." Léger was not interested in animating nature or characters. He wanted to "animate" the canvas itself, which has to "live" on the inanimate wall it hangs on. Contrast is the motive for the static aspect of objects, the inexpressive "masks" the characters seem to wear. The cold and hard nature of the human forms contrast with the warmth of the bright colors they rest against. The anatomy of the image takes precedence over the anatomy of the objects and the statuesque massiveness of the forms. This reenforces the stasis of the composition, to the exclusion of all dynamism. The sketches are sometimes more appealing in their imperfection, with all their "parasites." They have charm, enthusiasm, and awkwardness, as well as the warmth of a first spurt of inspiration. The final canvas, the "great machine," may be closer to the perfection that Léger sought, but it has lost a good part of its seductive value in the process.

In this respect we think back to the unfinished portrait of Bonaparte that the painter David executed in the space of three hours. It has more nervosity, realism, and seductive power than the monumental *Coronation* ("Sacre") that took him three years to do. We also think of Seurat whose "little sketches," painted subjects, are veritable flights of Impressionism that he then transformed into giant canvases using the mathematical formula of Pointillism, which had the same cooling effect.

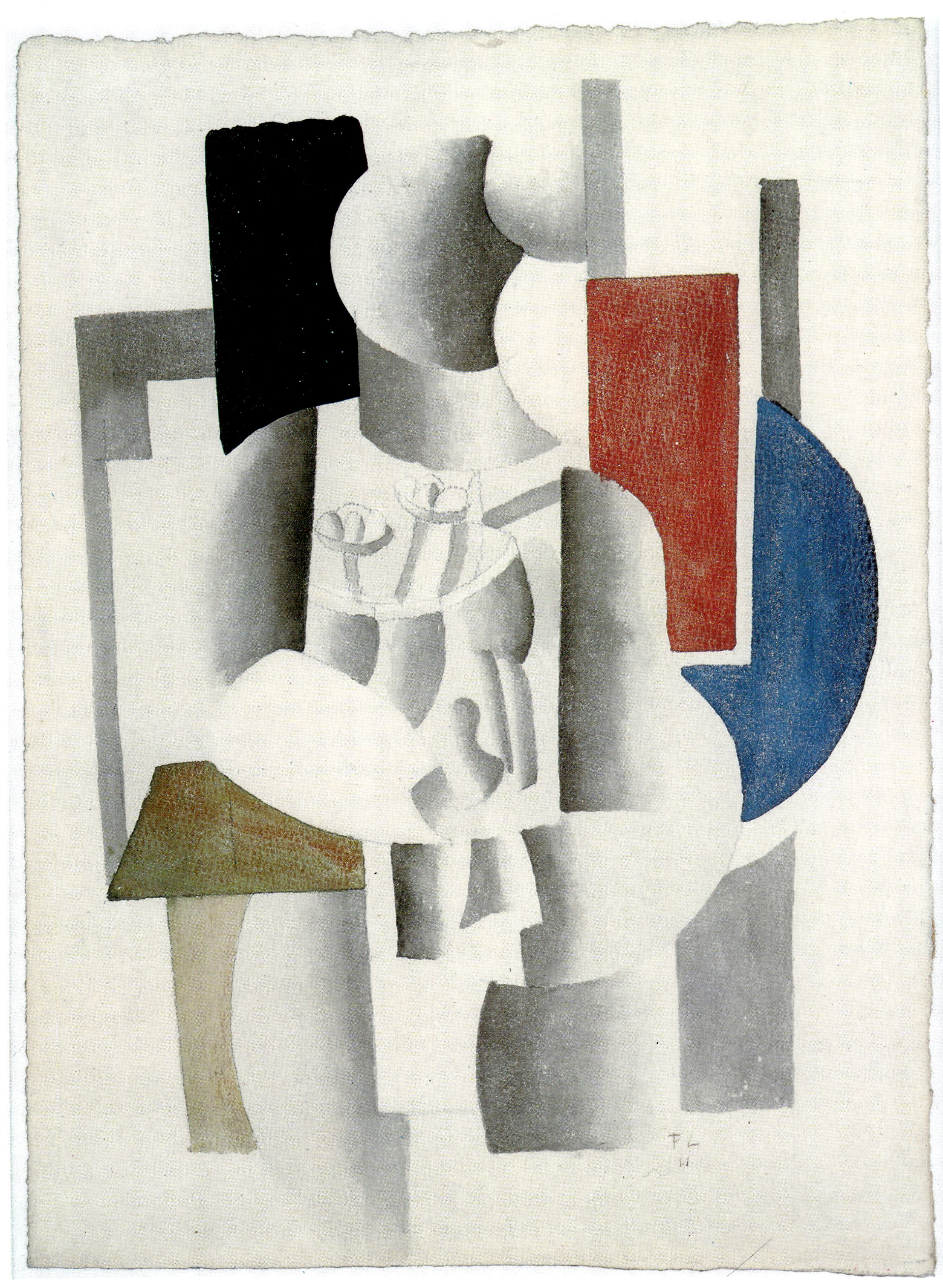

114. WOMAN WITH A FLOWER POT
1921—Gouache, 37 × 26 cm
Private collection

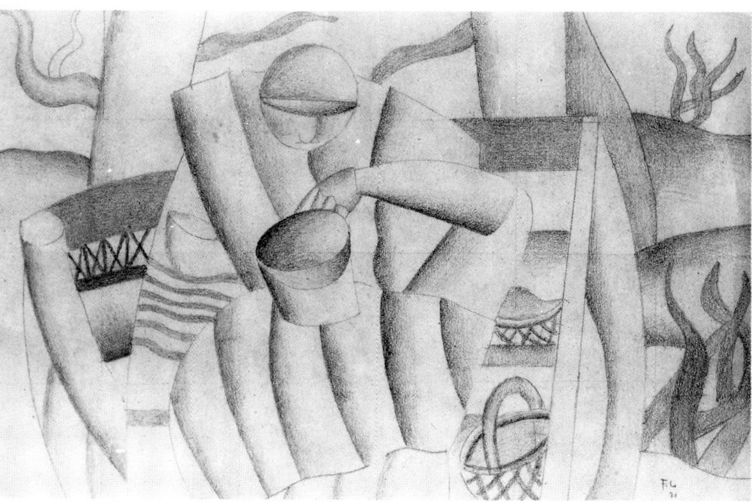

115. TWO FISHERMEN
1921—Pencil drawing, 10 × 14.5 cm
Private collection

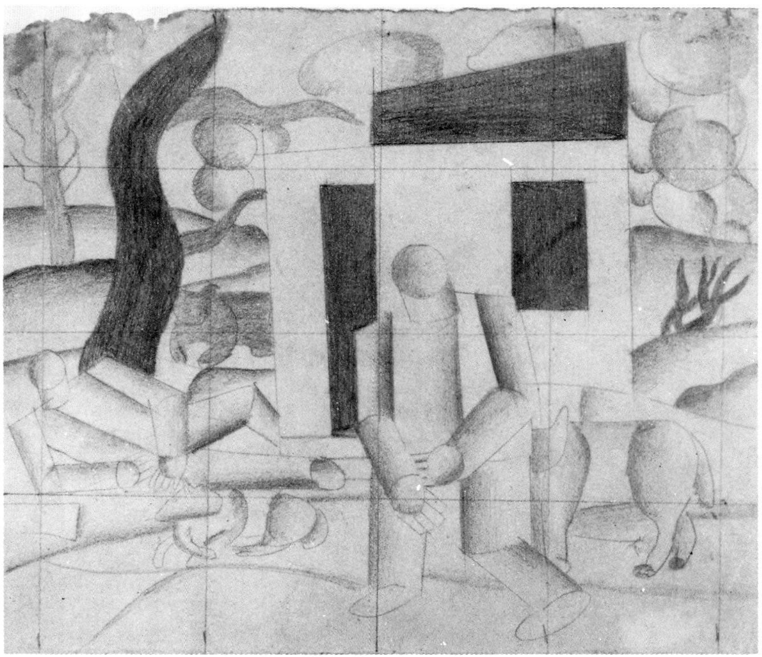

116. ANIMATED LANDSCAPE
About 1922—Pencil on paper, 26 × 31 cm
Private collection

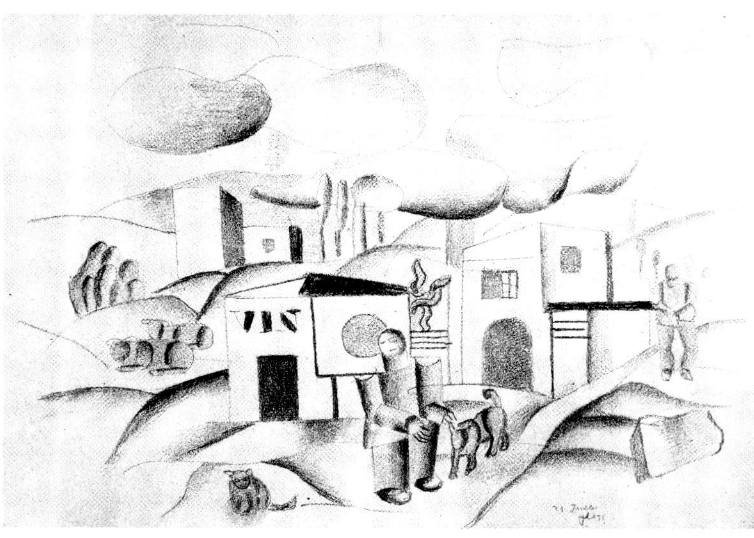

117. ANIMATED LANDSCAPE
1921—Pencil on paper, 25.5 × 37 cm
Musée National Fernand Léger, Biot

## Animated landscapes

Ill. 115 to 118

Between 1920 and 1922, Léger worked on a series, *Animated Landscapes*, in which the backgrounds portrayed leisure environments that were never totally separate from the industrial landscape. The "animated" landscapes were populated with human beings and animals, with factory smokestacks peeking out from a corner of the canvas and cutting the blue sky with polluted grays. The overall effect of these canvases, however, is bucolic, and markedly contrasts with the robotic aspect of the erect or relaxing characters. Garaudy interprets Léger's continued use of robotization as the artist's intention to create a link between the characters and the geometric forms that are the product of their work (straight lines of roads, rectangular houses, etc.). Even the great forest of 1909–10 was "animated" with woodcutters and altered by their hatchets. The mechanical period extended into the landscapes, which were marked, partitioned, and denatured by telegraph poles, metallic structures, and billboards. The *Animated Landscapes* are modern and industrialized, and they alone render a random dog or cow more "human." Man, however, is not humanized at all. Once again, he is ensconced in metallic gear, which makes him appear ready for a walk on the moon. People are painted in gray, deprived of eyes, devoid of expression. They are composed of mechanical parts, representing the world of work inscribed in a decor that is rich with color. In this way, Léger juxtaposed the rural and industrial worlds. A cow, a horse, or a dog are contrasted with the figurative spirals of industrial smoke. "The hard values underline the softer values," Léger would often say. He would refer to "villages that the billboards colored," the "landscapes with factory smoke through which trains and airplanes pass, or where cranes and machines operate." It was man's transformation of nature that interested him, not nature per se. "I assert that the billboard, a modern element that cuts through a soft and sentimental countryside, is the reason for modern art, and a magnificent one. It is a contrast." Léger's social preoccupations are present, as always, and *Animated Landscapes* could just as well be called "Awaiting the Paid Vacation"!

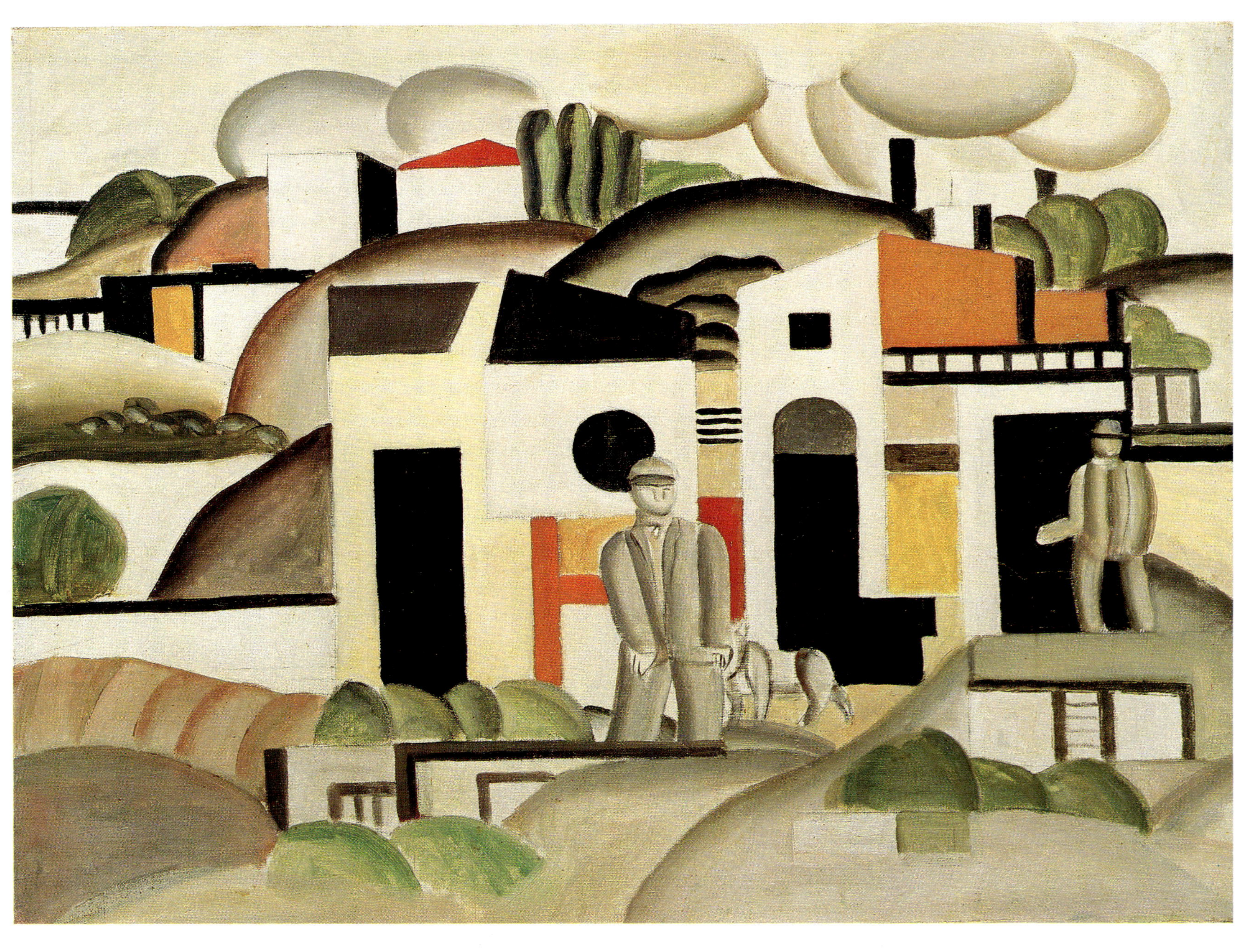

118. ANIMATED LANDSCAPE
1921—Oil on canvas, 50 × 65 cm
Private collection

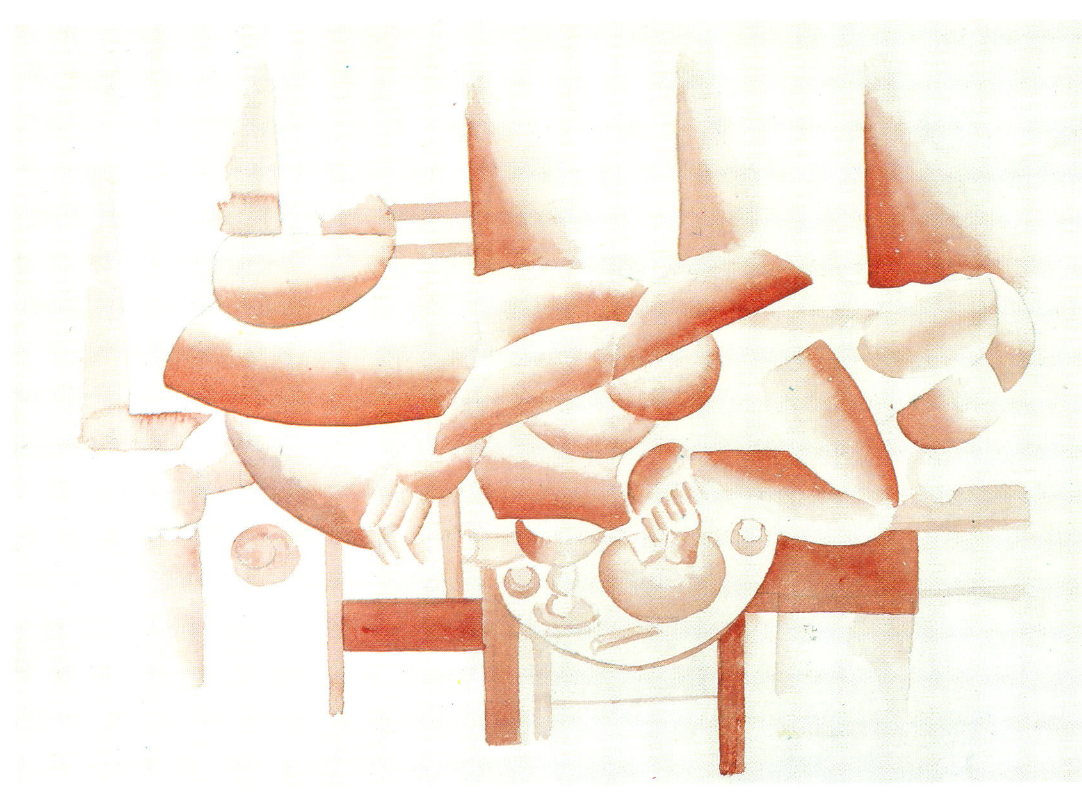

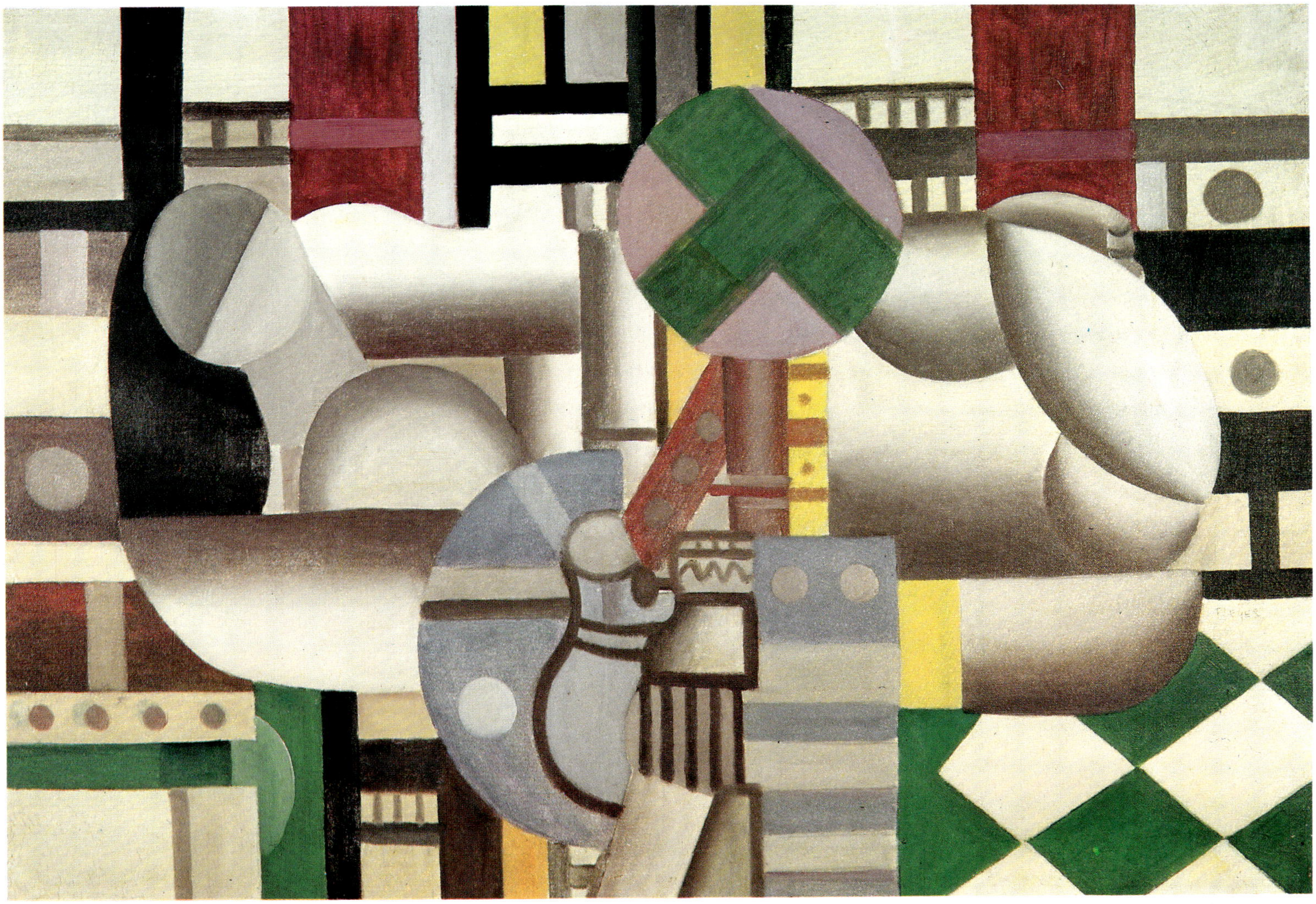

119. RECLINING WOMAN (STUDY FOR *THE LUNCH*)
1920—Watercolor on paper, 49 × 60 cm
Lionel Prejger collection, Paris

120. WOMAN AND STILL LIFE
1921—Oil on canvas, 65 × 92 cm
Gallery of Modern Art, Edinburgh

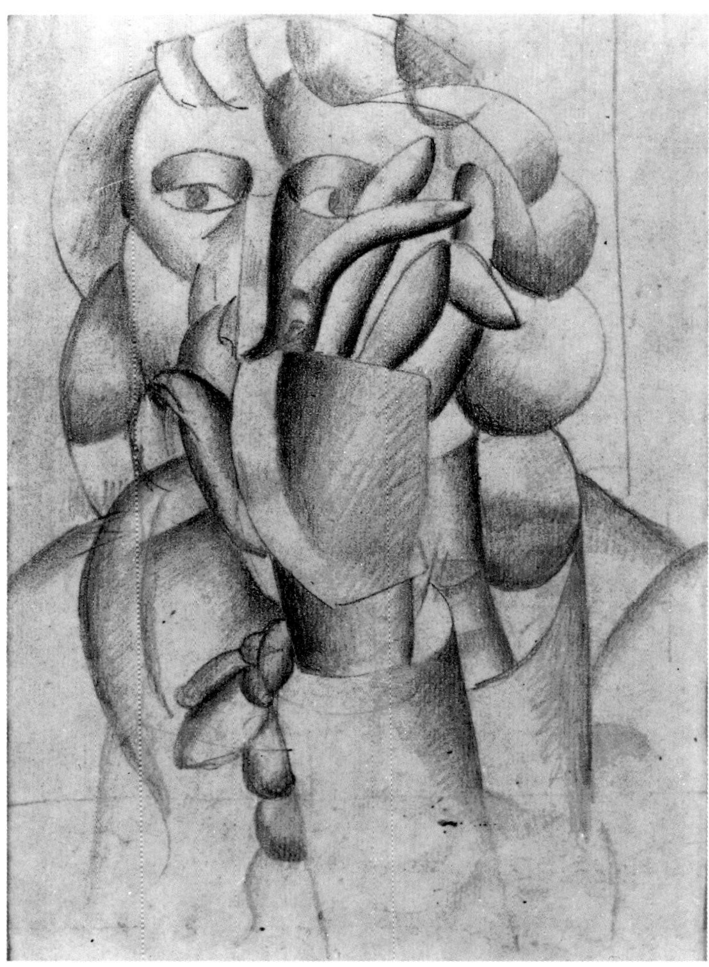

121. HEAD AND HAND
1920—Graphite pencil on paper, 30.9 × 19.9 cm
Musée National d'Art Moderne, Centre Georges Pompidou, Paris

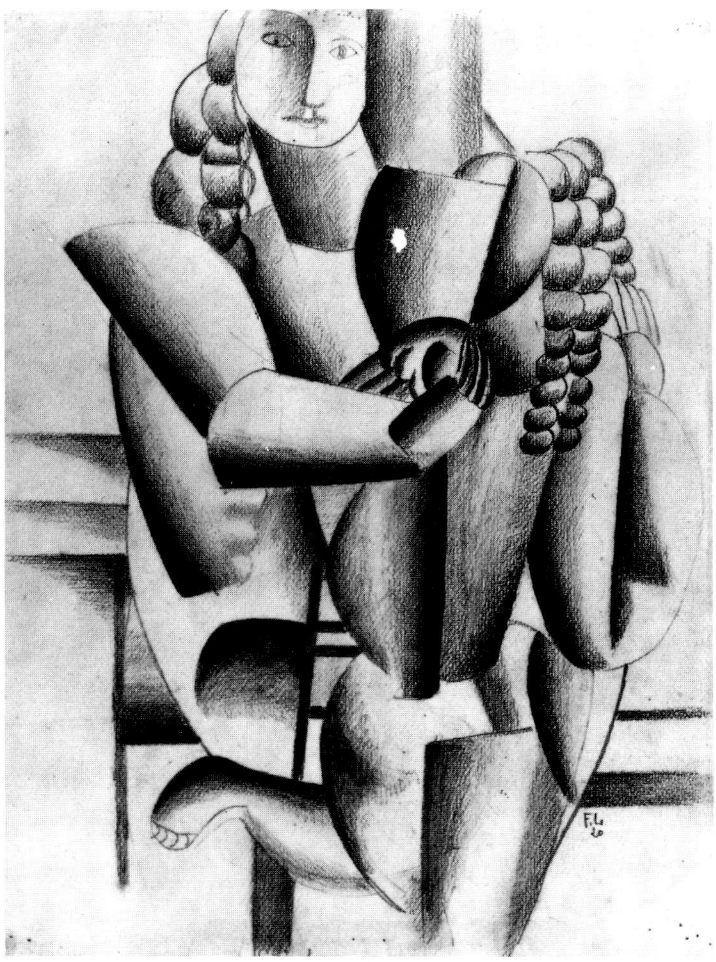

122. TWO WOMEN
1920—Pencil on paper, 41 × 30 cm
Musée National d'Art Moderne, Centre Georges Pompidou, Paris
Gift of Louise and Michel Leiris

## Be beautiful and keep your mouth shut

Léger's rediscovery of man was at the highest level —but not when it came to woman as subject: the nude woman, the giant woman, the woman at home and not in the workplace, the woman with cylindrical and round vases as breasts, woman colored in tones that remind us of cascading hair, full fruit forms that are juxtaposed to various body parts. In the midst of his interiors, the women were modeled giants with enormous thighs and arms like columns, and shoulders like pediments. They seem like architectural monuments. Their fluted hair, like sculpted stone, is the scrolls of an Ionic capital, and their breasts, stomachs, thighs, and kneecaps, even their faces, are spheres meant to contrast with the rigid, geometric lines of the decor. Léger was searching for the most effective formula, be it in robots, statues, or monuments. At this point he had not yet accepted the human being as a complete object; i.e., as a real man or a real woman. That would come during the

*Reading* ("La Lecture") period, even though the Ill. 242
women would lose some of their hair! His characters are not quite machines, and yet they do not seem endowed with life, either. There is a bit of the Frankenstein element in Léger's characters. They are bodies rebuilt from disparate parts and they more or less resemble humans without really being human. And they are not "bicycles" or "keys" either.

None of these giants is portrayed as a "working
woman," be she disconnected like *The Woman at the* Ill. 104
*Mirror* in 1920 ("La Femme au miroir") or portrayed
in the hieratic style like *The Big Lunch*, 1921 ("Le Ill. 125
Grand Déjeuner") or *Women in an Interior* (both the Ill. 128
1921 and 1922 versions). The woman at the mirror & 129
is making herself beautiful, and the others are totally idle, perhaps holding a flower or reclining on a couch in the manner of Madame Récamier: Be beautiful and keep your mouth shut. . .

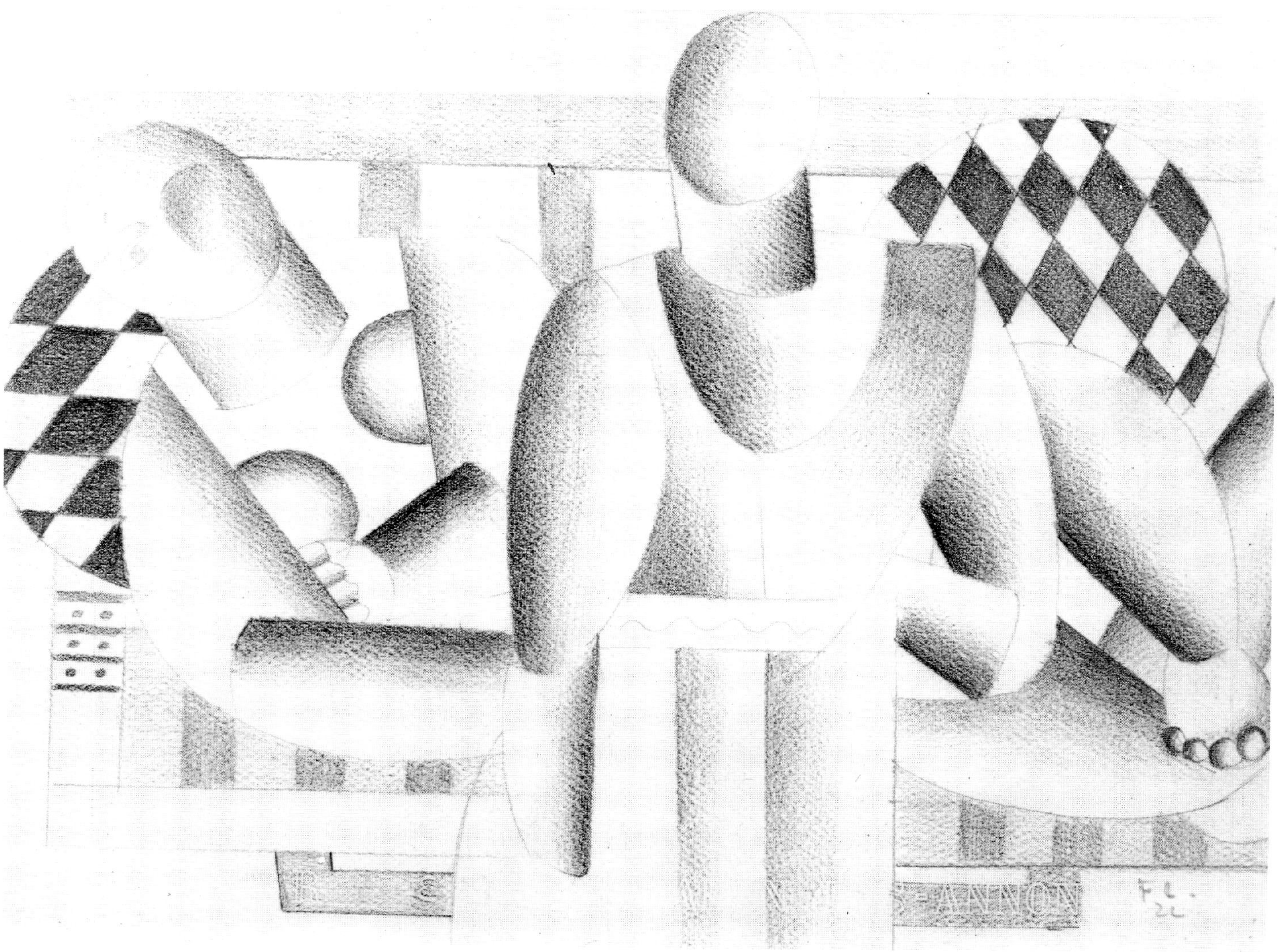

123. TWO WOMEN
1922—Pencil on paper, 24 × 33 cm
Lionel Prejger collection, Paris

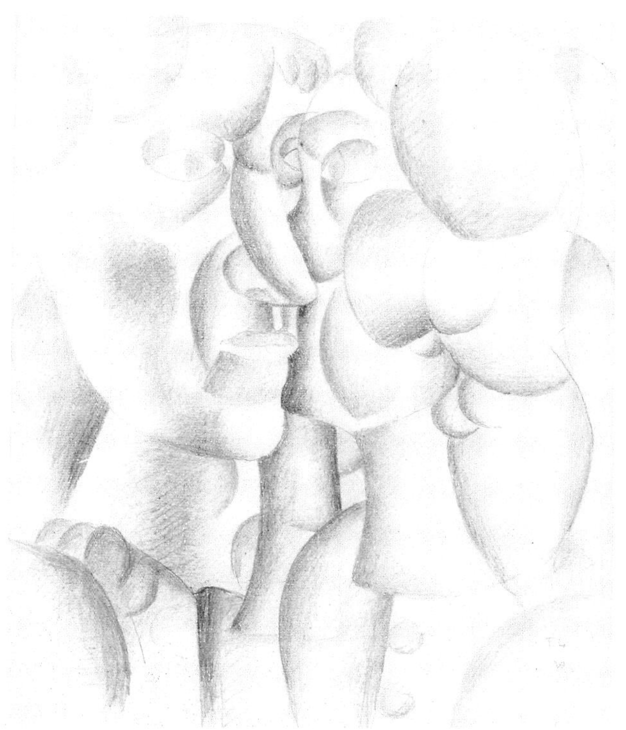

124. TWO HEADS
1920—Graphite drawing, 40 × 30 cm
Private collection

### *Le Grand Déjeuner* in the wink of an eye Ill. 125

It is as if Léger was giving a friendly wink to all his great predecessors who arranged their solemn and theatrical rituals on canvas using monumental nude women: Poussin, David, Ingres, Puvis de Chavannes, Gauguin; all the painters whom Léger particularly liked. Léger knew that his own "women" were eternal, like those of his predecessors, but also very contemporary. The bodies of Léger's nudes were trivialized. The faces were stereotypes, the environments were down to earth, and the colors were crude. Léger's nudes had no archaic qualities. They were marked by the modern world, sculpted by the machine, just like the other objects that surrounded them. Their forms were not naturalistic and had maintained only the essentials, just like the useful objects on the table at the center of *Le Grand Déjeuner*.

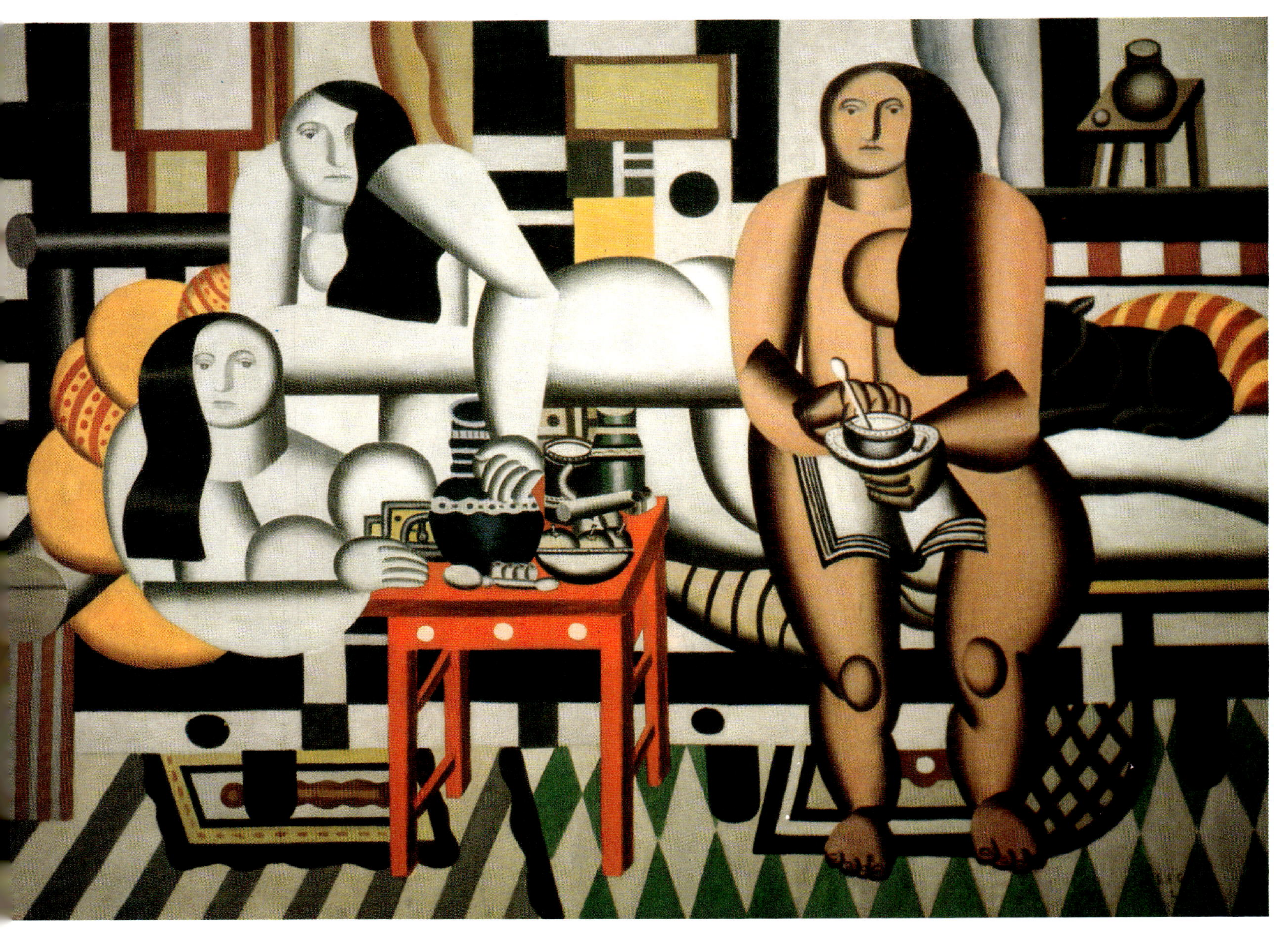

125. LE GRAND DÉJEUNER
1921—Oil on canvas, 183.5 × 251.5 cm
Museum of Modern Art, New York
Mrs. Simon Guggenheim Fund

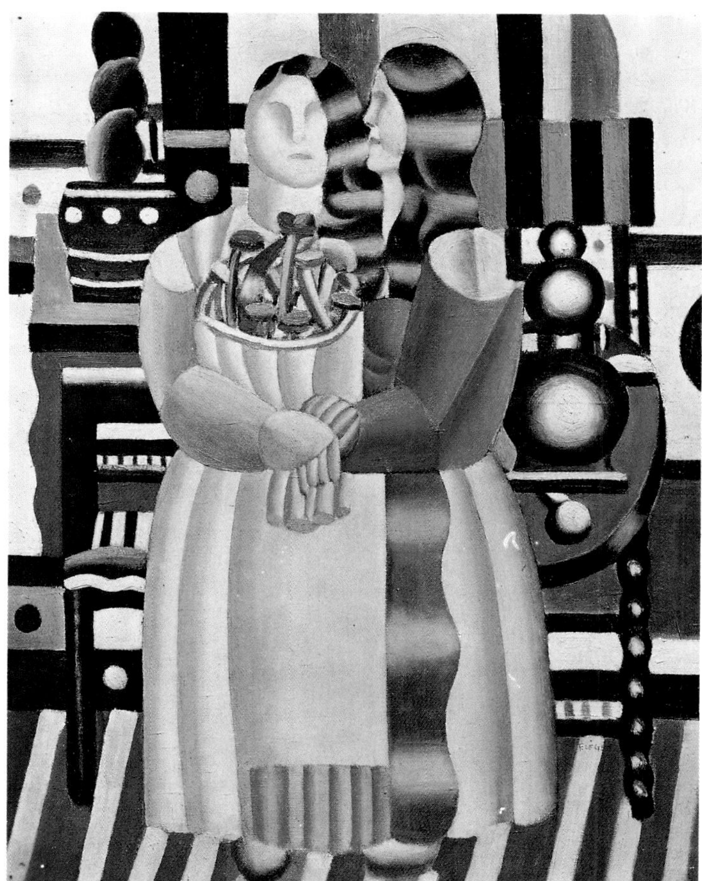

126. TWO WOMEN WITH TABLE AND CHAIR
1921—Oil on canvas
Private collection

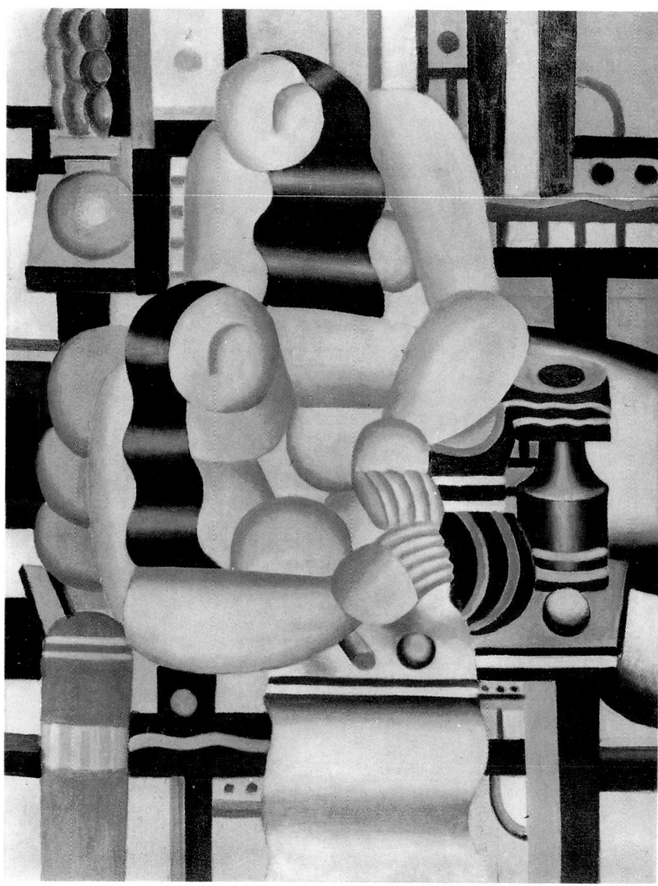

127. THE LUNCH (FRAGMENT, SECOND VERSION)
1921—Oil on canvas, 92 × 65 cm
Musée National d'Art Moderne, Centre Georges Pompidou, Paris
Gift of Louise and Michel Leiris

Ill. 126 to 130

## The monumentality of the domestic women

Nadia Léger spoke of how Léger had the impression of coming closer to life during the "giant" period, and how he thought that the working class would better understand his painting. "Just ask the maid," he said, when his wife was dubious: "When we got her to look up from her broom, she looked up at the painting and said, 'Are they sisters?' She meant that these feminine forms resembled each other like sisters. This comment shook Léger to the core. It was hard for me to imagine that a young girl of seventeen could have so shocked a colossus like Léger. He became very sad."

This did not discourage Léger from pursuing his work. He was stubborn and had no remorse. He adamantly refused to compose in the tradition of "good taste," and preferred to paint bald women in order to meet the dictates of a round form, if it were needed in that space. The characters in these paintings gradually attain a monumental scale and are there to break with the traditional concept of man's individuality. The painter tries to depersonalize them to the point at which they take on emblematic value and become "types." He is not searching the mirror of the soul in the human face, as did so many of those before him. Instead, he makes the world of objects the mirror of man's power.

Picasso deconstructed women as well as guitars. During this same period he went from his *Demoiselles d'Avignon* to a "neoclassical" harem. He returned to archaic and mythological sources, sketching giants with full but delicate lines in the purest tradition of Ingres or Raphael! This "neo-something" recycling was of no interest to Léger, who strived for modernism. Nonetheless, Léger's monumental style echoed Picasso's, as well as that of the very bourgeois Matisse. The whole period called for monumental things.

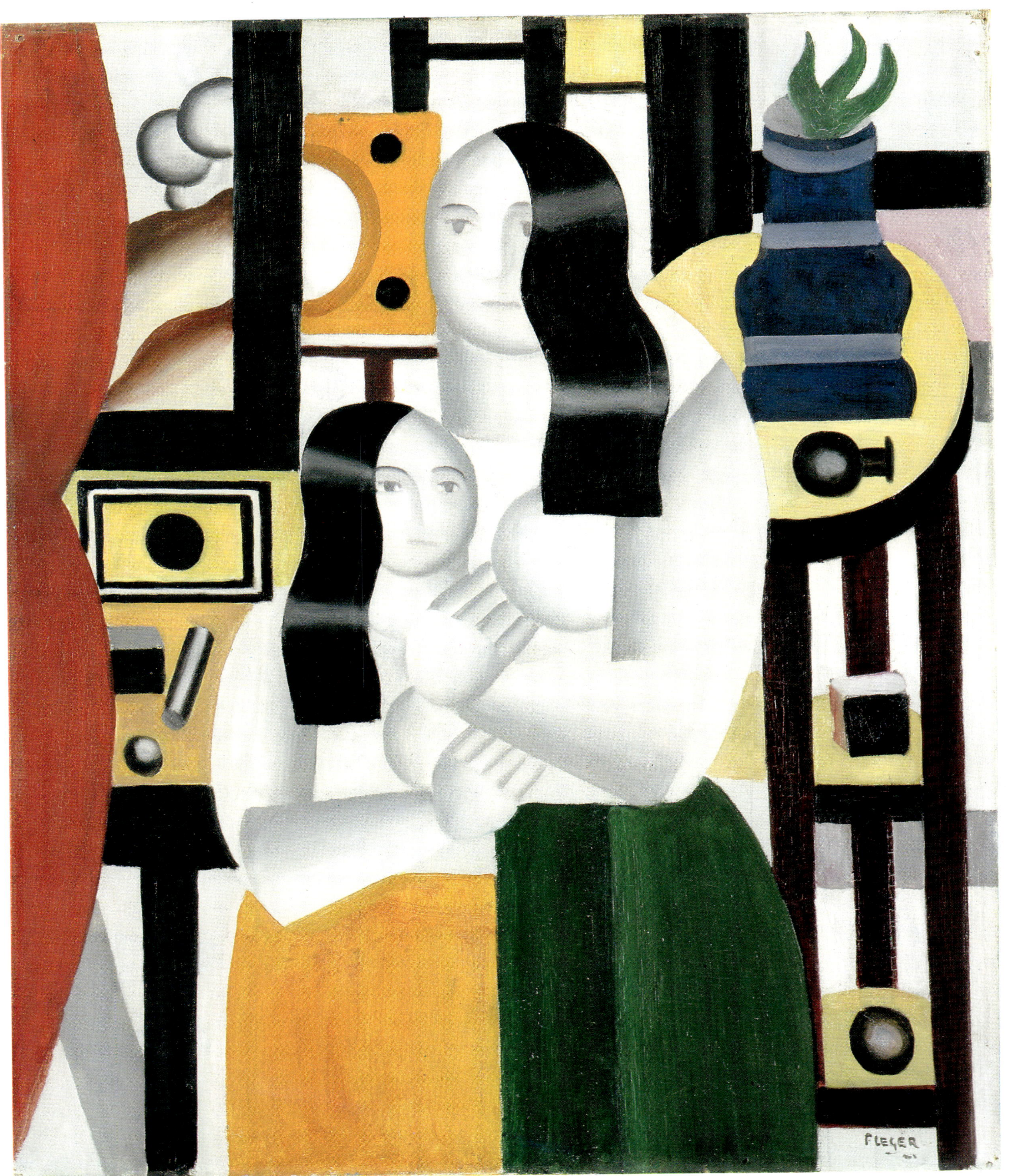


128. TWO STANDING WOMEN (WOMEN IN AN INTERIOR)
1922—Oil on canvas, 65 × 54 cm
Musée National d'Art Moderne, Centre Georges Pompidou, Paris
Gift of Jacques Zoubaloff

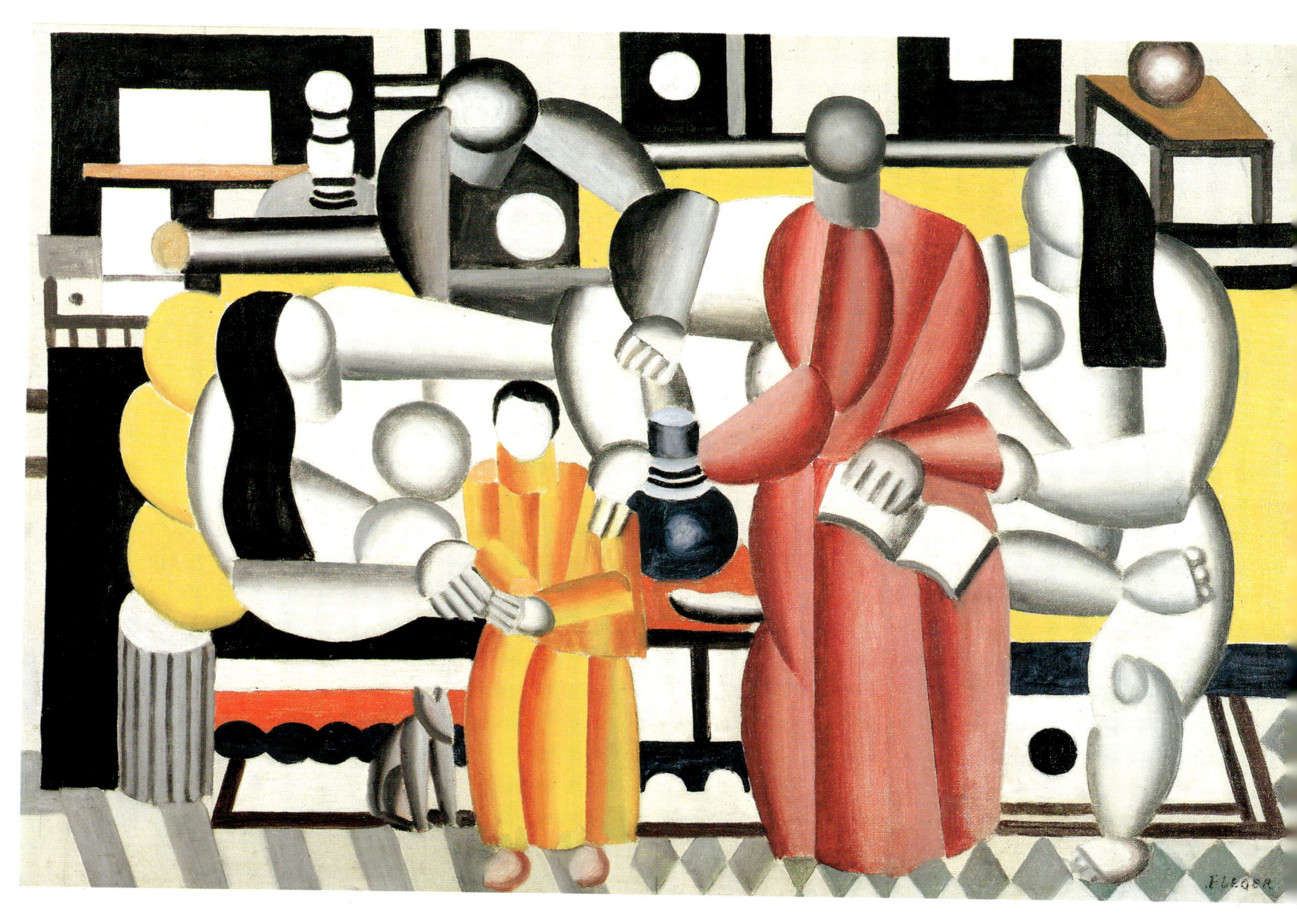


129. WOMEN IN AN INTERIOR
1921–22—Oil on canvas, 65 × 92 cm
Musée National d'Art Moderne, Centre Georges Pompidou, Paris
Bequest of Eva Gourgaud

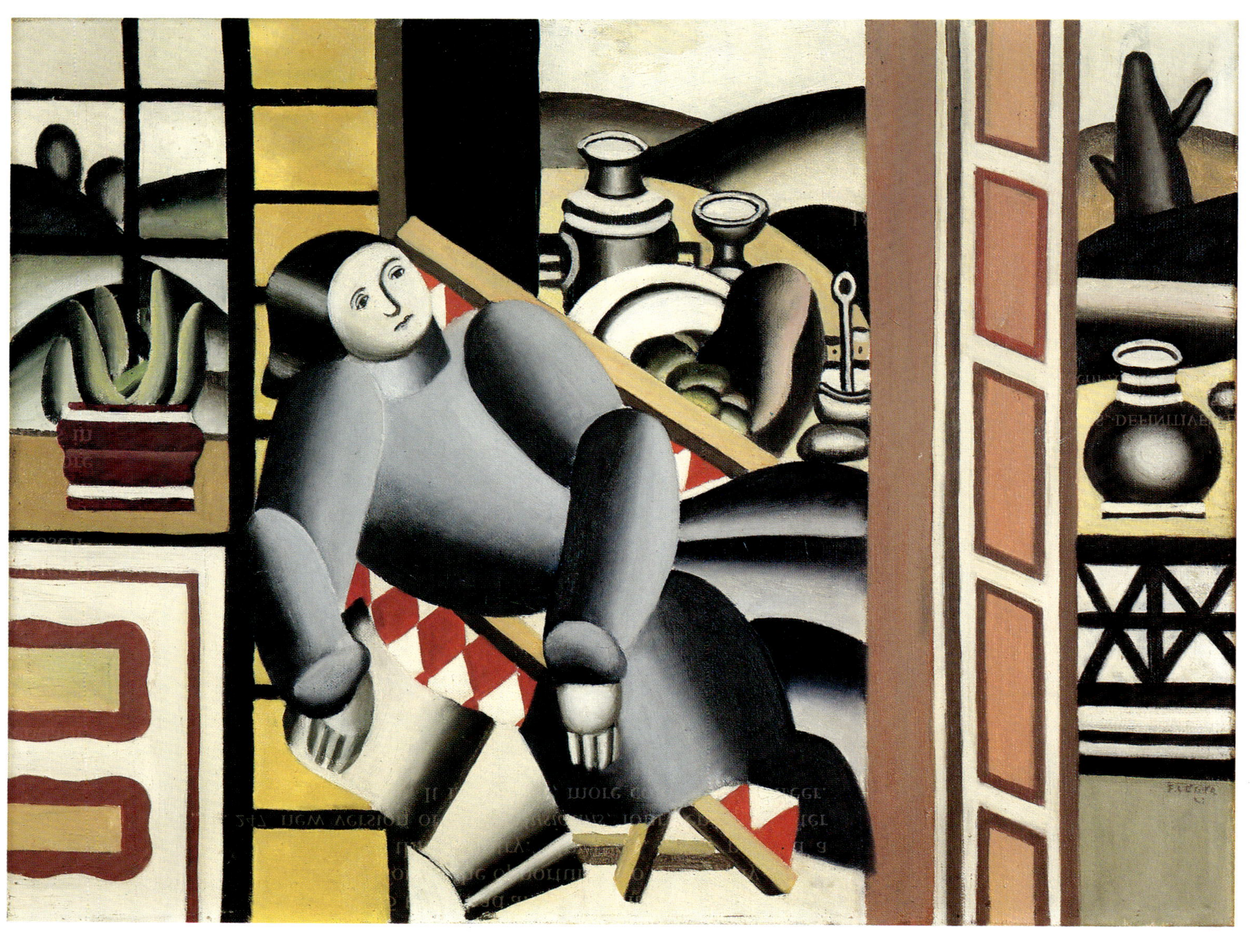

130. STUDY FOR *WOMAN AND CHILD*
1922—Oil on canvas, 50 × 65 cm
Louise Leiris Gallery, Paris

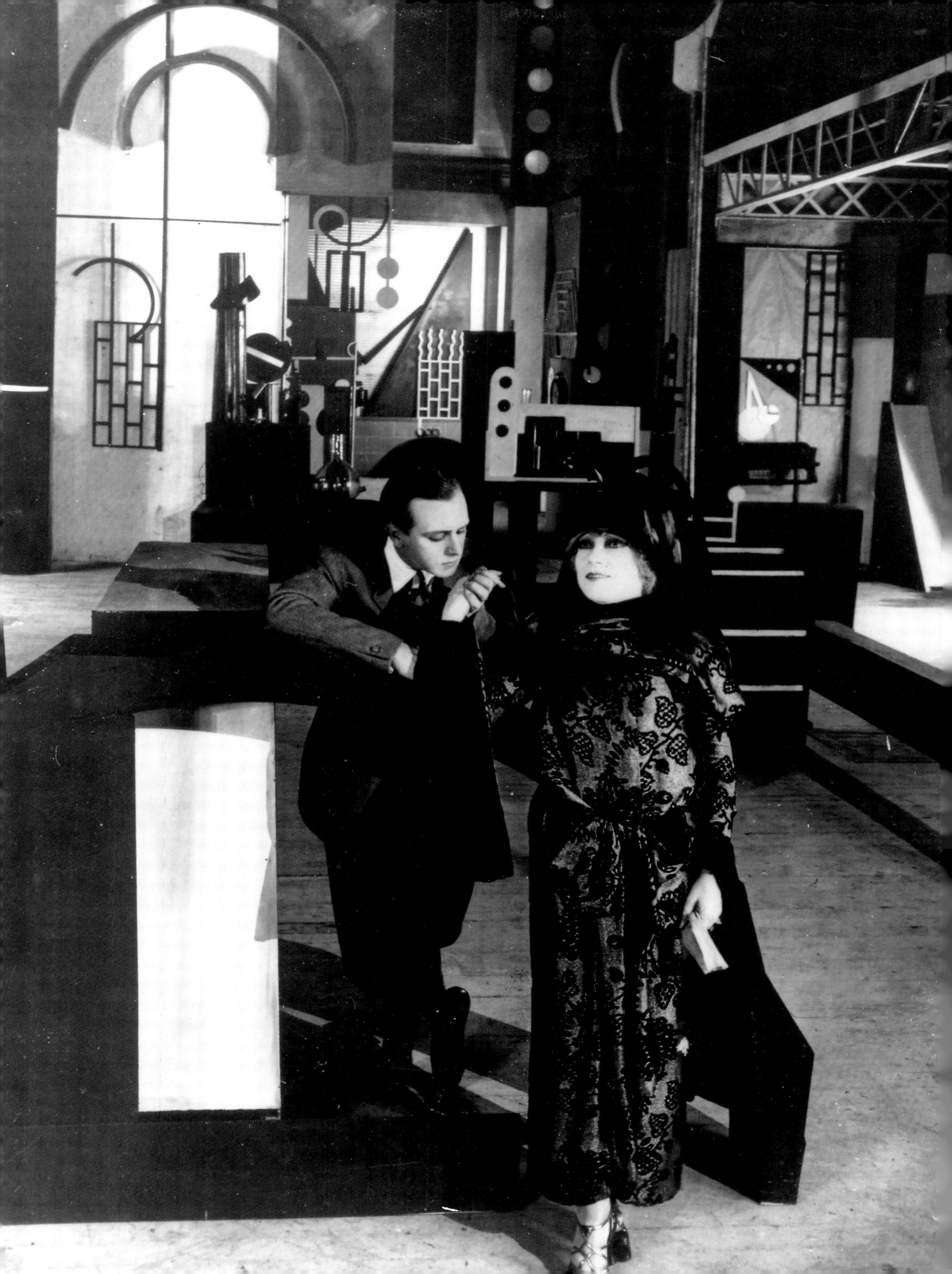

# The Temptation of the Cinema and the Attraction to Set Design

As he pursued his path of *modern imagist,* Léger developed a passion for the cinema. At one point he even considered giving up painting to work full time in film. In 1922 and 1923, Rolf de Maré and Jean Börlin called on him to decorate their Swedish Ballet: Honegger's *Skating Rink* in 1922, and Darius Mil-
Ill. 142 haud's *The Creation of the World* ("La Création du
Ill. 143 monde") in 1923. This first contact with set design familiarized Léger with new modes of expression at the same time that he was grappling with the plastic problems of movement. In "Spectacle and Cinema" he paid tribute to Rolf de Maré, "director of the Swedish Ballet, who was the first in France to have the courage to accept a production without any human forms on the stage—everything is done with machinery and the play of light; and to Jean Börlin, whose company was condemned to the role of moving scenery. When he took on the *Creation of the World,* he dared to present the public with the first truly modern set as technique. It was an immediate success with the public, despite the fact that the official critics wandered off into useless commentary about it."

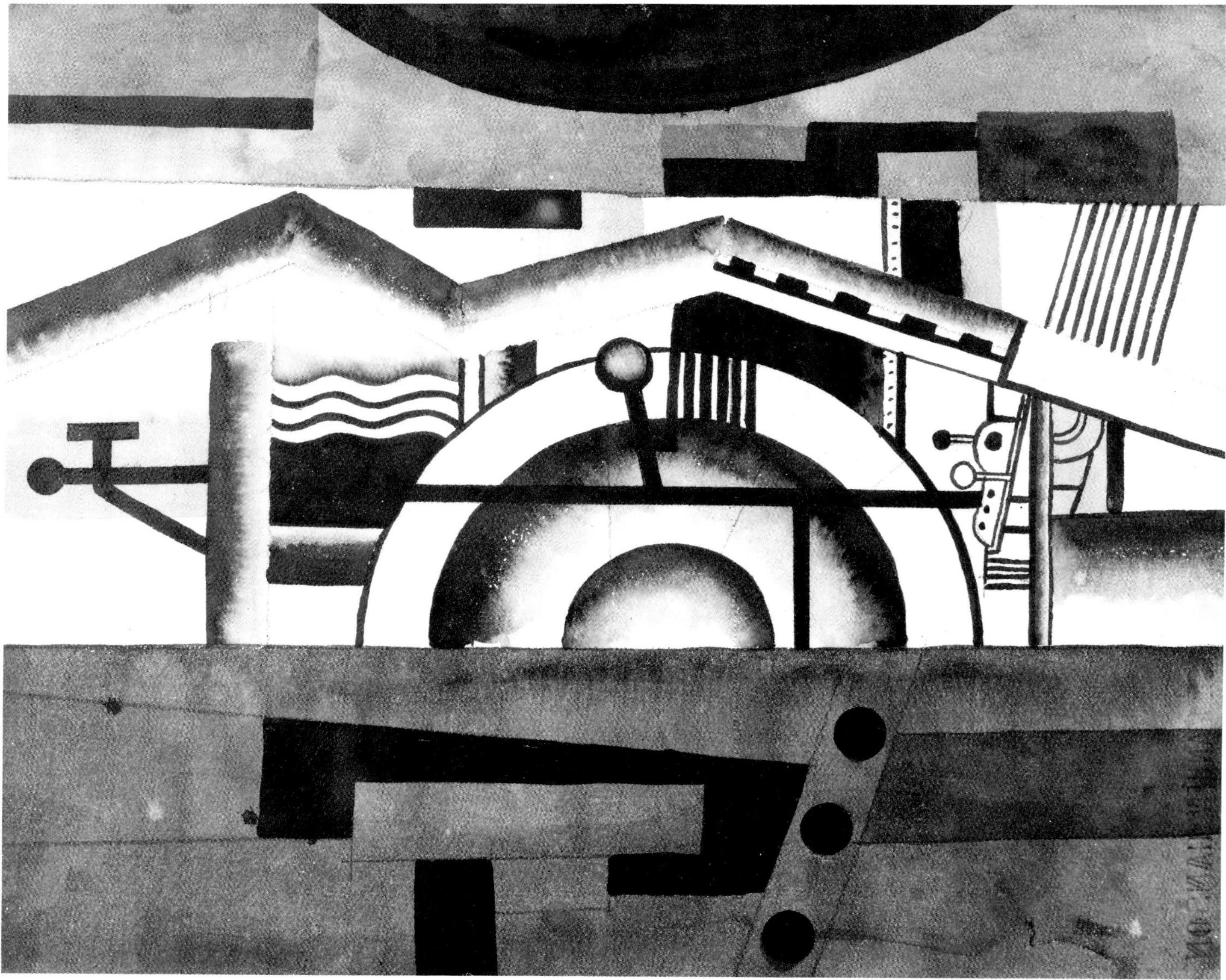

132. MODEL FOR THE SET DESIGN OF *INHUMAN* BY L'HERBIER
1922—Wash and China ink on paper, 30.5 × 58.5 cm
Lionel Prejger collection, Paris

131. PHOTO OF THE FILM *INHUMAN* BY MARCEL L'HERBIER
1923—Set design by Fernand Léger

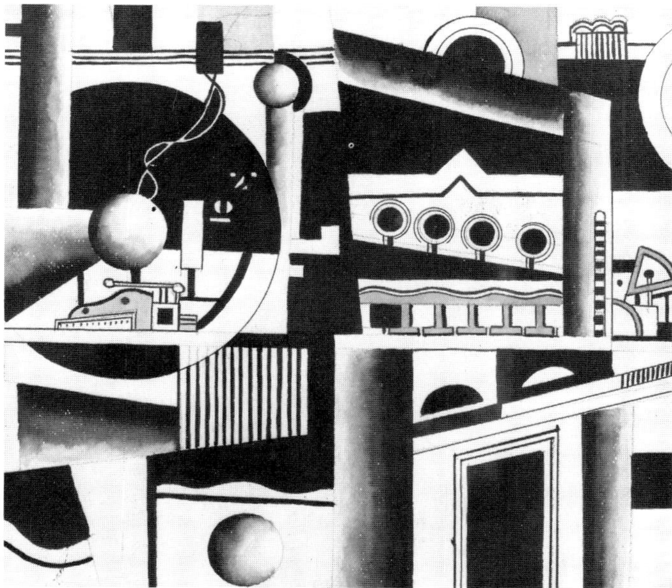

133. MODEL FOR THE SET DESIGN OF *INHUMAN* BY L'HERBIER
1922—Wash and China ink on paper, 29 × 34.5 cm
Lionel Prejger collection, Paris

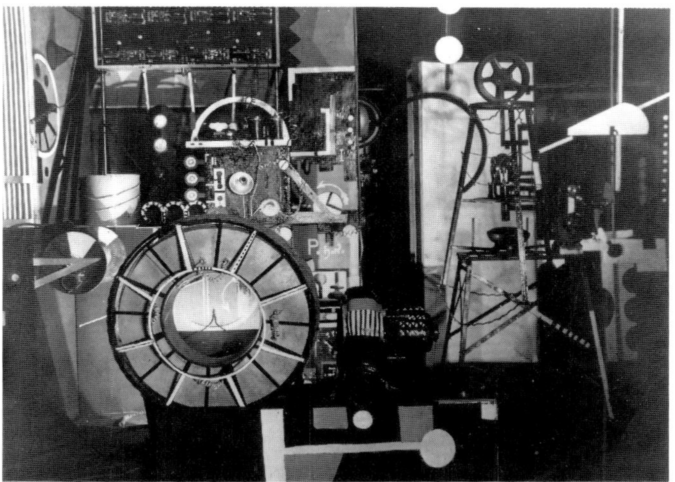

134. SET DESIGN FOR *INHUMAN* BY L'HERBIER, THE LABORATORY WITH THE DEVICE FOR VIEWING THE WORLD

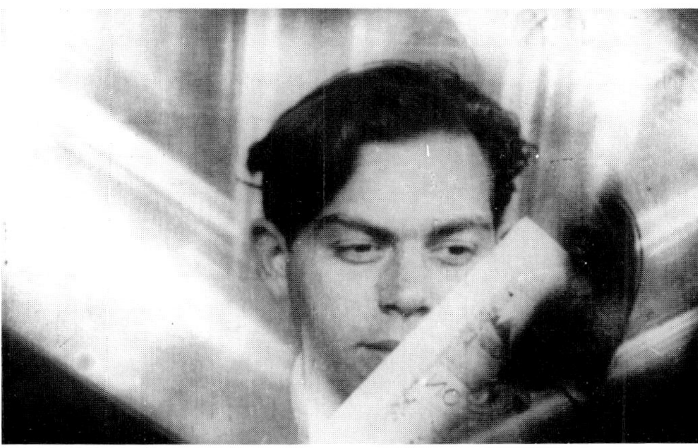

135–136. PHOTOS FROM THE FILM BY FERNAND LÉGER *LE BALLET MÉCANIQUE*, 1924

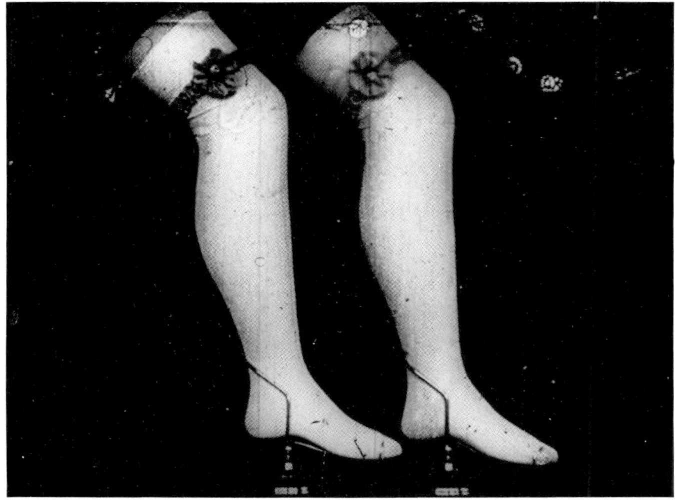

In *Skating Rink*, Léger used his system of contrasts to oppose the immobility of the set with the dynamism of the dancers, accenting the contrast between the stationary sky, pieces above the stage, and a uniform color beneath. In *The Creation of the World*, he tried to unite painting and dance through the interplay of mobile decorative elements. To achieve this he used African sculpture and masks as models. The same play of color that he used in his paintings allowed him to model the scenic space for the choreography. Painting thus took on the role of a principal performer.

It was the cinema, however, that had a decisive effect on Léger, allowing him to confirm the validity of his study of forms and objects. He had been an attentive spectator in the moviehouses before he began his first collaboration behind the camera. He and his poet friend Blaise Cendrars worked on *The Wheel* ("La Roue") with director Abel Gance. Léger stated that "the mechanical element had a preponderant role in the production, becoming *the main character, the lead actor.* It was to Abel Gance's credit that he so successfully conveyed the *object-as-actor* to the public. . . . The object-as-actor was presented in all aspects with an infinite variety of means: close-ups, fixed or mobile mechanical fragments. When these fragments were shot at eighteen or fewer frames per second, the images had an accelerated rhythm that touched on *simultaneity* when projected onto the screen. The human object was eliminated or reduced to insignificance through fragmentation. As a spectator, you are sad to see this *mechanical element* disappear, and then you impatiently wait for it to reappear. It's a subtle thing. It appears like projected light rays in a long, anguishing drama of great import. It's conveyed with uncompromising realism. The plastic significance is just as great. It is deliberately there, and framed with care. It seems to me that the consequences of this are enormous, both in the present and for the future."

In the beginning, cinema copied theater or the novel, but as far as Léger was concerned, "cinema is the Machine Age. Theater is the era of the horse and buggy. They'll never blend, and that's a good thing, because it's a deplorable mix." With *The Wheel*, Abel Gance achieved something that had already existed for some time in modern art: the fragmentation of the object and the figurative value of the object *as* object. To again quote Léger: "Gance's *The Wheel* lifted cinematic art to the level of the plastic arts." This new vision had to be "imposed." Léger used the term "imposed" each time he applauded the accomplishments of Rolf de Maré or Abel Gance. Experience had shown him that the common man could not be counted on to voluntarily take an interest in something new that disturbed his old habits.

In 1923, Léger collaborated with the young Claude Autant-Lara and Mallet-Stevens on the set designs Ill. 131 to 134

137. SET DESIGN OF THE LABORATORY FOR THE FILM *INHUMAN* BY L'HERBIER, 1923.

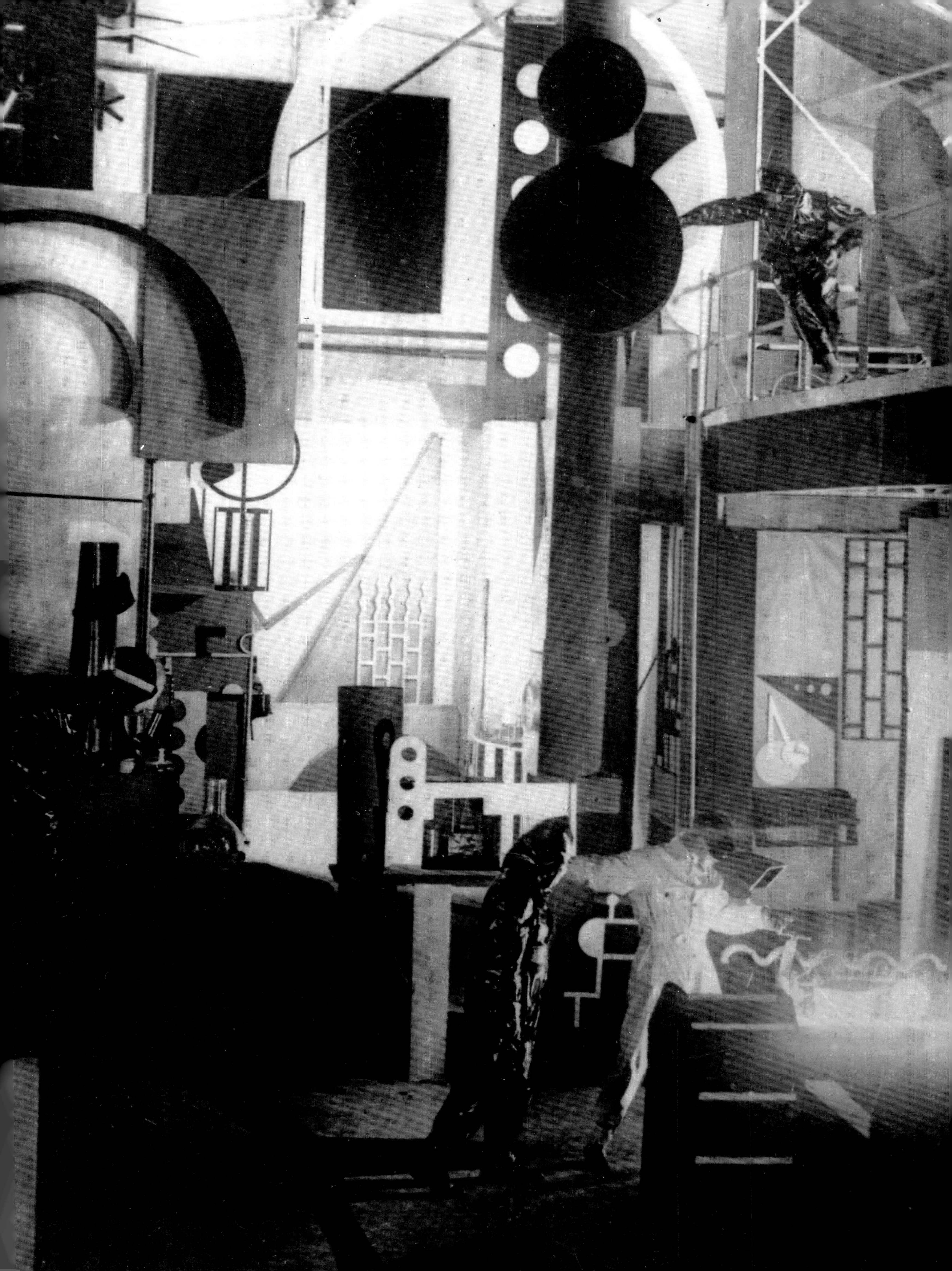

for Marcel L'Herbier's film *Inhuman* ("L'Inhumaine"), which was adapted from the book by Pierre Mac-Orlan. The film *imposed* the plastic emotion on the viewer by simultaneously projecting "image fragments" in quick succession, in the same manner as did Jean Epstein's *Faithful Heart* ("Coeur fidèle"), Moujoskine's *Kleim*, and L'Herbier's other film, *Rogue's Gallery* ("Galerie des monstres"). The moving trains of Cendrars and Gance and Epstein's travelling carnival were perfectly matched with the regular themes of Léger's paintings. So were the machine-works of L'Herbier's laboratories. "It's all figurative. The image alone works on the viewer who receives it, is moved by it, and is conquered by it. It's a beautiful victory over a public who has always applauded and reacted to sentimental and literary dramas."

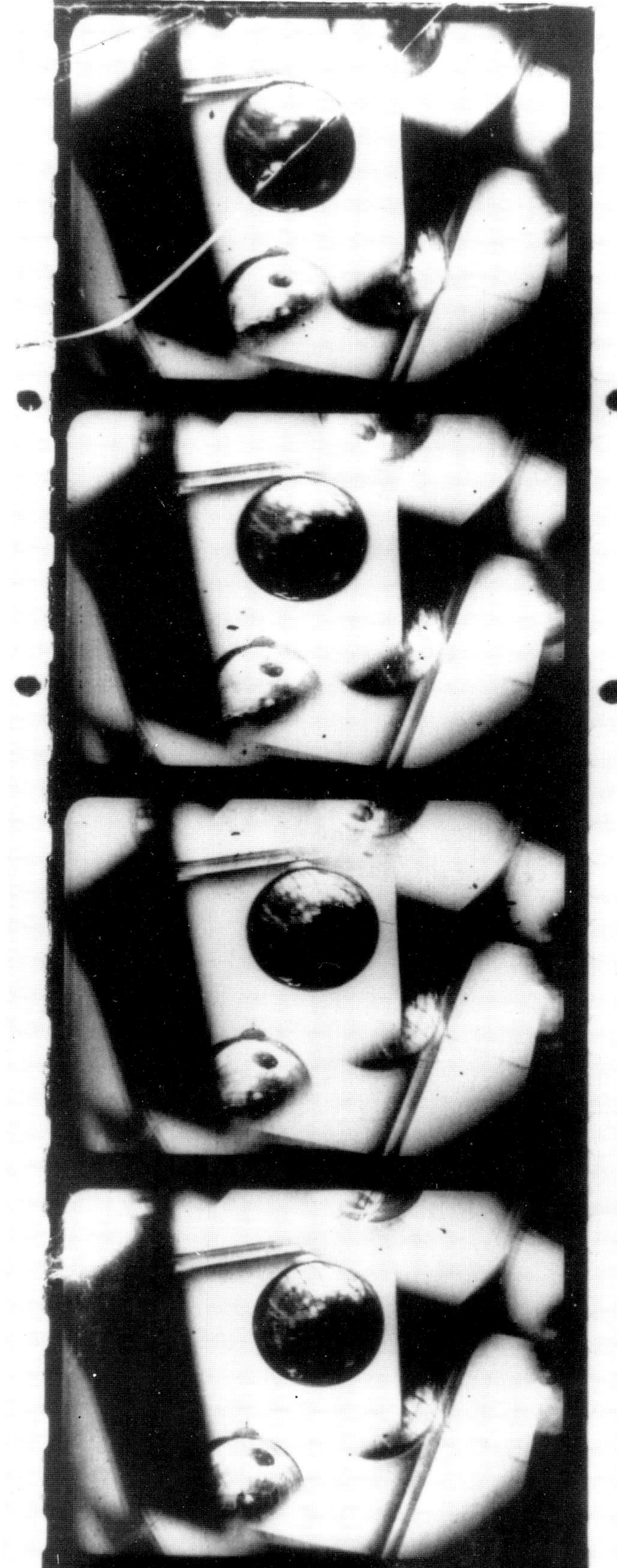

Encouraged by the experience, Léger applied to film the same process of transformation that he had applied to painting. Once the "subject" had been eliminated in favor of "pictorial reality," he then completely dispensed with the scenario. The object and object-fragment took over: "the pinky nail of my wife's left hand." This was done according to an editing techique based on the repetition of certain shots. Action photography, made possible with the advent of portable cameras, was also used. Film scholar Georges Sadoul wrote of Léger in an article entitled "Léger and the Invention of the Camera-Brush" (not to be confused with the *camera stylo*, "camera-pen," of the New Wave during the late 1950s and '60s): "With Léger, we have for the first time a painter who uses the camera instead of a paintbrush, chalk, or sketch pencil to replace the 'important subject' with the 'object,' which is the current concern of painting. In opposition to natural elements such as the sky, the trees, and the human body, Léger addresses the things that man has created, and uses them as the basis of a new realism in art."

Ill. 135 & 136 Ill. 138 to 140 Léger best expressed what he wanted to do: "I'm going to speak to you a bit about the *Ballet Mécanique*. The story is simple. I directed it in 1923 and 1924. At the time I was working on canvases with *isolated objects* in similiar conditions to those I was working with in film. Painters had already *destroyed the subject*. In avant-garde films it was a matter of destroying the descriptive scenario. I thought that *the object*, treated in similar fashion to what I was doing in painting, would also have a filmic value. That was

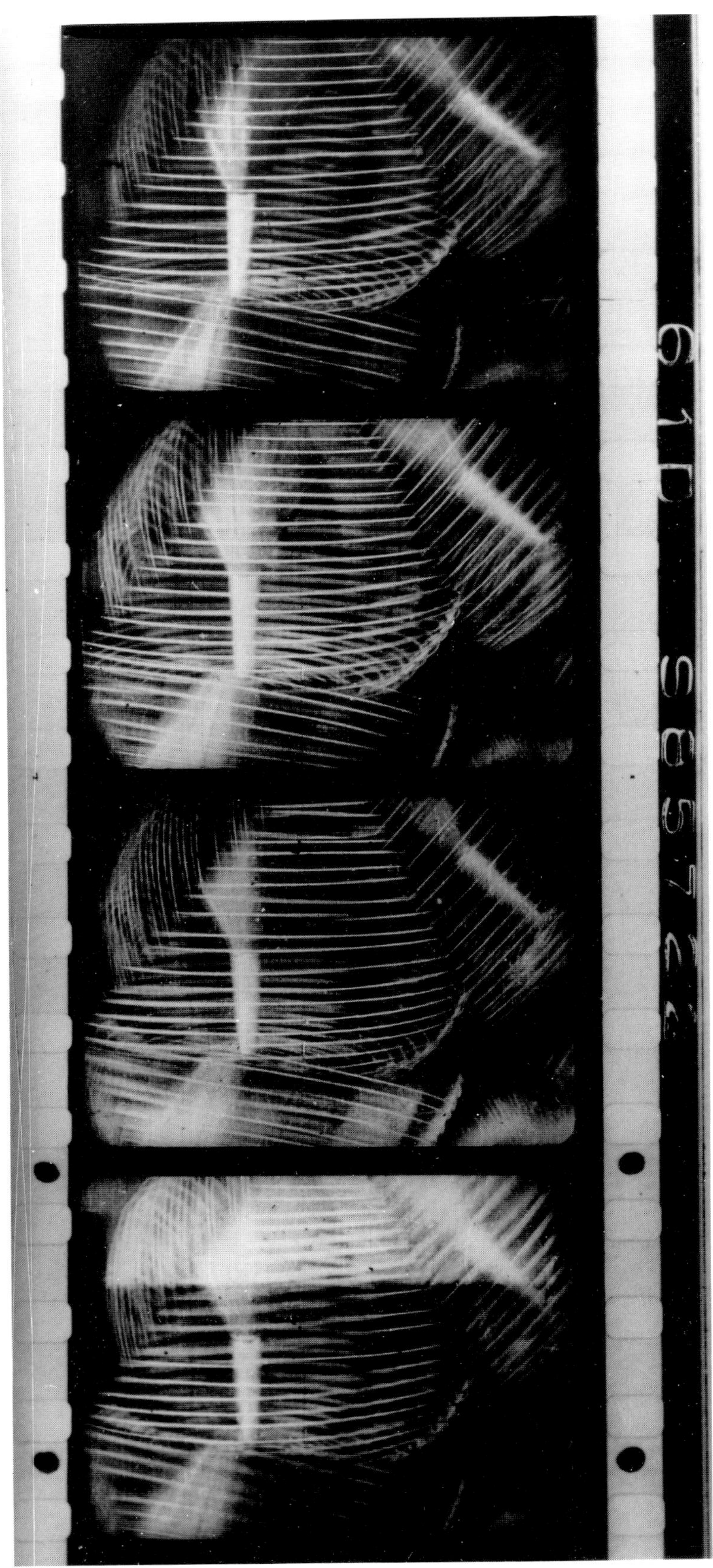

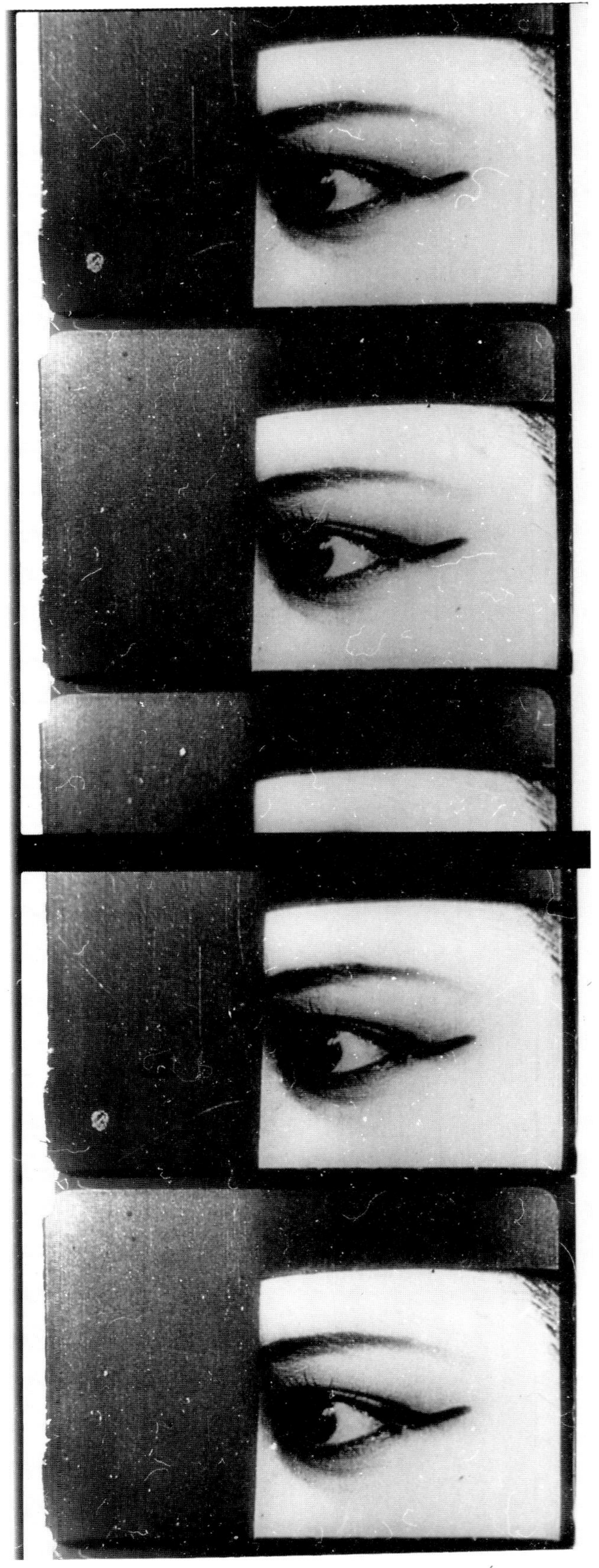

138 to 140. FRAMES FROM THE FILM BY FERNAND LÉGER *LE BALLET MÉCANIQUE*, 1924

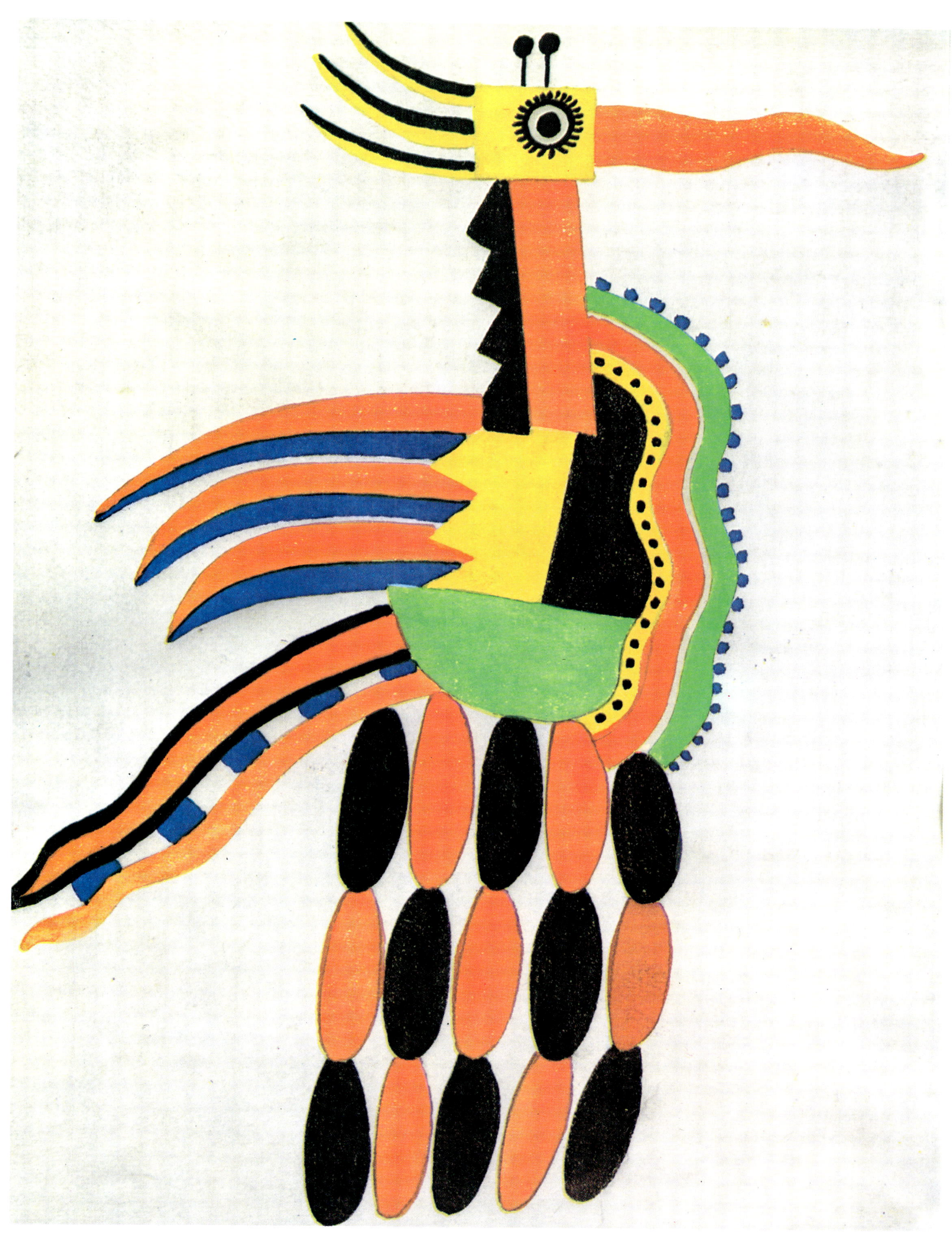

141. COSTUME FOR *THE CREATION OF THE WORLD* BY D. MILHAUD
1923—Gouache
Document Koreografiska Instituet, Stockholm

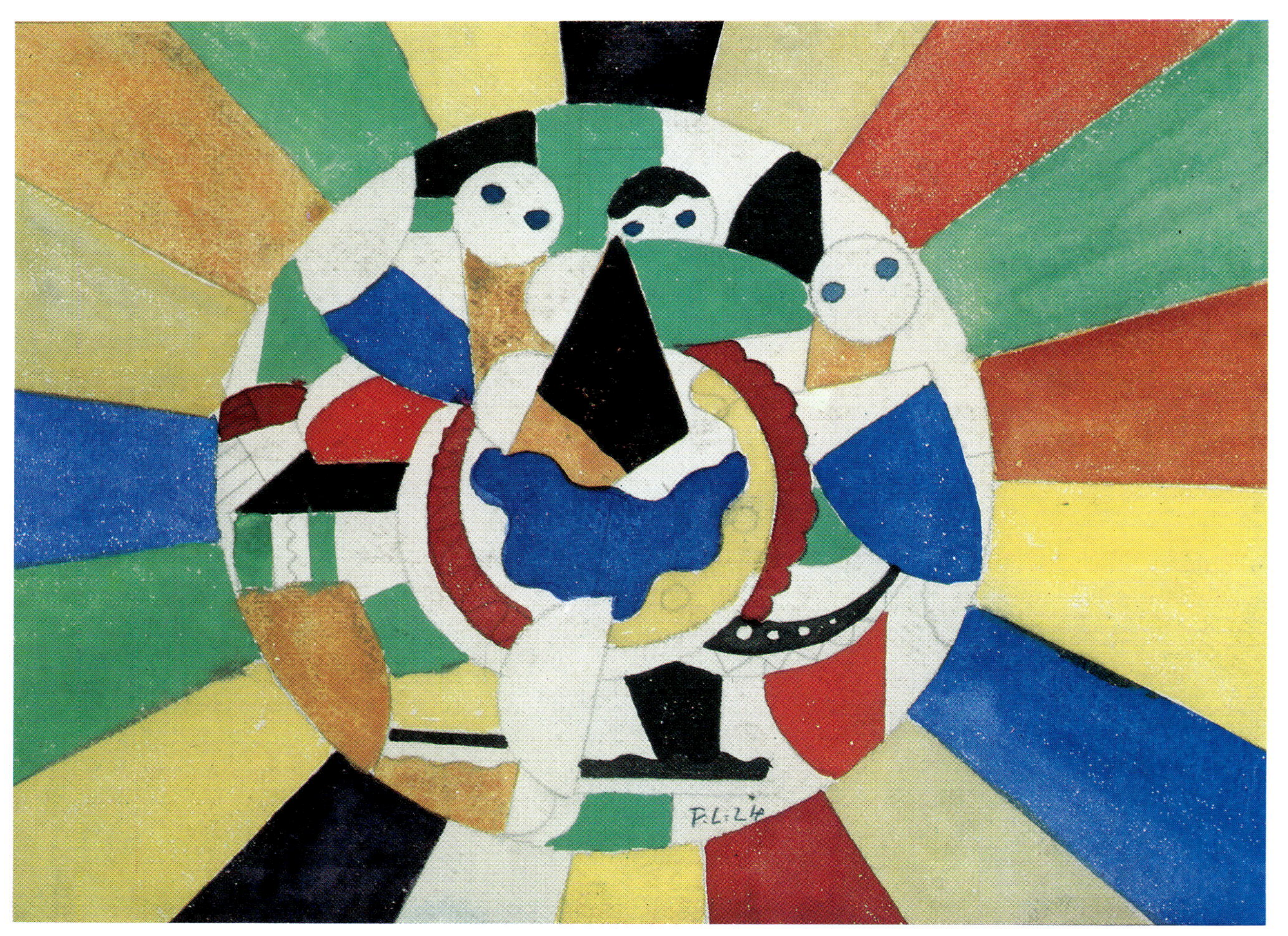

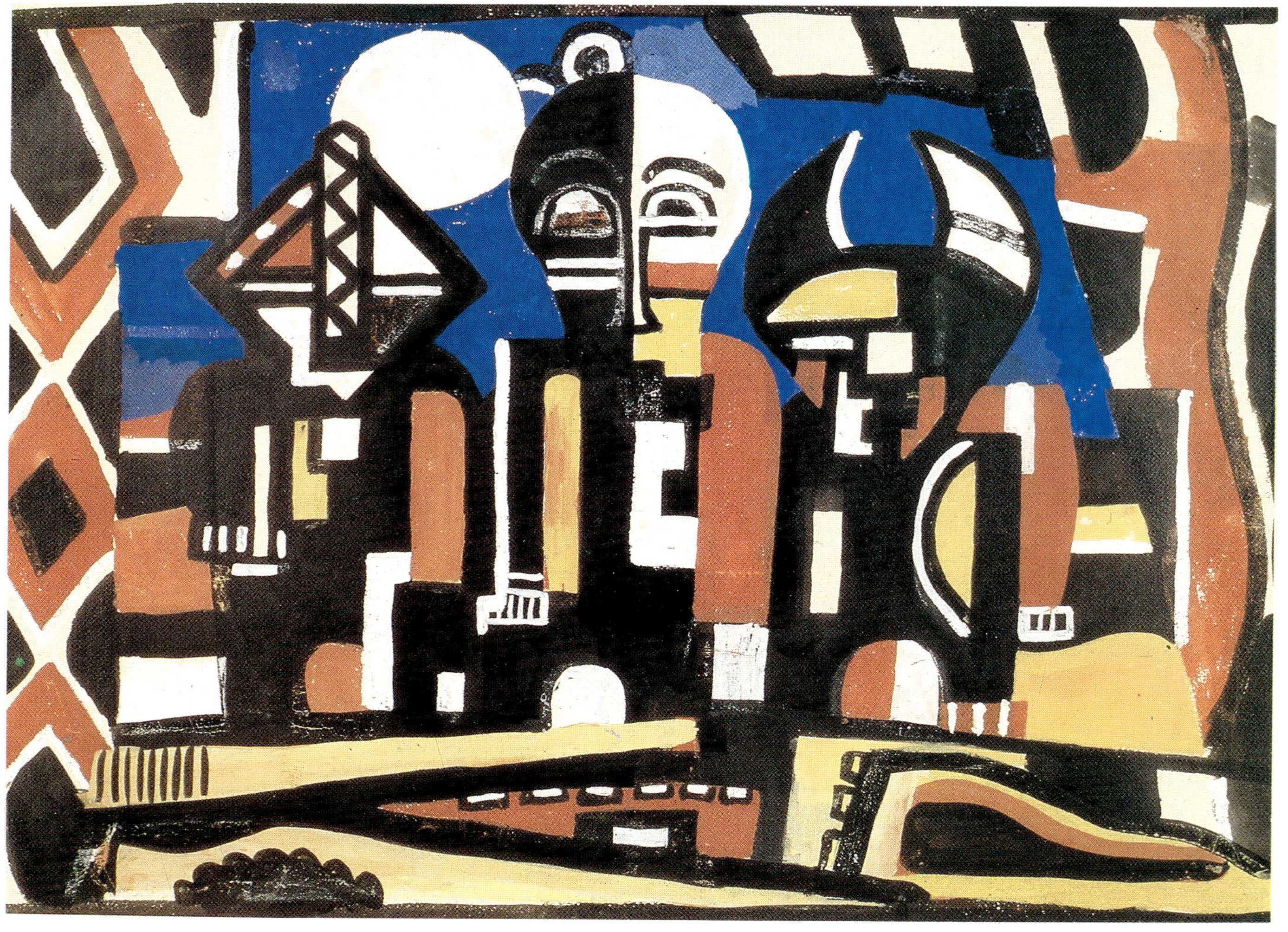

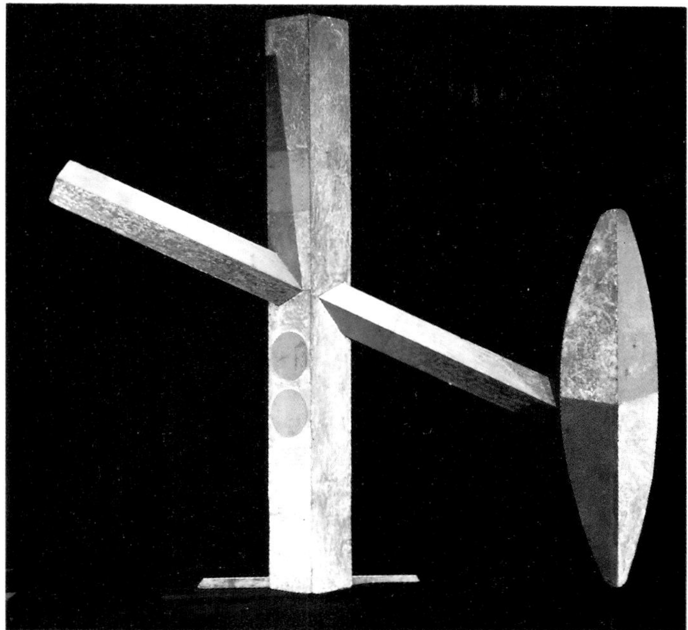

144

142. SET DESIGN FOR *SKATING RINK*, SWEDISH BALLET BY ROLD DE MARÉ AND ARTHUR HONEGGER
1924—Gouache, 24 × 22 cm
Collection of Mr. and Mrs. Adrien Maeght

143. PROJECT FOR THE SET DESIGN OF *THE CREATION OF THE WORLD*
1922—Gouache, 41 × 57 cm
Private collection

SCULPTURES FOR THE BALLET *THE STEEL STEP* BY S. PROKOFIEV
1948—Aluminum

144. AIRPLANE TAIL
Maximum height 330 cm

145. SKYSCRAPER
Composed of four superimposed elements, height 604 cm, width 185 cm.

147. CUBIST CHARLOT (CHARLIE CHAPLIN) FOR *BALLET MÉCANIQUE*, 1924

my starting point on the film. I took very common objects that I transposed to the screen by giving them *very deliberate* and calculated movement and rhythm. I wanted to contrast objects. To do this in film I used slow motion and sped up takes, as well as fixed-frame or static takes. *The entire film is built on this.* I used the *close-up*, a cinematic invention. The *object-fragment* also served me. In isolating it I was able to personalize it. All this allowed me to treat objectivity as a very real and new figurative actuality. Documentaries and the newsreels are filled with these beautiful 'objective facts.' It is all a matter of knowing how to present them. We are experiencing the *advent* of the object. The object is even imposing itself in the *shop windows* that decorate the streets.

"A flock of moving sheep, seen from a high angle and projected onto a full screen, is like an unknown body of water. It shakes up the viewer. *That's what I call objectivity.* Fifty female thighs gyrating in unison, projected in close-up on the screen, is also objectivity. Making the *Ballet Mécanique* cost me about 5,000 francs and created a lot of problems for me in the editing. The repetitions of movement were difficult to control. I had to deal with very precise mechanical measurements in terms of frames. Take the 'Woman climbing a Staircase' 'La Femme qui monte l'escalier', for example: First I wanted to stun the audience, and then slowly create uneasiness in them. Ultimately I wanted to exasperate them. . . . 'Woman on a Swing' ['La Femme à la balançoire'] is a *postcard in motion*. . . . It was a period characterized by experience, research, and random or chance occurrences. That period is perhaps coming to an end now. It continues in the cartoon, which has unlimited po-

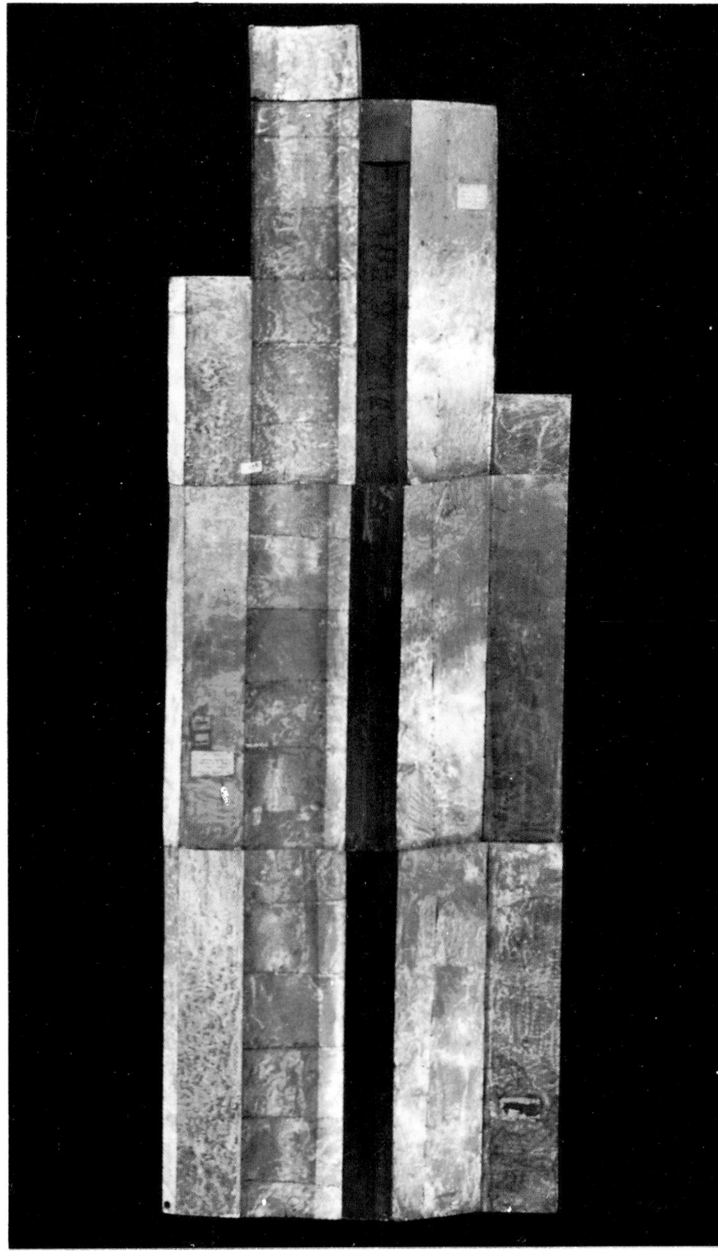

145

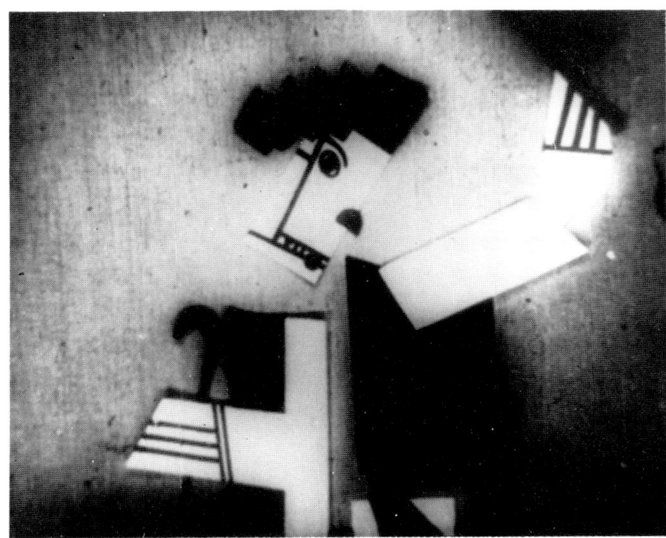

146. SPIRAL
Height 380 cm, width 200 cm

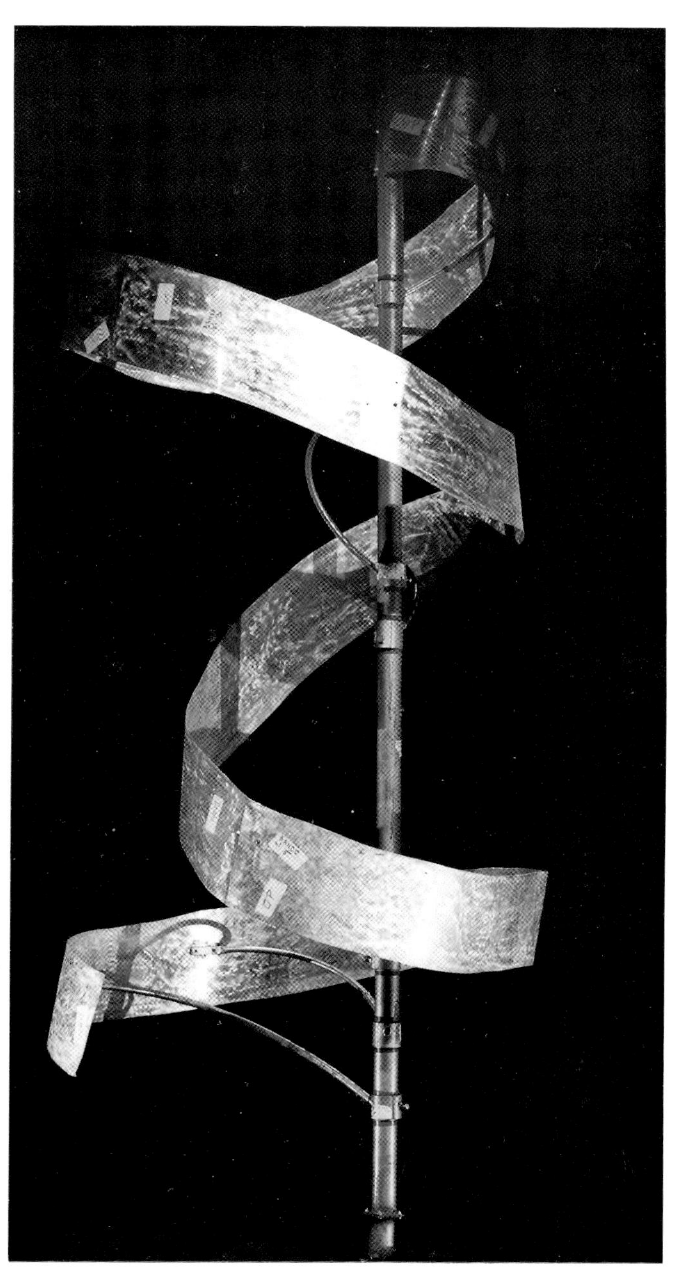

147

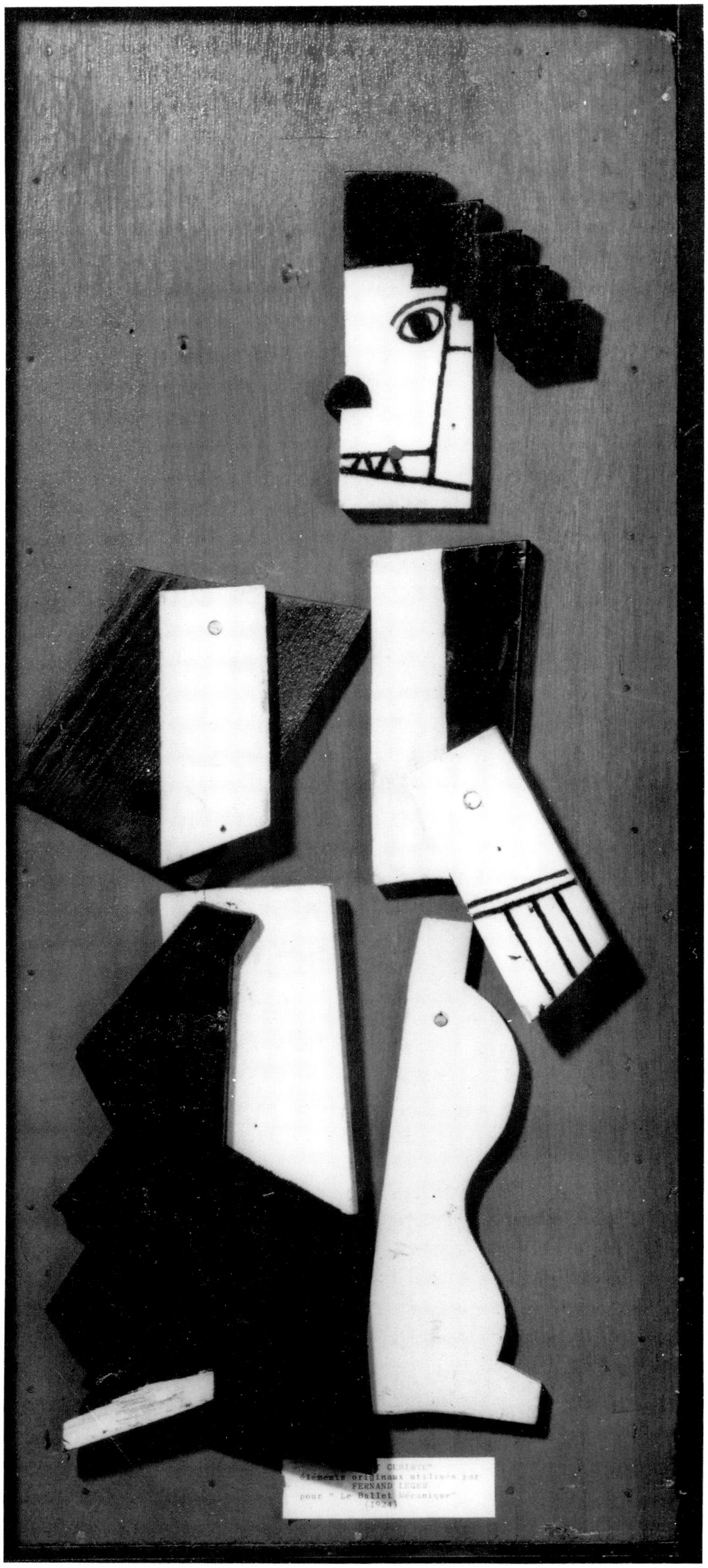

148. CUBIST CHARLOT, ORIGINAL ELEMENTS USED FOR *BALLET MÉCANIQUE*
1924—Nailed assemblage of painted wood, 74 × 34 cm
Musée National d'Art Moderne, Centre Georges Pompidou, Paris

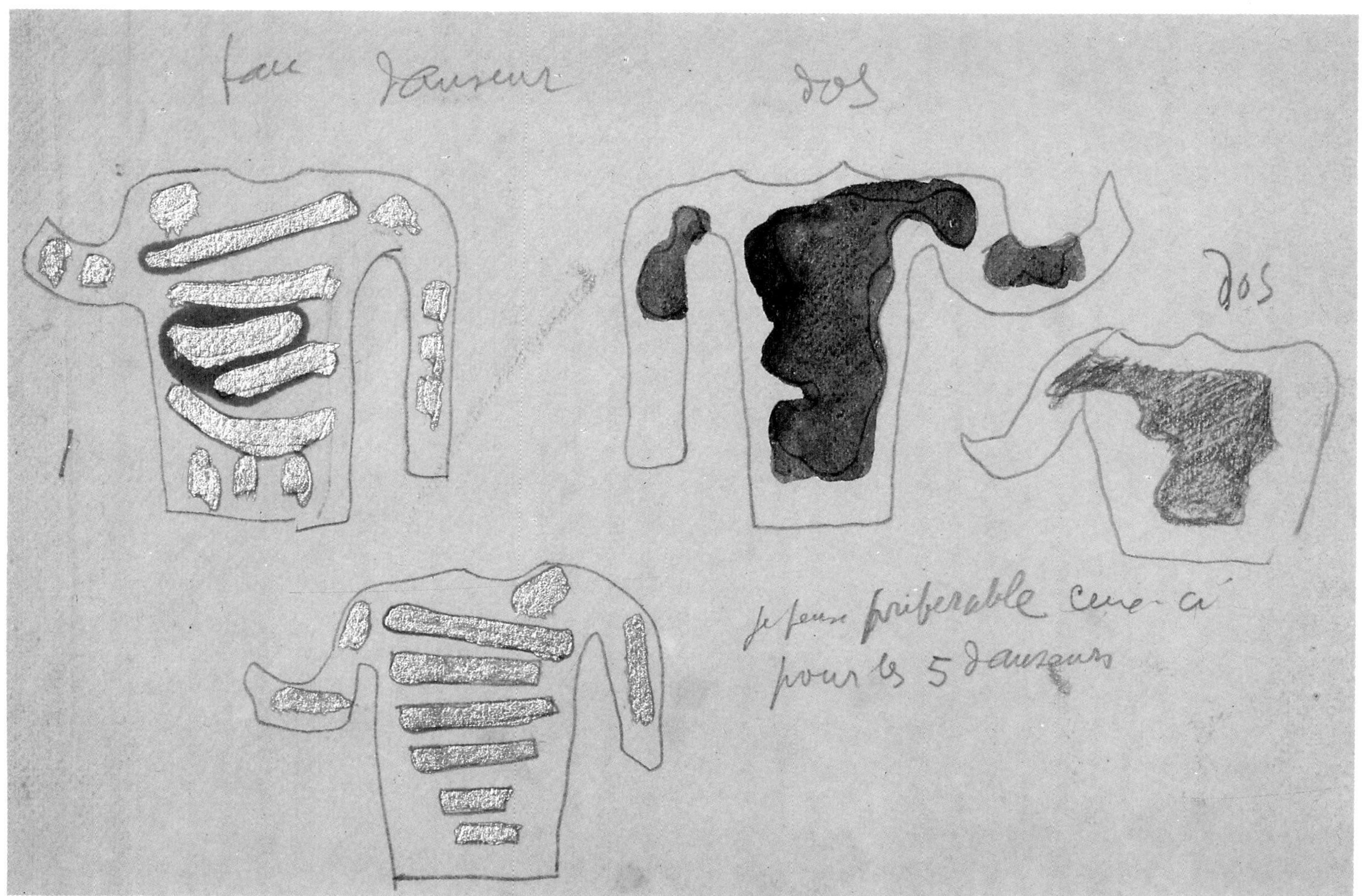


149. PROJECT FOR THE COSTUMES OF THE BALLET *THE STEEL STEP*
1948—Annotated sketch, enhanced with watercolor, 18 × 29 cm
Private collection

tential for the expression of fantasy and humor. The cartoon is taking over the reins."

Léger believed that film could channel "true emotion," as opposed to projecting mere "ornamentation," which covers and hides truth. "Diplomats invented the monocle so that their expressions would not betray them. A pair of pants is true when it has no pleats. Politeness was invented to conceal the true nature of the merchandise. . . ." On the other hand: "the button of a false collar, magnified one hundred times on the screen, becomes a radiant planet. A new lyricism of the transformed object has been brought into being. Plastic expression will be built upon this new truth." Léger was right. American Pop Art, in portraying the objects of consumer society, and in itself producing objects of consumption, was a direct outcome of Léger's cult of the object.

Léger dreamed of a film that would record "any ordinary couple, any kind of job, for a period of twenty-four hours." This is exactly what Andy Warhol would do fifty years later in films like *Sleep*, which runs for six and a half hours and shows a sleeping man; or in *Kiss*, which runs for an entire day and projects two mouths joined in close-up with the same simplicity that the Lumière brothers used in filming "Baby's First Taste" ("Le Goûter de Bébé"). Léger dreamed of an acute visual inquiry in which nothing would escape the eye of the camera during a twenty-four hour period: "work, silence, intimacy, and love. The film would be projected without any editing. I think it would be such a horrible thing that everyone would flee from the screening room to call for help, as if some global catastrophe had befallen them."

Léger's last creation for the theater was the set design Ill. 15
for *Bolivar*, an opera by Milhaud presented in 1950. to 15
Prior to this he had collaborated on *David's Victory* ("David triomphant") composed by Serge Lifar in 1937. At the time of *David's Victory*, Léger began to depart from the mechanical rhythm that characterized *Skating Rink* and *The Creation of the World*, and moved toward more flexible and modulated forms. In *Bolivar*, Léger gave us a hint that he was sensitive to the fact that, without moving away from realism, the art of the day was taking on more abstract aspects. With regard to *Bolivar*, however, he continued to apply his basic precepts for theater and film to the opera: "to break with the visual aspects of the stage and the audience, and to use human material at the expense of the individual, who had to be made to disappear; to create an invented stage on which hu-

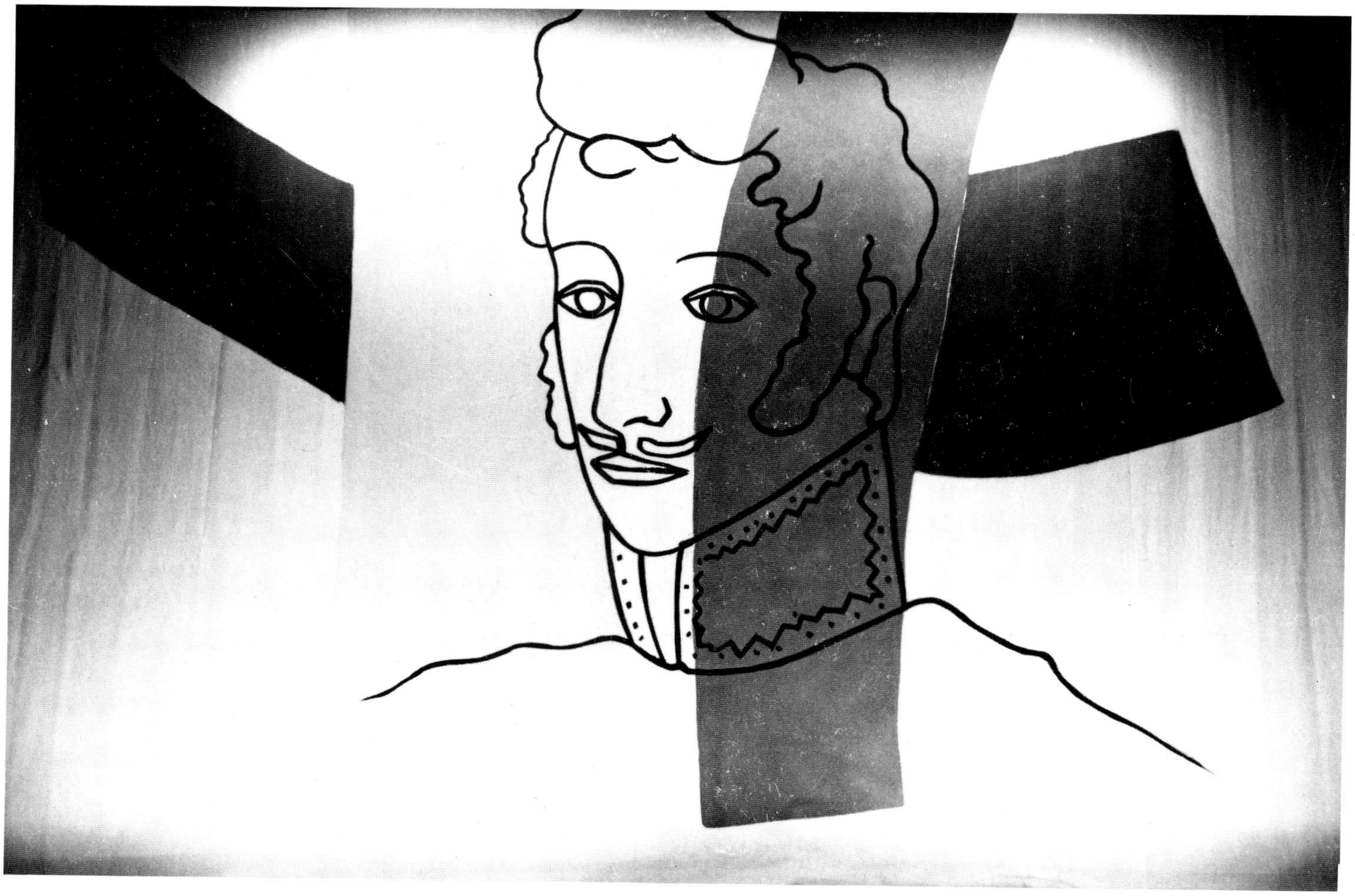

man material held a value comparable to the object and to the set design."
In 1950, Léger freely applied all of his old recipes to *Bolivar*: canvases in which forms and colors were contrasted; animated objects-as-characters that contribute to the "motion" within the framework of the stage. The curtain was treated as a separate, colored entity. The vocabulary of sets and costumes was dictated by the same things we find in his canvases, except for the monumental dimension. This was achieved by the very nature of opera itself.

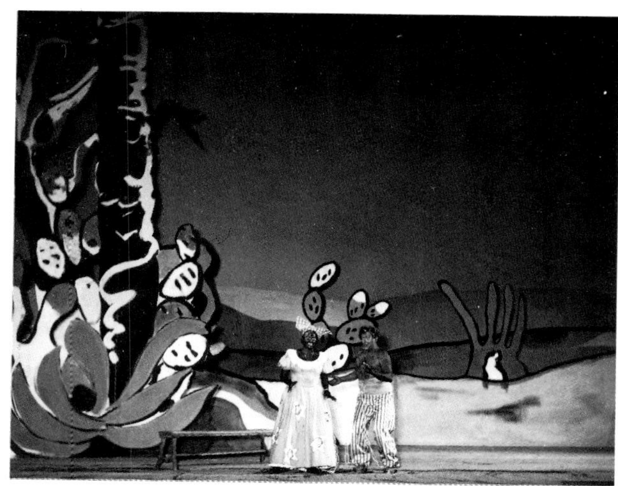

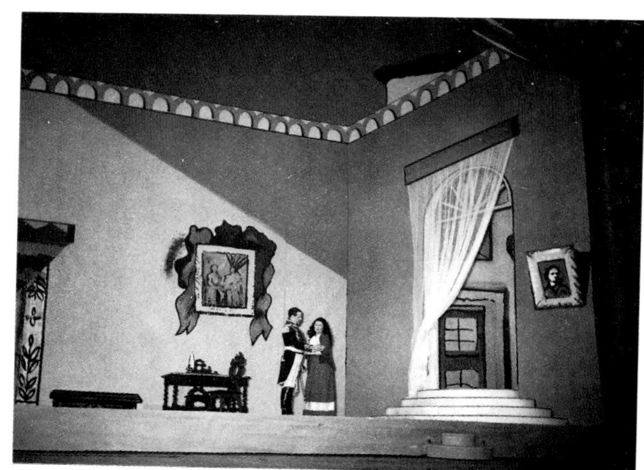

150 to 152. *BOLIVAR*, OPERA BY D. MILHAUD AND SUPERVIELLE
1950—Set design by Fernand Léger

153. POSTER FOR THE "OBJECTS" EXHIBIT AT THE VIGNON GALLERY
1934 — 40 × 30 cm

# GALERIE VIGNON

17, Rue Vignon, 17

# OBJETS

PAR

# FERNAND LÉGER

## GOUACHES-DESSINS 1933-34

RACINES - SILEX - QUARTIER DE MOUTON - TIRE-BOUCHON
VASE - PANTALON - MORCEAU DE BŒUF - FROMAGE - NOIX
ETC.

**16 AVRIL au 28 AVRIL 1934**

**VERNISSAGE : 16 Avril**
**de 16 heures à 20 heures.**

# From Purism to Pop Art, or the Triumph of the Object

"Cubism was a Purist movement," wrote the painter Amédée Ozenfant in 1919 in the review *L'Élan*, which he had founded the previous year with Charles-Édouard Jeanneret, better known as Le Corbusier. After *L'Élan*, the two theoreticians of Purism founded *L'Esprit nouveau*, where they would develop the ideas of the movement that tried to shift the current esthetics of Cubism and Orphism. They were convinced that Cubism needed defending against the misunderstanding and distortions that were taking place since the middle class, in particular, and then Art Deco had adapted it as an esthetic. Ozenfant and Le Corbusier wanted to "purify it" so it would regain its initial impact. The two friends cowrote the text. *After Cubism* was published in 1918, and called for the return to order and clarity, the rejection of anecdotes, the limitation of color, and absolute objectivity. The major precepts of Purism demanded the prohibition of gratuitous liberties in painting. It advocated a type of plastic perfection that used the machine as a model because of its perfect authenticity.

Léger found a great deal of appeal in this credo, and, except for the color aspect, it fit his own intent at that moment. The Purist equation, however, did not take into account Léger's good peasant sense or his sensual and generous nature. For these reasons, the paths of Léger and the Purists converged and diverged.

Ill. 154 In terms of painting, the theories of Ozenfant and Le
Ill. 155 Corbusier never amounted to more than decorative
geometrization, overlapping forms, and an economy of contour that quicky turned into systematized lines. Purist compositions were almost exclusively still lifes that favored the bottles, cups, and glasses that could be found in coffee houses. Only the lines of certain classical objects like vases or musical instruments were slightly more nuanced through the interplay and modulation of softer shades. The Purists were closer to Picasso, Gris, and Braque's brand of traditional Cubism, with an orientation towards Abstraction. Purism was not very appealing when applied to painting. Its theories were better suited to architecture.

Ill. 156 Purism was nonetheless representative of a "moment" in Léger's work. Brief as that moment may have been, his friends Le Corbusier and Ozenfant appreciated his responsiveness and welcomed him with open arms when they met him in 1920. The height of this collaboration took place between 1921 and 1925, at the time when Léger found a concrete and public application for Purism. He showed at the Decorative Arts Exhibit in 1925.

His friends realized that he was more advanced in his field than they were, but they expected him to apply his work to their new constructions. Le Corbusier praised Léger in *Cahiers d'Art* in 1933: "At that moment Léger had painted his 'mechanical canvases' and was pursuing his discovery of the modern world. He felt able to participate as a painter in the major wave that was increasingly pervading contemporary architecture: innumerable new objects were being brought forth as a result of a new way of thinking; the production of the day pulled us out of the past and projected us into a new cycle." This newness was "in the air," and Léger instinctually picked up on it; he was heartbroken being alone in the ivory tower of painting. Life was fomenting in the real world, and he wanted to be a part of it. He was out and about all over the place with his friend Cendrars, and for years the two of them took their fill of the postwar world.

Picasso and Braque had discovered the poetry that lay buried in everyday objects. Bistro and coffeehouse items became a form of deep cultural expression. Then an enlightened élite opened their eyes and admitted that these painters had discovered something. A magnificent outpouring of work ensued. Léger and Cendrars, however, marched to the beat of a different drummer, and their instincts led them elsewhere. Another vision was in the process of being born. Léger felt the commotion at the Aviation Show after the war: the startling appearance of new parts, forms, and colors that were arranged in a different way, an outburst of something totally novel. With the automobile came the garages and gas stations, along with walls covered with advertisements. The dull palette of bistros (decorated in fake wood, false marble, and fluted ornaments) was being replaced with a range of vibrant geometrical lines. It was as clear as daylight: geometry was having a rebirth, a Renaissance!

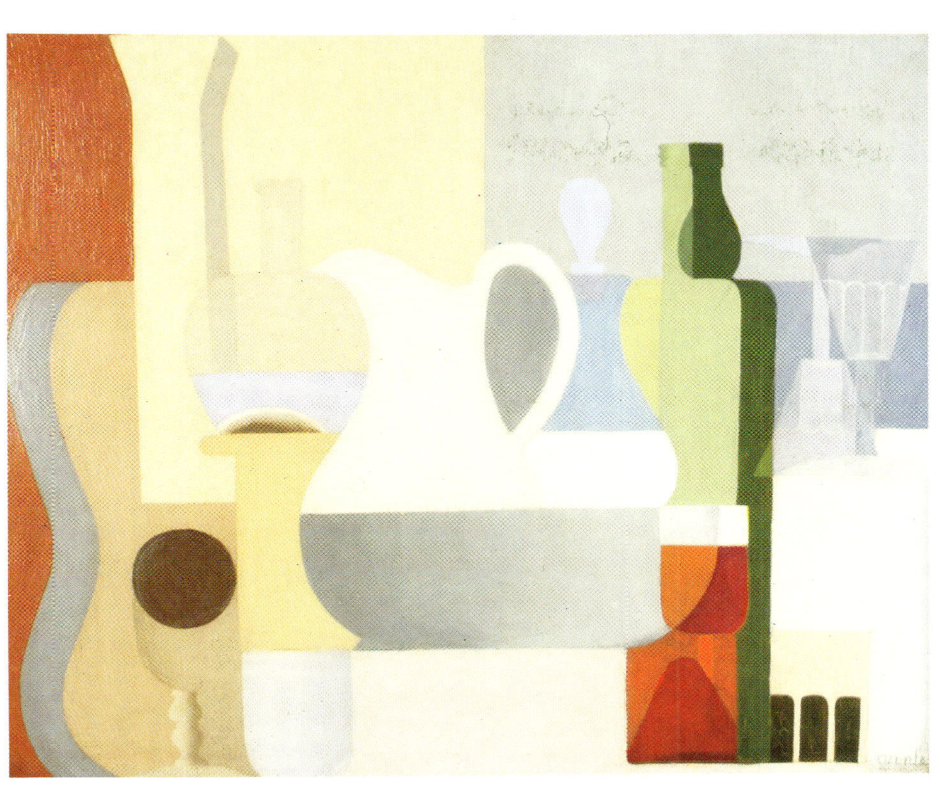

154. OZENFANT: *STILL LIFE*
1925—Oil on canvas

155. LE CORBUSIER: *STILL LIFE ''LÉONCE ROSENBERG''*
1922—Oil on canvas, 65 × 81 cm
Musée National d'Art Moderne, Centre Georges Pompidou, Pari

156. STILL LIFE
1924—Oil on canvas, 92 × 60 cm
Beyeler Gallery, Basel

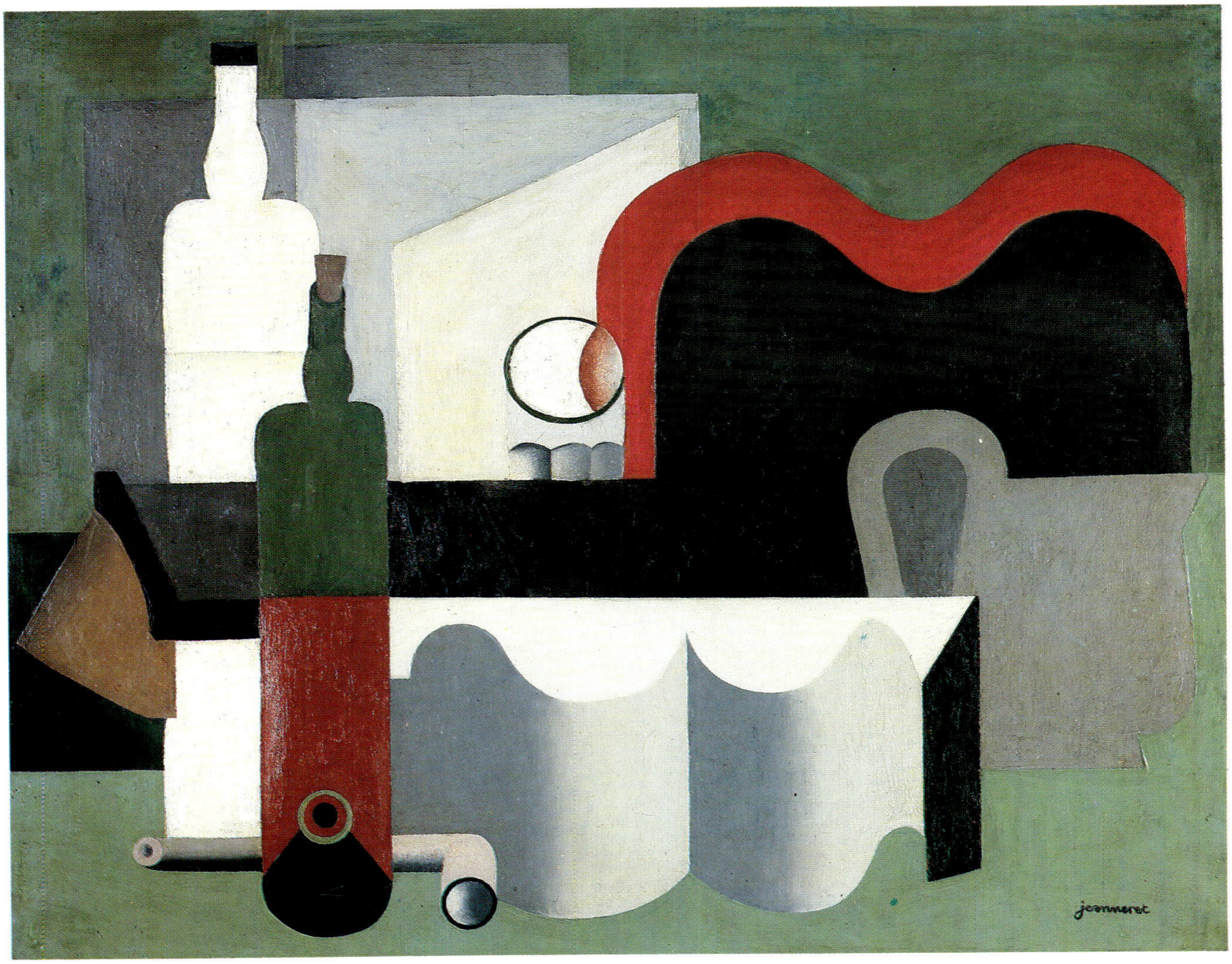

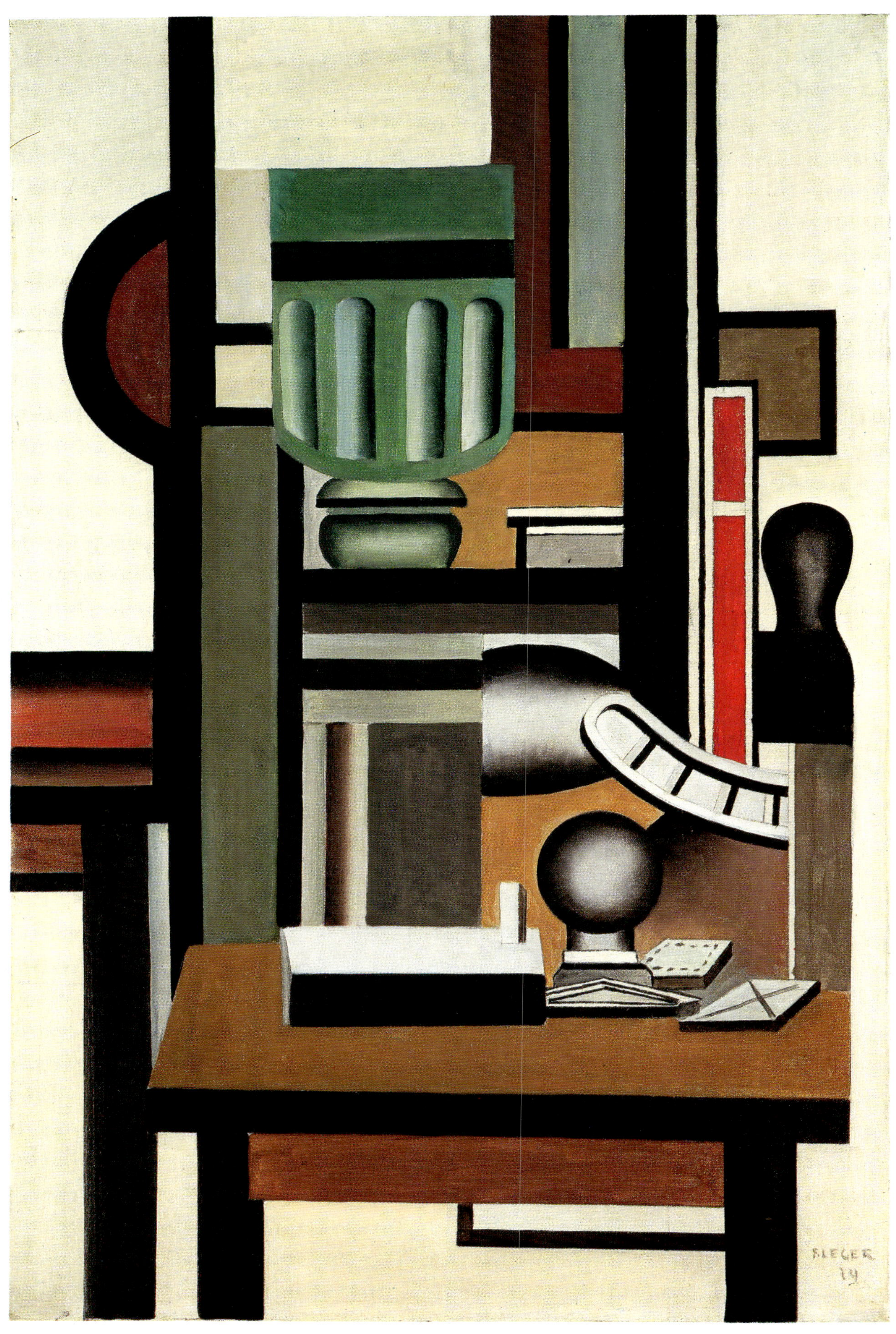

F.LEGER
19

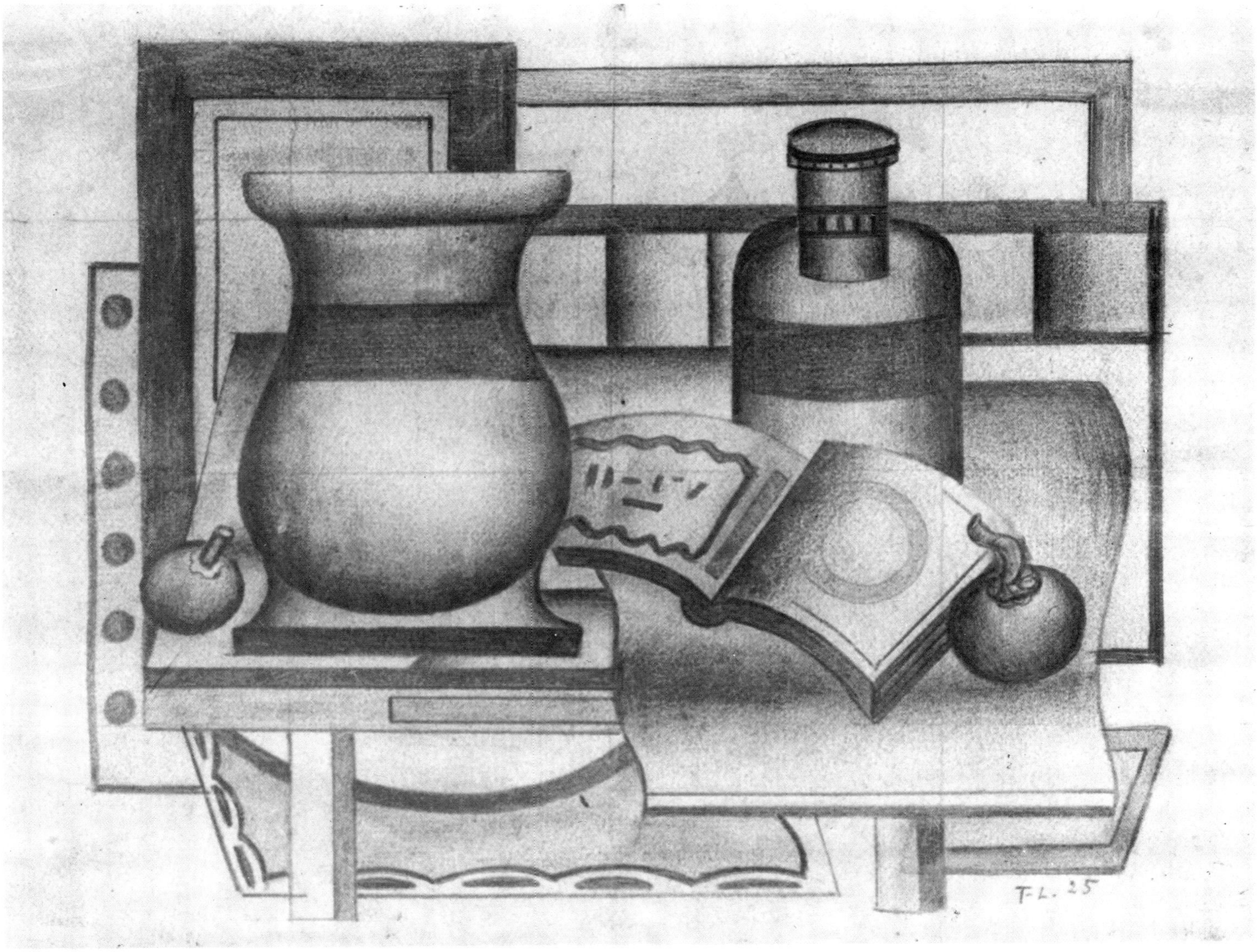

157. STILL LIFE ON TABLE
1925—Pencil drawing, 30 × 38 cm
Private collection, Paris

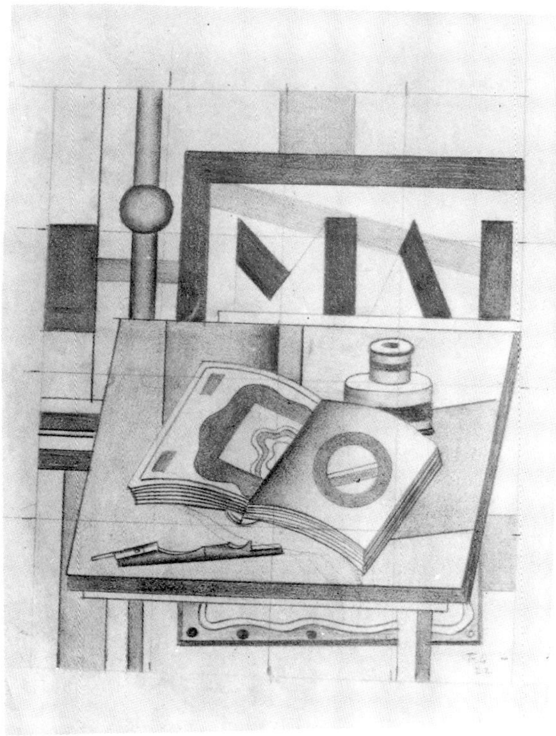

158. BOOK, INKWELL, AND PEN
1922—Pencil on paper
Private collection

As a painter, Léger assessed this pictorial event in which colors no longer ornamented forms. The purely specific attributes of color were used in composition to capture the eye of the viewer. Léger learned a great lesson from this.

Color became an autonomous agent, an art form in itself. It harkened back to an earlier time when painting was closer to architecture. Léger went beyond the tumultuously mechanical diagonal lines of his sketches. He leaped into the architectural dimension, which for him was expressed in the movement of color—"the scientifically magnificent movement of color on a wall, the play of light and the ensuing movement of form."

During the early 1920s, Léger enjoyed the support of a small élite who shared his convictions in one or more ways. Art between the two world wars was a nonstop, bubbling cauldron. Berlin, Paris, and Moscow were in perpetual dialogue and became the three major creative poles for the Western world. It was an extraordinary period for all the art forms—architec-

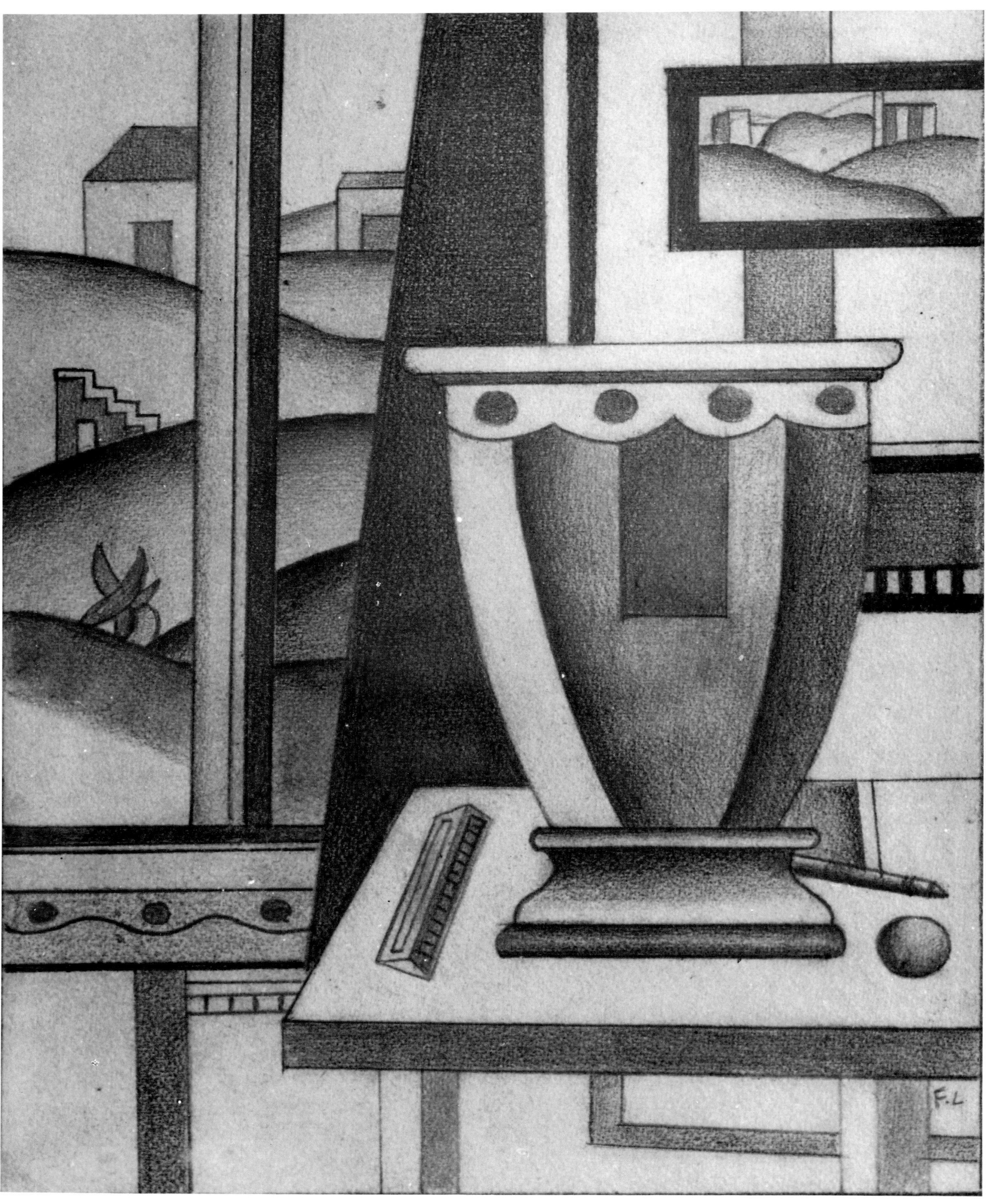


159. INTERIOR AND WINDOW
About 1924—Pencil on paper
Private collection

ture, painting, sculpture, graphics, theater, cinema, and photography. Generous social ideas promoted art for the good of the greatest number of people. From East to West, graphics invaded public spaces. Mayakovsky's slogan echoed Léger's own desire: "the street will be our paintbrushes, and the town squares will be our palettes." A new race of artists was born. Were they Constructivists, Neo-Plasticists, Purists, or members of the Bauhaus, all were striving towards a new golden age for mankind.

"We must understand that art and life are no longer two separate domains," wrote the Dutchmen van Doesburg and van Eesteren in the essay entitled "Towards Collective Building" (*De Stijl,* IV): "As soon as painters realize that a universal language is called for, they will abandon individualism for universal principles, and produce a cohesive style of work. As a result of the new relationship between the artist and society, the new style will be recognizable in all objects." These words could prove dangerous. If they deviated from their intended meaning or were misused, some would start blaming the individualists, and others would want to punish the "deviationists" and "degenerates."

"Attention, all architects, sculptors, and painters. We must all return to the craft! There is no such thing as *professional art.* There is no basic difference between the artist and the artisan. The artist is an inspired artisan, in whose hands craftsmanship becomes art. Art is born from a rare spark of light or a strong will, along with a state of heavenly grace. Nonetheless, every artist must possess technical competence, which is the true source of creative imagination. Let's join to form a new sort of enterprise, a corporation without the separation of classes. Let's abolish the barrier of disdain between the artisan and the artist. Together we will conceive of and engender an architecture of the future in which painting, sculpture, and architecture will be a single entity. With the hands of millions of workers a crystal symbol of this new faith will be constructed skyward."

Walter Gropius, in *The Bauhaus Manifesto* (1919), is the author of the above lyrical flight of idealism, which tends to bring everyone into agreement on everything. This marks a turning point in the history of art. It might have been possible in Moscow, where the brothers Gabo and Pevsner, both sculptors who were also involved with architecture, published the *Realist Manifesto* in 1920, which laid down the basic principles of Constructivism. Spatial construction was to be considered more in sculptural terms than as architecture: "We affirm that the only possible way to model space is from the inside out, using depth. It is impossible to go from the outside in, using volume." This echoes *L'Esprit nouveau,* in which the Purists wrote: "Architecture has nothing to do with different styles. The Louis XV, XVI, XIV or Gothic styles are to architecture what a feather in a hat is to the appearance of a woman—it's sometimes pretty, but nothing more." In the fourth part of their *Manifesto,* the Russians stated: "We reject the decorative line. We demand that each line in a work of art indicate lines of the internal strength of the subject." Then came Malevich in his 1924 *Suprematist Manifesto*: "We Suprematists are looking for allies in the struggle against past forms."

During this period the word *robot* was invented. It originated from the Czech word *robotnik* ("worker") and was coined by author and journalist Karel Capek. Paul Klee called his machine-men (*Analysis of Various Perversities,* 1922). In turn, Raoul Hausmann warned everyone in 1921: "We are in the space between two worlds. Not having quite broken with the traditions of the past and not quite ready to give shape to a new world, we are in a perfect situation for satire, grotesquerie, and caricature, where clowns and dolls as forms of expression are there to show us to what extent life has become mechanical. It is as if we are inhabited by puppets; the situation is real, and must allow us to think and feel that there is another kind of life."

Aldous Huxley in *Brave New World* was on the lookout, too, as well as Fritz Lang in his film *Metropolis* (1926), which spoke of a profound unease in modern urban society, a division between the race of landowners who lived in their paradisical gardens and the workers who labored in the underground. These workers were drudges of the machine, alienated beings, slaves of Moloch. All the writings that sprouted during this period prove that even the best intentions often contain potentially dangerous pitfalls. When Le Corbusier stated that "the ocean liner is the first step in the realization of a world organized according to the new way of thinking (*esprit nouveau*)," it is only a short step to the transformation of the ship into a monastery, and from the monastery into large urban dormitories.

Not to stray too far from the subject of painting—Léger admitted that the object he so cherished, and that is the foundation of his work, must be isolated and put in the spotlight in order for it to assume its full value: "five pairs of stockings presented on a color background have more impact than two hundred of them piled next to each other." Merchants quickly understood this with regard to their display windows, and the advertisers understood this in terms of their billboards. It was what Léger referred to as "the advent of the object."

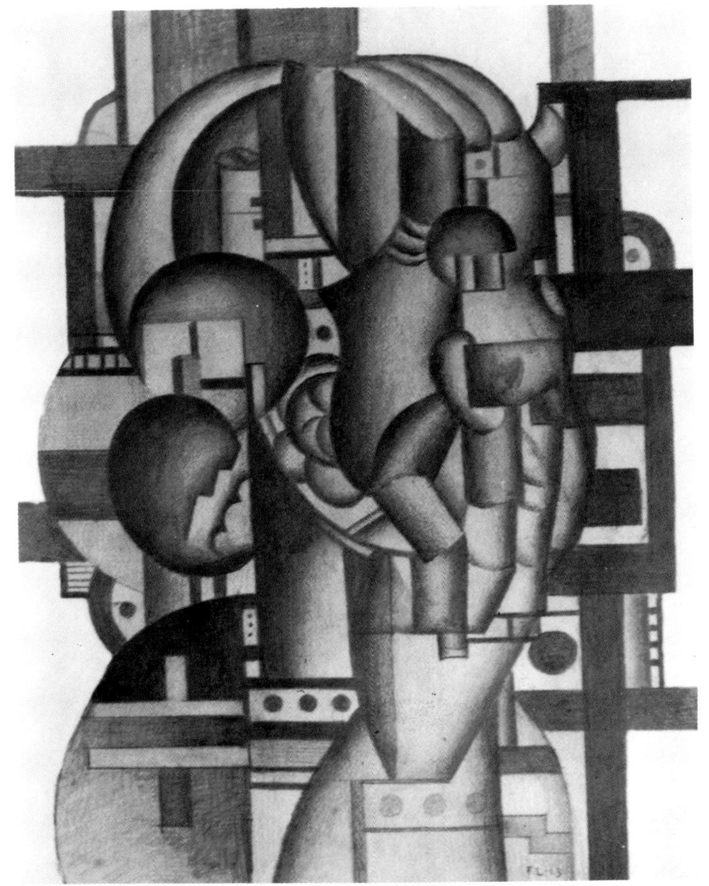

160. COMPOSITION
1923—Pencil on paper
Private collection

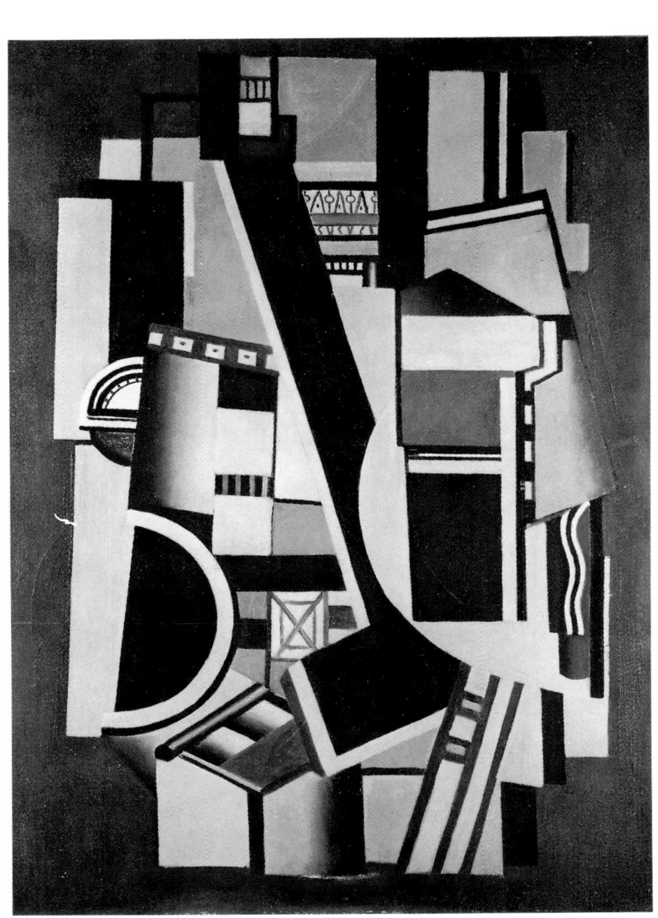

161. MECHANICAL ELEMENTS ON A RED BACKGROUND
1924—Oil on canvas, 92 × 65 cm
Musée National Fernand Léger, Biot

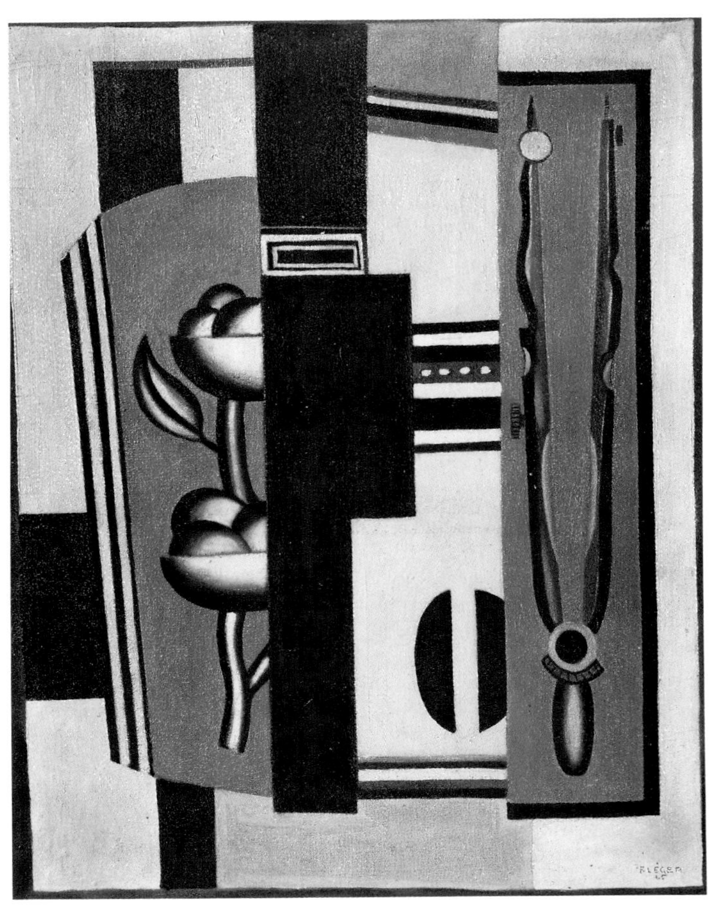

162. STILL LIFE WITH COMPASS
1925—Oil on canvas, 65 × 50 cm
Private collection

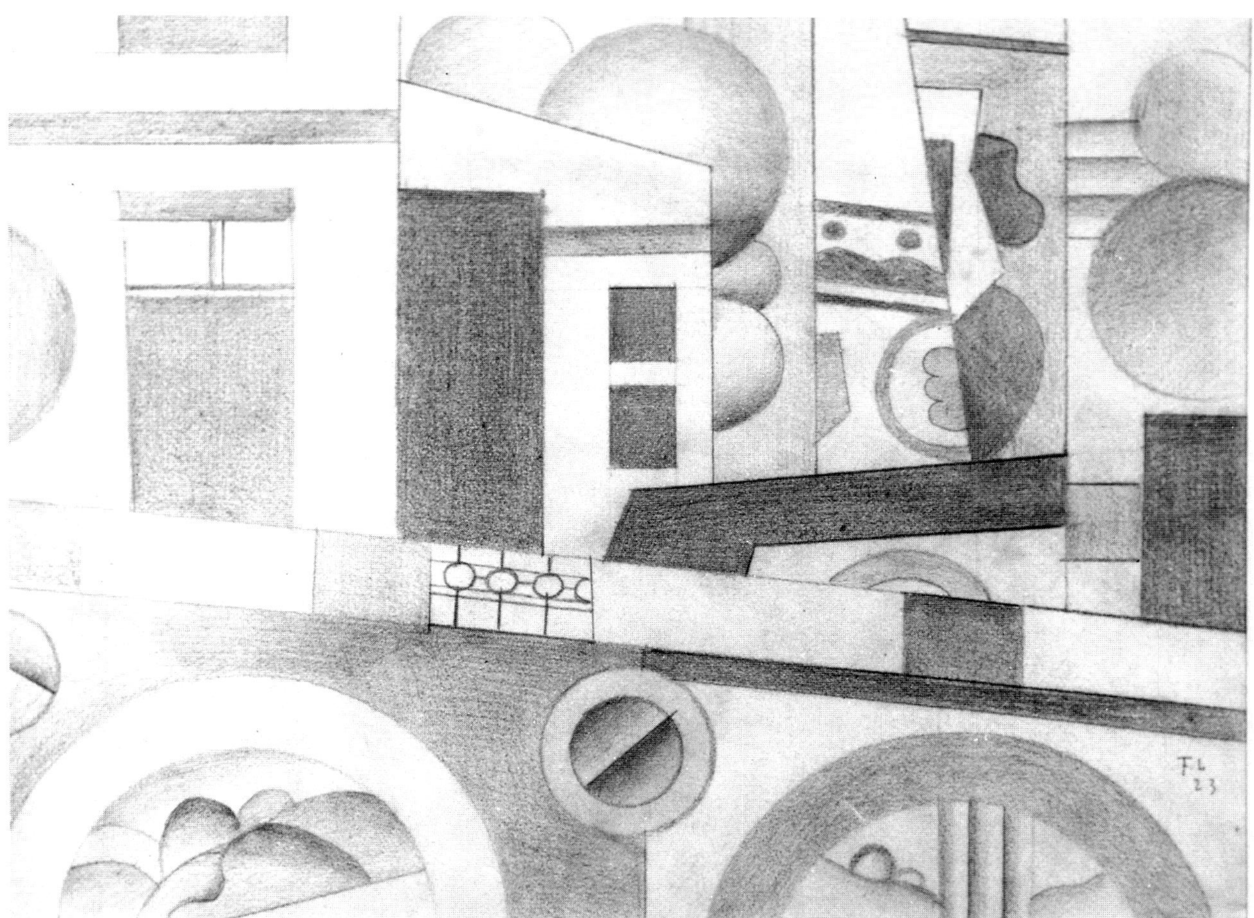


163. ARCHITECTURE-LANDSCAPE
1923—Pencil on paper, 25 × 32.5 cm
Private collection

**More beautiful than the Venus de Milo: a gas meter**

There is a story about how one day in 1925 Léger, having agreed to speak to a study group at the Sorbonne, arrived with a gas meter that he unwrapped and ceremoniously displayed on a table: "Ladies and gentlemen, this is much more interesting than the Venus de Milo!" Léger, as a good art historian, went on to explain the developments that led to his statement. He thought of artistic evolution since the start of the twentieth century as an ongoing battle between the concept of "the subject" as the Italian Renaissance had understood it, and "the object" and "pure tones" that dominated modern ideas of art. He went on to note that the notion of "the object" is not something new. It existed in the high periods of Egyptian, Assyrian, Greek, Roman, and Gothic art. The "moderns" developed it, isolated it, and tackled the ensuing consequences. The "obligatory subject" that dominated all of Renaissance art had been broken and was no longer acceptable. Now that the subject had been destroyed, it was necessary to find something else. The object and pure color became the replacement value. The same *object* that had been imprisoned in the *subject* was liberated, and out came pure color, which became the *leading character* in the new pictorial works.

In *The Siphon* (1924), the siphon is the "main character" of the painting. Léger had already been isolating his giants by "sticking" them against backgrounds, but here he began to isolate the object and Ill. 164
personalize it in the process.

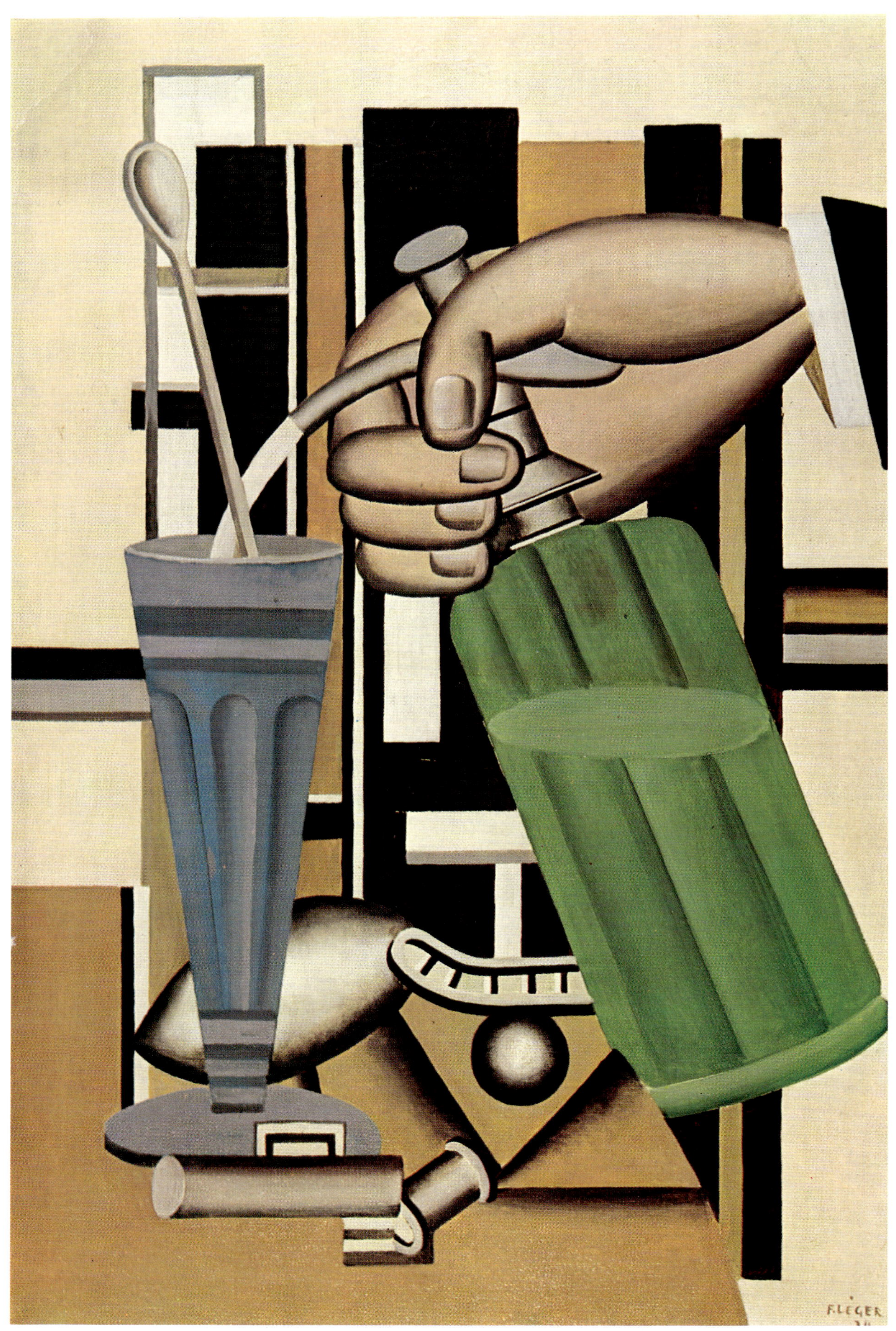


164. THE SIPHON
1924—Oil on canvas, 64.8 × 45.7 cm
Albright-Knox Art Gallery, Buffalo

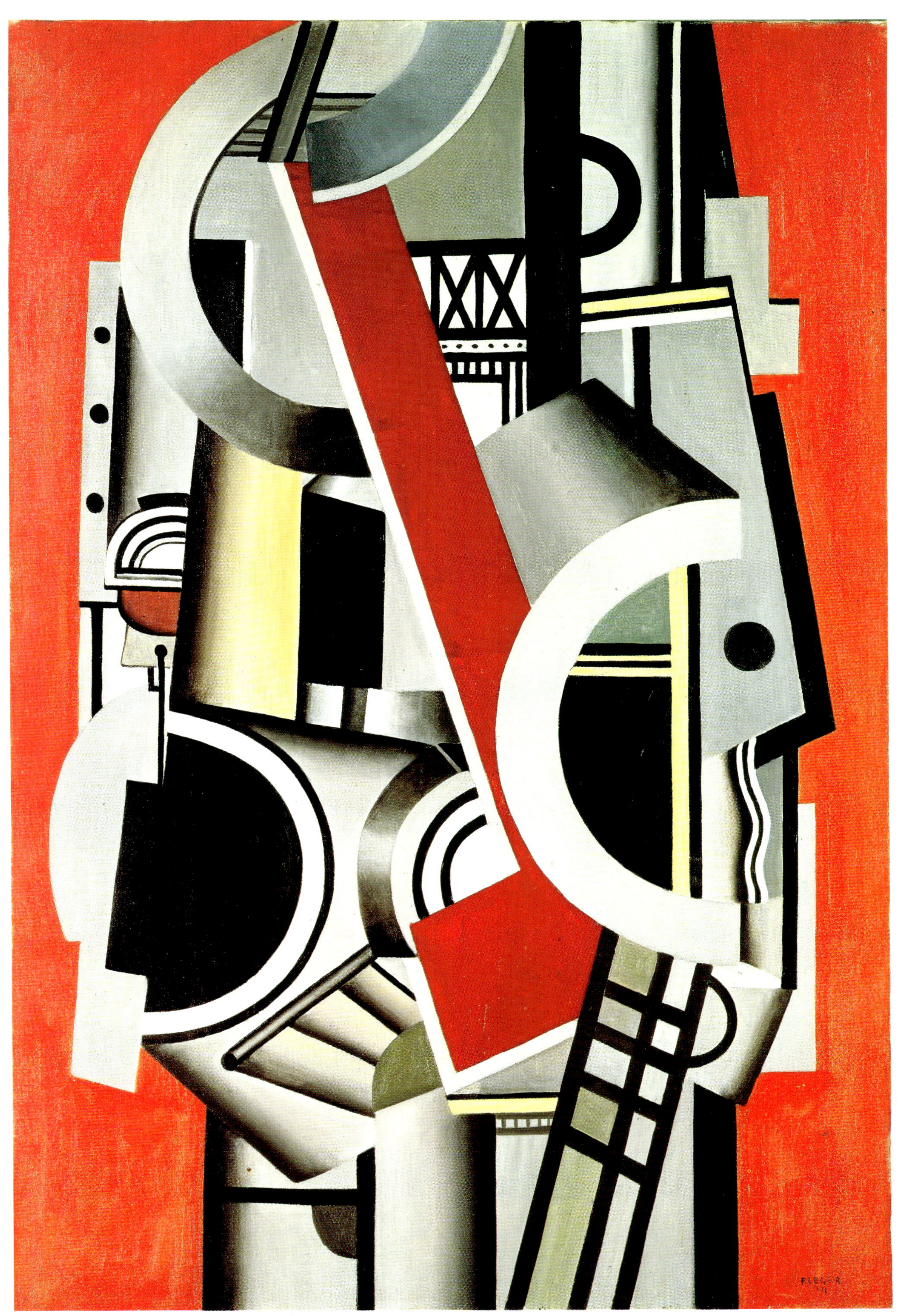

165. MECHANICAL ELEMENTS
1924—Oil on canvas, 146 × 97 cm
Musée National d'Art Moderne, Centre Georges Pompidou, Paris
Bequest of Eva Gourgaud

166. COMPOSITION WITH POST
1925—Oil on canvas, 92 × 73 cm
Oeffentliche Kunstsammung, Kunstmuseum, Basel
Gift of Raoul de la Roche

167. MOVEMENT WITH BALL BEARINGS
1926—Oil on canvas, 146 × 114 cm
Oeffentliche Kunstsammung, Kunstmuseum, Basel
Gift of Raoul de la Roche

168. CORKSCREW ON A BLUE BACKGROUND
1932—Oil on canvas, 54 × 65 cm
Private collection

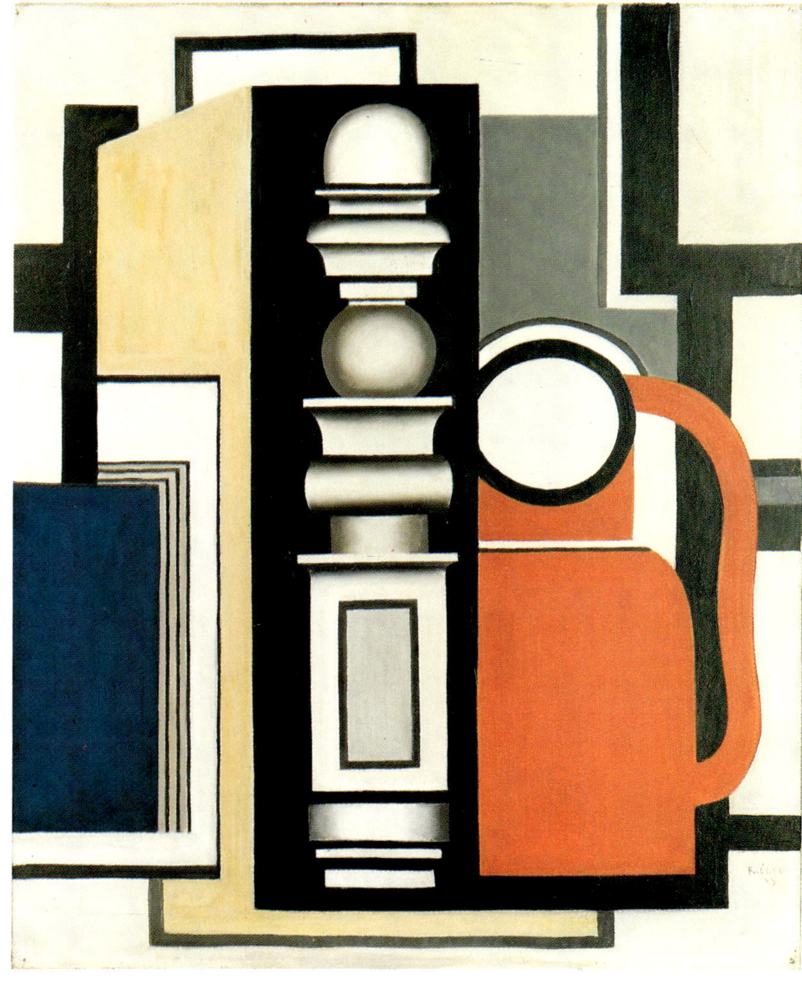

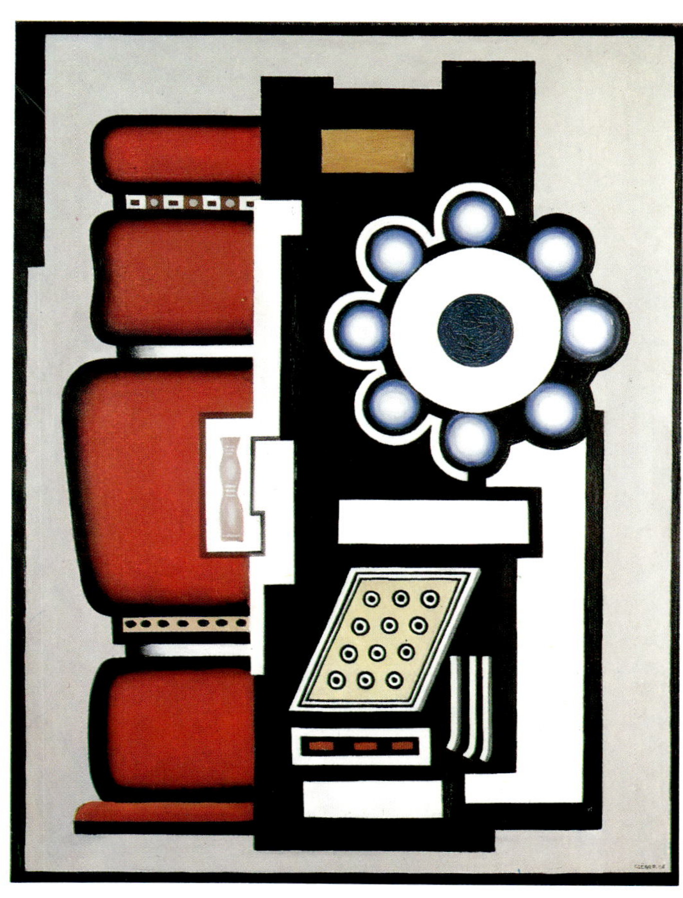

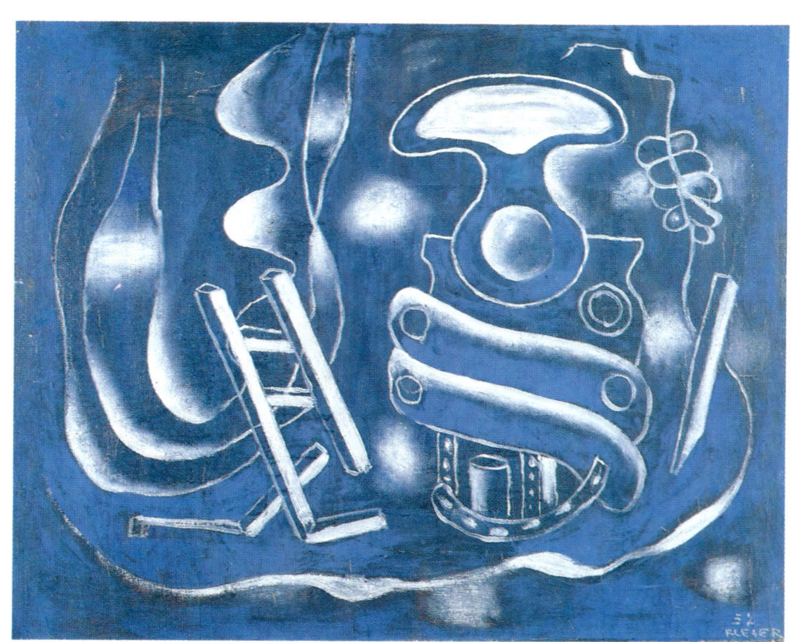

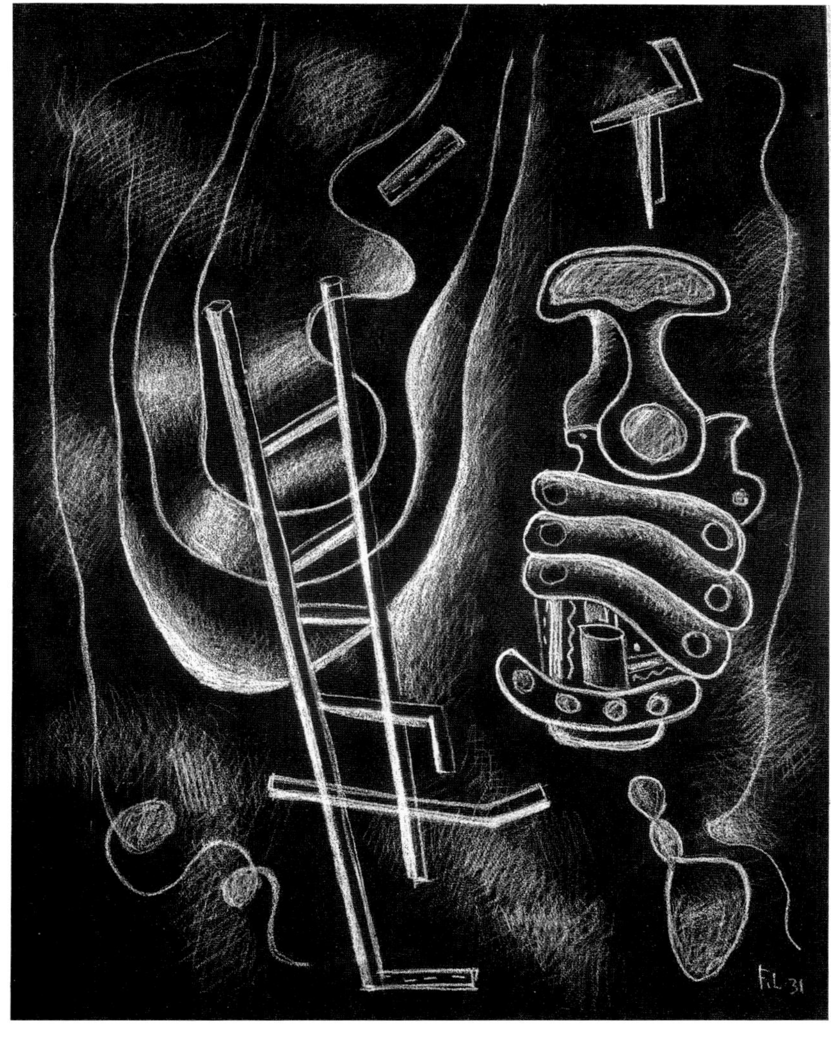

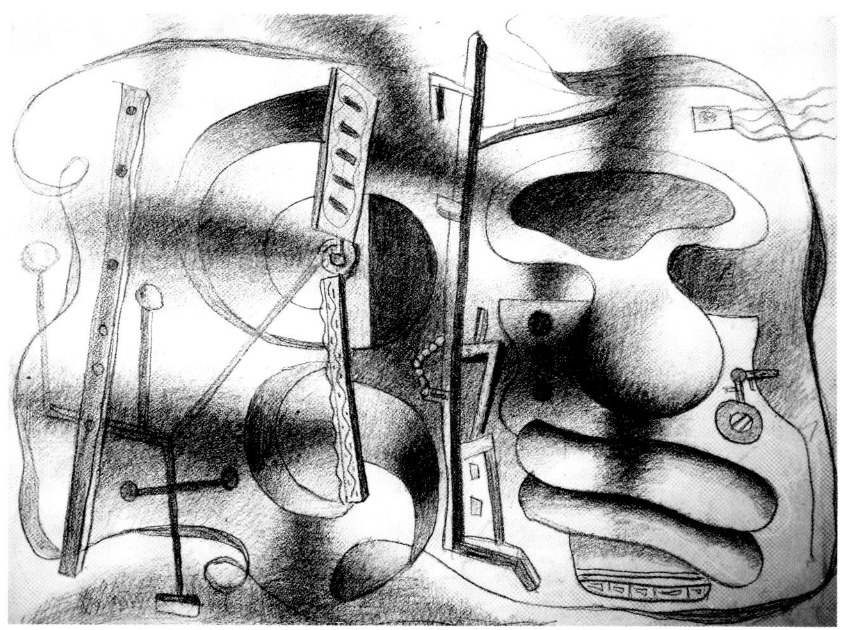

## A catalogue of objects in space

Ill. 169 to 172

Department store catalogues were the primary source of Léger's "objects in space." He used a technique similar to the one that the Douanier Rousseau used when he chose his exotic flowers and fruits from the pages of the Vilmorin catalogues. Léger also found his raw materials during his walks through the Paris streets. He would stroll along the Boulevard Voltaire or the avenues of Belleville, and he would look into shop windows at the strange assortments of hats, tools, and umbrellas. A crumpled piece of paper lying in the gutter, an old glove on a garbage can, an abandoned rag. . . It makes us think of raw art (*l'art brut*) that would come years later with Jean Dubuffet, and also of the first novels of Alain Robbe-Grillet. At first Léger would meticulously sketch these objects with pencil, and then transpose them onto his canvas. When he and his friend Ozenfant opened their atelier together in 1924 the first rule that their students learned was to "sketch objects with the greatest precision."

Léger explained the process that led to his sketches and later paintings: "I'm standing in front of a landscape of trees, sky, and clouds. Only the tree interests me, so I'm going to study it and extract its plastic potential: the bark is often expressive, the movement of the branches is dynamic, and the leaves have decorative value. The plastic richness of the tree is sacrificed in the *canvas which treats the tree as subject.* By isolating the tree, it becomes the needed material for renewing current pictorial expression."

The Impressionists had started the fight, and the modernists took the baton. Léger had been working with this long before he became involved in film, but in his passion for the object, cinema did allow him "to go faster," thanks to the "close-up."

The cinematic technique of the close-up helped Léger resolve his problems of composition. In order to avoid relationships between objects that lessened the visual impact, he wanted to project them into space, thus isolating them further by eliminating all supporting devices: "I made objects in space to be sure of my objects. I felt that I couldn't put my object on a table without lessening its value as an object. . . . I took the object and eliminated the table. I put this object in the air, without perspective and with no supports. Then I had to liberate color to a greater extent."

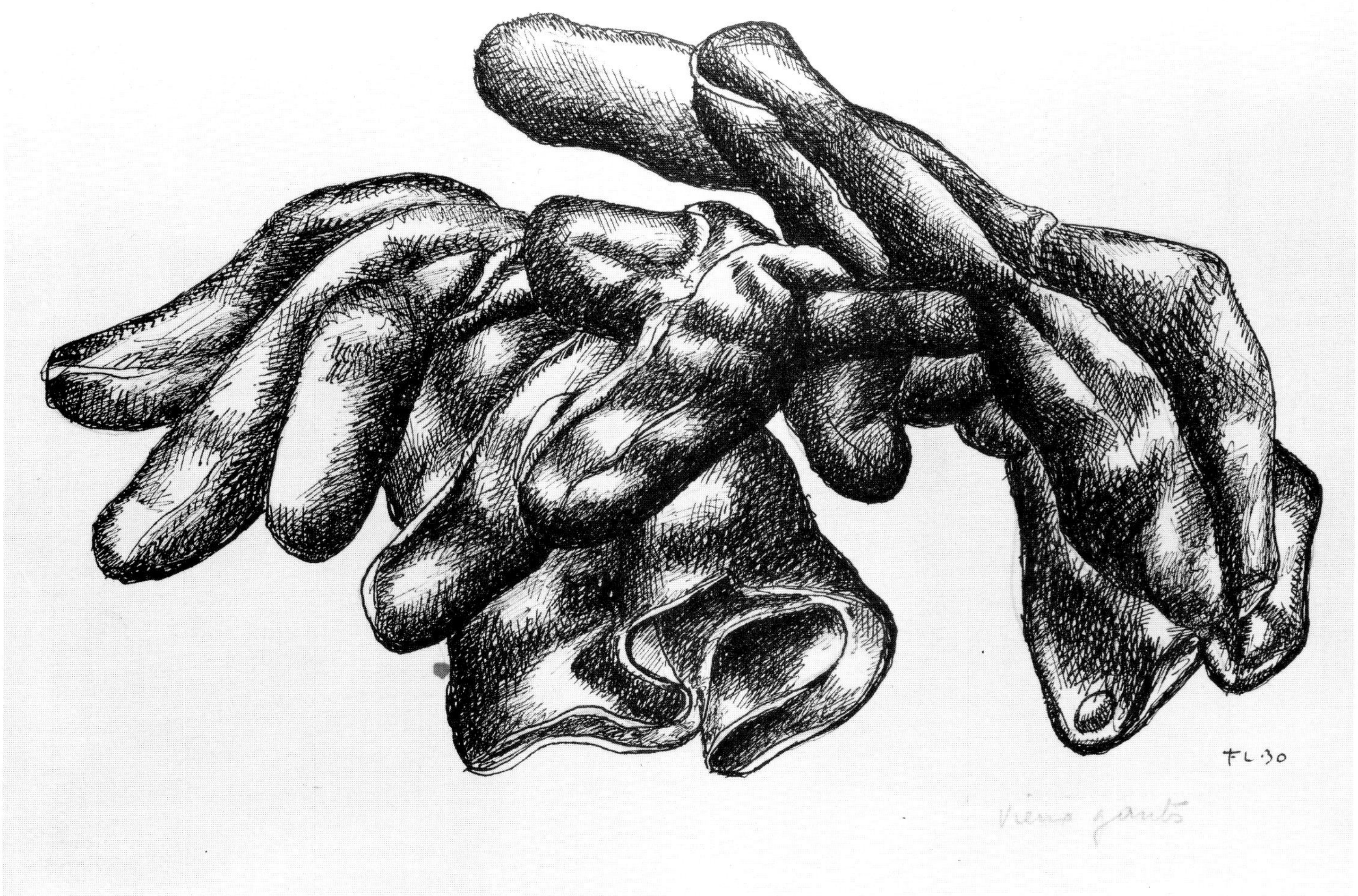

169. COMPOSITION WITH CORKSCREW
1931—Chalk, 65 × 50 cm
Louise Leiris Gallery, Paris

170. COMPOSITION WITH CORKSCREW
About 1930—Pencil on paper, 48 × 63 cm
Musée National Fernand Léger, Biot

171. OLD GLOVES
1930—China ink drawing, 24.8 × 32.5 cm
Q.L. Collection, Paris

172. BELT
1930—Pencil on paper, 26.5 × 18 cm
Q.L. Collection, Paris

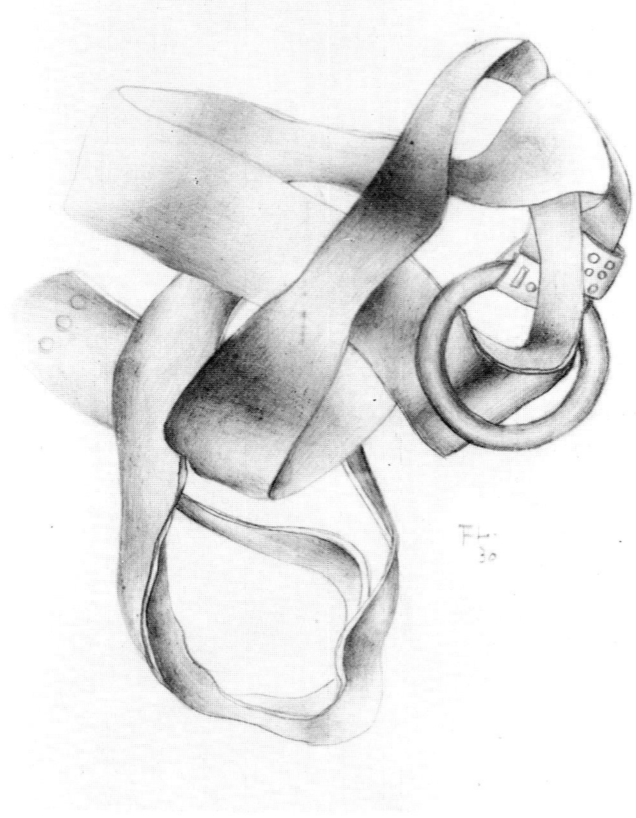

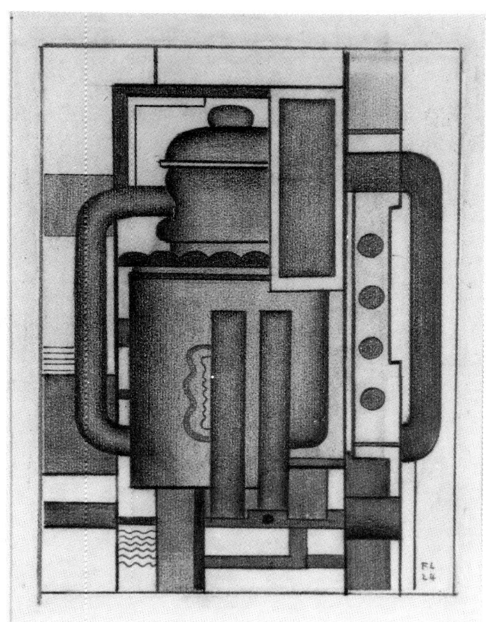

173. STILL LIFE
1924—Pencil drawing, 30.5 × 22.5 cm
Private collection

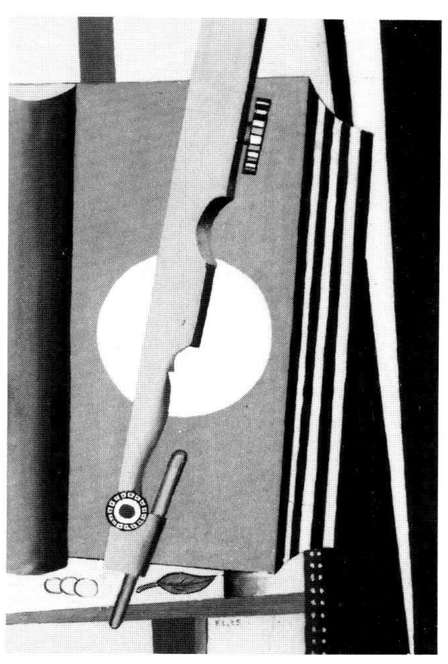

174. COMPASS
1925—Gouache, 36 × 25 cm
Private collection

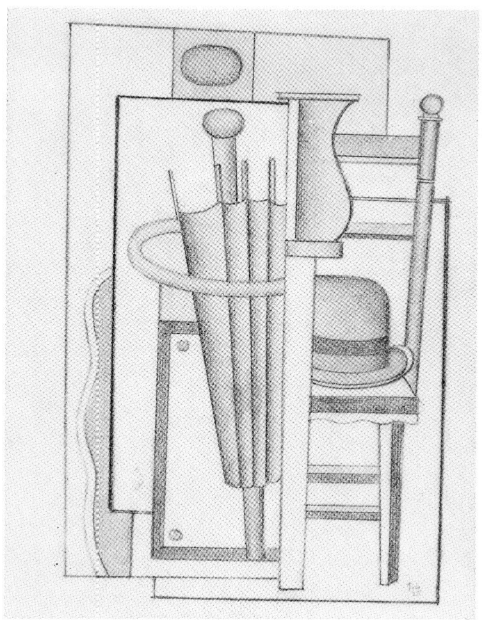

175. COMPOSITION WITH UMBRELLA AND HAT
1925—Pencil on paper, 30.5 × 23 cm
Lionel Prejger collection, Paris

### The new realism of the object or its fragment

During this period, Léger conceived of his canvases as a film montage. He used the montage technique to present objects, were they vases, compasses, umbrellas, hats, mechanical elements, corkscrews, or purely abstract objects. They were juxtaposed, divided, or contrasted images, such as an object and a form, a mechanical detail and a profile, a bunch of grapes and a mask, a root and a flint, a rack of meat and a rope. Léger expressed this love of concrete reality, which he found in films: "There's a new realism in the way of perceiving the object or its fragment."

Be careful not to mistake these combinations with Surrealism. Even André Breton, the leader of the Surrealist movement, was not able to bring Léger into the fold. Léger's combinations had nothing to do with Lautréamont's "encounter of an umbrella and a sewing machine on an operating table." Instead, they were an expression of Léger's own particular use of "freeze frames" in his 1924 film *Ballet Mécanique* and
Ill. 165 painting *Mechanical Elements* (Eléments méca-
Ill. 176 niques); *The Top Hat* ("Le Haut de forme"), *Umbrella*
Ill. 174 *and Hat* ("Parapluie et chapeau"), and *The Compass*
("Le Compas") in 1925; *The Yellow Triangle* ("Le Ill. 179
Triangle jaune") in 1926; *Profile, Vase, and Key* Ill. 193
("Profil, vase et clé") and *Composition of Four Hats* Ill. 209
("Composition aux quatre chapeaux") in 1927; *Still*
*Life with Plaster Mask* ("Nature morte au masque de Ill. 190
plâtre"), and *Seashell and Profile* ("Coquillage et pro- Ill. 192
fil") in 1928; *Cluster of Grapes* ("La Grappe de raisin") Ill. 210
in 1929; *Composition with Yellow Cameo* ("Composi- Ill. 189
tion au camée jaune") in 1931; *Corkscrew on a Blue*
*Background* ("Le Tire-bouchon sur fond bleu") in Ill. 168
1932. All the above were projections in space. The unexpected relationships between things have nothing in common with the unconscious, automatic associations that come into play with Surrealism.

Léger's associations were totally conscious and deliberate. They stemmed from the will of the artist to compose figurative harmonies or contrasts and to create a rhythm. From his "objects in space" to "contrasting objects," Léger composed his canvases in pursuit of the greatest possible plastic intensity. For him this was the highest expression of his sense of reality.

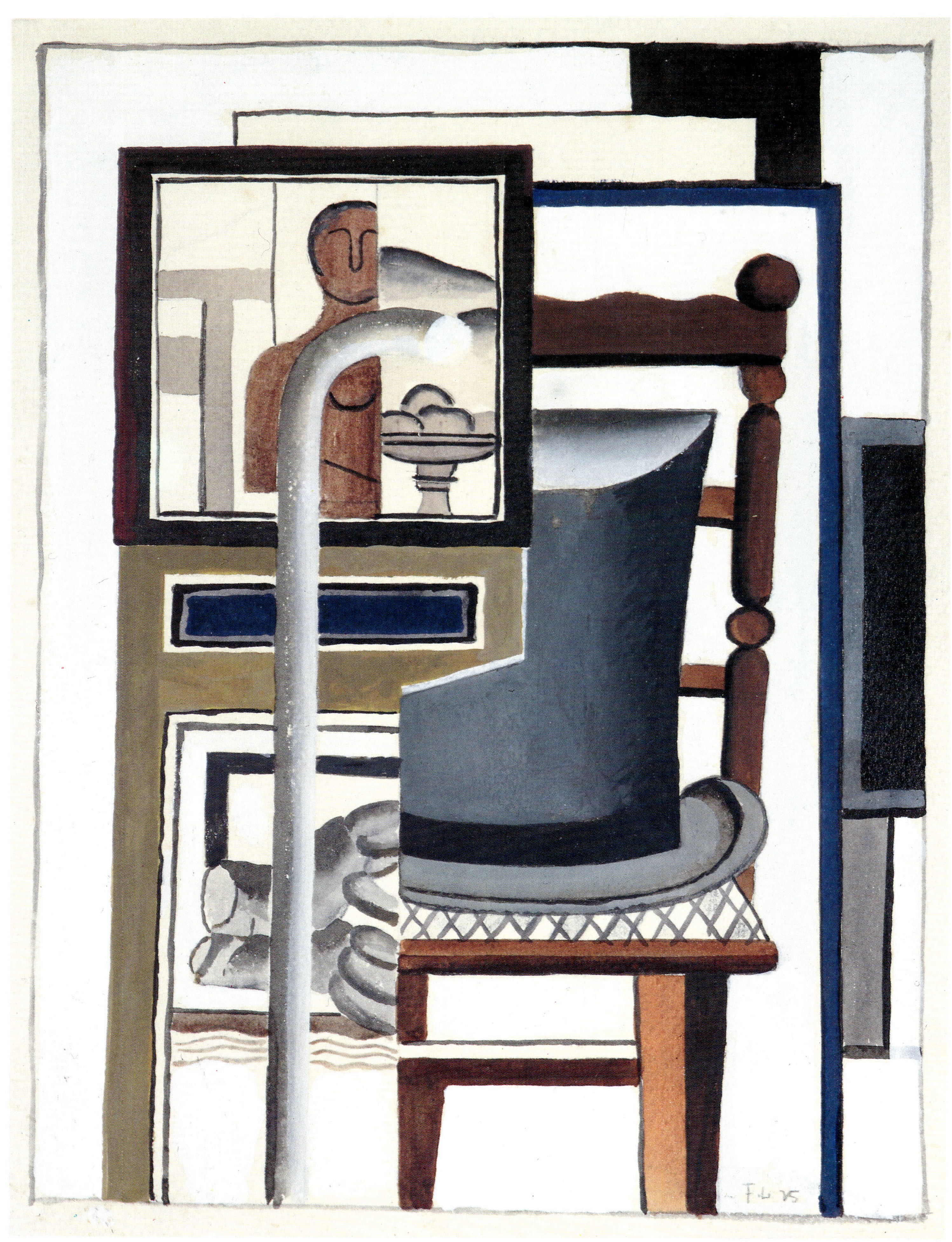

176. TOP HAT
1925—Gouache and China ink, 27 × 20 cm
Lionel Prejger collection, Paris

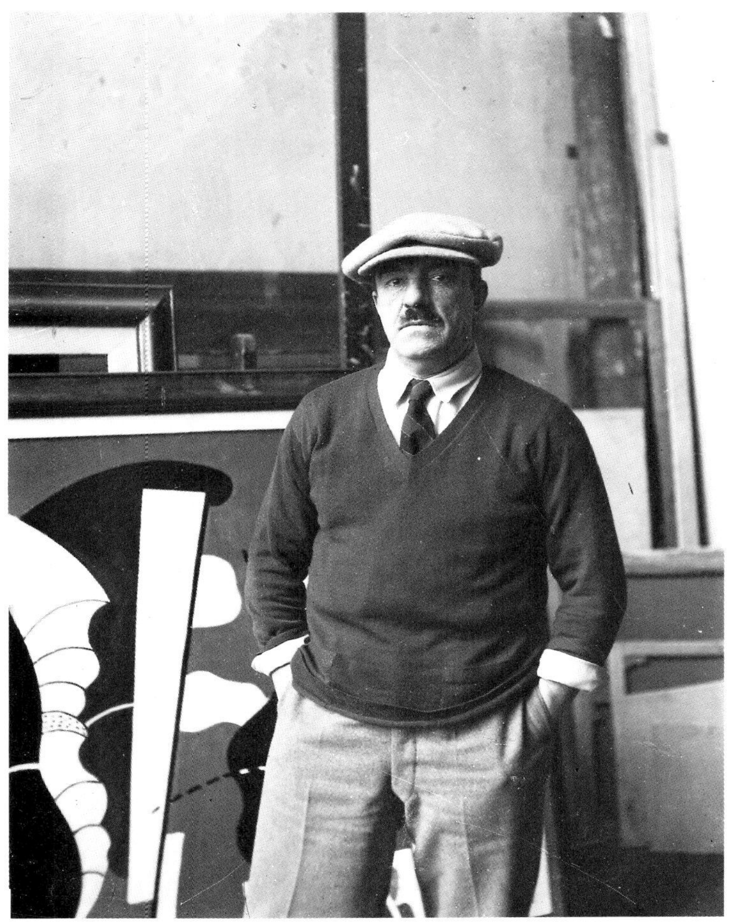

177. FERNAND LÉGER ABOUT 1930.

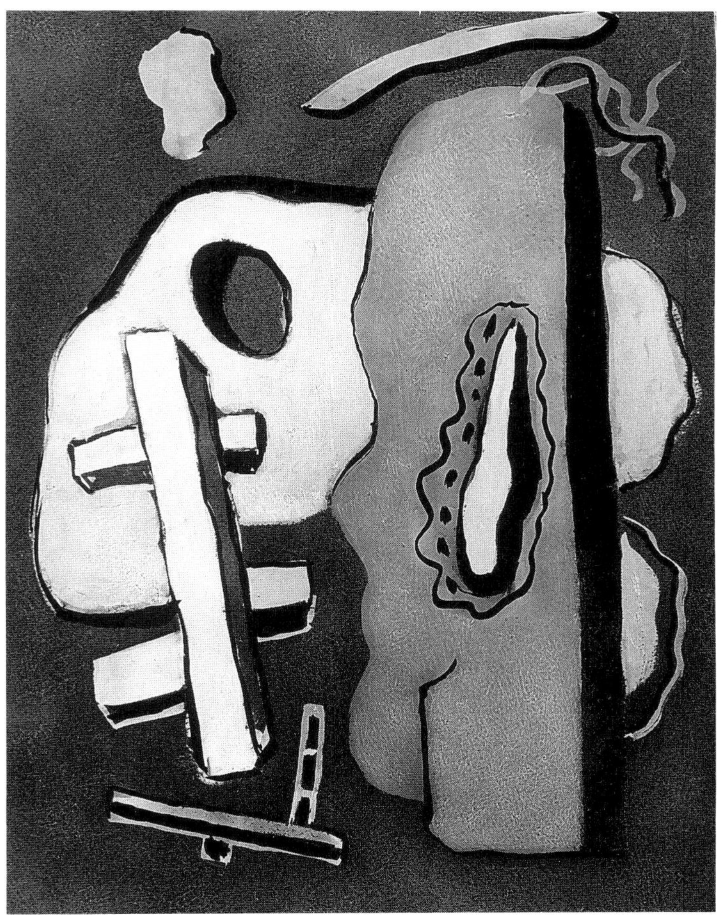

178. ABSTRACT COMPOSITION
About 1932—Oil on canvas, 42 × 36 cm
Private collection

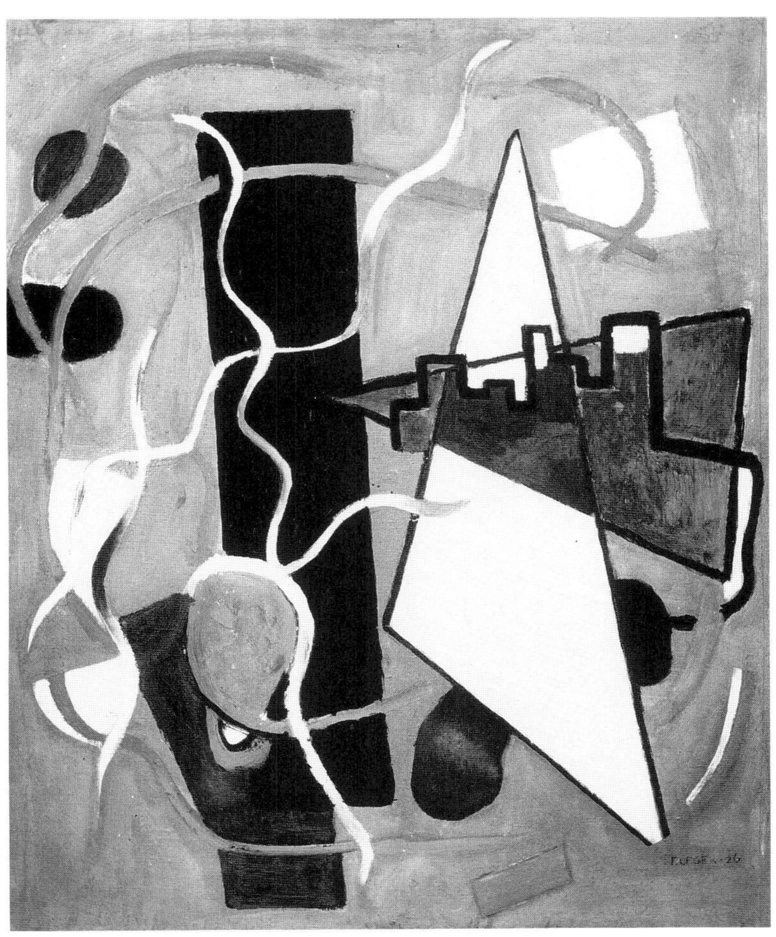

179. YELLOW TRIANGLE
1926—Oil on canvas, 65 × 54 cm
Private collection

## At the frontier of Abstraction

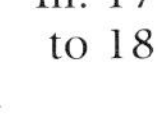

Ill. 17 to 18

In the same way that Léger had always remained on the fringe of Cubism without totally engaging in that radically new concept, he kept his distance from Abstraction. This did not prevent him from praising Mondrian and Neo-Plasticism. Léger thought of Abstraction as total freedom, and once he had mastered it, he used it to do something else, like sketching roots.

He did pay his dues to Abstraction, and even returned to it from time to time. He exhibited his work with Mondrian and Herbin at the "Effort Moderne." At the request of Michel Seuphor, he exhibited with the "Circle and Square" group. He even saw his work removed from the International Decorative Arts Exhibit in 1925 because of its abstraction! It was a design for the vestibule of "a French embassy" designed by Mallet-Stevens.

"Abstraction is a misguided concern." As geometric abstraction became more radical, Léger encouraged other artists to escape from its geometric carcass. He never participated in "Abstraction-Creation" and even took an "unfavorably neutral" position towards it. He considered Mondrian the artist who pushed

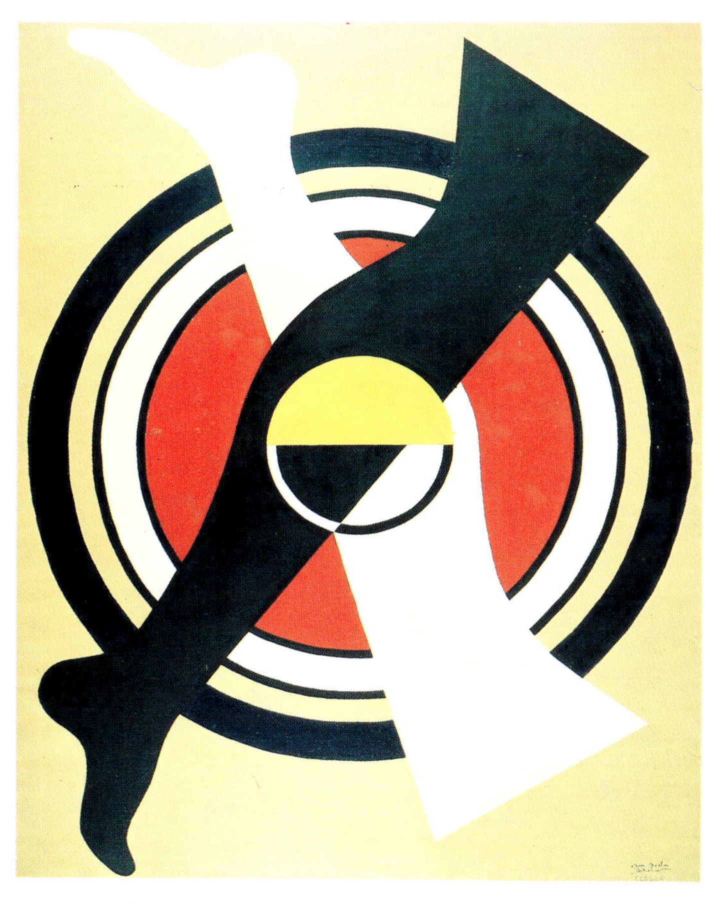

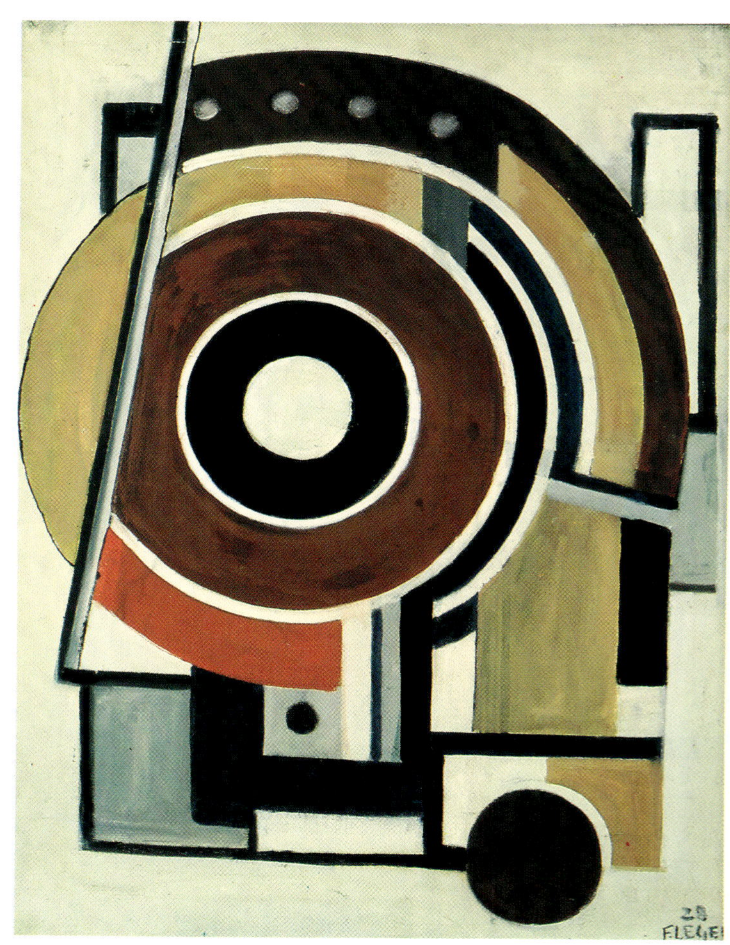

180. TRIBUTE TO DANCE
1925—Oil on canvas, 160 × 120 cm
Collection of Mr. and Mrs. Adrien Maeght

181. CIRCULAR COMPOSITION
1928—Oil on canvas, 65 × 50 cm
Collection of Mr. and Mrs. Adrien Maeght

Purism to its ultimate limits, to the point of total deprivation. The true purist was not Ozenfant or Le Corbusier, but Mondrian. "It was the necessary outcome of Purism. Neo-Plasticism had created an indisputable 'plastic event.' It had to happen. It did happen. . . Whether one likes it or not is irrelevant. I applaud those Northern European artists for their faith and unselfish spirit. Faced with the current *anything goes, as long as it will sell,* these men held their ground and continued their work in spite of the world's inability to understand. They were right, because they were dealing with certain preoccupations of a period that had aspirations in so many directions."

Note that Léger spoke of the Abstractionists in the past tense, thus defining their limitations, as well as their accomplishments. "Pure abstraction pushed to the extreme in this *new way of thinking* was the trump card that had to be played. . . . Since 1912, the *colored surface* has been haunting the innovators, who

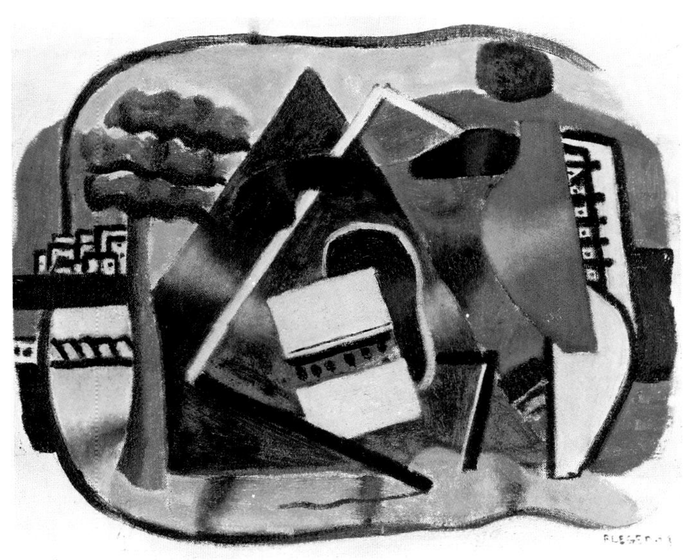

182. EIGHT FORMS
1929—Oil on canvas, 38 × 46 cm
Louise Leiris collection, Paris

183. STILL LIFE
1927—Watercolor and pencil sketch, 17 × 14.5 cm
Private collection

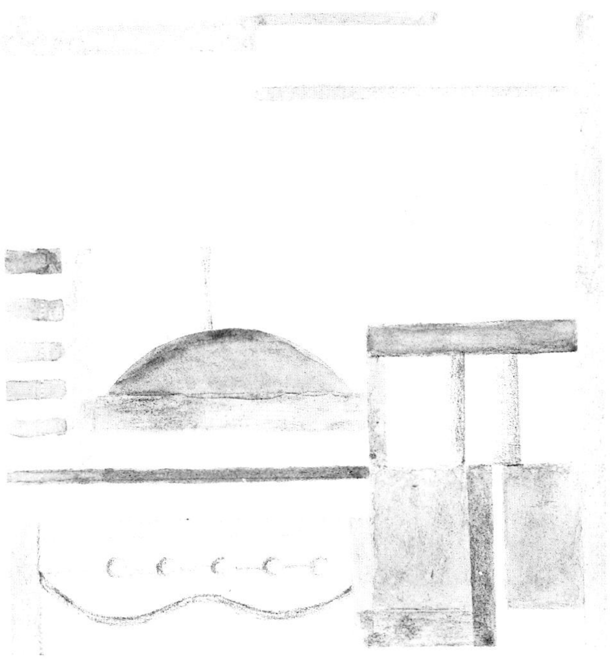

184. COMPOSITION
1929—Gouache
Private collection

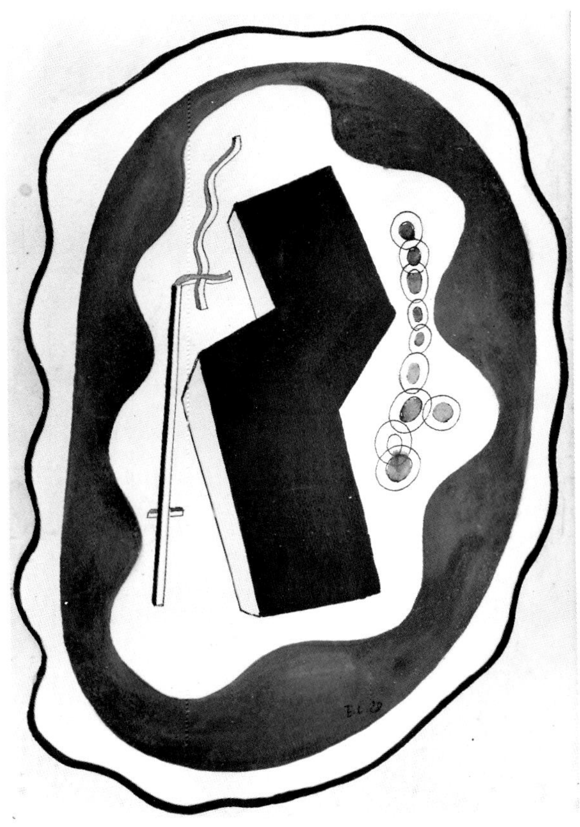

have audaciously used it as the 'leading character'; geometrical inscription strictly limits this, and keeps color from coming out; color has been locked in, and held fixed, static. . . . The cult of geometrically *balanced* color has been pushed so far that one gets the impression that all bets are off: *rien ne va plus*.''

Léger used abstractions in a totally different way. He used it from time to time in his easel painting, in works that he referred to as *Variations of Objects*
Ill. 187 (1930) or *Abstract Composition* (1932). The elements
Ill. 178 of these works resemble something, although it is not clear what. Most important, abstraction for Léger was liberating. It had to make color move instead of holding it captive and motionless. Absolute abstraction did not exist for Léger: Green will always be a tree. Blue will always be the sky. A red square and a yellow square is decorative art, advertising, and store windows.

All great artists realize that they must make public

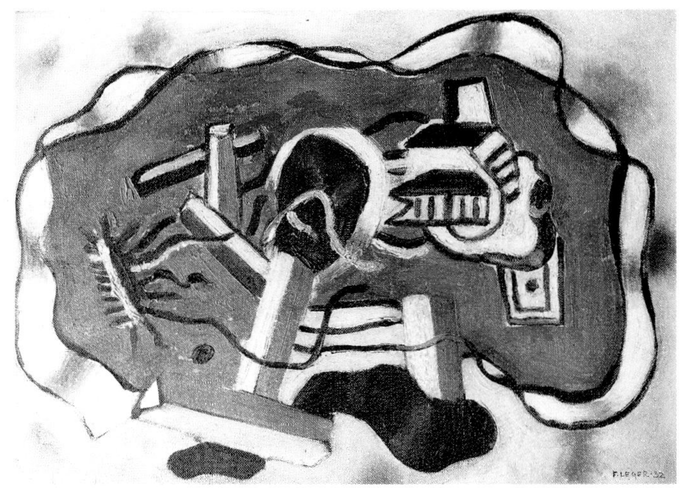

186. COMPOSITION
1932—Oil on canvas

185. VARIATION OF FORMS
1930—Pen sketch, 30.5 × 23 cm
Private collection

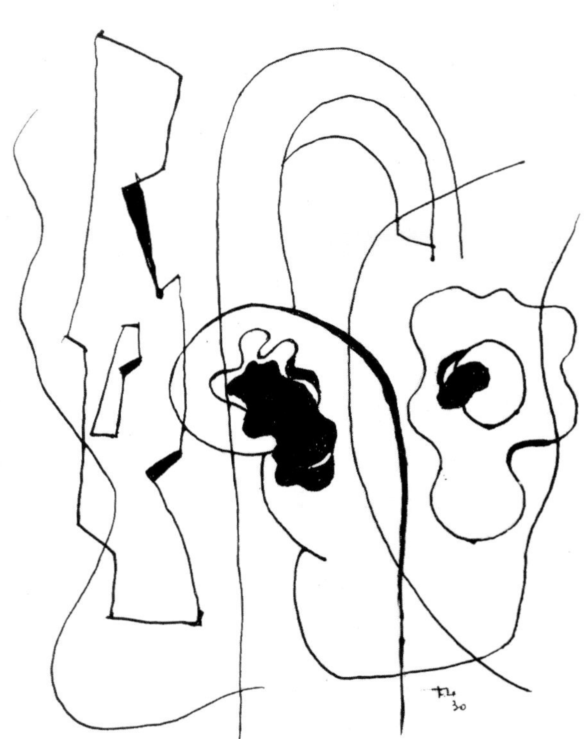

187. OBJECTS
1930—Oil on canvas, 46 × 38 cm
Private collection

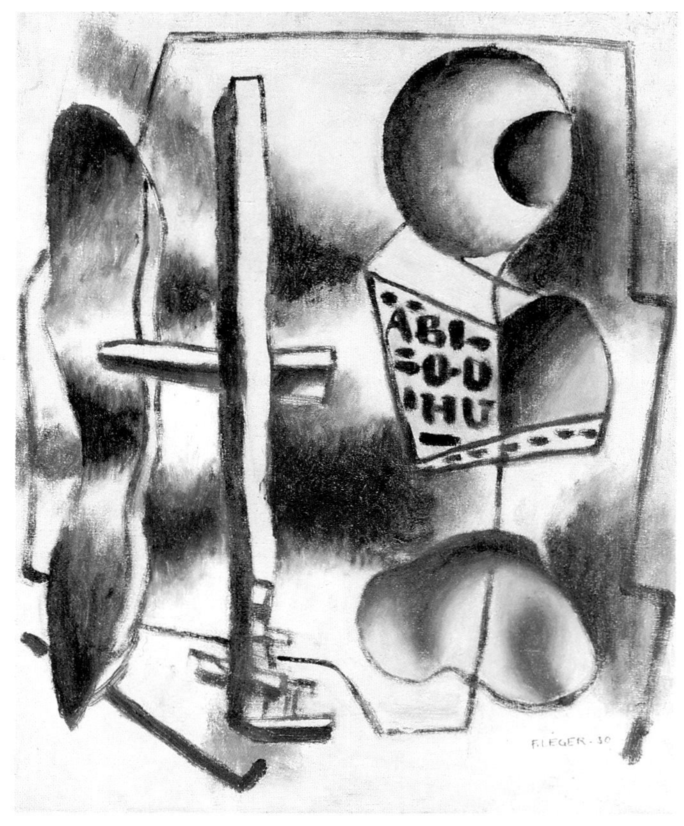

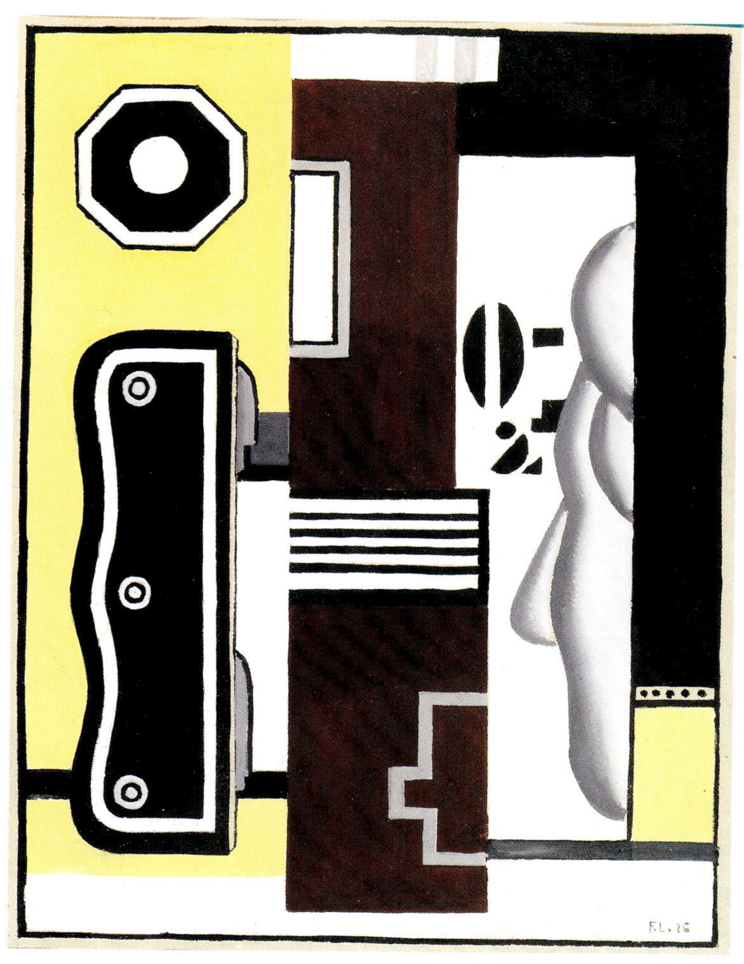

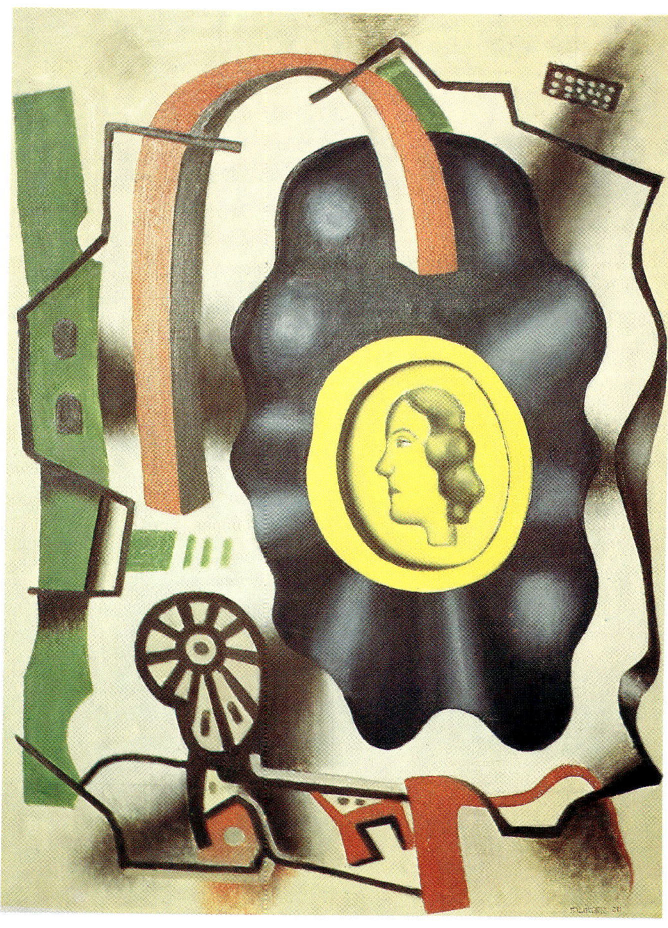

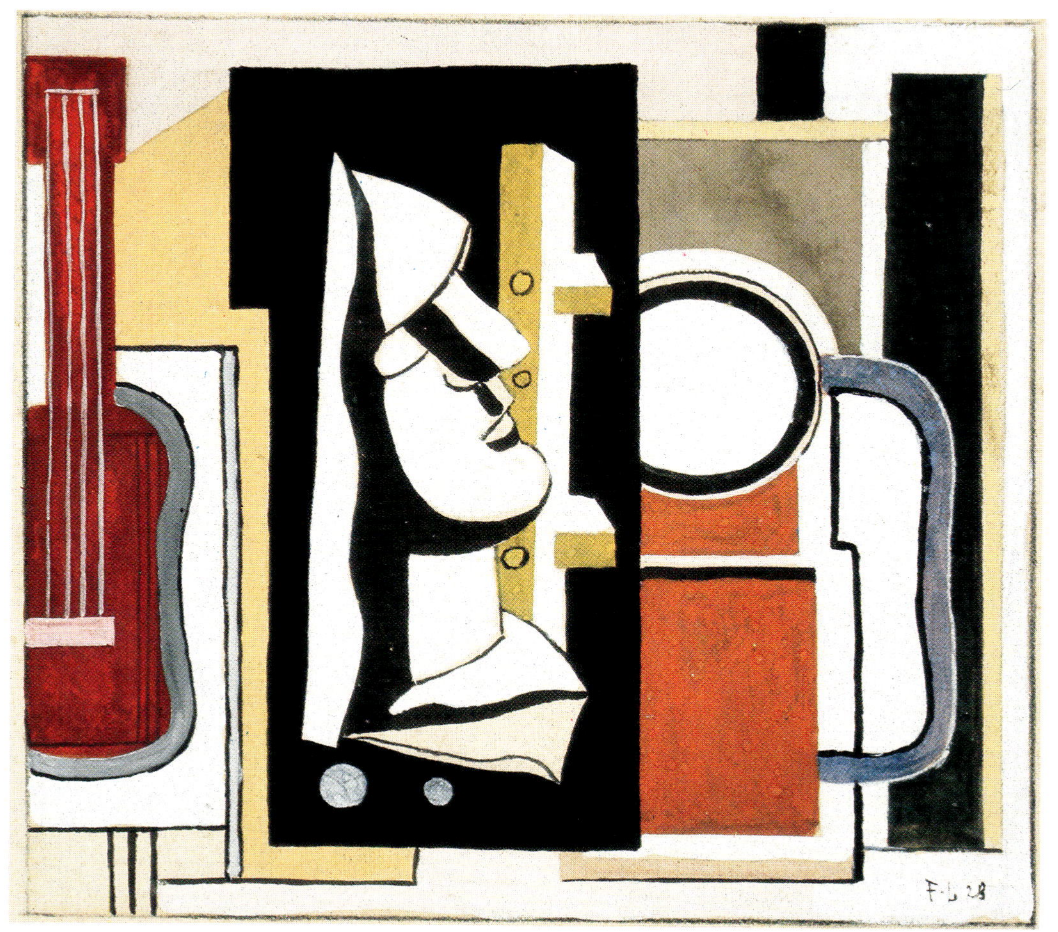

188. PROFILE
1926—Gouache and ink, 44 × 31 cm
Private collection

189. COMPOSITION WITH YELLOW CAMEO
1931—Oil on canvas, 92 × 65 cm
Louise Leiris Gallery, Paris

190. STILL LIFE WITH PLASTER MASK
1928—Gouache, 24.5 × 27 cm
Private collection

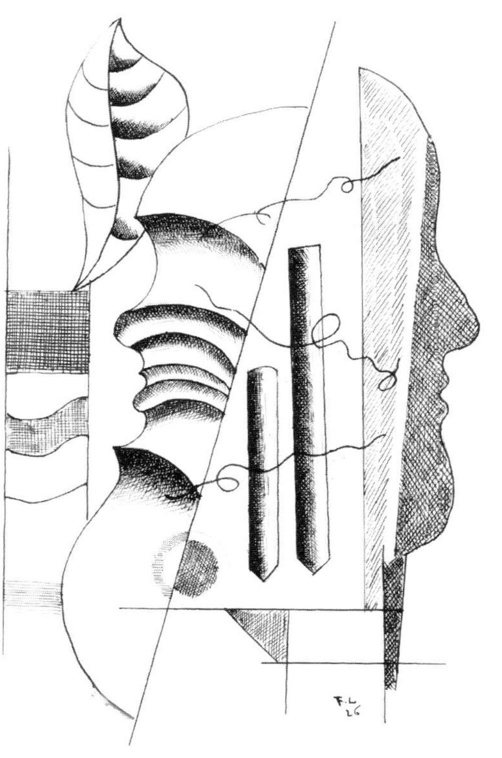

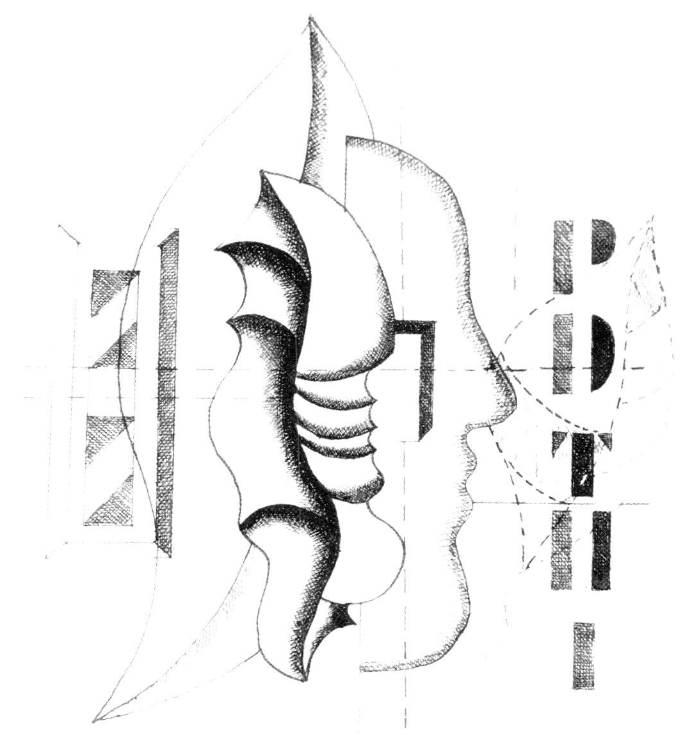

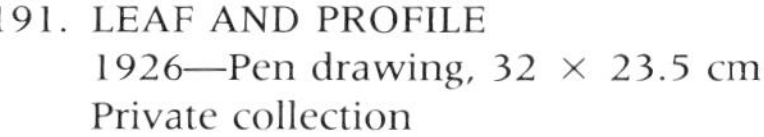

191. LEAF AND PROFILE
1926—Pen drawing, 32 × 23.5 cm
Private collection

192. SEASHELL AND PROFILE
1928—Pen drawing, 31 × 23.5 cm
Private collection

193. PROFILE, VASE, AND KEY
1927—Pen-drawing, 33 × 26.5 cm
Louise Leiris Gallery, Paris

appearances to promote their art. Salvador Dalí was the archetype of the artist-critics and journalists expected a verbal tirade from, and they avidly devoured all that he babbled about. In the end, what always surprised people most was Dalí's good sense and the real depth behind his outbursts. Léger, in his own rugged way, also "delivered" for the critics and press. He knew that Picasso owed a good deal of his public fame to publicity and the scandals that some of his paintings created. He also knew that Picasso had fun with this. In the 1981 catalogue for the exhibit at the Georges Pompidou Center, "Fernand Léger: The Poetry of the Object, 1928–1934," Christian Derouet elaborated on the "repartee" Léger offered to the press and the different poses he assumed for photographers: "He would clutch the easel, making sure that the canvas was upside down; he would ask his most beautiful models to pose nude in his studio; he would surround himself with charming and controlled middle-class ladies in order to highlight his own peasant and roguish side."

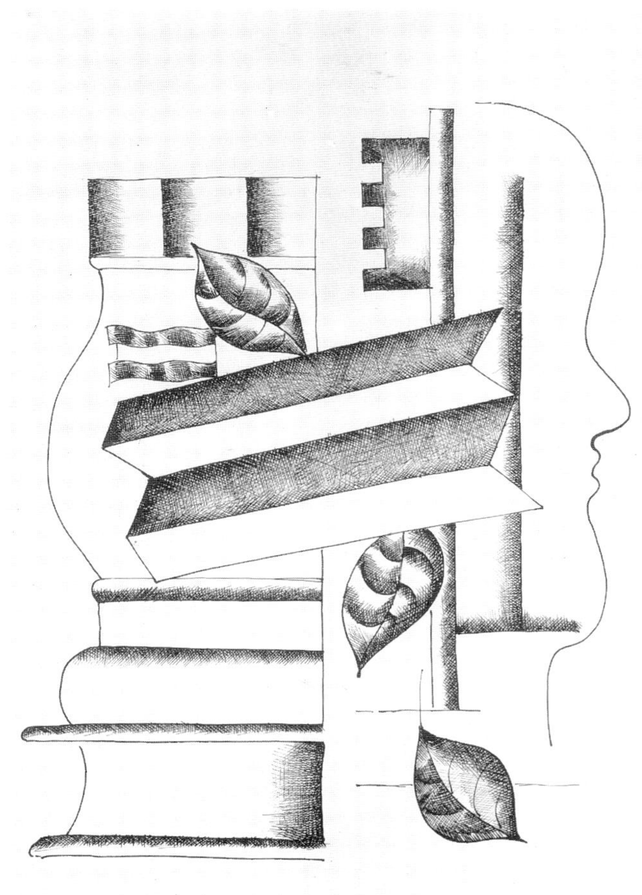

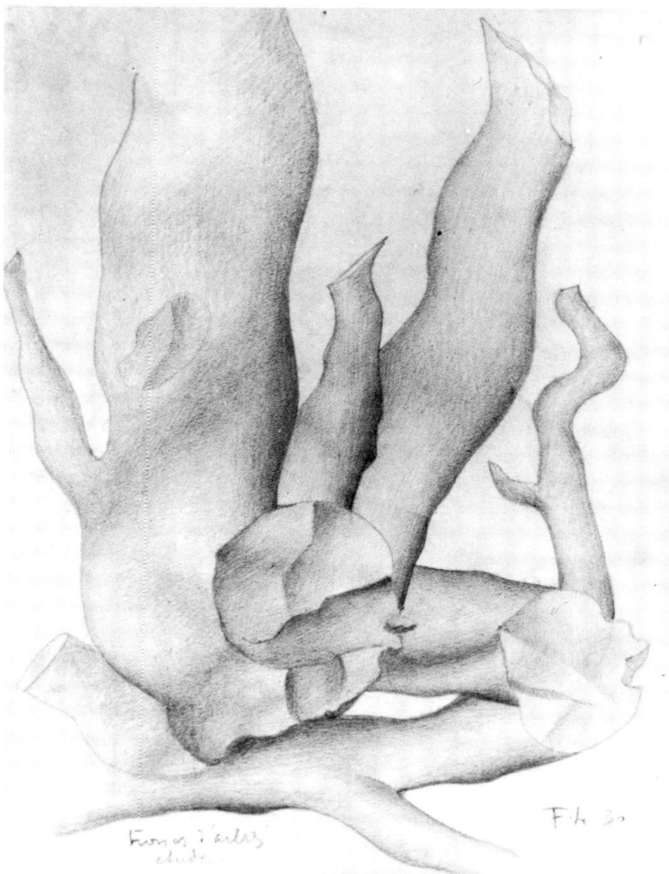

194. TREE TRUNK, STUDY
1930—Pencil on paper
Private collection

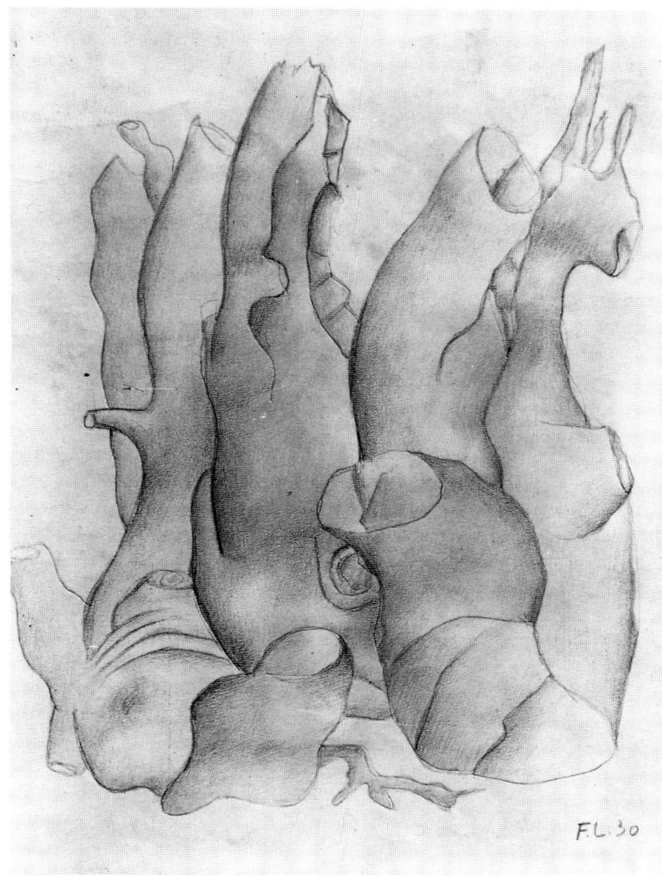

195. BRANCHES
1930—Pencil on paper, 29 × 21 cm
Louise Leiris Gallery, Paris

### The engineering student's dressing table

To annoy the critics who no longer knew how to classify him, Léger called his exhibit of gouaches and sketches at the Vignon Gallery (1933–34) "Objects."
Ill. 153 On the poster for the exhibit he included the follow-
Ill. 201 ing inventory: Roots, flint, rack of lamb, corkscrew,
to 207 vase, pair of pants, chunk of beef, cheese, nuts, etc. Needless to say, the critics could not make head nor tail of this, and wound up using explanations such as "half-figure, half-grape . . . it 'fluctuates' a bit"; the traits of "an 'admirable artisan' who takes the same intelligent and deliberate care with everything he represents . . . be it a pair of gloves, the roots of a pear tree, a fragment of the moon, or a piece of flint. . . . The name given to the exhibit constitutes a subtle provocation, in the manner of fervent advocates of pure intelligence or of engineering students at the Polytechnical School." To be described as a "polytechnician" by the *Beaux-Arts* review in 1934 must have been cause for Léger to rejoice, since he was self-taught!

Christian Derouet provides the following insight: "Léger wanted to have fun with his dealers, who were hoarding his works without being able to place them. . . . He organized an exhibit of sketches that had no relationship to his canvases; he emptied his pockets to outdo all those who had profited from reducing him to a mere mechanic, a specialist of rods and pistons; he was fed up with theories of form and color, so he threw his key ring, handkerchief, nut shells, flint stones, and corkscrews right under the noses of the critics. He used the occasion like the practical-minded Normandy peasant he was to make a salad of *found objects* and scatter them about everywhere. He used his impressive stature and corpulence to become a spokesman for all those well-informed persons in the arts who were fed up with the Surrealist, Neo-realist, and Abstractionist bugaboos." In short, Léger used this exhibit to air all his gripes. The show, with all its strange sketches, ran as a countercurrent, and let it be known that Léger situated himself "elsewhere." This meant that he was removed from conformist Realism, from the petty games of Surrealism, and from the extremists of Abstraction like Mondrian or

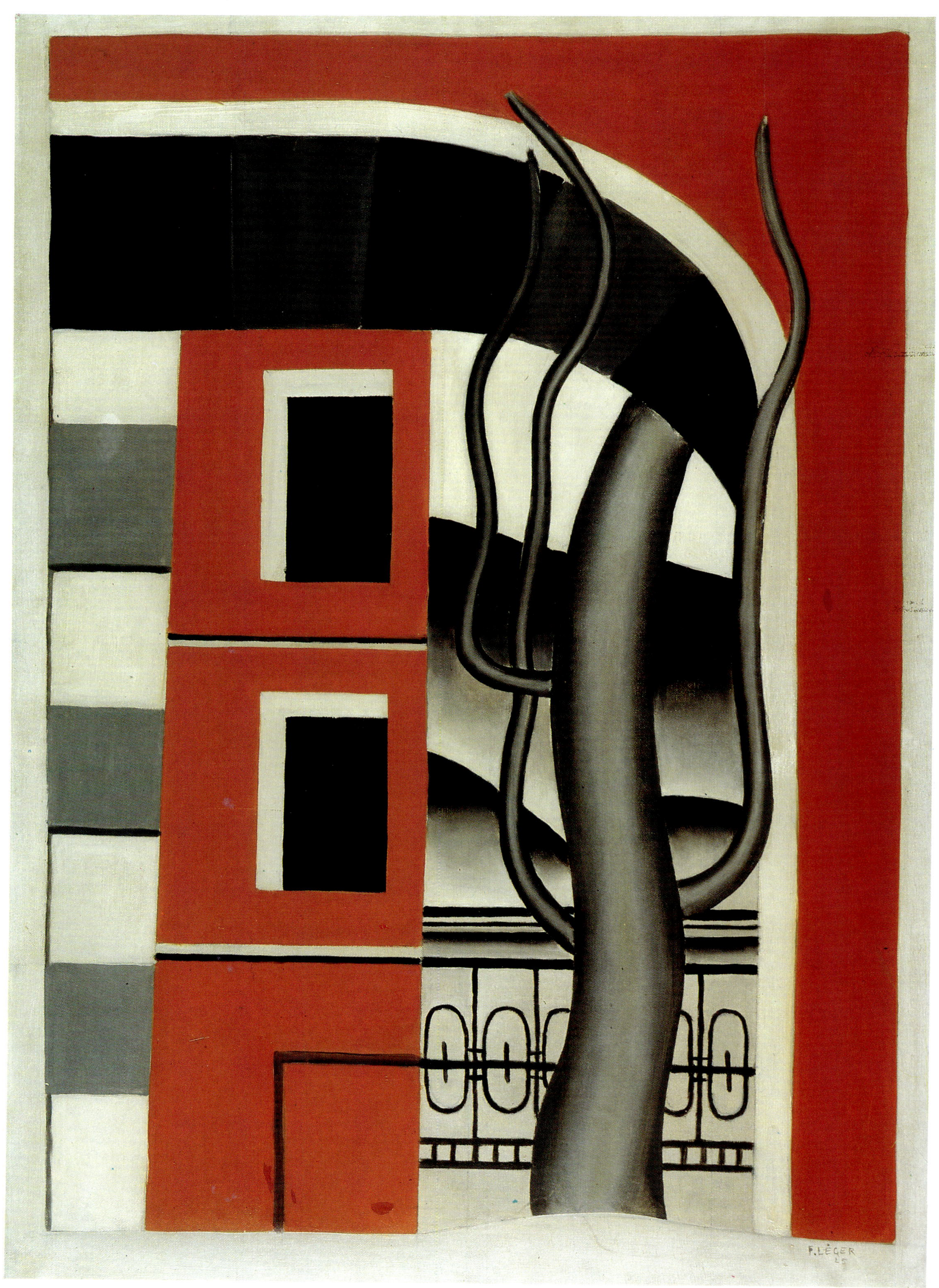


196. LANDSCAPE
1925—Oil on canvas, 92 × 65 cm
Louis Carré Gallery, Paris

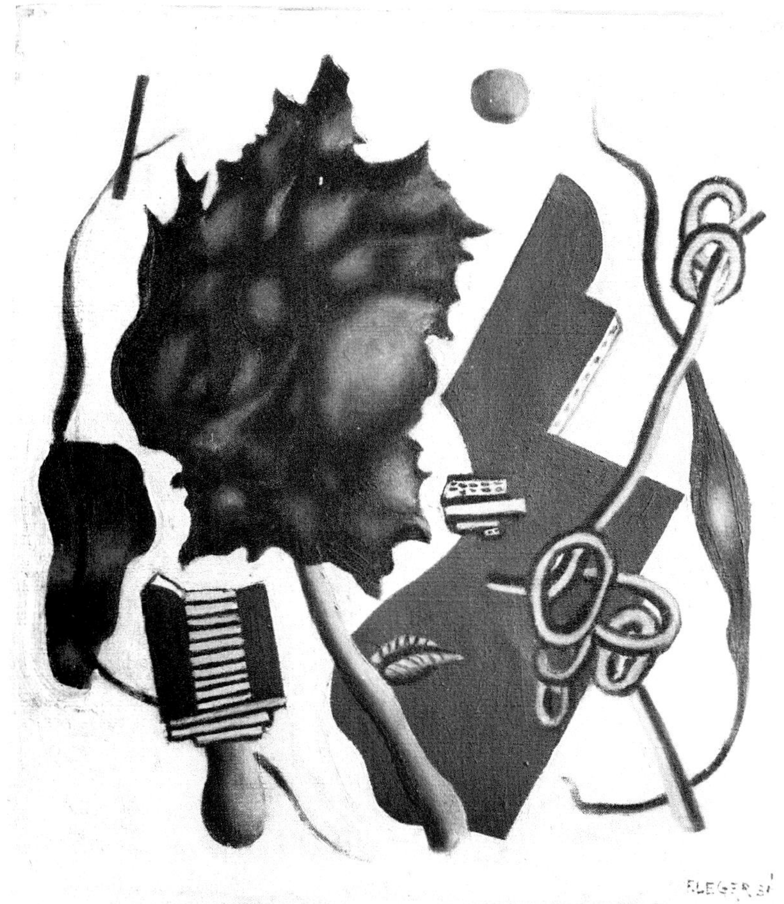


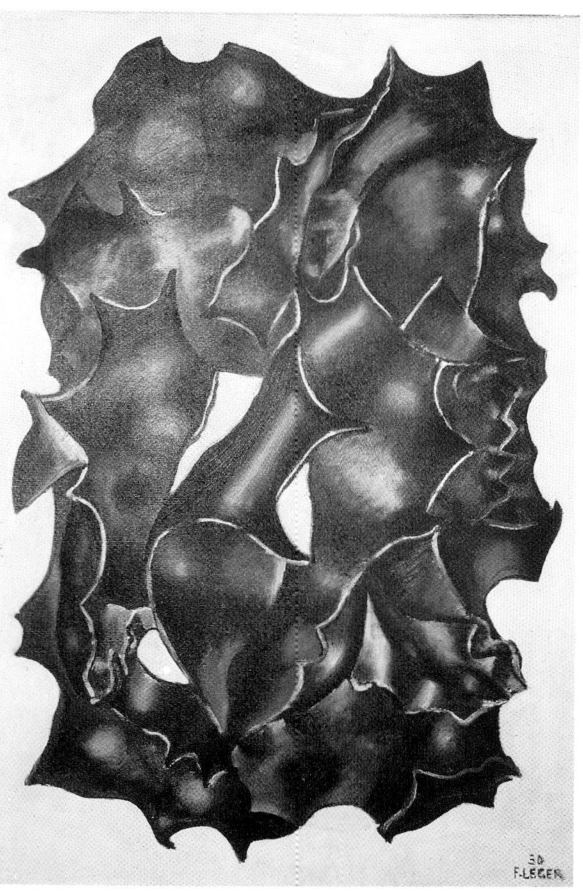


197. COMPOSITION WITH LEAF
1931—Oil on canvas
Private collection

198. HOLLY LEAF
1930—Oil on canvas, 92 × 60 cm
Private collection

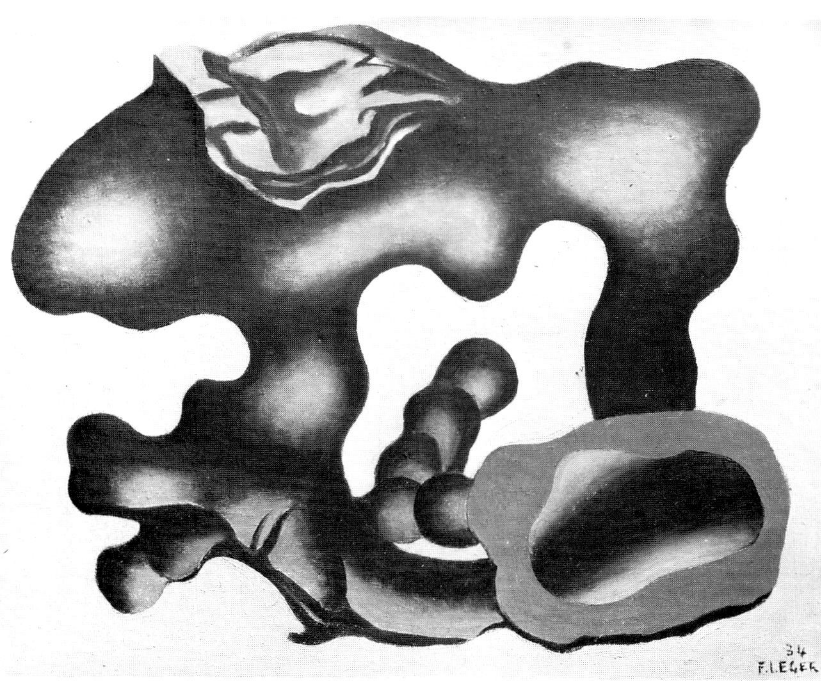


199. ROOT
1934—Oil on canvas, 54 × 65 cm
Louise Leiris Gallery, Paris

Herbin whose efforts he appreciated but whose limits he acknowledged.
Maurice Jardot, who knew Léger well through Kahnweiler at the Louise Leiris Gallery, also thought that this exhibit of objects was Léger's way of settling some accounts once and for all. "Contrary to the general tendency to downplay the importance of the object, current trends in thought were elevating the object to its rightful place, thanks to Freud and Marx. The purists of the "Esprit Nouveau" appreciated Léger's randomly found objects, but invited him to direct his attention to elitist themes in his selection of natural and mechanical objects! Léger seemed to be calling for more simplicity and sincerity."
In Berlin, Lissitzky and Ilya Ehrenburg published a review called "*OBJECT*" in three langauges (Russian, German, and French). In *Cahiers d'Art* ("Art Notebooks"), Christian Zervos dedicated a long study in four parts to what he titled "The Importance of the Object in Today's Painting" ("L'Importance de l'objet dans la peinture d'aujourd'hui"). Léger was the subject of the fourth part. Finally, from 1931 to 1936, four exhibits in four different Parisian galleries showed objects by Arp, Breton, Eluard, Ernst, Giacometti, Miró, Paalen, Tanguy, and others. The majority of these objects were paltry, makeshift things put together by poets, Surrealists, and Dadaists.

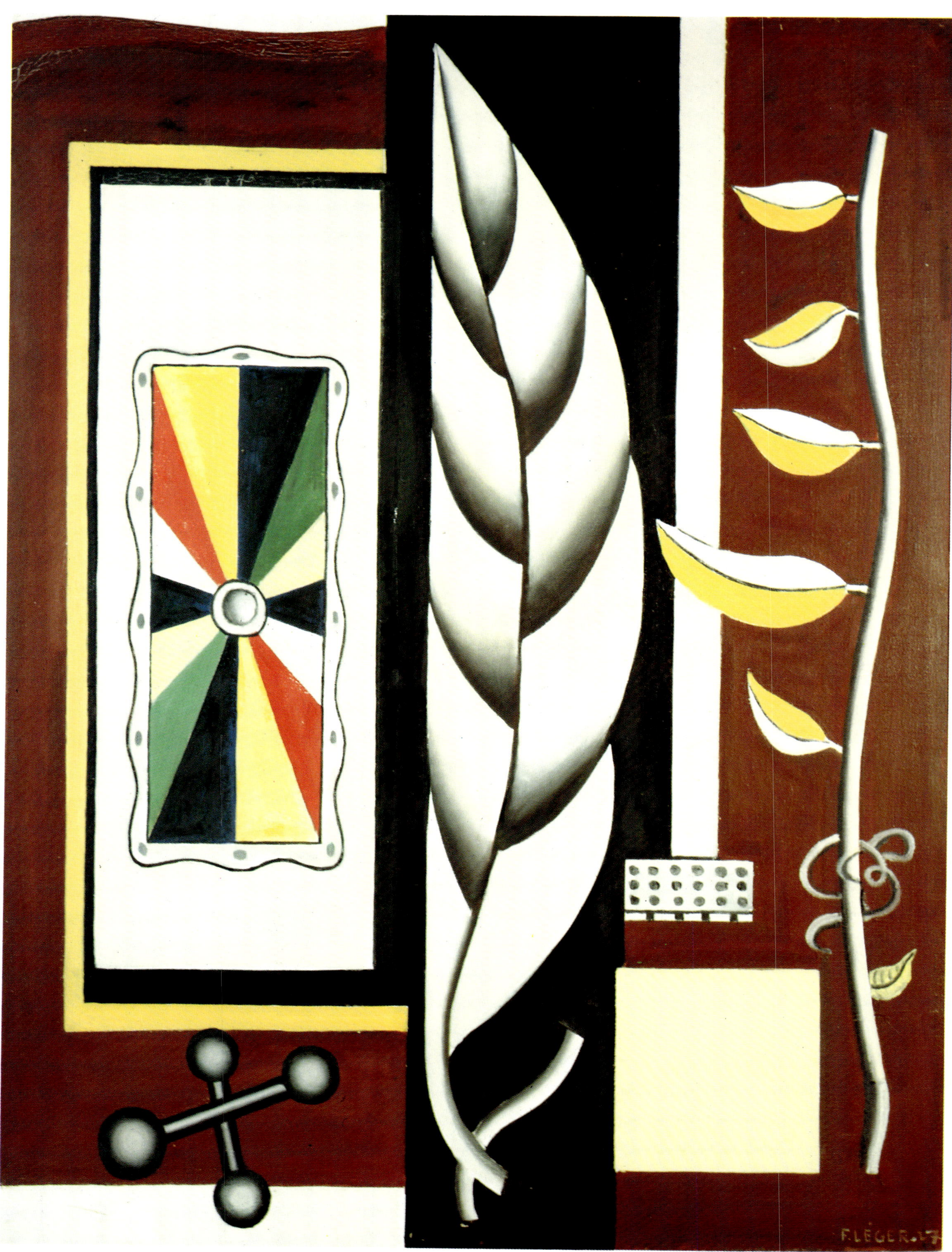


200. COMPOSITION WITH LEAF
1927—Oil on canvas, 130 × 97 cm
Musée National Fernand Léger, Biot

8

## Sketches in the manner of Dürer

Léger made the defense of "his" object, which was under attack from all fronts, the basis of an esthetic and almost a moral war. Léger's object is "interior, taught, deep-down, tight." It must reflect the plastic flair, the dry aspect, the perfect "polish" that gives the work its beauty and dignity. In a letter he wrote: "twenty-five sketches in five days, sketches with very fine detail 'in the manner of Dürer,' tightly drawn—splendid, even wicked—they are wicked."

Léger, who so loved color, wound up loving grayness thanks to his sketches: "subtle tones . . . what power in the absence of color; the stiffness of an old pair of pants with an enormous, gnarled gray hand—the pebbles—the tree trunks—I find them with no seductive value—it's beautiful or it's nothing—color disgusts me—it's too easy." This is quite surprising coming from Léger, but the poet's eye is ever present: in a train, "boredom makes me a keen observer of a small clump of chiffon caught on a large, polished, copper nail. Because this piece of chiffon is ruffled by a draft of air, its movement becomes an infernal dance . . . there are moments when it is like an insect caught by its foot who is struggling to free itself. At other moments the chiffon is caught in a different kind of air current that stretches it out flat, and then it all starts over again, the elegant seduction, feminine gracefulness caught on a nail—it implores and starts up again in a fury." The works that were exhibited in the "Objects" show were deliberately free of all industrial manufacture. They were "documents" that Leger would one day incorporate into his compositions. Maurice Jardot wrote: "These works have a way of positioning themselves within the limits of what is possible, and this confers on them a certain raw sense of nobility: the figurative object, trivial by nature, is always solitary, isolated in space." It was a world of silence and peace, of poetry and sweetness. It was Léger without any frills, in a raw and refined state, in a state of suspension before a large "composition" pinned him down and obliged him to take "definitive" action.

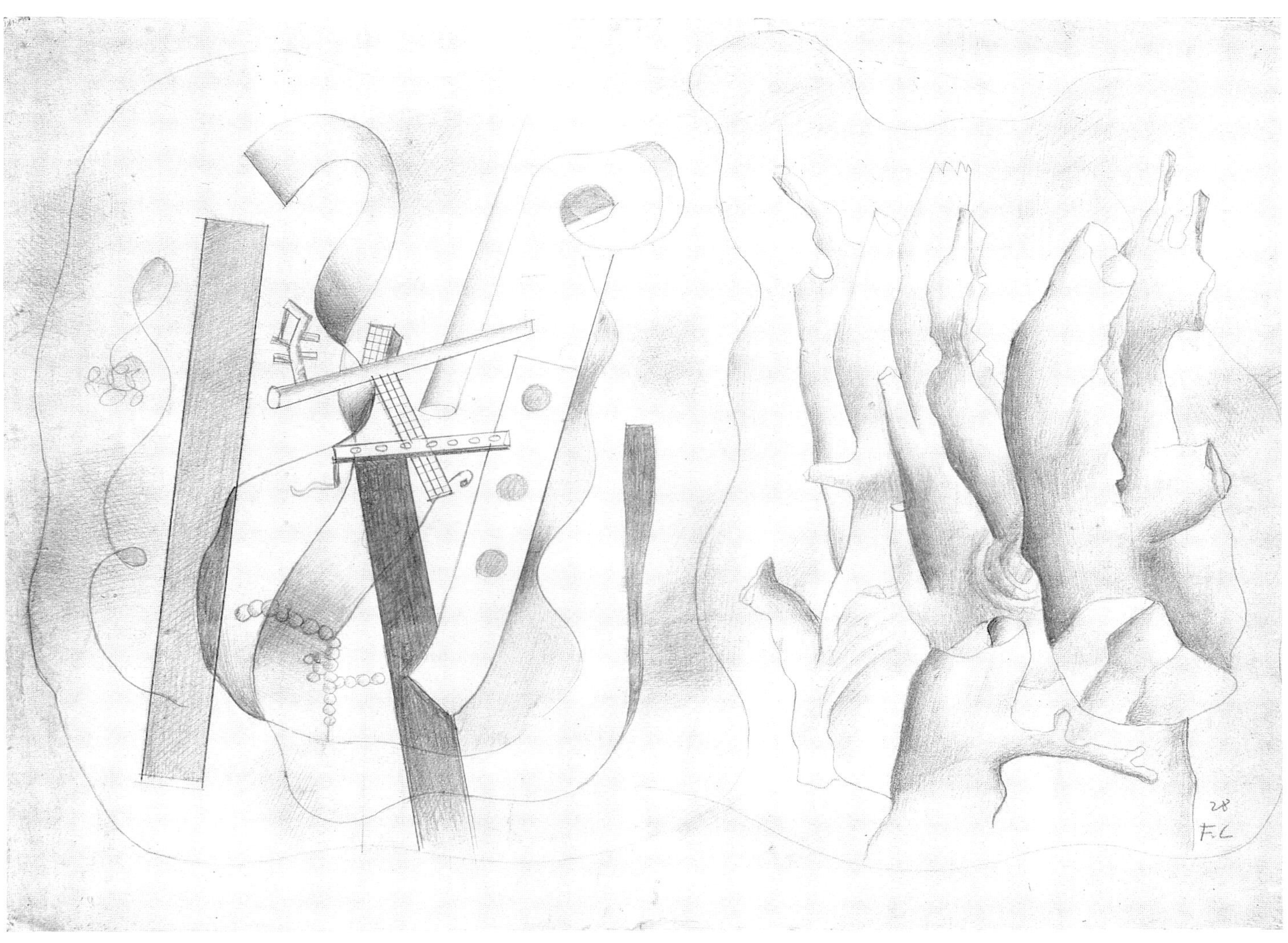


201. COMPOSITION WITH ROOT
1928—Pencil on paper, 37.5 × 52 cm
Louise Leiris Gallery, Paris

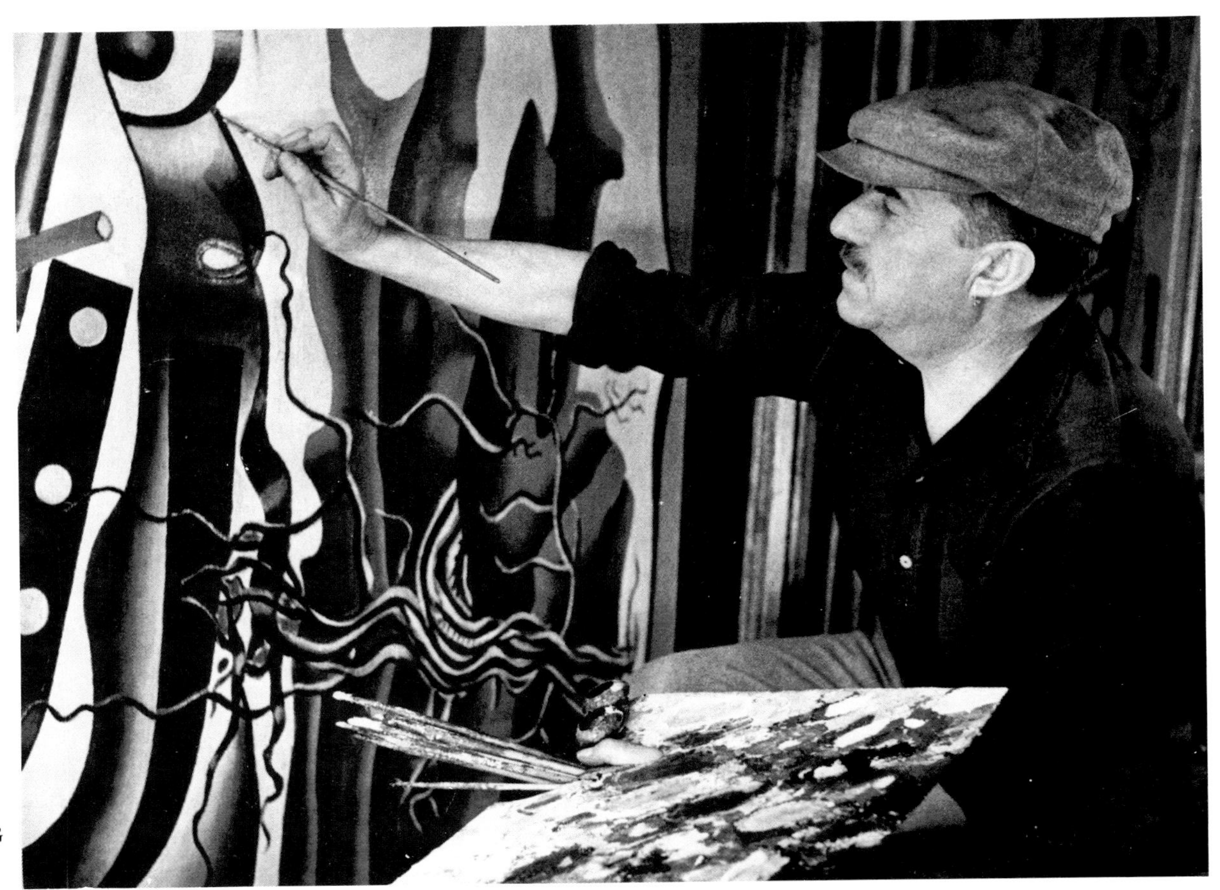

202. FERNAND LÉGER PAINTING
About 1930
Photo by Limot

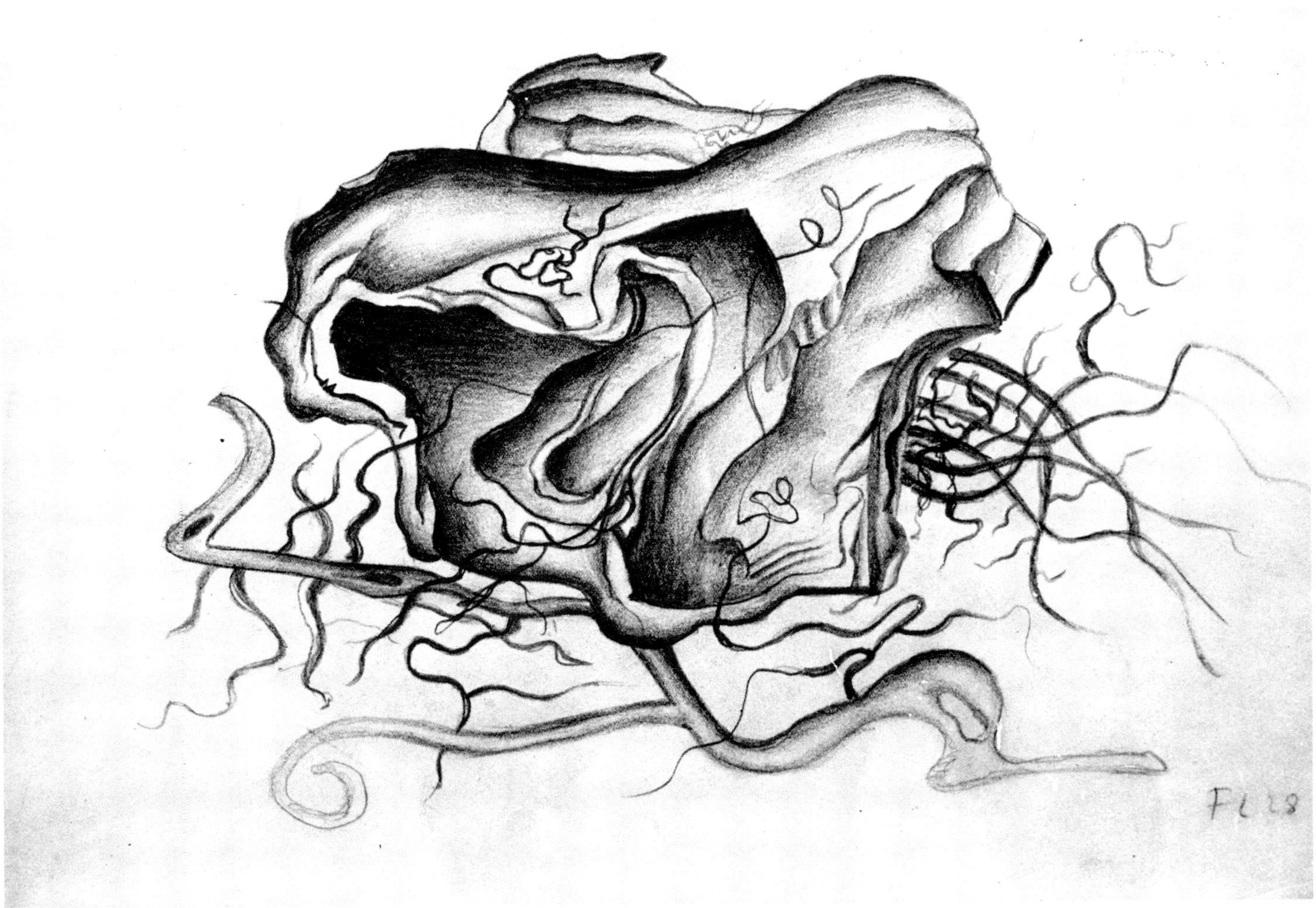

203. ROOT
1928—Pencil drawing, 26 × 37 cm
Louise Leiris Gallery, Paris

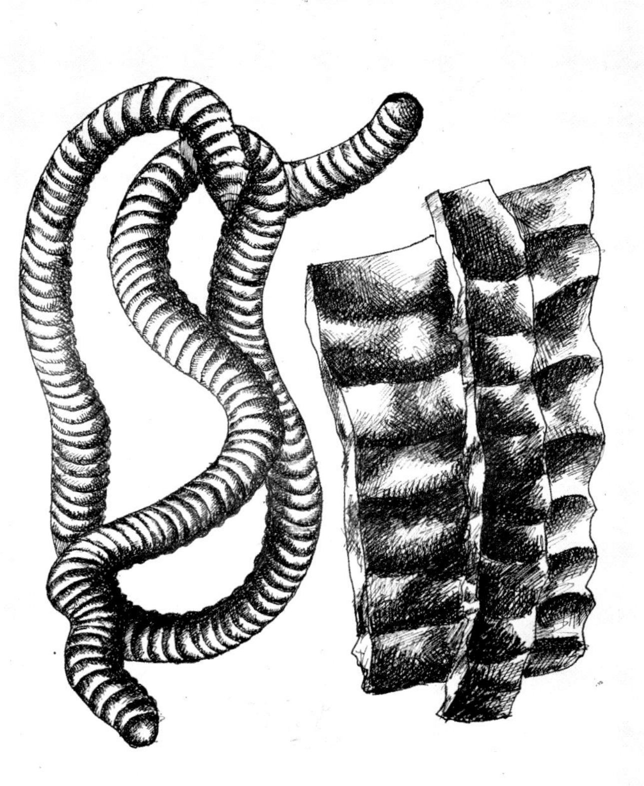

204. ROPE AND HAUNCH OF BEEF
1933—China ink on paper, 37.3 × 31.5 cm
Musée National d'Art Moderne, Centre Georges Pompidou, Paris

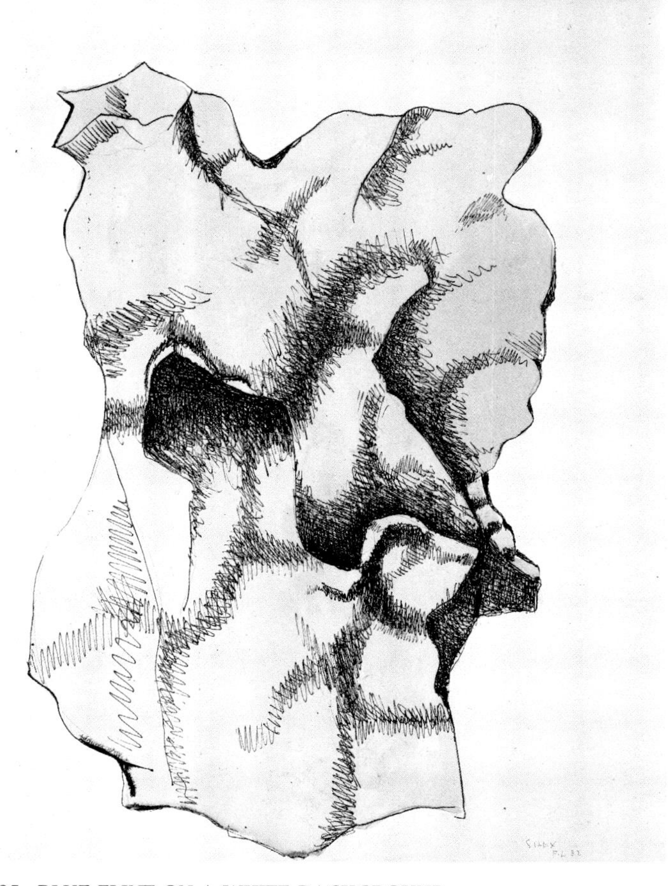

205. BLUE FLINT ON A WHITE BACKGROUND
1932—Gouache and ink, 62 × 48 cm
Louise Leiris Gallery, Paris

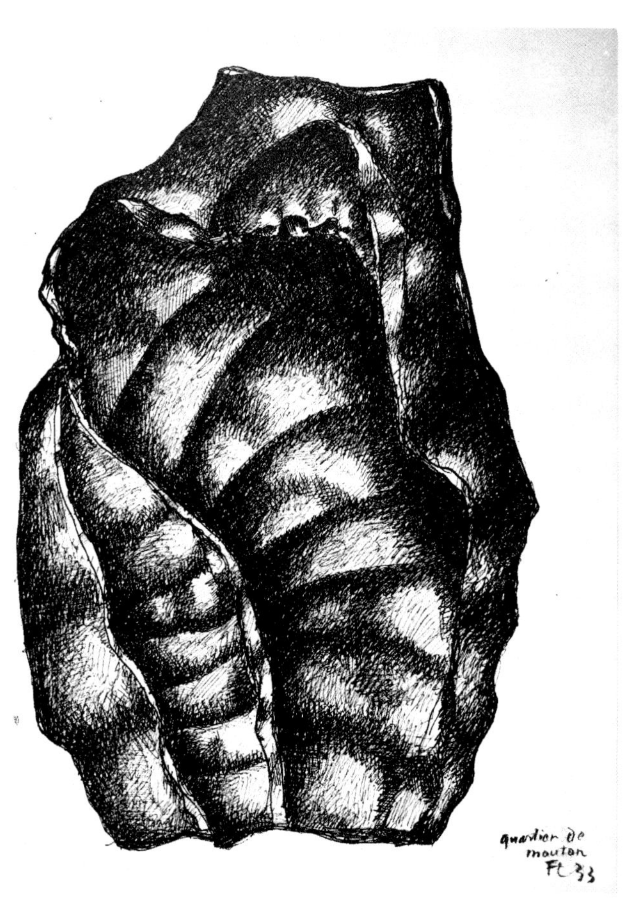


206. RACK OF LAMB
1933—Ink drawing, 40 × 30.5 cm
Musée National d'Art Moderne, Centre Georges Pompidou, Paris

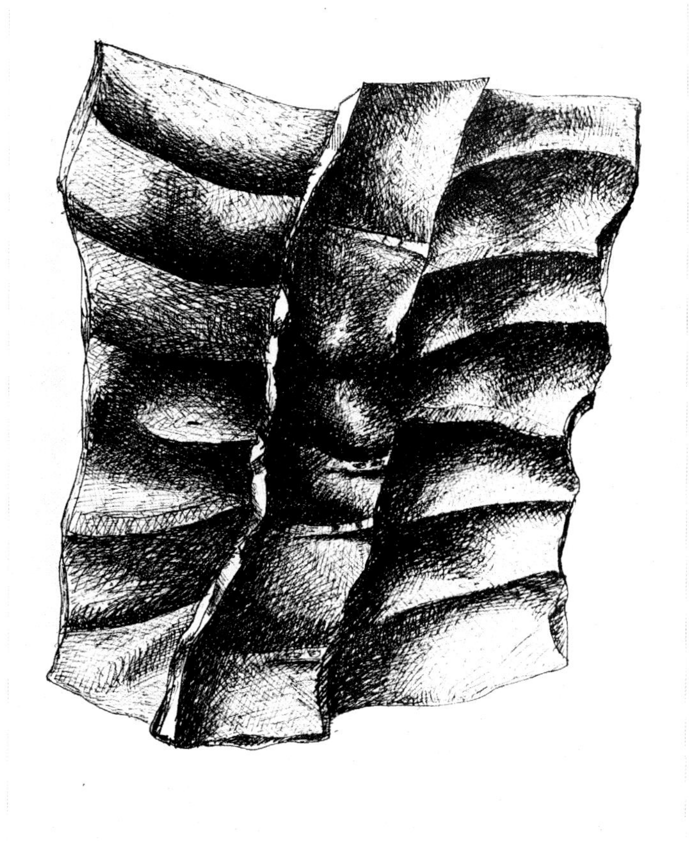

207. HAUNCH OF BEEF
1933—Ink drawing, 36.5 × 30 cm
Private collection

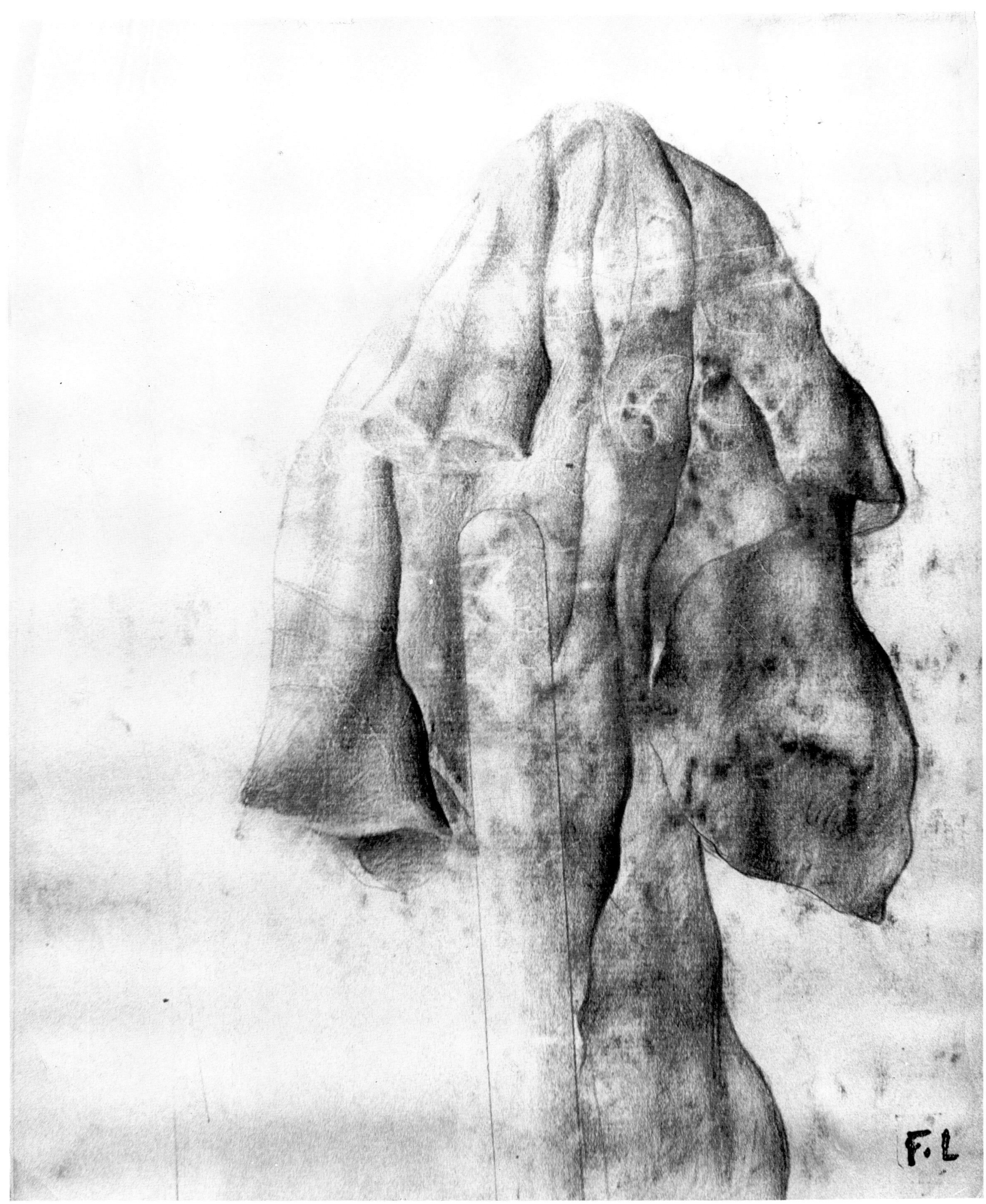


208. STUDY FOR DRAPERY
1930—Graphite on Ingres paper, 27 × 21 cm
Musée National d'Art Moderne, Centre Georges Pompidou, Paris
Gift of Claude Bernard

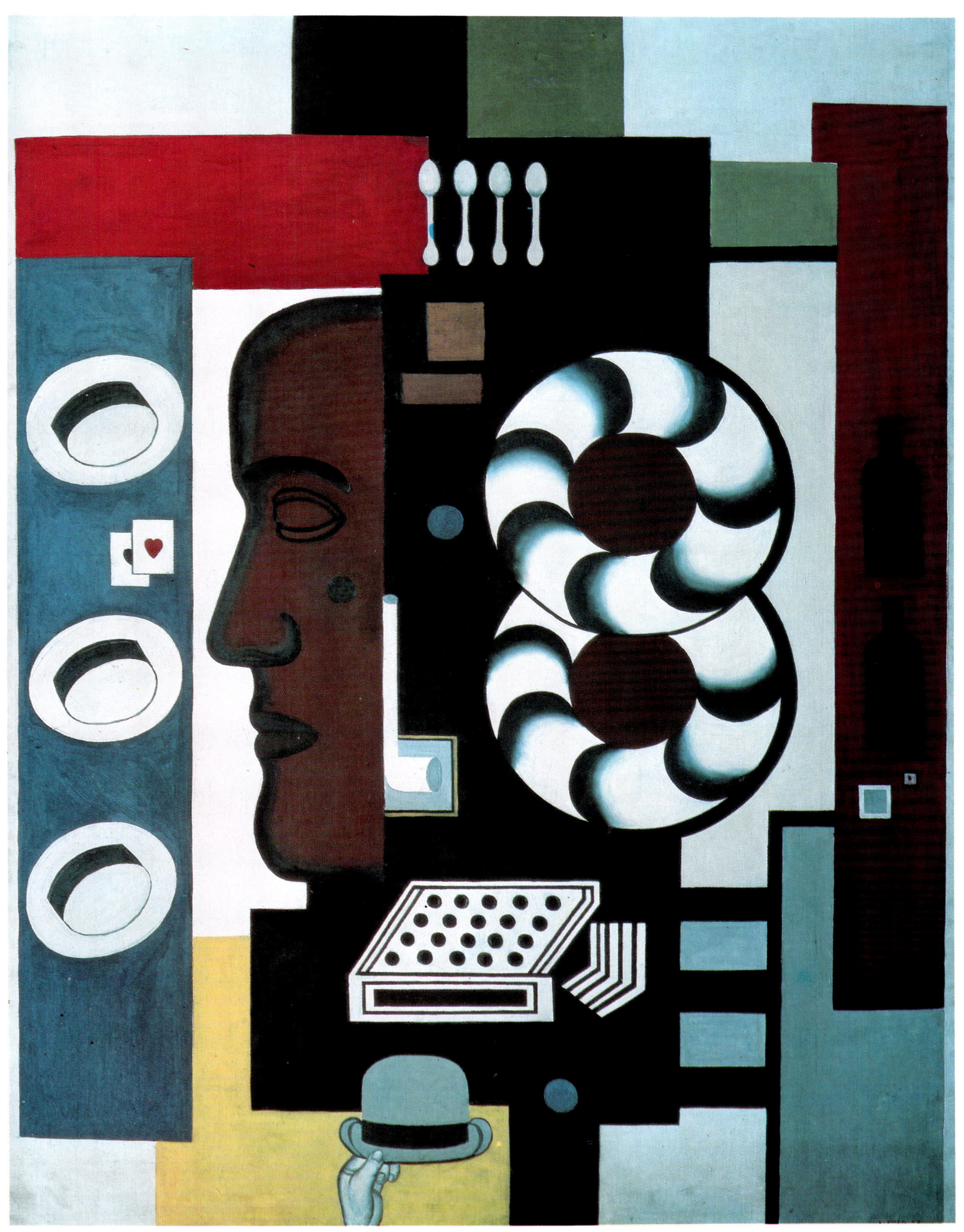

209. COMPOSITION WITH FOUR HATS
1927—Oil on canvas, 248 × 185 cm
Musée National d'Art Moderne, Centre Georges Pompidou, Paris

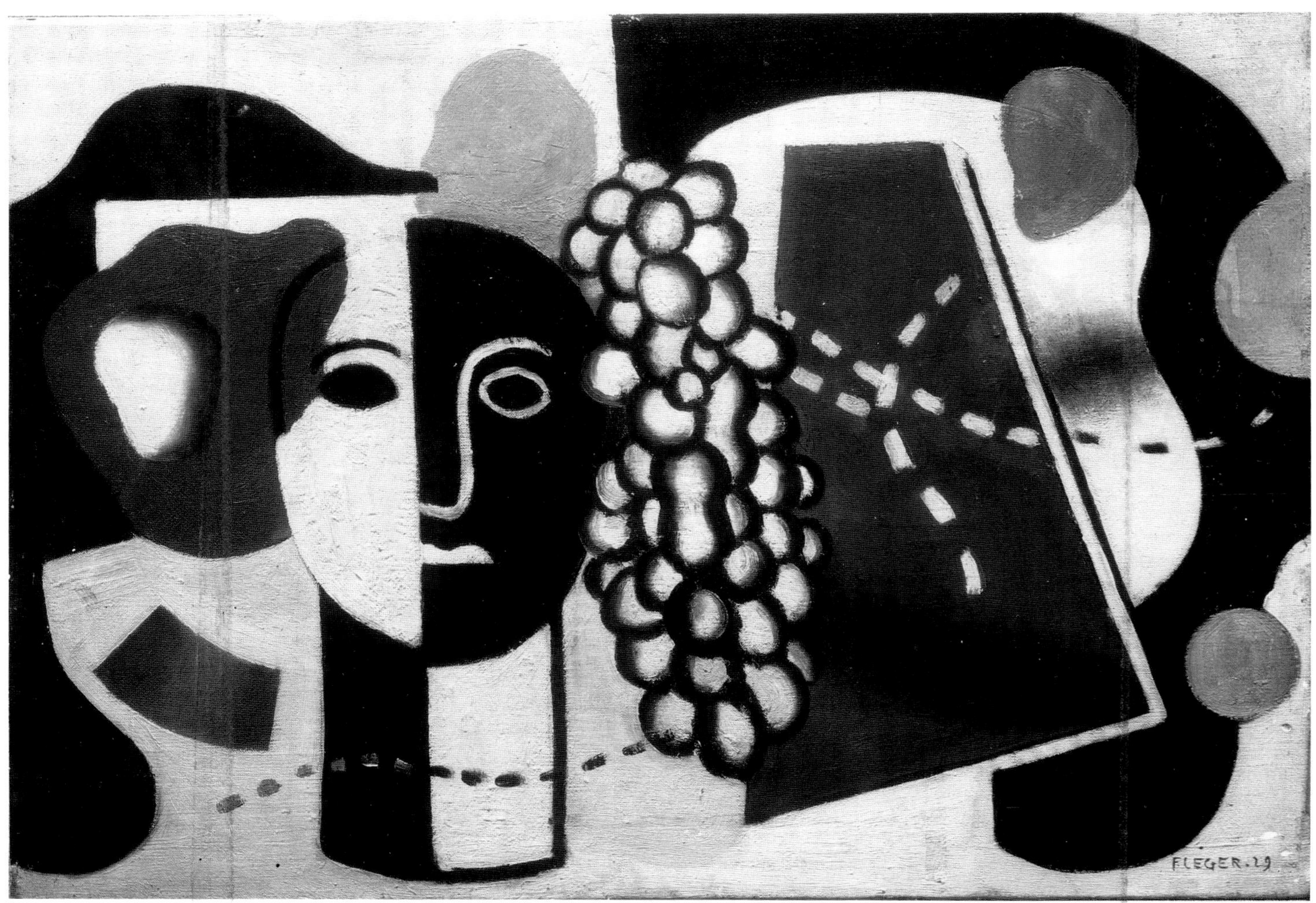


210. CLUSTER OF GRAPES
1929—Oil on canvas, 46 × 65 cm
Musée National d'Art Moderne, Centre Georges Pompidou, Paris
Gift of Louise and Michel Leiris

## A loving encyclopedia of objects

Pl. 222 *Mona Lisa with Keys* ("La Joconde aux clés"), *Dancers*
Pl. 227 *with Keys* ("Danseuses aux clés"), and *Composition*
Pl. 217 *with Umbrella* ("Composition au parapluie") were
Pl. 228 Léger's major works of this period. They had great impact: "I am for an art that smokes like a cigarette, that smells like a pair of shoes. . . . I am for an art that is put on and taken off like a pair of pants, that gets holes in it like a pair of socks, that is eaten like a piece of cake, or disdainfully abandoned like debris. . . . I am for the art of teddy bears, guns, beheaded rabbits, and popping umbrellas. . . . I am for an art that's inspected by the American government . . . ready-cooked art, thoroughly cleaned art . . . more edible art, ham-art, chicken-art, tomato-art, banana-art, apple-art, turkey-art." This is *not* Léger speaking, but his descendant, Claes Oldenburg, one of the bastions of American Pop Art, who envisioned "a loving encyclopedia of objects": sinks, electric plugs, ties, shoes, and even price tags . . . Campbell's Soup cans by Andy Warhol, pinups by Roy Lichtenstein, breasts and giant lips by Tom Wesselman, immense buttered slices of bread or titanic pickles by James Rosenquist, containers of French fries or soft toilets by Claes Oldenburg are all the offspring of *Mona Lisa with Keys*. Aragon wrote of Léger: "There's more wonder in a coffee grinder than in all the angels in heaven."

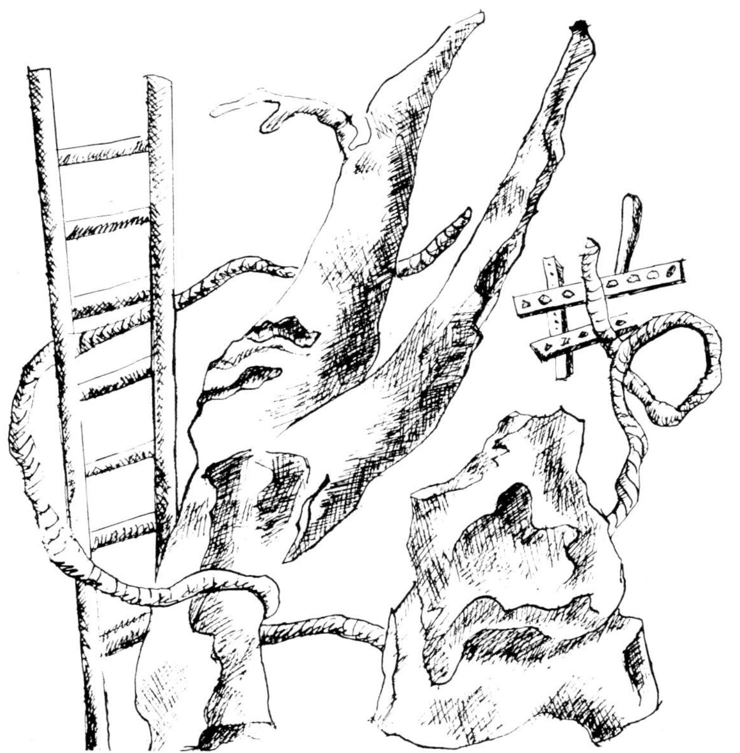

211. COMPOSITION WITH LADDER
1931—Ink drawing, 31.5 × 25 cm
Private collection

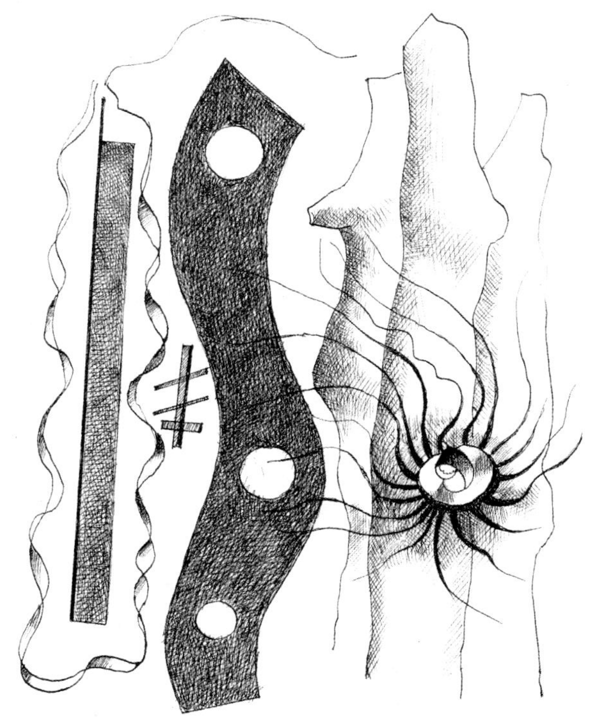

212. COMPOSITION WITH TREE TRUNK
1932—China ink drawing, 41.5 × 31.5 cm
Private collection

**What difference is there between the Mona Lisa and a bottle of Coca-Cola?**

Were the Pop Artists Léger's children? No doubt they were, but via advertising and publicity, and in a purely American context. Warhol earned his living in the early days doing posters for I. Miller Shoes and dressing windows for department stores like Bonwit Teller in New York. Rosenquist painted giant outdoor advertisements, which he would later incorporate into his paintings. Advertising imagery, the ravenous appetites of consumer society, the childishness of cartoons, the refusal to become an adult, and the passion for hygienic nudes wrapped in cellophane was what the major "stars" of Pop Art had in common. "Made in Europe" gave way to "Made in the USA," but the Pop credo, like Léger's, implied that any kind of object was virtually a work of art. (Warhol suggested exhibiting bank notes instead of canvases, so that everyone would know the price of the artwork.) From this point of view there is no difference at all between the Mona Lisa and a bottle of Coca-Cola. Were these painters the purveyors of modern life that Léger was waiting for?

The Americans had their European counterparts: Gnoli, an Italian, and Stämpfli, who was Swiss, also used the cinematic technique of close-up, the "part of the whole," which Pop Art made its principal mode of expression after advertising and after Léger. Gnoli, who died of cancer at the age of thirty-seven, only had time to leave us some exceptional enlargements of buttonholes, neckties, hems, ladies' pumps, and curls of hair—which would have delighted the Léger of bicycles and keys.

Stämpfli went from a wide-angle technique to close-up, as if zooming in on the details: an automobile in its entirety to a fender, then a wheel, then a tire, and finally the tread of a tire. The tire ended up resembling a mountain, and the tread of it took on characteristics of infinity. This reminds us of Léger, who worked in the same way with a tree, and in the techniques he used when making *Le Ballet Mécanique.* Stämpfli also directed films, one of which was as interminable as a Warhol film. The only subject was yellow or white bands that materialized from traffic on a highway.

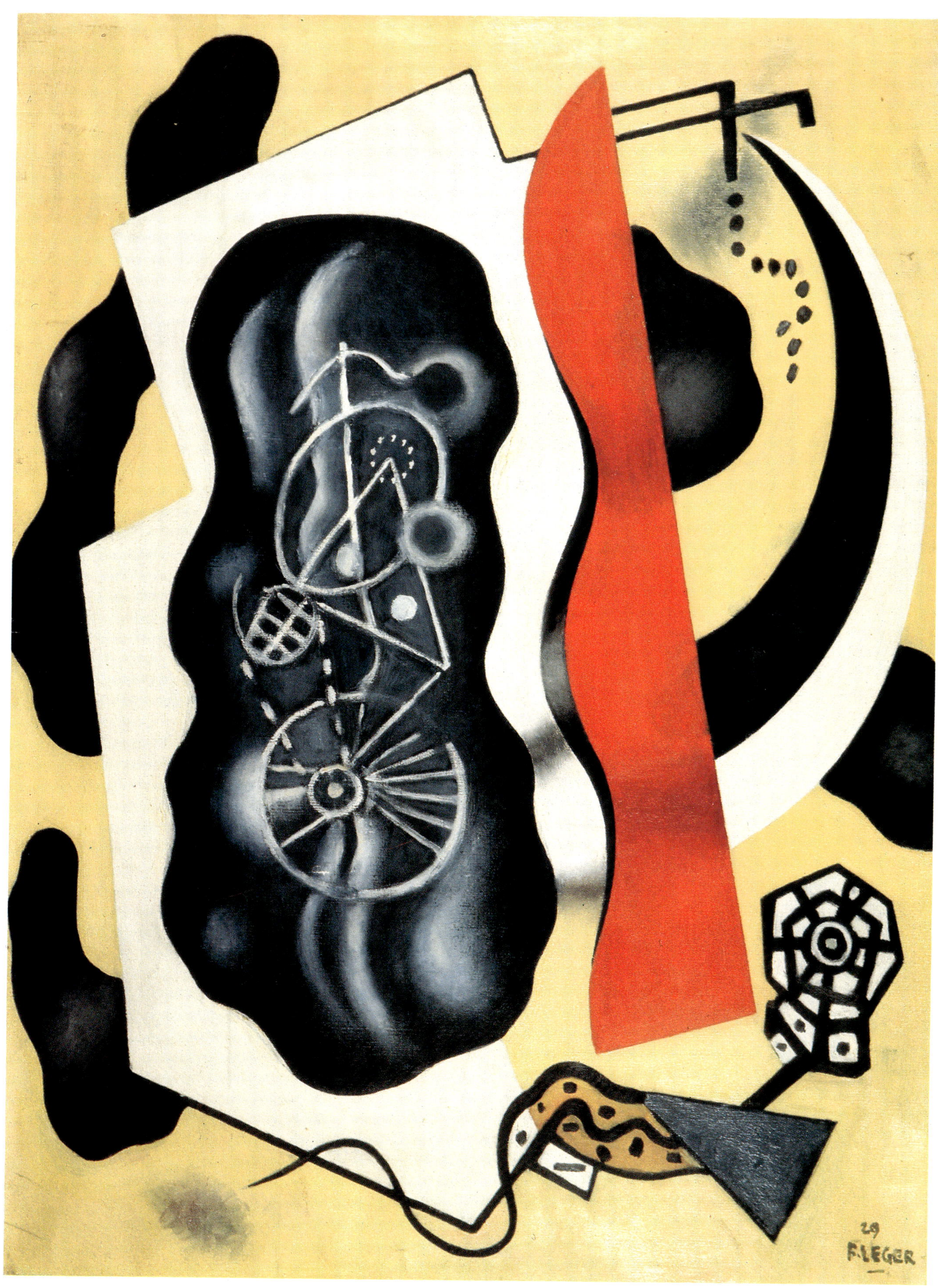


213. BICYCLE ON A BLUE BACKGROUND
1929—Oil on canvas, 92 × 65 cm
Private collection

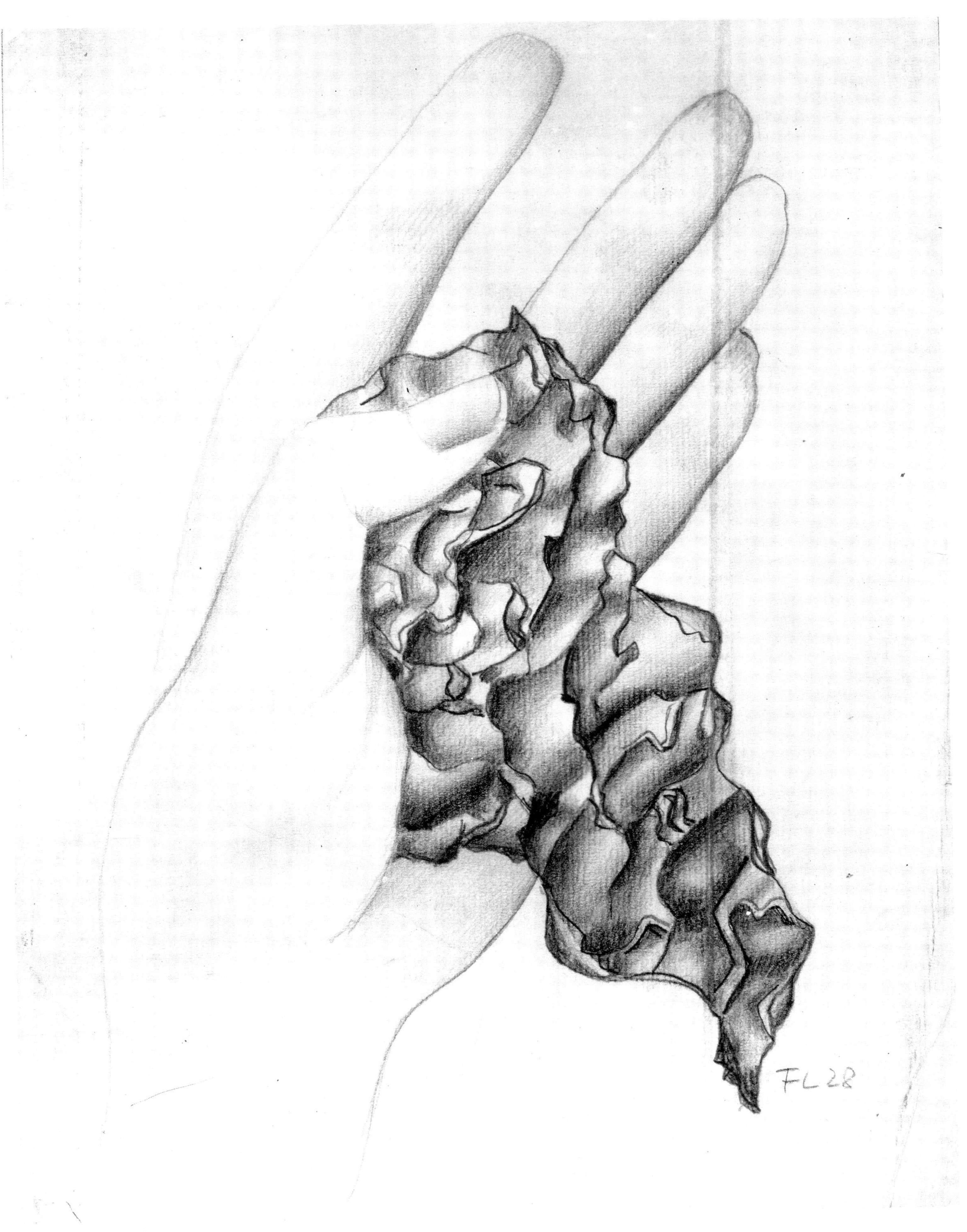


214. HAND AND PAPER
1928—Pencil on paper, 31.8 × 24.4 cm
Louise Leiris Gallery, Paris

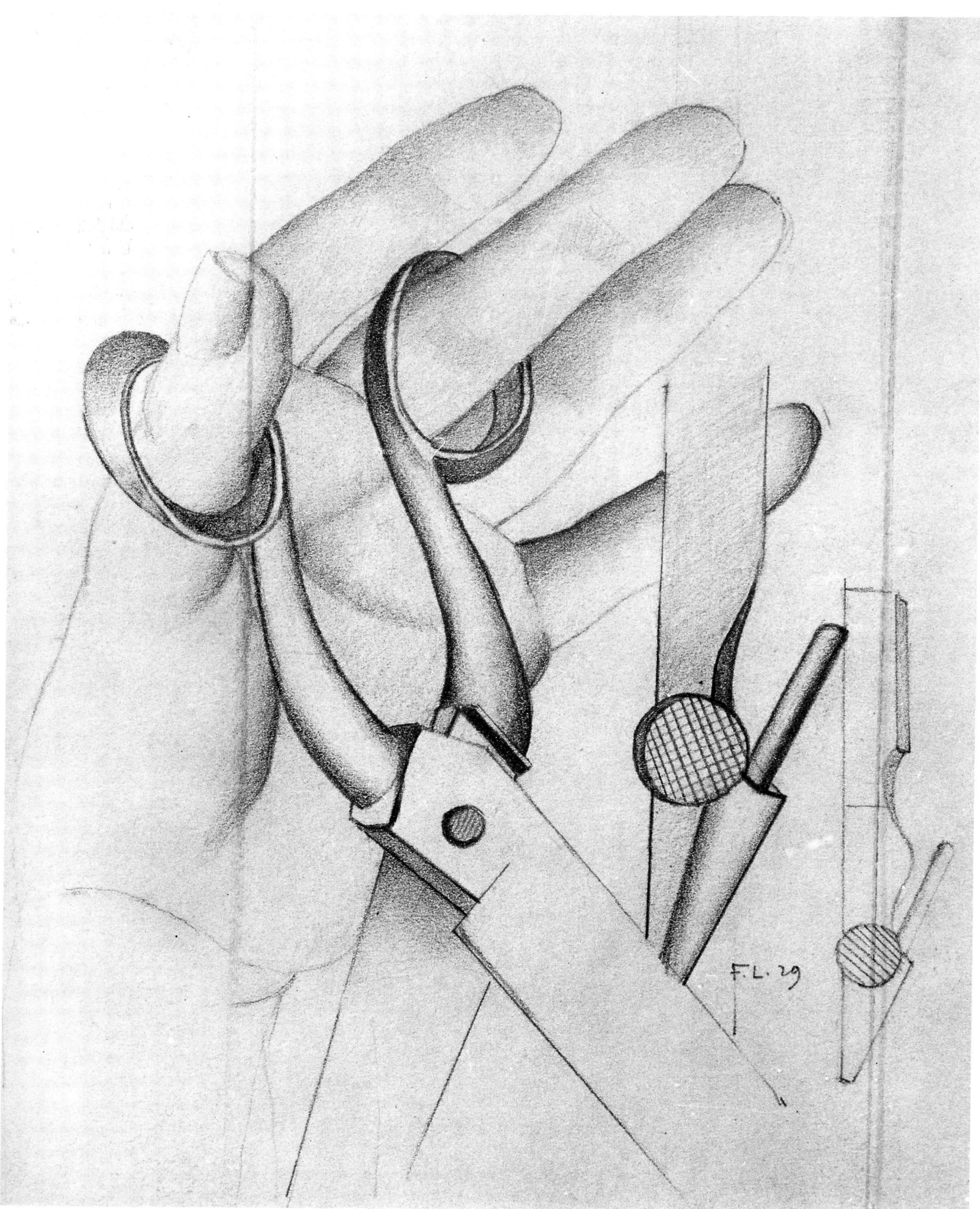


215. HAND AND SCISSORS
1929—Pencil on paper, 30 × 24 cm
Musée National Fernand Léger, Biot

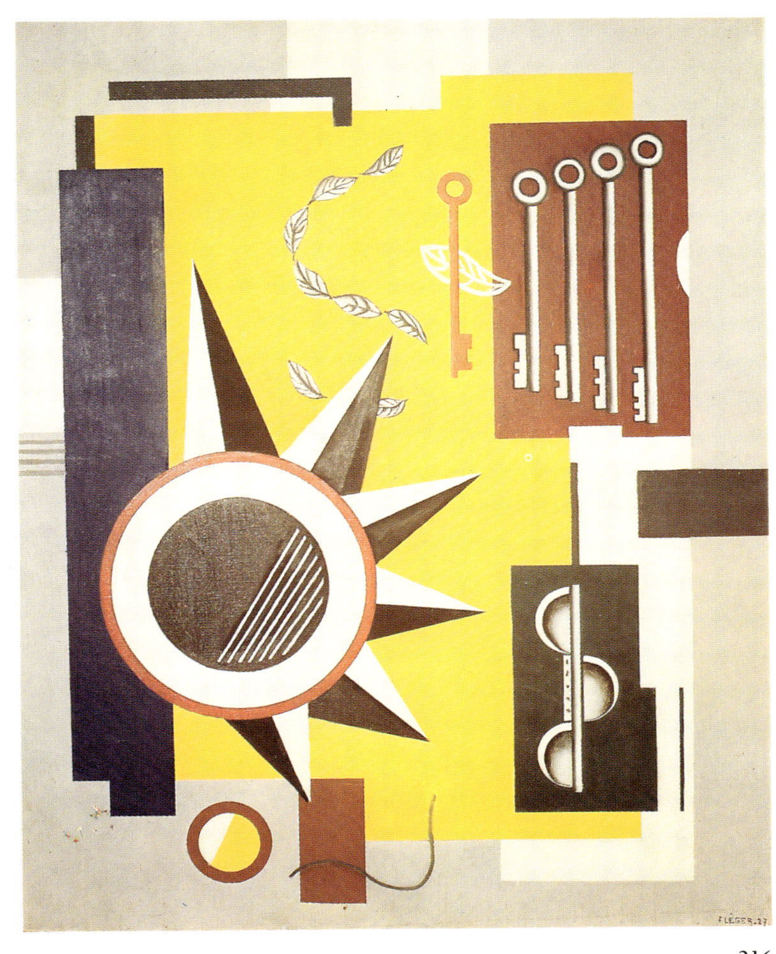

216

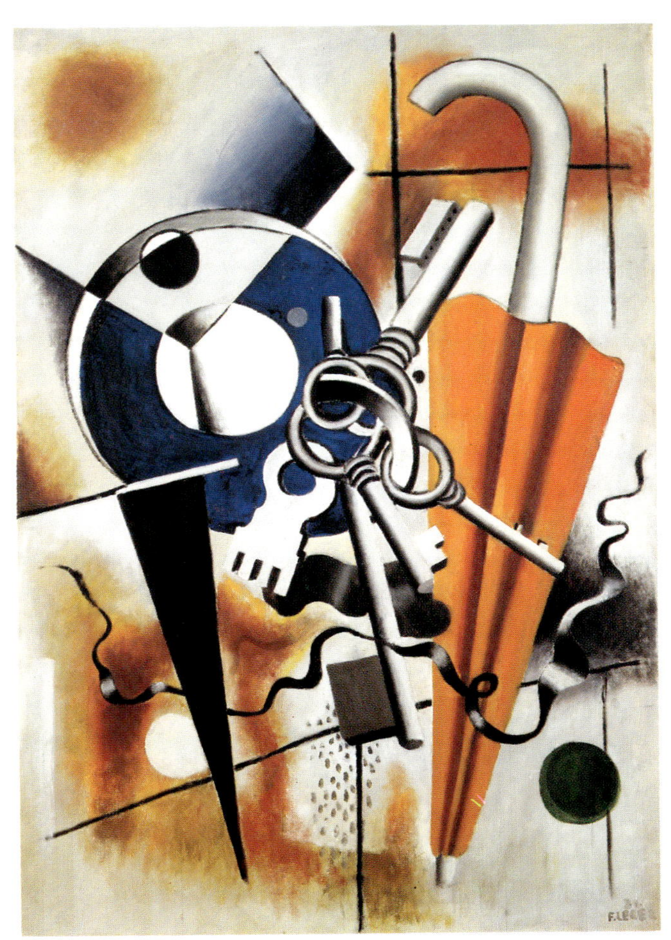

217

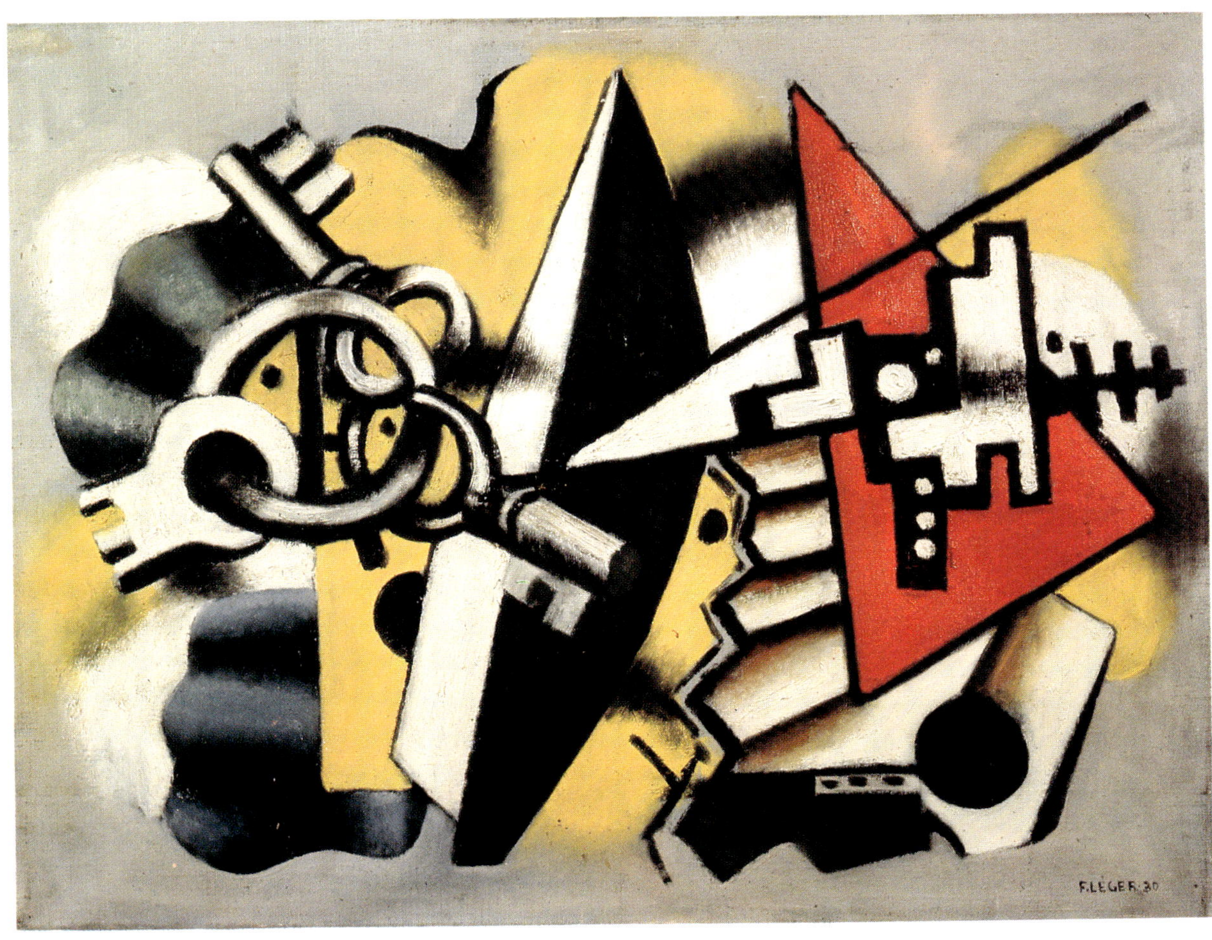


218

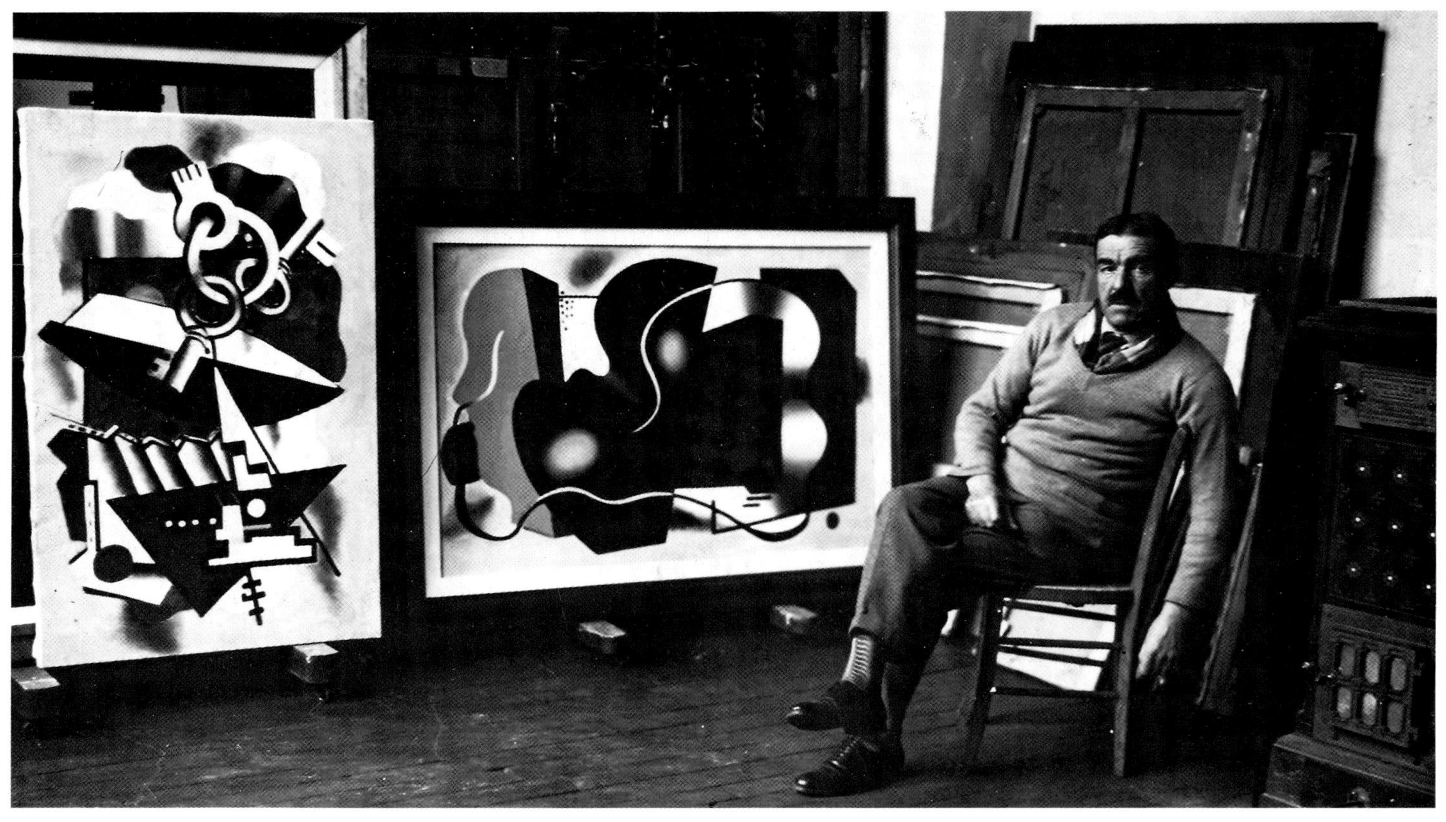

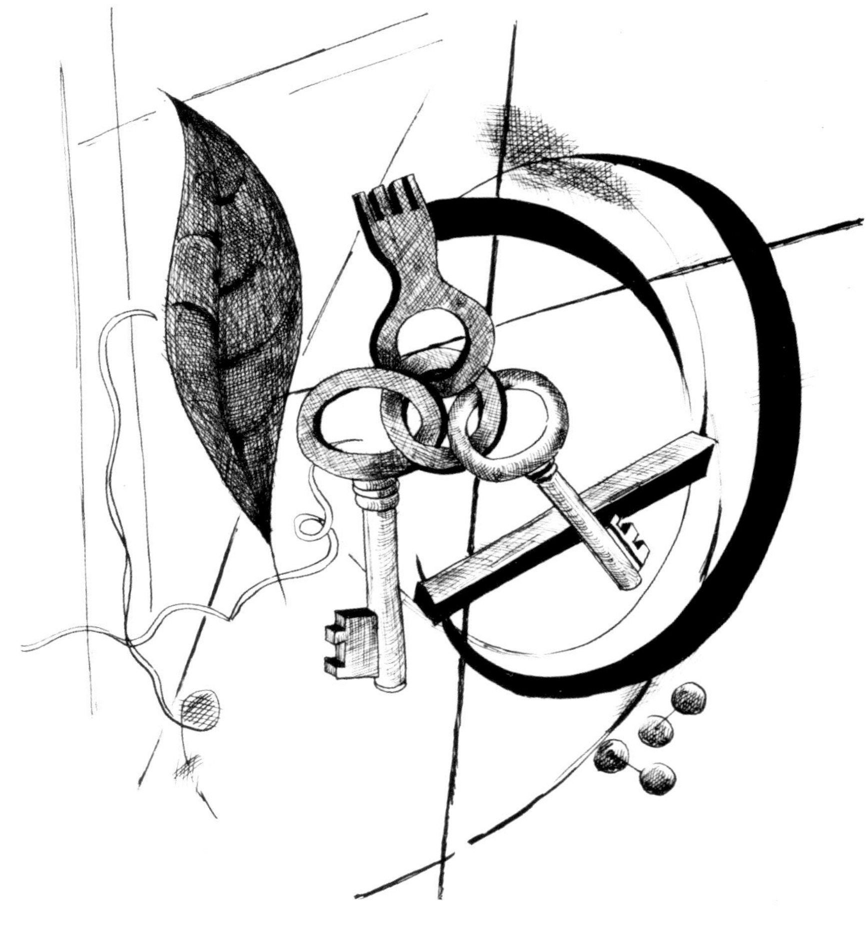

216. COMPOSITION NO. 1
1927—Oil on canvas, 162 × 130 cm
Private collection

217. COMPOSITION WITH UMBRELLA
1932—Oil on canvas, 130 × 82 cm
Louise Leiris Gallery, Paris

218. COMPOSITION WITH KEYS
1930—Oil on canvas, 50 × 65 cm
Private collection

219. FERNAND LÉGER IN HIS STUDIO, 86 RUE NOTRE-DAME-DES-CHAMPS, IN PARIS
About 1932
Photo by Seuphor

220. COMPOSITION WITH KEYS
Around 1929—China ink drawing, 37 × 31 cm
Private collection

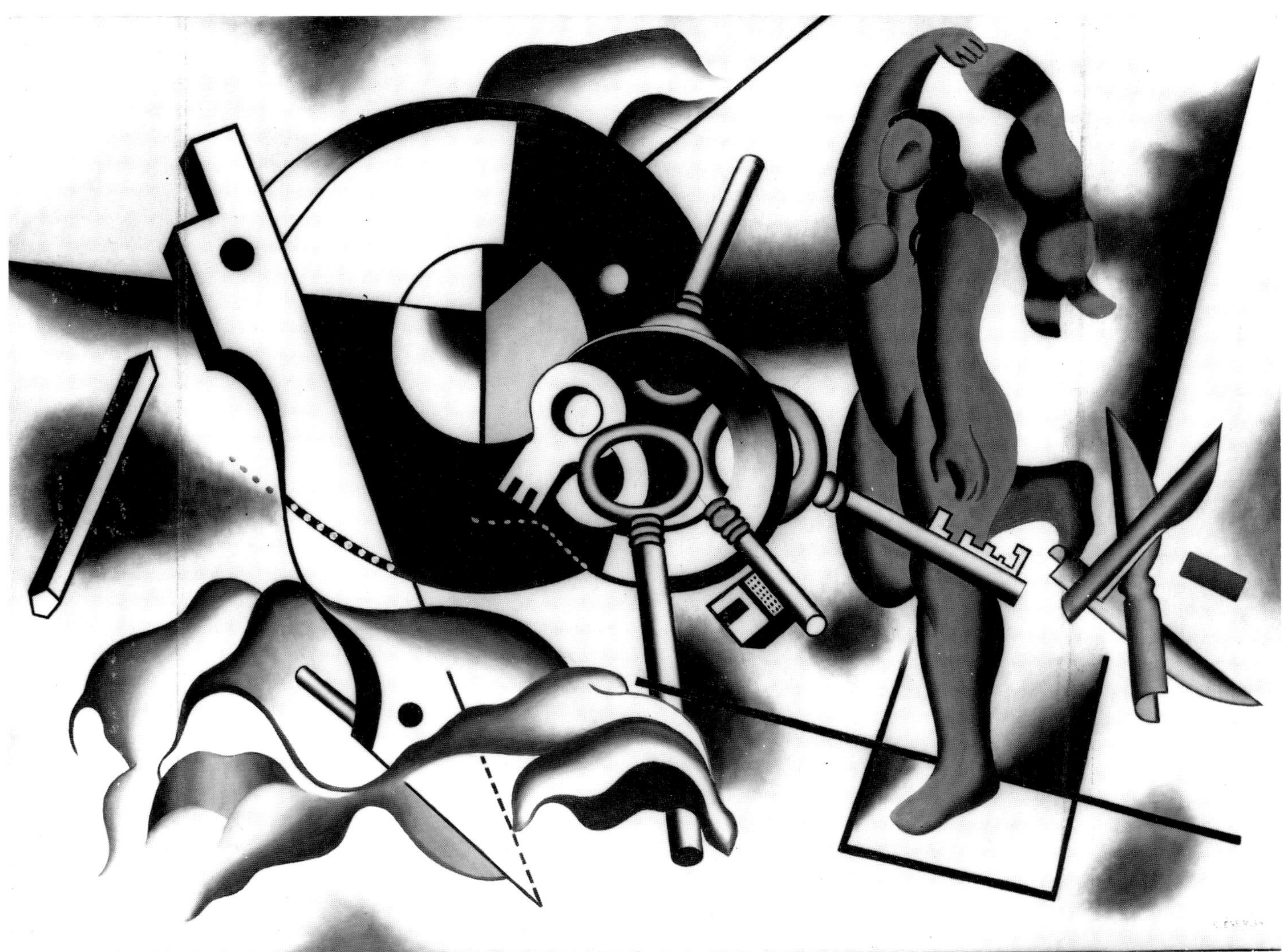

221. CONTRASTING OBJECTS
1930—Oil on canvas, 97 × 130 cm
Musée National d'Art Moderne, Centre Georges Pompidou, Paris
Gift of Paul Rosenberg

Ill. 222 **A story of contrast**

"If you want a story of contrast, here's a good one: One day I painted a ring full of keys on a canvas, my own set of of keys. I didn't know what I was going to put next to it. I needed something totally contrary to the keys. When I finished working, I went out. Barely had I taken a few steps and what do you think I saw in the window of a shop? A postcard of the Mona Lisa! I suddenly understood that she was what I needed to contrast with the keys. That's how I came to put her on the canvas. When I finished painting her, I also painted a can of sardines. It made for such a sharp contrast! It's a painting that I won't sell, because I must keep it for myself. . . . It was the riskiest canvas I had ever done in terms of contrasted objects. The Mona Lisa is an object just like other objects, as far as I'm concerned." Despite this lovely little story, there is no doubt that Léger had an old account to settle with the Mona Lisa, and he must have been quite pleased to put one over on Leonardo da Vinci and kill another bird with the same stone: traditional "good taste." To show that one object is as good as another, he painted his bunch of keys many times more—in combination with an umbrella, with a dancer flying in space, and with various women who had no earthly attractiveness.

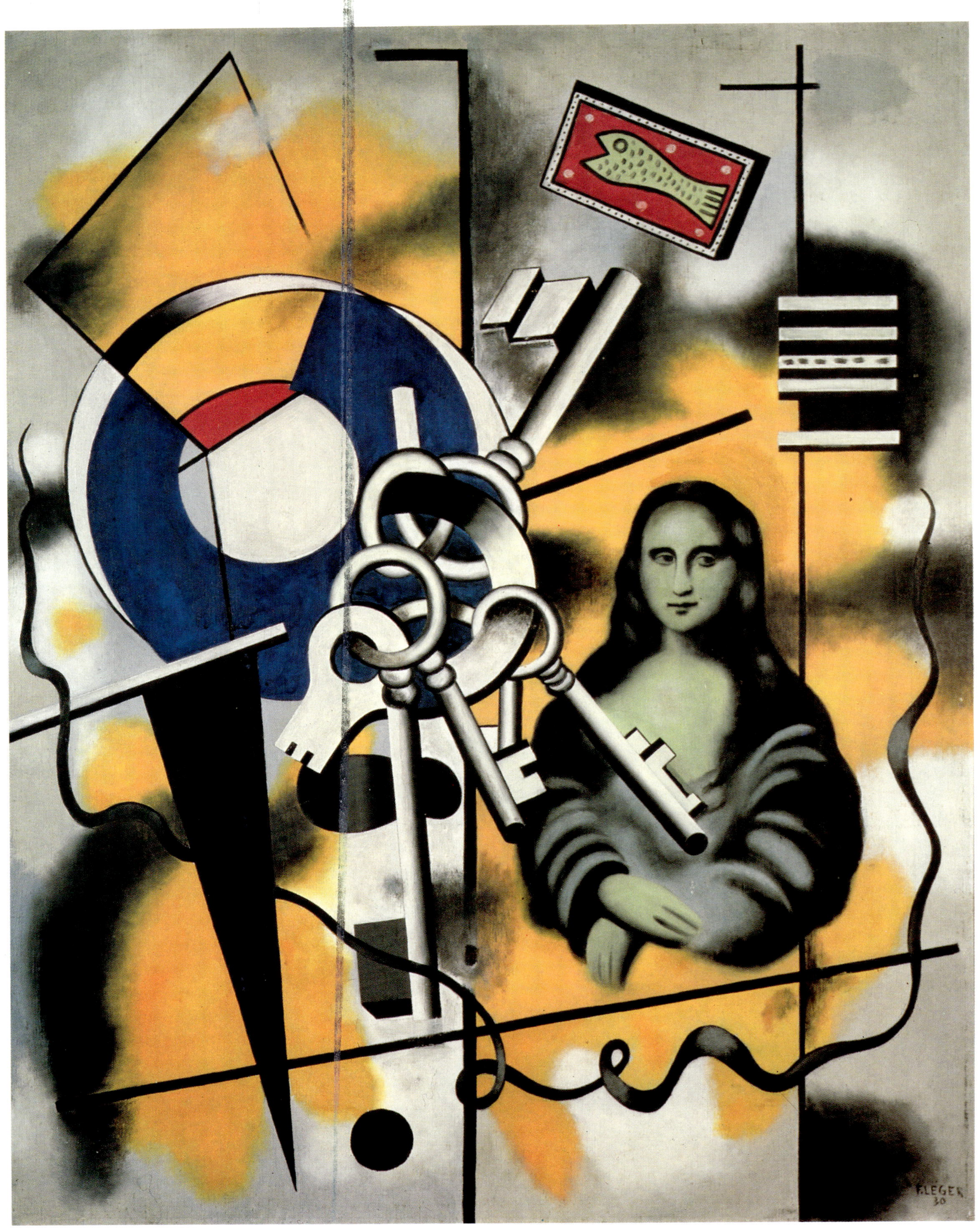


222. MONA LISA WITH KEYS
1930—Oil on canvas, 91 × 72 cm
Musée National Fernand Léger, Biot

## A certain gratuitous aspect

It is difficult to use the expression "gratuitous" in terms of American Pop Art, since it sells for such a fortune. Unlike American Pop artists, however, who did not know when enough was enough, Léger sensed in the 1930s the danger of gratuitousness in his own art. He undoubtedly felt that there was too much facility, too much repetition, and too much comfort in presenting objects, forms, and characters floating about in space at the whim of various decorative combinations or organized contrasts. He may have felt he was moving away from reality in focusing in on *things*. It was time for Léger to return to things more human, to rediscover "the voice of the people," to return to more "popular" paintings, to rejoin the worker whom he had been neglecting for
Ill. 240 far too long. In his *Decorative Project for a Physical Culture Stadium* (1935), he had already begun to bring in man's use of objects in space. A new array of angels would alight on his canvases: gymnasts, divers, acrobats, and other builders who were dear to Léger's heart.

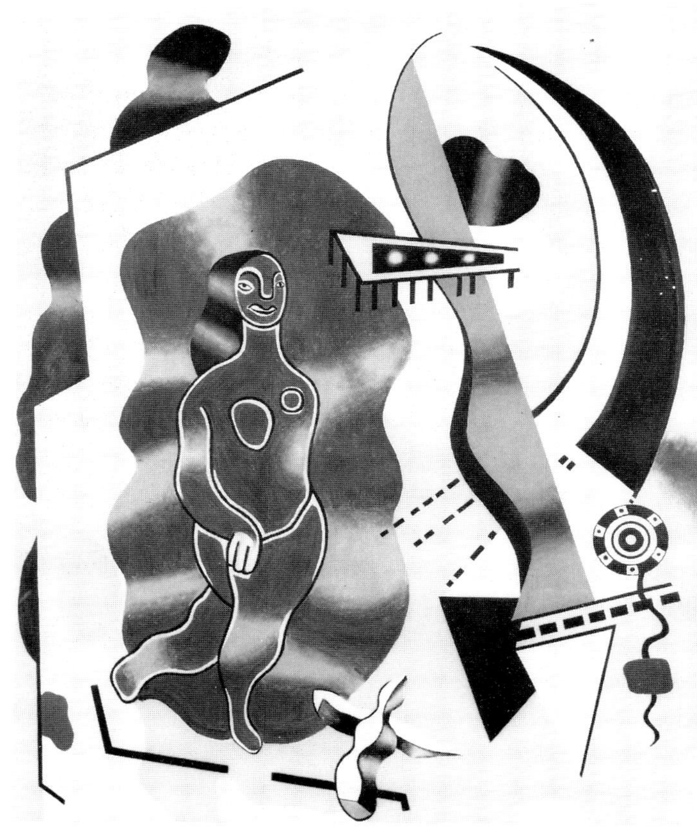

223. BLUE DANCER
1930—Oil on canvas, 146 × 114 cm
Musée National d'Art Moderne, Centre Georges Pompidou, Paris
Gift of Paul Rosenberg

224. COMPOSITION WITH TWO WOMEN
1930—Oil on canvas, 54 × 81 cm
Private collection

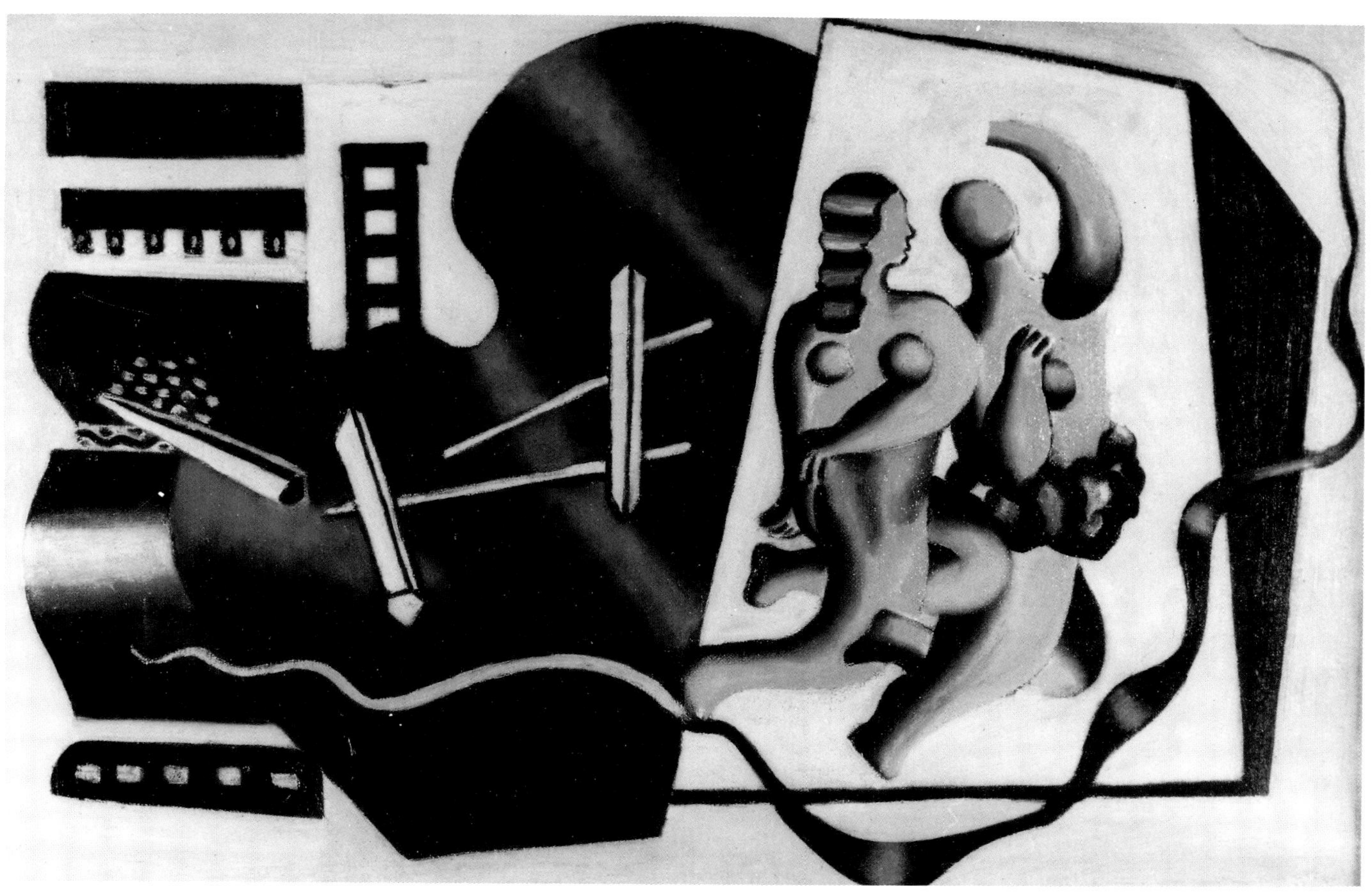

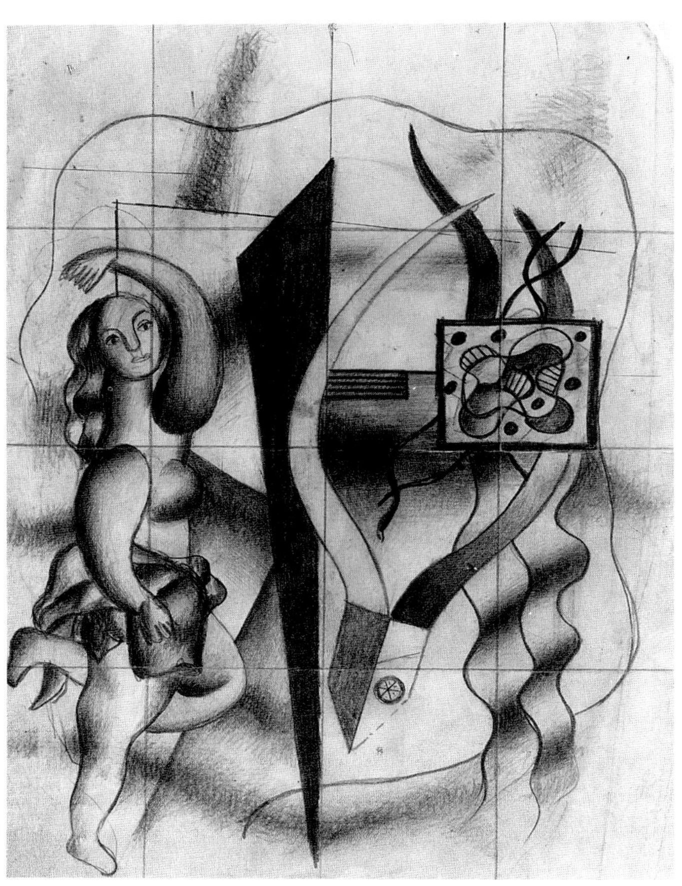

225. THE DANCER
1930—Pencil on paper, 27 × 21 cm
Louise Leiris Gallery, Paris

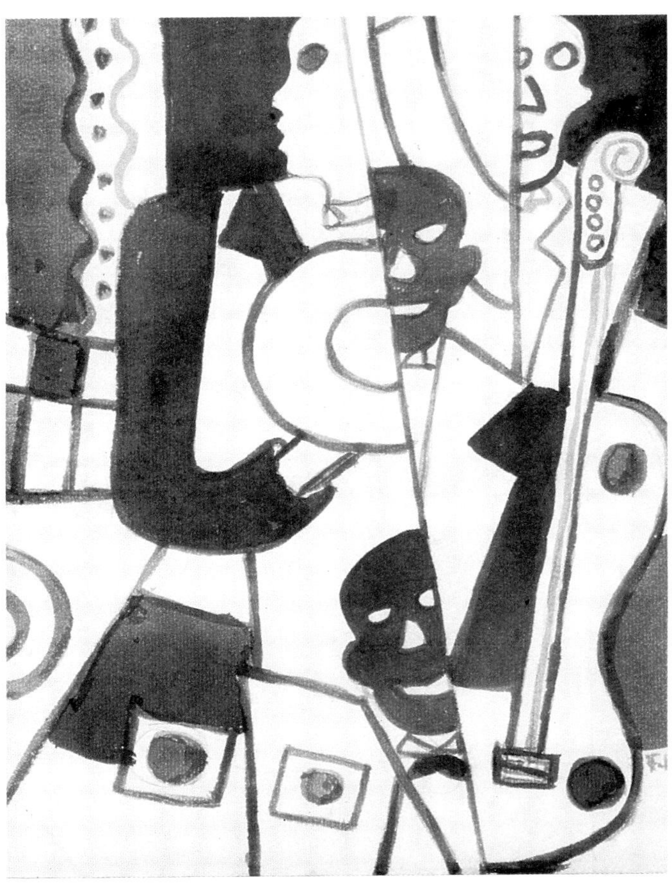

226. JAZZ
1930—Wash and violet ink, 30.5 × 22 cm
Private collection

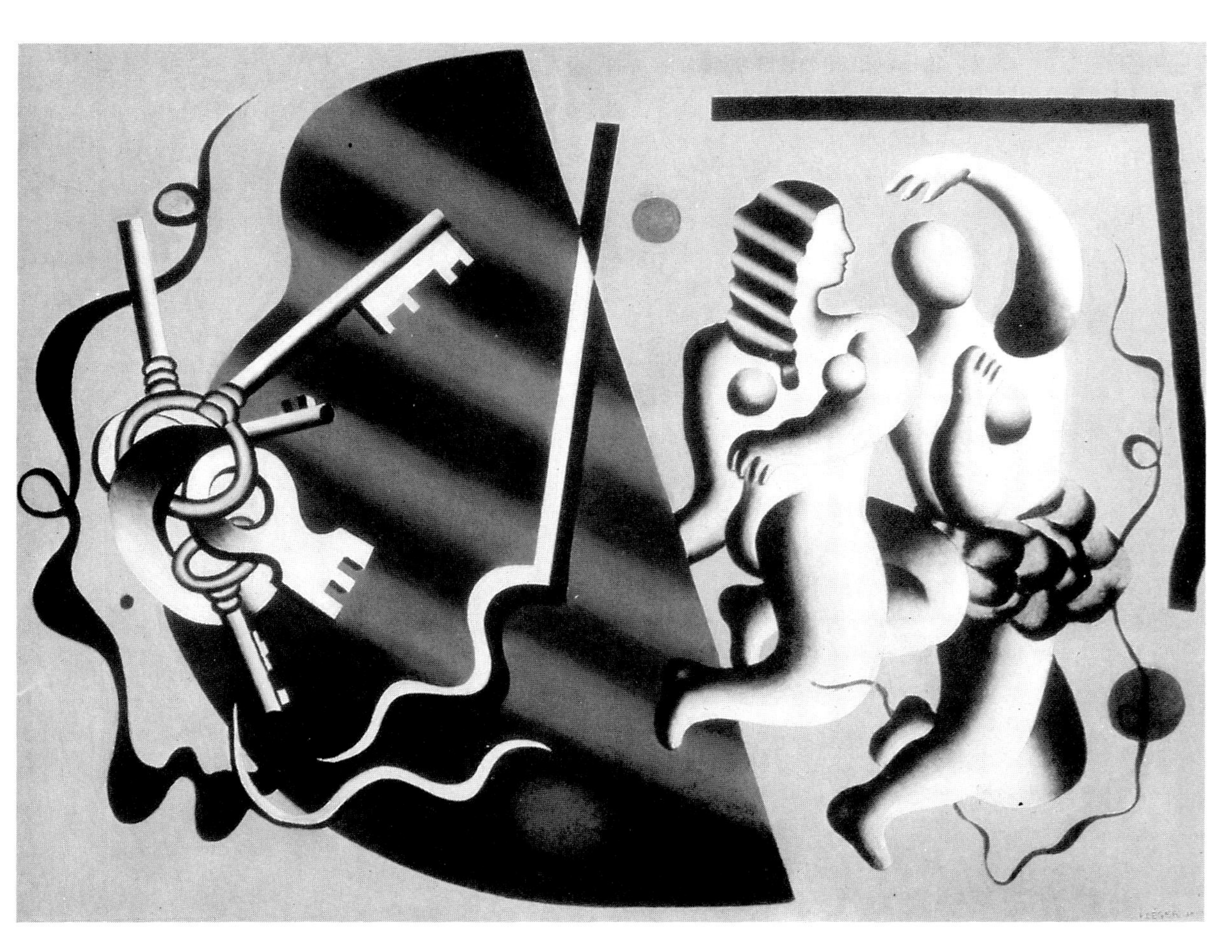

227. DANCERS WITH KEYS
1930—Oil on canvas, 97 × 130 cm
Private collection

228. DANCERS WITH KEYS
1930—Oil on canvas, 183 × 250 cm
Moderna Museet, Stockholm

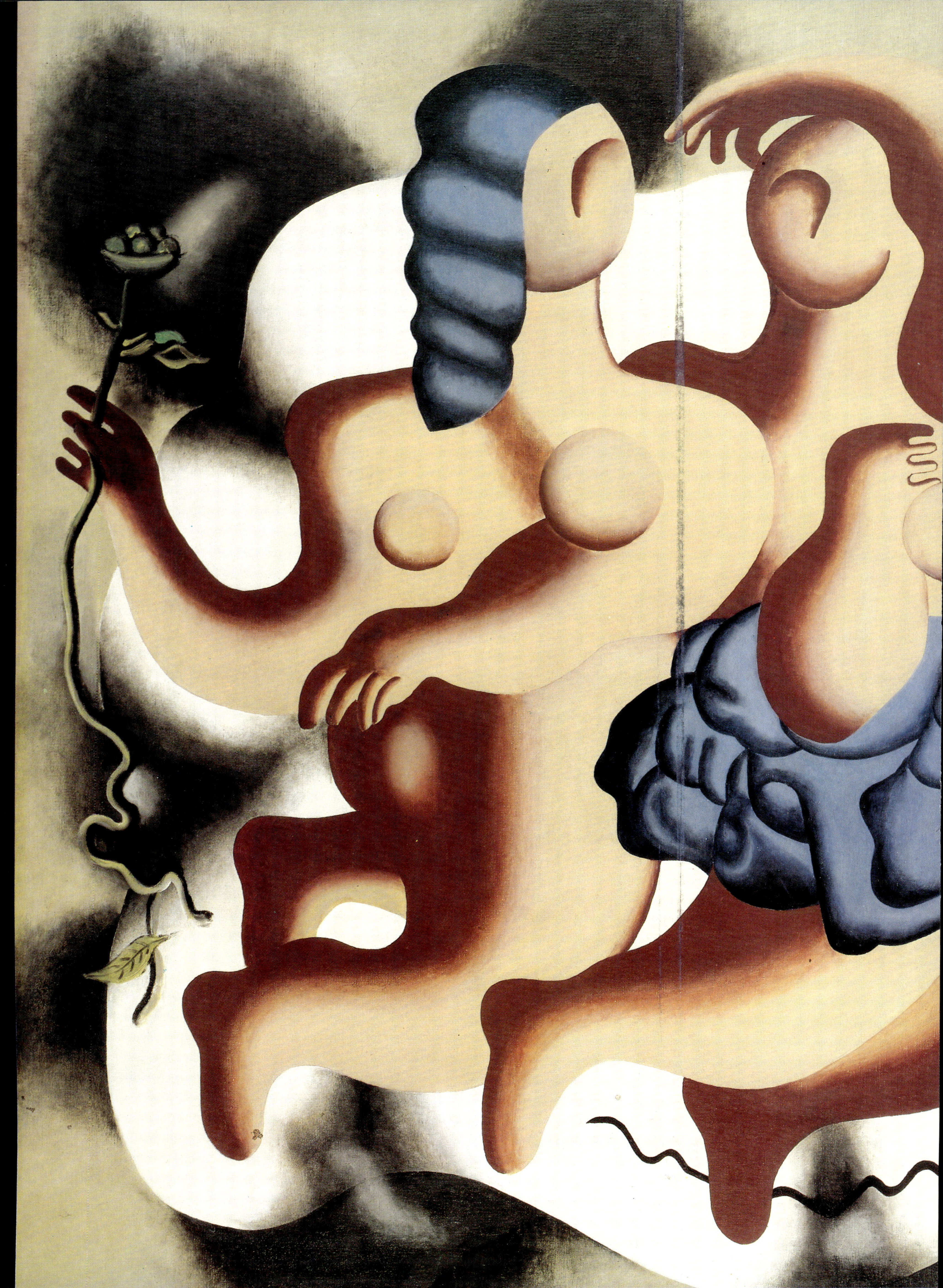

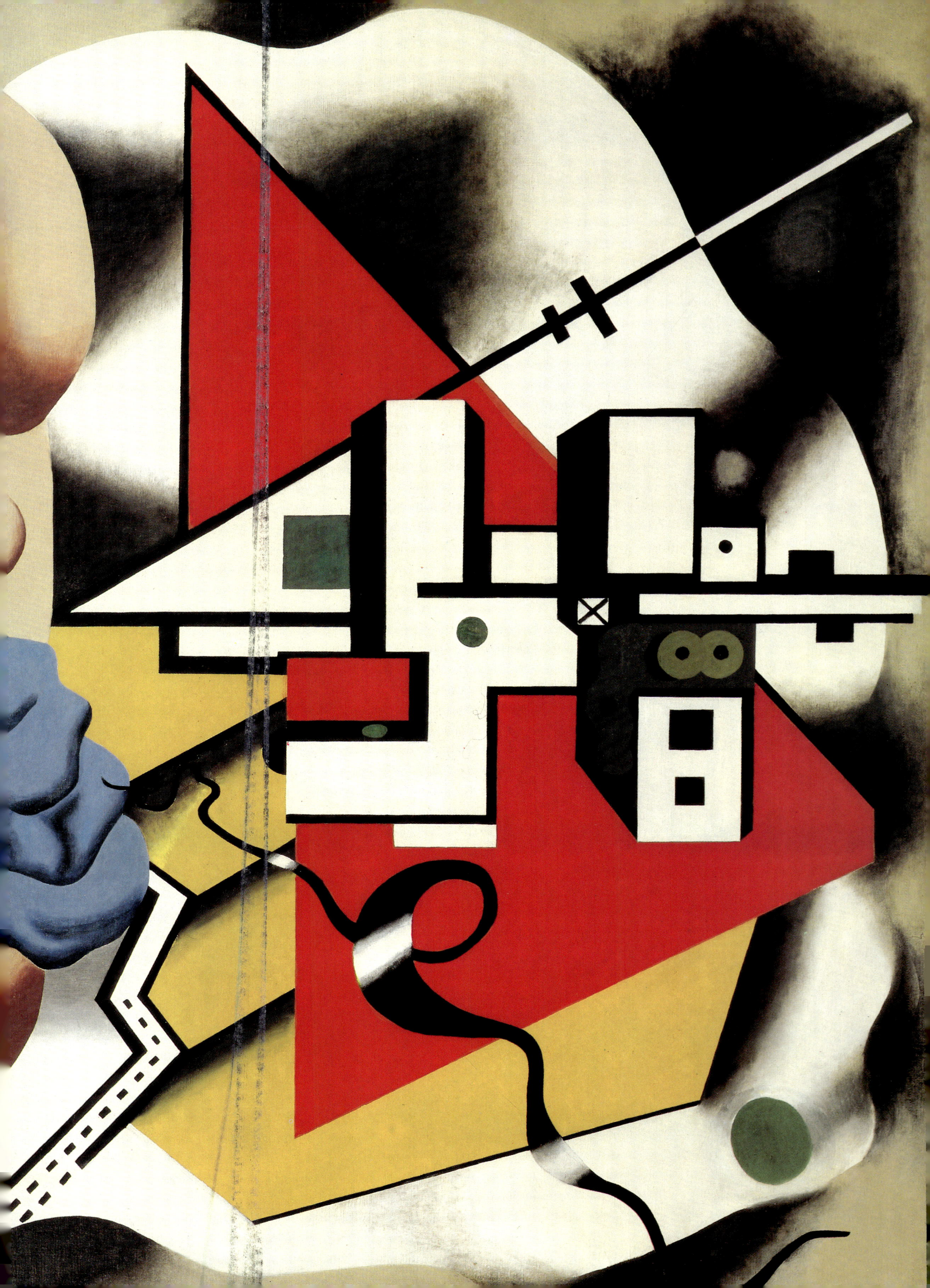

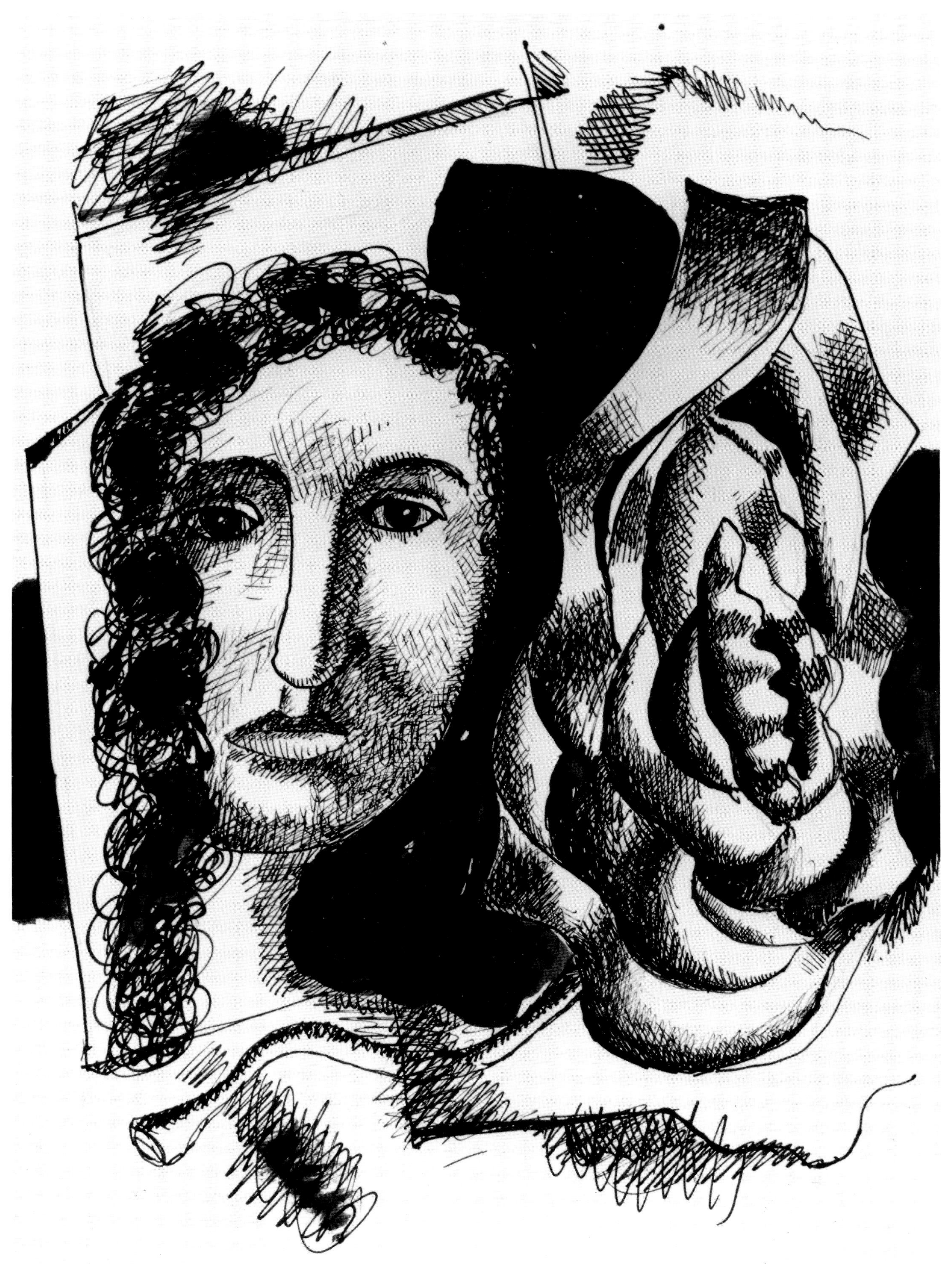

229. WOMAN'S HEAD
1935—China ink drawing, 31 × 23 cm
Private collection

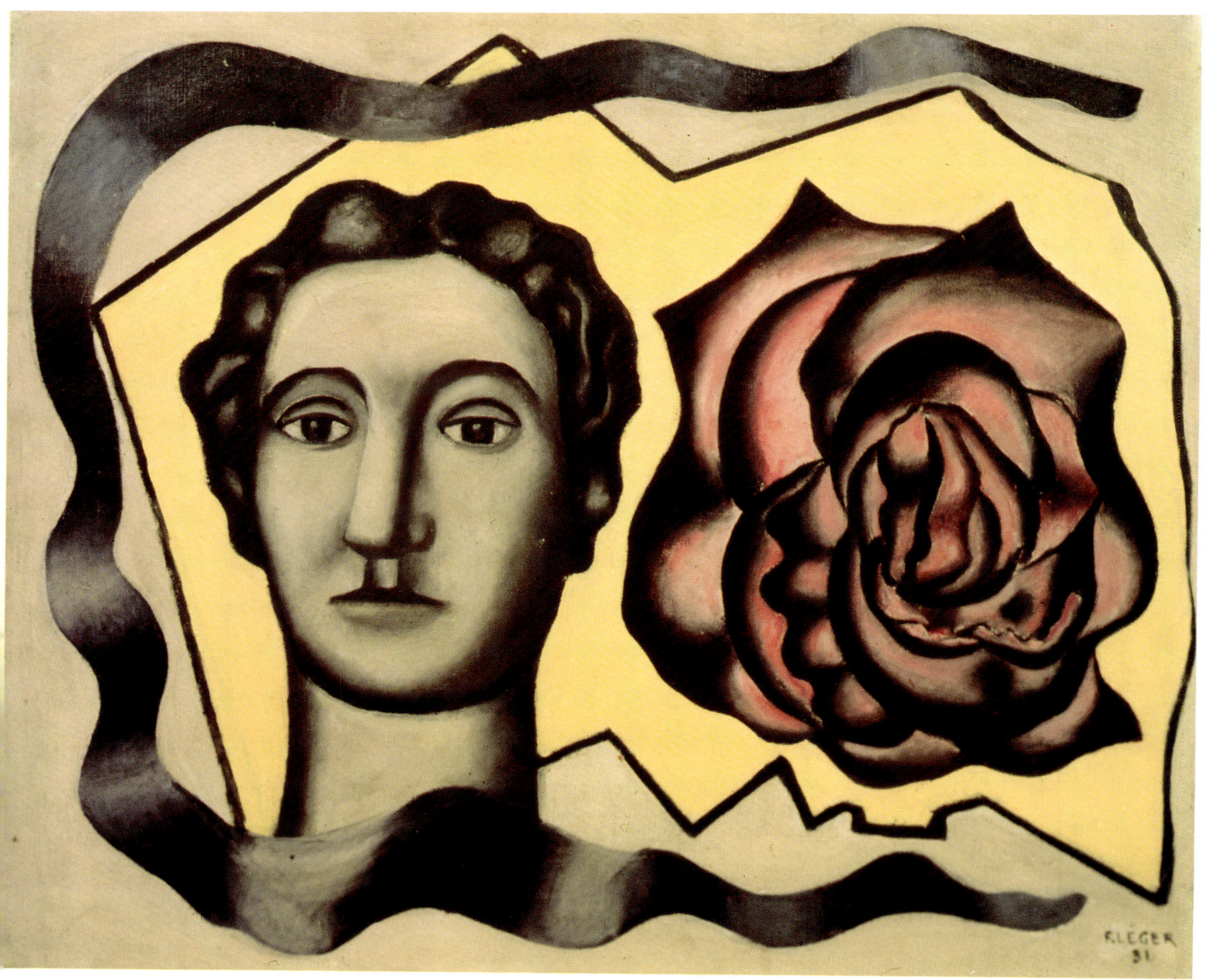


230. ROSE AND FACE
1929–31—Oil on canvas, 54 × 65 cm
Collection of Mr. and Mrs. Adrien Maeght

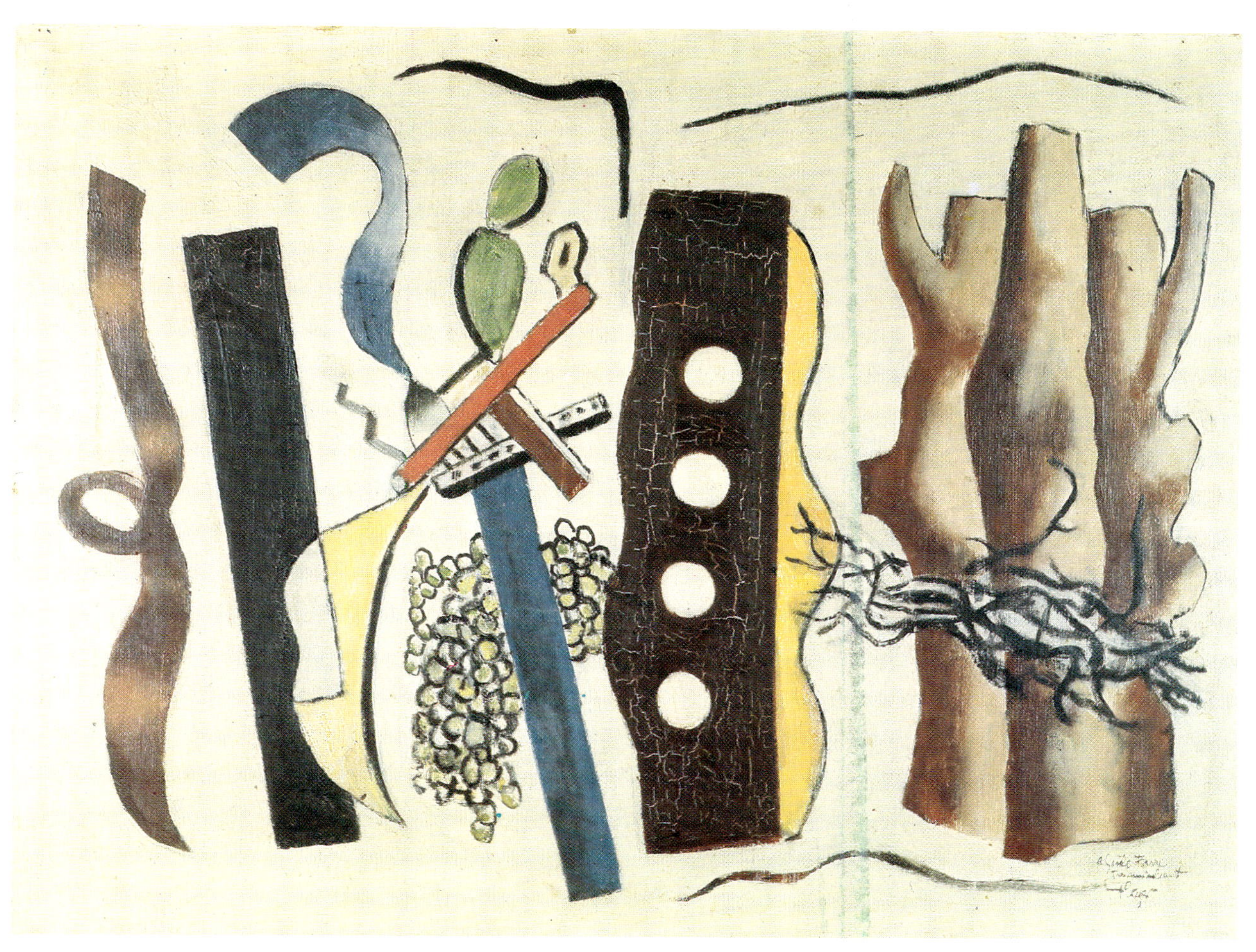

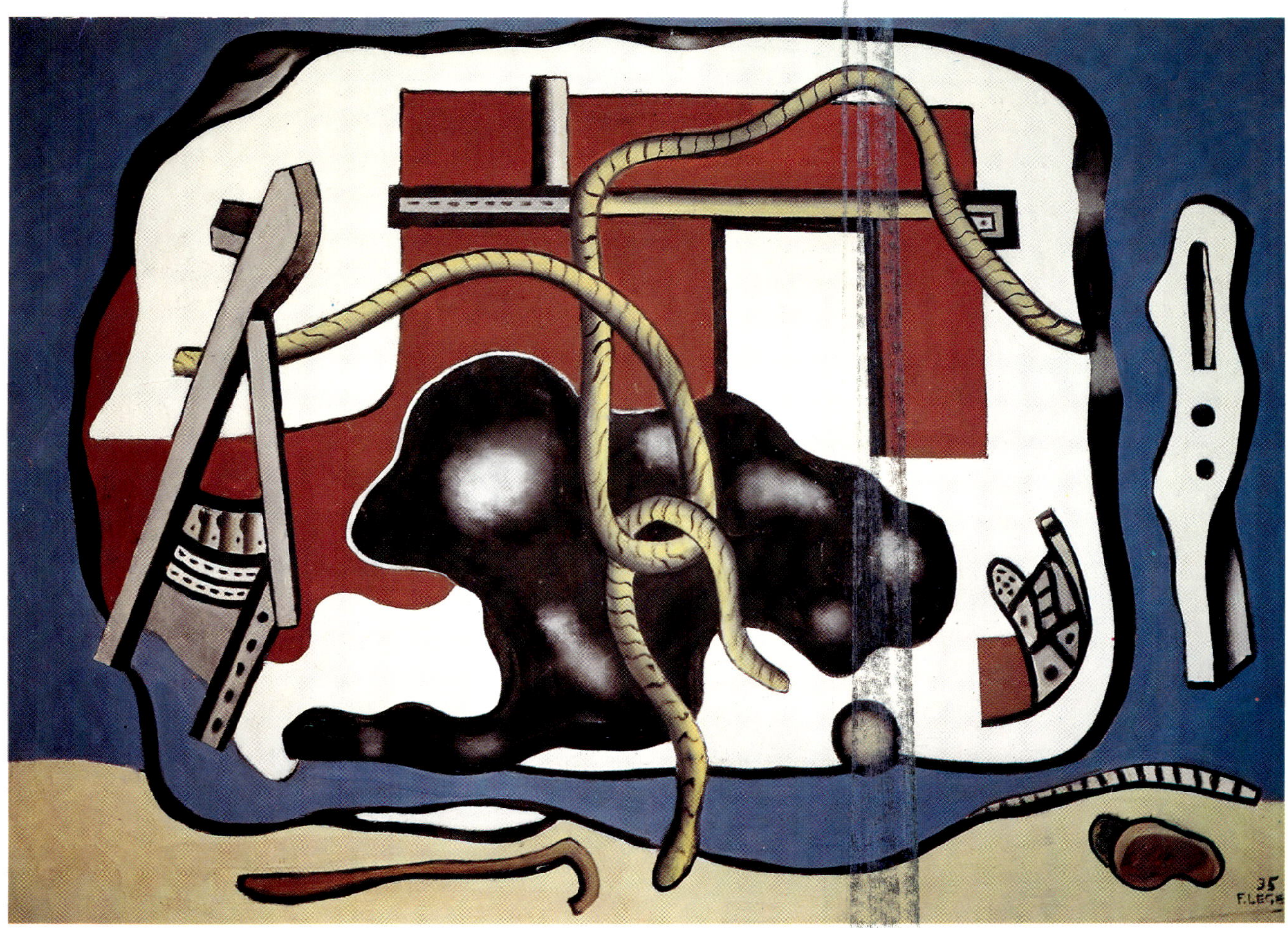


231. COMPOSITION
About 1932—Oil on canvas, 50 × 65 cm
Private collection

232. COMPOSITION ON BLUE BACKGROUND
1935—Oil on canvas, 97 × 130 cm
Private collection

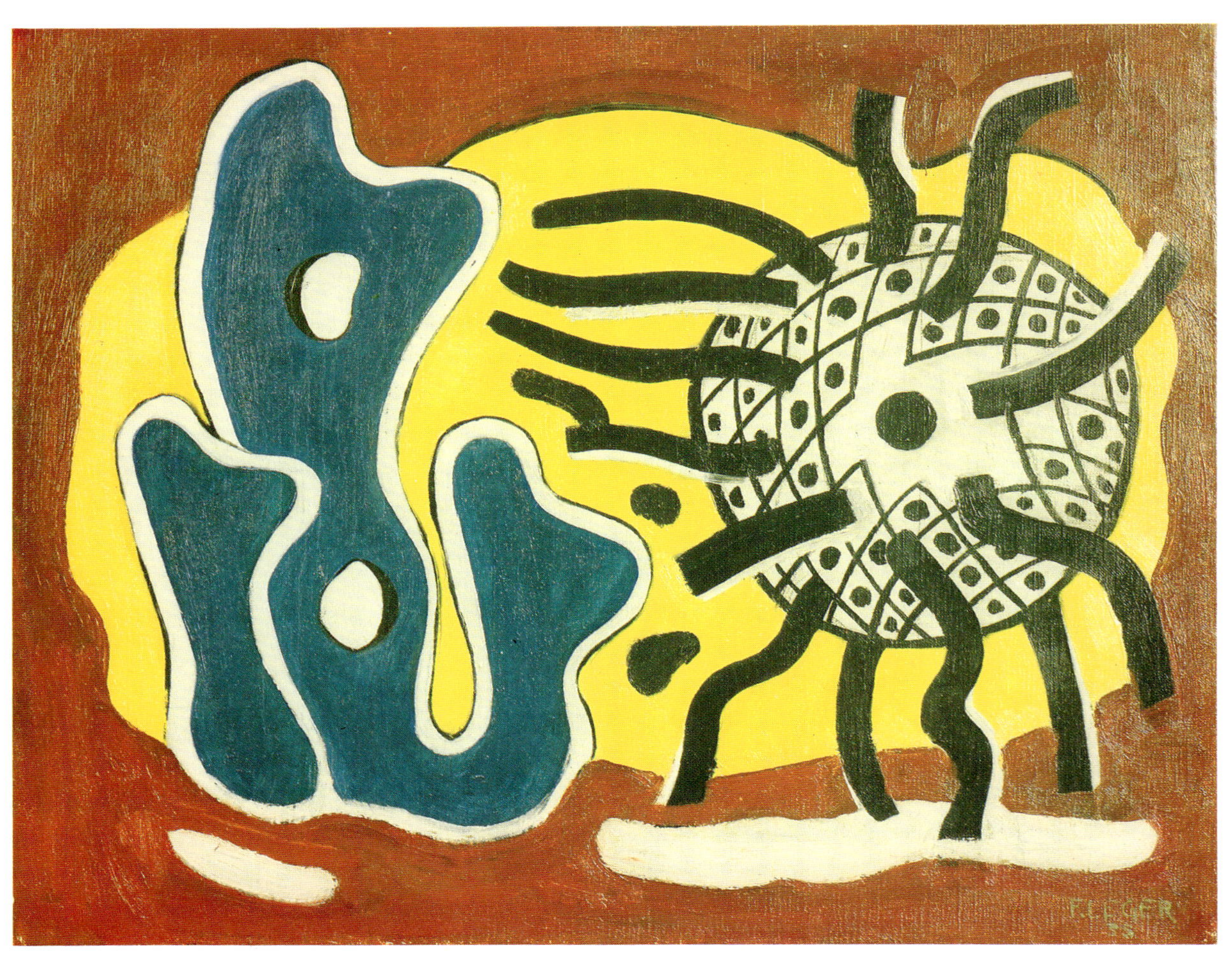


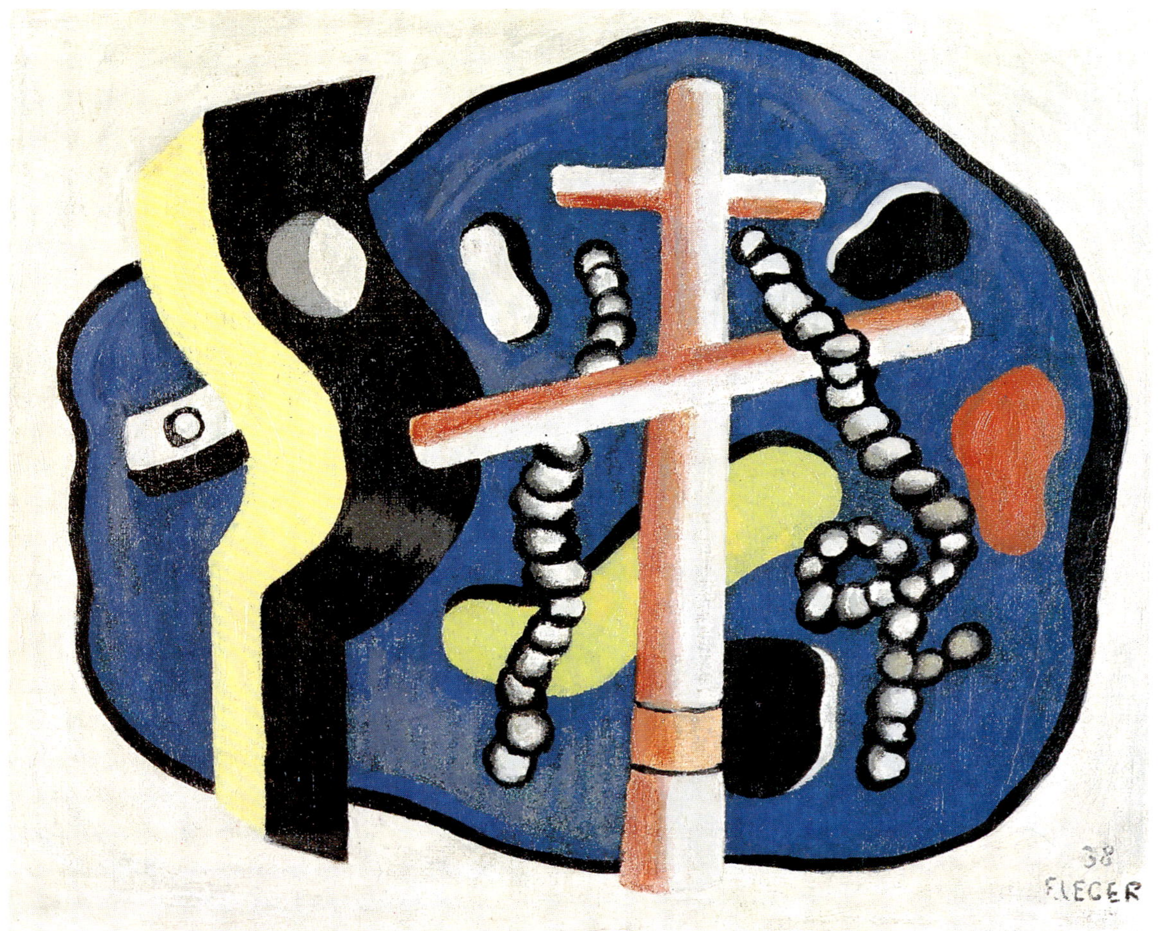


233. COMPOSITION
1935—Oil on canvas, 33 × 41 cm
Private collection

234. STILL LIFE WITH ROPES
1938—Oil on paper remounted on cardboard, 54 × 64.5 cm
Private collection

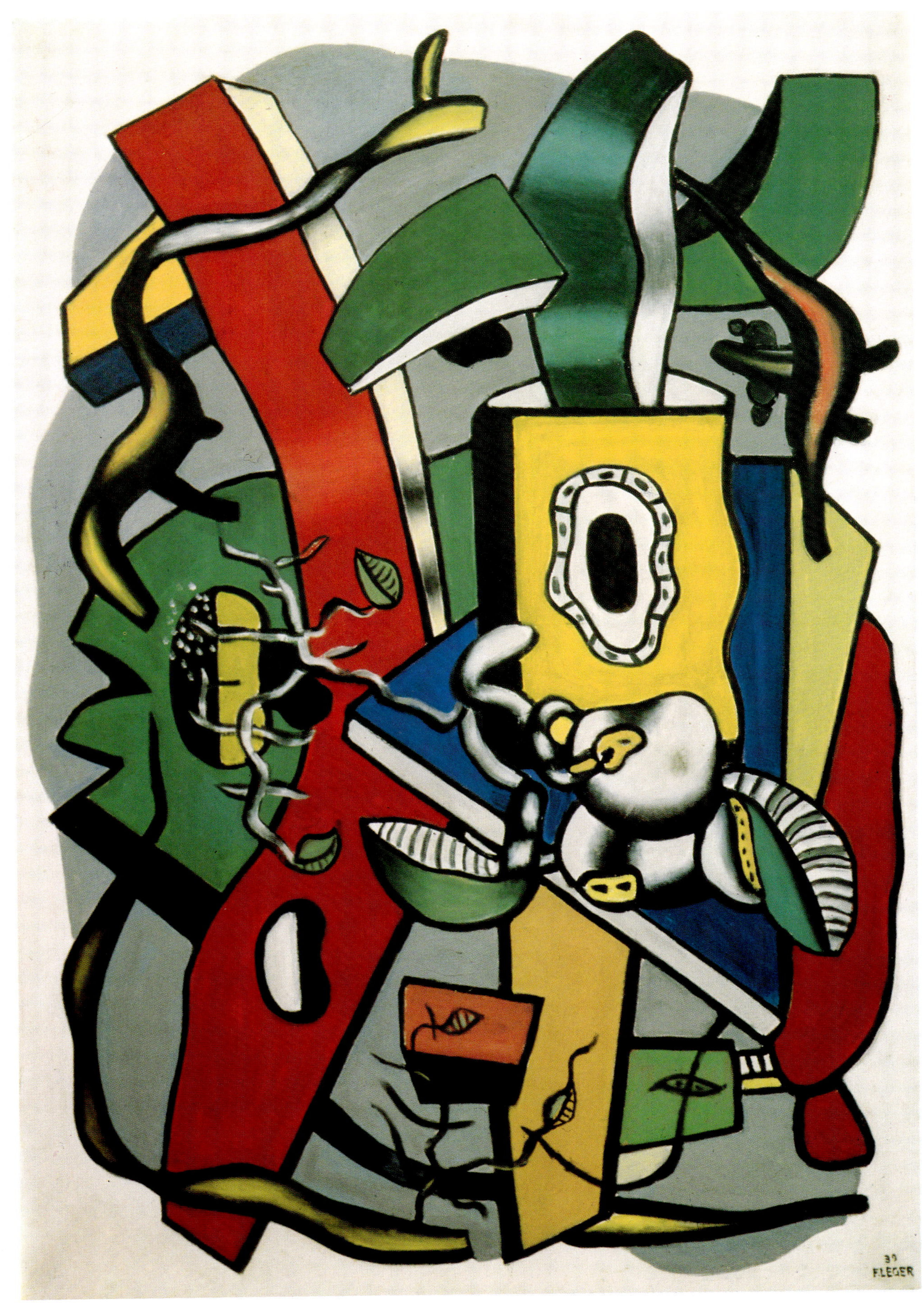


235. STILL LIFE
1938–39—Oil on canvas, 130 × 89.5 cm
Private collection

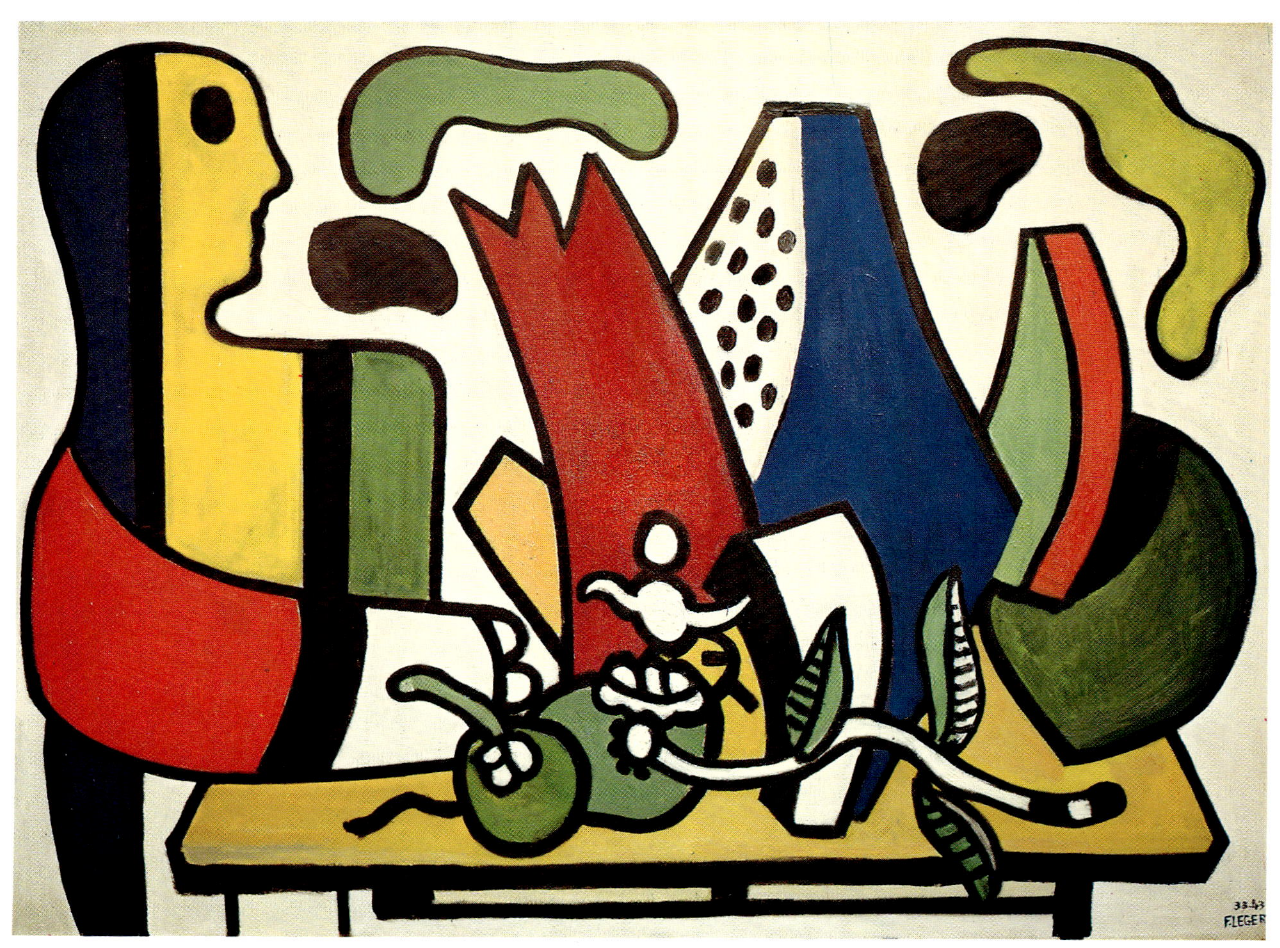


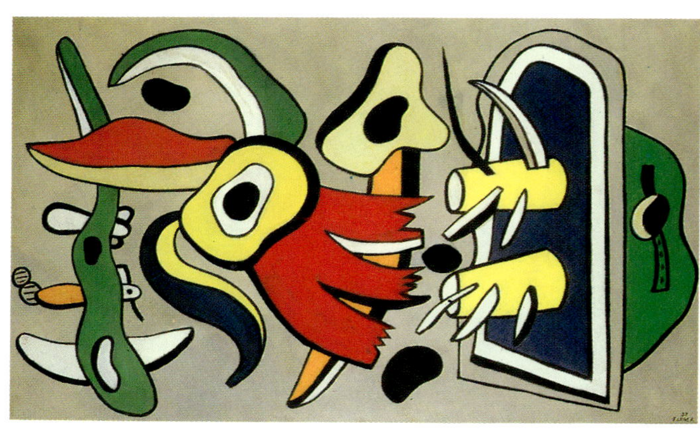

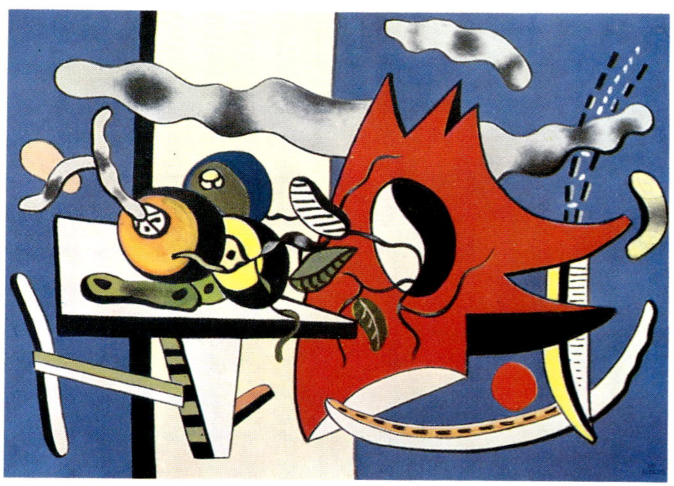

236. MAN WITH STILL LIFE
1938–43—Oil on canvas, 97 × 130 cm
Louise Leiris Gallery, Paris

237. POLYCHROME BUTTERFLIES
1938—Oil on canvas, 81 × 130 cm
Private collection

238. COMPOSITION ON BLUE BACKGROUND
1938—Oil on canvas, 64.8 × 91.4 cm
Beyeler Gallery, Basel

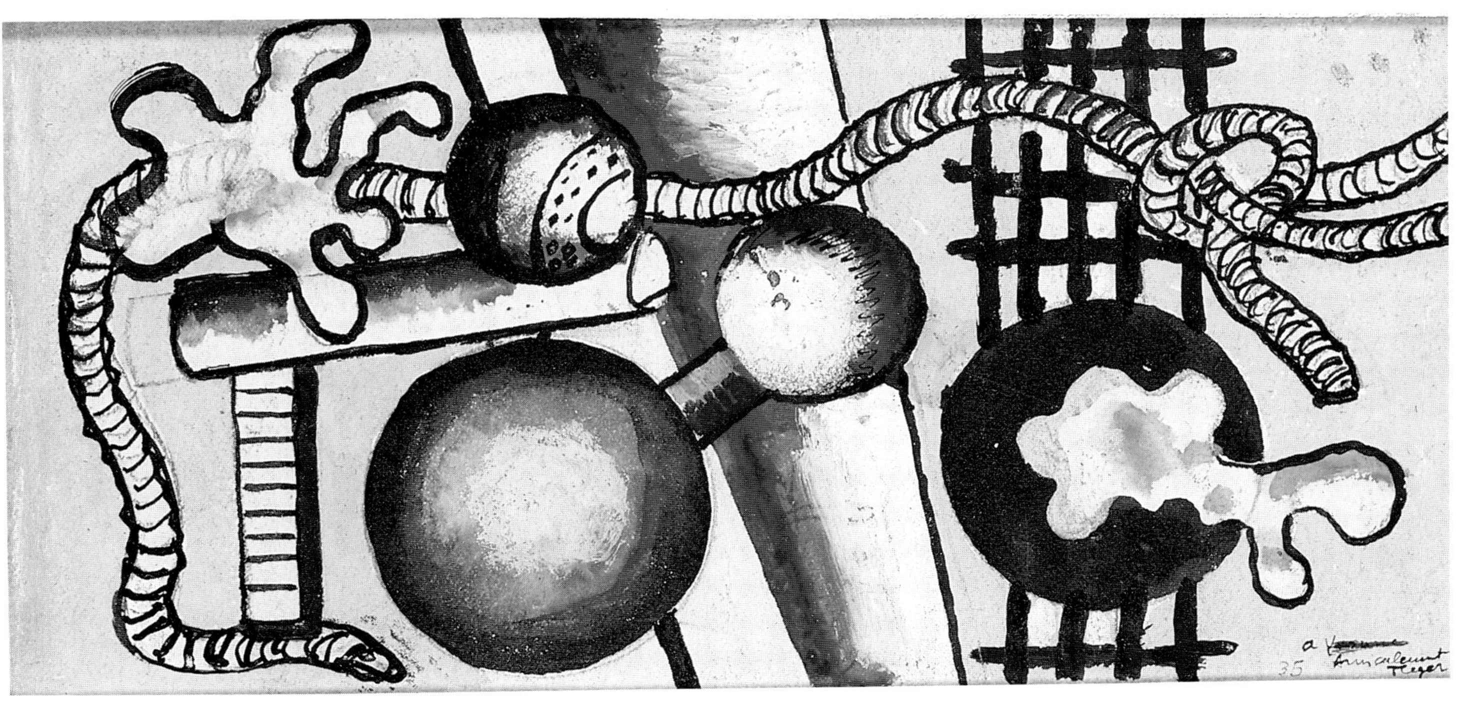

239. STUDY
1935—Gouache, 9.7 × 19.9 cm
Private collection

240. DECORATIVE PROJECT FOR A STADIUM
1935—Gouache, 23.5 × 35.5 cm
Private collection

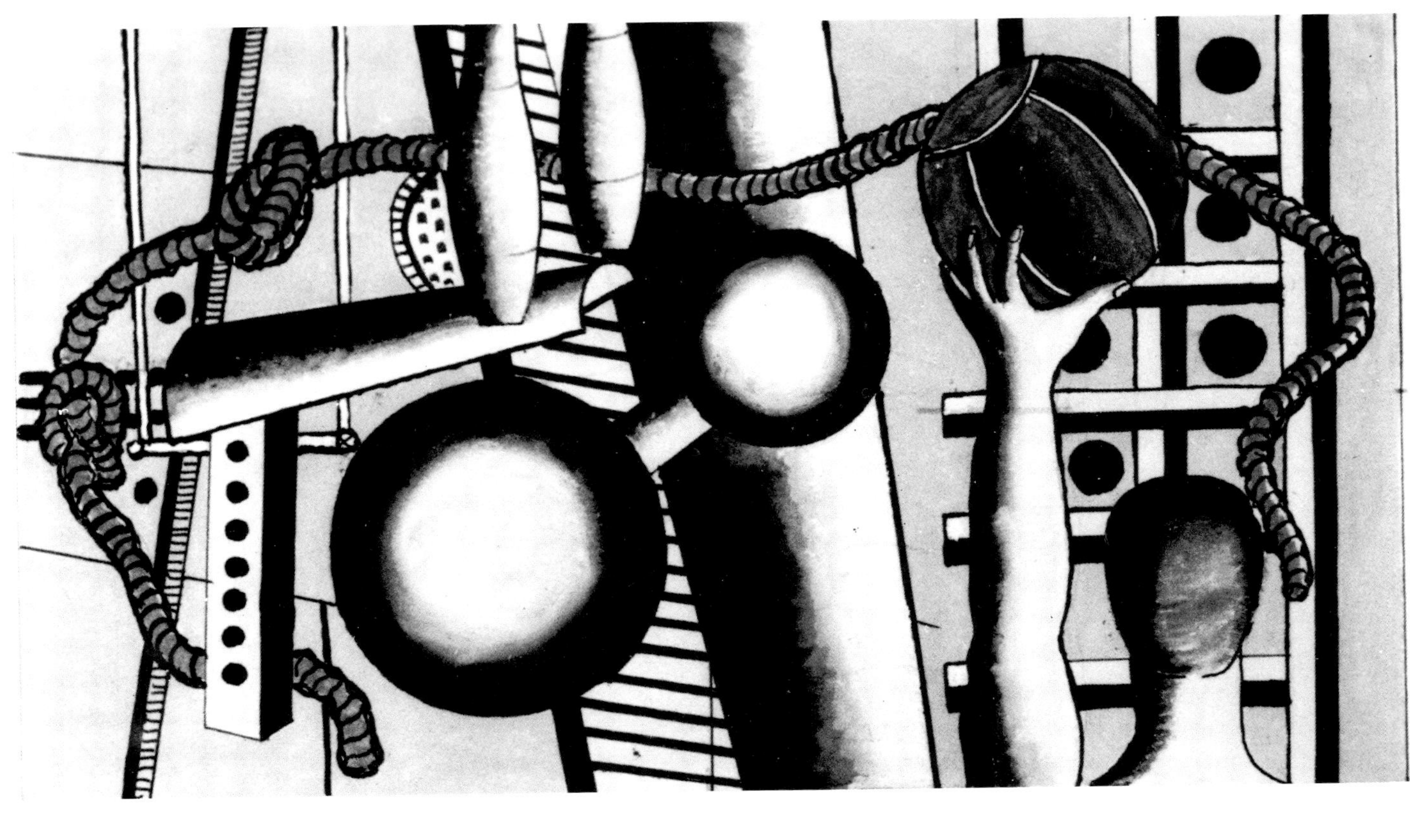

# Return to the Human Form

"I remember that I was short on cash when I brought
Ill. 242 *Reading* ["Le Lecture"] to Rosenberg. He looked at the painting and said to me: 'But the woman has no hair! Be reasonable, and give her a little hair. She looks like she's been plucked, and it's unpleasant to look at.' He was insistent. With all the good will in the world, I just couldn't put hair on the woman. I couldn't. At the place where her head went I needed a clean, round form. I didn't do it on purpose! I just couldn't put hair on her head."

During the period of this anecdote (around 1924), Léger had already travelled a path that led from the anonymous robot in its purity and hardness to more human characters with recognizable traits. But his need to use the face as just one among many elements of the painting made it impossible for him to treat it any other way than as a decorative object, regardless of how much this displeased people. Léger did not want to be dominated by the subject. A break with sentimental painting was the only way for him to create a beautiful object on the canvas. He had his "professional conscience" to reckon with, just as the early masters did.

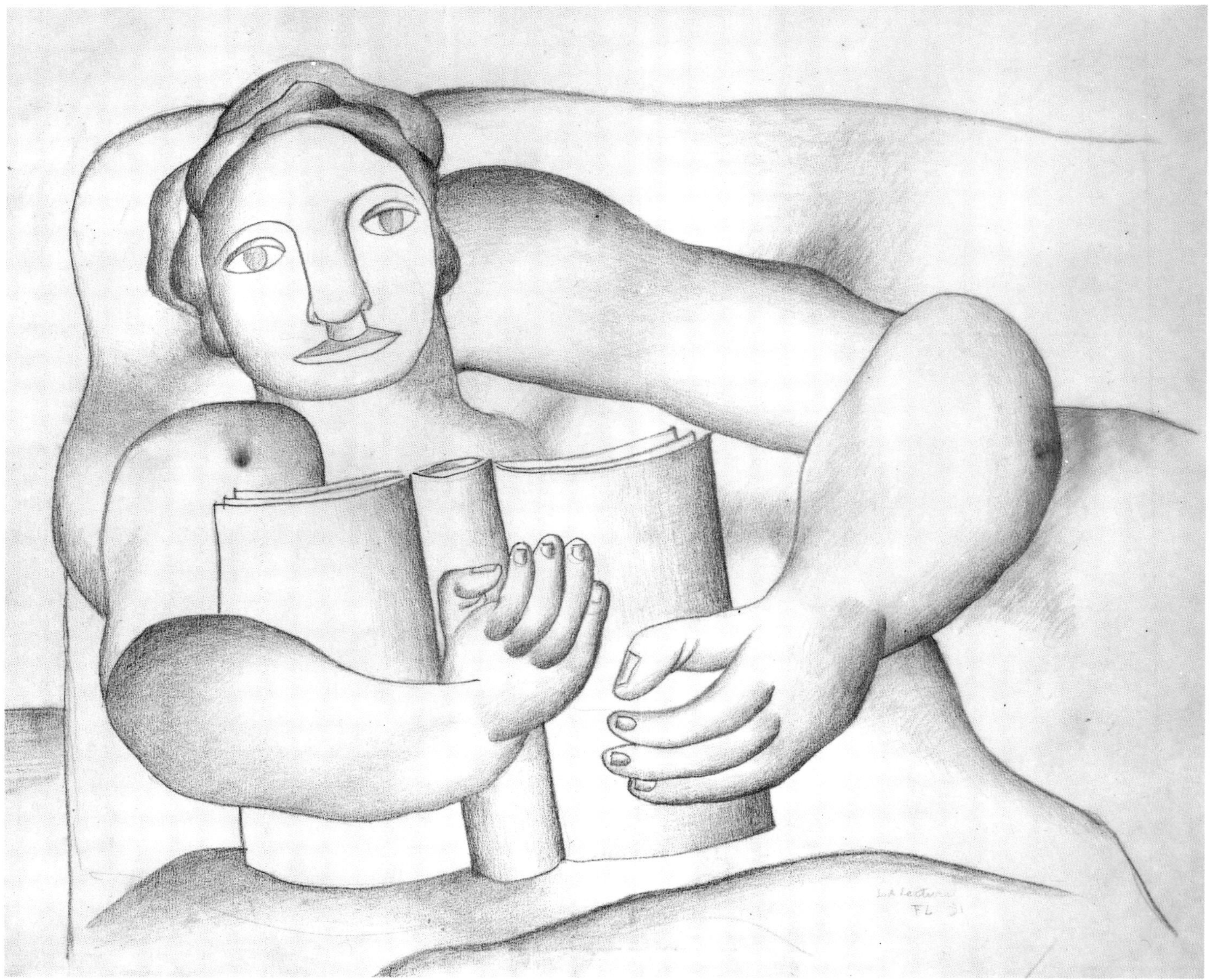

241. STUDY FOR *THE READER*
1931—Graphite on paper, 52.1 × 61 cm
Musée National d'Art Moderne, Centre Georges Pompidou, Paris

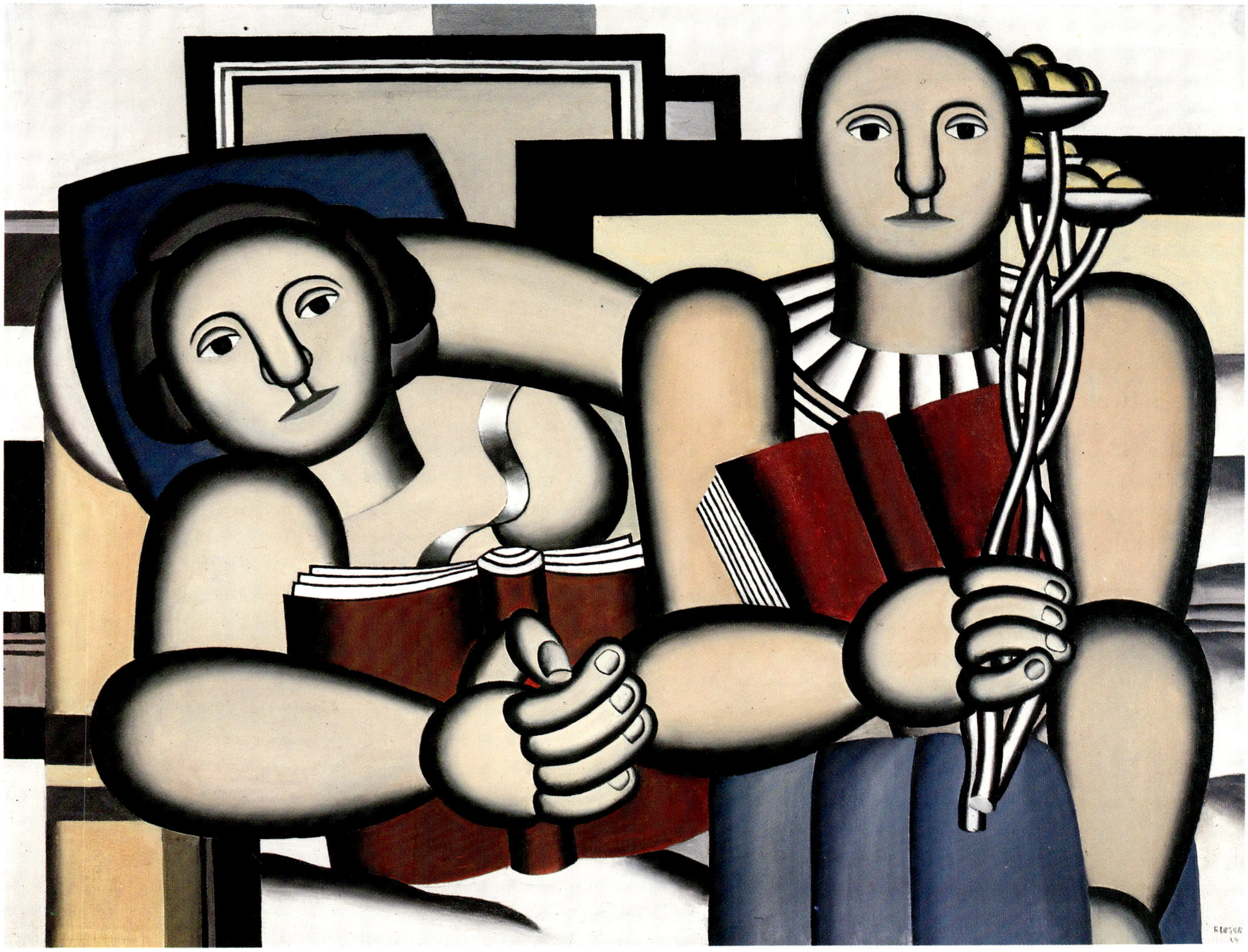

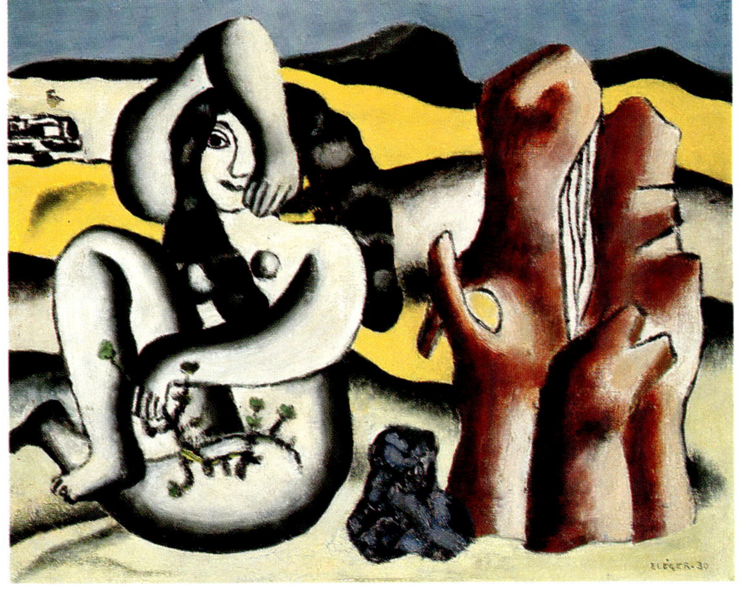

242. THE READER
1924—Oil on canvas, 114 × 146 cm
Musée National d'Art Moderne, Centre Georges Pompidou, Paris
Gift of Eva Gourgaud

243. BATHER WITH TREE TRUNK
1930—Oil on canvas, 37.5 × 45 cm
Louise Leiris Gallery, Paris

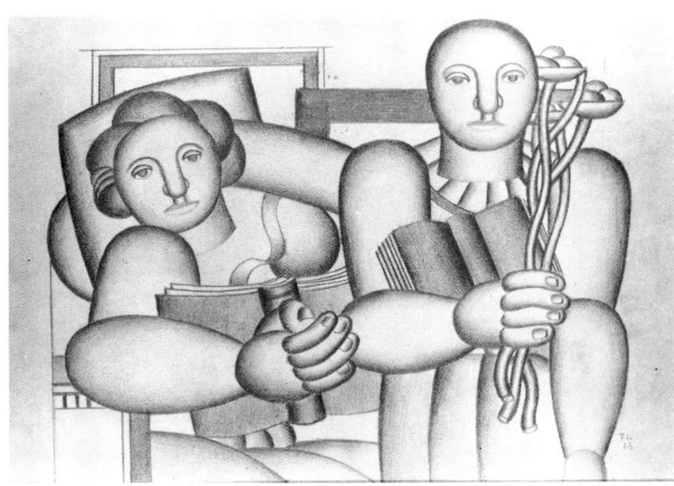

244. STUDY FOR *THE READER*
1923—Graphite on paper, 27 × 37 cm
Musée d'Art moderne, Villeneuve-d'Ascq
Gift of Geneviève and Jean Masurel

### The bald reader

Ill. 242 The anecdote of the "bald" woman in *Reading*, the
1924 painting, is significant because it comes at a turning point in Léger's artistic life. The period during which he was preoccupied uniquely by the isolation of objects, the human body included, and the focus on volumes and contrasts, was on the verge of becoming a new period in which his characters would start to live, to do things (read, for instance), be reflective, and dream, rather than be round, soulless forms stuck to a rigid geometric background. Despite Léger's need to get closer to the common man and follow him in the workplace and during his leisure time, Léger had no intention of abandoning his fundamental plastic studies. This is what attracted him to Chaplin, rather than an actor like Douglas Fairbanks: "Douglas is predictable, but Charlot rarely is. If one solidly attaches human material to the mobile decorative material, there is room for surprise. The surface increases tenfold, and the background comes alive, as well." This lesson from film marked Léger profoundly, and prompted his quest for the precise balance between the living element and the decorative element that one sees when looking at his painting of the "sisters."

To advance his system, Léger reverted to the juxtaposition of a completed landscape (not merely a geometric landscape) with a form that starts to move.
Ill. 243 *Bather with Tree Trunk* ("La Baigneuse au tronc") in
1931 is not only a charming painting, but a key work. His precisely sketched objects—rumpled fabrics, tree roots, branches, and stones—virtually reappear on the canvas. We begin to see how the inanimate and hieratic giants of the preceding period have been transformed into a gracious and lively bather. Her body is modeled. Stiff arms and legs have given way to the position of a dancer who seems to be in motion. Her volumes are exaggerated, as if to fill the canvas, but she has discovered liberty and escaped from a schematic context. Even her hair has escaped that sculpted marble aspect, and flows freely in disarray over her shoulders. The spheres are still present, but she does not need to be "bald" any more. Contrast is there, but it is softened and generous: the vegetable mass next to the bather seems to echo her. Léger treats us to his vision of two beautiful plants that seem to have sprung up together from the same earth. Trees fascinated Léger just as women did. "No two trees are alike. Trees are my great passion! I'm relaxed when there are trees around me. I'm so tempted to paint them, but I know that I'll never be able to paint them like I see them. How could I possibly give them more expression than they already have?" The same Léger who had deliberately deprived his objects and characters of all personality became preoccupied with giving "expression" to a tree! We are at the threshold of a new Léger. It is a new harvest from the same source.

Little by little, Léger was beginning to reconcile himself with the notion of the "subject." The same Léger who had severely criticized the Italian Renaissance allowed the subject to gradually impose itself in his painting. *The Bather* is one of the first canvases in which Léger stops being obsessed by the object so that he can incorporate it again in a "melodious ensemble" that is close to nature. Was this the same Léger who wanted to pursue Cézanne's atonalities? Léger's return to the subject was not a contradiction. Quite the contrary. It was the logical evolution that we saw starting in the 1920s with the character compositions. We can even trace it as far back as *Nudes in
the Forest* (1909–10). The importance of history thus Ill. 39
becomes clearer in terms of Léger's work.

After embarking once again on his quest for the com-
mon man, Léger met his *Three Musicians* ("Les Trois Ill. 245
Musiciens"), 1930. It is our initiation into a new phase of his work, since for the first time he is expressing the "voice of the people." From man-as-abstract-robot to women-as-stereotyped-statues and then to active, living characters who are real, it is important to realize that one phase could not have happened without the preceding one. Contrast is still there, even though it is reduced to a minimum between the musicians and their instruments: the lines of the strings on the base fiddle and the stops on the accordion contrast with the roundness of the musicians' shoulders, the bowler hat, and the mouth of the trombone. The haughty and dignified giants without social reference who were deprived of all
individuality in *The Big Lunch* have merely become Ill. 125

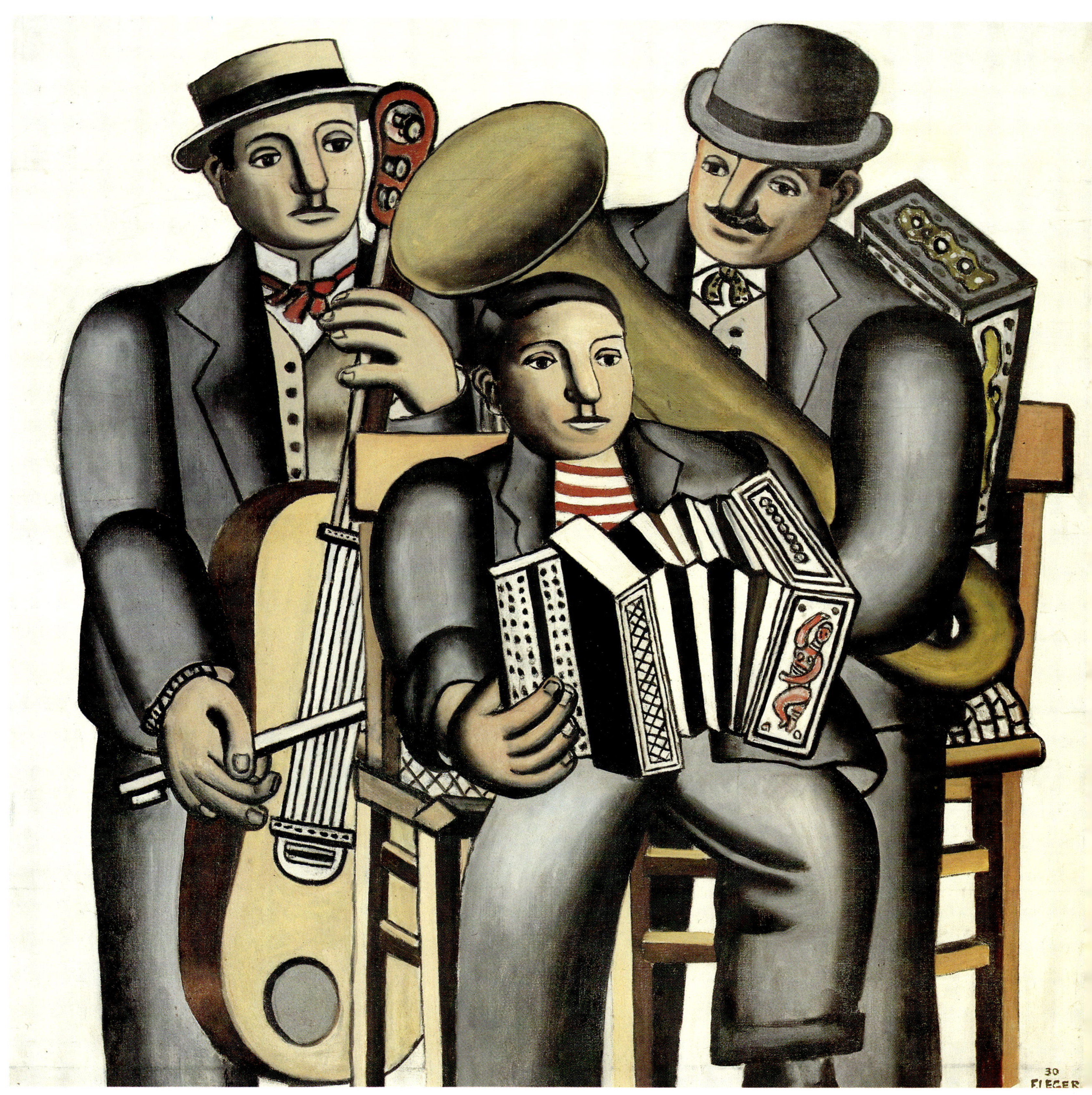


three working-class men practicing their trade, which happens to be music. They are in Sunday dress and depicted with a care for detail that reminds us of the works of the Douanier Rousseau. From the cravats to the moustache and vest buttons, the same quality of "naive" art comes through in a warm, friendly way.

Léger always identified with the simple men he had met in the trenches between 1914 and 1917. Although he had collaborated on the set designs for ballets, he had always preferred the working-class dance halls. He never tired of the clarity of "instinct" in them: "The bourgeois and decadent aristocratic milieus must be avoided at all costs. There's nothing

245. THREE MUSICIANS
1930—Oil on canvas, 72 × 72 cm
Von der Heydt-Museum, Wuppertal

to gain and everything to lose with that kind of people; the mechanism of their existence is based on a *minimal amount of life.* The rough and hard aspects of working-class life, with all its tragedies and comedies, is where I feel most at home."

Between 1925 and 1930, Léger went to the dances on the Rue de Lappe, where colors and contrasts abounded: "The majority of people whom one meets are young, and neatly dressed, working-class people. White shirts—without detachable collars—limit their features at shoulder level. That gives the effect of a medallion. Only there have I seen men's profiles. The girls stand out because of their eyes and the dryness of their matted hair. When they dance they clearly detach themselves from the naked white walls of the dance hall, and their forms have great figurative value. You can see the whole of them when they stand or lean against the wall or sit with their elbows on the tables. They are like workers who are relaxing."

Léger saw "Légers" everywhere. Everything he looked at with interest took on the attributes of his vision of the world. "It's in those kinds of milieus that one must search for the origins of a new French choreography. That's the only place it can be found."
To paraphrase Léger, we could also say that it is in
Ill. 245 *Three Musicians* that we find the origins of the material that would grow into *The Circus* ("Le Cirque") in 1950, *Acrobats and Musicians* ("Les Acrobates et les
Ill. 333 to 336 musiciens") in 1953 or *The Big Parade* ("La Grand Parade") in 1954. Ideas took a long time to germinate with Léger. Even though they seemed to disappear momentarily, it would only be to gather strength when they reappeared. While Léger was living in the United States, he said to J. J. Sweeny with
Ill. 246 regard to *Three Musicians*: "It's based on a sketch I did in 1925 that I had always wanted to transcribe to oils, but I found the opportunity to do so only after I arrived in this country." In 1944, Léger painted a
Ill. 247 new version of *Three Musicians,* fourteen years after the first one. It is sweeter, more colorful, and freer.

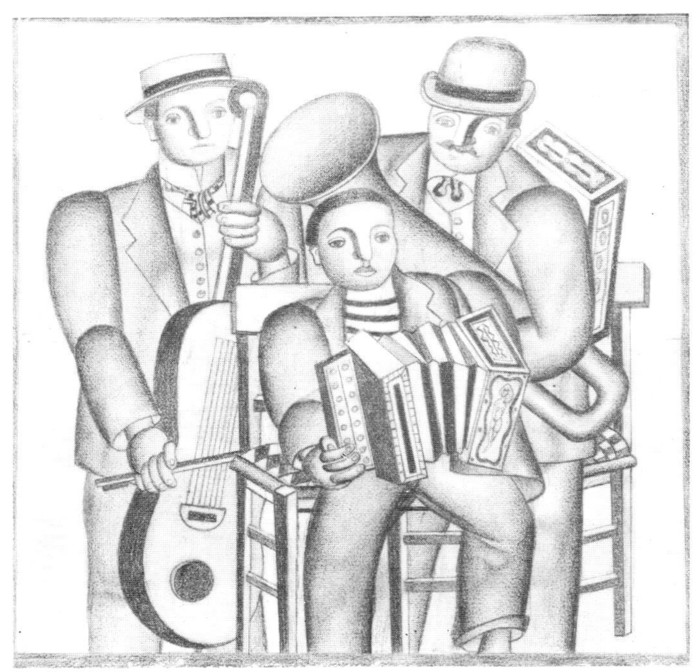

246. THREE MUSICIANS
1925—Pencil-on-paper drawing, 35 × 36 cm
Lionel Prejger collection, Paris

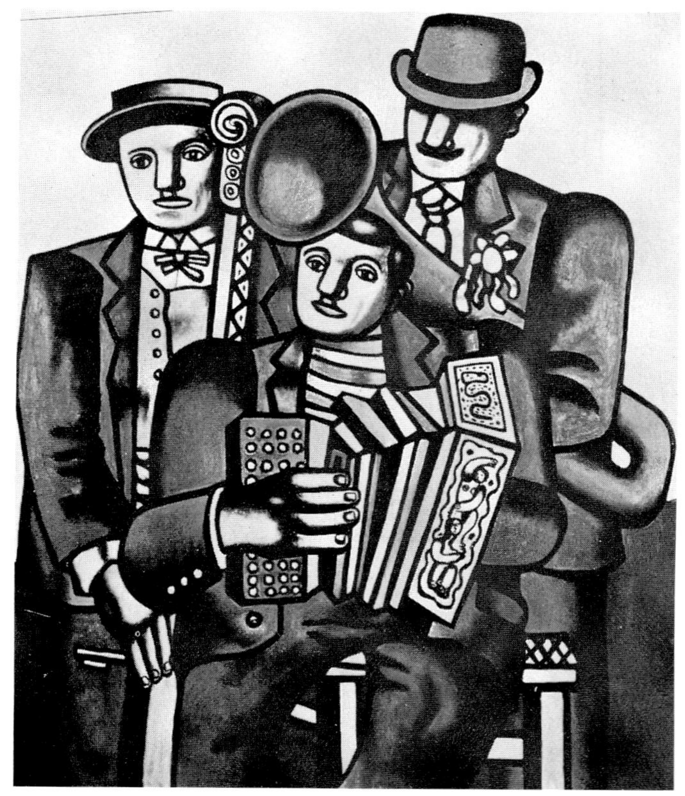

247. THREE MUSICIANS, DEFINITIVE VERSION
1944—Oil on canvas, 174 × 145.5 cm
Museum of Modern Art, New York

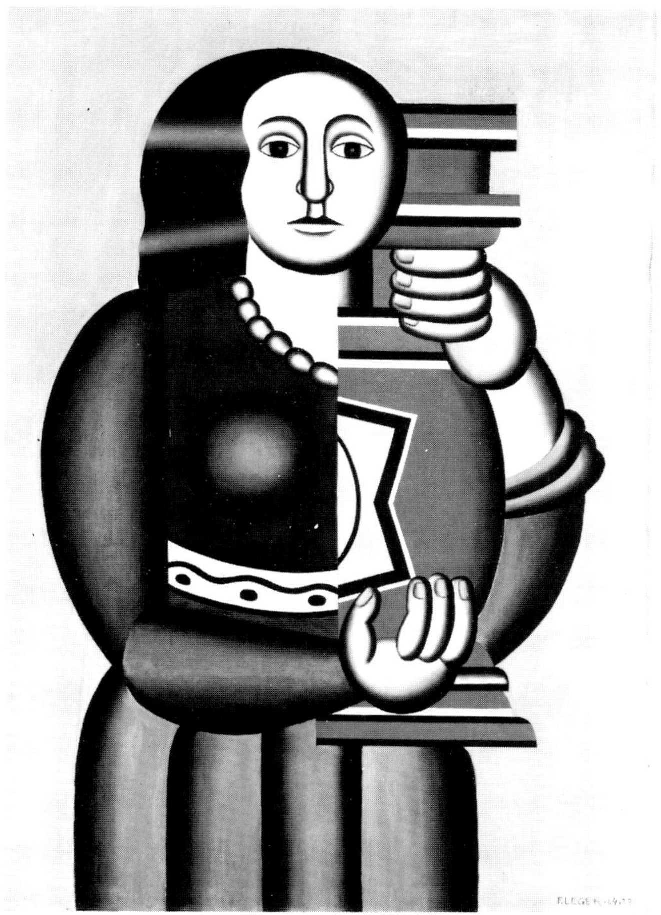

248. WOMAN HOLDING A VASE
1924–27—Oil on canvas, 131 × 89.5 cm
Oeffentliche Kunstsammlung, Kunstmuseum, Basel

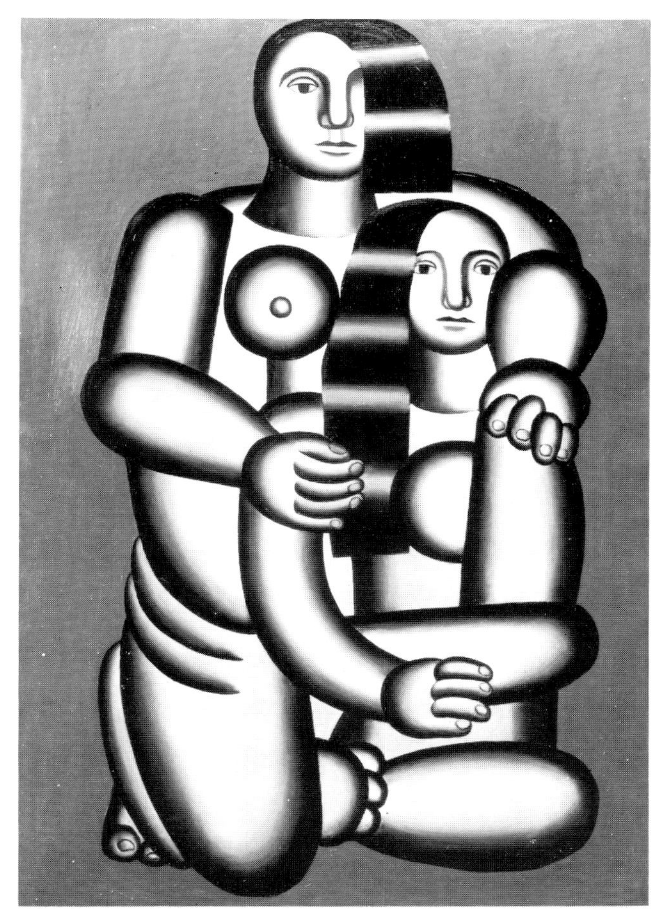

249. NUDES ON RED BACKGROUND
1923—Oil on canvas, 146.5 × 98 cm
Oeffentliche Kunstsammlung, Kunstmuseum, Basel

### The obsession with close-ups

What Léger actually did was to synthesize all his phases, all his discoveries. His nudes done in the
Ill. 251 1920s, *Three Women on Red Background* ("Trois
Ill. 249 Femmes sur fond rouge") in 1927, for example, are more than figurative studies. Léger's choice of color and his inflation of human forms give them an imperious, ostentatious, and eloquent aspect. They are on the scale of Greek and Roman antiquities. All of these paintings reflect Léger's obsession with the close-up. Léger referred to it as a "diabolical invention": "A foot on the large screen is as moving as a face. . . . A new lyricism of the transformed object has been brought into being. The plastic arts will build upon these new events, this new truth." The choice of a large format for multiple characters, such as *Composition with Three Figures* in 1932, was a synthesis whose cycle would continue until 1945 when
Ill. 250 Léger painted *The Big Julie* ("La Grande Julie"). *Mona
Ill. 222 Lisa with Keys* was also representative of a synthesis in Léger's work in which he divided elements of the canvas into two groups. He used a type of dialetic with the very deliberate opposition of clearly formulated, contrasting themes: faces and roses, bathers and tree trunks, Marie the acrobat and coat hanger, Adam and Eve, big Julie and bicycle, and so on.

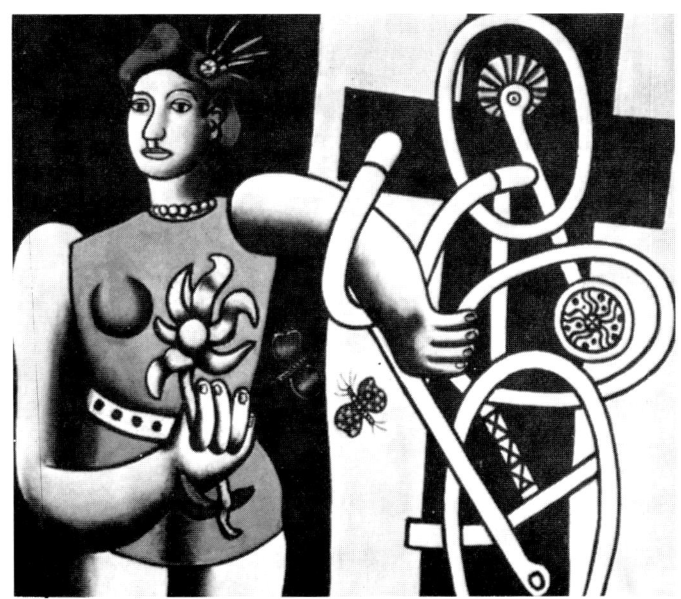

50. THE BIG JULIE
1945—Oil on canvas, 102 × 127 cm
Museum of Modern Art, New York

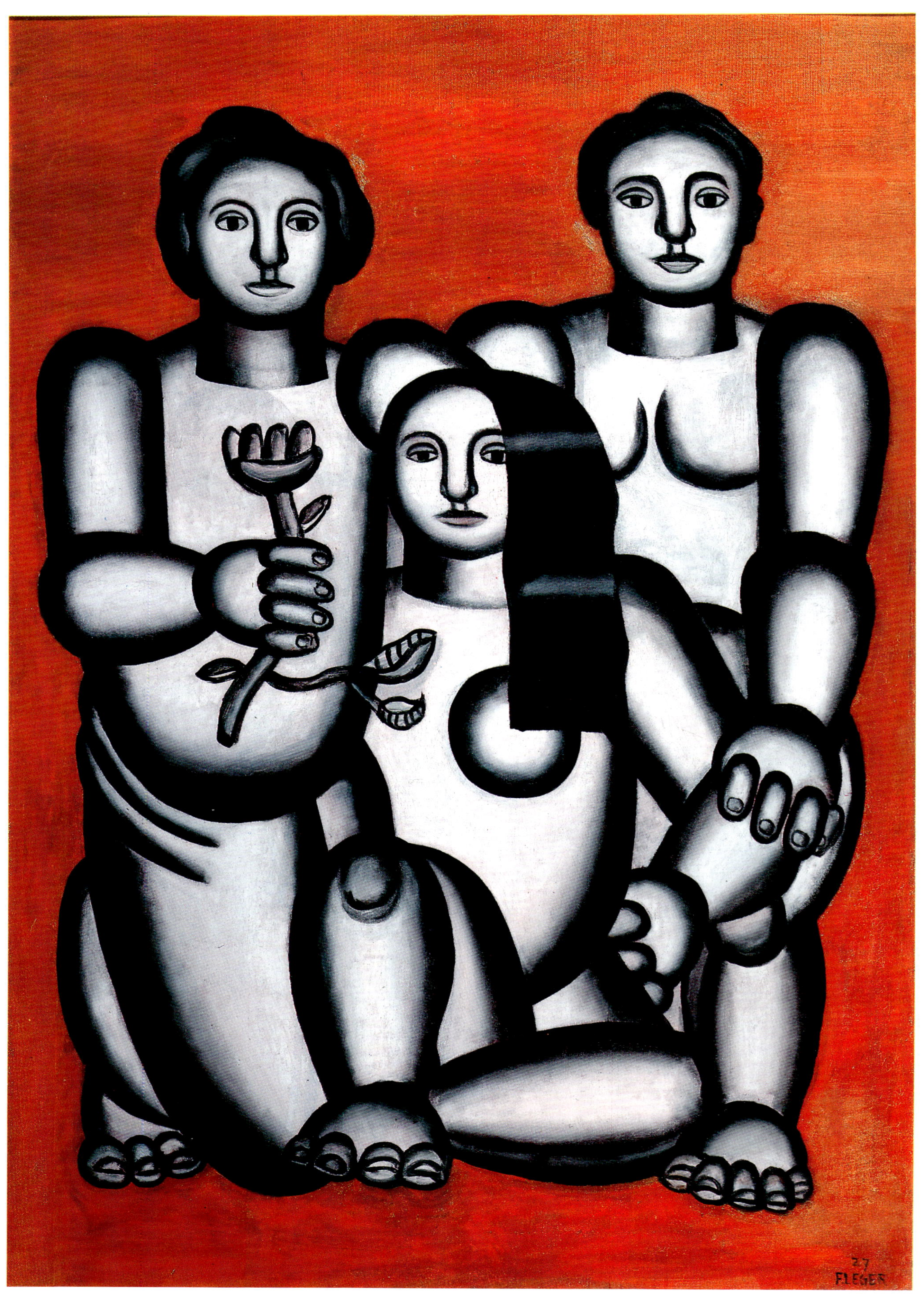


251. THREE WOMEN ON RED BACKGROUND
1927—Oil on canvas, 139 × 96 cm
Musée d'Art Moderne, Saint-Étienne

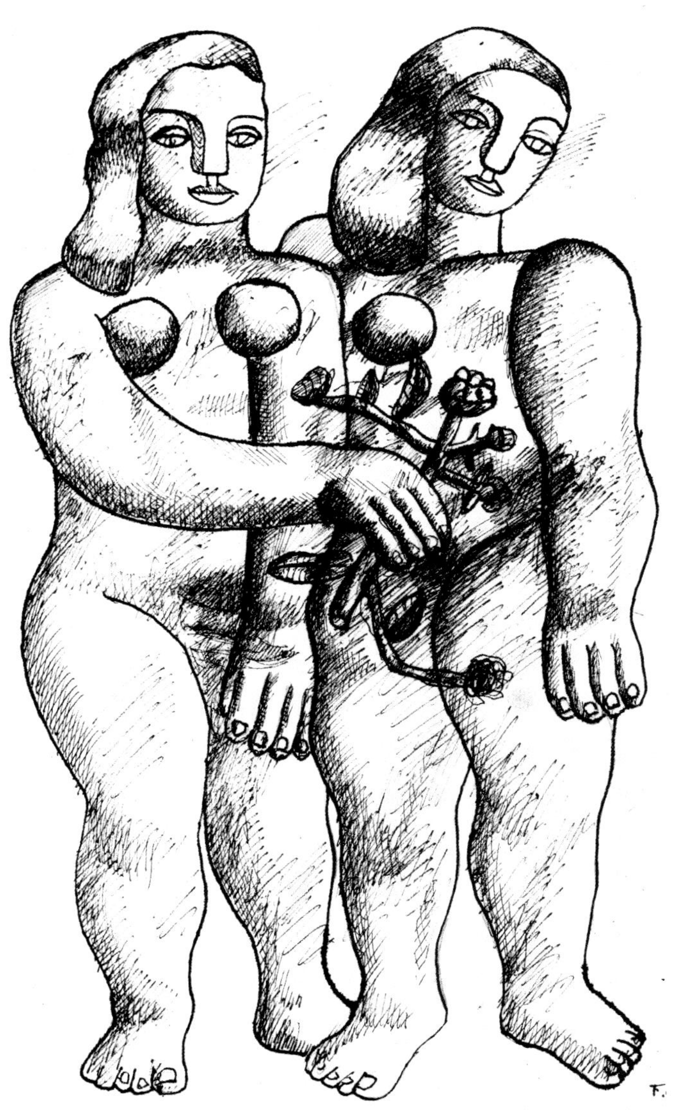

252. TWO SISTERS
1939—Pen drawing, 42 × 28
Private collection

## The naturalism of ugliness

Ill. 254 In 1935, Léger painted *The Two Sisters* ("Les Deux Soeurs"). He painted two ugly women to prove a point: he would not fall into the same trap as Leonardo da Vinci. Léger's paintings would remain
222 "trump cards" like his *Mona Lisa*, and would not allow themselves to become new phases of the Renaissance. Beauty as a subject had to be formally forbidden because it would destroy the canvas! "If a subject or an object is beautiful, it's no longer the raw material. It's already a plastic value, and therefore unusable; the only thing left to do would be to look at it and admire it." This was Léger's logic!

This naturalism of ugliness that prompted Léger to paint four-fingered hands on his two charming "fatties" was also an effort to bring him closer to real-life people. Léger foresaw what would come in magazine and television advertising, the commercials that bombard us with beautiful dream-women to sell cars to men, and dirty rags to sell detergent to homemakers. He sought to avoid it in his own work. The sisters whom Léger's maid had seen when she looked at his *Three Women* would become a reality in *The Two Sisters*. Léger drew on ordinary people for his examples. Nonetheless, the magic of Léger's brushstrokes and the enormousness and monumental character of his forms make *The Two Sisters* a superb work of art. They almost *become* beautiful. They are neither abstract nor identical. If they do resemble each other, it is because they are real-life siblings, as the title indicates. He contrasts the heaviness of their bodies with his favorite flower, the rose. There is power in this strange combination of violence and tenderness. The blend of naturalness and unreality in his figurative syntax proves Léger's command, his clarity of intent. Twenty years later he would use the same subject in
*Three Sisters*, in which the family will have grown to Ill. 326
include a young boy sitting on the lap of the reclining sister and playing the accordion. Instead of a yellow decor, he would paint a blue decor, but the same power, tenderness, and poetry of the first painting would come through.

253. TWO WOMEN
1934—Ink drawing
Private collection

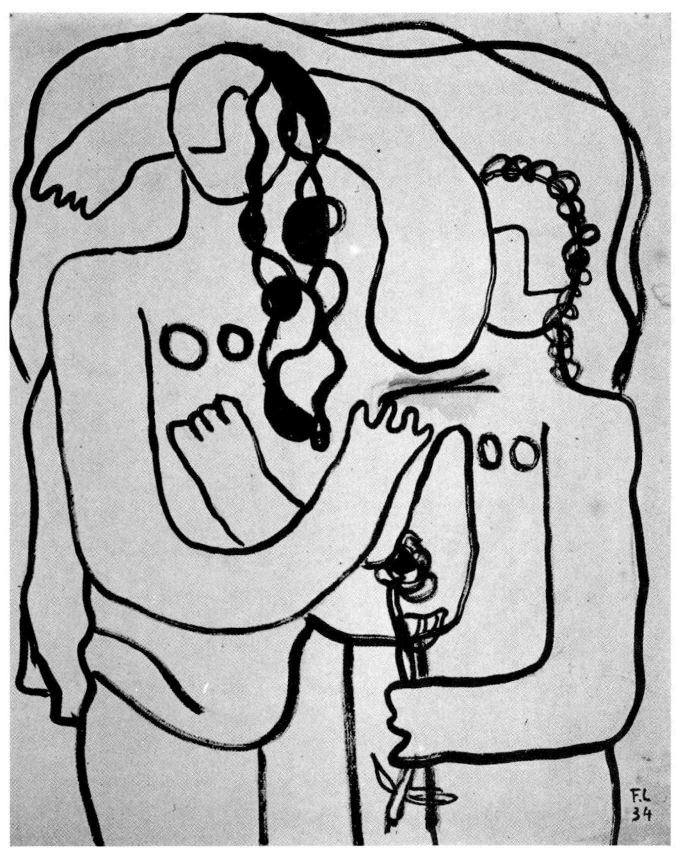

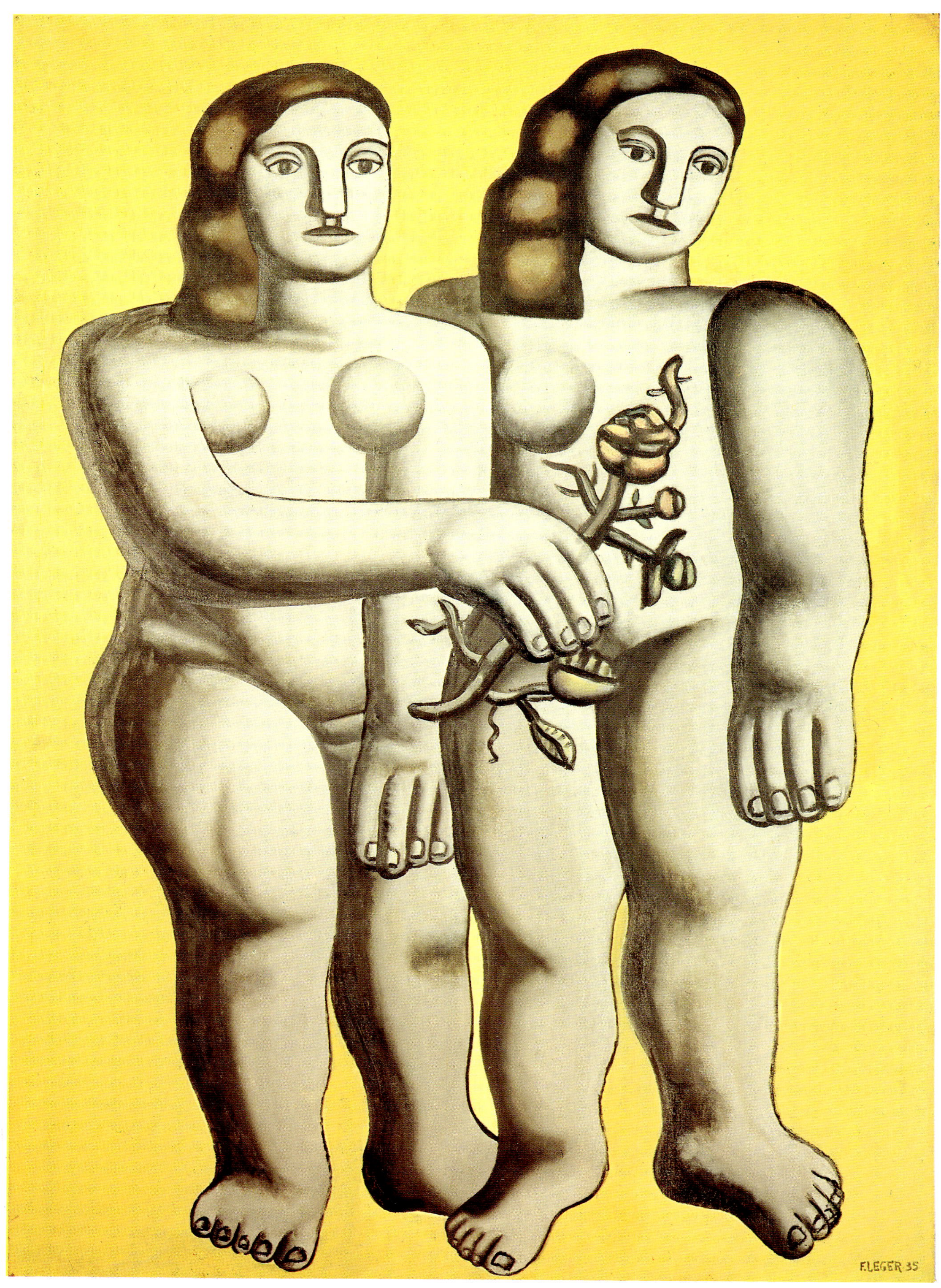


254. TWO SISTERS
1935—Oil on canvas, 162 × 114 cm
Staatliche Museen, Nationalgalerie, Berlin

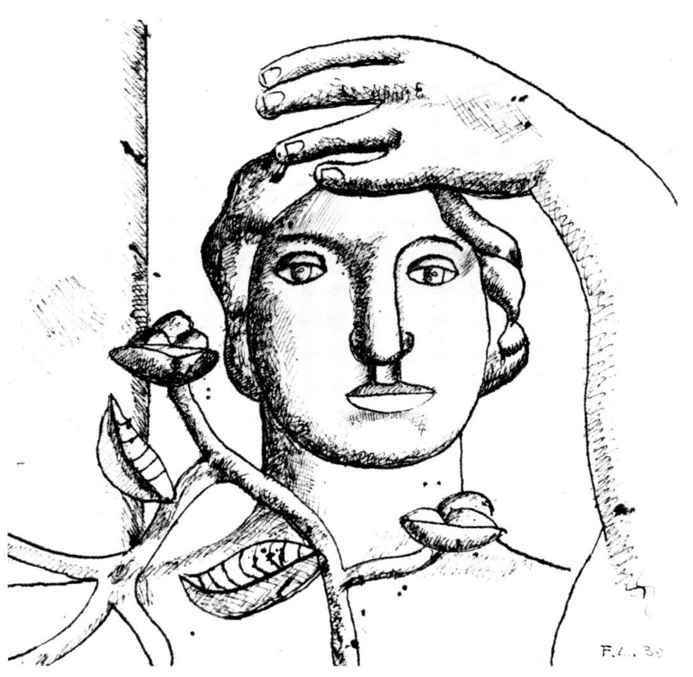

255. HEAD, HAND AND FLOWER
1939—Pen drawing
Private collection

Léger was conscious of renewing his ties with the great classical tradition of figurative painting, even though he was not totally ready to admit it. He did, however, remain objective: "The painters of the Italian Renaissance reproduced the human body. The modern painter, however, must confront different problems. . . . As far as I'm concerned, I 'invent' human form in a freer way than the Renaissance artists. I'm more in the tradition of the romantic art of the cathedrals and the primitive art that preceded the Italian Renaissance. . . . Later on, people will realize that this art isn't so very revolutionary and that it's closer to old tradition."

256. HEAD AND HAND
1939—Pen drawing, 31.5 × 40 cm
Private collection

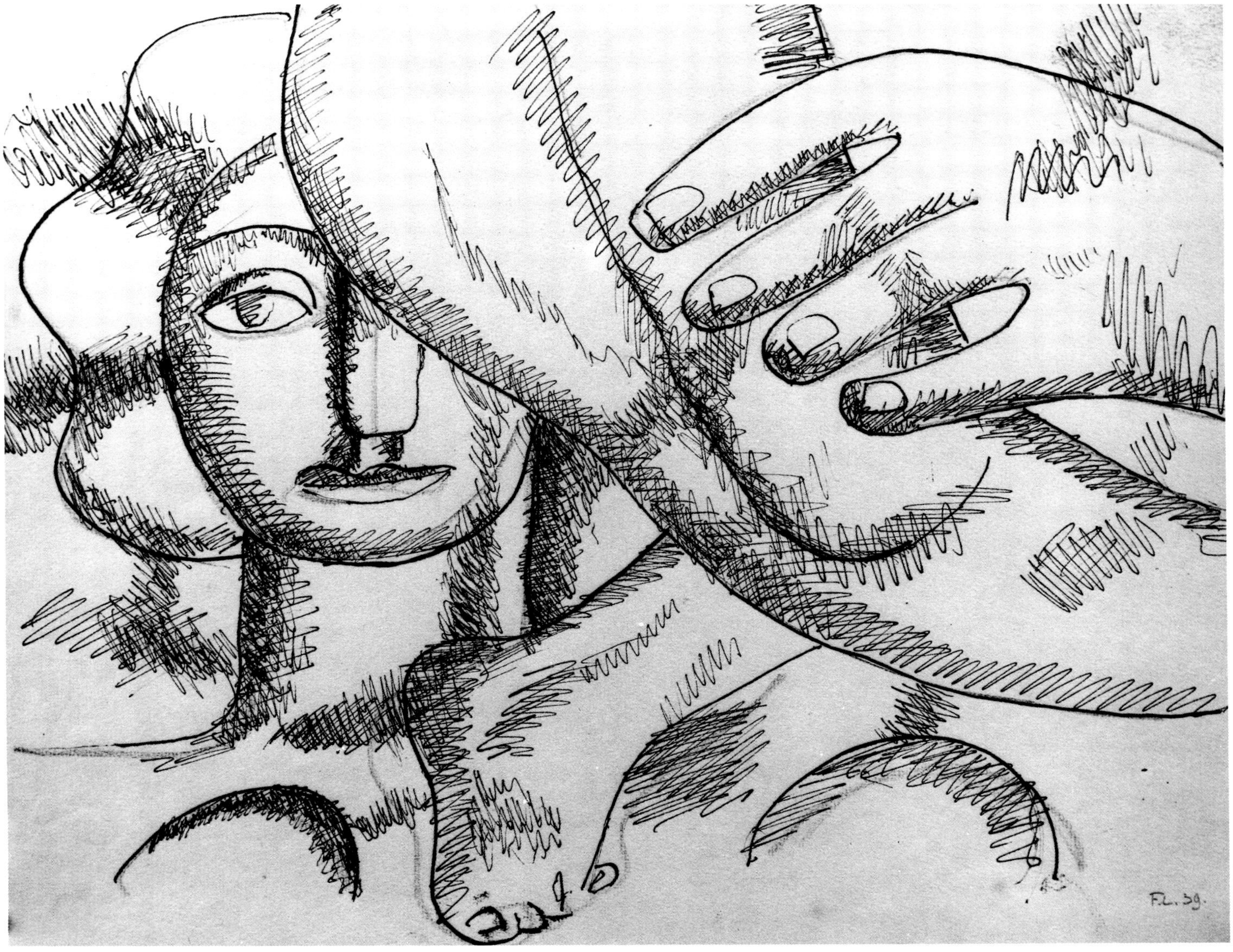

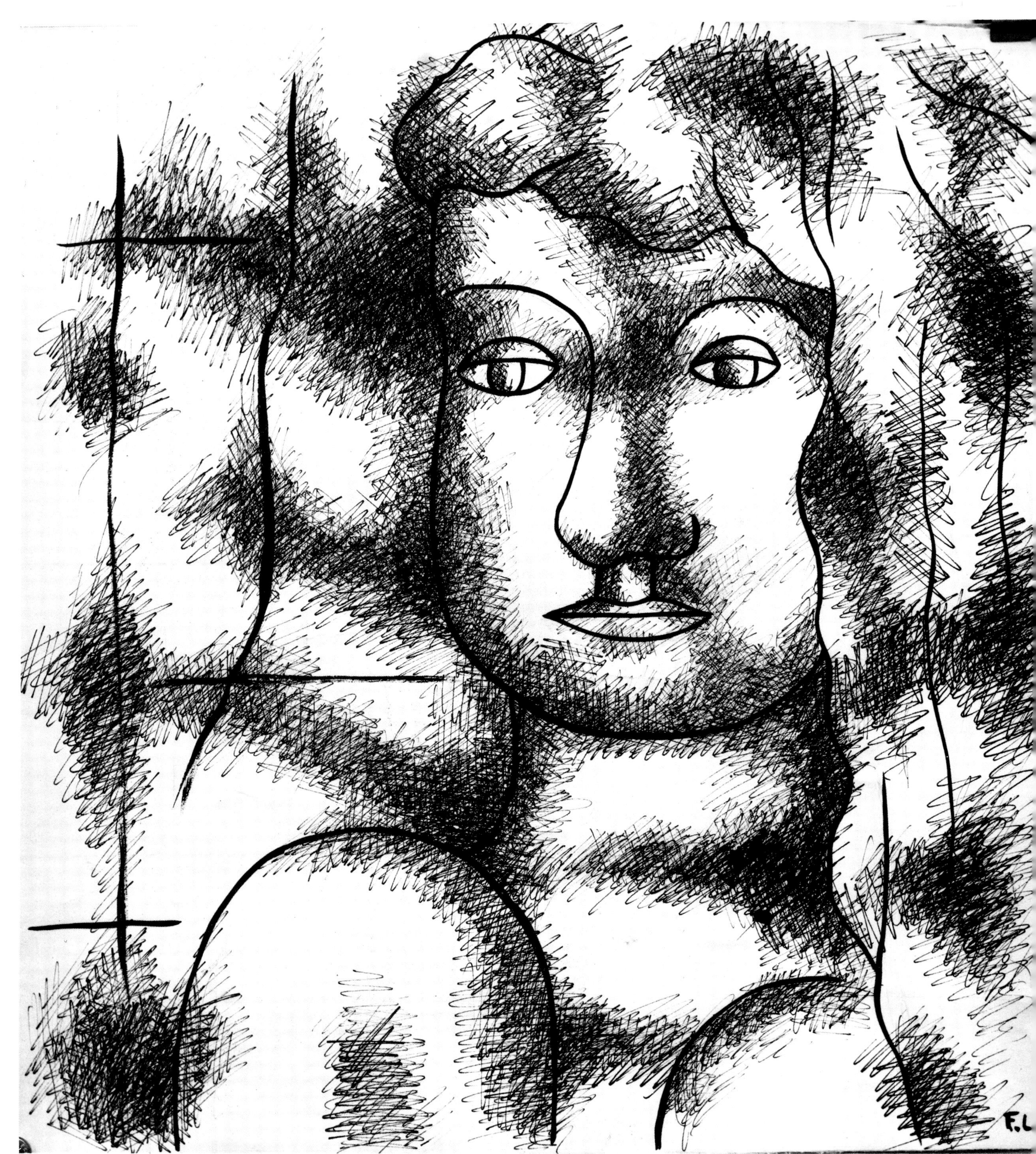


257. FACE
About 1938—Pen drawing, 42 × 37 cm
Private collection

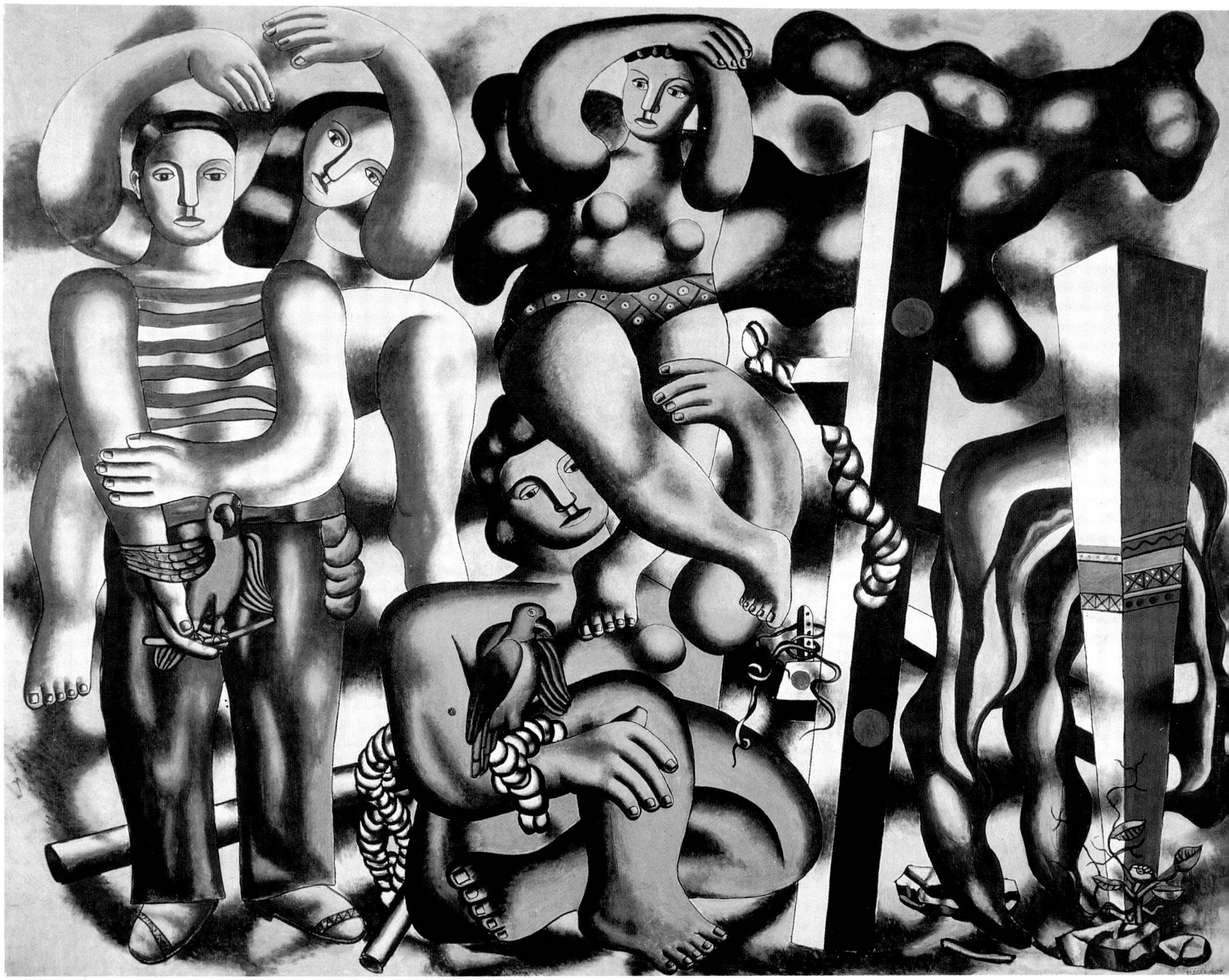

258. COMPOSITION WITH TWO PARROTS
1935–39—Oil on canvas, 400 × 480 cm
Musée National d'Art Moderne, Centre Georges Pompidou, Paris

## I'm working on my biggies

Léger did not give up his monumental scale, but it became monumental scale in movement: an acrobat
Ill. 259 flourishing a dance step, like *Marie, the Acrobat* ("Marie, l'acrobate") in 1934, for example. Léger attached great importance to this painting as proof of his evolution and the success of his methods. He worked for several years on it: "I'm working on my biggies. It's long and slow." All the ingredients were there in a new form: space, the acrobat, the cloud, geometry, the wrinkled fabric.

The total fusion of these elements occurred in the large *Composition with Two Parrots* ("Composition aux Ill. 258
deux perroquets"), 1935–39, with studies dated 1933 and 1937. It was the peak of this synthetic phase, which united all the ingredients: the vertical distribution of mass, the alteration between fullness and emptiness, light zones and dark zones, ample and undulating rhythms, and contrapuntal curves. Each painting was a kind of ballet of flexible, elastic forms that were suspended in space, dancing in the middle of nowhere.

The *subject* got a hold on Léger and never relinquished him, regardless of how much Léger defended

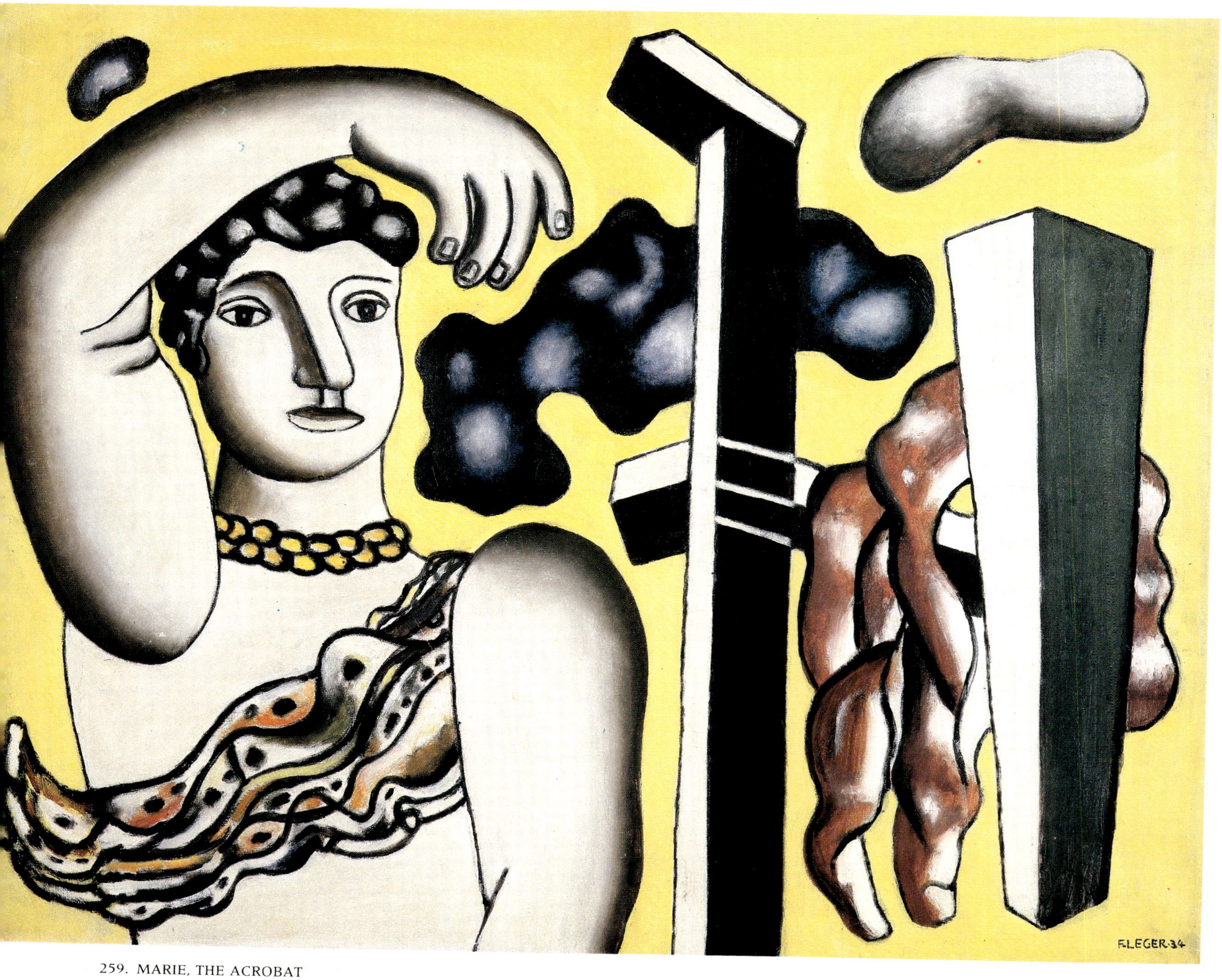

259. MARIE, THE ACROBAT
1934—Oil on canvas, 73 × 92 cm
Louise Leiris Gallery, Paris

himself: "I take on big subjects, but I must repeat the fact that my painting is still object-painting. It started
l. 260 in 1936 with *Adam and Eve*. My characters continued to be more humanized, but I am still working within the context of the plastic fact, and not eloquence or romanticism." Léger's paintings were far from such
l. 165 earlier titles as *Mechanical Elements.* Adam and Eve came straight out of the Bible and landed on Léger's canvas as acrobats in leotards with tattoos on the arm. They stood in a very proletarian Eden holding Léger's typical flower, which was his representation of the "tree of knowledge." Even the serpent was present. He was wound around the acrobat's stick. It was a perfect anecdote, an illustration that would fit very well into the Book of Genesis!

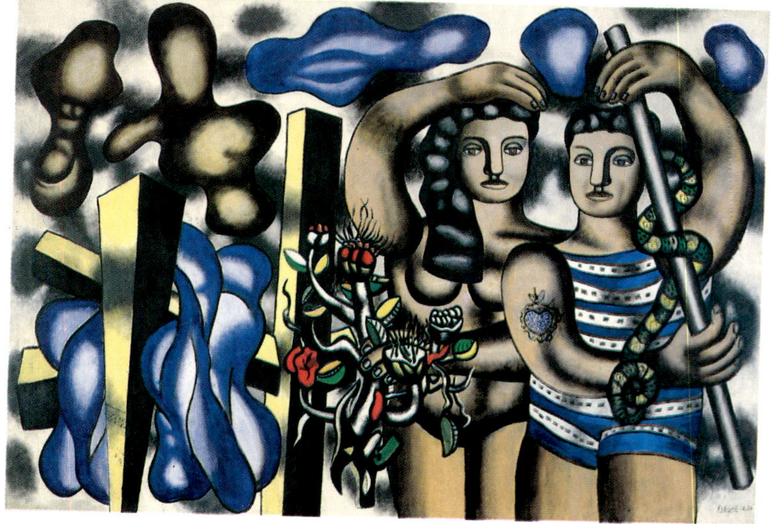

260. ADAM AND EVE, DEFINITIVE VERSION
1935–39—Oil on canvas, 228 × 324 cm
Kunstsammlung Nordrhein Westfalen, Düsseldorf

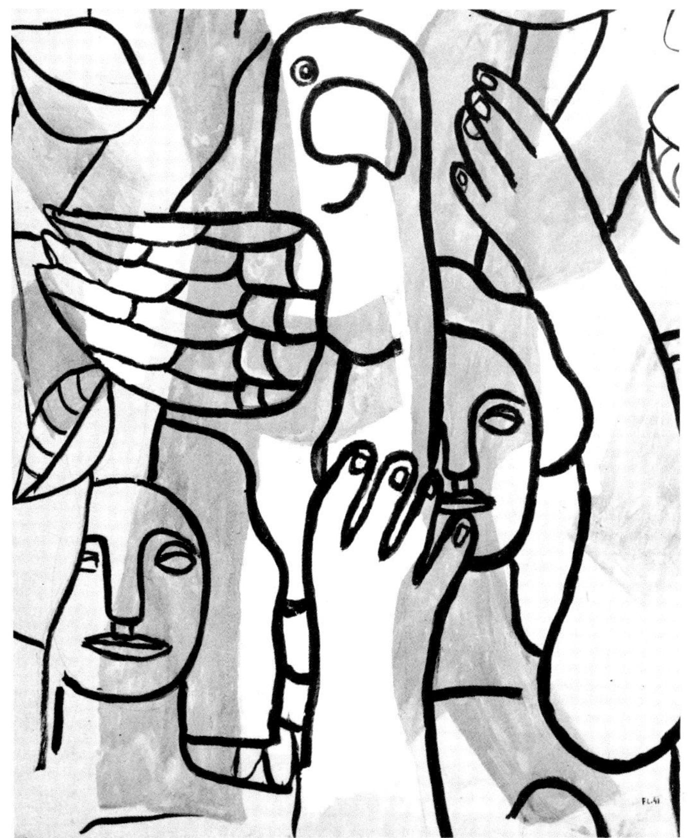

261. TWO WOMEN WITH PARROT
1941—Gouache, 114 × 91 cm
Private collection

## The color liberated from the floodlights

Those close to Léger tell of how, in the midst of his biggies, he was looking for the small detail, an element that would contrast with all that monumentality. He was tired of the flower. Someone he knew had made a little stuffed parrot and gave it to him. Léger started parading it from one canvas to the next until he found the right place for it. That became the series of his "parrot paintings." Thanks to Léger, the little winged creature became a giant and monumen-
Ill. 261 tal bird of prey.

There was another reason why *Two Women with Parrot* ("Les Deux Femmes au perroquet") in 1941, and *Two Women with a Bird* (1942) marked a new revolution. This was the first time that Léger pushed his study of color to the limit, and dissociated color from the drawing. The two women are there with the giant parrot in the midst of the trees and bushes, but the colors are elsewhere. There are red bands of color or green bands of color, blue bands and yellow bands—color has escaped, and taken its freedom. Léger did not like the role of jailer that Mondrian was so fond of.

"I completely separated color from the drawing; this gives another movement, an intense dynamism." He would apply autonomous color to numerous can-
vases until *The Big Parade* in 1954. The story of how I
this idea came about is worth telling. He had already visited the United States in 1931, and returned to live there during World War II. He was in the United States from October 1940 to December 1945, when he returned to France. In the streets of New York, and on Broadway in particular, he explained: "I was struck by the play of color from the colored floodlights that swept through the streets to advertise things. I was talking to someone. He had a blue face. Twenty seconds later his face turned yellow. One color came, then another arrived, and he became red, then green. I lifted my head and looked at the buildings. They were striated with bands of color. That really made an impression on me. The changing colors on the faces, this color projected from spotlights, was liberated, *free.* It was in space. I wanted to do the same thing on my canvases." Let us remember the time when Léger wanted to paint the city in different colors. Now it was the city that streaked his canvases with colors.

262. HANDS
1939—Pen drawing, 40 × 31.5 cm
Private collection

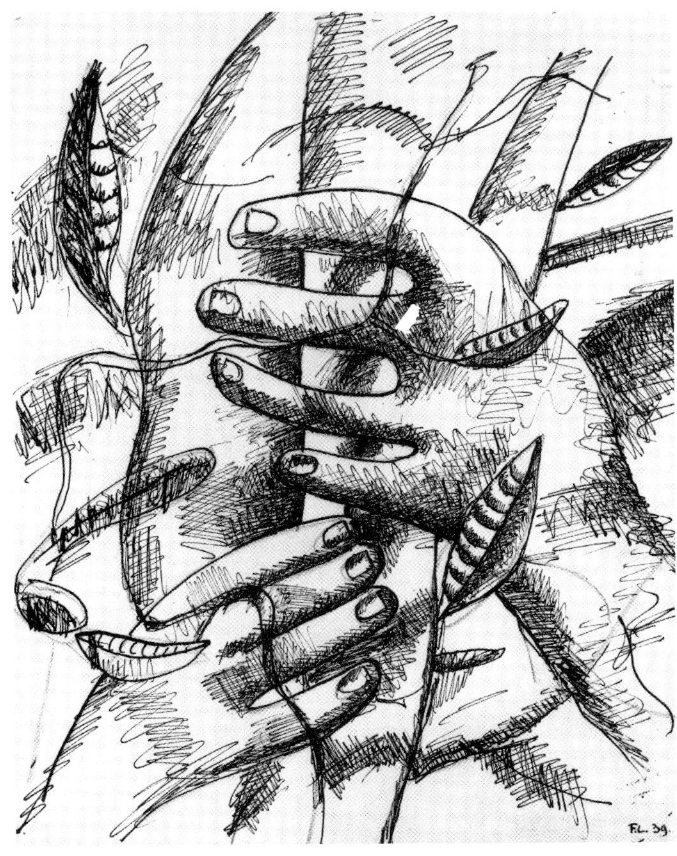

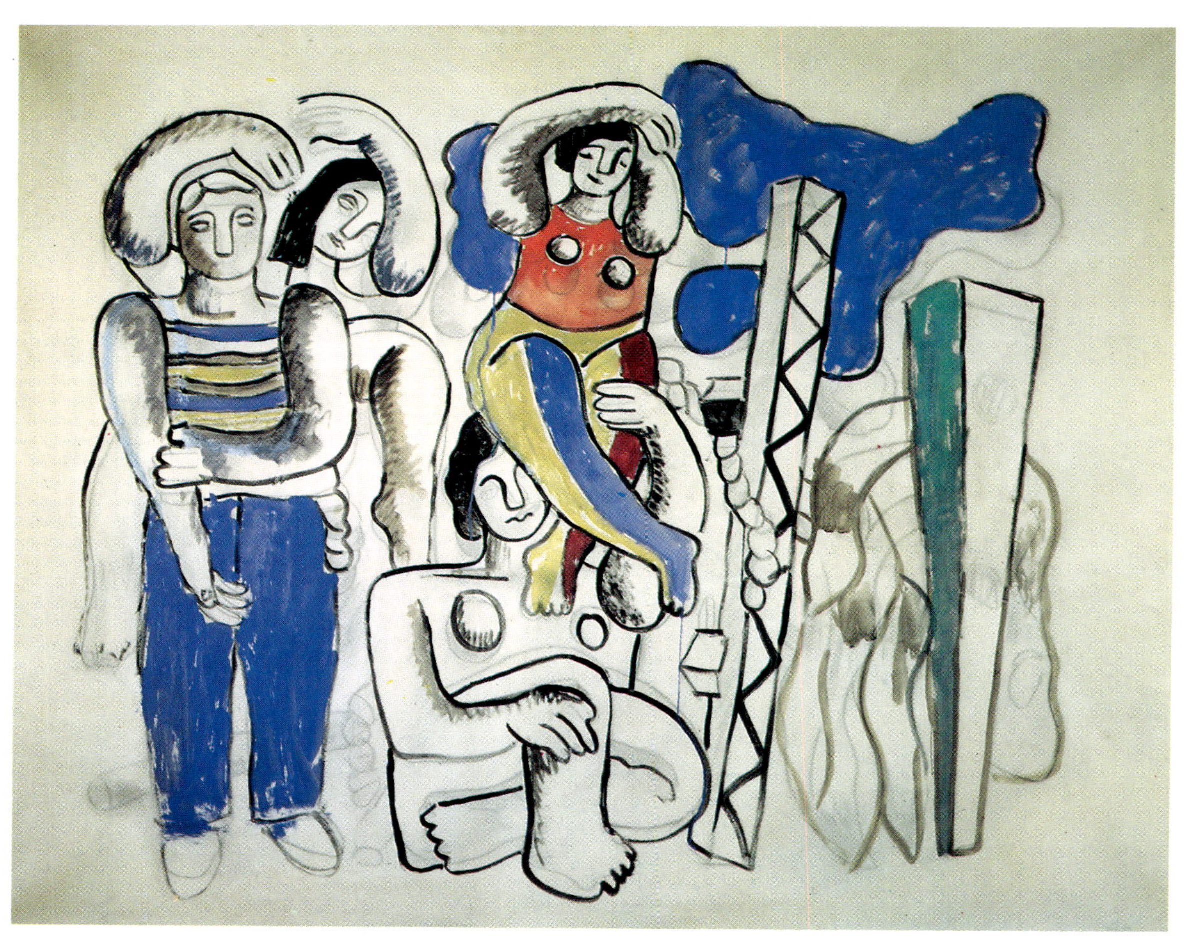

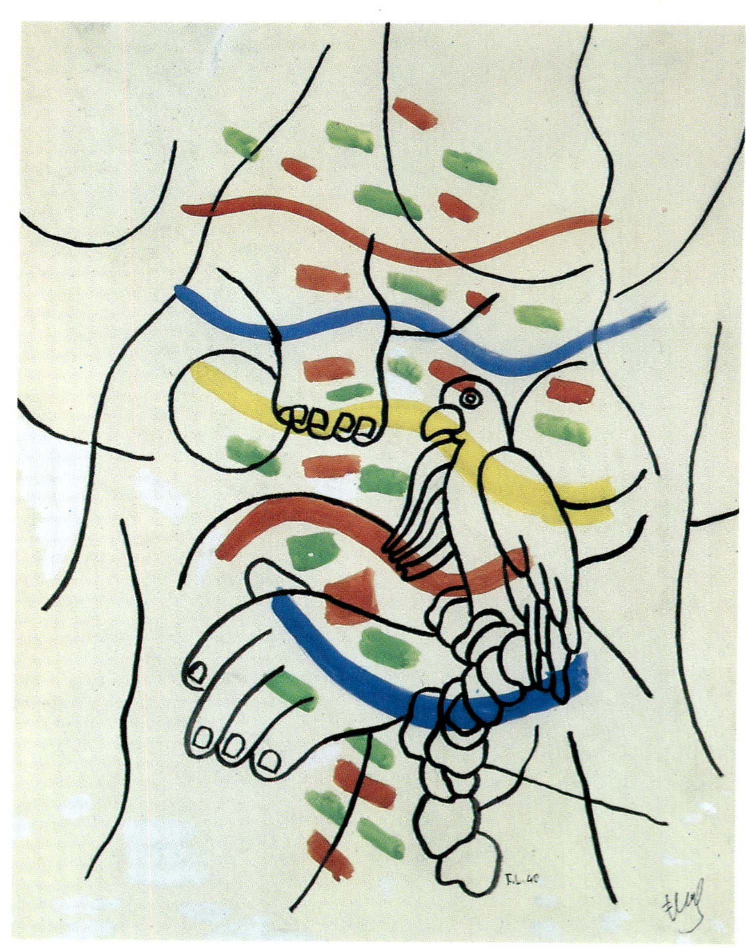

263. COMPOSITION WITH PARROT
About 1935—Gouache and graphite on paper, 152 × 189 cm
Collection of Mr. and Mrs. Adrien Maeght

264. TWO WOMEN WITH PARROT
1940—Gouache, 53 × 42 cm
Collection of Mr. and Mrs. Adrien Maeght

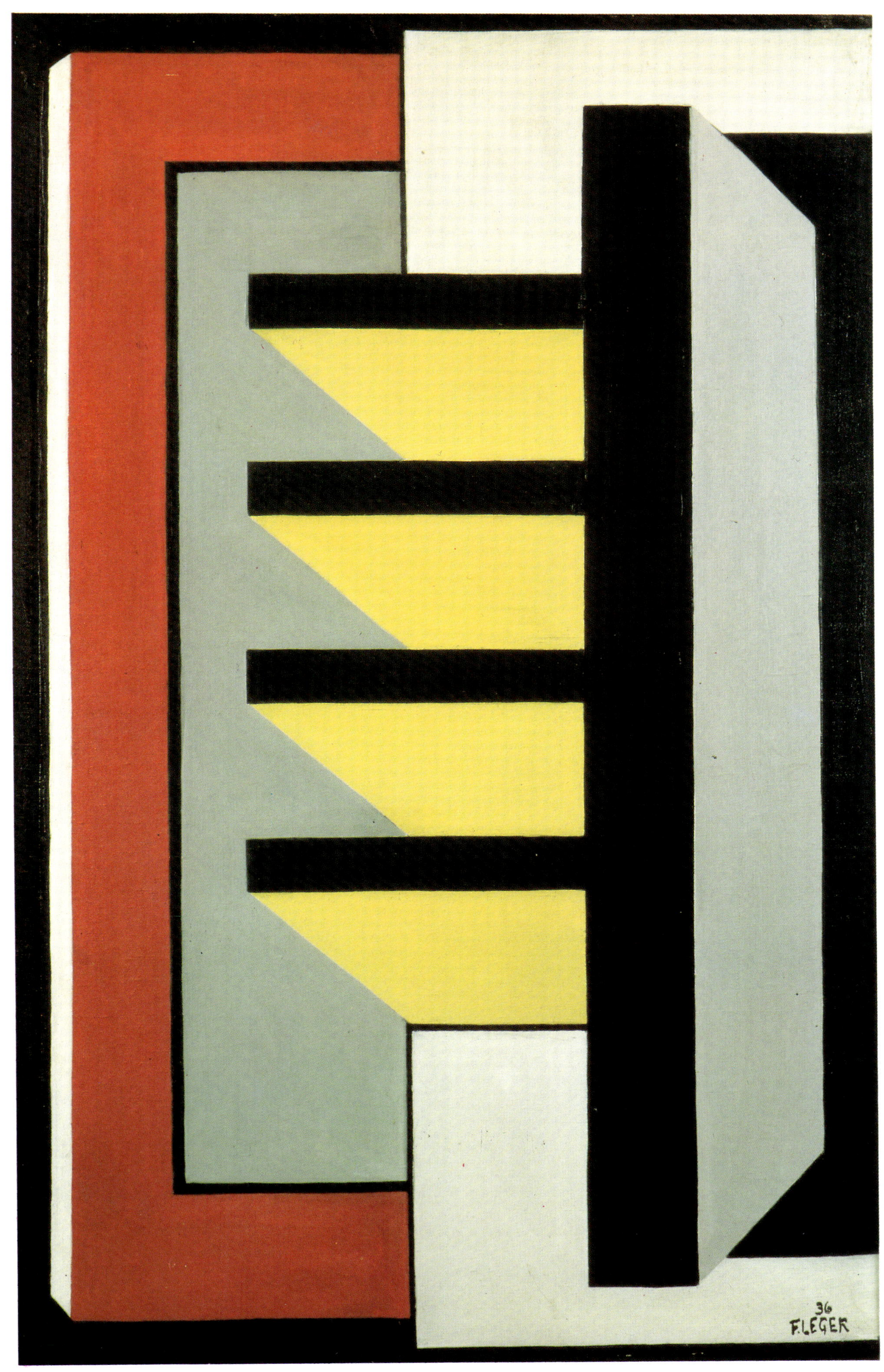


265. MURAL COMPOSITION
1936—Oil on canvas, 130 × 80.5 cm
Private collection

# Monumental Language

"During the Exposition of 1937 I thought of hiring 300,000 unemployed workers to clean up all the houses of Paris. The idea was to create a 'surprising event' for the visitors: an all-white Paris. At night, large spotlights would flood the city with vibrant, moving colors. Why not? My project was not accepted. Nonetheless, it was the only way of creating a new event on the scale of an international show." André Malraux, who became minister of culture under Charles de Gaulle, would recall Léger's proposal. "Why would a minority of the ruling classes own our paintings and derive all the benefits from them?" Léger asked. Everyone should benefit from the magic of color and form: let's get the paintings into the streets, comrades, so that everyone can profit from them! "A naked wall is *a dead surface.* A colored wall is *a living surface.*" Léger's architect friends were very taken with Léger's witty monumental paintings, even when their formats were not large. In particular, they were captivated by some of his abstract compositions in pure color that he painted between 1921 and 1925. Léger himself admitted that he had not composed in the spirit of easel painting, and he was burning to bring color and architecture into play. He wanted to do murals in color, "either as a decorative companion piece, or as a destruction of the wall." He felt both were possible. The Decorative Arts Exhibit of 1925 provided him the occasion to present one of these to the public. It was the embassy project of Mallet-Stevens, the pavilion in the "Esprit Nouveau" ("new spirit") of Le Corbusier. "Reactions were naturally mixed," noted Léger, disillusioned. "But the impact had been made and the consequences are taking place."

Léger had proposed to create a feeling of space, to break the color barriers in terms of the confining limits of walls. He wanted walls of different colors that corresponded to the various abstractions that he attached to them. This included interior walls as well as exterior walls. "The apartment that I will refer to as 'an inhabitable rectangle' will be transformed into an 'elastic rectangle.' A yellow wall disappears (the destruction of the wall). The new possibilities are numerous. A black piano, for example, in front of a pale yellow wall creates a visual shock that can diminish the feeling of dimension." Color had a major social role to accomplish. It contributed to enveloping the monotonous everyday realities. It dressed reality. The humblest objects could be and were calling out for color to change the way people perceived their real purpose. "Let's try to continue this effort towards space and liberation in the architecture of the future. Color is a powerful means of action. It can destroy a wall or decorate a wall. It can make the wall recede or advance. It creates a new space. . . . The goal is to attain perfect beauty through the balance of *new plastic forces.* This is what modern architecture must attempt to achieve."

266. MURAL COMPOSITION
1926—Oil on canvas, 130 × 97 cm

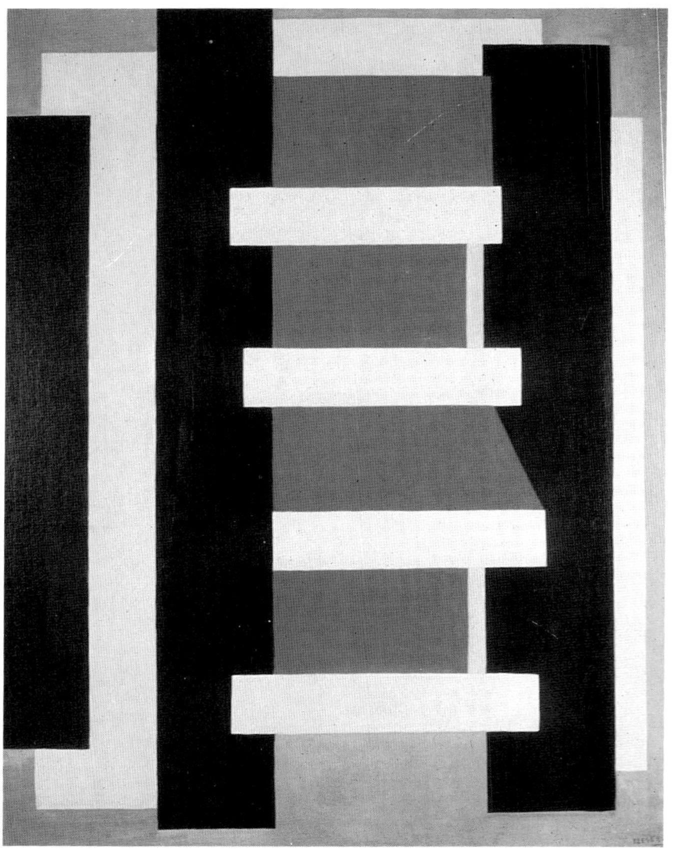

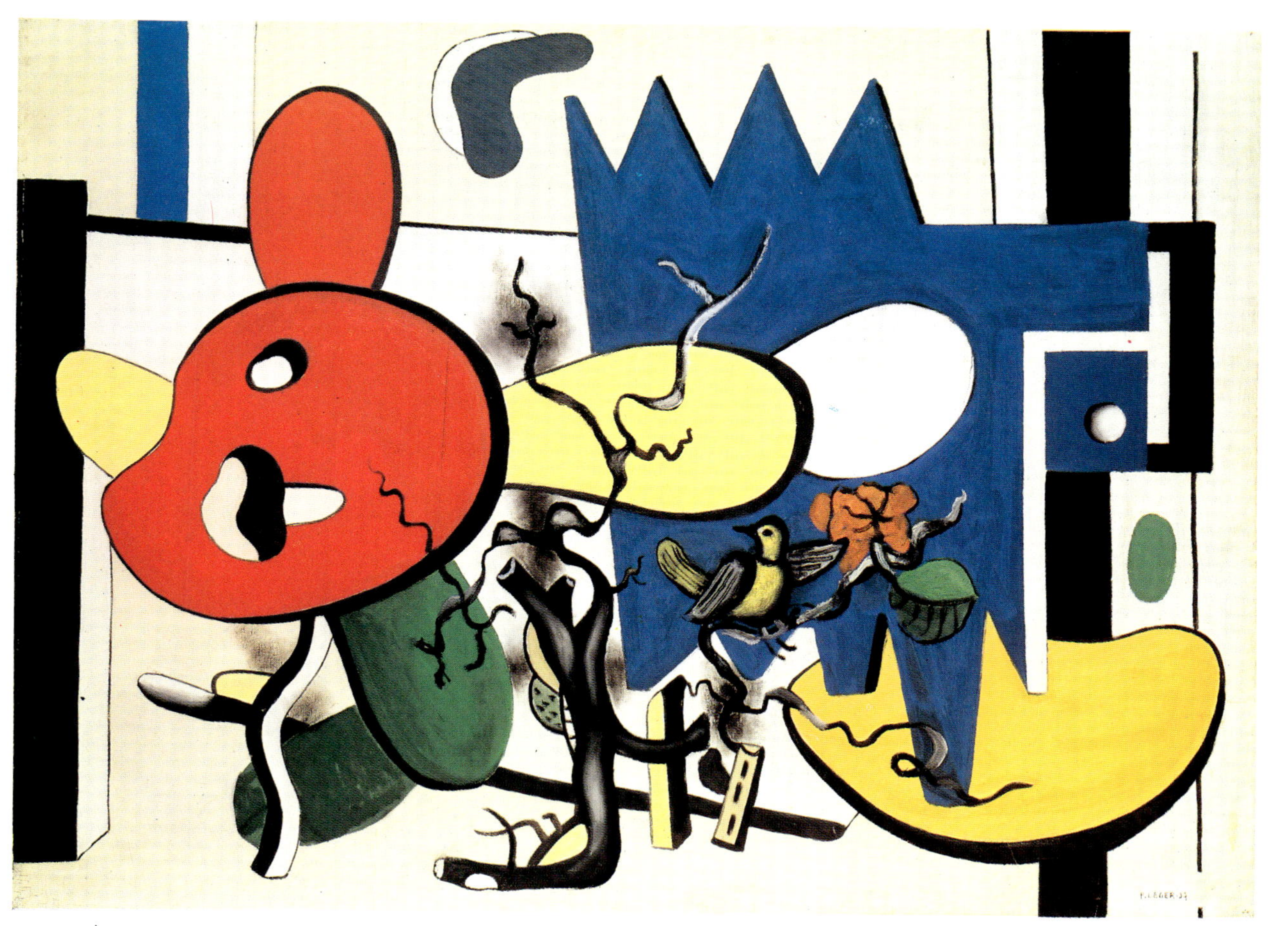

267. COMPOSITION WITH YELLOW CANARY
1937—Oil on canvas, 97 × 130 cm
Beyeler Gallery, Basel

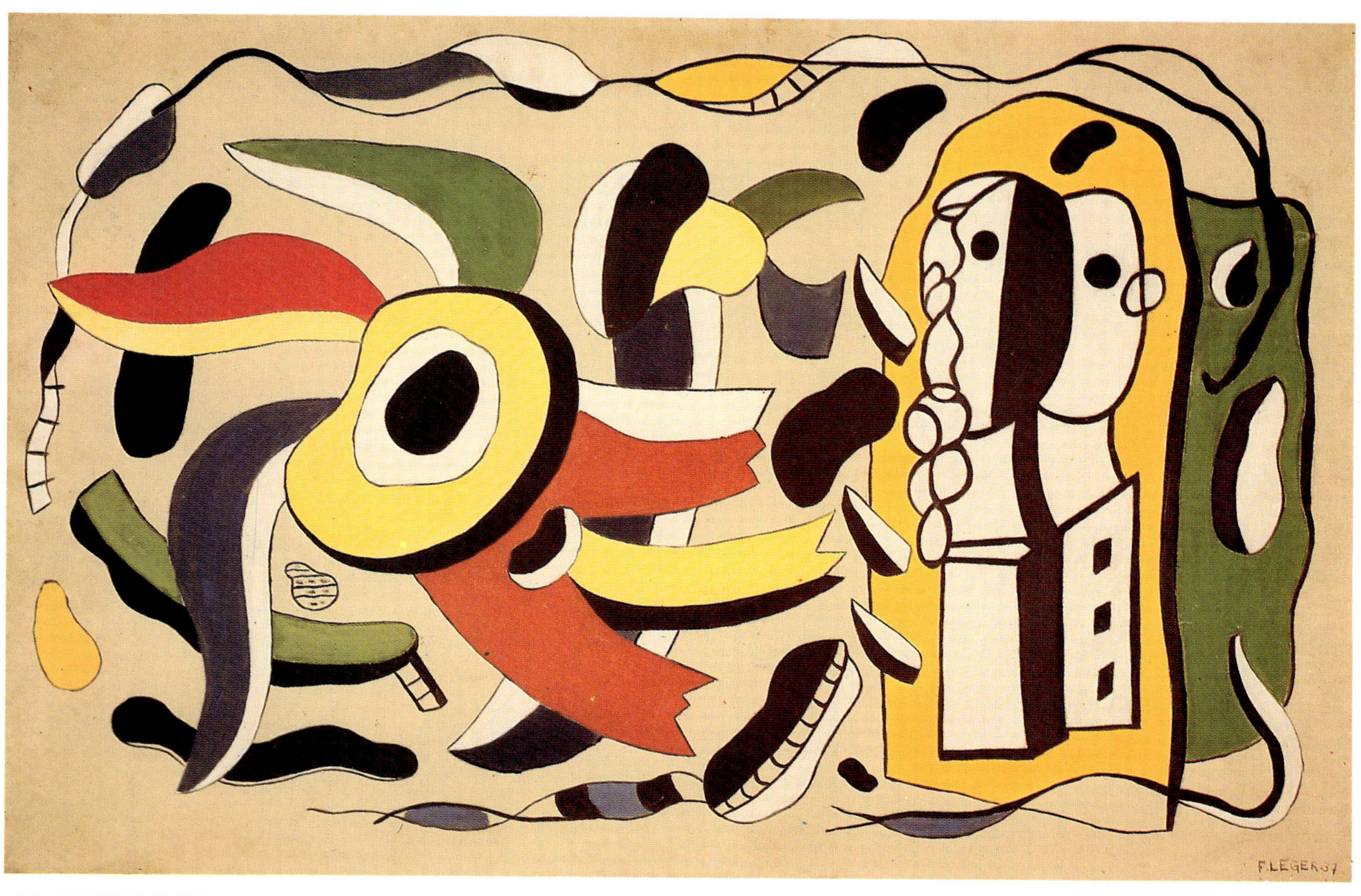


68. TWO DUMMIES
1937—Oil on canvas, 60 × 92 cm
Louise Leiris Gallery, Paris

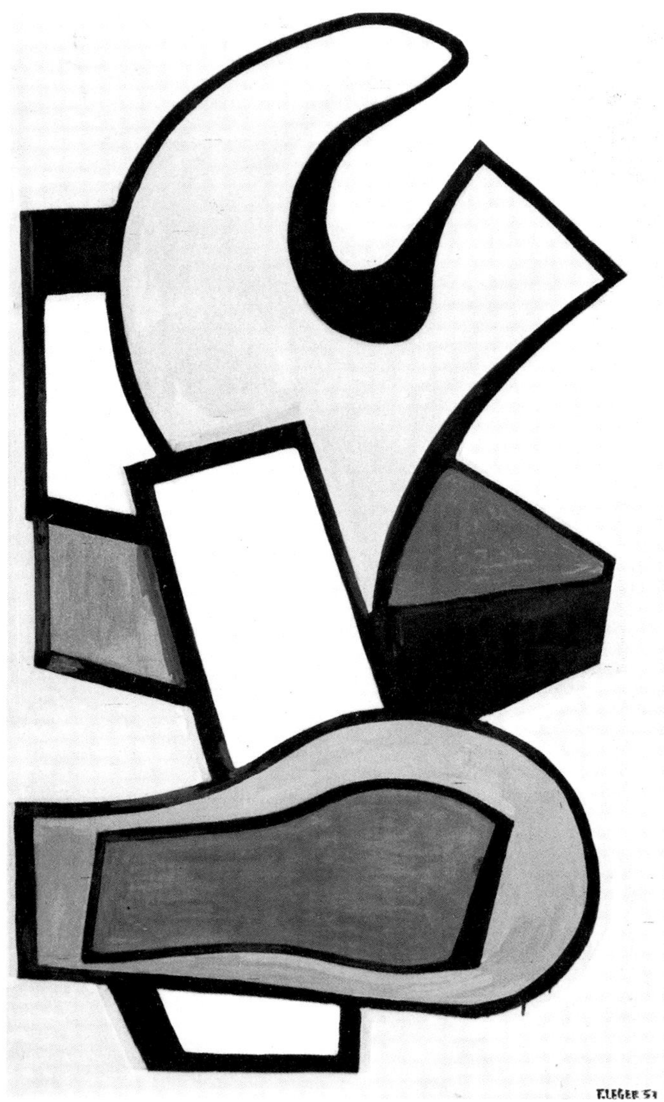

269. MURAL COMPOSITION
1953—Oil on canvas, 147 × 88 cm
Private collection

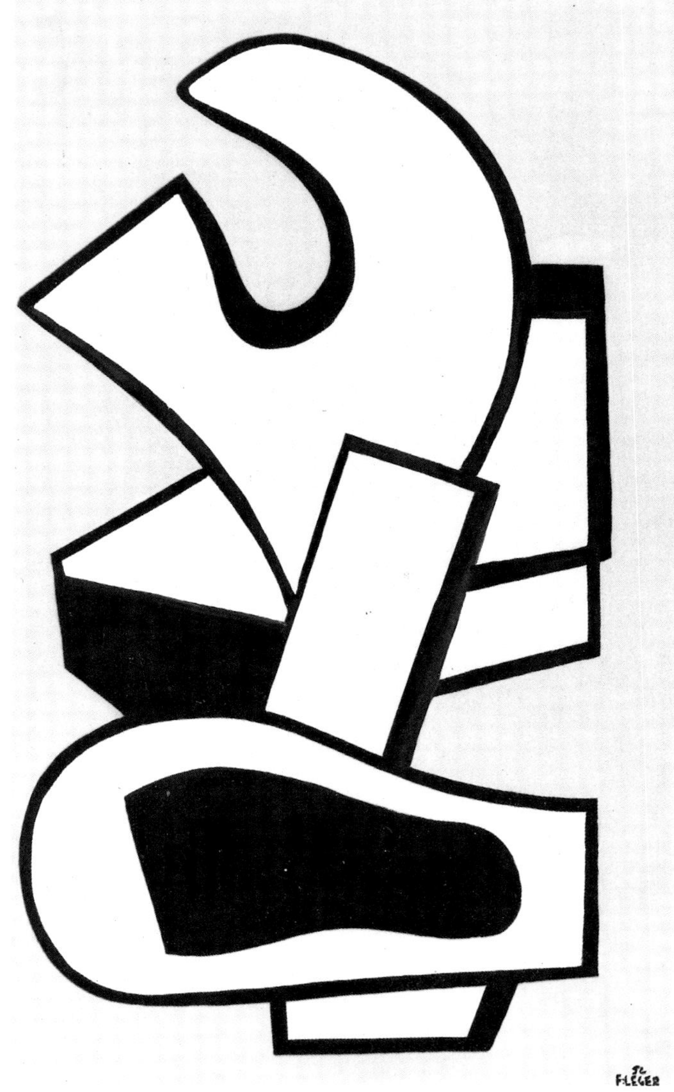

270. MURAL COMPOSITION
1952—Oil on canvas, 148 × 90 cm
Musée National Fernand Léger, Biot

Léger was always careful to separate his easel paintings from his *Studies for Architectural Adaptations* and *Projects for Mural Compositions.* Nonetheless, these two procedures did not contradict each other. They went
Ill. 125 hand in hand. The monumentality of *The Big Lunch*
Ill. 254 or of *Two Sisters* conferred a silent grandeur on his paintings that related (to quote André Verdet) "the sacred works of the Archaics of the high cosmic civilizations."

In tandem with this "monumental and static" period, Léger worked on and realized his architectural "contrivances." In his easel paintings, he returned to the subject and the human form in movement, while in his mural paintings he confirmed an abstract perspective.

Léger not only clearly established the separation of the genres, but their complementary nature, as well: "As a general rule, pure color and geometric form alone do not support easel painting. Abstraction demands immense surfaces, walls. . . . I would even go as far as saying that easel painting is often limited. Mural painting, however, has no dimension. They are two different fields. My first mural paintings were for Le Corbusier. They blend with architecture: where lies the contrasted rhythm of free colors, a decorative function, an amplification of space, and a need for luminosity. . . . Abstract art is a necessity today. It is going to animate interior walls as well as exterior walls. I think that my easel paintings will be all the more possible and realizable, especially as my architectural collaboration will be abstract."

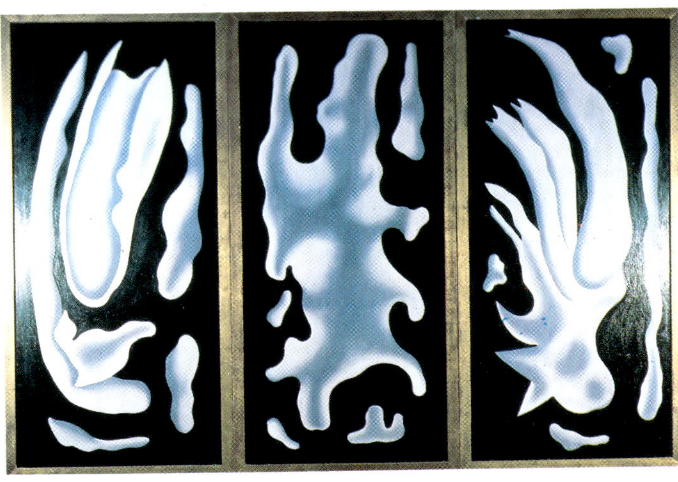

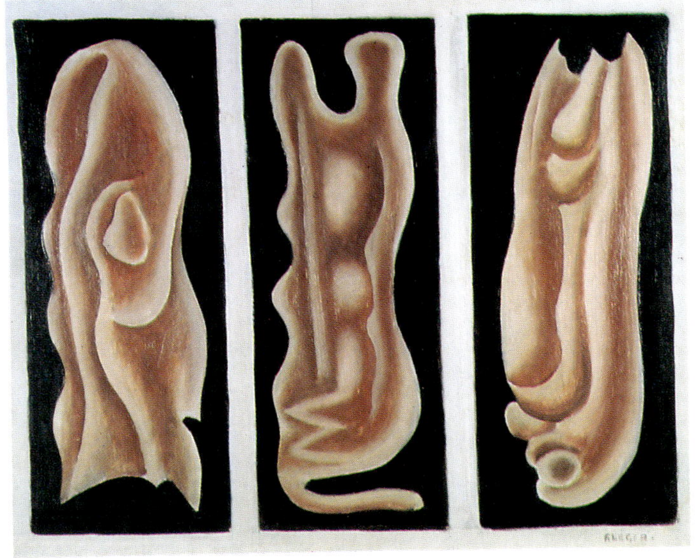

271. LARGE COMET TAILS
1930—Oil on canvas, 201 × 75 cm
Collection of Mr. and Mrs. Adrien Maeght

272. COMET TAILS
1930—Oil on canvas, 54 × 65 cm
Collection of Mr. and Mrs. Adrien Maeght

273. PROJECT FOR MURAL PAINTING FOR THE STEAMSHIP *VULCANIA*
1951—Oil on canvas, 112 × 196 cm
Musée National Fernand Léger, Biot

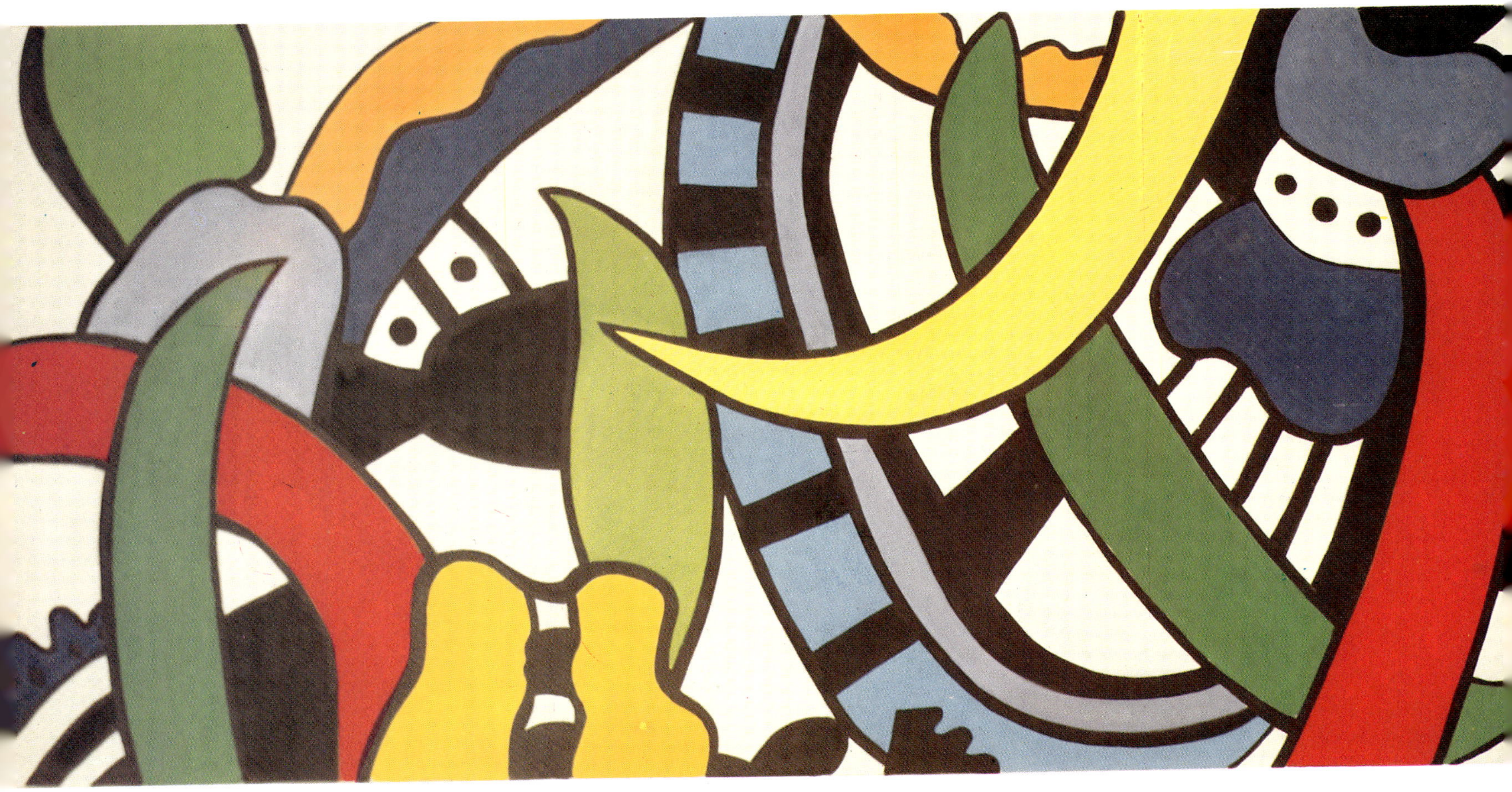

274. GOUACHE A 619
Gouache, 22.3 × 23 cm
Private collection

275. MURAL PAINTING FOR THE FRENCH PAVILION AT THE MILAN TRIENNIAL
1951—Oil on canvas, 45 × 74 cm
Private collection

276. PLANE IN THE SKY
1939–52—Oil on canvas, 60 × 92 cm
Musée National Fernand Léger, Biot

277. PROJECT FOR A MURAL PAINTING
1952—Oil on canvas, 114 × 195 cm
Musée National Fernand Léger, Biot

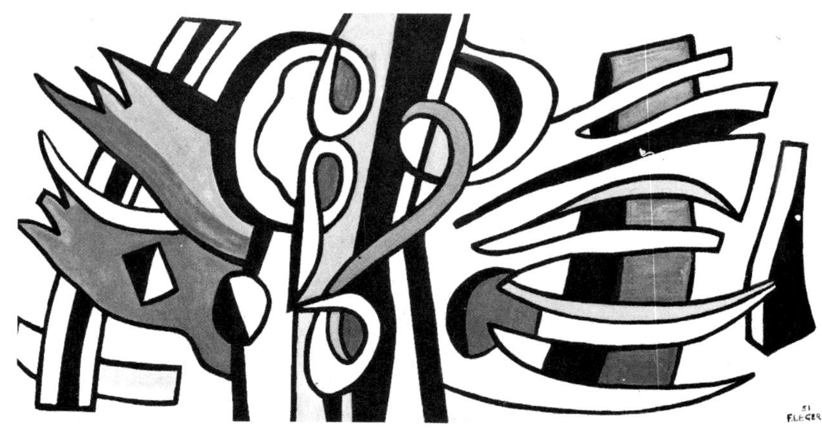

275

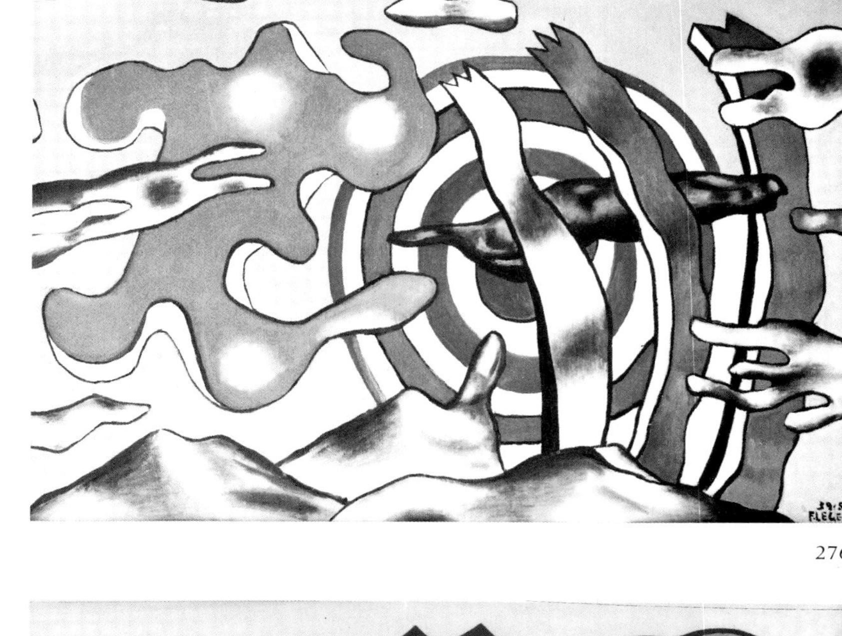

276

274

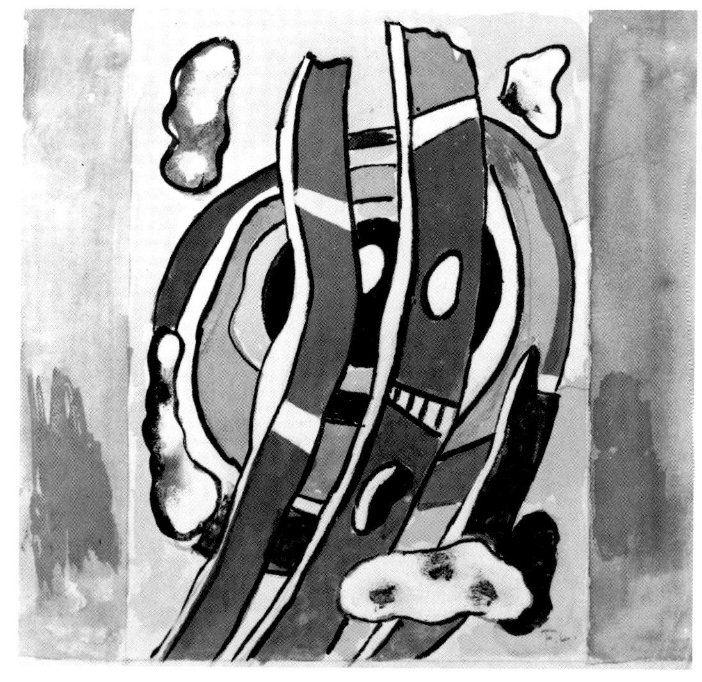

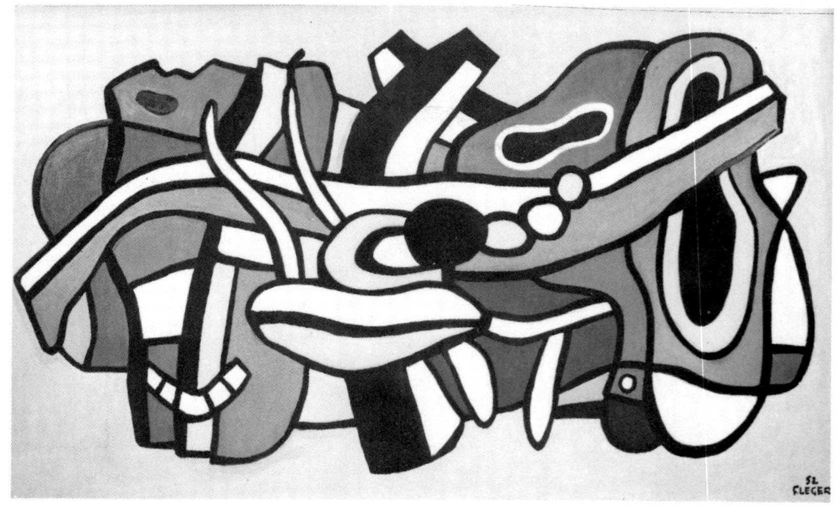

277

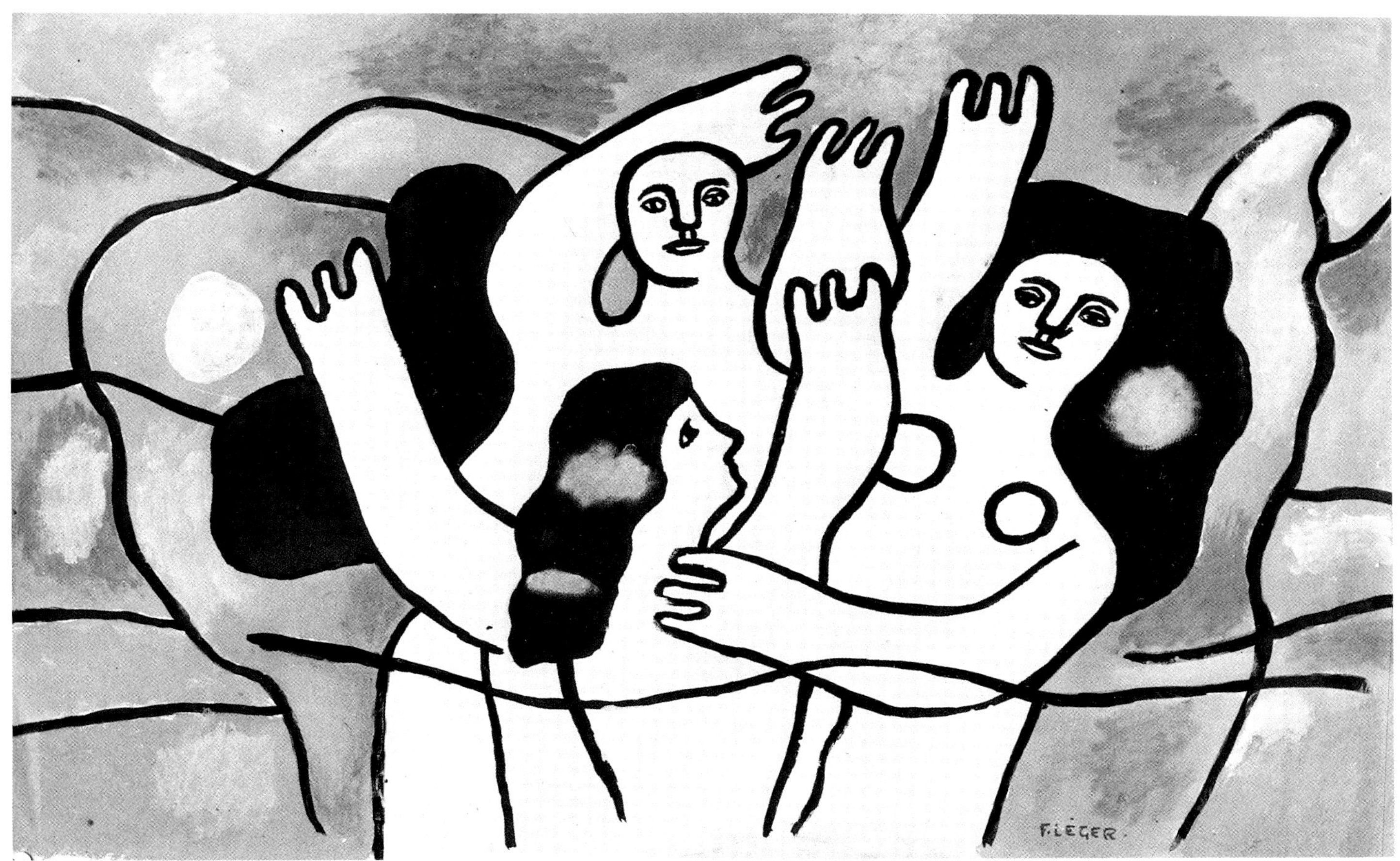


278. JOY OF LIFE ON ORANGE BACKGROUND
About 1955—Gouache, 48 × 75 cm
Private collection

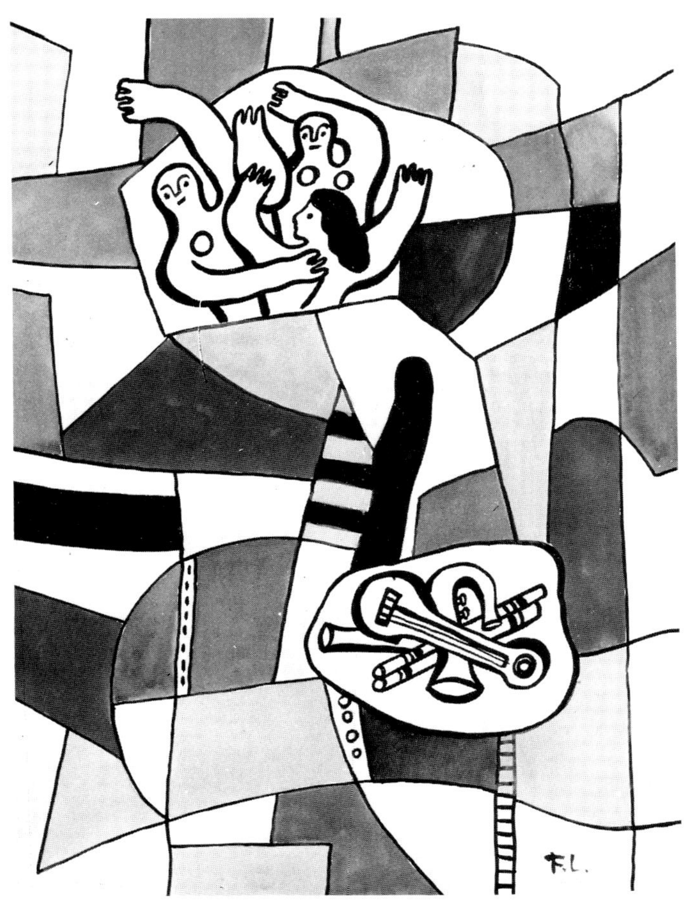


279. SÃO PAULO
About 1953—Gouache, 50 × 40 cm
Private collection

### The São Paulo Opera

International recognition of Léger's monumental concepts came in 1954, when the architect Niemeyer
asked him to draw up plans for a decorative mosaic Ill. 279
for the auditorium of the São Paulo Opera. The great Ill. 280
Brazilian architect had been strongly influenced in his early years by the work of Le Corbusier, and used contrasting rectangular volumes and curves throughout his career. He also used reinforced concrete with glass and steel elements. He brought into play the relationship between the impact of mass and the colored mosaic murals that he incorporated into his structures as well. A case in point is his Chapel of Saint Francis of Assisi in Belo Horizonte, Brazil.
It was very sad, with Léger at his peak he would die the following year, thus leaving this superb project unfinished. He had started to combine *abstraction* with a memory of "men in space" that we find in
paintings like *La Danse* (1942). He did this with com- Ill. 290
pelling contrast.

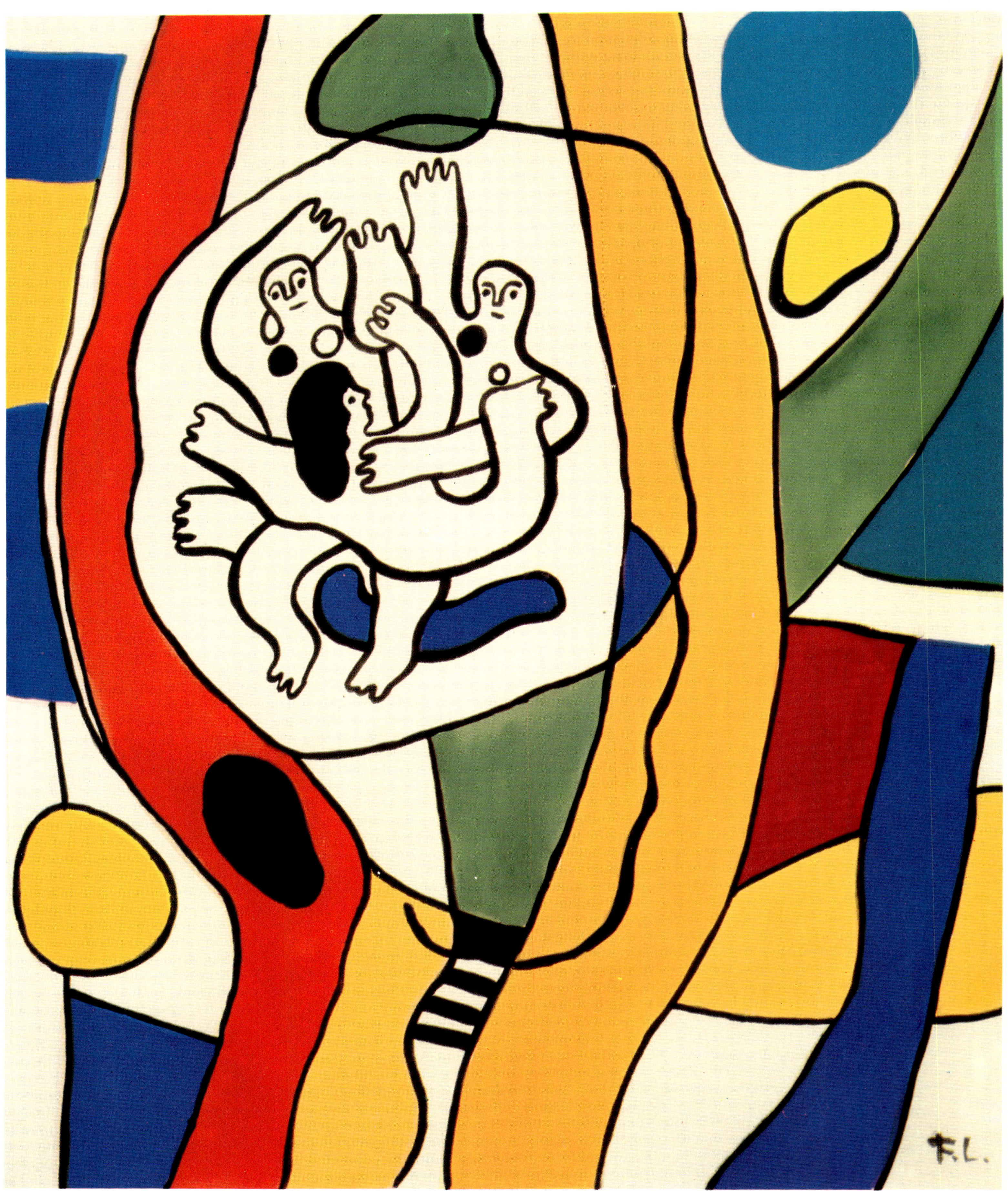


280. MODEL FOR THE SÃO PAULO OPERA
1954—Gouache, 65 × 50 cm
Private collection

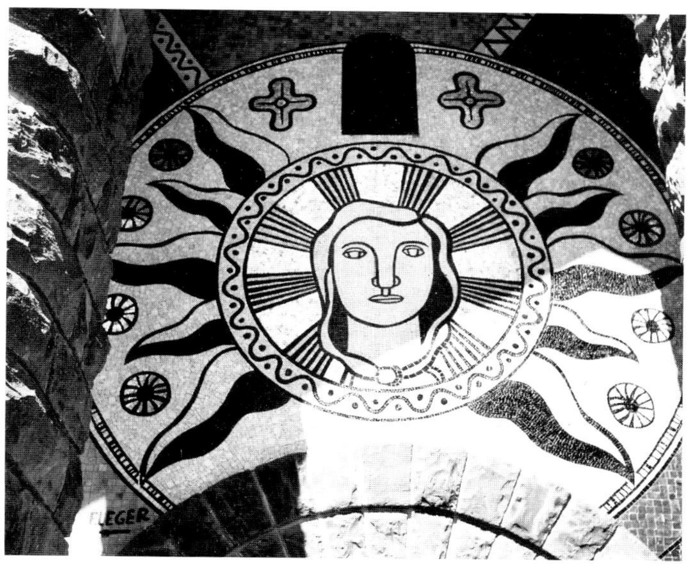

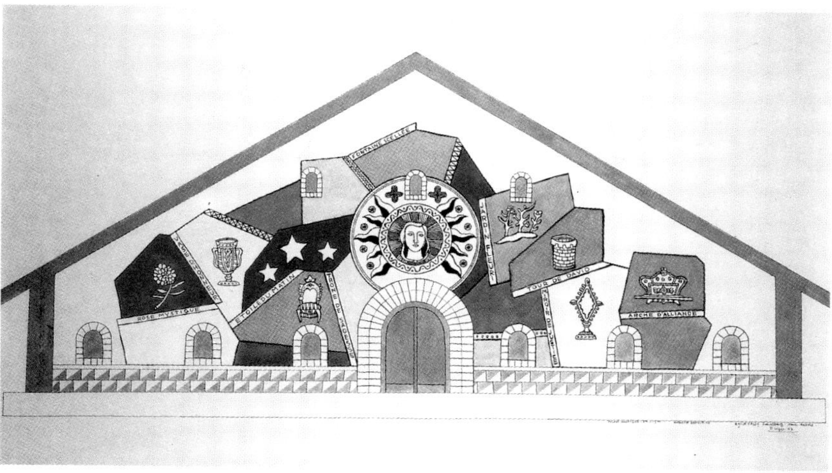

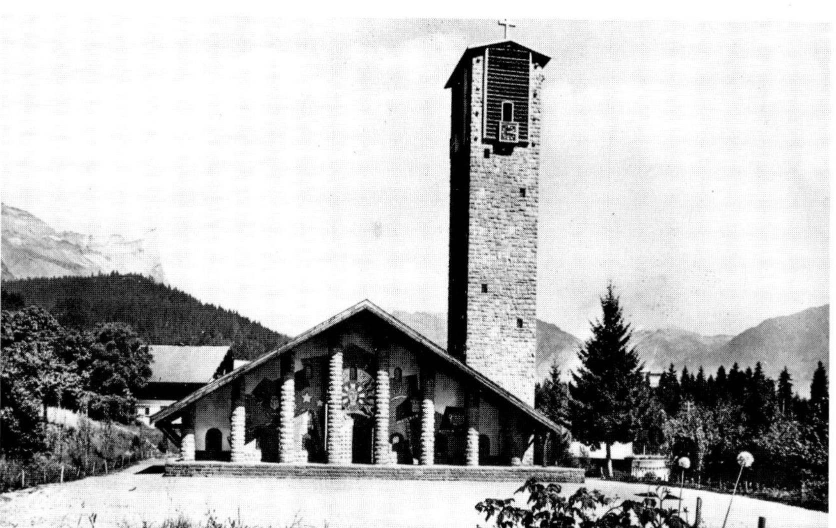

281. MOSAIC TYMPANUM FOR THE CHURCH OF NOTRE-DAME-DE-GRÂCE, IN ASSY, HAUTE-SAVOIE

282. MODEL FOR THE FACADE OF THE CHURCH OF NOTRE-DAME D'ASSY

283. CHURCH OF NOTRE-DAME D'ASSY

Nonfigurative monumentality dominated the work Léger did in 1925 with Mallet-Stevens and Le Corbusier, and again in 1936 in *Power Transmission* ("Transport des Forces"), a fresco for the Palais de la Découverte (The Palace of Discovery) science museum in Paris. This abstract work helped prepare Léger for his interior design of the Rockefeller House in New York in 1938, and for the mural painting for the Brussels World's Fair in 1935.

Murals were a permanent part of Léger's work. The
more they tended towards abstraction, the more one
could imagine them done in monumental dimen-
sions. His early visionary works, such as *The Big* Ill. 96
*Tugboat*, *Discs*, or *The Card Game*, already contain Ill. 99
these elements. It was not only that the paintings Ill. 66
were impregnated with the feeling of the monu-
mental. There were also numerous compositions
that dealt with large subjects, such as *Leisure: Hom-* Ill. 321
*age to Louis David*, *The Country Outing* ("Partie de Ill. 322
compagne"), *The Camper* ("Le Campeur"), or *The* Ill. 325
*Builders*. Despite the large format of these canvases, Ill. 311
these paintings are, above all, easel paintings. Léger
himself attested to this: "Despite what people
think, it is not possible to transpose paintings like
*The Country Outing* or *The Builders* onto the wall. It
has nothing to do with the actual size of a canvas.
I have often done tiny, abstract watercolors as a
preliminary approach to a large, decorated surface.
These small formats can be enlarged without any
damage to the final work, because their composi-
tion is calculated in relationship to the wall, a sur-
face of large dimensions. If, however, I try to
transpose a painting like *The Builders* onto the wall,
I would unavoidably produce an effect of gigan-
tism. . . . As I have said many times, easel painting
has one set of principles, and monumental painting
another set. Sometimes, and I am now speaking in
terms of the subject-painting, they do coincide. I
am thinking in particular of a painting like *Adam* Ill. 260
*and Eve*, and of certain of my paintings that make
very minimal use of color and form, the ones with
very "straight" lines, certain canvases I did in the Ill. 287
*Divers* series. . . Even in *Big Parade* there are some Ill. 336
possibilities for mural transposition. All this may seem minor, but it is very important. The more my paintings remain in the plastic context of what I have referred to as *object painting*—where all the elements are treated with equal pictorial value, are emotionally expressionless, and do not have any one predominant element—the more possibilities they will have for opening up into murals."

Despite his plastic ideals and his faith in the monumental, Léger had very few occasions to collaborate with the architects. A singular destiny had ordained that Léger, materialist thinker and leftist artist, would
receive the opportunity to realize one of his most
beautiful projects from the Roman Catholic church. Ill. 281
Unable to make secular art, he made sacred art. The to 283

building of the church at Assy allowed him to make optimal use of his passion for the mozaic murals he had discovered in Ravenna, Italy.

Between 1935 and 1940, Léger received several government commissions. The first was for the mural decoration of the French Pavilion at the Brussels World's Fair in 1935. Two years later, he and his students did the vast *Power Transmission* panel for the Palace of Discovery. The mural celebrates science and electricity. In 1940, the Ministry of Education commissioned another decorative project for a civil aviation center near the city of Nancy, but it was cancelled because of World War II. Léger then went back to his paintings and gouaches, which remind us of the works he did during World War I: *Cockade*
Ill. 71 ("La Cocarde"), *Crashed Airplane* ("L'Avion brisé"), *Helices.*

In the 1950s, Matisse was working on the decoration for his Rosary Chapel of Vence, and Le Corbusier was working on his own chapel in Ronchamp. Léger was also participating in this revival of sacred art. He did the stained glass windows for the Church of the Sacred Heart of Audincourt, for which Bazaine made a mosaic. This project came about after the mosaic façade that he had done for the church in Assy and just before the limpid and serene stained glass windows he made for the church in Courfaivre (1953–54). There were also projects to be done for the University of Caracas, and the models for a large ceramic mosaic for the administrative building of Gaz de France in Alfortville. Art critic Pierre Descargues told the story of Léger's seventeen stained windows in slabs of glass and cement illustrating the "objects" of the Passion of Christ for the church in Audincourt: Léger showed his models in gouache to the people of the town to see how they felt about them. Their reaction was enthusiastic. As they looked at his watercolors, they exclaimed: "Well, there sure is color! When the light hits them, they're gonna *fart fire.* It's gonna be thunderous!"

The model for the ornamental front of the Fernand Léger Museum in Biot was initially intended for the Olympic stadium in Hanover, Germany. It was enlarged to one hundred times its size and was a tribute to youth and sports. It is composed of mosaics and polychrome sculpture. In his grand dream of public and collective art, Léger considered integrating the arts of fresco painting, stained glass windows, tapestry, and sculpture. For him they were all integral parts of the monumental environment. In 1949, he founded a ceramic workshop in Biot to manufacture polychrome sculpture and bas-reliefs. One of these ceramic murals, *Women with a Parrot* ("Femmes au perroquet"), which was done during Léger's lifetime, now sits in the gardens of Colombe d'Or in Saint-
Ill. 338 Paul. His *Polychrome Flower* ("Fleur polychrome") that he made with his own hands decorates the Pompidou Center.

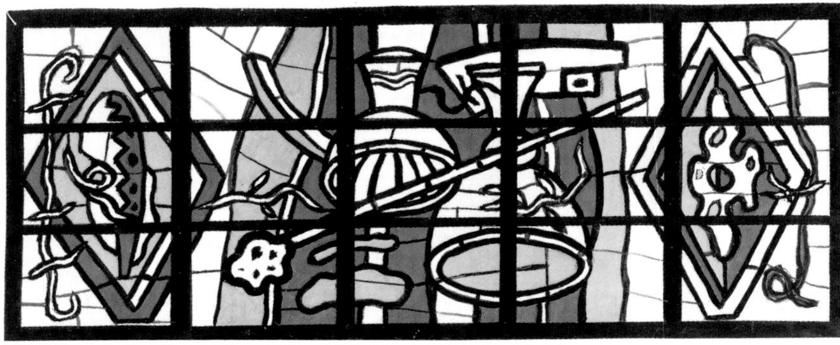

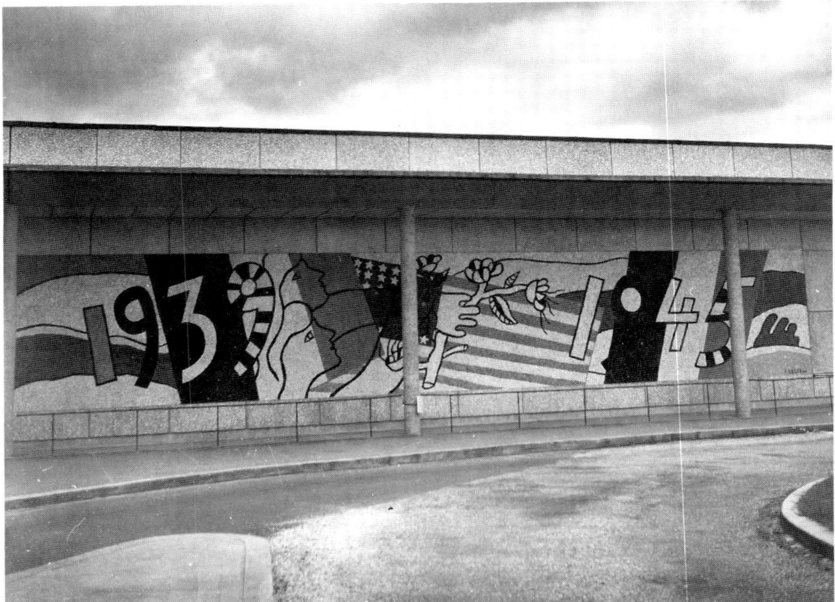

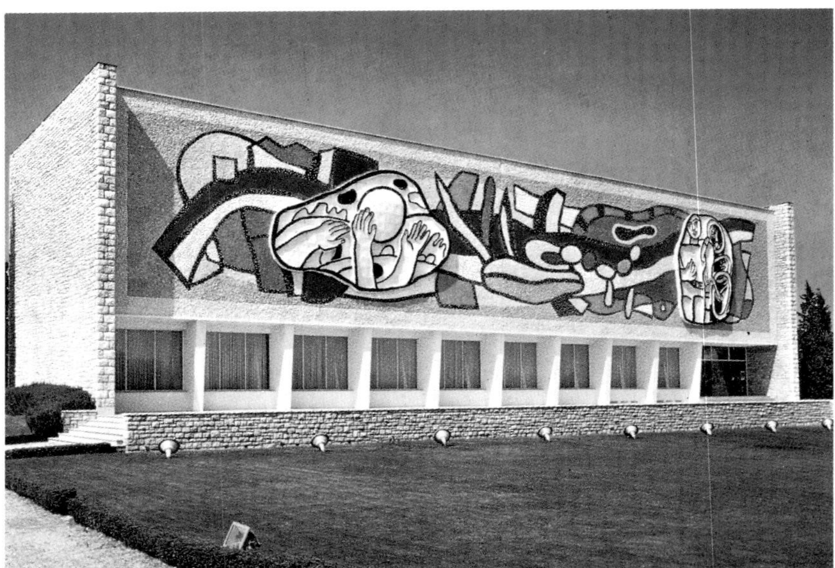

284. MODEL FOR THE STAINED GLASS WINDOWS OF THE CHURCH OF THE SACRED HEART IN AUDINCOURT, CHALICES AND SPONGE AT THE TIP OF A REED
1950—Gouache, 37 × 92 cm
Musée National d'Art Moderne, Centre Georges Pompidou, Paris

285. MOSAIC BY FERNAND LÉGER FOR THE MEMORIAL HOSPITAL AT SAINT-LÔ, MANCHE
1955—Photo by Lapad

286. THE FERNAND LÉGER MUSEUM IN BIOT

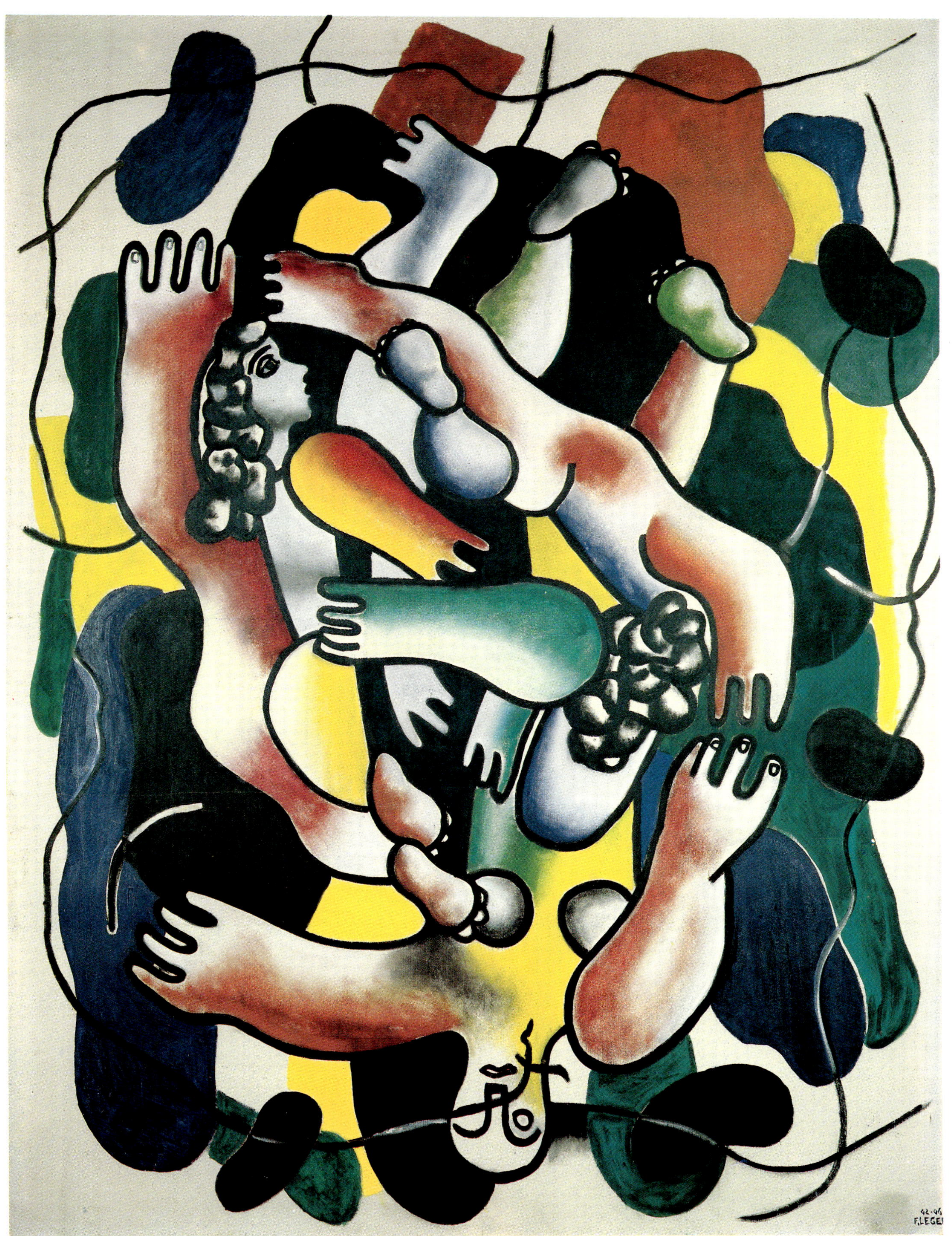


287. POLYCHROME DIVERS
1942–46—Oil on canvas, 250 × 185 cm
Musée National Fernand Léger, Biot

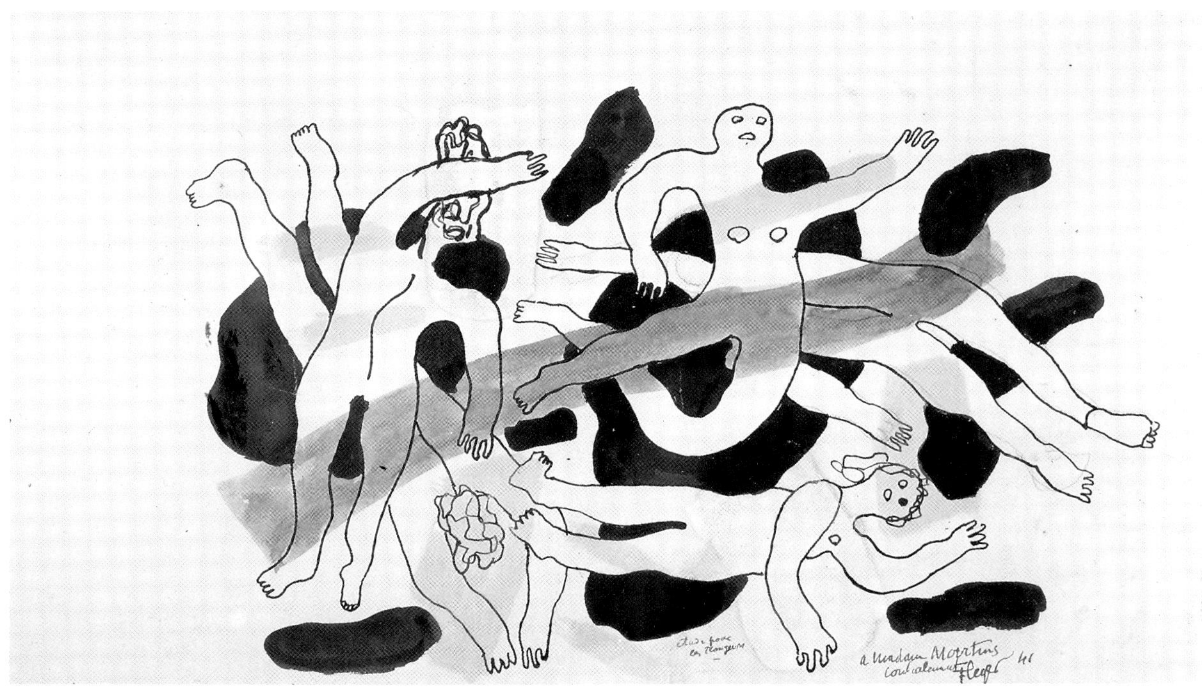

288. ACROBATS (STUDY FOR *THE DIVERS*)
1941—Watercolor sketch, 26 × 44 cm
Private collection

# The New York Years

"The most colossal spectacle in the world. . . . Life at its height. It hit the ceiling, overshot the target . . . crisis!" In New York, Léger had the impression that he was living inside one of his own paintings! "It's the apotheosis of vertical architecture; a sturdy combination of architecture and ruthless bankers driven by greed. An unknown and unintended elegance comes out of this geometric abstraction. Squeezed within two metal angles are windows, numbers that go skyward, rigid numbers that are overcome by a distorted perspective." Léger never tired of telling about what he saw and experienced during the war. The spectacle of the United States created a battle between the lyrical and the epic when he described houses that were higher than cathedrals. "New York with millions of luminous windows. . . How many windows? What German will be able match these statistics?"

Léger felt at home in New York. He left Marseilles in October 1940. When he arrived in New York Harbor, he found that the Statue of Liberty, France's gift to the United States, was extremely modest, "forgotten at the threshold to this new, audacious, and vertical continent. You can barely see her torch. She's stretching out her arm in vain. She sheds a bit of light like a night lamp over enormous moving things, indifferent and majestic forms that cast a shadow over her."

Within a very short time, Léger got a teaching position at Yale University, along with Darius Milhaud, Focillon, and André Maurois. He also taught at Mills College in California. Darius Milhaud remembered that Léger's lectures "were not easy for a decent woman to translate, especially when he'd exclaim: 'Then came the Renaissance. It was all fucked up.' " To avoid risky questions, he always said: "I can speak [English], but I don't understand!" He exhibited his work with Rosenberg. At Pierre Matisse's house he met the majority of artists temporarily exiled in the United States: Masson, Tanguy, Matta, Breton, Zadkine, Max Ernst, Chagall, Mondrian, Ozenfant. . . All this talent would pollinate America.

America, however, would not transform Léger's palette, colors, themes, or ideas. Everything that he did during his exile had already been determined before he left France. At best, he would experience the unleashing of New York's brutal power, uncontrollable energy, and virulence. In characterizing the excesses of the country, he would say: "It's very young. Swallow a sword and keep smiling, cut off your finger because it's dirty. . . . From A to Z, that's what America's about."

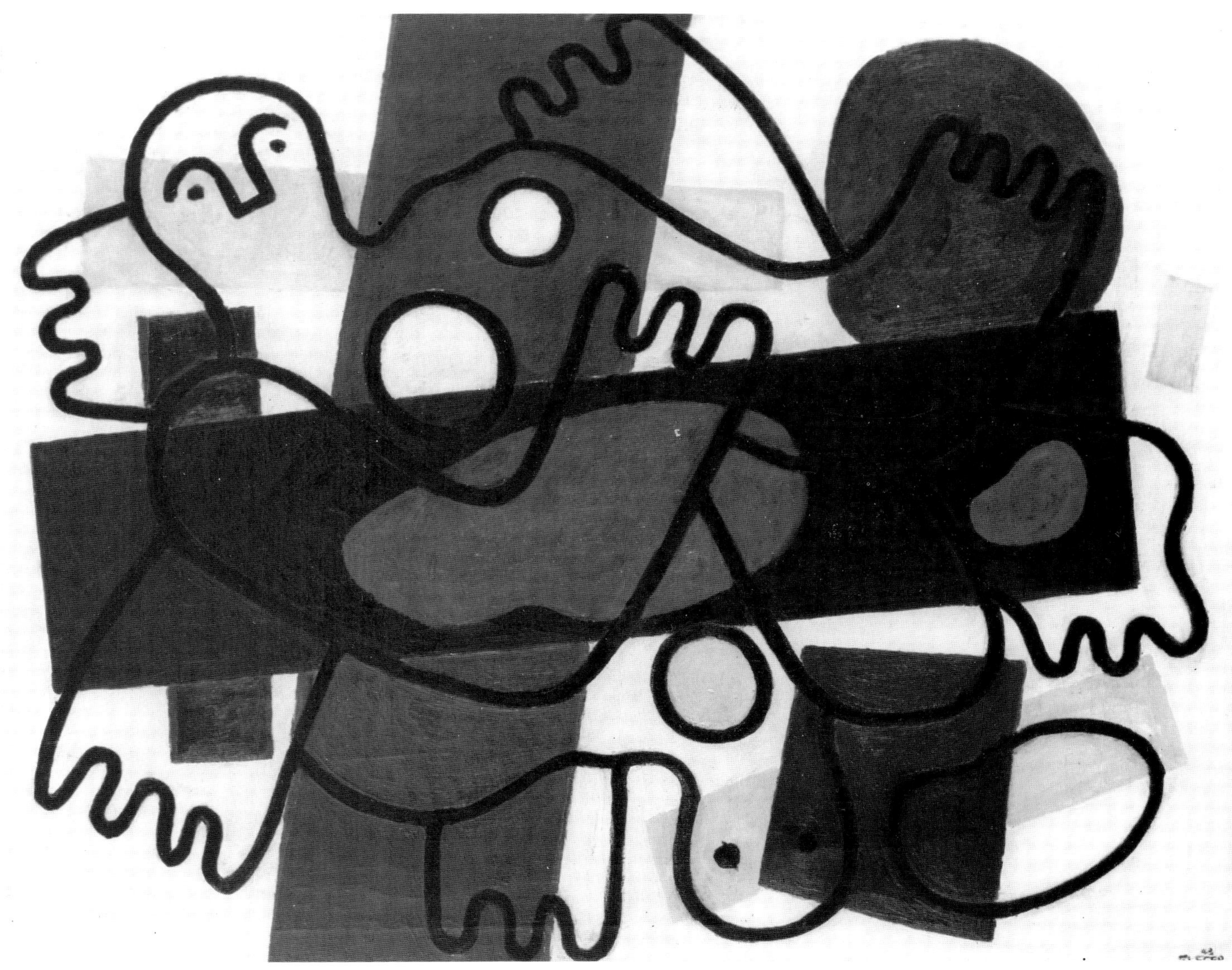

289. DIVERS IN RED AND BLUE
1943—Oil on canvas, 73 × 91 cm
Private collection

Ill. 125 *Le Grand Dejeuner*, *Composition with Two Parrots*, and
Ill. 258 *The Divers* illustrate the profound unity of his meth-
Ill. 287 ods. He had completed the launching pad for his
Ill. 297 spacecraft, and it was time to send man into space: "My true creative evolution (men in space) started in Paris in 1936–1937 with my painting *Composition with Parrots*. Three years of work preceded this painting. The same evolution is continuing here in the U.S. with *The Acrobats* ["Les Saltimbanques"] and *The Divers* (1941–1942). It's a dynamic cycle that impels me to project human groups into space. Nobody, as far as I know, has ever been able to solve this problem." Léger called upon his good old ally, color, to solve it. He tried to use it in all its forms: black modeled against colored backgrounds, polychrome bodies against a black background, and mixtures of colored and polychrome flat tints. He finally
Ill. 261 discovered the method in *Parrots*, which was part drawing and part color.

Louis Aragon knew that Léger's "exterior color" did not come from Broadway, but from the circus: "Fernand Léger was the first to take the big step, the first to make the brutal decision. In terms of precedents, at least, it goes without saying that the theory of exterior color comes from the music halls or the circus where the light from the spotlights determines everything. What was white becomes red, thanks to the work of man as electrician. . . . It was a necessary outcome that the lessons learned from floodlights extend into the streets . . . so that the complete separation of form and color could take place on the painter's canvas. In turn, the canvas would become its own system, expressing the painter's will. This is what is occurring in Fernand Léger's painting."

Was Léger able to launch his man into space, thanks to the variety of formal means he had at his fingertips? One thing is sure: a certain static element that characterized his mural painting breaks loose in his divers, acrobats, and overlapping dancers. It is the kind of stasis that is associated with movement. It is not the movement of falling bodies, but of forms that seem to turn like discs, and therefore seem immobile.

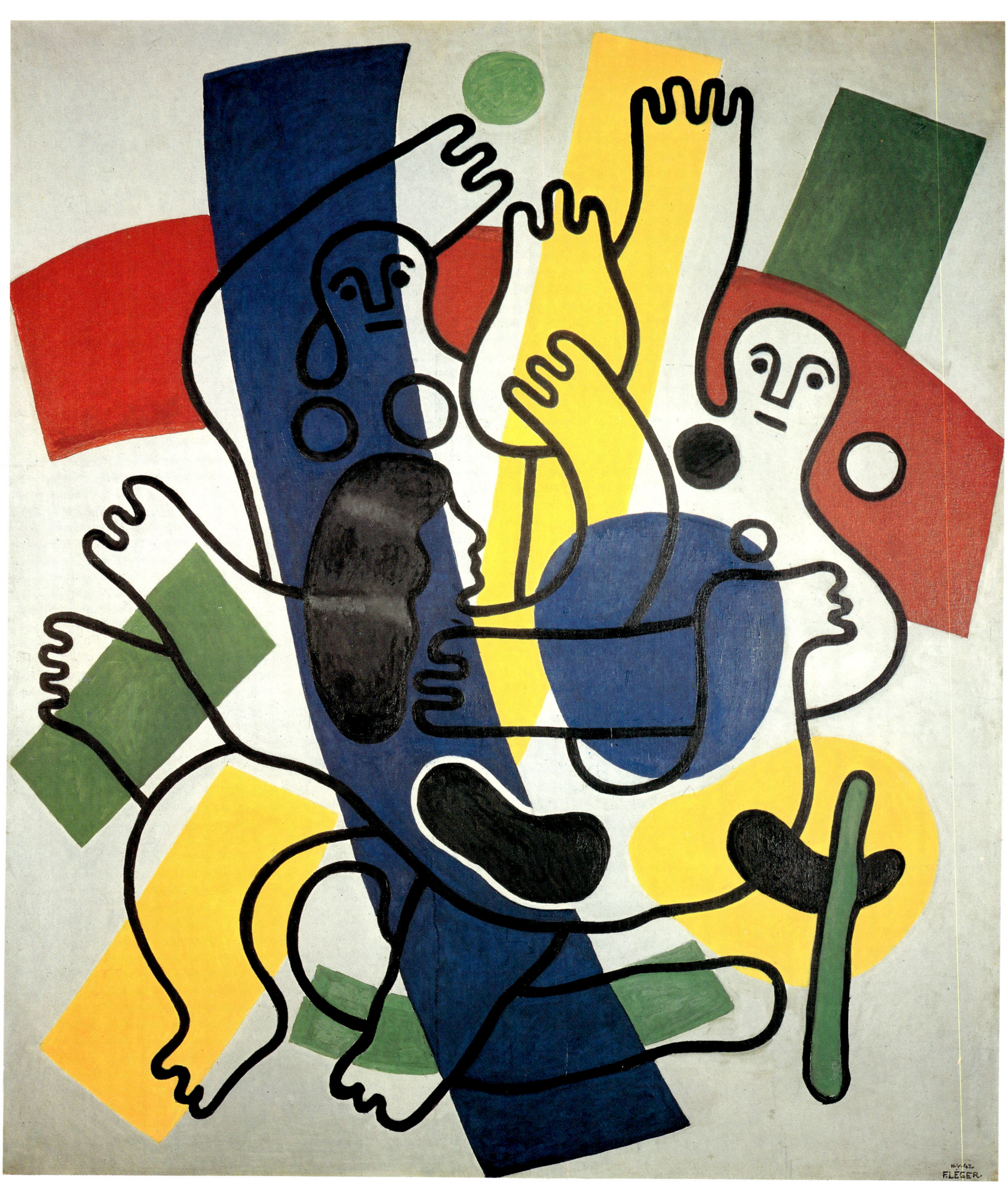


290 THE DANCE
1942—Oil on canvas, 183 × 154 cm
Louise Leiris Gallery, Paris

## Cannibalistic nature

Léger was thoroughly enchanted to discover that in the affluent U.S.A., where economics dictated that old engines were to be discarded rather than repaired, "one could find tons of abandoned machines with flowers cropping up from within, and birds perching on top of them. I'm looking for the shock value between natural elements and mechanical elements, between birds, for example, and invented geometrical forms."

During the summer Léger made frequent trips to Rouses Point in northern New York State, near Lake Champlain. The valley reminded him of his native Normandy countryside. In upstate New York he discovered abandoned farms, harrows, shearers, plows, sowing machines, and tractor tires. They were half-buried in the earth and invaded by weeds. "You don't see this sort of thing in Europe," Léger commented, while profiting from his discovery. He used it to contrast what was violent with what was pastoral through the contrast between flowers and rusty machinery: "I painted a series of American landscapes, inspired by the contrast between an abandoned machine that had turned into rusty metal, and the vegetation that was devouring it. Nature was literally eating up the machinery. You could see it disappearing under the wild flowers and greenery. The opposition between this heap of twisted metal and the wild daisies had a lively and endearing charm about it."

There is a joyous music that emanates from the paint-
ings of this period, among which are *The Forest*, 1942; Ill. 298
*Flowers in a Mechanical Element* ("Les Fleurs dans un
élément mécanique"), 1943; *The Tree in the Ladder* Ill. 299
("L'Arbre dans l'échelle"), 1943–44; *The Black Wheel* Ill. 291
("La Roue noire"), 1944; and *Romantic Landscape* Ill. 294
("Paysage romantique"), painted in 1946. These
paintings combine luxurious and fragrant flowers
with machine parts or useless tools. Even the various
*Roots* ("Racines") that Léger painted in 1941, which Ill. 292
border on abstraction, are full of joy. They seem to have a music of their own, independent of any references to nature. During the New York years, Léger was no longer confronting realism with abstraction. Instead, he was fusing them in a frenzy of colored intensity. This was the real influence of America, a form of excess in expressing the pure joy of being alive. There is no doubt that the frenetic and nerve-racking New York lifestyle strongly impressed Léger, and played an important part in his unleashing of colored intensity.

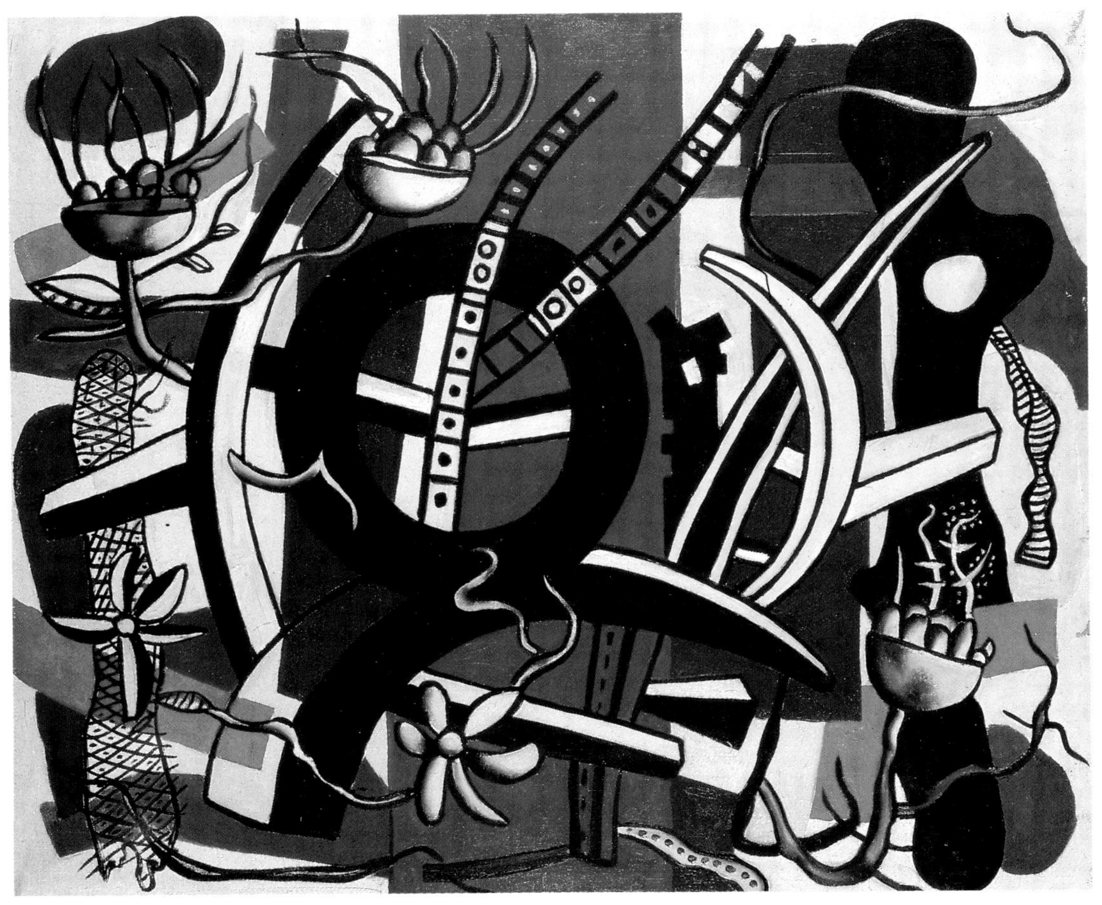

291. THE BLACK WHEEL
1944—Oil on canvas, 112 × 127 cm
Louis Carré Gallery, Paris

292. BLACK ROOT
1941—Oil on canvas, 177 × 122 cm
Collection of Mr. and Mrs. Adrien Ma

293. PROJECT FOR A MURAL COMPOSI
FOR *THE DIVERS* ON A YELLOW
BACKGROUND
1941—Gouache, 44 × 30 cm
Private collection

294. ROMANTIC LANDSCAPE
1946—Oil on canvas, 66 × 91 cm
Louise Leiris Gallery, Paris

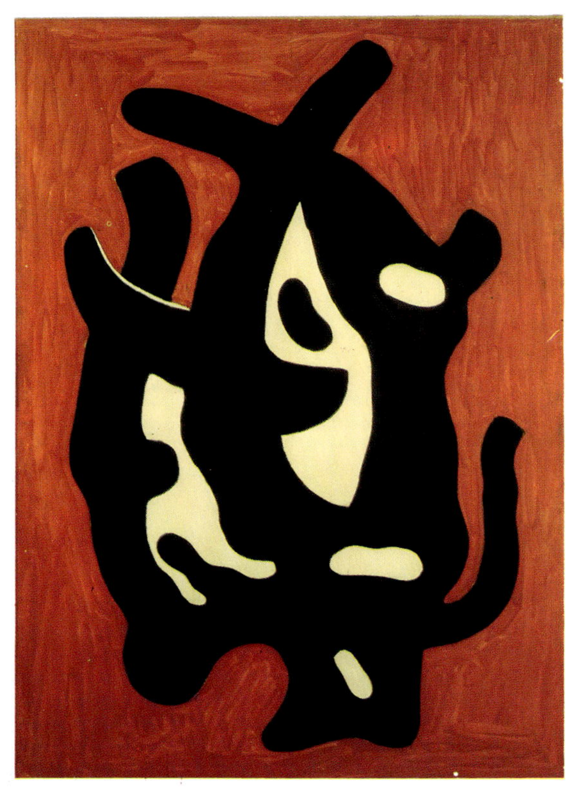

292

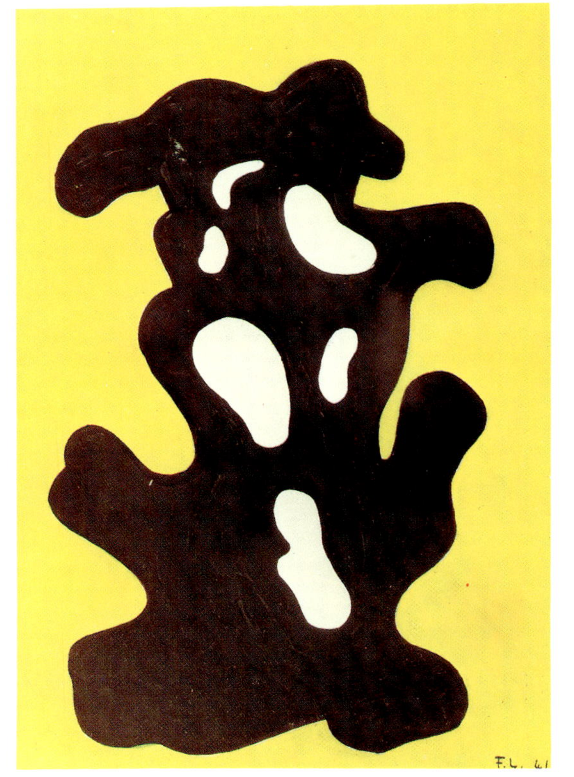

293

294

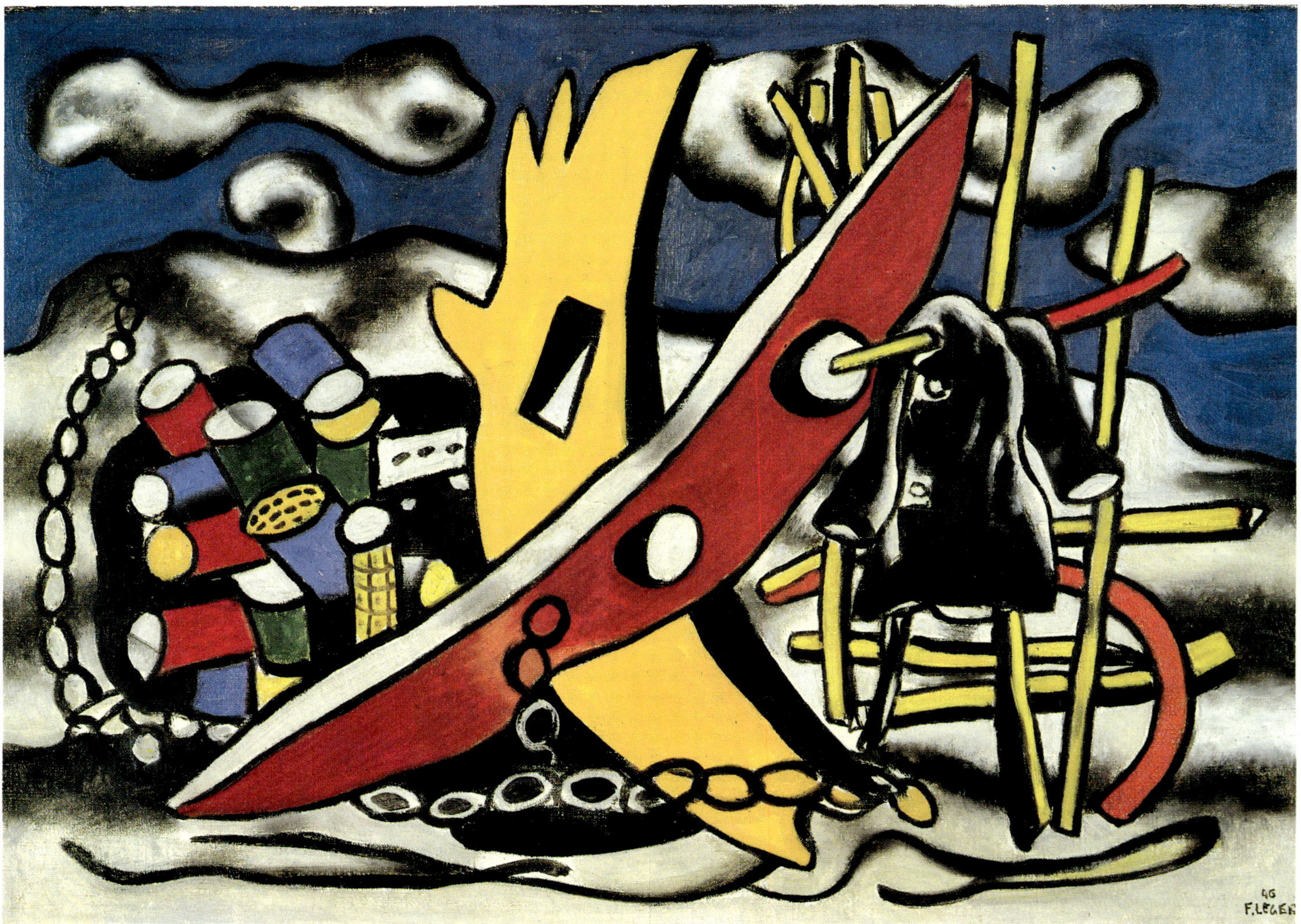

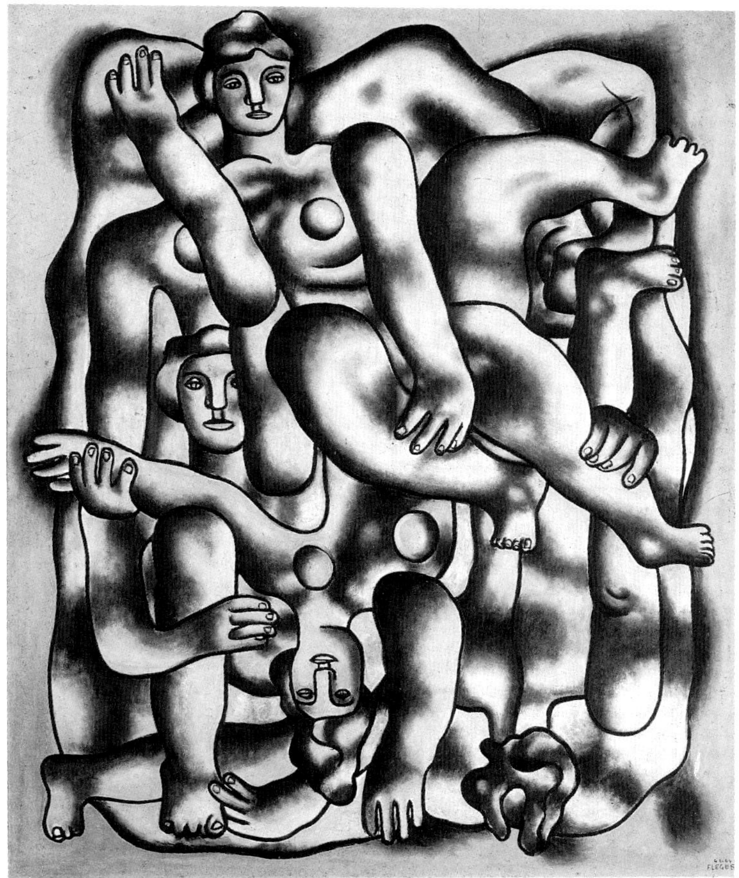

295. ACROBATS IN GRAY
1942–44—Oil on canvas, 183 × 147 cm
Musée National d'Art Moderne, Centre Georges Pompidou, Paris

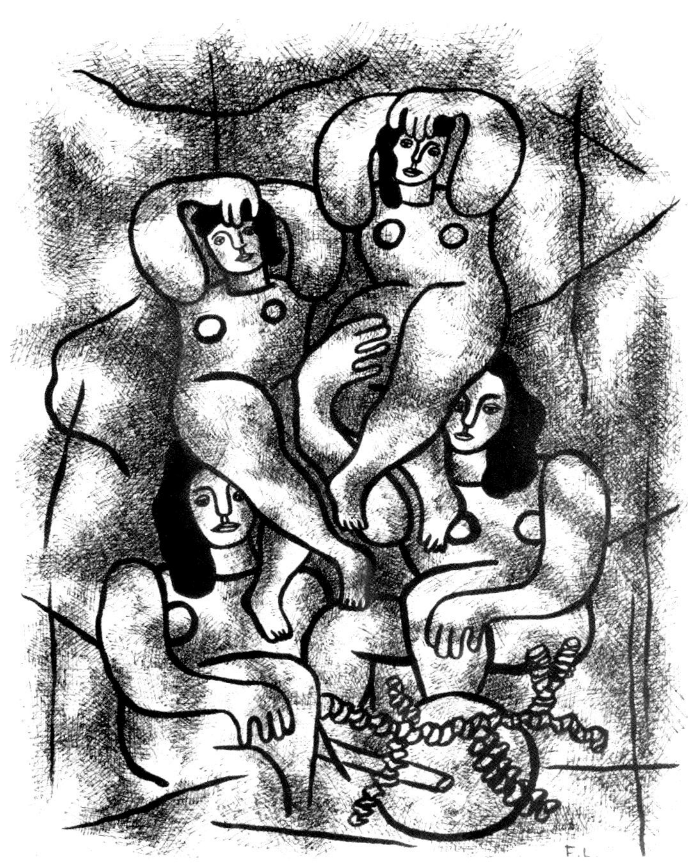

296. THE ACROBATS, STUDY
1940—Pen drawing, 64 × 44 cm
Collection of Mr. and Mrs. Adrien Maeght

### Truer than Michelangelo

Ill. 287 *Divers* was one of Léger's newest and most spectacular paintings of this period. He conceived the idea
Ill. 297 for the painting in Marseilles in 1940, when he watched five or six people diving. "I'm about to leave for the United States, and I go one day to the swimming pool. The divers weren't just five or six people, but hundreds all at once. Try to distinguish them! Whom does that head belong to, and what about that leg, or that arm? I couldn't tell any more. Well, then I dispersed all these body parts on my canvas. In so doing, I think I portrayed more truth than Michelangelo did when he studied the muscles of each body part in detail. I've seen the characters he painted on the ceiling of the Sistine Chapel. They don't fall. They're stuck to every corner of the entire chapel. You can even distinguish their toenails. I give you my word that when the boys from Marseilles dove into the water, I had no time at all to see the details. My divers drop."

Léger's statement about the influence of New York on his work is categorical. In a study done by *Cahiers d'Art* on the theme, "What influence do environmental events have on the creative act?" Léger responded that his evolution was not influenced by his temporarily being transplanted to another country. He was influenced only by the general spirit of the times. "With regard to my own work and my current circumstances, living in exile in the United States . . . my work is continuing and developing independently of my geographical situation. . . . The surroundings don't influence me one bit. A work of art is the result of an inner state and owes nothing to a pictorial exterior. Maybe the rhythm of New York or the climate here allows me to work faster, but that's about it."

After the objects that fly in space, Léger painted bodies that fall in space. Could it be that he had not finished settling accounts with the Italian Renaissance? Could it be the gravity of Hell that pulled his bodies down from the heavenly ceilings of the Sistine Chapel? How could he validly attack Michelangelo's meticulous "naturalism"?

Werner Schmalenbach noted that Léger's divers do not really fall because one could just as easily turn the canvas upside down: "Léger transformed the cascading bodies into a stable composition, whose center of gravity is not on the bottom of the canvas, but rather just about in the center of the canvas." There is the impression of a certain stasis that we see in his mural paintings. There is no doubt about it: Léger was dealing with the same problem as his illustrious predecessors: Michelangelo's giants who float on the ceilings of the Sistine Chapel, as well as Rubens with his human clusters, and Tiepolo with his human bodies in space.

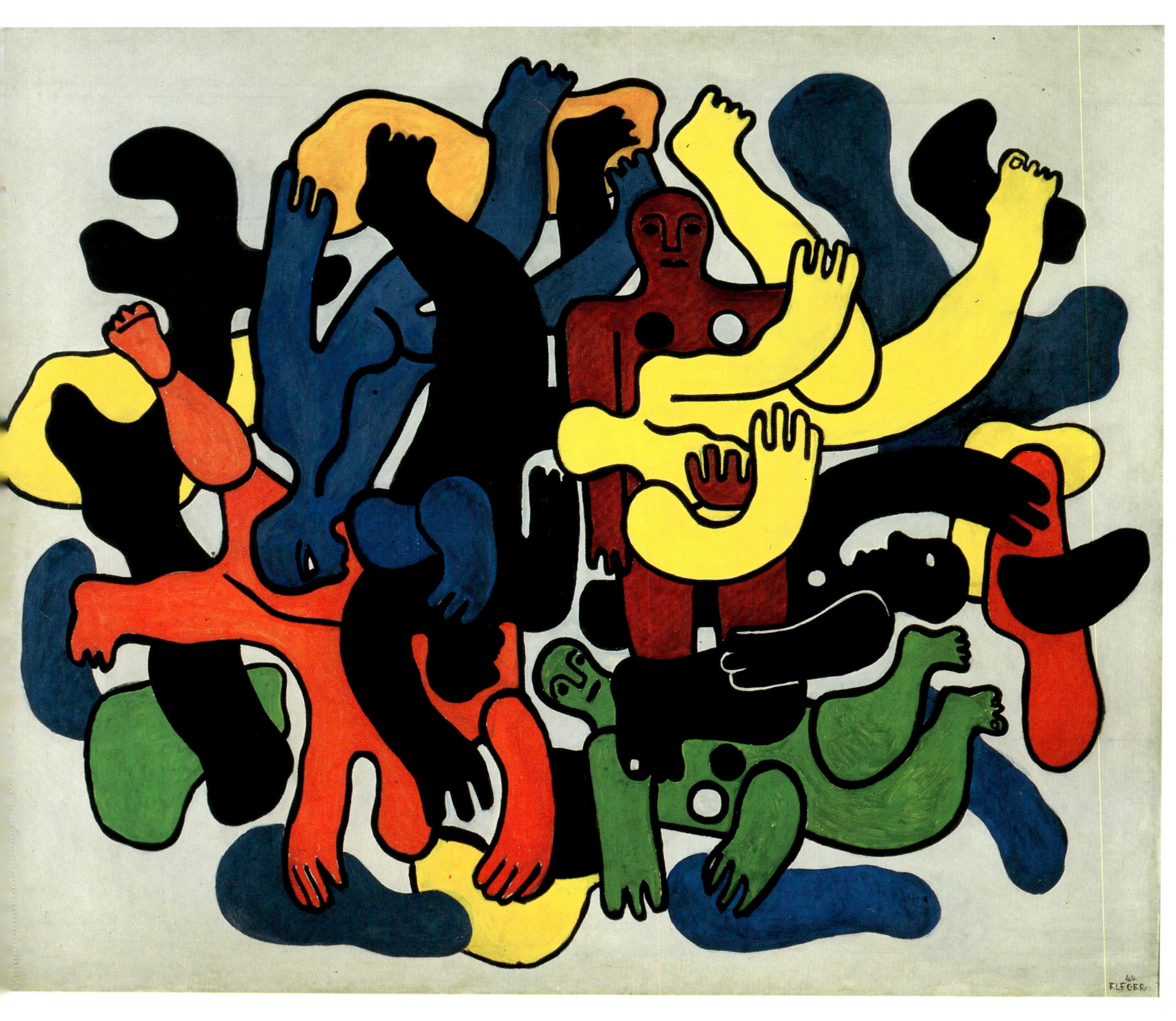


297. THE BIG BLACK DIVERS
1944—Oil on canvas, 186 × 221 cm
Musée National d'Art Moderne, Centre Georges Pompidou, Paris

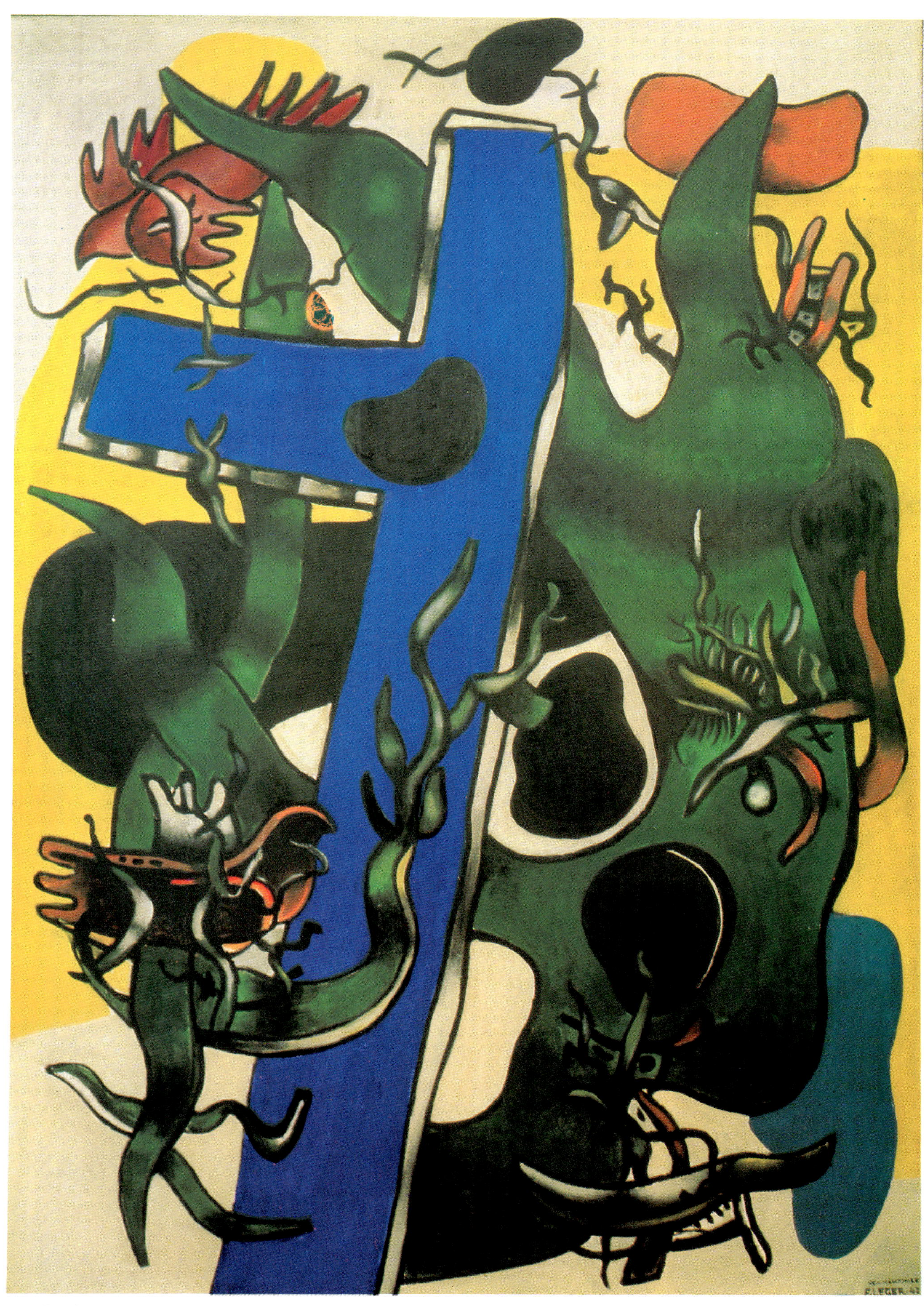

298. THE FOREST
1942—Oil on canvas, 182 × 127 cm
Musée National d'Art Moderne, Centre Georges Pompidou, Paris

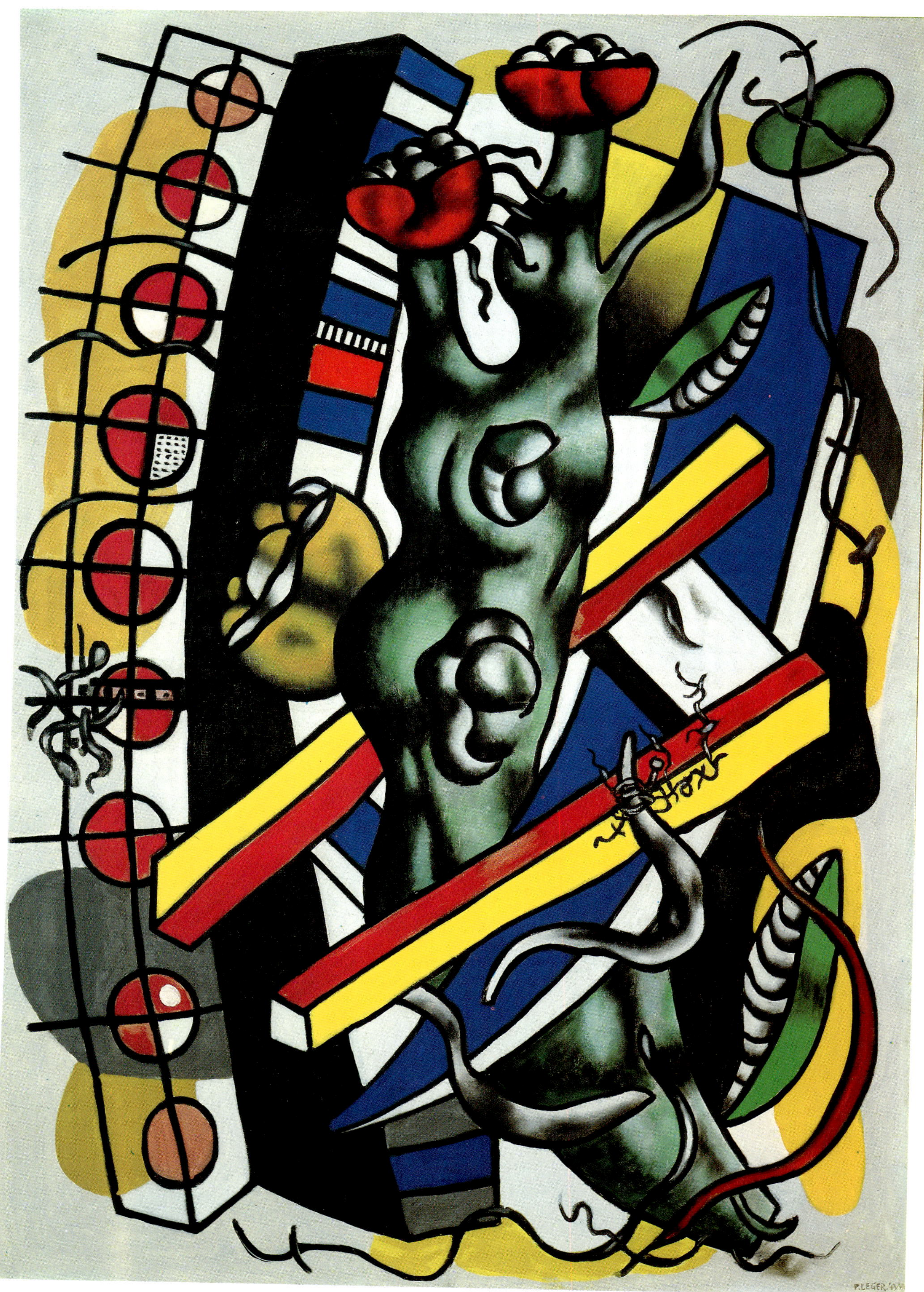


299. THE TREE IN THE LADDER
1943–44—Oil on canvas, 182 × 125 cm
Louise Leiris Gallery, Paris

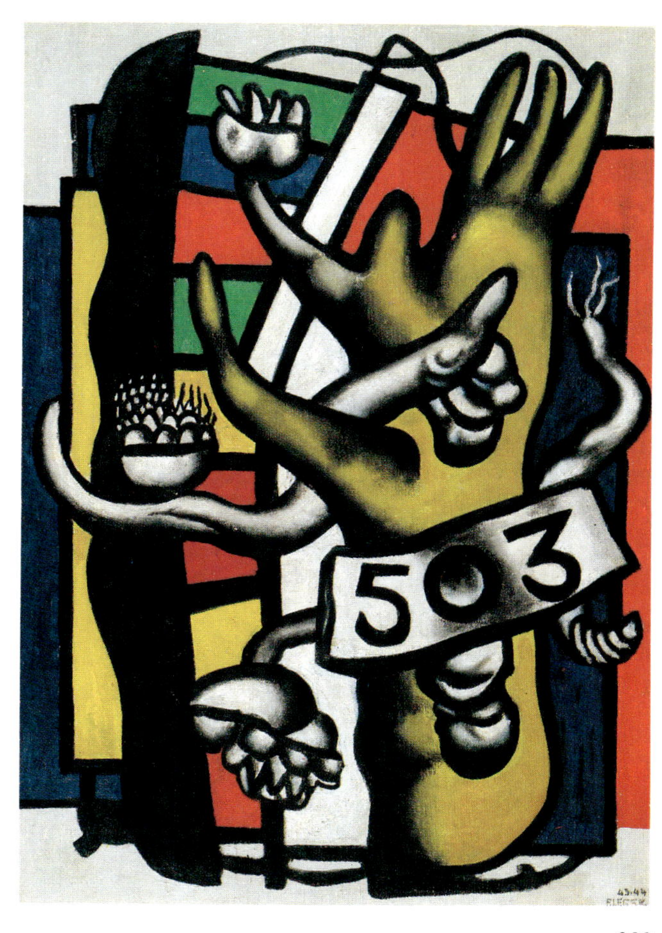


300

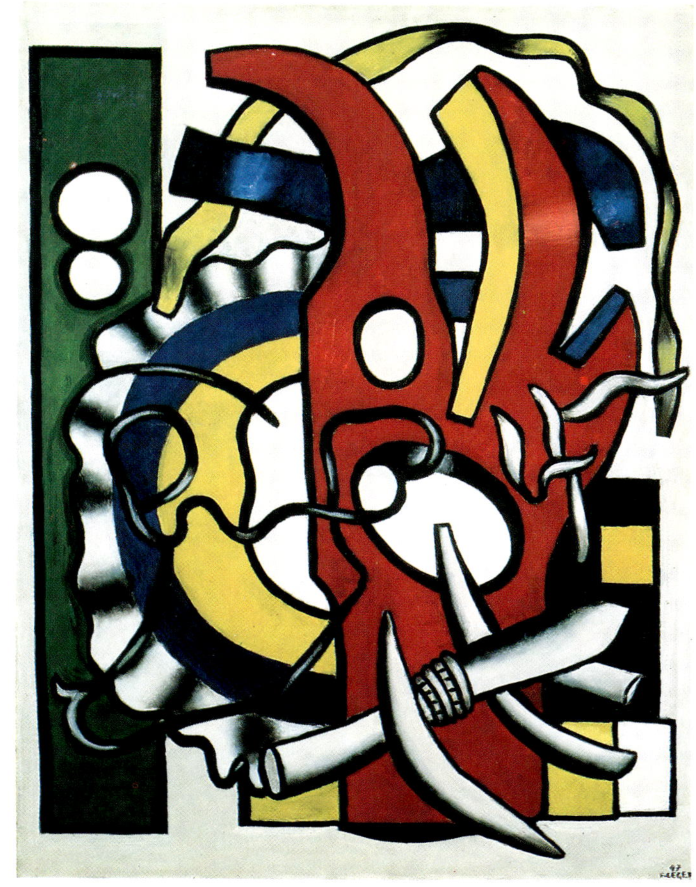

301

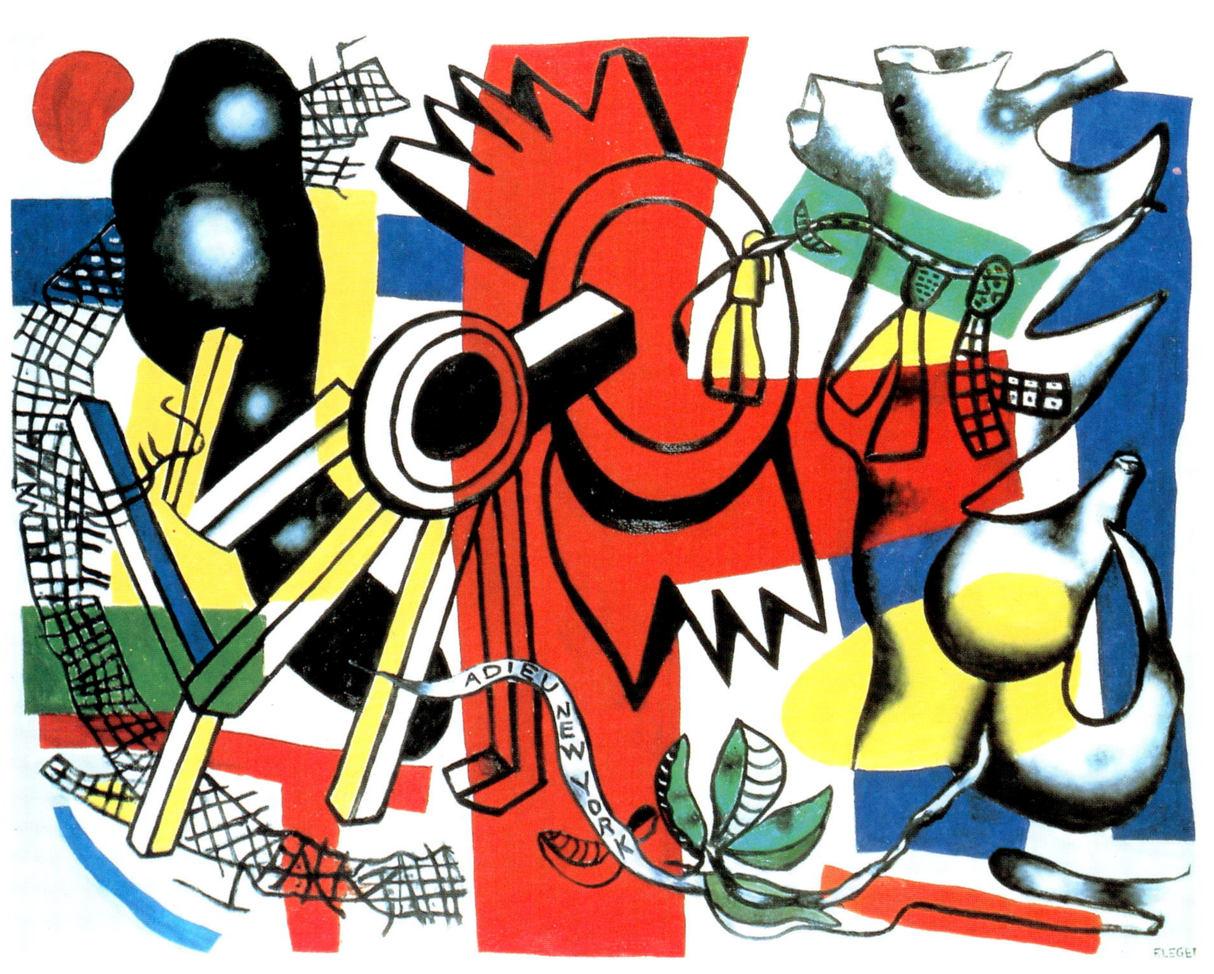


302

300. 503
1943–44—Oil on canvas, 94 × 66 cm
Louise Leiris Gallery, Paris

301. COMPOSITION WITH KNIFE
1947—Oil on canvas, 130 × 87 cm
Collection of Mr. and Mrs. Adrien Maeght

302. FAREWELL, NEW YORK
1946—Oil on canvas, 130 × 162 cm
Musée National d'Art Moderne, Centre Georges Pompidou, Paris

303. COMPOSITION WITH BASKET
1950—Oil on canvas, 65 × 50 cm
Private collection

304. MAN WITH MELON
1943–44—Oil on canvas, 125 × 111.5 cm
Private collection

### Tear down New York

It was not so much a *discovery* that the American landscape offered Léger, but rather the new raw material for his unending study of contrasts. It allowed him to multiply the oppositions between nature and machines. When Leger escaped war-ravaged Europe for the bucolic life in the United States, he was already in his sixties. Besides, he had already done Verdun under Marshal Pétain's command. One war

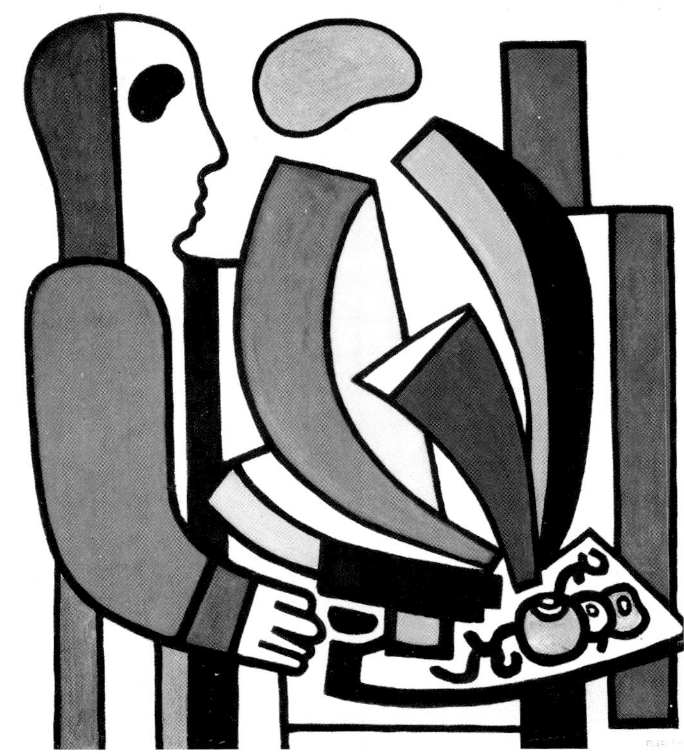

304

303

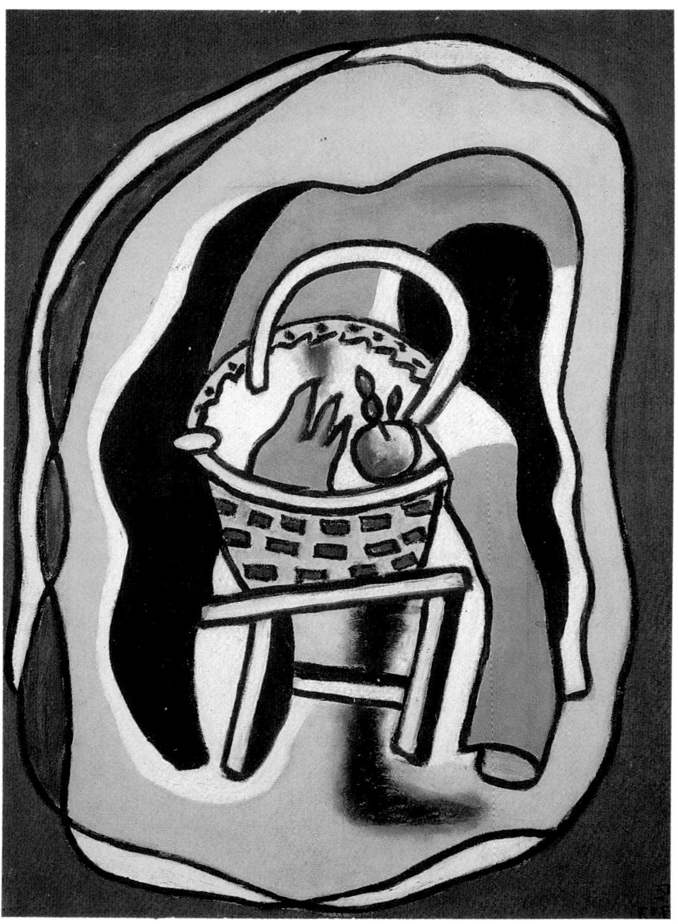

in a lifetime is enough! Léger even lampooned Pétain and wrote him a project proposal in 1931 that called for the destruction of New York . . . so that the city could be rebuilt entirely in transparent, translucent glass with blue, red, and yellow storeys for each building. . . An unprecedented enchantment! "Tear down New York! It's impossible for Pétain not to have been tempted, even for a few seconds. What a magnificent task for the artillery! The Americans would have been the first to applaud it. . . Engineers have recently found a way of making glass with *sour milk.* It's much cheaper than cement. The problems are unbelievable! All the American cows would be working to rebuild the city!"

### Farewell, New York Ill. 302

When Pierre Descargues visited Léger in 1946 at his atelier on Rue Notre-Dame-des-Champs, the artist showed him a canvas: "That's America, my latest painting. It's called *Farewell, New York.* That's written on a streamer. You know, the U.S.A. is a country with an infinite amount of garbage. People throw things away rather than repair them. See here, all those bits of rusty metal, machine arms, and even neckties. What I enjoyed while I was over there was painting canvases that exploded with all that sort of stuff."

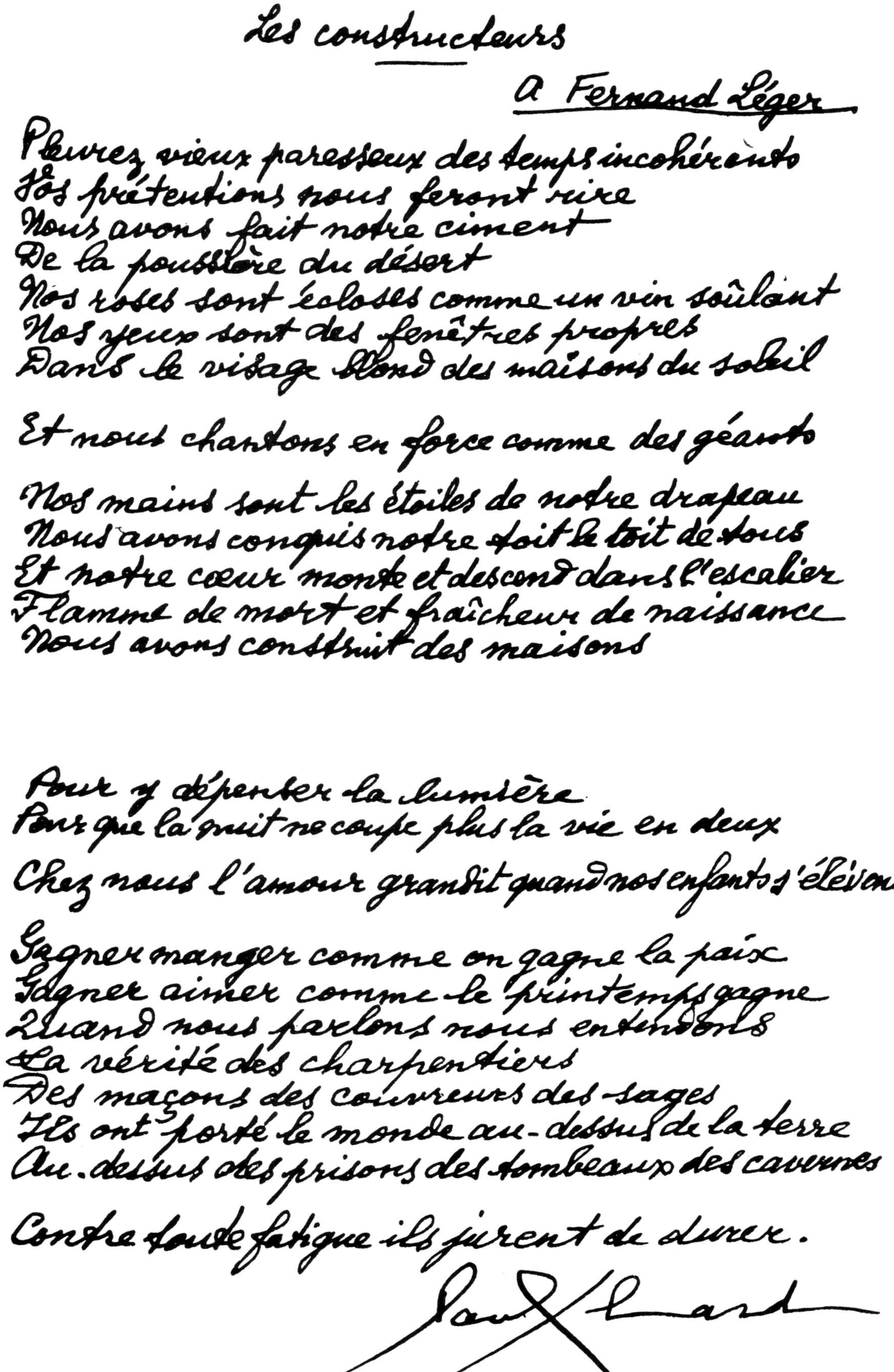

# Les constructeurs

*à Fernand Léger*

Pleurez vieux paresseux des temps incohérents
Vos prétentions nous feront rire
Nous avons fait notre ciment
De la poussière du désert
Nos roses sont écloses comme un vin soûlant
Nos yeux sont des fenêtres propres
Dans le visage blond des maisons du soleil

Et nous chantons en force comme des géants

Nos mains sont les étoiles de notre drapeau
Nous avons conquis notre toit le toit de tous
Et notre cœur monte et descend dans l'escalier
Flamme de mort et fraîcheur de naissance
Nous avons construit des maisons

Pour y dépenser la lumière
Pour que la nuit ne coupe plus la vie en deux

Chez nous l'amour grandit quand nos enfants s'élèvent

Gagner manger comme on gagne la paix
Gagner aimer comme le printemps gagne
Quand nous parlons nous entendons
La vérité des charpentiers
Des maçons des couvreurs des sages
Ils ont porté le monde au-dessus de la terre
Au-dessus des prisons des tombeaux des cavernes

Contre toute fatigue ils jurent de durer.

Paul Eluard

305. POEM BY PAUL ELUARD: "THE BUILDERS" DEDICATED TO FERNAND LÉGER, 1950

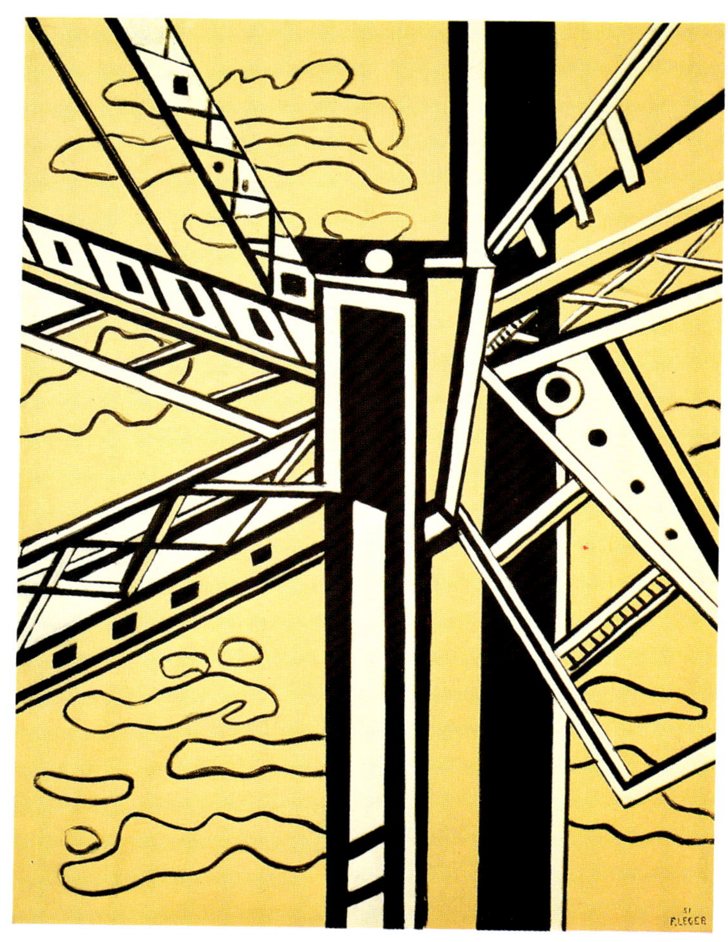


306. MECHANICAL ELEMENTS IN SPACE
1951—Oil on canvas, 130 × 97 cm
Louise Leiris Gallery, Paris

307. THE BUILDERS ON BLUE BACKGROUND
1951—Gouache and ink, 49.5 × 65 cm
Louise Leiris Gallery, Paris

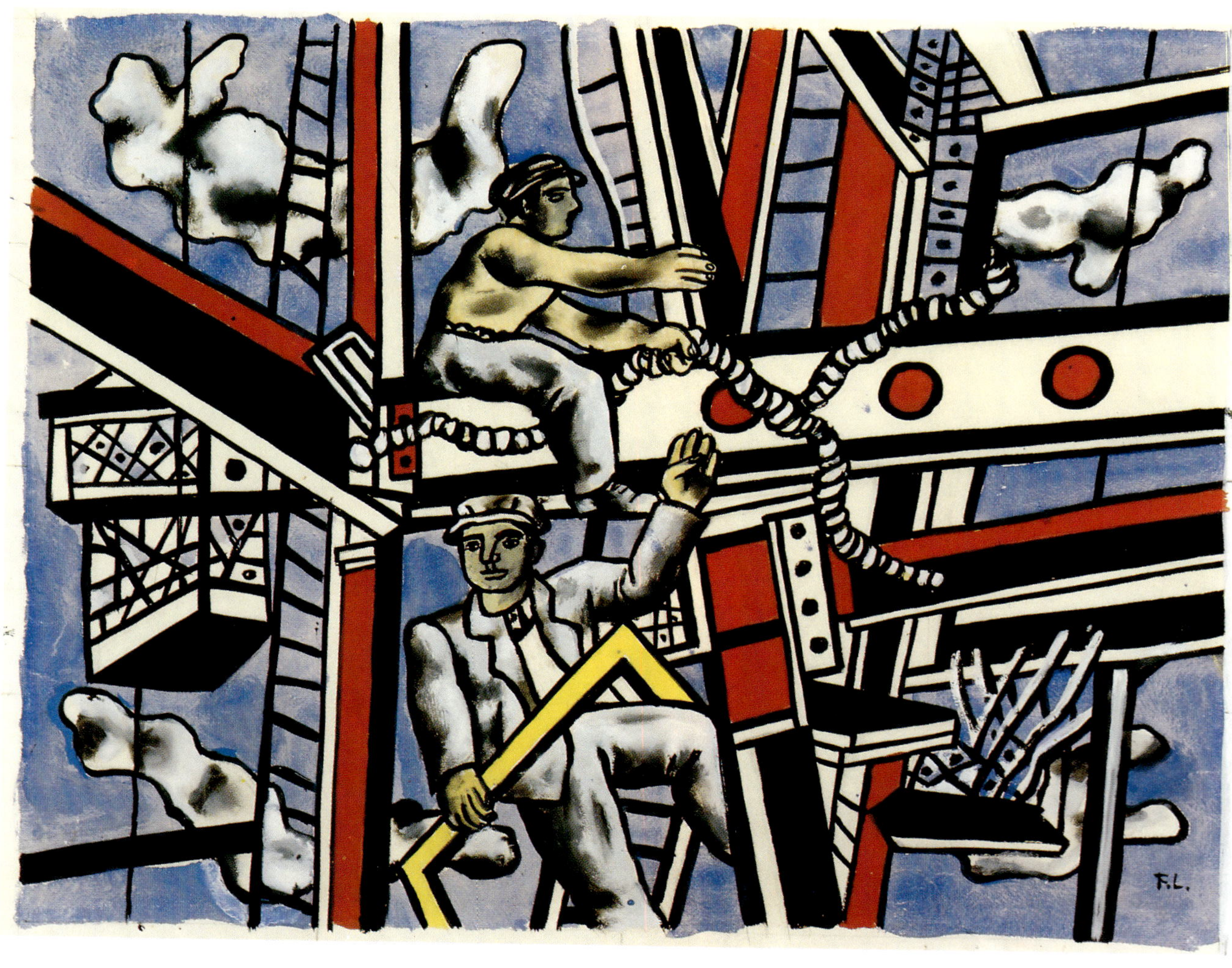

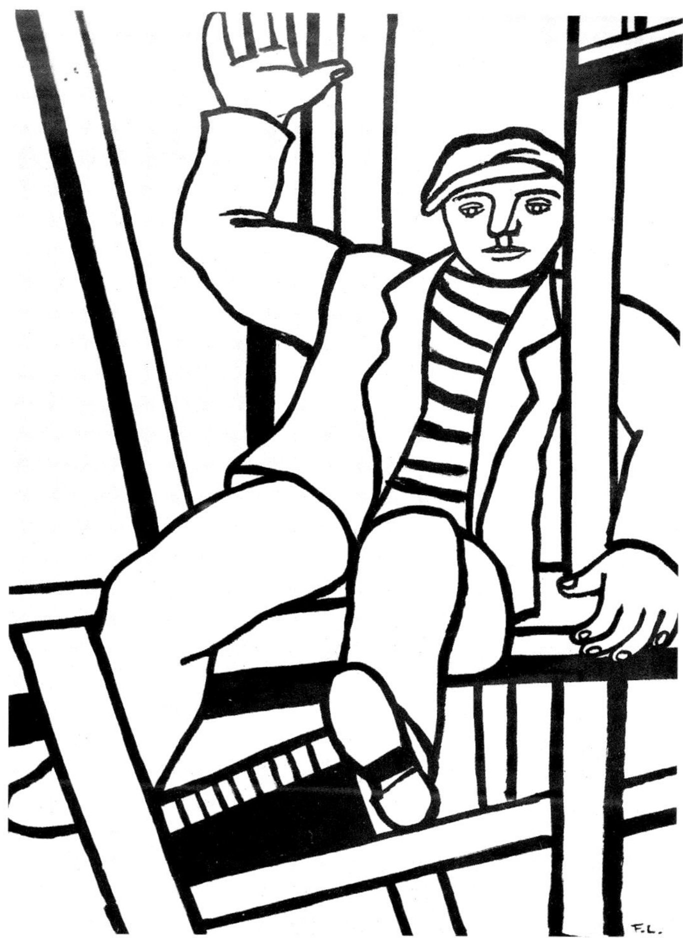

308. THE BUILDERS: CHARACTER
1950—Ink drawing, 77 × 52.5 cm
Musée National Fernand Léger, Biot

## Ill. 306 to 311 *The Builders*

Léger's return to France marked the definitive presence of man in his paintings, and his definitive return to the subject. With regard to human beings in his paintings, Léger explained that "in my latest canvases where figures connected to subjects are present, you may find that the human figure has a tendency to become the primary object. Only the future will tell whether this is better, or if it's a mistake. In any case, contrasted values still dominate my work and must justify this evolution." In terms of the subject, Léger emphasized that "we've got to be clear on what I mean by the word 'subject.' *I don't paint subjects. I paint contrasts.* I'm a painter. I don't write descriptive literature."

*The Builders* is the most famous postwar example, as well as the most disliked, of Léger's "contrasts." Léger was still dreaming of painting his working-class canvases for working-class people, and thought he had found a good opportunity to establish a dialogue with his dear comrades at the same time that he was erecting his idea of a monument to them. The idea came to him on his way to Chevreuse: "There were three high-tension electrical pylons being built near the highway. Perched on top, there were men at work. I was struck by the contrast between these men, the metallic architecture, and the clouds in the sky. The men looked so small, as if lost in a rigid, hard, and hostile maze. I wanted to render that in an uncompromising way. I examined the exact value of the human factor, the sky, the clouds, and the metal. If the forms of my workers are more varied, if I'm moving closer to individualizing the characters, it's because I want to maximize the violent contrast between them and the metallic geometry in which they are situated. . . . Modern subjects, be they social or something else, are valid as long as this law of contrasts is respected. Our everyday life is made up of contrasts. They must become part of our current preoccupations."

Léger stuck to his principles. If *The Builders* is close to human, it is only to accentuate the contrast between the human and the mechanical world. Yet something important has changed since Léger's period of "mechanical elements" in which he subordinated man-as-robot to the machine. With his new approach to the world, Léger in a certain way had liberated man from the technical constraints. Although it is undeniable that these little men in his series of builders do not have any more importance than the steel beams, they do move freely within the geometric framework.

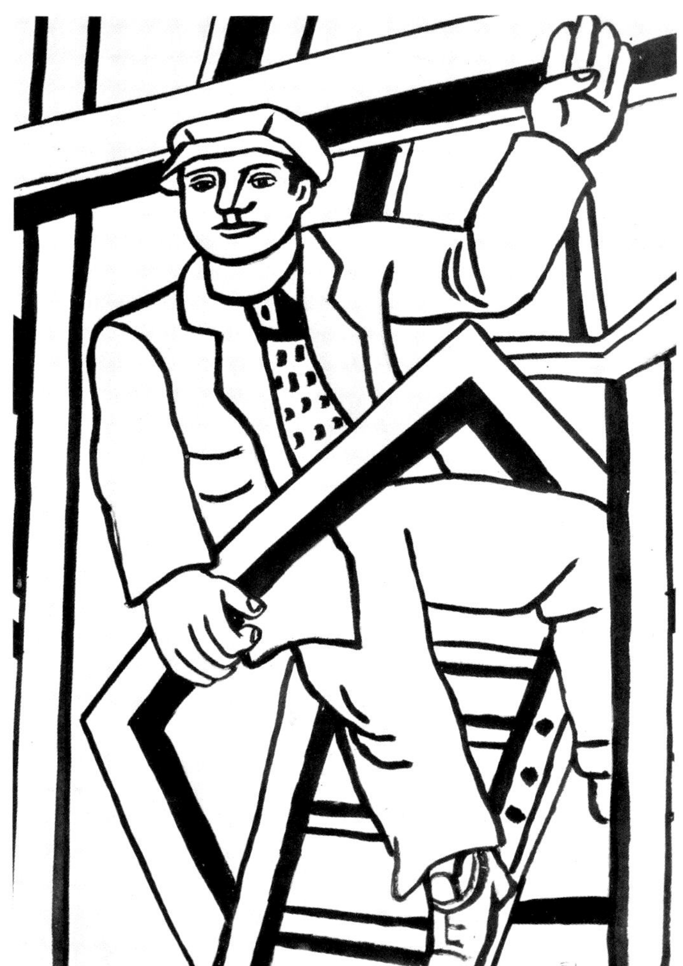

309. THE BUILDERS: CHARACTER WITH A FRAME
1951—Ink drawing, 77.5 × 52.5 cm
Musée National Fernand Léger, Biot

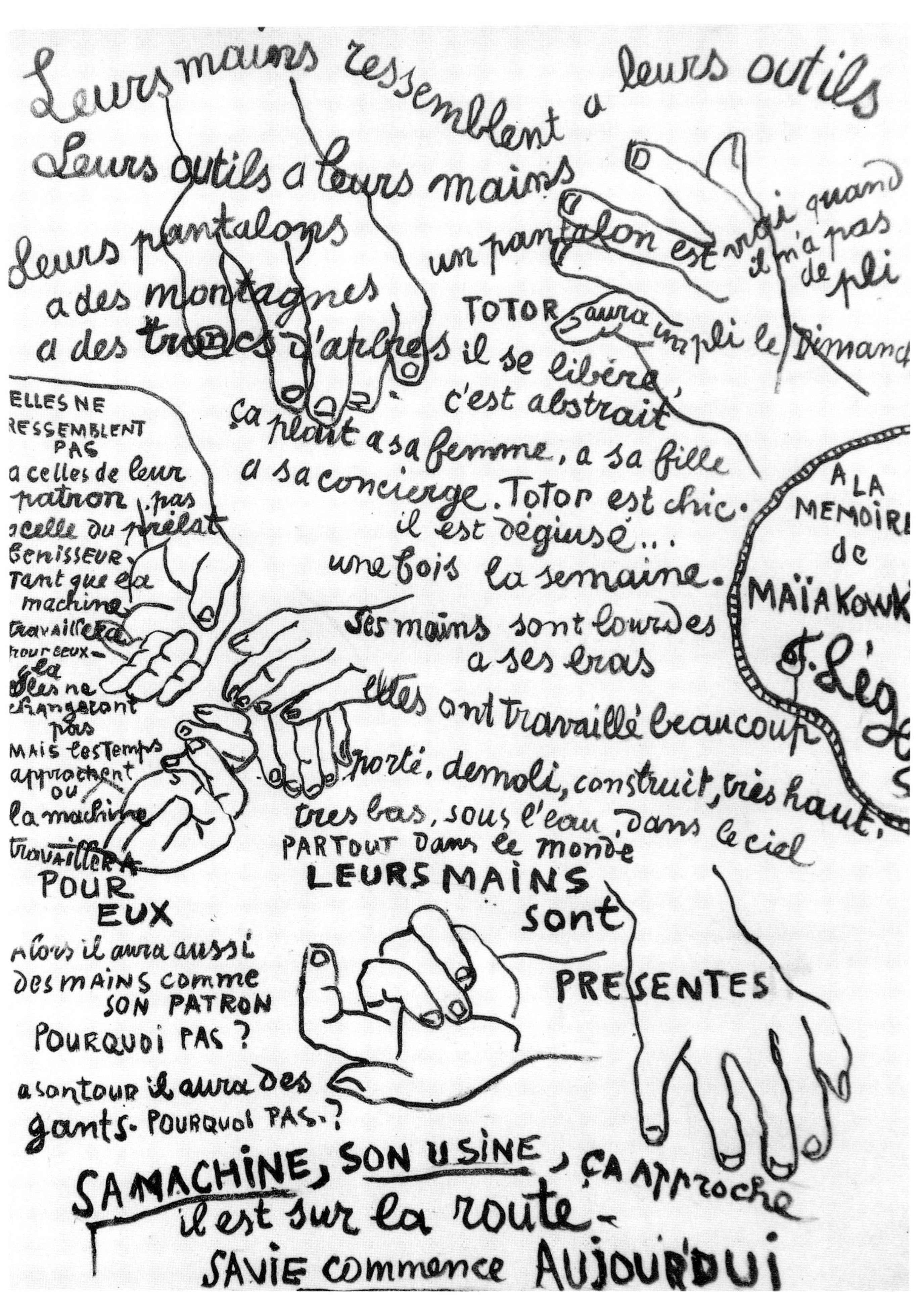


310. "THE HANDS," A POEM DEDICATED TO THE MEMORY OF MAYAKOVSKY
1950—Oil on canvas, 80 × 130 cm
Private collection

311. THE BUILDERS, DEFINITIVE VERSION
1950—Oil on canvas, 300 × 200 cm
Musée National Fernand Léger, Biot

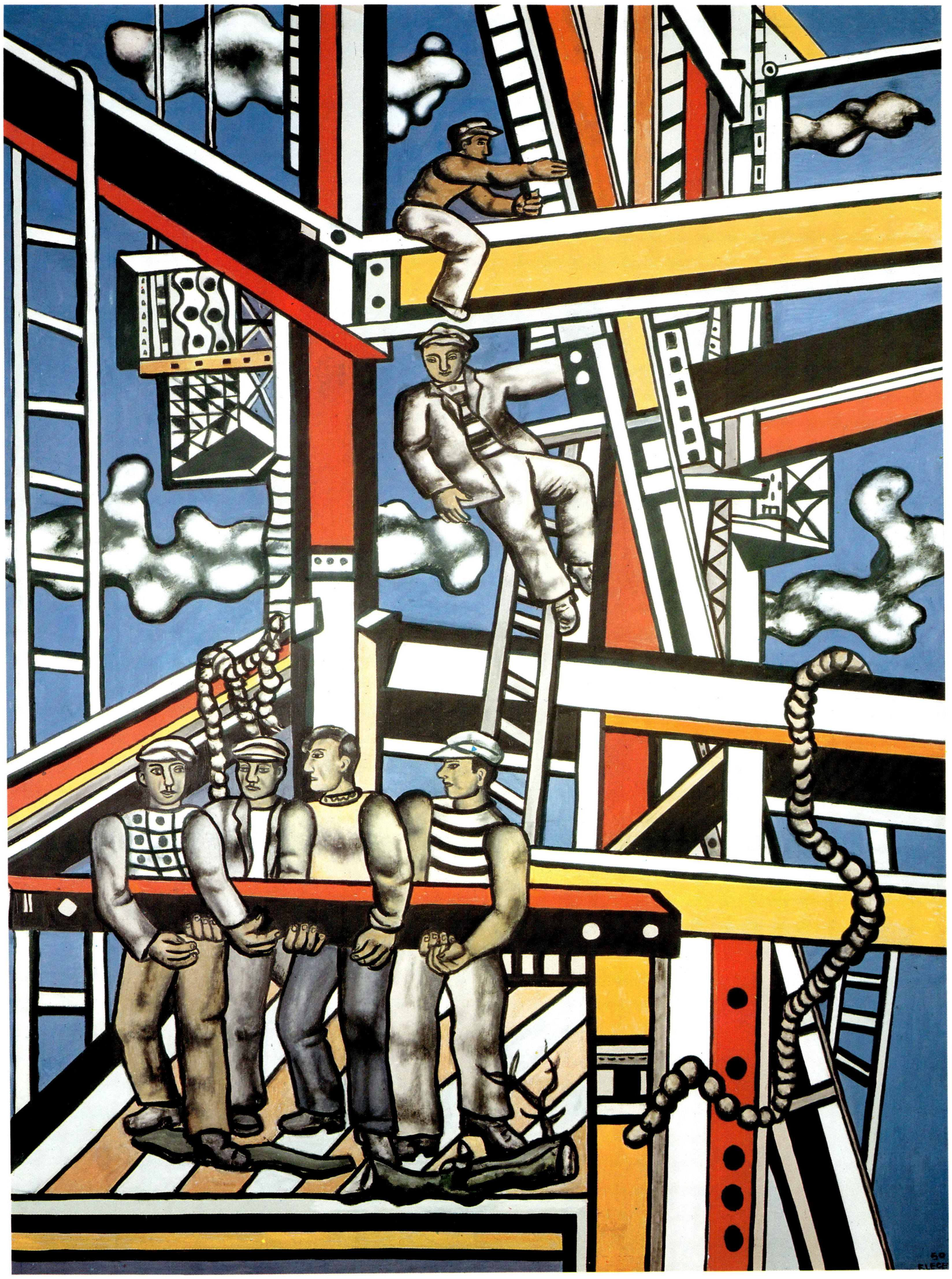
50

## The canteen of the Renault car factory

To find out if what he had done was enough to seduce the working class, Léger hung *The Builders* on the wall of the canteen at the Renault factory: "At noon, the guys arrived. They looked at the paintings while they were eating. Some of them made pokes at the paintings: 'Get a load of those guys. They couldn't work with the kind of hands they got.' The workers were making value judgments based on comparison. My canvases amused them, but they didn't understand anything. I listened to them and sadly swallowed my soup.

"Eight days later I went back to eat at the canteen. The mood had changed. The guys weren't laughing anymore. They weren't talking about the paintings either. However, a good many of them were looking up to glance at my paintings before dropping their eyes back to their plates. Could they be intrigued by the canvases? Who knows? Then, when I was about to leave, a chap came over to me and said: 'You're the painter, aren't you? You'll see. After they take your paintings away my buddies are gonna realize it. All they're gonna see is the bare walls in front of them; they're gonna realize what your colors are all about.' That was good to hear!"

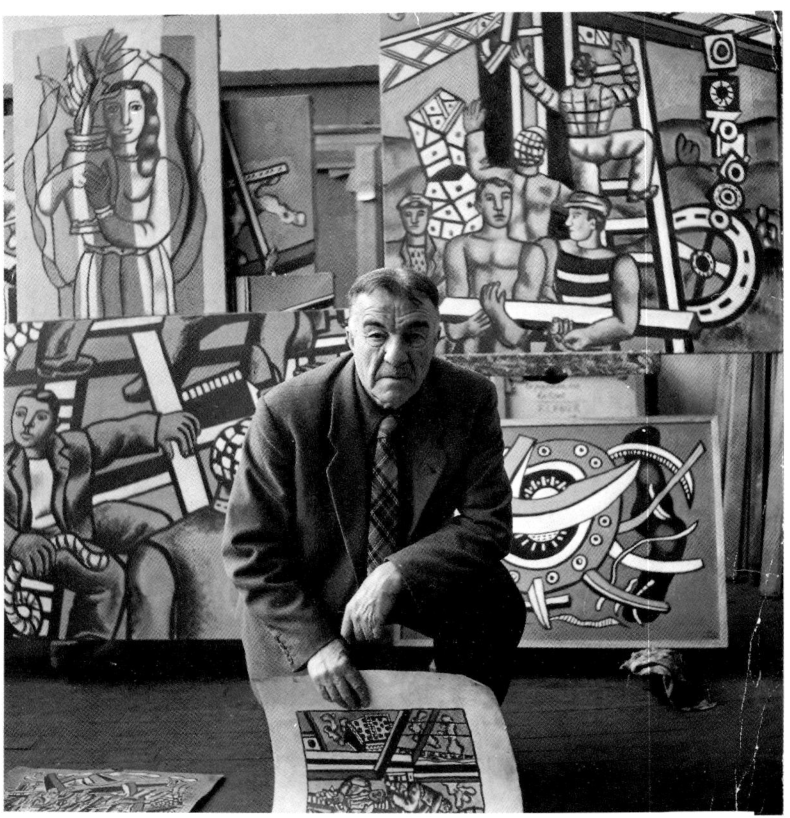

313. LÉGER IN FRONT OF *THE BUILDERS*
1951—Photo by Maywald

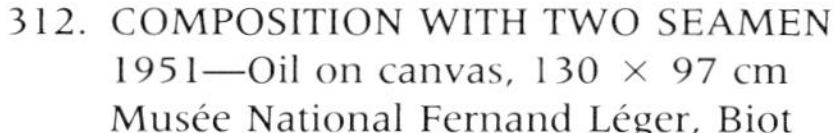

312. COMPOSITION WITH TWO SEAMEN
1951—Oil on canvas, 130 × 97 cm
Musée National Fernand Léger, Biot

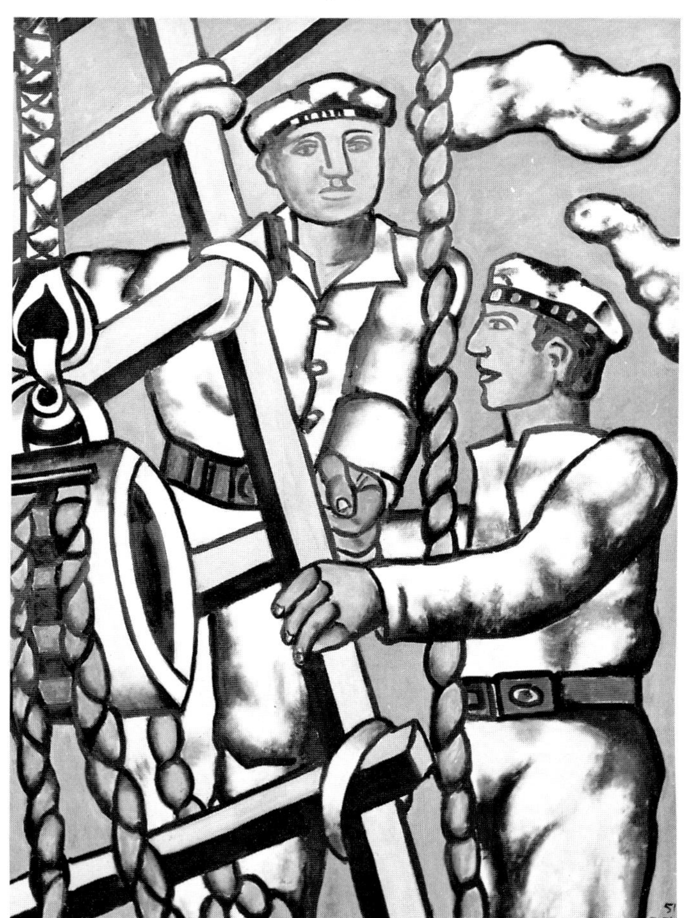

314. CHARACTERS IN A TRUCK
1955—Ink on paper, 65 × 50 cm
Musée National Fernand Léger, Biot

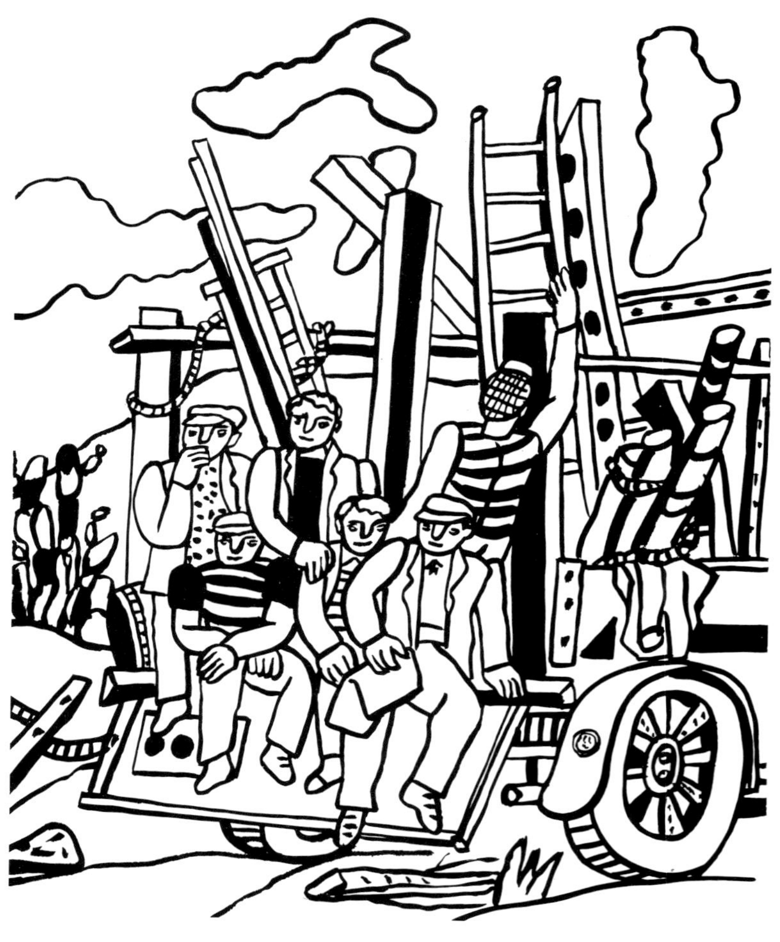

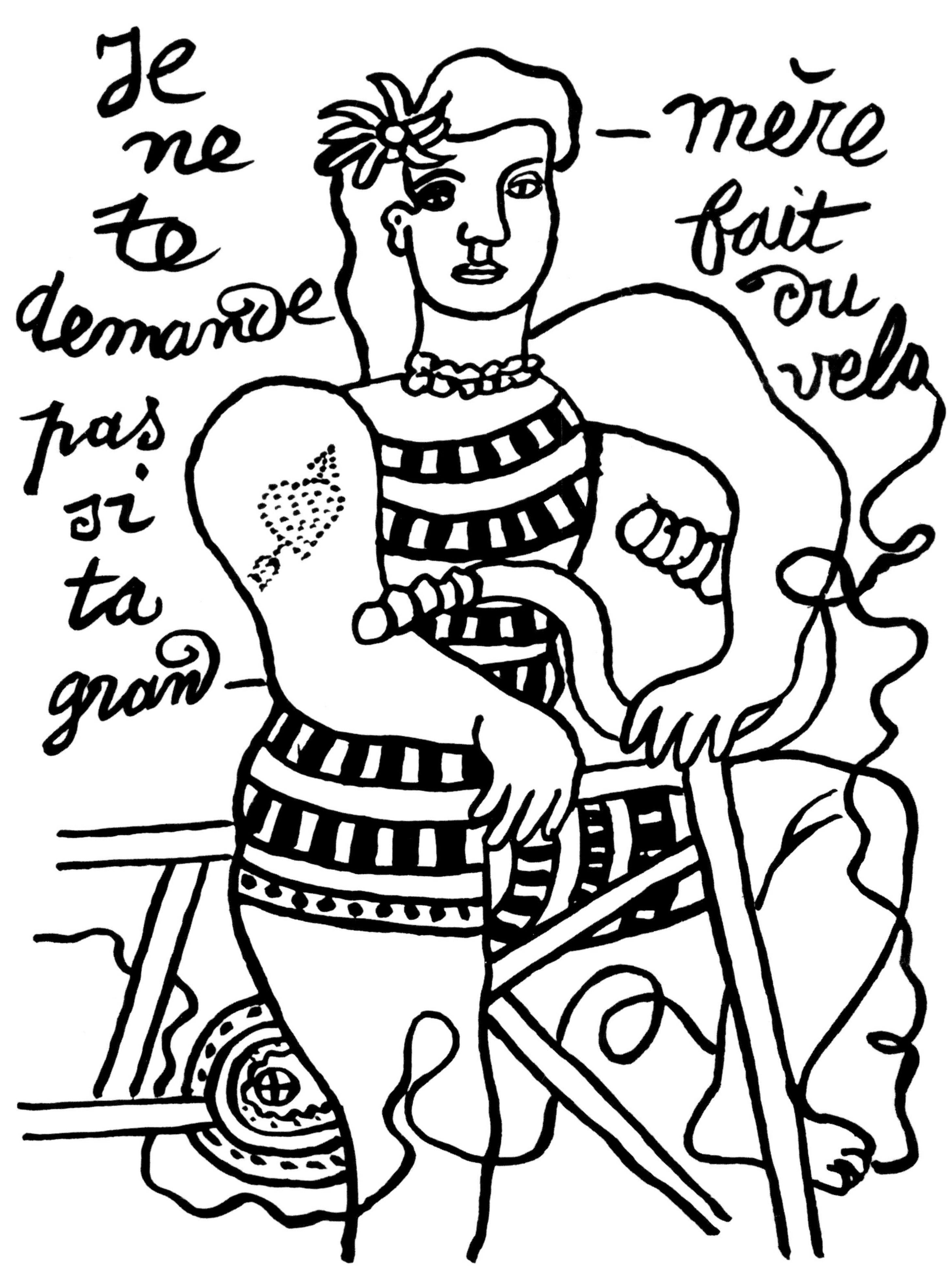


315. EXCERPT FROM THE BOOK *THE CIRCUS*
*I'm not asking you if your grandma rides a bike*

# Country Outing

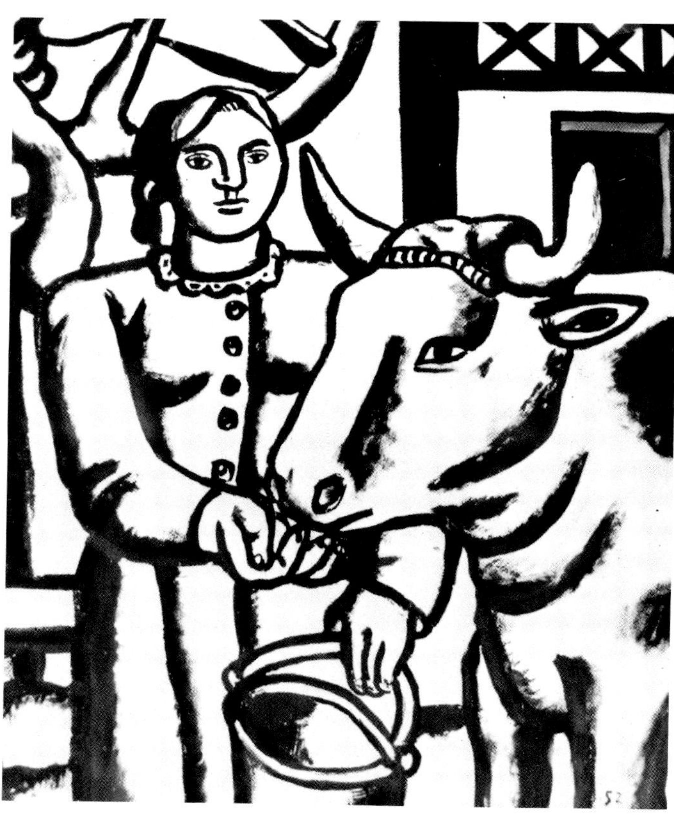

316. THE FARM MAIDEN
1952—China ink and gouache, 57 × 51 cm
Private collection

In 1939 Léger wrote: "The case of David is probably going to come to the surface. What young person today is strong enough to solve the problem in the human and plastic sense? I think about the early masters, and about the ordinary people as well. In
l. 100 that sense, there's a change. After I painted *The Me-*
l. 247 *chanic, Musicians, Big Lunch,* and *The City,* I was often
l. 125 troubled by all these major issues. I was touched by
Ill. 92 some of the paintings by the early Italian masters (Carpaccio and Bellini), but we have escaped from that field of painting. Let me get back to David, because he was the one who came close to the Ingres-Delacroix solution—by the application of contrasts, pure tones, and the organization of forms. What David did was possible after thirty years of small paintings. Therefore, let's enlarge the problem. Four apples on a table become ten characters in plastic action. A face, an eye, or a foot could be substituted, as long as the overall orchestration of the painting is done well. They thus become a variety of values, as opposed to having anecdotal value."

In 1912 the good-natured Douanier Rousseau took Léger and some other friends with him to see the exhibit of David's portraits at the Petit Palais in Paris. "We all discounted the event, because we had no interest in David at the time." In 1933 Léger told Raymond Cogniat, "Imagine what lessons we've learned from Ingres, and from David, too. David has been sorely misunderstood and underestimated. I've just gone to Versailles for the sole purpose of taking another look at David's work. He's a very great painter, and Rousseau, who was so pure and full of instinct, knew this."

There were five years in between *Leisure: Homage* Ill. 321
*to Louis David* (1948–49), a veritable painting- Ill. 322
manifesto, and *Country Outing* ("La Partie de cam- to 325
pagne") and *Camper,* both painted in 1954. Both periods dealt with the same subject, and were probably inspired by the painter's memories of a paid vacation that dated back to 1936. Between these two periods is the transition from conventional and static composition to a vibrant and natural reality, populated with more realistic and spontaneous characters. Between the two periods we see all the difference that exists between a posed photo with a cardboard studio background, and a spontaneous outdoor snapshot.

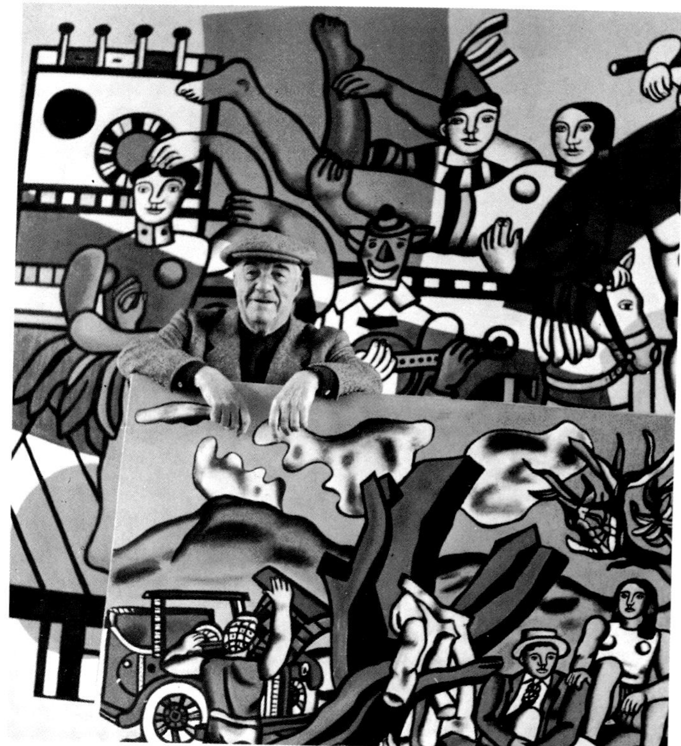

317. FERNAND LÉGER POSING WITH HIS CANVASES *COUNTRY OUTING* AND *THE BIG PARADE*
About 1954—Photo by Robert Doisneau

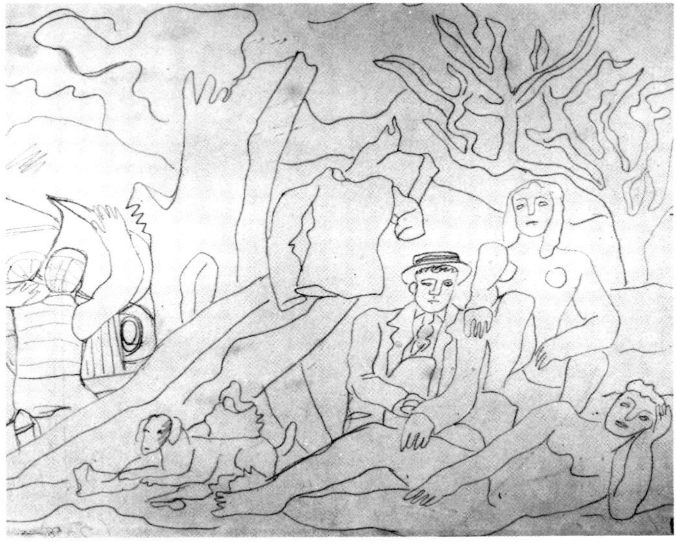

318. SKETCH FOR *COUNTRY OUTING*
About 1954—Drawing, 23 × 44 cm
Musée National Fernand Léger, Biot

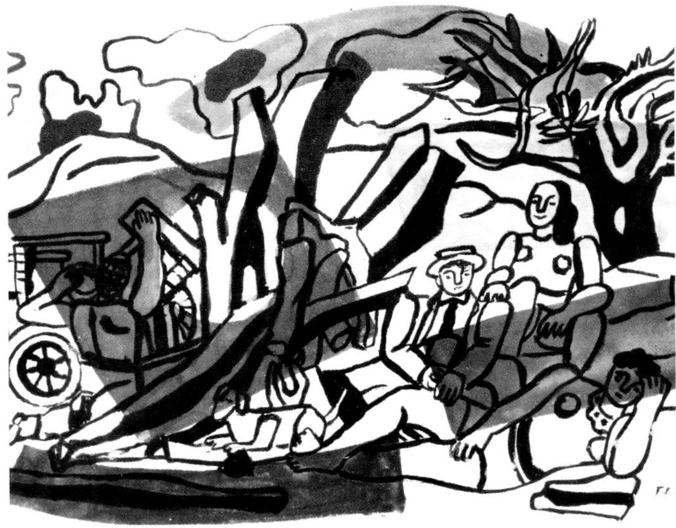

319. STUDY FOR *COUNTRY OUTING*
1953—Gouache, 40 × 55 cm
Private collection

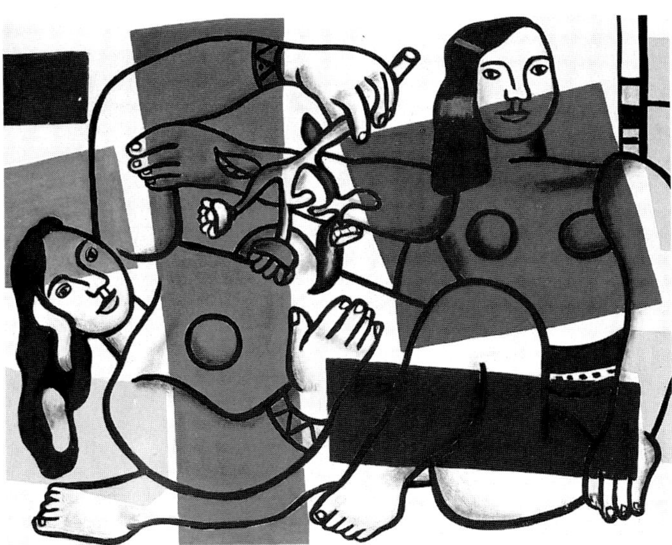

320. TWO WOMEN HOLDING FLOWERS, DEFINITIVE VERSION
1954—Oil on canvas, 97 × 130 cm
Tate Gallery, London

### The Pietà of Leisure

In *Homage to Louis David*, the men and women are of Ill. 321
the same species as *Three Musicians* or *Big Julie*. In Ill. 247
other words, Léger wanted to make idealized "types" Ill. 250
that were representative of the human condition of his day. Everything is simplified in these paintings: contours, colors, scenery. He is dominated by the "naive" spirit, and the vignettes could just as well be called "Liberty, equality, fraternity . . . leisure."
Serenity dominates in *Country Outing* and *Camper*. Ill. 322
Leisure had outgrown the status of an inalienable Ill. 325
and egalitarian right to be fought for. It had become an acquired form of happiness, and the goal was to make the best possible use of it. It was the revenge of the worker to be able to "do nothing," *farniente*. Liberty is the key word. It seems to have increasingly guided Léger back to some "Golden Age," a time when the world was a better place.

*Homage to Louis David* was an absolutely necessary step for Léger. He rendered a tribute to David as the creator of *Brutus* and *Marat*, as the Revolution's bard, the poet of the Empire: a return to classicism, the austerity and sobriety of republicanism, the absence of romanticism and sentimentality, the clarity and architectural structure of his work.

The reclining woman at the bottom of *Homage to Louis David* is Léger's complicitous wink at David. The woman is in the same position as Marat in his bath, and just like Marat, she is holding a paper in her hand. Léger insisted on making the intent of this tribute clear: "I wanted to mark the return to simplicity, to an art that is direct, and that everybody could understand without having to be subtle. . . . I was impressed with David because he was an anti-impressionist. He took imitative art as far as it could go, and it's for this reason that the atmosphere of the Renaissance is completely absent from his paintings. I feel that David is closer to me than to Michelangelo, especially in his portrait work. I like the spareness of David's work. I like it in Ingres' work as well. It was my path, and for this reason David's work immediately touched me." Léger was still speaking in terms of ideas and intentions. David's "spareness" is quite modified in the variegated outfits, smiling faces, and little flowers that sprout up all over Léger's canvas. The birds are doves, in the manner that Picasso was painting them in 1949, as symbols of peace. It is clear that Léger was dominated by the will to convey happiness and peace.

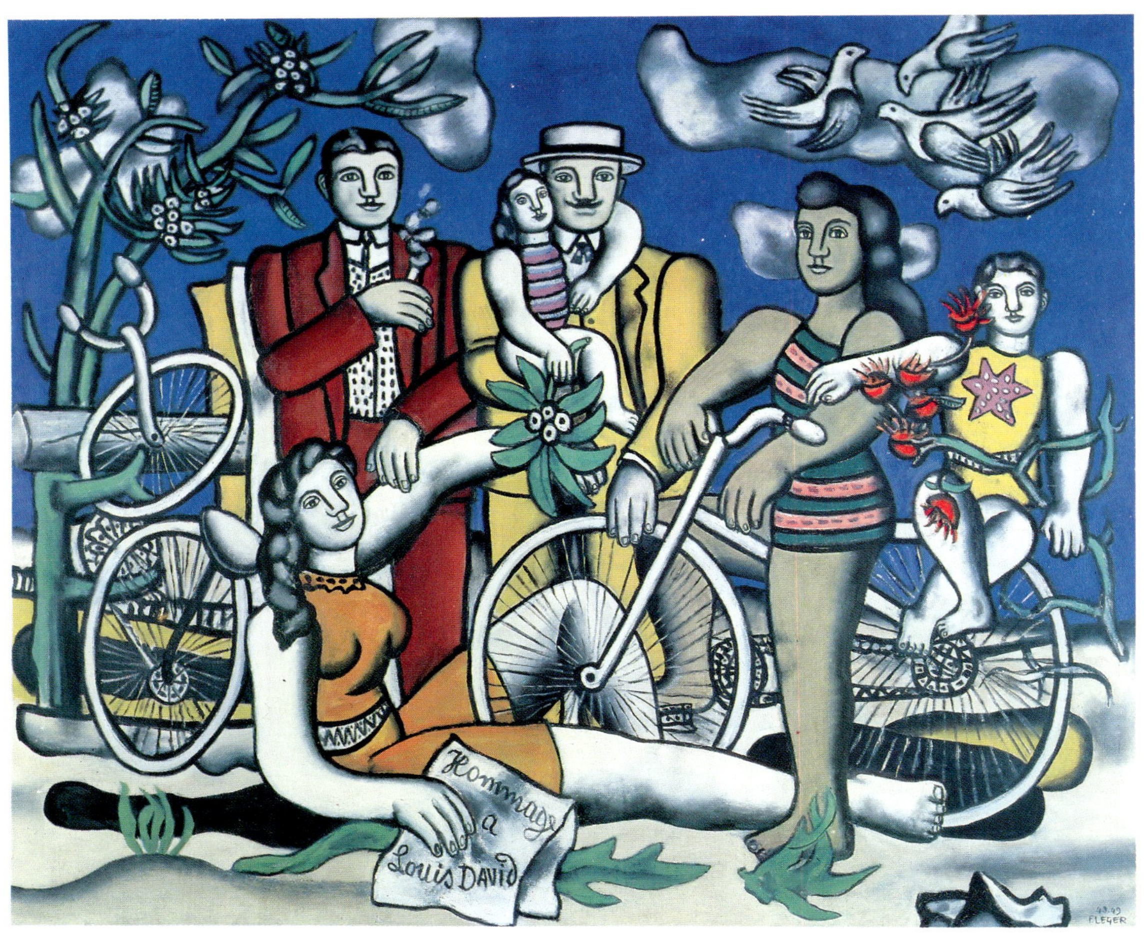


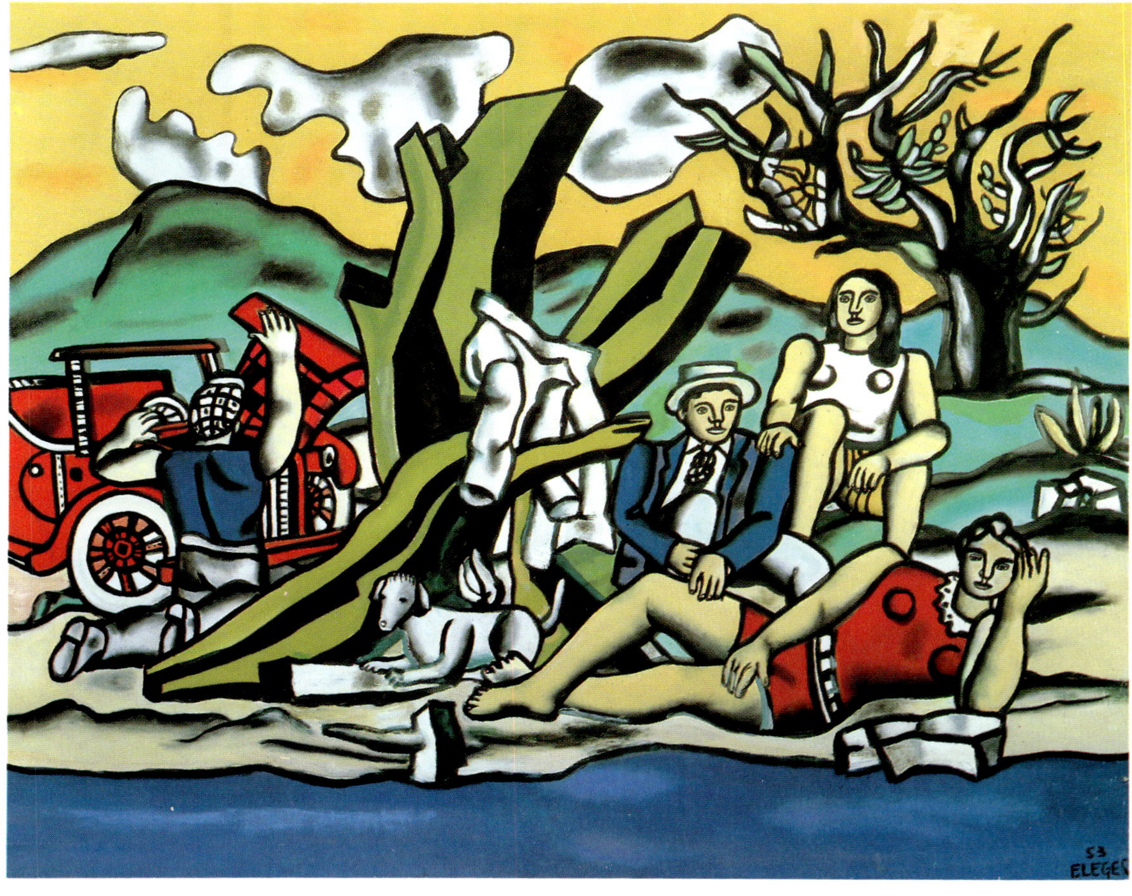

321. LEISURE: HOMAGE TO LOUIS DAVID
1948–49—Oil on canvas, 154 × 185 cm
Musée National d'Art Moderne, Centre Georges Pompidou, Paris

322. COUNTRY OUTING, SECOND VERSION
1953—Oil on canvas, 130 × 161 cm
Musée d'Art Moderne, Saint-Étienne

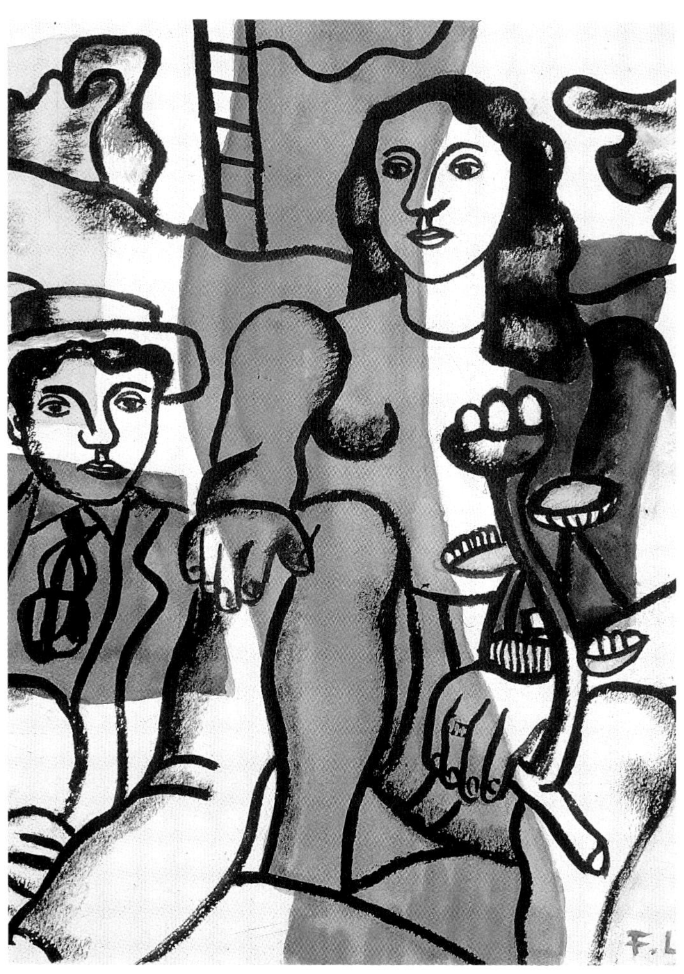


323. STUDY FOR *COUNTRY OUTING*
1952—Gouache, 28 × 22 cm
Private collection

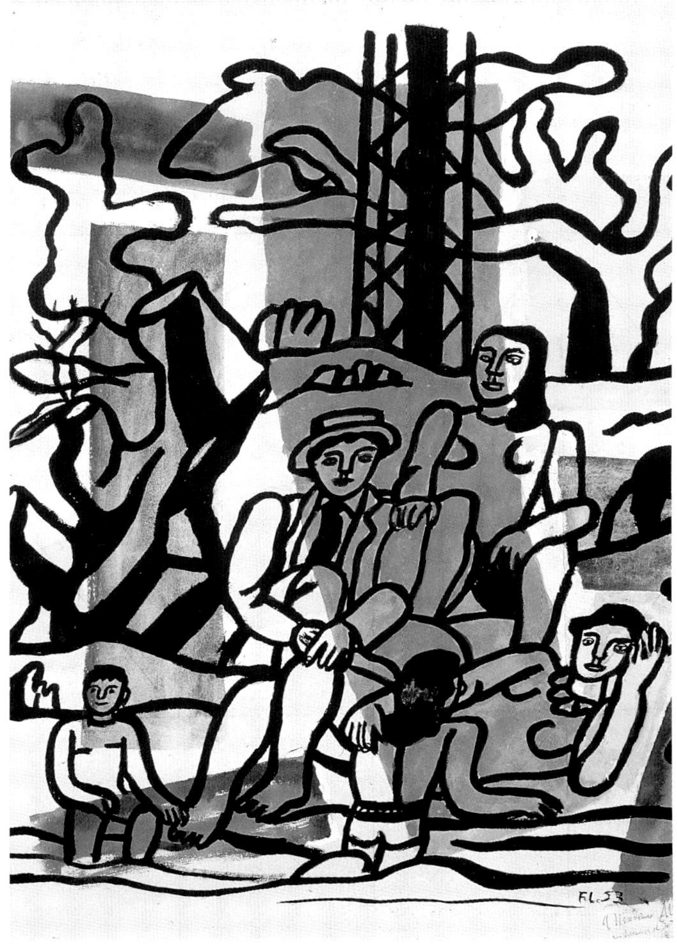


324. STUDY FOR *COUNTRY OUTING*
1953—Gouache on paper; 84 × 48.5 cm
Collection of Mr. and Mrs. Adrien Maeght

## Capturing happiness in flight

Ill. 318 to 325 The concept for *Homage to Louis David* is quite different from the concept for *Country Outing* and *Camper*. The last seems to evoke Manet, a very different ancestor of Léger's, and his painting *Déjeuner sur l'herbe*. No doubt Léger recalled Manet's idyllic painting, in which two fully dressed "dilettantes" are chatting in the company of a nude woman—who is meant to be the model and the mistress—while another "girlfriend" is bathing in the background. Léger venerated Manet, who for him was one of the most important renewers of painting, an artist who knew how to portray simple people on canvas. Léger was no longer trying to impose the will for happiness, as he was in *Homage to Louis David*. He was affirming happiness, the kind of happiness that he captured in flight. . . The characters are no longer standing in rows. They are dispersed about the canvas, kneeling, sitting, bending, lying down. There is even a character who is seen from behind as he takes care of his car. Faces are no longer seen frontally, as in the works that came before, but in profile or in three-quarter views.

Serenity began to soften Léger's rigid and willful intent. Although anecdote replaced his professed faith in substituting different plastic values, his art did not become "social realism." The mastery of his means and the power of his inspiration protected him from this. He knew his campers and hikers well. He watched them pass by his window at the end of every week. Georges Bauquier notes that "Léger lived at the Porte d'Orleans, which was the southern entrance to Paris. Because the countryside wasn't far, it would have been impossible for him not to see those who had labored hard all week heading out for more pleasurable pursuits. Léger enjoyed seeing the masses pass by. Their gaiety was contagious and so was their warmth and humanness. It had to do with the simple joys of simple people, the need to relax and unwind, to break with the constraints of everyday life. This is expressed in *Country Outing* and *Camper*, which also perhaps express the serenity experienced by Léger himself."

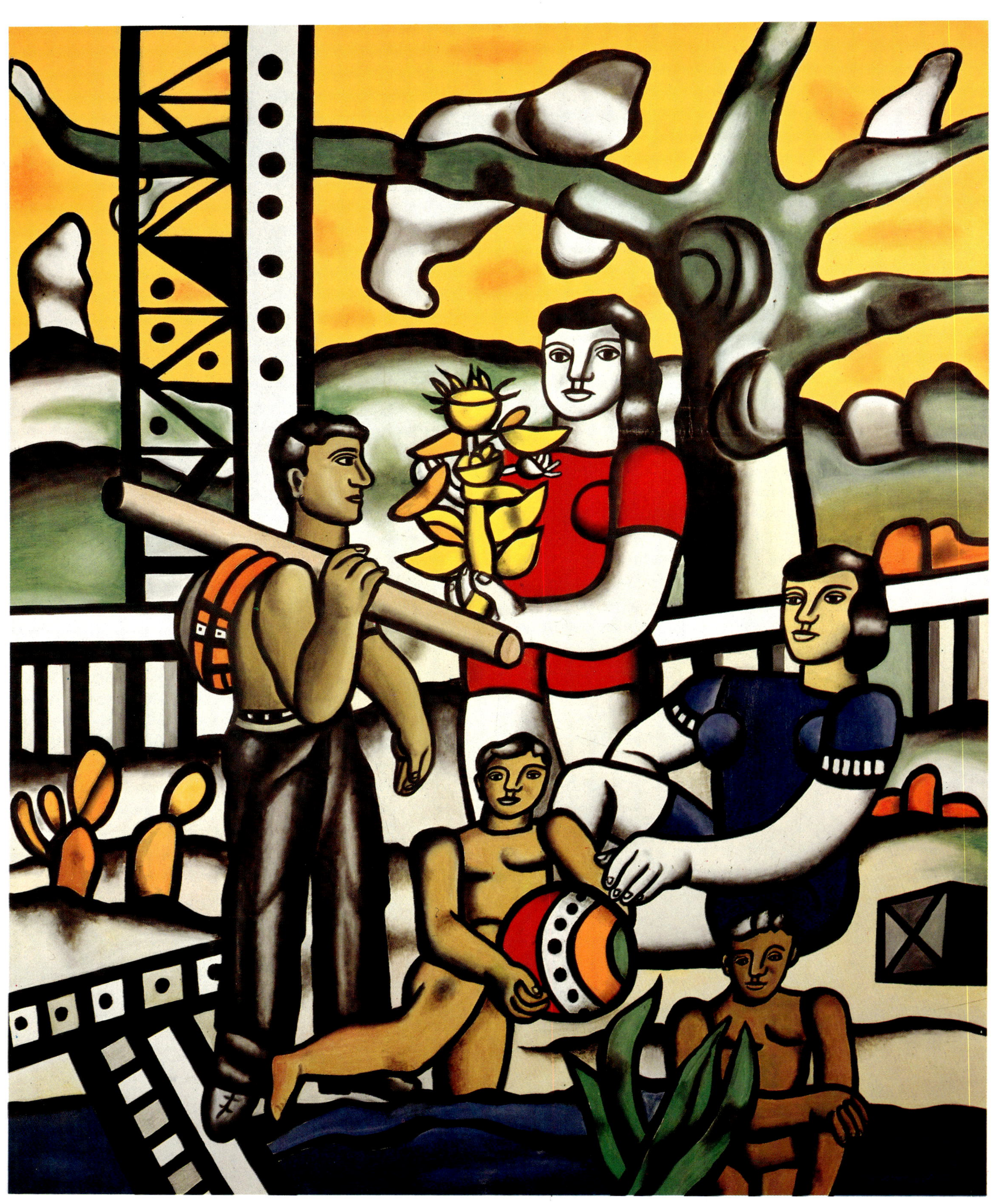

325. THE CAMPER
1954—Oil on canvas, 300 × 245 cm
Musée National Fernand Léger, Biot

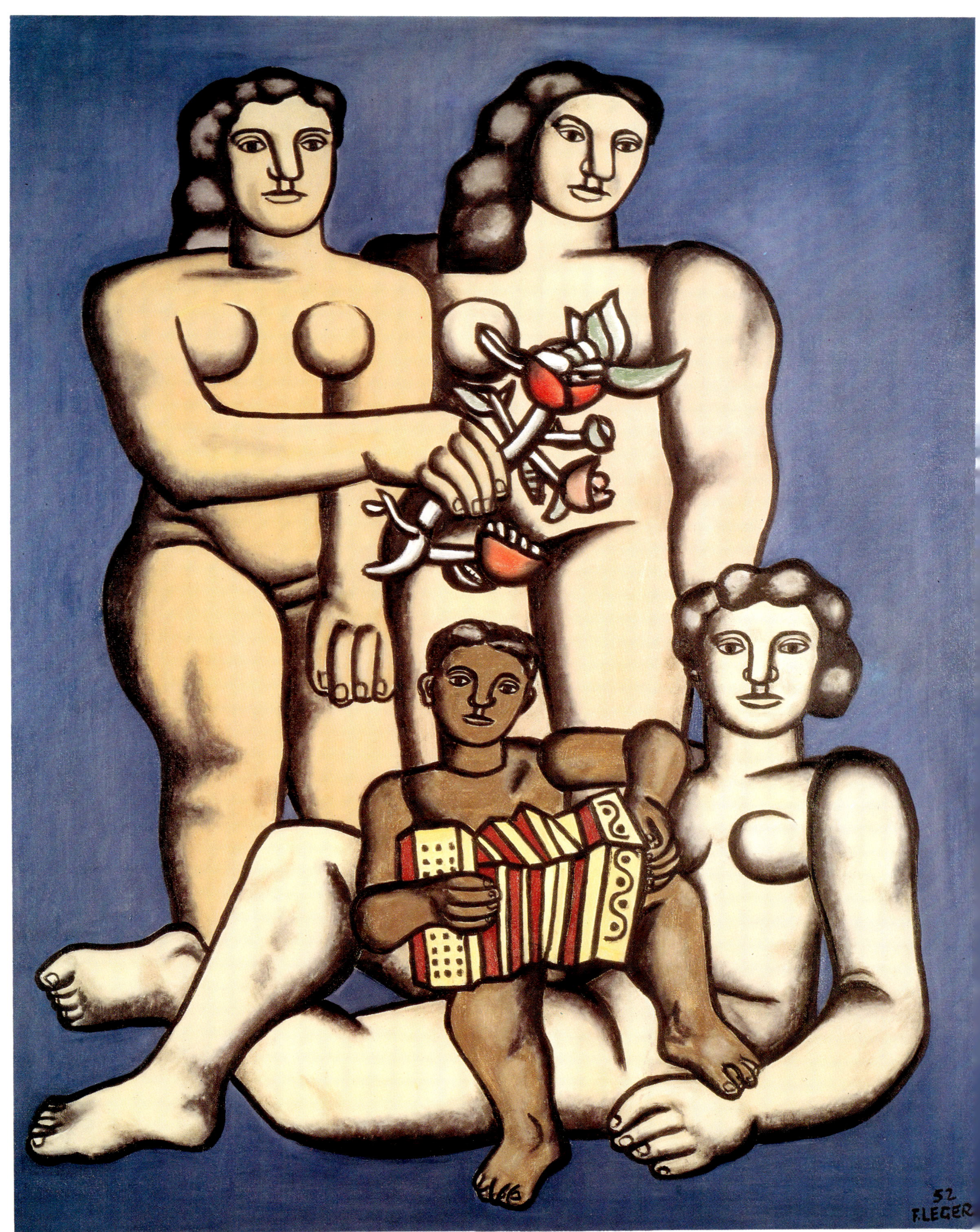


326. THREE SISTERS
1952—Oil on canvas, 162 × 130 cm
Staatsgalerie, Stuttgart

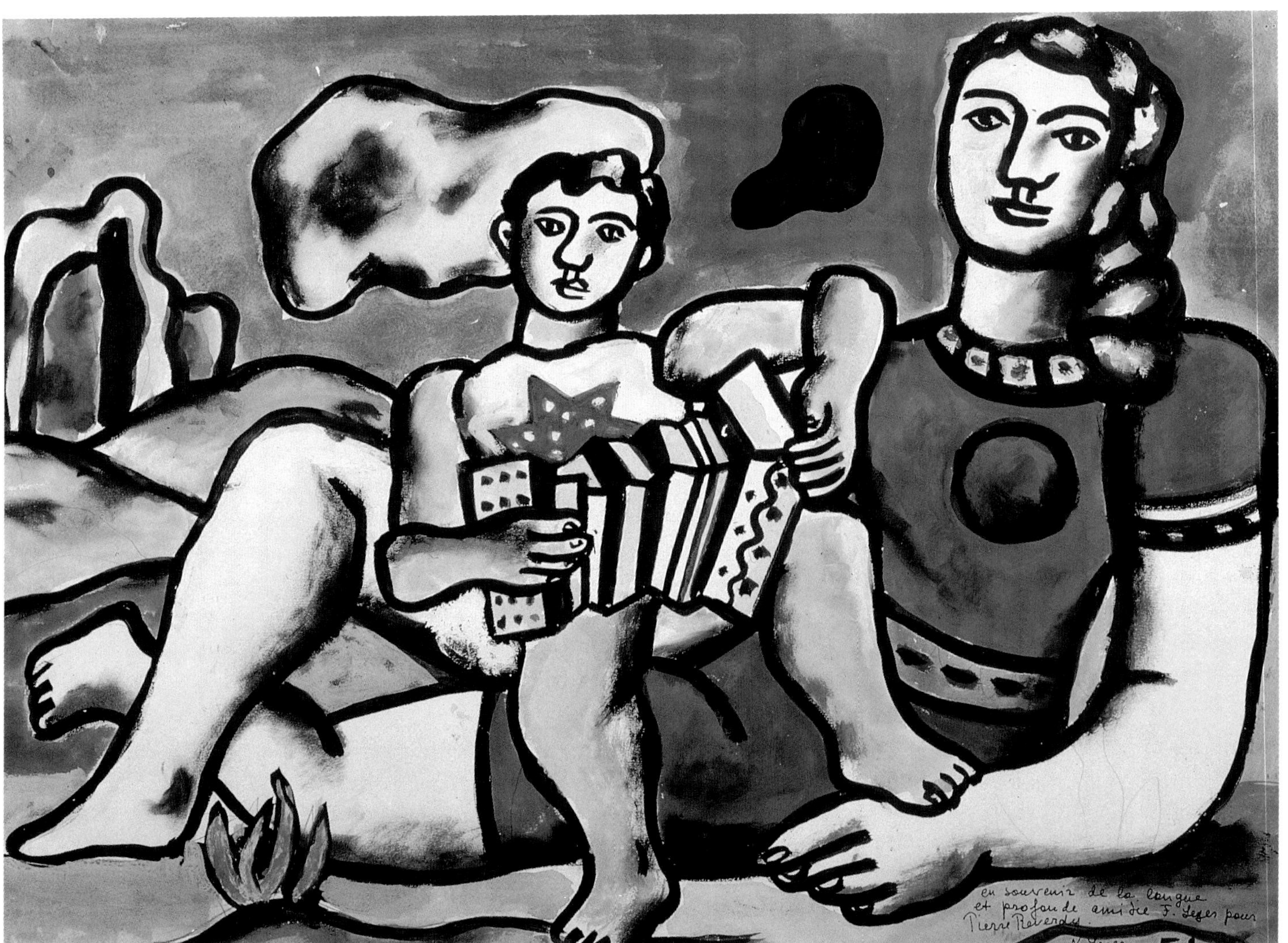


327. MOTHER AND CHILD WITH ACCORDION
1951—Gouache, with dedication, 50 × 65 cm
Collection of Mr. and Mrs. Adrien Maeght

## Plastic effects give character to the painting

Léger moved without bias from the theme of work to the theme of leisure time, as if in a diptych. Likewise, the care that the painter took in portraying people in their own particular context or in their various activities was translated onto the canvas in the language and style that he had achieved. With
Ill. 321 regard to *Homage* in particular, but also in terms of all the paintings that followed and that relate to leisure themes, Roger Garaudy offers the following judgment: "It's a simple and talkative imagery, like that of the *Pietà* of Avignon (David's *Death of Marat* has been referred to as the 'Pietà of the Mountagnards'), of *Horace's Oath*, or the paintings of the Douanier Rousseau. The characters in *Homage* create emotion in us, not so much because of the gesture of the child who is holding onto his father's neck or the relaxed state of the young, reclining girl, but because of the figurative organization of the painting as a whole. The strongly modeled composition, which is elongated far beyond the limits of anatomy, gives the impression of serenity and peaceful tenderness without any sense of bombast or grandiloquence." (There are three extra vertebrae in Ingres' *Grand Odalisque*, a painting much admired by Léger!) "The flower at the point where the diagonals of this rectangle inter-
sect resembles the flower in *Big Julie* and has the same Ill. 250
activating function: at the center of the canvas it is like the axle or hub around which the composition turns. . . . This painting is an illustration of the major theme of Léger's realism: It is the plastic element that gives character to the painting."

This was not the first time that Léger's paintings disconcerted the public. *Homage* and *Country Outing* even took Léger's admirers by surprise. In his desire to create simplicity and to make his work more accessible, he was accused of a lack of subtlety in these paintings. The works were referred to as "historical paintings adapted to the modern subject" of leisure time for the masses. Pierre Descargues saw them as an encounter between Sunday strollers and circus folks. It is true that the circus and the cycle are often closely related themes in Léger's work. The *circle* was a magical and "fabulous adventure" for Léger: "Since the earth is round, how can you expect a performance within a square?"

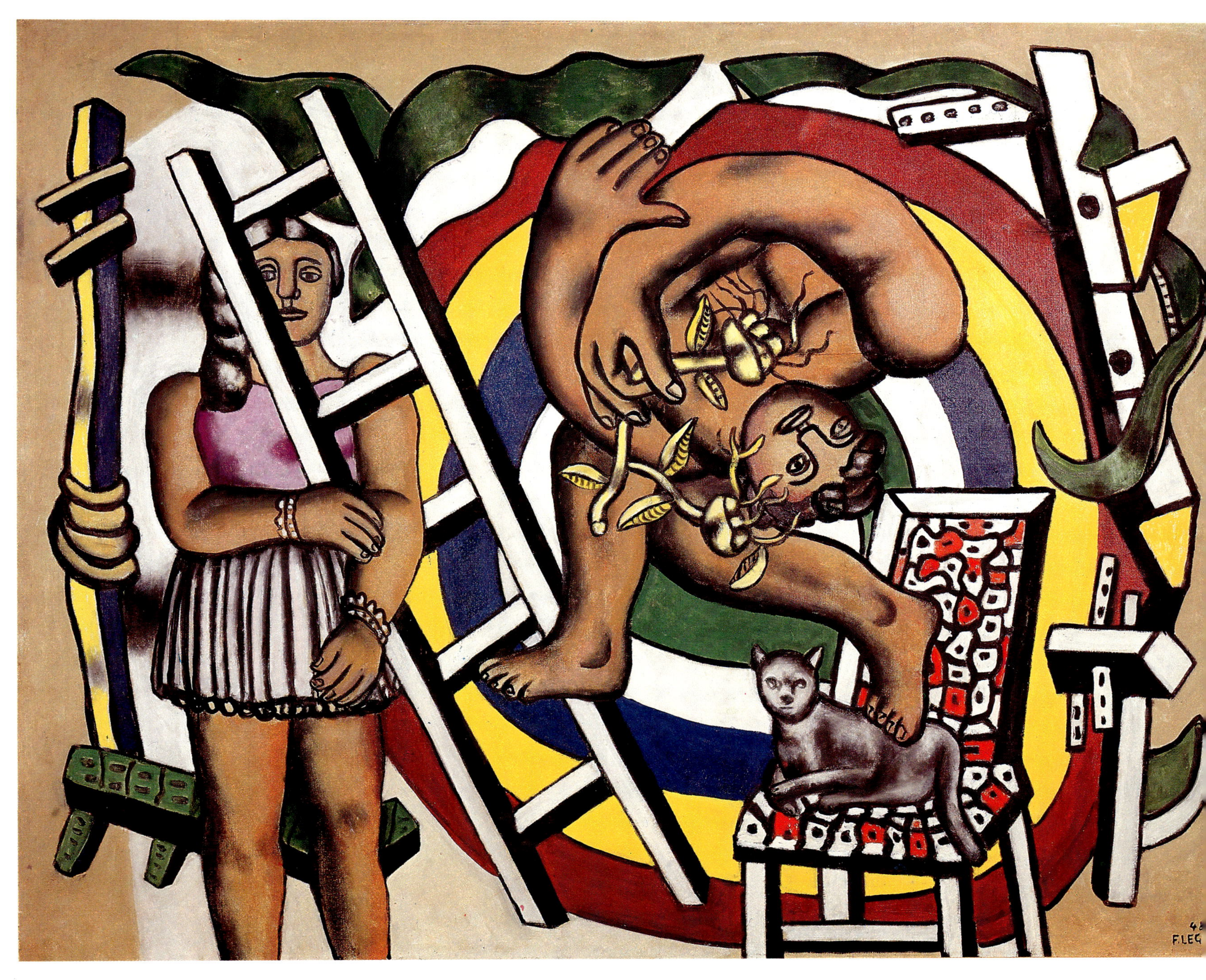

328. ACROBAT AND HIS PARTNER
1948—Oil on canvas, 130 × 162 cm
Tate Gallery, London

# The Big Parade

Ill. 329 From 1918 on, the circus was an omnipresent theme
to 336 in Léger's work. He even composed and illustrated a
Ill. 24 book entitled *Circus*. That book has generously con-
Ill. 25 tributed to the quotations and illustrations used for
this book. The last cycle of his work, *The Big Parade* ("La Grande Parade"), was preceded by many
Ill. 328 works, the most important being *The Acrobat and His Partner* ("L'Acrobate et sa partenaire") in 1948. Léger gave us his own analysis of this work: "I go through periods where my paintings are static. During other periods I only paint with curves: those are my dynamic periods. But some of my paintings have both static *and* dynamic elements. In *The Acrobat and His Partner*, the acrobat and the disc that encircles him represent movement. The flower that he is holding in his hand is entirely composed of curves, and heightens the impression of movement. So does the form of the cat that is sitting on the chair. The straight lines of the chair, along with the straight lines on the same side at the edge of the canvas, as well as the ladder and the acrobat's partner, constitute the static part of the painting. The static part and the dynamic part are in violent contrast. The more contrasts there are in a painting, the stronger the painting. The fewer contrasts there are, the more melodious it is: I'm anti-melodious."

Despite Léger's "anti-melodious" stance, the painting is a powerful and masterful synthesis of his art. This makes *The Acrobat and His Partner* a very pleasurable and "melodious" experience for us to see. It does this without sacrificing "good bourgeois taste," which so often happened with "proletarian art," or the "socialist realism" favored by the Communist Party and Stalin, and dear to Hitler as well.

In *The Acrobat and His Partner* there are faraway traces of *Discs* from 1918, and *Circular Forms* by Robert Delaunay. Léger replaced the geometrical disc with the circus ring. The painting is the synthesis of the studies, themes, and techniques that Léger perfected dur-
ing the period between *Three Musicians* and *Divers*, Ill. 245
and between *Big Julie* and *Homage to Louis David*. The Ill. 287
knot was tied: every painting that followed *The Ac-* Ill. 250
*robat and His Partner* would integrate the totality of Ill. 321
the painter's work, down to the smallest detail.

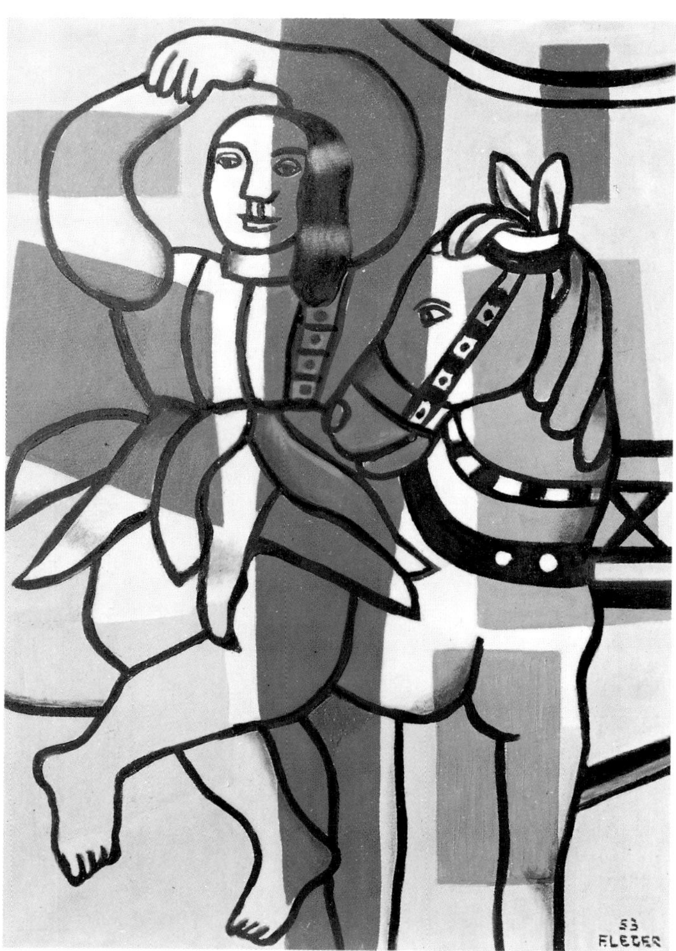


329. THE BAREBACK RIDER
1953—Oil on canvas, 92 × 65 cm
Louis Carré Gallery, Paris

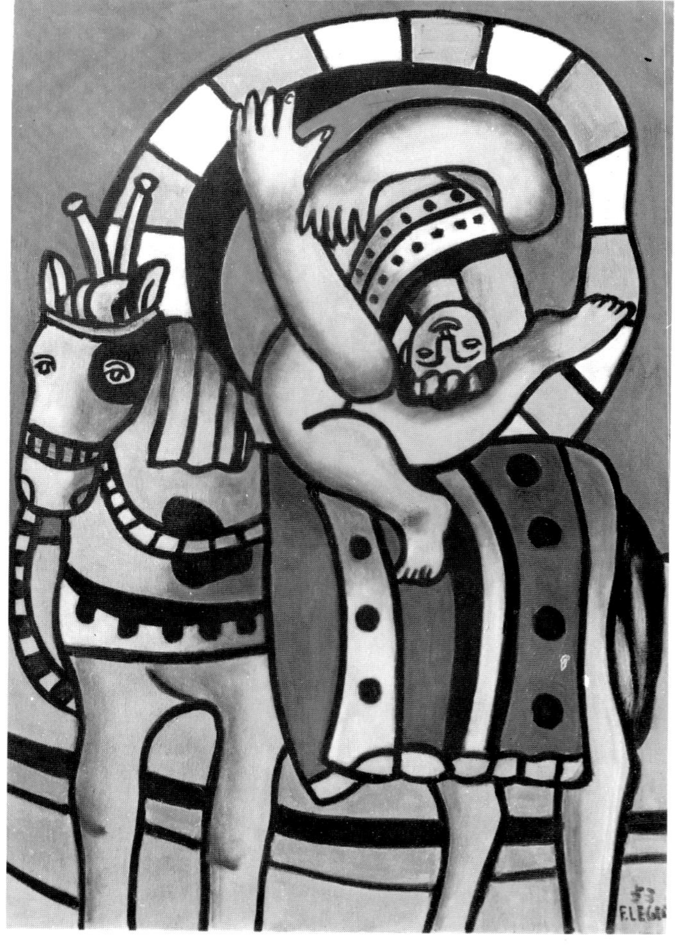

330. ACROBAT ON HORSEBACK
1953—Oil on canvas, 92 × 65 cm
Louis Carré Gallery, Paris

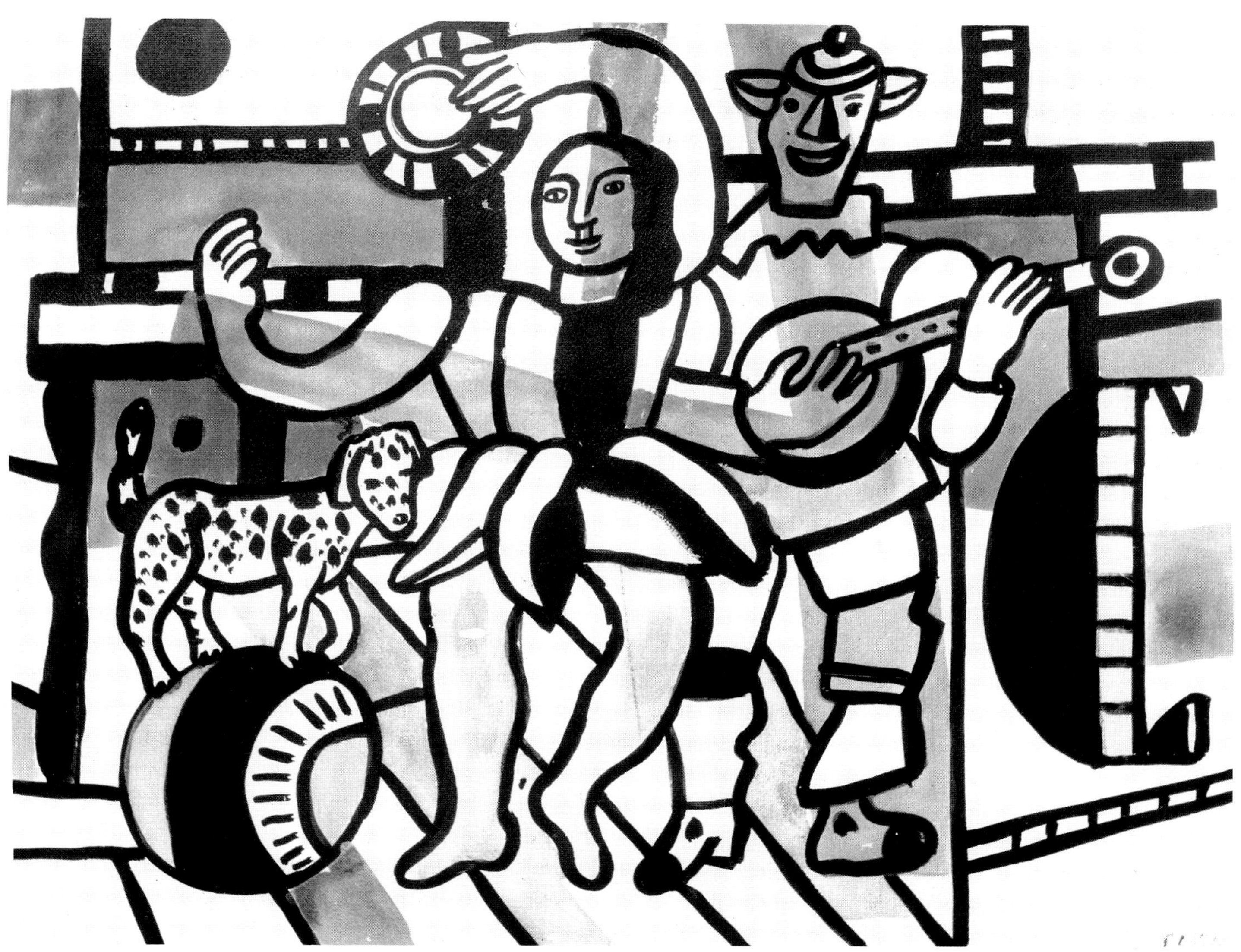

331. DANCER WITH DOG
1952—Gouache, 41 × 50 cm
Musée National Fernand Léger, Biot

### *The Big Parade*

Ill. 333 to 336 *The Big Parade* is not only the apotheosis of the representation of the circus, but the apotheosis of Léger's artistic life, the "bouquet of flowers" that is shot off at the end of the fireworks display. It is the grand finale, the ultimate synthesis of all his previous research. Instead of being a last will and testament, it is another manifesto, another door opened wide for younger generations of artists to enter. Léger is standing at the threshold, extending a welcoming hand to them. Instead of being the culmination of old age, the state of peaceful serenity that crowns a fertile career, *The Big Parade* is an extraordinary artistic renewal, a bridge that spans the gap between the twentieth century's artistic pioneers and future generations. It is a bridge that is built as solidly as they come.

This unique role makes Léger the fourth great one of his era. He was both an avant-garde innovator and a great classical master, an attentive observer of everyday life and a builder of the future. He knew how to dress this seemingly self-deprecating technical civilization of ours in the most joyous colors. His works are as modern as they are spiritual. They stand up next to the Etruscan frescoes of Tarquinia, with whom they share the same robust solidity and indestructible freshness. They have a strange resemblance to the art that presided over the spandrels of Romanesque churches. They are animated in a similar vein. They are primitive and dense. We are beholden to him for the red and yellow tractors that color the fields, the multicolored gas pumps that line our highways. It is no accident that his artistic life ends in fanfare after *Country Outing* (1953) and *The Big Parade* (1954). Ill. 322 His work contains the high iconography of men in hard-working and joyous fraternity. *The Big Parade* provides the seed from which the common man could henceforth derive his symbols.

Léger best described this synthesis in his own words: "If I sketched circus people, acrobats, clowns, and jugglers, it's because for over thirty years I've been interested in what they do. My interest dates back to the time when I was designing Cubist costumes for Fratellini. I did a quantity of sketches and studies for *The Big Parade*. That's because I'm a classicist: If my first sketches are always impulsive, it doesn't mean I don't know where I'm going or don't know the means I'll use to get there. There's an entire year
Ill. 332 between the first version of *The Big Parade* and the
Ill. 336 final version. That time corresponds to a long effort to elaborate and synthesize my intent. With the help of more new sketches, I thought about and worked through the slightest transformation in a painstaking way. One minor structural change can influence the equilibrium of the painting as a whole, and for this reason I often had to rework the entire canvas. Color was married to form in the first version. In the final version you can see what power and spirit I've conveyed by using colors outside the forms."

The great contrast of the composition is found in the circle that evokes the circus ring, as we see in *The Acrobat and His Partner*. It balances the rectangular Ill. 328
flat tints. The hub of the painting is the large capital C stenciled in black. It is the first letter in the word "circus." It is also the equivalent of the green flower at the center of *Homage to Louis David*. The rest of the Ill. 321
canvas is organized like a "parade" and mixes together young girls, dancers, the three musicians, the divers, and even the camper. They are disguised for the occasion as clowns, acrobats, and circus musicians. The accessories are recognizable: the telegraph poles, the halter on the horse, and the rope from *Decorative Project for a Stadium*. "My studies are pon- Ill. 240
derous," said Léger, as if to apologize. "I am extremely slow in my work. I don't know how to improvise. The more knowledgeable I become about this, the more I realize that I am a classicist. I have a long preparatory process. First I make a whole series of sketches; then I do studies in watercolor; and finally I move to the canvas. However, when I do move to the canvas, I attack it with 80 percent confidence. I know where I'm headed."

332. THE BIG PARADE, FIRST VERSION
1952—Oil on canvas, 181 × 212 cm
Private collection

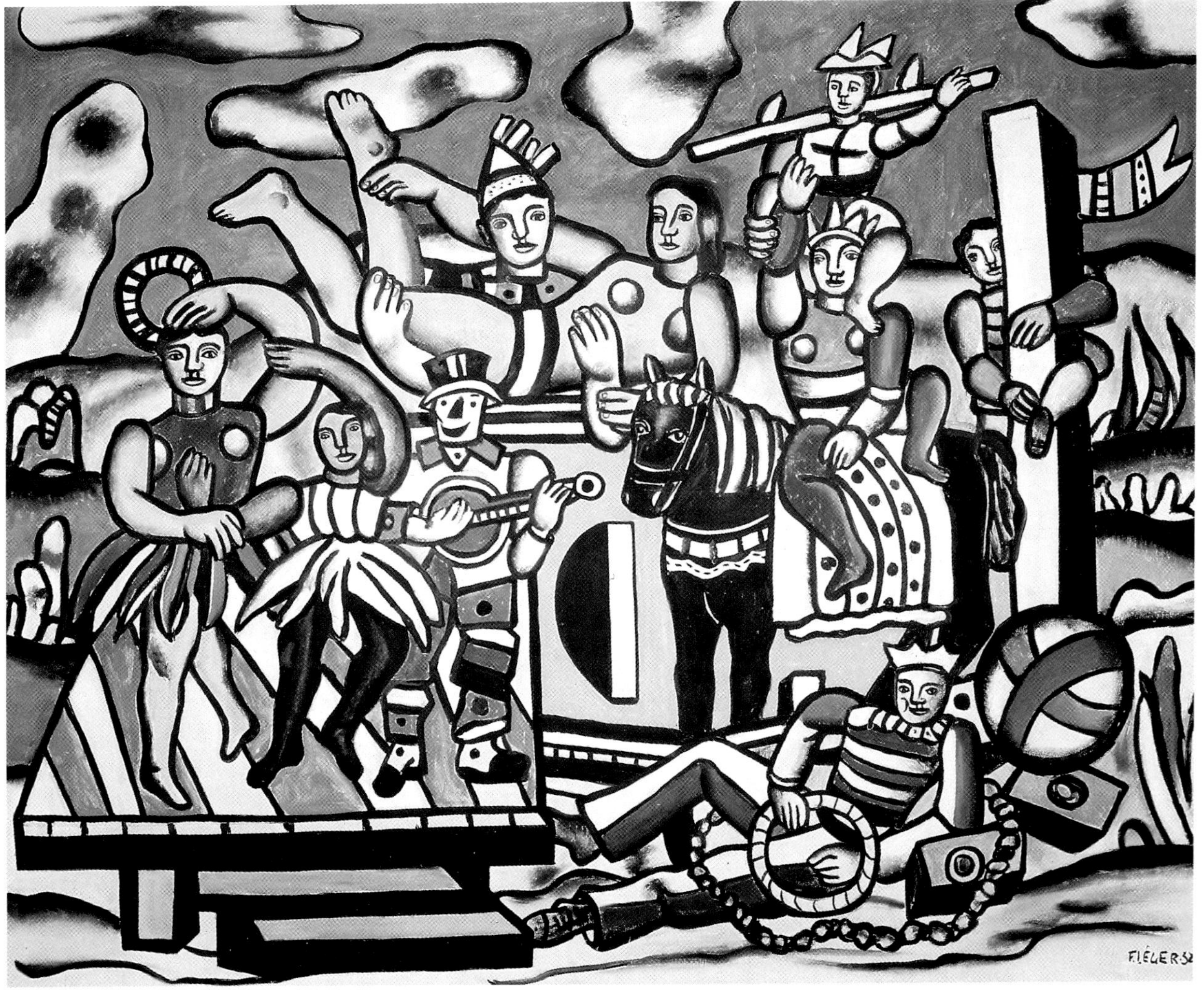

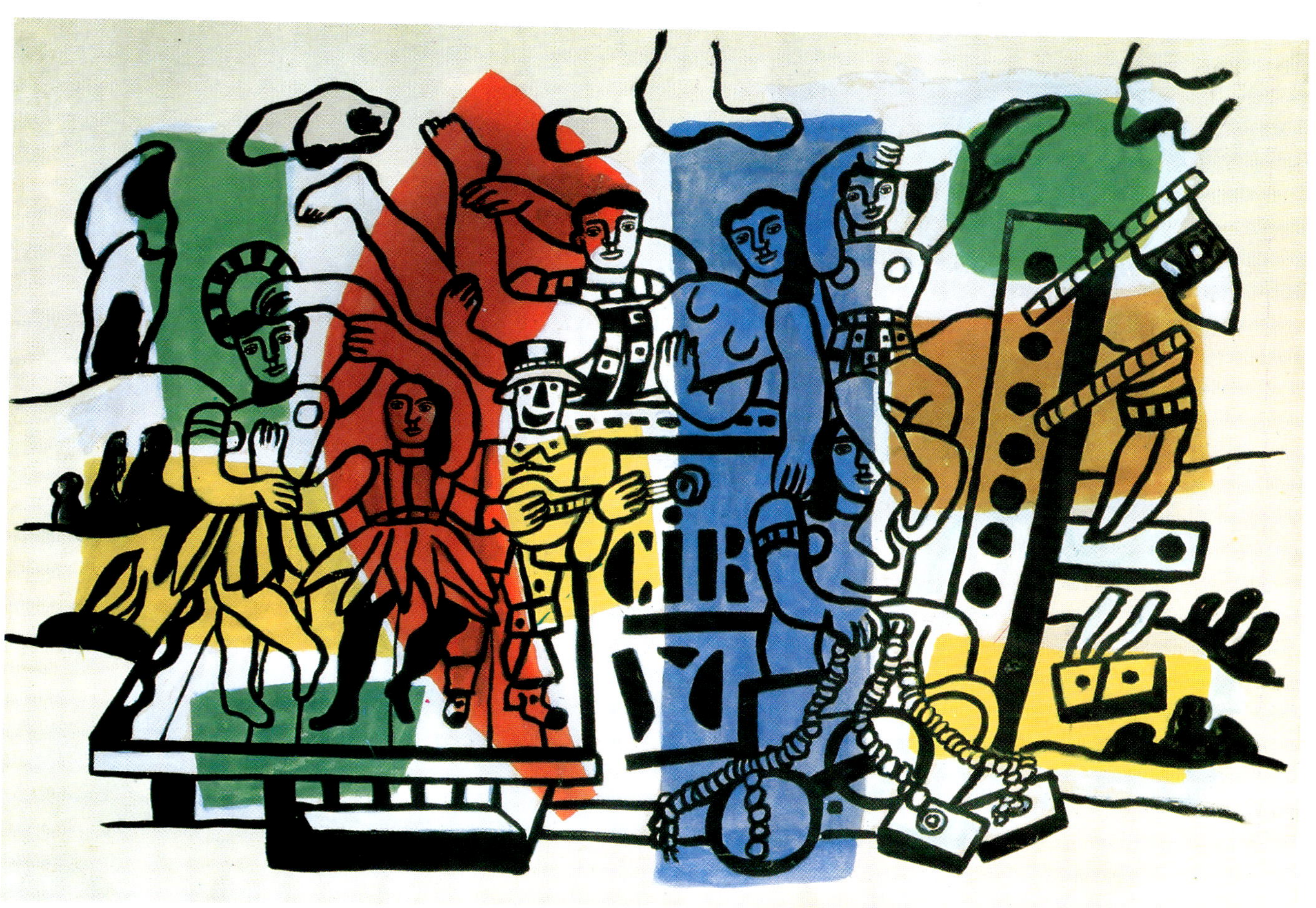


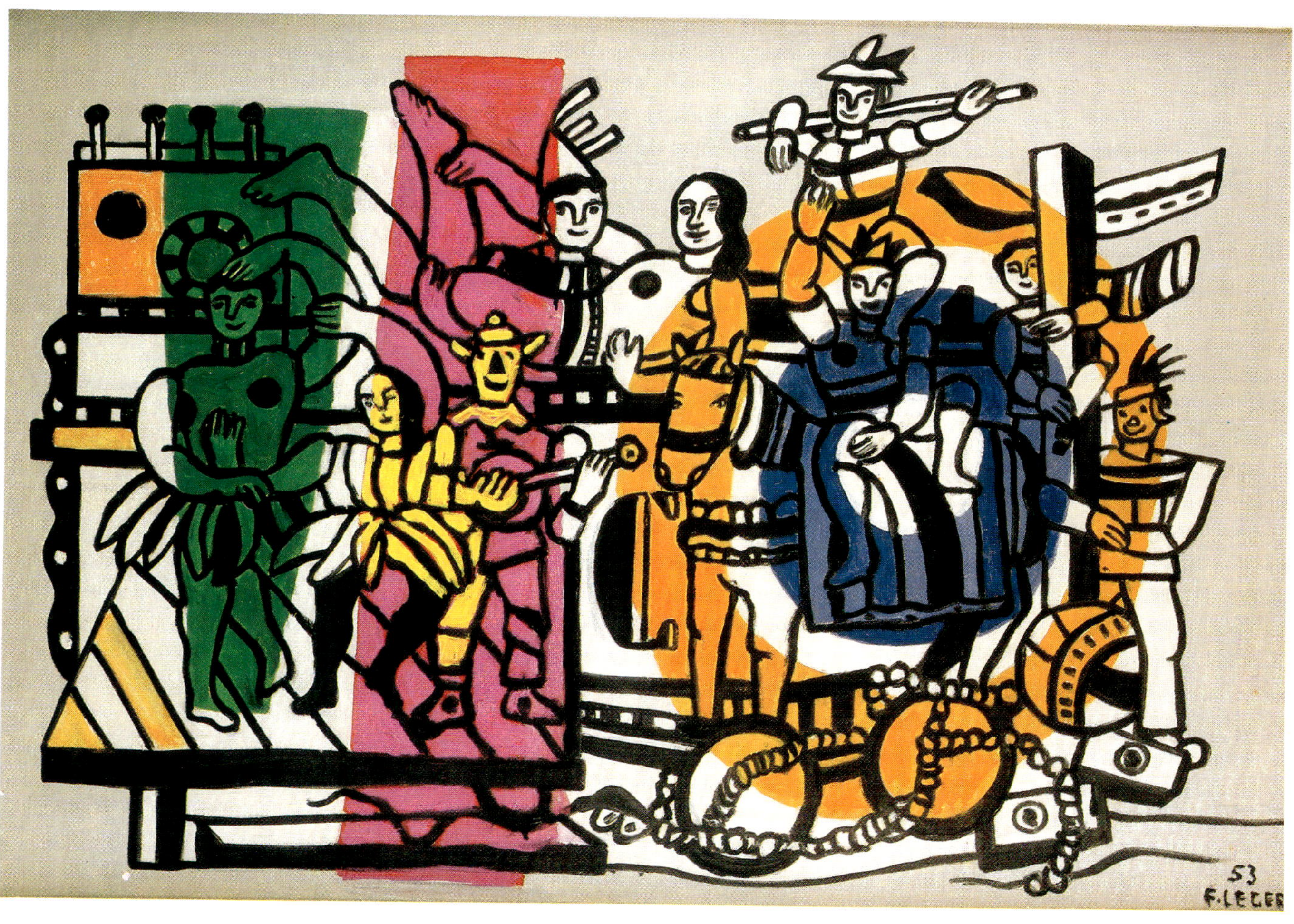


333. STUDY FOR *THE BIG PARADE*
1953—Gouache on paper, 70 × 105 cm
Collection of Mr. and Mrs. Adrien Maeght

334. THE BIG PARADE, SKETCH
1953—Oil on canvas, 65 × 92 cm
Private collection

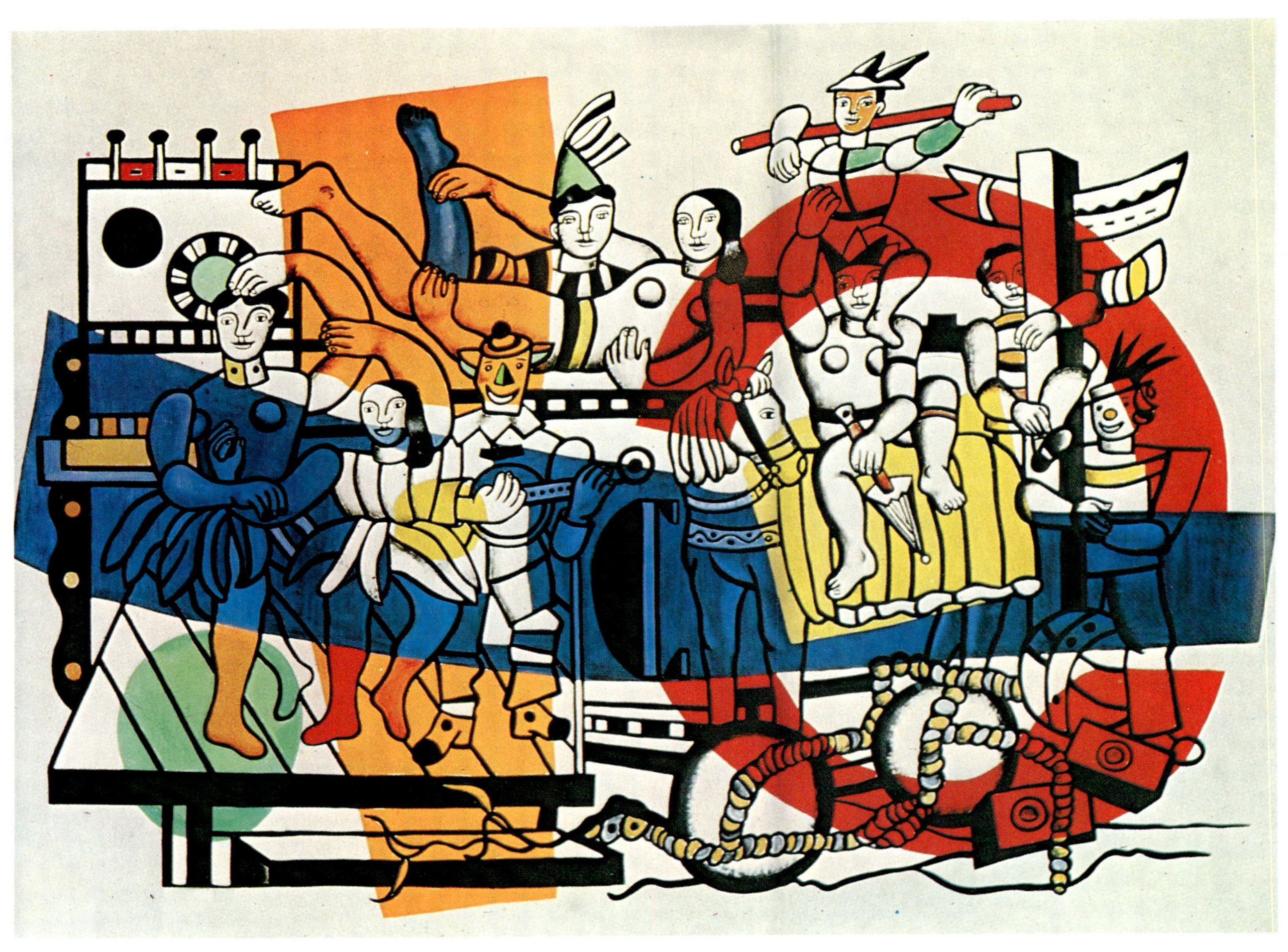

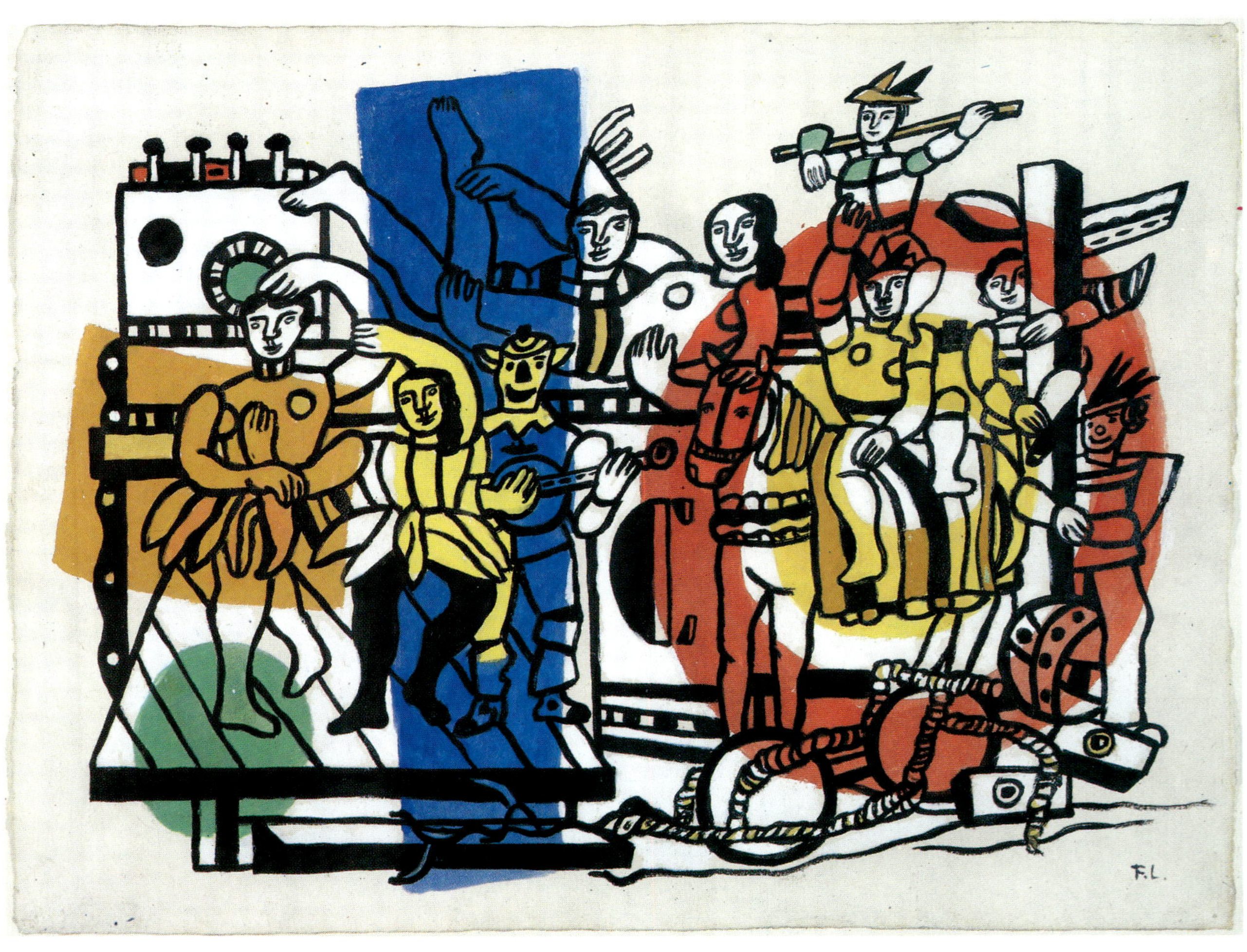


335. THE BIG PARADE (EXTERIOR COLORS)
1953—Gouache on paper, 49.5 × 65 cm
Louise Leiris Gallery, Paris

336. THE BIG PARADE, DEFINITIVE VERSION
1954—Oil on canvas, 300 × 480 cm
Solomon R. Guggenheim Museum, New York

## The final apotheosis

Léger as a "classicist" falls gloriously into the ranks of David, Ingres, and Manet. *The Big Parade* is Léger's own parallel to David's *Coronation*. The work is monumental not only in terms of its dimensions, but in terms of the language, spirit, and influence of the painted mural: "Large volumes of color on a large surface. . . . We're facing forward towards the future, and the future is a collective phenomenon. Yes! It is becoming apparent through certain social and artistic indicators that we're on the threshold of a renewal in mural painting. Monumental art can and must use this new concept and enlarge on it. . . . The young architects who are building a new Europe have seen and understood this. It is an art that must find expression in the vast architectural enterprise. We come back to what I have already stated: It is static in expression. It respects the wall along with the dynamic concept that destroys the wall. . . . It allows not only for measure and equilibrium, but for invention and rhythm, as well."

Léger was motivated by the belief in a better world. His "realistic idealism" is deliberately oriented towards objectivity in color, form, space, and time. He did not merely want to paint reality, but to act on this reality. It is useless to contrast Léger's "earthly" credo with Kandinsky's "spirituality in art" or Malevich's "Suprematism." To the extent that one can pass judgment: the medium was the same. Just the paths differed. Léger had transcended "art for art's sake." He elevated art in the modern world to the level of a moral dictate. When someone aspires to this, it is possible to get there. Each person must fill in the gaps. The nature of modern art is to inspire participation in the viewer. Léger was not the proselyte of a new religion. He limited his field of influence to a socialist perspective of society, independent of any kind of formal or official doctrines.

Léger's only failure was in the short term. He was unable to seduce the public he so passionately wanted to reach. To break through the "glorious isolation of the artist" Léger did not resort to professional and personal scandals, or to the other techniques used by Dalí and Picasso. He could look at himself the way that Cézanne looked at himself: as "an almond tree that bears fruit in season," someone able to satisfy and encourage the deep aspirations of modern society through a kind of painting that was solid, easily comprehensible, and accessible to everyone. His painting grew out of the "popular imagery" that illustrated and celebrated modern life.

Léger found himself up against the general public who preferred sentimental models and prefabricated subjects to artistic invention, television soap operas, and B movies to experimental film. The objective art of Léger demanded an effort that the public just was not yet ready to make. While Léger continued to work and wait for his dream and life's ambition to come true, collectors and dealers were the first to speculate on him and gather up his paintings. Maybe the public will begin to realize that Léger was indeed a painter of merit now that they see what exorbitant prices his paintings and even his pencil sketches command at public auction. The public needs guarantees and reassurances that the painter is or was a genius. Today's price tags on van Goghs and Picassos are closely linked to the popularity of these artists.

Gently and capriciously swaying on his bicycle as he travelled the curving road, Léger could feel contented. He was "in order with nature." He was able to find the surprises of childhood, which he expressed in large natural spectacles of clouds, waves, the sun, and the moon. He held on to the things in life that constitute its real value, the happiness of being alive, the riches of creation. He was finally able to dream that he was not a revolutionary figure at all, but someone who was "accepted," inscribed in the "general will," incorporated into things as they are, without effort and in the most natural way.

He had his own unique way of challenging us in the most affectionate or brutal way. He could crack the protective shells we tend to surround ourselves with, these useless shells that we think can ward off death or harm, and that, in reality, limit us and constrict us. These walls are formed by our lack of understanding, our indifference, ignorance, transitory feelings, and the desire for social recognition and fame: "What good is it to have eyes in the back of our heads," asked Léger, "if we can just as easily turn our heads around? Heads . . . these round and mobile forms we have with eyes and mouths mounted on necks that are round like tree trunks. All this could be accomplished whether it be within a restricted space, or on an unlimited surface. Straight lines could occur where there are no straight lines. Birds and airplanes could harmoniously evolve in a sky that gently descends towards the horizon.

"We are experiencing space more than ever before. Man is growing and expanding in all directions; there's a competition to escape and leave behind all earthly constraints, to flee what is solid and concrete. A nervous mobility is taking over the world. Everything is moving and escaping from traditional constraints . . . the safety net of the flying acrobats is disappearing; it's becoming a life in which game birds are soaring and rifles are being aimed.

"And yet, we tend to want to go backwards, to see life run in reverse, like a movie: all the traditional sanctuaries and safe havens return, the lights are extinguished, the hierarchies and inexplicable mysteries are reestablished, and we once again find respect for the great natural forces." For Léger, "the birds will always be marvelously dressed in color, progress is a meaningless word, and a cow that nourishes the world will always move at three kilometers an hour."

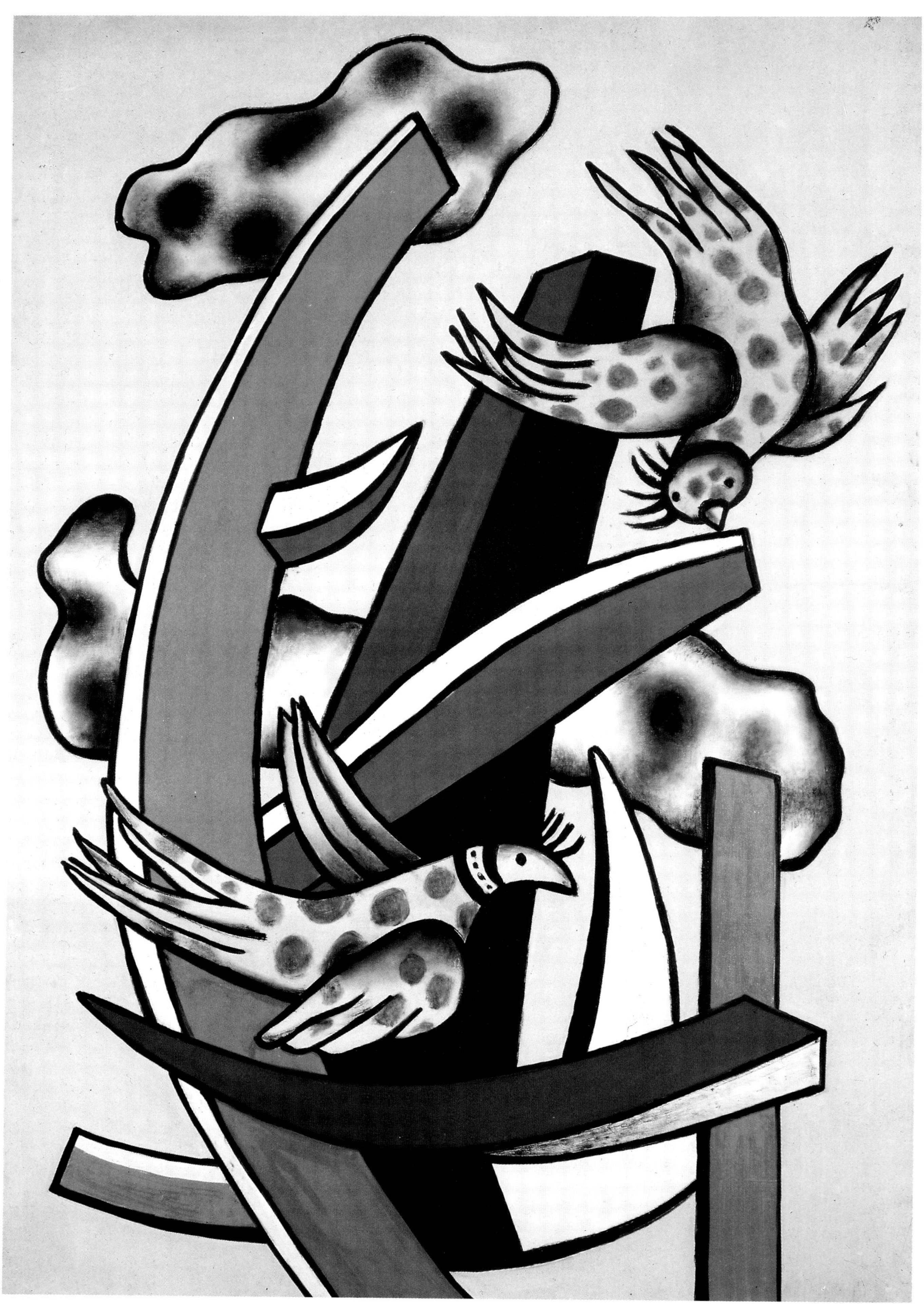

337.
COMPOSITION WITH BIRDS AGAINST A YELLOW BACKGROUND
1955—Oil on canvas, 130 × 89 cm
Musée National Fernand Léger, Biot

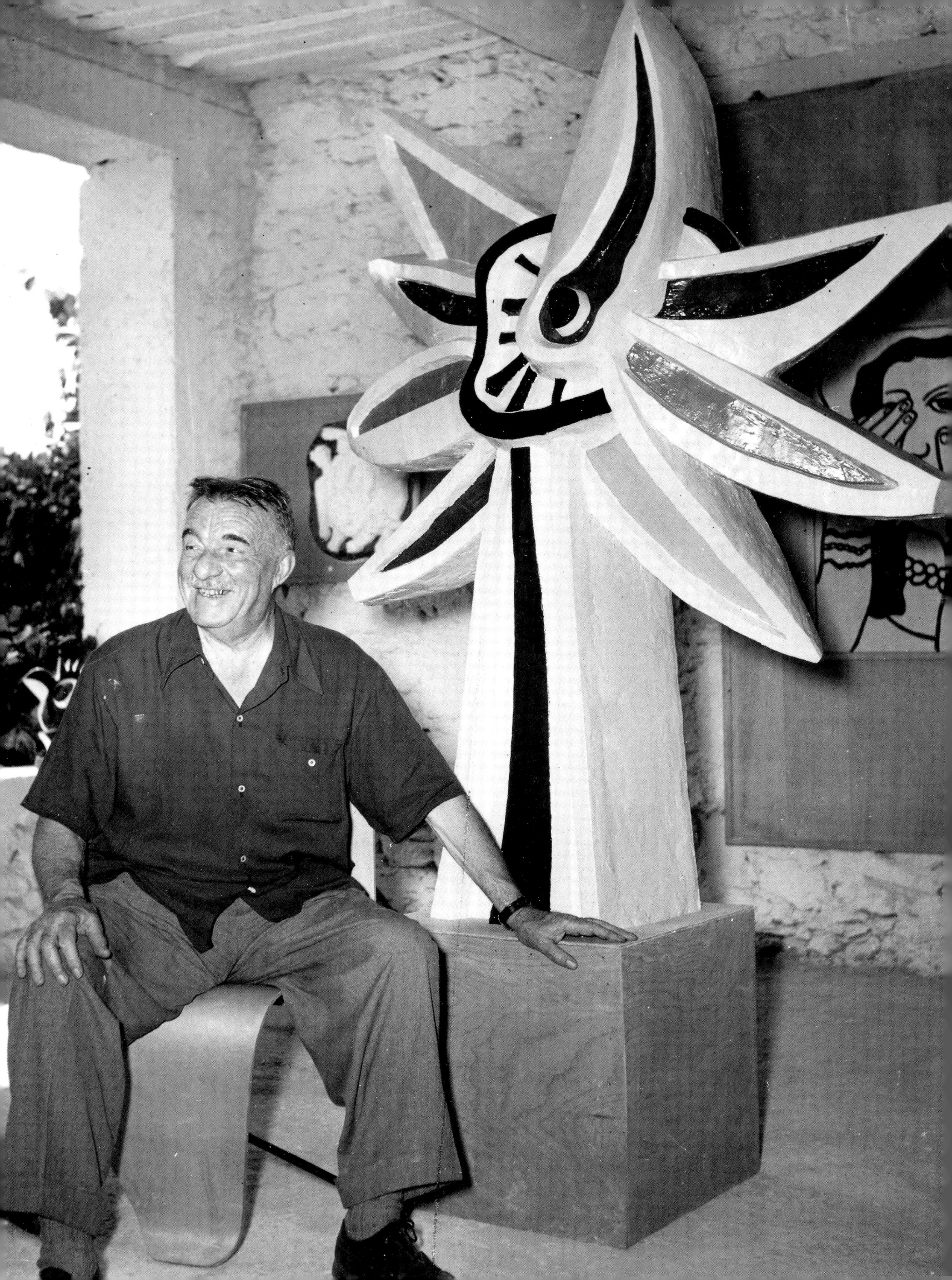

## BIOGRAPHY

*with contemporary events in the life of F. Léger*

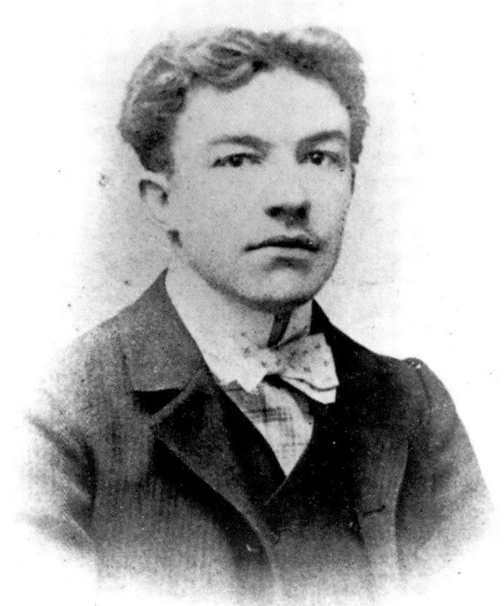

339. LÉGER IN PARIS, ABOUT 1901

**1881** Fernand Léger was born on February 4 in Argentan, Normandy, the year of Picasso's birth. His father, Henri-Armand Léger, who raised livestock, died several years later. His mother, Marie-Adèle Daunou, lived on her farm in Lisores until her death in 1922.
*If a fairy hovered over his work desk, it had to be a metallic one named the Eiffel Tower, which a few years later would initiate metal into architectural technique. It was also the era of linotype, the first automobiles, and the beginning of "moving images," which would become cinema. In 1881, Paul Sedille builds the Paris department store Le Printemps, and the broad Parisian boulevards are illuminated by electricity. 1882: The first Edison electric power station. The Lumière Company is bringing the cinematic image into focus. 1883: The Brooklyn Bridge is built with steel cables that have a span of 481 meters. Karl Marx dies. 1884: William Morris founds the Socialist League. 1885: The first skyscraper is built in Chicago. Louis Pasteur discovers the rabies virus. 1886: Koenen demonstrates the tensile strength of iron and the shrinkage of concrete. 1887: Artists protest against the Eiffel Tower. E. Henard presents his project for a moving sidewalk for the 1889 World's Fair. The automatic telephone. 1889: The Paris World's Fair, the Eiffel Tower, the Ferris wheel, the Machinery Exhibit, automobiles that run on gas. The Second Workers' International.*

**1890–1896** Léger studies at the elementary school in Argentan, and then at a parochial school in Tinchebray.
*Invention of the diesel engine, the wireless telegraph; discovery of the X-ray. Georges Mélies opens his motion picture studio. Horta applies the iron framework to his "People's Center" ("Maison du Peuple"). First major workers' May Day demonstration on May 1, 1890. In 1892, Cézanne paints his* Bathers *("Baigneuses") and his* Mount Sainte Victoire *("Montagne Sainte Victoire")*

**1897–1899** With the consent of his uncle, Léger studied architecture in Caen.

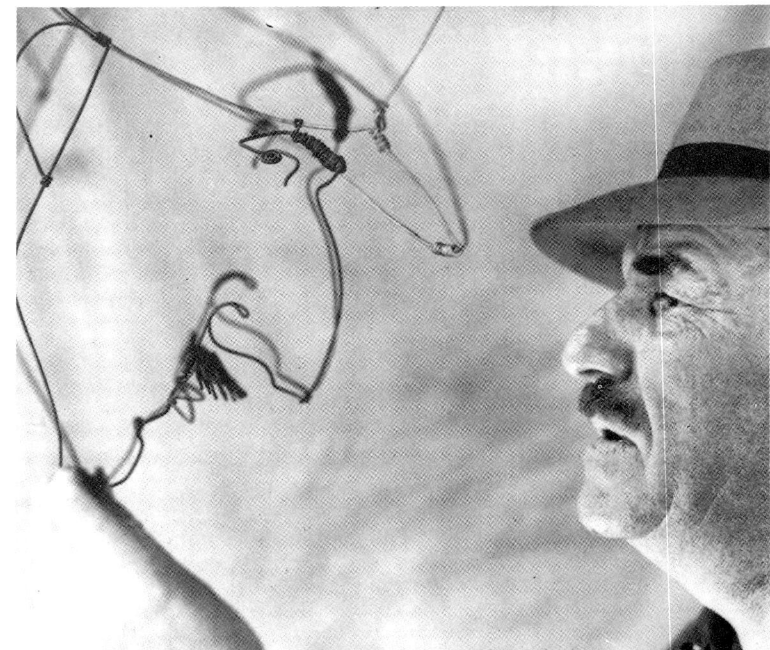

340. LÉGER AND HIS PORTRAIT IN WIRE BY CALDER, ABOUT 1931

*Ader makes the first flight in an airplane. Monet paints his first* Water Lilies. *Zola publishes* J'accuse *("I Accuse").*

**1900** Léger arrives in Paris and gets a job as an architectural draftsman.
*Picasso's first stay in Paris. The height of Art Nouveau, or Modern Style. Gaudi builds his labyrinth at the Guëll Park in Barcelona. Planck formulates his quantum theory, and Freud publishes* Die Traumdeutung.

**1902–1903** Léger does his military service as a sapper in the Second Engineer Corps stationed in Versailles.
*Picasso's first exhibit in Paris. Mélies makes the film* Voyage to the Moon *("Un Voyage dans la lune"). Perret introduces concrete into residential architecture.*

**1903** Léger is accepted at the School of Decorative Arts, but rejected by the Beaux-Arts. He follows the courses of Gérôme as a free student, and then goes to the atelier of Gabriel Ferrier. He also frequents the Académy Julian and the Louvre museum.
*In Paris the Salon d'Automne is founded, and the first exhibit is a Gauguin rétrospective. "Die Brücke" is born in Dresden.*

**1903–1905** Léger struggles to get by: he shares a studio on Avenue de Maine with a friend from Argentan, the painter André Mare. He works for an architect as a draftsman, and touches up photos for a photographer. He paints his first canvases.
*Einstein comes out with his theory of relativity. Pierre and Marie Curie receive the Nobel Prize in physics for the discovery of radium. The physiologist Pavlov receives the Nobel Prize in medicine.*

**1905** Léger moves into the Ruche ("beehive") on Passage Dantzig in Montparnasse.
*Einstein discovers photons.*

**1906–1908** Léger is ill and goes to spend the winter with a friend at Belgodère in Corsica. He paints landscapes that he classifies as "being in the Impressionist style." He is very much influenced by the Cézanne Retrospective at the Salon d'Automne in 1907, after returning to Paris.
*Picasso finishes the* Demoiselles d'Avignon. *Auguste Lumière uses color for motion pictures. The first vacuum tubes. Adolf Loos publishes* Ornament and Crime.

338. LÉGER AND HIS SUNFLOWER IN POLYCHROME CEMENT 1953–54—Photo: Associated Reporters

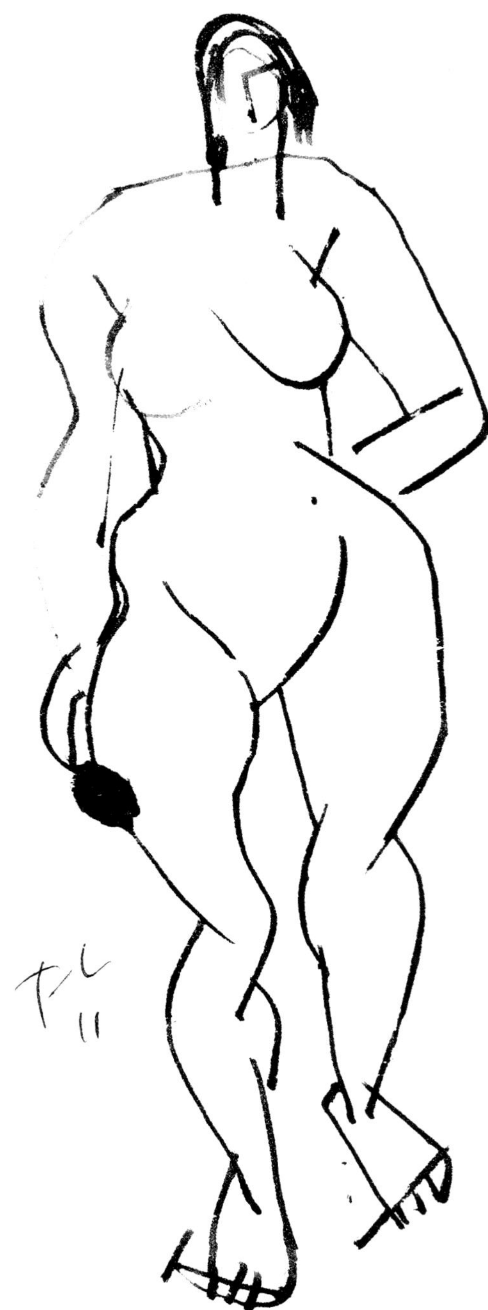

341. NUDE
1911—Ink drawing, 32 × 25 cm
Louise Leiris Gallery, Paris

**1909** At the Ruche, Léger meets Archipenko, Lipchitz, Soutine, Chagall, and then Robert Delaunay and Henri Rousseau. Rousseau has a major influence on Léger. His paintings are "popular" and removed from the things that were preoccupying the avant-garde. Frequent visitors at the Ruche are Max Jacob, Apollinaire, Raynal, Cendrars. Léger reacts against Impressionism. In *The Seamstress* we see the influences of Cézanne and Rousseau.
Le Figaro *publishes Marinetti's* Manifesto of Futurism. *Premiere of Diaghilev's Ballets Russes. Blériot flies across the English Channel. In New York, the work of Gilbreth inaugurates the systematic study of forms in movement. The first German garden-apartment complex at Hellerau near Dresden. Duralumin invented.*

**1910** Kahnweiler, who is already supporting Picasso and Braque, takes an interest in Léger's work and buys paintings from him. Léger moves into 14 Avenue du Maine, and then 13 Rue de l'Ancienne Comédie, where he starts his series *Roofs*. He works on *Wedding*. He visits Jacques Villon in Puteaux. The Puteaux group, which becomes the "Section d'Or" (The Golden Section), includes Delaunay, Le Fauconnier, Gleizes, André Mare, Picabia, Marie Laurencin, and Valensi.
*Stravinsky's* The Firebird *("L'Oiseau de Feu"). Founding of the Austrian Werkbund.*

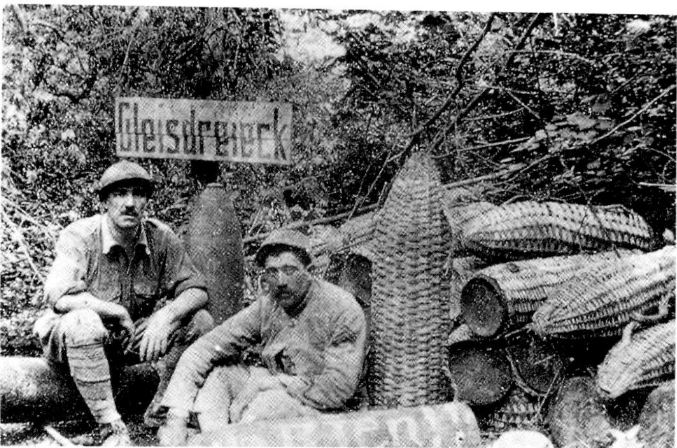


342. LÉGER IN THE "THE KRAUT WOODS" ("BOIS DES BOCHES") IN 1914

**1911** Léger shows his independence from Cubism and presents his series, *Nudes in the Forest,* which receives raves at the Salon des Indépendents. *Wedding* is shown at the Salon d'Automne, and he paints *The Smokers* ("Les Fumeurs"). The word "Tubism" is used when critics describe his paintings. He collaborates with Rouault, La Fresnaye, and Duchamp-Villon on the presentation of a "kitchen" and an "office" conceived by André Mare for the Salon d'Automne.
*It is the height of the Cubist period. The "Blaue Reiter" show in Munich. Gropius introduces the glass wall into industrial architecture. Husserl publishes* Idées directrices pour une phénoménologie pure *("Guidelines for Pure Phenomenology").*

**1912** Léger shows *Woman in Blue* ("La Femme en bleu") at the Salon d'Automne, and *The Smokers* at the Indépendents. First solo show at Kahnweiler. Participates at the second salon of the Section d'Or at the "Jack of Diamonds" exhibit organized by Malevich in Moscow.
*Mondrian and Malevich are living in Paris. Beginnings of Synthetic Cubism. Duchamp and Villon exhibit a "Cubist House" at the Salon d'Automne. Kandinsky publishes* The Spiritual in Art. *Shoenberg eliminates the tonal system in* Pierrot lunaire. *The Balkans War.*

**1913** Atelier 86 on Rue Notre-Dame-des-Champs that Léger would keep throughout his life. Exclusive contract with Kahnweiler. Lectures at the Wassilieff Academy: "The Origins of Contemporary Painting and Its Representative Value." Participates in the Armory Show in New York. The debut of "Contrasting Forms."
*Delaunay paints* Simultaneous Discs. *Apollinaire publishes* Cubist Painters *and* Alcools. *Malevich paints the first Suprematist work. Tatlin and Rodchenko found Constructivism. Rayonnist Manifesto. Sant'Elia: Project for the "Città Nuova." Creation of the Stravinsky's* Rite of Spring *("Sacre du printemps"). Niels Bohr's theory of atomic or bits. First production line at Ford in Detroit.*

**1914–1916** A new lecture at the Wassilieff Academy, "Current Pictorial Activity." Léger paints *The Fourteenth of July 1914* ("Le 14$^{e}$ juillet"), *The Alarm Clock* ("Le Réveille Matin"). Mobilized into the engineer corps on August 2. Stationed at the front in Argonne for two years. Serves as stretcher-bearer at the Battle of Verdun. Sketches in the trenches and in the barracks. The war brings him into

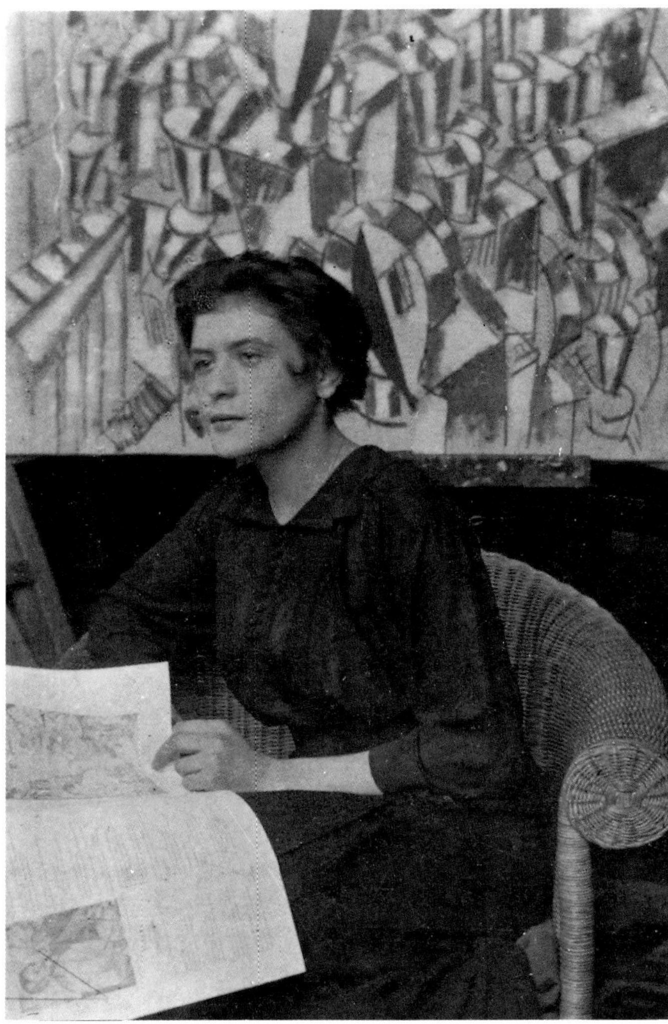

343. JEANNE LOHY DURING THE PERIOD OF *CONTRASTING FORMS*

contact with the common folk, "the people," and he is captivated by the breech of a 75 millimeter in the sunlight. During a furlough in 1916, Apollinaire introduces him to the films of Charlie Chaplin, and he paints *Soldier with a Pipe*, the first of his works that make Pierre Abraham refer to him as "the herald of the people." He is gassed in September while on the front lines at Verdun.
*During this time, away from the front, Marcel Duchamp does his ready-mades and Mondrian his neo-plastic paintings. In Zurich, Hans Arp pursues abstraction in his works. In 1915, Malevich launches the Suprematist Manifesto. In 1916, Freyssinet builds the hangars at Orly Airport and Frank Lloyd Wright builds the Imperial Hotel in Tokyo. Stainless steel is invented. P. Scheebart publishes "Architecture in Glass."*

**1917** Léger is hospitalized in Villepinte. He takes advantage of opportunity and paints *The Card Game*. His off-duty soldiers are already his future *Builders*.
*Van Doesburg and Mondrian found the review* De Stijl *in Leyde, the Netherlands. The Dada Gallery opens in Zurich. Rietveld: blue and yellow chair. Eric Satie's ballet "Parade" is performed in Paris. The Fratellinis at the Mérdrano Circus. Einstein's "Theory of the Universe."*

**1918–1919** Intensive work. Léger wants to paint the new city in colors and to acknowledge the speed and violence of urban and industrial civilization: *The Discs, City, Mechanical Elements, The Acrobats, Typography, The Mechanic.* Illustrations for the books of Blaise Cendrars: "I Killed" and "The End of the World, Filmed by the Notre-Dame Angel." In 1918 he marries Jeanne Lohy.
*Armistice at Rethondes, the end of World War I. Death of*

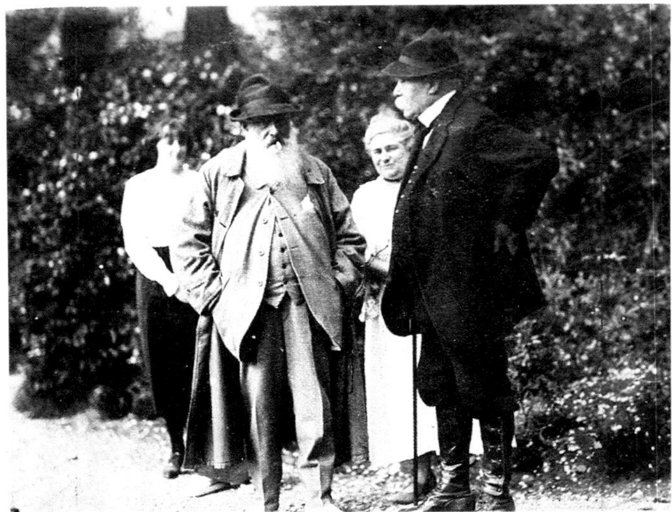

344. CLAUDE MONET AND GEORGES CLEMENCEAU AT THE TIME OF *THE WATER LILIES*

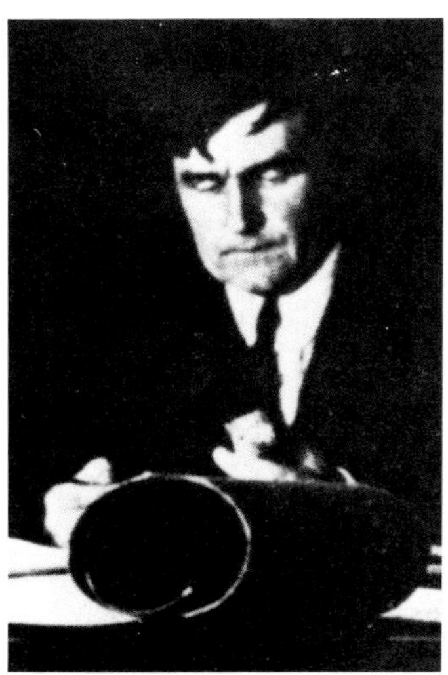

345. MALEVICH IN PETROGRAD IN 1923.

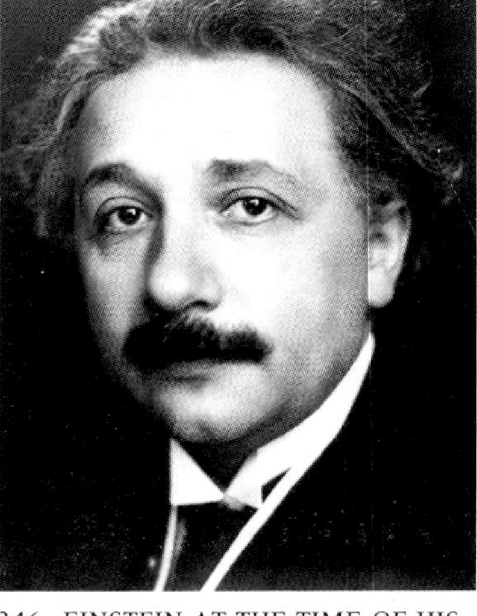

346. EINSTEIN AT THE TIME OF HIS THEORY OF RELATIVITY

*Apollinaire. Czar Nicholas II executed. Le Corbusier and Ozenfant publish* After Cubism, *the Purist Manifesto. Max Ernst's collages. Jazz introduced in Europe. In 1919, Gropius founds the Bauhaus in Weimar. The Taut brothers in Magdebourg speak out in favor of multicolored architecture. Mies van der Rohe: project for a skyscraper in glass and steel. Rutherford splits the atom. Proust receives the Goncourt Prize for* Within a Budding Grove *("A l'ombre des jeunes filles en fleur"). Wiener and Lang make the film* The Cabinet of Dr. Caligari. *Wilhelm II abdicates. Paul Valéry authors* Crisis in Thought *("La Crise de l'esprit").*

**1920** Léger joins with Le Corbusier. He paints *The Waiter* ("Le Garçon de café"), *Woman at the Mirror* ("La Femme au miroir"), *The Staircase* ("L'Escalier").
*The first photomontages of the Dadaists and photograms of Moholy-Nagy and Man Ray. Ozenfant and Le Corbusier found the review called* L'Esprit nouveau, *which will be published until 1925. Klee is a teacher at the Bauhaus. Tatlin's drawing for the monument to the Third International. Malevich's architectonics. The brothers Gabo and Pevsner publish their "Manifesto of Constructivist Realism." Mondrian's "Neo-Plasticist Manifesto." First radio broadcasts. The discovery of penicillin.*

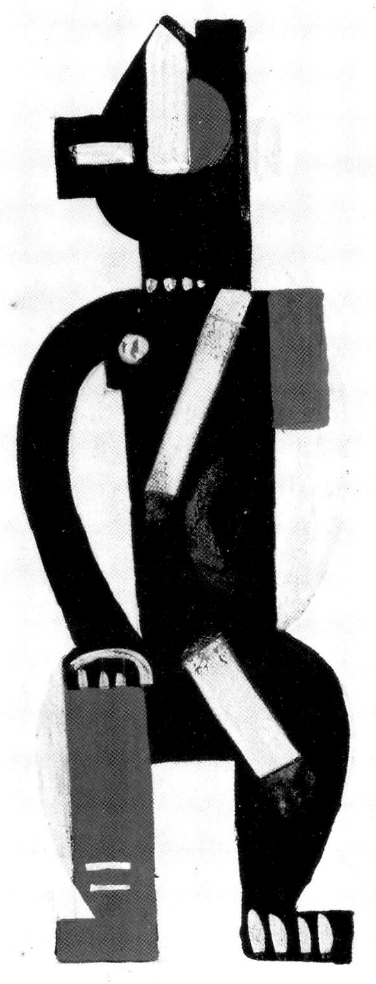

347

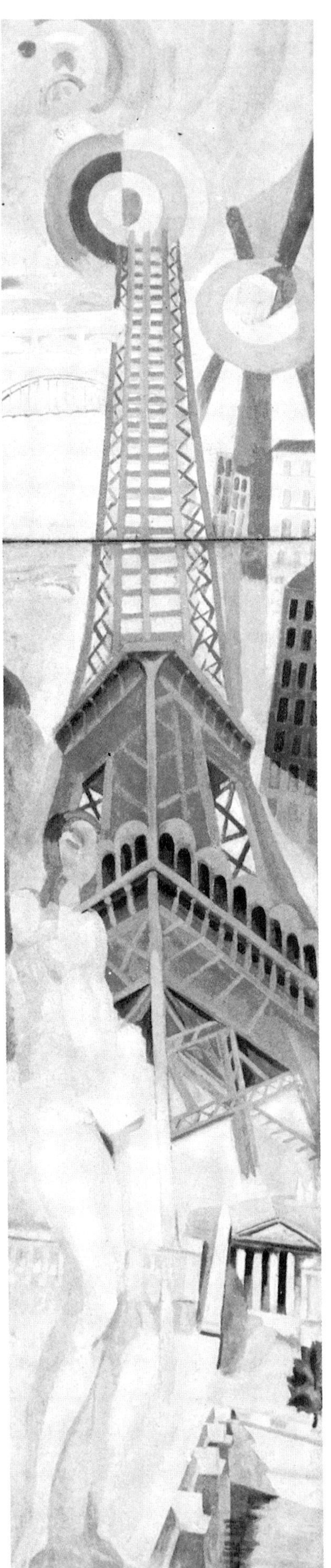

348

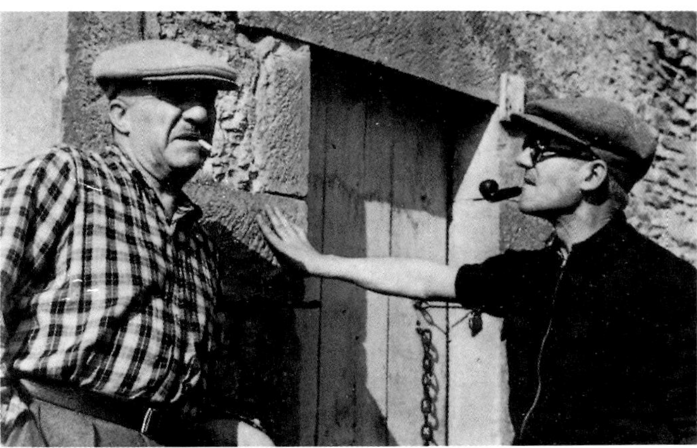

349.

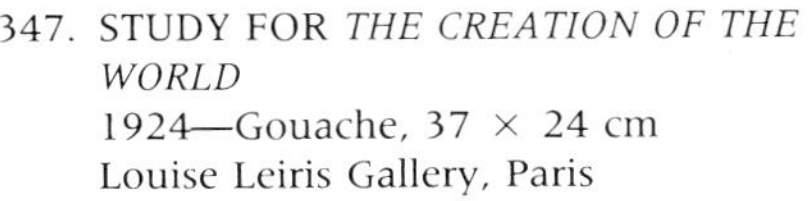

347. STUDY FOR *THE CREATION OF THE WORLD*
1924—Gouache, 37 × 24 cm
Louise Leiris Gallery, Paris

348. ROBERT DELAUNAY: *WOMAN AND THE TOWER*
1925—Oil on canvas, 450 × 94 cm
Deutsche Bank Collection, Düsseldorf

349. LÉGER AND LE CORBUSIER AT VÉZELAY, IN 1938

**1921** Léger works with Cendrars on *The Wheel* ("La Roue"), a film by Abel Gance. He paints *Animated Landscapes* ("Paysages animés"). He illustrates Malraux's *Paper Moons* ("Lunes en papier"). He meets the De Stijl group, van Doesburg and Mondrian.
*Severini publishes* From Cubism to Classicism. *V. Eggeling and H. Richter make the first abstract films. Van de Velde does the designs for the Kröller-Müller Museum in Otterlo. The astronomical physicist Eddington restates the problem of the universe in* Space, Time, and Gravitation. *Einstein receives the Nobel Prize in physics for his theory of relativity. Elie Faure publishes* Modern Art. *Sun Yat-sen is president of the Chinese Republic.*

**1922** *Women in an Interior.* Set decoration, costumes, and the curtain for *Skating Rink* for the Swedish Ballet of Rolf de Maré with the music of Darius Milhaud. He inherits the farm in Lisores upon his mother's death and will continue to go there on a regular basis. He settles in Fontenay-aux-Roses. He finishes *Woman and Child* ("Femme et enfant"). *Kandinsky and Moholy-Nagy teach at the Bauhaus. Moholy-Nagy and L. Kassak publish* Buch neuer Künstler *using reproductions by Léger, Malevich, Le Corbusier, Picasso, Schwitters. J. J. P. Oud builds the De Unie restaurant in Rotterdam. James Joyce's* Ulysses *is published. (It will be translated into French in 1929). Niels Bohr receives the Nobel Prize in physics for his work on the structure of the atom. Mussolini comes to power in Italy. Russia takes the name of the Union of Soviet Socialist Republics.*

**1923** Léger's *The Big Tugboat* ("Le Grand Remorqueur"), *The Train Station* ("La Gare"). A new work for Rolf de Maré, set design and costumes for *The Creation of the World*—the libretto is by Cendrars, the music is by Milhaud. He collaborates on the set design for the film *Inhuman* ("L'Inhumaine") by Marcel L'Herbier, along with Mallet-Stevens, Cavalcanti, and Claude Autant-Lara, with music by Milhaud.
*Le Corbusier publishes* Towards an Architecture *("Vers une architecture"). The De Stijl Exhibit in Paris. Schwitters founds the review* Merz. *Auguste Perret builds the Church of Raincy, and Le Corbusier does the "Maison La Roche" in Auteuil. Louis de Broglie lays down the principles of wave mechanics. Tokyo is destroyed by an earthquake.*

**1924** Léger produces and directs the first film without a screenplay: *Le Ballet Mécanique,* with photographs by Man Ray and Dudley Murphy, and music by G. Antheil. For a time Léger thinks about abandoning painting for film. He paints *The Siphon* and *Reading.* He opens a free studio with Ozenfant, Marie Laurencin, and Exter. He lectures at the Sorbonne. He travels to Italy and is very enthusiastic about Ravenna.

*Klee, along with Kandinsky, Feininger, and Jawlensky, forms a group known as Les Quatre Bleus. André Breton publishes the "Surrealist Manifesto." Death of Lenin.*

**1925** International Decorative Arts Exhibit: Léger and Delaunay decorate work together on abstract panels for the entrance hall of the pavilion of a "French embassy" designed by Mallet-Stevens, and the first mural paintings for the pavilion of Le Corbusier's "Esprit Nouveau." Léger, with the help of Le Corbusier, wants to color the interiors and exteriors of the habitats: as contrasts, "inhabitable rectangles," "elastic rectangles." "A light blue wall retreats, extending the space; a black wall closes in. A yellow wall disappears." Lecture at the Collège de France on the "Esthetics of the Machine."
*Eisenstein:* The Battleship Potemkin.

**1926–1927** Exhibits in New York at the Anderson Galleries, then at the Brooklyn Museum. Exhibits in Paris at Galerie des Quatre Chemins. His first retrospective at the Salon des Indépendents. His attention increasingly drawn to "objects-as-emblems."
*Deslaw directs the film* The March of the Machines. *Fritz Lang directs* Metropolis. *Beginnings of experimental television. Zervos founds the* Cahiers d'Art *("Art Notebooks"). Brinkmann and Van der Vlugt build the Van Nelle factory in Rotterdam. Heidegger publishes* Sein und Zeit *("Being and Time").* The Jazz Singer, *first sound film in the United States. Lindberg flies across the Atlantic. Monet donates his* Water Lilies *to the French government and dies in December 1926.*

**1928** Léger travels to Berlin for his show of 100 works at the Flechtheim Gallery. He lectures on the theme of "Currents" ("Actualités"), which he dedicates to Le Corbusier. He exhibits at the Galerie de l'Effort Moderne. A variety of still lifes with leaves, plaster masks, hats, profiles.
*Dalí and Buñuel make the film* An Andalusian Dog *("Un Chien Andalou"). The C.I.A.M. (International Congress of Modern Architecture / Congrès Internationaux d'Architecture Modernes) established in Switzerland. Poelzig builds the I. G. Farben factory in Frankfurt. Einstein formulates the unified field theory. Heisenberg formulates the uncertainty principle. Freyssinet invents prestressed concrete. Breton:* Surrealism and Painting *("Le Surréalism et la Peinture"). Malraux's* The Conquerors *("Les Conquérants"). D. H. Lawrence's* Lady Chatterly's Lover. *Ravel's* Bolero.

**1929** Numerous sketches of objects, *Bicycle against a Blue Background* ("Le Vélo sur fond bleu"), which provided a means of renewing his interest in the inventory of "objects." These objects, however, are floating in space. They are "levitating."
*The International Exhibit of Abstract Art in Zurich. Museum of Modern Art (MOMA) founded in New York. Leduc holds the first patent for jet propulsion. The stock market crash on Wall Street.*

**1930** Léger's *Mona Lisa with Keys* ("La Joconde aux clés"), *Dancers* ("Danseuses"), *Three Musicians* ("Les Trois Musiciens") open the door to what will become Pop Art, and return to a realism that revolves around the human form. Now bodies are grappling in space. He exhibits in London at the Leicester Galleries. He becomes friendly with Calder.

*Moholy-Nagy composes his first "space modulators" in London. The death of Russian poet Mayakovsky. Le Corbusier's project for "Ville Radieuse" (Radiant City). Ginzburg's project for Moscow as a "green city." Mermoz crosses the South Atlantic by plane. Louis de Broglie receives the Nobel Prize in physics for his theory of wave mechanics.*

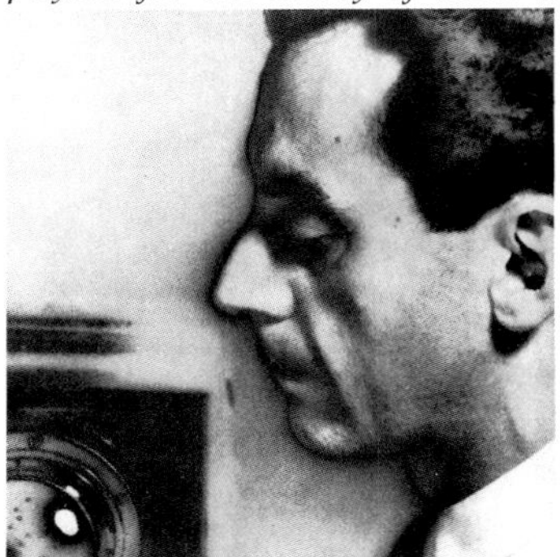

350. MAN RAY AT THE TIME OF *LE BALLET MÉCANIQUE*

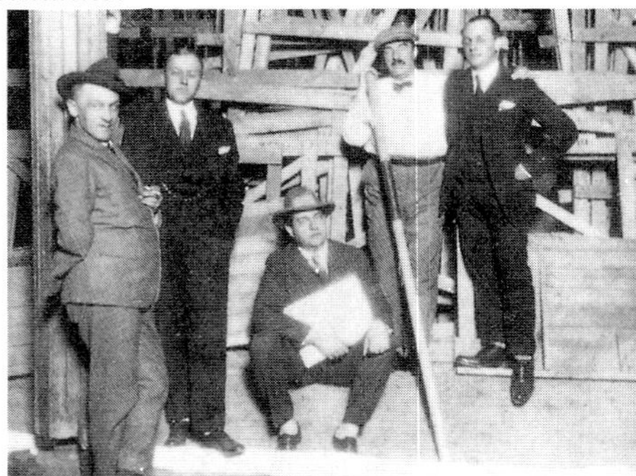

351. BLAISE CENDRARS, DARIUS MILHAUD, FERNAND LÉGER, L. BÖRLIN, ROLF DE MARÉ

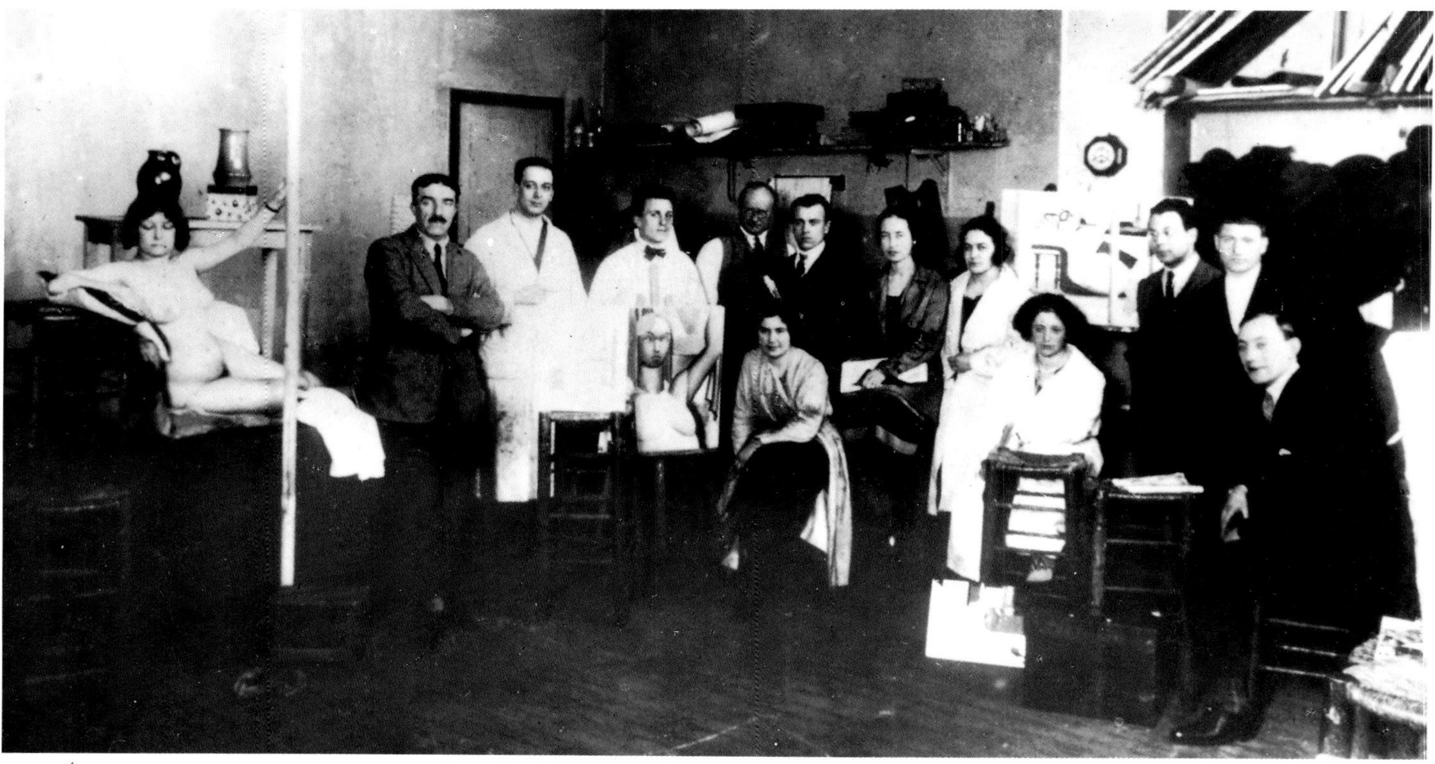

352. LÉGER'S STUDIO, ABOUT 1924

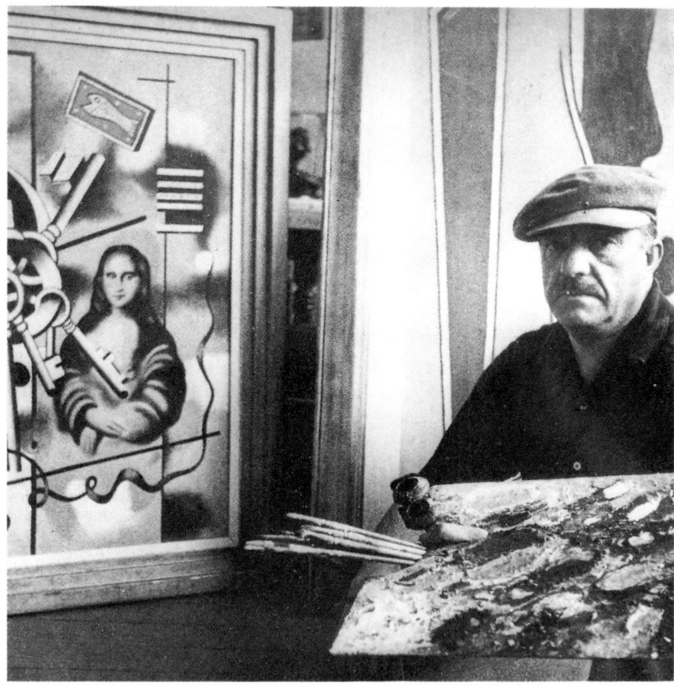

353. LÉGER AND *THE MONA LISA WITH KEYS,* IN 1930

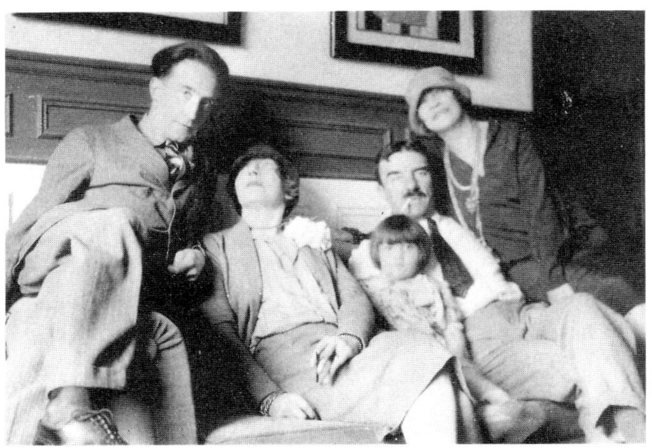

354. DUCHAMP, LÉGER, AND THEIR WIVES, IN 1928

**1931** *The Bather* ("La Baigneuse"). Léger spends the summer in Austria at the home of his friends the Murphys. First trip to the United States (New York and Chicago). Exhibits at the John Becker Gallery and at the Durand-Ruel Galleries.
*The end of Russian Constructivism. The death of van Doesburg. The dissolution of De Stijl. In film: Chaplin makes* City Lights, *Pabst makes the* Three-Penny Opera, *Cocteau makes* Blood of a Poet, *René Clair makes* The Million. *The building of Rockefeller Center in New York. The Spanish Republic comes into being. The Japanese invade Manchuria.*

**1932** Léger does the sign for the Grande-Chaumière. He travels to Sweden and Norway. His work is exhibited in New York and at the Valentine Gallery.
*The Abstraction-Creation group is formed in Paris. Calder's mobiles are shown. The Bauhaus is moved to Berlin. Landovsky's project for a "rocket city" (ville-fusée). Chadwick discovers the neutron. The birth of electron microscopy. Céline authors* Voyage au bout de la nuit (*"Journey to the End of the Night"*).

**1933** Léger goes to Zurich for a large exhibit of his work at the Kunsthaus. He travels to Greece with Le Corbusier for the conference of the C.I.A.M. While returning to France on the ship *Paris II,* he gives a lecture, "Architecture in a Life Context" (L'Architecture devant la vie).

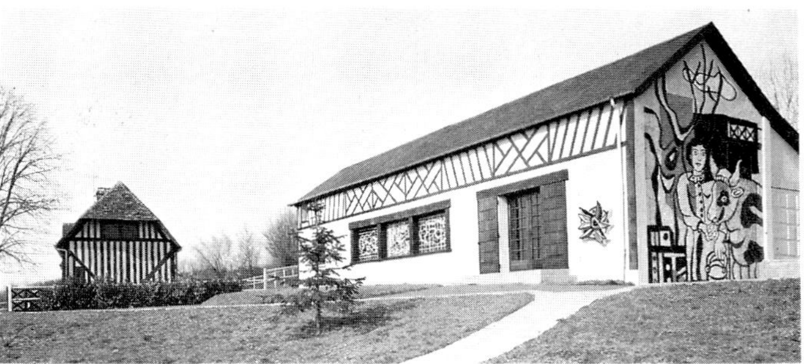

355. THE FARM IN LISORES, IN CALVADOS, WHICH BECAME AN ART GALLERY DECORATED WITH THE MOSAIC *THE MILKMAID AND THE COW*

*Hitler becomes chancellor of Germany. Stalin is in power. The Nazis order the closing of the Bauhaus. Klee returns to Bern, Switzerland. Kandinsky moves to Paris. Élie Faure publishes* The Life of Forms *("La Vie des formes"). Exhibit in Chicago: "A Century of Progress." Dalí:* The Terrifying and Edible Beauty of Modern Style *("De la beauté terrifiante et comestible du style moderne). Malraux:* The Human Condition *("La Condition humaine"). Aldous Huxley:* Brave New World. *Joliot-Curies produce artificial radioactivity. Invention of the photoelectric cell. In China: the Long March. Roosevelt is president of the United States.*

**1934** Léger's "Objects" gouaches and sketches exhibited at the Vignon Gallery in Paris—"Roots, flints, rack of lamb, corkscrew, vase, pair of pants, chunk of beef, cheese, nuts." Spends the summer in Antibes. In August he goes to London to collaborate on the sets for a film by H. G. Wells, *The Shape of Things to Come.* In September he goes to Stockholm for his show at the Modern Gallery. The museum in Göteborg buys *Woman at the Dressing Table* ("Femme à la toilette"). He lectures at the Sorbonne: "From the Acropolis to the Eiffel Tower."
*The "Art and Machines" exhibit at the MOMA in New York. Gaston Bachelard publishes "Le Nouvel esprit scientifique" ("The New Thinking in Science"). Lewis Mumford's* Technics and Civilization. *Caldwell's* God's Little Acre.

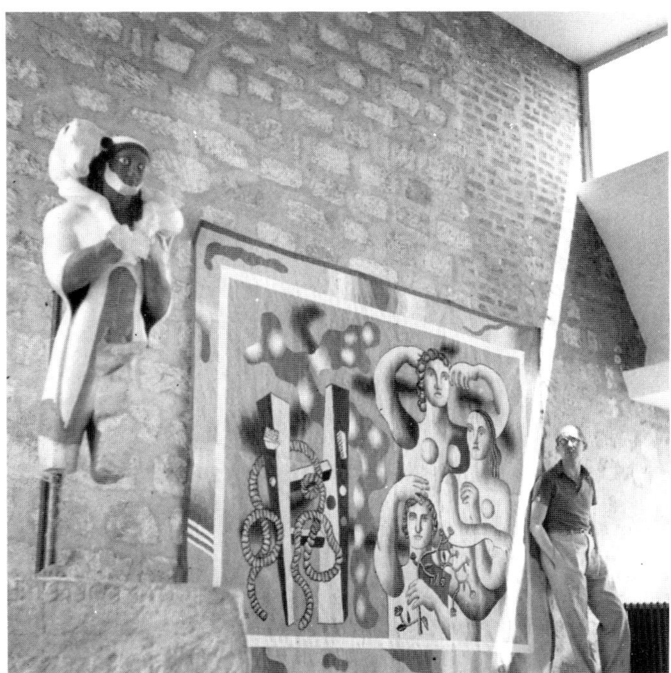

356. LE CORBUSIER IN HIS STUDIO NEXT TO A LEGER TAPESTRY AND HIS COPY OF *THE ARCHAIC MOSCOPHORE,* IN 1935

**1935–1936** The period of the sculptural Giants, the *Two Sisters, Adam and Eve*. Léger travels to Brussels where he presents the decoration for the physical culture stadium designed by Charlotte Perriand for the World's Fair. His second trip to the United States, this time with Le Corbusier. Exhibits at MOMA in New York and at the Art Institute of Chicago.
*Le Corbusier publishes ''La Ville Radieuse''* (''The Radiant City''). *Schwitters emigrates to Norway. Wright builds his ''House on the Waterfall.'' Stakhanovism in the U.S.S.R. The New Deal in the U.S.A. Racial laws in Germany. Italy attacks Ethiopia. Construction of the Moscow subway. The death of Malevich. In 1936: Chaplin makes* Modern Times. *The outbreak of the Spanish Civil War. Picasso is director of the Prado in Madrid. The Popular Front in France. The discovery of oil in Saudi Arabia.*

**1937** Léger does the sets for *David Triumphant*, Serge Lifar's ballet for the Opera, with music of Mussorgsky and Debussy. He organizes the decorations for a trade union celebration at the Vélodrome d'Hiver (Winter Gardens). Mural painting at the Palais de la Découverte science museum in Paris: *Power Transmission*. Léger prefers the Aviation Show to the Louvre museum. He lectures in Antwerp, "Color in the World." He travels to Helsinki, Finland, for the opening of his exhibit at the Artek Gallery, and befriends Alvaar Aalto. He wants to change the color of Paris, scrape the buildings, illuminate the Eiffel Tower, paint the gasoline pumps in lively colors.
*Picasso paints* Guernica. *Le Corbusier publishes* When Cathedrals Were White *(''Quand les cathédrals étaient blanches''). Moholy-Nagy opens the ''New Bauhaus'' in Chicago (today it is the Art Institute of Design). The Museum of Non-Objective Painting is founded in New York. Gropius is the director of the Harvard School of Architecture in Cambridge, Massachusetts. Costa, Niemeyer, Reidy, Leão, and Moreira build the National Ministry of Health and Education in Rio de Janeiro. The Japanese capture Beijing.*

**1938–1939** The summer in Vézelay with Le Corbusier. Léger's third trip to the United States: he decorates the apartment of Nelson A. Rockefeller, Jr., in New York. He stays in Provincetown with Dos Passos, and on Long Island with the architect Harrison. He gives a series of eight lectures, "Color in Architecture," at Yale University and at Columbia University. In Paris he does the set design for *Birth of a City*, a play by J. R. Bloch presented at the Vélodrome d'Hiver in Paris. The music is by Milhaud and Honegger.
*The International Surrealism Exhibit in Paris. Jean Renoir makes* La Grande Illusion *(''The Great Illusion''). Jaspers publishes* Existenz Philosophie. *Delaunay organizes the first Salon des Réalités Nouvelles (''New Realities Show''). Bourbaki publishes the theory of combinations. Atomic fission. Great Britain and France declare war on Germany.*

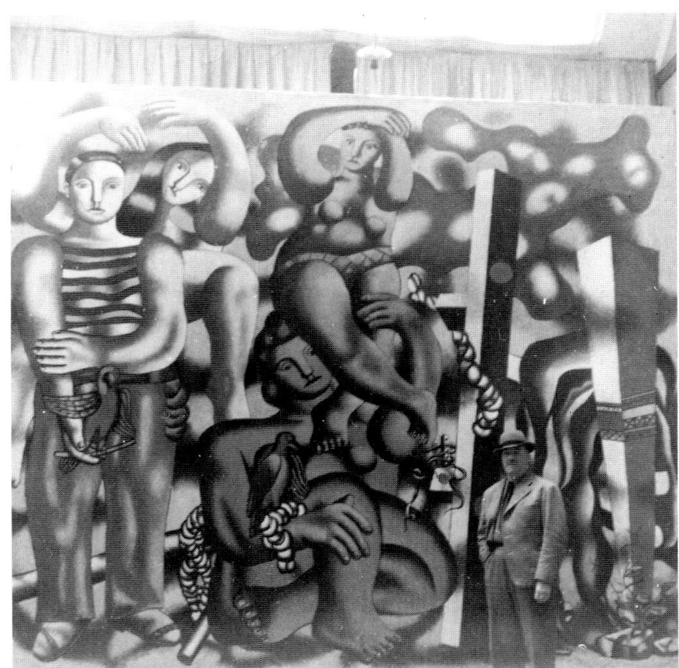

357. LÉGER AND HIS *GIANTS IN SPACE*, ABOUT 1935–39

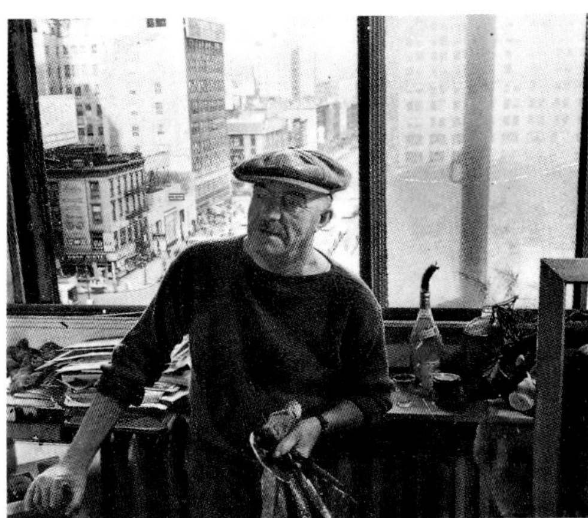

358. LÉGER IN HIS NEW YORK CITY STUDIO, 1940–45

**1940–1945** In October 1940, Léger leaves Marseilles fc the United States. He teaches at Yale University along with Milhaud, Focillon, and André Maurois. The Museum of Modern Art in New York exhibits his *Composition for Two Parrots*, which marks the appearance of "outside" color, and the influence of the colored spotlights used for advertising on Broadway. He paints in the following order: *The Divers* series ("Les Plongeurs") between 1941 and 1944, *The Forest* ("La Forêt") in 1942, and *Big Julie* in 1945. He teaches at Mills College in California, where he organizes an exhibit. He strikes up a friendship with R. P. Couturier. He exhibits with Paul Rosenberg in New York (1942) and meets the majority of exiled artists at the home of Pierre Matisse: Masson, Tanguy, Matta, Breton, Zadkine, Ernst, Chagall, Mondrian, Ozenfant. He directs the sequence "The Girl with the Manufactured Heart" for the film *Dreams That Money Can Buy*, directed by Hans Richter. Léger exhibits in 1945 at the Fogg Art Museum in Cambridge, and at the Valentine Gallery and the Samuel P. Kootz Gallery in New York.
*Fermi frees nuclear energy and builds the first atomic pile, a discovery of very grave consequences. Pollock, Motherwell, and Baziotes exhibit in New York. At the same time in Europe artistic groups are dismantled and the museums are closed. Camus publishes* 'L'Étranger' *(''The Stranger'') and* Le Mythe de Sisyphe *(''The Myth of Sisyphus'') in 1942.* L'Être et le Néant *(''Being and Nothingness'') by Sartre in 1943. Merleau-Ponty's* Phénomenlogie de la perception *(''Phenomenology of Perception'') in 1945. Marinetti dies in 1944, and Mallet-Stevens in 1945. The atomic bomb. The Yalta Conference. Germany and Japan surrender. In December 1945, Léger returns to France.*

**1946** Exhibit of works from America at the Galerie Carré in Paris. Léger paints *Adieu New York* ("Farewell, New York"). R. P. Couturier asks him to compose a mosaic ıor the facade of the church in Assy in Haute-Savoie. He delivers a lecture at the Sorbonne, "Work and Culture."
*The inauguration of the Picasso Museum in Antibes. In Paris, Fougeron takes charge of a movement favoring Socialist Realism. A new generation of Constructivists: Dewasne, Deyrolle, Vasarely. The first of the Informals: Wols, Fautrier. Airplane breaks the sound barrier.*

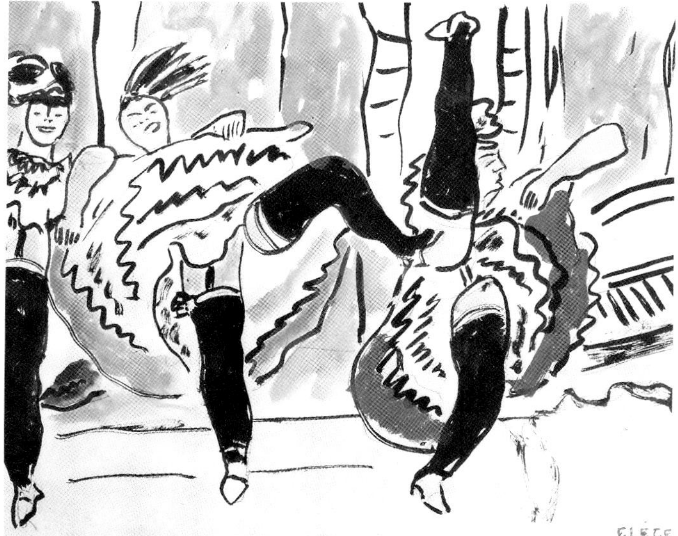

359. MOULIN ROUGE
1954–55—Gouache, 32.4 × 51.3 cm
Louise Leiris Gallery, Paris

**1947** A stay in Normandy. A portrait of Paul Éluard. Exhibits with Calder in Amsterdam and Bern.
*Marshall Plan. Indochinese War. The Partition of Palestine.*

**1948** Set design for *Steel Steps* ("Pas d'acier"), music by Prokofiev, for the Ballets of the Champs-Élysées. Léger and his students do the decoration for the International Congress of Women at the Porte de Versailles in Paris. He participates in the Peace Conference in Wroclaw, Poland. He participates in a debate on current art in Brussels and in Antwerp along with Bazaine and Diehl for the Friends of Art.
*Establishment of the Cobra Group. The first geodesic domes of Fuller. Wiener formulates the principles of cybernetics. The first transistor. Establishment of the State of Israel. Assassination of Gandhi.*

**1949** Léger Retrospective at the Museum of Modern Art in Paris. Text and illustrations for the book *Le Cirque* ("The Circus") published by Tériade. Illustrations for Rimbaud's *Illuminations*. Costumes and set design for the opera *Bolivar* by Milhaud. The first ceremics with his student Roland Brice in Biot.
*Le Corbusier takes on the "Maison du Fada" (House of Fada), a housing complex in Marseilles. Jean Prouvé produces twenty-five houses manufactured in aluminum. Pierre Schaeffer's concrete music.*

**1950** Death of Jeanne Lohy. Léger finishes *The Builders* ("Les Constructeurs"), which accompanies a poem dedicated to the memory of Mayakovsky, "The Hands of the Builders": "Their hands resemble their tools, / Their tools, their hands, / Their pants are like mountains, like tree trunks, / a pair of pants is real and true when it has no pleats. . . ." He exhibits at the Tate Gallery in London. A mosaic for the crypt of the American Memorial in Bastogne. The consecration of the church in Assy.
*The Korean War.*

**1951** Léger is present at the Triennial of Milan for which he paints a large composition. Installment of the seventeen windows in stained glass and cement and tapestry for the church of Audincourt (in Doubs). The first polychrome sculpture exhibited at the Louise Leiris Gallery in Paris.
*Inauguration of the Chapel of the Rosary in Vence, which was conceived and realized by Matisse.*

**1952** In February he marries Nadia Khodossevitch, a student at the Academy in 1924, then his assistant. He moves to the Gros Tilleul in Gif-sur-Yvette. He gives a lecture in Bern on architecture and color on the occasion of his exhibit at the Kunsthalle. He exhibits at the Musée d'Antibes, at the Berri Galleries, at Louis Carré in Paris, and at the Sidney Janis Gallery in New York. He travels to Venice to participate in the Twenty-sixth Biennale. Panels and costumes for Janine Charrat's ballet presented in Amboise on the occasion of Leonardo da Vinci's 500th birthday.
*The death of Paul Éluard. The death of George VI. Elizabeth II becomes queen of England. Ionesco's "The Chairs." Schaeffer publishes "In Search of Concrete Music" ("À la recherche d'une musique concrète").*

**1953** Léger works on *Country Outing* ("La Partie de campagne") and begins work on the series *The Big Parade* ("La Grande Parade"). Travelling exhibit in Japan, at the MOMA in New York, at the Art Institute of Chicago, and in San Francisco. Conference in Brussels, "Modern Painting." Illustration for the poem "Liberty" (Liberté) by Paul Éluard. *Landscapes of the Seine-et-Oise* ("Paysages de Seine-et-Oise").
*Wright elaborates his plans for the Guggenheim Museum in New York. Le Corbusier builds the the courts of law in Chandigarh. Bachelard publishes* Rational Materialism *("Le Matérialisme rationnel"). Robbe-Grillet's* The Erasers *("Les Gommes"). Samuel Beckett's* Waiting for Godot. *Messiaen composes* The Awakening of the Birds *("Le Réveil des oiseaux"). The death of Stalin. Eisenhower is president of the United States.*

**1954** Mosaics and stained-glass windows for the University of Caracas, Venezuela. Stained-glass window for Innocente Palacios. Stained-glass windows for the church of Courfaivre in Switzerland. *Country Outing* and *The Big Parade* are the mainstay of the exhibit at the Maison de la Pensée Française. Preparatory studies for the Memorial Hospital of Saint-Lô designed by the architect Nelson, which will be opened in 1956. Project for a mosaic composition for the auditorium of the Opera in São Paulo, designed by the architect Niemeyer.
*The death of Matisse. Candela builds the church of Santa Maria Miraculosa in Mexico; the walls are covered with polychrome mosaics. Elyot Noyes invents the "bubble house," which links up to another one of Léger's ideas. The first nuclear power plant in the U.S.S.R. Dien Bien Phu. The beginning of the Algerian revolt. Nasser becomes leader of the Egyptian state.*

**1955** Léger is awarded the Grand Prize at the São Paulo Biennial. Ceramic sculpture and mosaics for the coking plant of Gaz de France in Alfortville. Trip to Czechoslovakia for the Congress of Sokols in Prague. Retrospective at the Museum of Lyon. Léger dies on August 17 at his home in Gif-sur-Yvette, the same year that Einstein, Beaumeister, Hofer, Pechstein, and Tanguy die. Homage to Fernand Léger at the Maeght Gallery.
*Le Corbusier finishes his church in Ronchamp, Haute-Saône. The beginnings of Pop Art, Cinétism in Paris. Launching of the first atomic submarine in the United States.*

**1956** Inauguration of the hospital at Saint-Lô. A Léger retrospective encompassing 222 works at the Museum of Decorative Arts in Paris. The first stone is laid for the Fernand Léger Museum at Biot. It will open on May 13, 1960. Publication of Léger's *My Travels* ("Mes Voyages"), with a poem by Louis Aragon.

## BIBLIOGRAPHY


### Works by Fernand Leger

Léger Fernand, *Le Cirque*, text and 60 lithos, Tériade, Paris, 1949.

Léger Fernand, *Propos et présence*, Gonthier-Seghers, Paris 1959.

Léger Fernand, *La Ville*, 29 lithos Tériade, Paris, 1959.

Léger Fernand, *Mes Vcyages* (with a poem by Aragon), 28 lithos, Éd. Français Réunis, Paris, 1960.

Léger Fernand, *Fonctiɀns de la peinture*, Gonthier, Paris, 1965.

### Works about Fernand Léger

Raynal Maurice, *Fernand Léger*, L'Effort Moderne, Paris, 1920.

Waldemar George, *Fernand Léger*, Gallimard, Paris, 1929.

Elgar Franck, *Léger, peintures 1911-1948*, Éd. du Chêne, Paris, 1948.

Cooper Douglas, *Fernand Léger et le nouvel espace*, Éd. des Trois Collines, Geneva, 1949.

Roy Claude, *Fernand Léger, Les Constructeurs*, Falaise, Paris, 1951.

Zervos Christian, *Fernand Léger, oeuvres de 1905 à 1952*, Cahiers d'Art, Paris, 1952.

Maurois André, *Mon ami Léger*, Louis Carré, Paris, 1952.

Jardot Maurice, *Léger, dessins*, Éd. des Deux Mondes, Paris, 1953.

Descargues Pierre, *Fernand Léger*, Éd. du Cercle d'Art, Paris, 1955.

Verdet André, *Fernand Léger, le dynamisme pictural*, Pierre Cailler, Geneva, 1955.

Jardot Maurice, *Fernand Léger, dessins*, Hazan, Paris, 1956.

Aragon Louis, *Fernand Léger, Constrastes*, Au Vent d'Arles, Paris, 1959.

Delevoy Robert, *F. Léger*, Skira, Geneva, 1962.

Garaudy Roger, *Pour un réalisme du XX^e siècle : dialogue posthume avec Fernand Léger*, Grasset, Pris, 1968.

*Hommage à Fernand Léger*, special edition of XX^e siècle, Paris, 1971.

*Rétrospective Fernand Léger*, catalog, Grand Palais, Paris, 1971–1972.

Néret Gilles, *Rétrospective Fernand Léger*, catalog, Tokyo-Nagoya-Fukuoka, 1971.

Cassou Jean et Leymarie Jean, *Léger, dessins et gouaches*, Éd. du Chêne, Paris, 1972.

Saphire Laurent, *Fernand Léger*, The Complete Graphic Work. New York, 1978.

Schmalenbach W., *Léger*, DuMont, Cologne, 1977.

Diehl Gaston, *Fernand Léger*, Paris, 1985.

*Léger et l'Esprit moderne*, catalog, musée d'Art moderne de la Ville de Paris, 1982.

Laugier Claude et Richet Michèle, *Œuvres de Fernand Léger*, Collection du Musée national Art moderne, Paris, 1981.

Bauquier Georges, *Fernand Léger*, Adrien Maeght Éditeur, Paris, 1987.

*Rétrospective Fernand Léger*, catalog, Fondation Maeght, Saint-Paul, 1988.

*Fernand Léger, œuvres sur papier*, catalog, Museum of Israel, Jerusalem, 1989.

Schmalenbach W., Bauquier G., Cooper Douglas et Moellet Magdaleina, *Fernand Léger*, catalog, Kunsthalle, Munich. 1988. 1989.

*Antologica Mostra Fernand Léger*, Palazzo Reale, Milan, 1989-1990.

Bauquier Georges, *Catalogue raisonné de l'œuvre peint de Fernand Léger* vol. I-II, Adrien Maeght Éditeur, Paris.


## FILMS

### Film directed by Fernand Léger with the collaboration of Dudley Murphy

*Le Ballet mécanique*, 1924.

### Participation of Fernand Léger in the design

*La roue* by Abel Gance, 1921-1924 (posters).

*L'inhumaine* by Marcel L'Herbier, 1923.

*The shapes of things to come* by H.G. Wells, 1934.

### Films about Fernand Léger

*Léger à son arrivée à Paris* by R. Hessen, 1924.

*Léger en Amérique (Leger in America—His new realism)* by T. Bouchard, 1942.

*Fernand Léger, les Constructeurs* by G. Bauquier, 1955-1956.

*Fernand Léger dans l'Art et les Hommes* by J.-M. Drot, 1955-1960.

*Léger dans Plaisirs des Arts*, by M. Mitrani, 1959.

*Fernand Léger* by T. Saytlor and J.P. Cordero, 1962.

*Why Leger?* by M. Gill; 1965.

*Le musée de Fernand Léger à Biot dans la couleur dans l'Art* by C. Vilardebo, 1967.

*Fernand Léger dans le Monde des Arts* by J.M. Berzosa and Y. Kovacs, 1971.

*Le dossier Fernand Léger* by D. Le Comte, 1975.

*Fernand Léger, le Constructeur, dans Écouter-Voir* by P. Gauthier, 1982.

*Le pas d'acier*, by U. Laugier, 1984.

*Fernand Léger* by J. Berthier.

*Fernand Léger et le temps présent*, Musée Fernand Léger.

360. SKETCH FOR *FOUR FIGURES*
1944—oil on canvas, 50 × 61 cm
Private collection

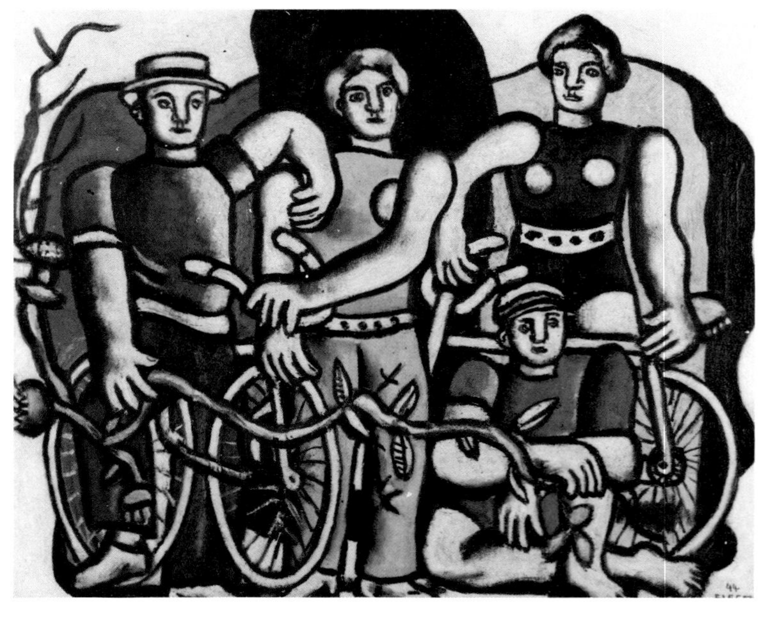

Sur mes cahiers d'écolier
Sur mon pupitre et les arbres
Sur le sable sur la neige
J'écris ton nom

Sur toutes les pages lues
Sur toutes les pages blanches
Pierre sang papier ou cendre
J'écris ton nom

Sur les images dorées
Sur les armes des guerriers
Sur la couronne des rois
J'écris ton nom

Sur la jungle et le désert
Sur les nids sur les genêts
Sur l'écho de mon enfance
J'écris ton nom

Sur les merveilles des nuits
Sur le pain blanc des journées
Sur les saisons fiancées
J'écris ton nom

Sur tous mes chiffons d'azur
Sur l'étang soleil moisi
Sur le lac lune vivante
J'écris ton nom

Sur les champs sur l'horizon
Sur les ailes des oiseaux
Et sur le moulin des ombres
J'écris ton nom

Sur chaque bouffée d'aurore
Sur la mer sur les bateaux
Sur la montagne démente
J'écris ton nom

Sur la mousse des nuages
Sur les sueurs de l'orage
Sur la pluie épaisse et fade
J'écris ton nom

Sur les formes scintillantes
Sur les cloches des couleurs
Sur la vérité physique
J'écris ton nom

Sur les sentiers éveillés
Sur les routes déployées
Sur les places qui débordent
J'écris ton nom

Sur la lampe qui s'allume
Sur la lampe qui s'éteint
Sur mes maisons réunies
J'écris ton nom

Sur le fruit coupé en deux
Du miroir et de ma chambre
Sur mon lit coquille vide
J'écris ton nom

Sur mon chien gourmand et tendre
Sur ses oreilles dressées
Sur sa patte maladroite
J'écris ton nom

Sur le tremplin de ma porte
Sur les objets familiers
Sur le flot du feu béni
J'écris ton nom

Sur toute chair accordée
Sur le front de mes amis
Sur chaque main qui se tend
J'écris ton nom

Sur la vitre des surprises
Sur les lèvres attentives
Bien au-dessus du silence
J'écris ton nom

Sur mes refuges détruits
Sur mes phares écroulés
Sur les murs de mon ennui
J'écris ton nom

Sur l'absence sans désirs
Sur la solitude nue
Sur les marches de la mort
J'écris ton nom

Sur la santé revenue
Sur le risque disparu
Sur l'espoir sans souvenirs
J'écris ton nom

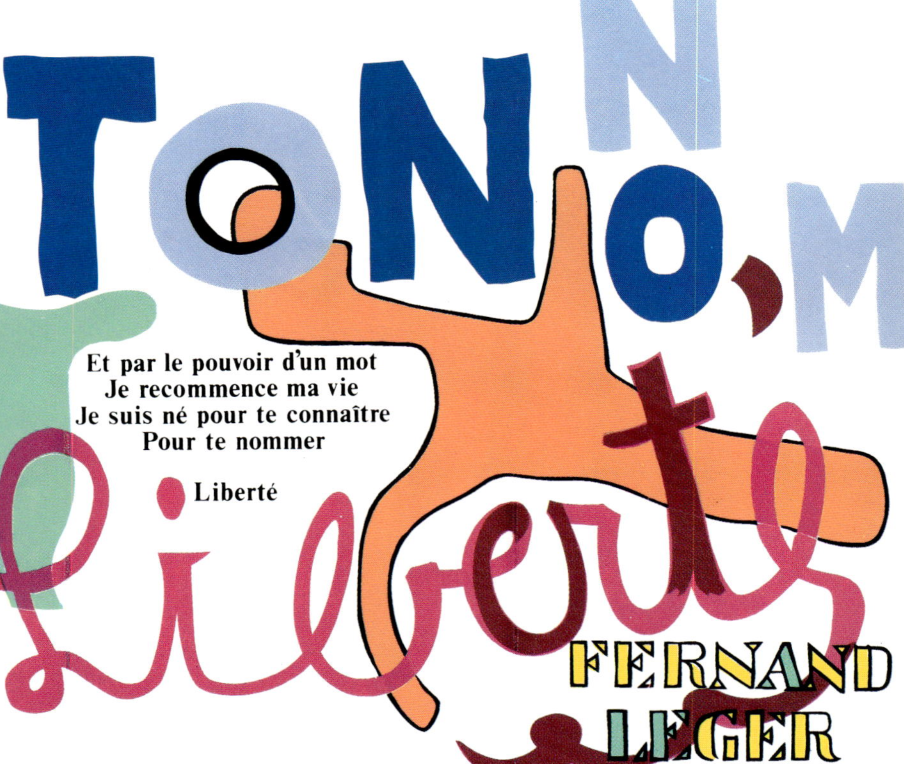


Et par le pouvoir d'un mot
Je recommence ma vie
Je suis né pour te connaître
Pour te nommer

Liberté

# Photo Credits

STEDELIJK MUSEUM, AMSTERDAM
Color Photograph: 108.

OEFFENTLICHE KUNSTSAMMLUNG, KUNSTMUSEUM, BASEL
(Photographie Hinz)
Color Photographs: 166, 167.
Black & White Photographs: 61, 77, 248, 249.

GALERIE BEYELER, BASEL
Color Photographs: 45, 48, 52, 156, 238, 267.

MUSÉE NATIONAL FERNAND LÉGER, BIOT
Color Photographs: 41, 96, 200, 287.
Black and White Photographs: 1, 10, 29, 33, 63, 117, 202, 215, 313, 317, 339.

KUNSTSAMMLUNG NORDRHEIN WESTFALEN, DÜSSELDORF
Color Photographs: 68, 260.

NATIONAL GALLERIES OF SCOTLAND, EDINBURGH
Color Photograph: 120.

TATE GALLERY, LONDON
Black & White Photograph: 320.

GALERIE ROSENGART, LUCERNE
Color Photograph: 106.

RIJKSMUSEUM KRÖLLER MÜLLER, OTTERLO
Color Photograph: 66.
Black & White Photograph: 39.

MUSÉE NATIONAL D'ART MODERNE, CENTRE GEORGES POMPIDOU, PARIS
Color Photographs: 38, 43, 46, 56, 58, 74, 87, 128, 129, 155, 165, 242, 297, 321.
Black & White Photographs: 40, 47, 67, 121, 122, 127, 148, 221, 223, 258, 284, 295.

RÉUNION DES MUSÉES NATIONAUX, PARIS
Color Photograph: 251.

CINÉMATHÈQUE FRANÇAISE, PARIS
Black & White Photographs: 131, 134, 135, 136, 137, 138, 139, 140, 146.

GALERIE JEANNE BUCHER, PARIS
Color Photographs: 71, 114, 231.
Black & White Photographs: 6, 8, 9, 12, 14, 16, 18, 55, 60, 70, 90, 93, 102, 110, 113, 126, 158, 159, 160, 162, 182, 184, 185, 191, 194, 197, 204, 252, 253, 255, 256, 262, 274.

GALERIE LOUIS CARRÉ & CIE, PARIS
Color Photograph: 196.
Black & White Photographs: 98, 291, 329, 330.

GALERIE LOUISE LEIRIS, PARIS
Color Photographs: 118, 130, 188, 217, 243, 259, 294, 299, 300, 307, 335.
Black & White Photographs: 15, 75, 83, 89, 153, 169, 171, 172, 193, 195, 199, 201, 203, 210, 214, 225, 341, 347, 359.

GALERIE ADRIEN MAEGHT, PARIS
Color Photographs: 32, 142, 180, 181, 209, 230, 235, 263, 264, 265, 271, 272, 292, 298, 301, 322, 333.
Black & White Photographs: 5, 112, 296, 324, 327.

ARCHIVES LIONEL PRÉJGER, PARIS
Color Photographs: 49, 80, 119, 176.
Black & White Photographs: 103, 123, 132, 133, 175, 246.

ÉTUDE FRANCIS BRIEST, PARIS
Color Photographs: 42, 234, 293.
Black & White Photograph: 124.

ÉTUDE GUY LOUDMER, PARIS
Color Photographs: 81, 97, 111, 143, 168, 233, 237, 334.
Black & White Photographs: 20, 22, 57, 64, 73, 78, 95, 115, 144, 145, 147, 149, 163, 183, 187, 211, 212, 220, 229, 239, 288, 289, 303, 323.

ÉTUDE HERVÉ POULAIN, PARIS
Black & White Photographs: 69, 226.

GAMMA, PARIS PHOTOGRAPHIC REPORTERS ASSOCIATION
Black & White Photograph: 338.

ROGER-VIOLLET, PARIS
Color Photographs: 125, 336.
Black & White Photographs: 4, 7, 109, 150, 151, 152, 161, 177, 186, 281, 283, 285, 337, 356.

STATENS KONSTMUSEER, STOCKHOLM
Color Photographs: 54, 91, 228.

STAATSGALERIE, STUTTGART
Color Photographs: 76, 326.
Black & White Photograph: 51.

KUNSTHISTORISCHES MUSEUM, VIENNA
Black & White Photograph: 44.

MUSÉE D'ART MODERNE, VILLENEUVE-D'ASCQ (Photo Muriel Anssens)
Color Photographs: 62, 100.
Black & White Photographs; 85, 105, 244.

VON DER HEYDT-MUSEUM, WUPPERTAL
Color Photograph: 245.

KUNSTHAUS, ZÜRICH
Color Photograph: 53.

AUTHOR'S ARCHIVES

Color Photographs: 37, 50, 59, 65, 72, 86, 99, 104, 154, 164, 189, 190, 213, 216, 218, 222, 232, 236, 254, 268, 273, 280, 290, 302, 306, 311, 325, 328.

Black & White Photographs: 11, 13, 17, 19, 21, 23, 26, 28, 34, 35, 36, 79, 82, 84, 88, 92, 94, 101, 107, 116, 157, 170, 173, 174, 178, 179, 192, 198, 205, 206, 207, 208, 219, 224, 227, 240, 241, 247, 250, 257, 261, 266, 269, 270, 275, 276, 277, 278, 279, 286, 304, 308, 309, 310, 312, 314, 316, 318, 319, 331, 332, 340, 342, 343, 344, 345, 346, 348, 349, 350, 351, 352, 353, 354, 357, 358.